Foundations of Business

2nd Edition

Foundations of Business

2nd Edition

William M. Pride
Texas A&M University

Robert J. Hughes
Richland College, Dallas County
Community Colleges

Jack R. Kapoor
College of DuPage

SOUTH-WESTERN
CENGAGE Learning

Australia • Brazil • Japan • Korea • Mexico • Singapore • Spain • United Kingdom • United States

Foundations of Business, 2e
William M. Pride, Robert J. Hughes, and Jack R. Kapoor

Vice President of Editorial, Business:
Jack W. Calhoun

Vice President/Editor-in-Chief:
Melissa Acuña

Senior Acquisitions Editor: Erin Joyner

Senior Developmental Editor:
Joanne Dauksewicz

Senior Content Project Manager:
Colleen A. Farmer

Marketing Communications Manager:
Sarah Greber

Media Editor: Kristen Meere

First Print Buyer: Miranda Klapper

Production Service: MPS Limited

Senior Art Director: Stacy Shirley

Senior Photo Manager: Deanna Ettinger

Internal and Cover Designer:
Craig Ramsdell

Cover Images: © Getty Images/Creative-Flickr

For product information and technology assistance, contact us at
Cengage Learning Customer & Sales Support, 1-800-354-9706

For permission to use material from this text or product,
submit all requests online at **www.cengage.com/permissions**
Further permissions questions can be emailed to
permissionrequest@cengage.com

Exam*View*® is a registered trademark of eInstruction Corp. Windows is a registered trademark of the Microsoft Corporation used herein under license. Macintosh and Power Macintosh are registered trademarks of Apple Computer, Inc. used herein under license.

© 2008 Cengage Learning. All Rights Reserved.

Cengage Learning WebTutor™ is a trademark of Cengage Learning.

Library of Congress Control Number: 2009936054

ISBN-13: 978-0-538-74451-5
ISBN-10: 0-538-74451-0
Instructor's Edition ISBN 13: 978-0-538-74634-2
Instructor's Edition ISBN 10: 0-538-74634-3

South-Western Cengage Learning
5191 Natorp Boulevard
Mason, OH 45040
USA

Cengage Learning products are represented in Canada by Nelson Education, Ltd.

For your course and learning solutions, visit **academic.cengage.com**

Purchase any of our products at your local college store or at our preferred online store **www.ichapters.com**

Printed in the United States of America
3 4 5 6 7 14 13 12 11

*To the Prides: Jim and Yvonne, Garrett and Kathy,
Melinda, Jonathan, and Carrie*

*To my mother, Barbara Y. Hughes; and my wife, Peggy,
and in memory of Pat Thomas*

*To my father, Ram Kapoor, and in memory of my mother, Sheela;
my wife, Theresa; and my children Karen, Kathryn, and Dave*

BRIEF CONTENTS

©Lidija Tomic

CONTENTS

©Grant Dougal

Part 3: Management and Organization 158

Part 5: Marketing 289

Preparing for Success with *Foundations of Business, 2e's* New Features!

Foundations of Business, 2e does much more than prepare you for success in future business courses. It equips you with a solid foundation for success in life—wherever your career may lead you. Known for its thorough yet succinct coverage, *Foundations of Business, 2e* delivers a survey of the major functional areas of business—management, marketing, accounting, finance, information technology—as well as covers such core topics as ethics and social responsibility, forms of ownership, small business, and international business.

Entertainment Giants Tune Into Hulu

Move over, YouTube: Hulu is here, and it's changing the world of online video. NBC Universal and News Corp. started Hulu as a joint venture to build a new website for streaming videos, with brief ads embedded, over the Internet. Both companies have a library of hit television shows and movies, NBC through its ownership of the NBC network and Universal Studios and News Corp. through its ownership of the Fox network and 20th Century Fox Studios.

The two equity partners envisioned Hulu as an online destination for viewing professionally-produced entertainment, distinct from the free videos—many created by consumers—on the wildly popular YouTube site. From the start, Hulu negotiated to include movies and television episodes from other networks and studios and offered advertising deals to companies seeking a large online audience.

Hulu was organized as a limited-liability company to give the partners more flexibility in managing the joint venture. As it turned out, this worked well because new equity partners have joined the venture over the years. Soon after Hulu was formed, Providence Equity Partners invested $100 million to become a part-owner. Hulu later attracted another key partner, Walt Disney, which invested millions in Hulu and added its ABC television programs to the site's fast-growing lineup of video offerings.

Today, Hulu offers premium entertainment content from many sources beyond its joint-venture partners, including MTV, PBS, Sony Pictures, Comedy Central, MGM, National Geographic, and Warner Brothers. Among the advertisers that air commercials during Hulu videos and display banner ads on the Hulu site are Best Buy, McDonald's, Visa, Nissan, Cisco, Johnson & Johnson, and Procter & Gamble. Hulu's rapid rise in viewership demonstrates that people are willing to sit through brief ads to watch their favorite shows streamed online, on demand. Can Hulu pass YouTube to become the most-viewed video site on the Internet? Can Hulu earn enough profit to reward the firms that own this joint venture? Tune in tomorrow.[1]

INSIDE BUSINESS

DID YOU KNOW?

Hulu is a joint-venture online entertainment destination where visitors view more than 300 million videos every month.

◀ **Inside Business Cases**
New! All-new opening cases about real business organizations drive home the relevance of the chapter concepts.

Many people dream of opening a business, and one of the first decisions they must make is what form of ownership to choose. We begin this chapter by describing the three common forms of business ownership: sole proprietorships, partnerships, and corporations. We discuss how these types of businesses are formed and note the advantages and disadvantages of each. Next, we consider several types of business ownership usually chosen for special purposes, including S-corporations, limited-liability companies, not-for-profit corporations, cooperatives, joint ventures, and syndicates. We conclude the chapter with a discussion of how businesses can grow through internal expansion or through mergers with other companies.

Sole Proprietorships

A **sole proprietorship** is a business that is owned (and usually operated) by one person. Although a few sole proprietorships are large and have many employees, most are small. Sole proprietorship is the simplest form of business ownership and the easiest to start. Some of today's largest corporations, including Ford Motor Company, H.J. Heinz Company, and Procter & Gamble Company, started out as tiny—and in many cases, struggling—sole proprietorships.

As you can see in Figure 4.1, there are more than 21.5 million sole proprietorships in the United States. They account for 72 percent of the country's busi-

1 LEARNING OBJECTIVE

Describe the advantages and disadvantages of sole proprietorships.

sole proprietorship a business that is owned (and

and employees or a group of investors to purchase the company

Concept Check

1. What happens when a firm makes a decision to grow from within?

2. What is a hostile takeover? How is it related to a tender offer and a proxy fight?

3. Explain the three types of mergers.

4. Describe current merger trends and how they affect the businesses involved and their stockholders.

time from new-product development and other vital business activities. This, they believe, is why U.S. companies may be less competitive with companies in such countries as Japan, Germany, and South Korea, where takeovers occur only rarely. Finally, the opposition argues that the only people who benefit from take-overs are investment bankers, brokerage firms, and takeover "artists," who receive financial rewards by manipulating U.S. corporations rather than by producing tangible products or services.

Most experts now predict that mergers and acquisitions during the first part of the twenty-first century will be the result of cash-rich companies looking to acquire businesses that will enhance their position in the marketplace. Analysts also anticipate more mergers that involve companies or investors from other countries. Regardless of the companies involved or where the companies are from, future mergers and acquisitions will be driven by solid business logic and the desire to compete in the international marketplace.

Finally, experts predict more leveraged buyouts in the future. A **leveraged buyout (LBO)** is a purchase arrangement that allows a firm's managers and employees or a group of investors to purchase the company. (LBO activity is sometimes referred to as *taking a firm private*.) To gain control of a company, LBOs usually rely on borrowed money to purchase stock from existing stockholders. The borrowed money is later repaid through the company's earnings, sale of assets, or money obtained from selling more stock.

120   Part 2: Business Ownership and Entrepreneurship

◄ Concept Checks

New! Concept checks at the end of each major topic test your understanding of the major issues discussed.

Get Flash Cards, Quizzes, Games, Crosswords and more @ www.cengage.com/introbusiness/pride

Test Yourself

Matching Questions

1. _____ It is an association of two or more business owners.

2. _____ A distribution of earnings to the stockholders of a corporation.

3. _____ This type of ownership is the easiest type of business to start.

4. _____ A person who invests only capital in a partnership.

5. _____ The concept of being personally responsible for all debts of a business.

6. _____ A business entity or artificial being with most of the legal rights of a person.

     j. partnership
     k. sole proprietorship
     l. unlimited liability

True False Questions

11. **T F** Unlimited liability is an advantage of a sole proprietorship.

12. **T F** Preferred stockholders elect the board of directors that manage the day-to-day business activities of a corporation.

13. **T F** Cooperatives are owned by their members.

14. **T F** A limited partner is responsible for any debts of the partnership, regardless of whether he or she was directly involved in the transaction that

◄ Test Yourself Quizzes

New! **Test Yourself** quizzes at the end of each chapter help you prepare for exams and gauge your mastery of key concepts and terminology.

APPENDIX A
Understanding Personal Finances and Investments

As the saying goes, "I've been rich and I've been poor, but believe me, rich is better." And yet, just dreaming of being rich doesn't make it happen. In order to be successful, you must be willing to invest the time and effort required to become a good money manager and a good investor. And don't underestimate how important you are when it comes to managing your money. No one is going to make you manage your money. No one is going to make you save the money you need to fund an investment program. These are your decisions—important decisions that literally can change your life.

Many people ask the question: Why begin an investment program now? At the time of publication, this is a very important question given the recent economic cri-

Two New Appendices!

New! Appendix A on Understanding **Personal Finances and Investments** is an especially helpful learning aid for you in these uncertain economic times.

New! Appendix B on Careers in Business provides valuable information on choosing and planning a career.

APPENDIX B
Careers in Business

Careers in Business

Words such as *excited, challenged, scared,* and *frustrated* have been used to describe someone involved in a job search. The reality, however, is that everyone who is employed must have looked for a job at one time or another, and survived. Although first-time employees often think that they will work for the same company for their entire career, most people change jobs and even careers during their lifetime. In fact, according to the Bureau of Labor Statistics, today's job applicants will change jobs over ten times. Therefore, the employment information that follows will be of lasting value. Let's begin our discussion with a look at the factors affecting an individual's career choices.

Preparing for Success with Technology for *Foundations of Business, 2e!*

◀ Student Website for *Foundations of Business, 2e*

A wealth of FREE resources are available to help prepare you for success in your Introduction to Business course. The student companion website offers a variety of study tools including:

- **Bonus Enrichment Chapters**
- **TWO sets of chapter quizzes**
- **Games**
- **Chapter Outlines**
- **And more!**

To access the student companion website:

1. Go to **www.cengage.com/ introbusiness/pride**.
2. Find your book.
3. Click on "Companion Site" under the 'Student' headline.

◀ CengageNOW™

Just What You Need to Know and Do NOW!

CengageNOW is an online product that includes a personalized learning path, an ebook, and much more! When you purchase CengageNOW with a new text you also receive access to the Business and Company Resource Center (BCRC) database. For more information, visit **www.cengage.com/now.**

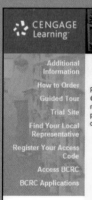

Business & Company Resource Center

Put a complete business library at your fingertips with **The Business & Company Resource Center.** The BCRC is a premier online business research tool that allows you to seamlessly search thousands of periodicals, journals, references, financial information, industry reports, company histories and much more.

- BCRC is conveniently accessible from anywhere with an Internet connection, allowing students to access information at school, at home, or on the 'go'.
- BCRC is a powerful and time saving research tool for students-- whether they are completing a case analysis, preparing for a presentation or discussion, creating a business plan, or writing a reaction paper.
- Instructors can use the BCRC like an online coursepack, assigning readings and research-based homework without the inconvenience of library reserves, permissions, and printed materials.
- BCRC filters out the 'junk' information students often find when searching the Internet, providing only the high quality, safe, and reliable news and information sources.

The Business & Company Resource Center can be packaged with any Cengage Learning textbook or coursepack at little or no additional cost. Use the resources on this page to learn more about this complete online information solution. To learn how you can include BCRC in your course, contact your local Cengage Learning representative.

BCRC Applications In Your Class

Combine BCRC with your favorite Harvard Business School Publishing cases and provide your students with a complete research tool for case analysis at no additional cost. Contact your Cengage Learning representative for additional information.

Easily assign homework, share articles, create journal lists, and save searches using BCRC Infomarks.

BCRC saves students valuable time and provides them a safe and reliable resource in which to hone their research skills and analytical abilities.

Click here to view some examples of how you can integrate BCRC into your course.

◀ Business & Company Resource Center

The Business & Company Resource Center is a premier online business research tool that allows you to seamlessly search thousands of periodicals, journals, references, financial information, industry reports, company histories and much more. Visit **www.cengage.com/bcrc** for more information.

WebTutor™

WebTutor is an epack that can be used with both WebCT® and Blackboard®. This content-rich, web-based learning aid reinforces chapter concepts and acts as an electronic student study guide. WebTutor provides interactive chapter review quizzes, writing improvement exercises, and flash cards of glossary terms.

▶ Business Plan Builder

This powerful, interactive online tool walks you step-by-step through the process of building a business plan—a skill that will benefit you throughout your career. The system provides informational modules about each part of the business plan and then prompts you to fill in the templates with information supporting your own business plan. Step by step, the program literally "builds" the business plan from the ground up!

Cengage Learning's Global Economic Watch

Lessons from real life right now

Acknowledgments

We would like to thank Marian Wood and Elisa Adams for their help on this edition, as well as Larry Flick of Three Rivers Community College for his work on the Instructor Manual, PowerPoints, and eLecture program. Our great thanks also go out to Theresa Kapoor, Dave Kapoor, Kathryn Thumme, Karen Tucker, Saleha Amin, Courtney Bohannon, and Vasuda Singh.

The quality of this book and its supplements program has been helped immensely by the insightful and rich comments of a special set of instructors. Their thoughtful and helpful comments had real impact in shaping the final product. **In particular, we wish to thank:**

John Adams, *San Diego Mesa College*

Harvey Bronstein, *Oakland Community College - Orchard Ridge*

Laura Bulas, *Central Community College - Hastings*

Mary Cooke, *Surry Community College*

Dean Danielson, *San Joaquin Delta College*

Gary Donnelly, *Casper College*

Karen Edwards, *Chemeketa Community College*

Karen Gore, *Ivy Tech Community College - Evansville*

Carol Gottuso, *Metropolitan Community College - Fort Omaha*

Eileen Kearney, *Montgomery Community College*

Robert Lupton, *Central Washington University*

John Mago, *Anoka Ramsey Community College*

Myke McMullen, *Long Beach City College*

Carol Miller, *Community College of Denver*

Jadeip Motwani, *Grand Valley State*

Mark Nagel, *Normandale Community College*

Dwight Riley, *Richland College*

Gail South, *Montgomery College - Germantown*

Leo Trudel, *University of Maine - Fort Kent*

Randy Waterman, *Richland College*

Leslie Wiletzky, *Pierce College - Ft.Steilacoom*

Anne Williams, *Gateway Community College*

Many talented professionals at Cengage Learning have contributed to the development of *Foundations of Business*, Second Edition. **We are especially grateful to**

Jack Calhoun,
Melissa Acuña,
Erin Joyner,
Joanne Dauksewicz,
Colleen Farmer,
Sarah Greber,
Kristen Meere,
Renee Yocum,
Jana Lewis,
Shanna Shelton,
and Kayti Purkiss.

Their inspiration, patience, support, and friendship are invaluable.

Exploring the World of Business and Economics

WHY THIS CHAPTER MATTERS. Studying business will help you to choose a career, become a successful employee, perhaps start your own business, and become a better-informed consumer and investor.

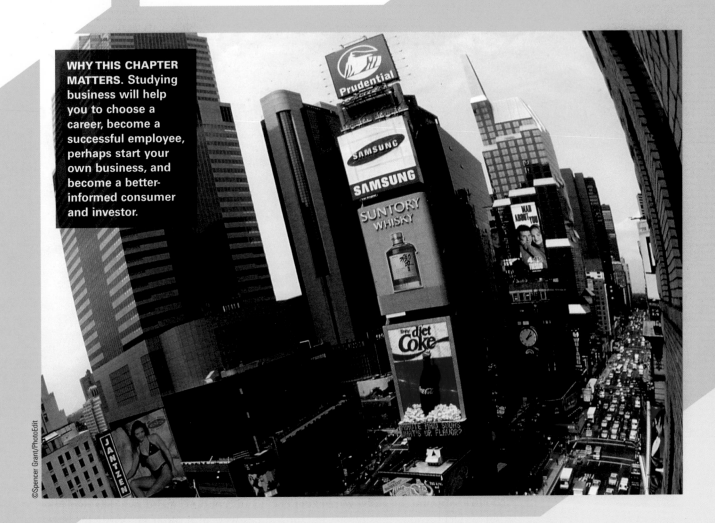

©Spencer Grant/PhotoEdit

LEARNING OBJECTIVES

1 Discuss your future in the world of business.

2 Define *business* and identify potential risks and rewards.

3 Define *economics* and describe the two types of economic systems: capitalism and command economy.

4 Identify the ways to measure economic performance.

5 Examine the four different phases in the typical business cycle.

6 Outline the four types of competition.

7 Summarize the factors that affect the business environment and the challenges American businesses will encounter in the future.

IBM Reinvents Its Future

International Business Machines (IBM) knows how to change with the times and technology. Founded in 1911 as the Computing-Tabulating-Recording Company, it originally made mechanical time-clocks and adding machines for U.S. and Canadian businesses. Today, IBM employs more than 400,000 worldwide, rings up $103 billion in annual revenue, and offers a wide range of information technology products and services for consumers and business customers.

The company has been reinventing itself year after year for nearly a century, entering new markets, filing new patents, and finding new paths to profit. IBM expanded into Europe, Latin America, and Asia during the 1920s. It introduced automated computing equipment in the 1940s and by the 1950s, it was manufacturing giant computers bundled with programs for billing, payroll, and inventory control. In 1960, IBM began tailoring computer and software packages to the needs of individual business customers, a move that launched the company into the lucrative market for technology services.

During the 1980s, IBM revolutionized business computing when it introduced the desktop personal computer. As the Internet Age dawned during the 1990s, the firm expanded into network servers and electronic commerce services. In 2005, it sold its PC business to Lenovo so it could focus on technology products and services for businesses of all sizes. Despite intense competition from Hewlett-Packard and other rivals, IBM has continued to prosper in the past decade by deemphasizing equipment in favor of more profitable software and services.

Whether the global economy expands or contracts, IBM is ready for all kinds of challenges and opportunities. It has $14 billion in cash to acquire compatible businesses, pay for advanced research, and construct new facilities. More than 70 percent of its skilled workforce is now located outside the United States, in nations where costs are low and growth is brisk. Every year, IBM files more than 4,000 patents and commercializes hundreds of scientific discoveries. In short, it's a century-old company that's always on the cutting edge.[1]

DID YOU KNOW?

With $103 billion in annual revenue, IBM has $14 billion in cash for acquiring businesses, paying for research, and building facilities.

Economic Crisis! Just two words, but these same two words will change the way that the world does business in the future. While the United States along with other countries around the globe were experiencing an economic meltdown that rivals the "Great Depression," businesses and individuals were also suffering. Virtually, every person was affected in some way by the economic crisis that began in late 2007. Just for a moment, think about the economic problems below and how they affect not only businesses, but also individuals.

- Unemployment rates approaching 10 percent
- Reduced consumer spending
- A slowdown in the homebuilding industry
- Automobile manufacturers file for bankruptcy
- A large number of troubled banks, savings and loan associations, and financial institutions on the verge of financial collapse
- An increasing number of business failures
- Depressed stock values that reduced the value of investment and retirement accounts for most individuals

In spite of the efforts of the federal government to provide the economic stimulus needed to stabilize the economy, the nation was still in the midst of recession when this text was published. Hopefully, by the time you read this material, the nation's economy will be improving. Still, it is important to remember the old adage, "History is a great teacher." Both the nation and individuals should take a look at what went wrong to avoid making the same mistakes in the future. Also, it helps to keep one factor in mind. Despite all of the problems described above, make no mistake about it, our economic system will survive. In fact, our economy continues to adapt and change to meet the challenges of an ever-changing world.

Our economic system provides an amazing amount of freedom that allows businesses that range in size from the small corner grocer to ExxonMobil to adapt to changing business environments. Within certain limits, imposed mainly to ensure public safety, the owners of a business can produce any legal good or service they choose and attempt to sell it at the price they set. This system of business, in which individuals decide what to produce, how to produce it, and at what price to sell it, is called **free enterprise**. Our free-enterprise system ensures, for example, that Dell Computer can buy parts from Intel and software from Microsoft and manufacture its own computers. Our system gives Dell's owners the right to make a profit from the company's success. It gives Dell's management the right to compete with Hewlett-Packard, Sony, and IBM. And it gives computer buyers the right to choose.

In this chapter, we look briefly at what business is and how it got that way. First, we discuss your future in business and explore some important reasons for studying business. Then we define *business,* noting how business organizations satisfy needs and earn profits. Next, we examine how capitalism and command economies answer four basic economic questions. Then our focus shifts to how the nations of the world measure economic performance and the four phases in a typical business cycle. We also outline different types of competition. Next, we look at the events that helped shape today's business system, the current business environment, and the challenges that businesses face.

Your Future in the Changing World of Business

1 **LEARNING OBJECTIVE**

Discuss your future in the world of business.

The key word in this heading is *changing.* When faced with both economic problems and increasing competition not only from firms in the United States but also from international firms located in other parts of the world, employees and managers now began to ask the question: What do we do now? Although this is a fair question, it is difficult to answer. Certainly, for a college student taking business courses or an employee just starting a career, or an unemployed worker looking for work, the question is even more difficult to answer. And yet there are still opportunities out there for people who are willing to work hard, continue to learn, and possess the ability to adapt to change. Let's begin our discussion in this section with three basic concepts.

- What do you want?
- Why do you want it?
- Write it down!

During a segment on the Oprah Winfrey television show, Joe Dudley, one of the world's most successful black business owners, gave the preceding advice to anyone who wants to succeed in business. And his advice is an excellent way to begin our discussion of what free enterprise is all about. What is so amazing about Dudley's success is that he started a manufacturing business in his own kitchen, with his wife and children serving as the new firm's only employees. He went on to develop his own line of hair-care products and to open a chain of beauty schools and beauty supply stores. Today, Mr. Dudley has built a multimillion-dollar empire and is president of Dudley Products, Inc. Not only a successful business owner, he is also a winner of the Horatio Alger Award—an award given to outstanding individuals who have succeeded in the face of adversity.[2] While many people would say that Joe Dudley was just lucky or happened to be in the right place at the right time, the truth is that he became a success because he had a dream and worked hard to turn his dream into a reality. Today, Dudley's vision is to see people succeed—to realize "The American Dream." He would be the first to tell you that you have the same opportunities that

free enterprise the system of business in which individuals are free to decide what to produce, how to produce it, and at what price to sell it

Spotlight

Who Makes the Most Money?

$100,000 Professional degree

$75,861 Bachelor's degree

$49,691 Some college, no degree

$39,426 High school graduate

Source: 2009 Statistical Abstract of the United States, p. 443.

he had. According to Mr. Dudley, "Success is a journey, not just a destination."[3]

Whether you want to obtain part-time employment to pay college and living expenses, begin your career as a full-time employee, or start a business, you must *bring something to the table* that makes you different from the next person. Ask yourself: What can I do that will make employers want to pay me a salary? What skills do I have that employers need? With these two questions in mind, we begin the next section with another basic question: Why study business?

Why Study Business?

The potential benefits of a college education are enormous. To begin with, there are economic benefits. Over their lifetimes, college graduates on average earn much more than high school graduates. And while lifetime earnings are substantially higher for college graduates, so are annual income amounts— see the Spotlight feature to the left.

The nice feature of education and knowledge is that once you have it, no one can take it away. It is yours to use for a lifetime. In this section, we explore what you may expect to get out of this business course and text. You will find at least four quite compelling reasons for studying business.

For Help in Choosing a Career What do you want to do with the rest of your life? Someplace, sometime, someone probably has asked you this same question. And like many people, you may find it a difficult question to answer. This business course will introduce you to a wide array of employment opportunities. In private enterprise, these range from small, local businesses owned by one individual to large companies such as American Express and Marriott International. There are also employment opportunities with federal, state, county, and local governments and with not-for-profit organizations such as the Red Cross and Save the Children. For help in deciding what career might be right for you, read Appendix B: Careers in Business, which appears at the end of this text.

In addition to career information in Appendix B, a number of additional websites provide information about career development. For more information, visit the following sites:

- Career Builder at **www.careerbuilder.com**
- Career One Stop at **www.careeronestop.org**
- Monster at **www.monster.com**
- Yahoo! Hot Jobs at **http://hotjobs.yahoo.com**

One thing to remember as you think about what your ideal career might be is that a person's choice of a career ultimately is just a reflection of what he or she values and holds most important. What will give one individual personal satisfaction may not satisfy another. For example, one person may dream of a career as a corporate executive and becoming a millionaire before the age of thirty. Another may choose a career that has more modest monetary rewards but that provides the opportunity to help others. One person may be willing to work long hours and seek additional responsibility in order to get promotions and pay raises. Someone else may prefer a less demanding job with little stress and more free time. What you choose to do with your life will be based on what you feel is most important. And the *you* is a very important part of that decision.

Managing Your Career

Interviewing the Interviewer

Part of getting ready for a job interview is practicing answers to questions such as "What are your strengths and weaknesses?" Being prepared with questions to ask the interviewer is just as important. If you have no questions, the interviewer may think you don't care about the job or haven't given much thought to the interview. Here are a few questions to keep the conversation flowing and help you make up your mind about a particular position:

- What are the main challenges I can expect to face in this job? (Learn as much as you can about potential problems upfront.)
- What skills and training are especially critical to success in this job? (See whether your qualifications fit the job.)
- What are the company's goals and how would an effective employee in this job help achieve those goals? (Find out where the company is headed and how this job contributes to its success.)

- Why is this job open at this time? (Learn whether the last person in this job was promoted, transferred, or let go.)
- How will you measure success in this job? (Understand how job performance will be assessed.)

One final question to ask, tactfully: "When do you expect to make a decision about hiring for this position?"

Sources: "Ask and Ye May Receive . . . That Job You Want," *Associated Press,* April 24, 2009, http://www.msnbc.msn.com/id/30314963/; Maureen Moriarty, "Workplace Coach: What Not to Do During the Job Interview," *Seattle Post-Intelligencer,* August 10, 2008, http://seattlepi.nwsource.com/business/374357_workcoach11.html; Marshall Krantz, "Nine Things to Ask Your Future Boss, the CEO," *CFO.com,* September 4, 2008, www.cfo.com.

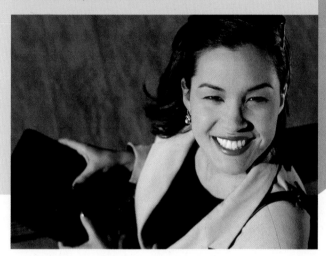

To Be a Successful Employee Deciding on the type of career you want is only a first step. To get a job in your chosen field and to be successful at it, you will have to develop a plan, or road map, that ensures that you have the skills and knowledge the job requires. You will be expected to have both the technical skills needed to accomplish a specific task and the ability to work well with many types of people in a culturally diverse workforce. **Cultural (or workplace) diversity** refers to the differences among people in a workforce owing to race, ethnicity, and gender. These skills, together with a working knowledge of the American business system, can give you an inside edge when you are interviewing with a prospective employer.

This course, your instructor, and all the resources available at your college or university can help you to acquire the skills and knowledge you will need for a successful career. But don't underestimate your part in making your dream a reality. It will take hard work, dedication, perseverance, and time management to achieve your goals. Communication skills are also important. Today, most employers are looking for employees who can compose a business letter and get it in mailable form. They also want employees who can talk with customers and use e-mail to communicate with people within and outside the organization. Employers also will be interested in any work experience you may have had in cooperative work/school programs, during summer vacations, or in part-time jobs during the school year. These things can make a difference when it is time to apply for the job you really want.

To Start Your Own Business Some people prefer to work for themselves, and they open their own businesses. To be successful, business owners must possess many of the same skills that successful employees have. And they must be willing to work hard and put in long hours.

cultural (or workplace) diversity differences among people in a workforce owing to race, ethnicity, and gender

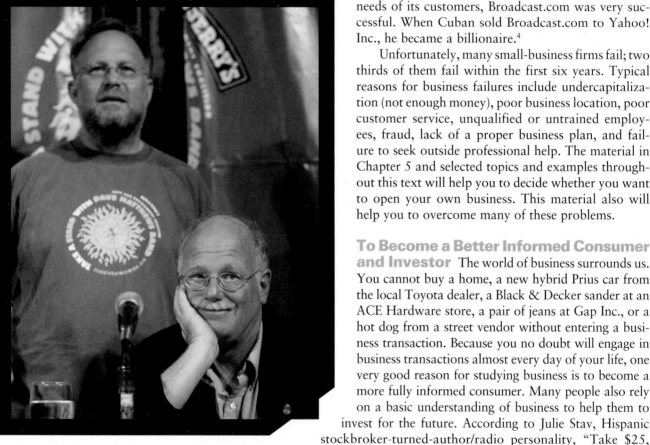

Meet Ben & Jerry. Back in 1978, Jerry Greenfield (left) and Ben Cohen (right) invested $8,000 and borrowed an additional $4,000 to start Ben and Jerry's Homemade Ice Cream in Burlington, Vermont. Today, over 30 years later, the one original store has grown into a chain of ice cream shops that delight customers with flavors like Turtle Soup, Neapolitan Dynamite, and Imagine Whirled Peace. Obviously, their business was a success—just ask any of their customers.

It also helps if your small business can provide a product or service that customers want. For example, Mark Cuban started a small Internet company called Broadcast.com that provided hundreds of live and on-demand audio and video programs ranging from rap music to sporting events to business events over the Internet. And because Cuban's company met the needs of its customers, Broadcast.com was very successful. When Cuban sold Broadcast.com to Yahoo! Inc., he became a billionaire.[4]

Unfortunately, many small-business firms fail; two thirds of them fail within the first six years. Typical reasons for business failures include undercapitalization (not enough money), poor business location, poor customer service, unqualified or untrained employees, fraud, lack of a proper business plan, and failure to seek outside professional help. The material in Chapter 5 and selected topics and examples throughout this text will help you to decide whether you want to open your own business. This material also will help you to overcome many of these problems.

To Become a Better Informed Consumer and Investor The world of business surrounds us. You cannot buy a home, a new hybrid Prius car from the local Toyota dealer, a Black & Decker sander at an ACE Hardware store, a pair of jeans at Gap Inc., or a hot dog from a street vendor without entering a business transaction. Because you no doubt will engage in business transactions almost every day of your life, one very good reason for studying business is to become a more fully informed consumer. Many people also rely on a basic understanding of business to help them to invest for the future. According to Julie Stav, Hispanic stockbroker-turned-author/radio personality, "Take $25, add to it drive plus determination and then watch it multiply into an empire."[5] The author of *Get Your Share,* a *New York Times* bestseller, believes that it is important to learn the basics about the economy and business, stocks, mutual funds, and other alternatives before investing your money. And while this is an obvious conclusion, just dreaming of being rich doesn't make it happen. In fact, like many facets of life, it takes planning and determination to establish the type of investment program that will help you to accomplish your financial goals.

Special Note to Students

It is important to begin reading this text with one thing in mind: *This business course does not have to be difficult.* In fact, *learning about business and how you can be involved as an employee, business owner, consumer, or investor can be fun!*

We have done everything possible to eliminate the problems that students encounter in a typical class. All the features in each chapter have been evaluated and recommended by instructors with years of teaching experience. In addition, business students were asked to critique each chapter component. Based on this feedback, the text includes the following features:

- *Learning objectives* appear at the beginning of each chapter.
- *Inside Business* is a chapter-opening case that highlights how successful companies do business on a day-to-day basis.
- *Margin notes* are used throughout the text to reinforce both learning objectives and key terms.

- *Boxed features* highlight environmental issues, career information, starting a business, ethical behavior, and the economic crisis.
- *Spotlight* features highlight interesting facts about business and society and often provide a real-world example of an important concept within a chapter.
- *End-of-chapter materials* provide a chapter summary, a list of key terms, discussion questions, a "Test Yourself" quiz, and a video case. The last section of every chapter is entitled Building Skills for Career Success and includes exercises devoted to exploring the Internet, building team skills, and researching different careers.
- *End-of-part materials* provide a continuing video case about the Finagle A Bagel company that operates a chain of retail outlets in the northeastern section of the United States. Also at the end of each major part is an exercise designed to help you to develop the components that are included in a typical business plan.

In addition to the text, a number of student supplements will help you to explore the world of business. We are especially proud of the website that accompanies this edition. There, you will find online study aids, including interactive study tools, practice tests, games for each chapter, flashcards, and other resources. If you want to take a look at the Internet support materials available for this edition of *Foundations of Business*.

1. Make an Internet connection and go to www.cengage.com/introbusiness/pride.
2. Click on the Book Companion Site link and choose Select a Chapter.

As authors, we want you to be successful. We know that your time is valuable and that your schedule is crowded with many different activities. We also appreciate the fact that textbooks are expensive. Therefore, we want you to use this text and get the most out of your investment. In order to help you get off to a good start, a number of suggestions for developing effective study skills and using this text are provided in Table 1.1. Why not take a look at these suggestions and use them to help you succeed in this course and earn a higher grade. Remember what Joe Dudley said, "Success is a journey, not a destination."

Concept Check

1. What reasons would you give if you were advising someone to study business?

2. What factors affect a person's choice of careers?

3. Once you have a job, what steps can you take to be successful?

TABLE 1.1: Seven Ways to Use This Text and Its Resources

1. Prepare before you go to class.	Early preparation is the key to success in many of life's activities. Certainly, early preparation can help you to participate in class, ask questions, and improve your performance on exams.
2. Read the chapter.	Although it may seem like an obvious suggestion, many students never take the time to really read the material. Find a quiet space where there are no distractions, and invest enough time to become a "content expert."
3. Underline or highlight important concepts.	Make this text yours. Don't be afraid to write on the pages of your text. It is much easier to review material if you have identified important concepts.
4. Take notes.	While reading, take the time to jot down important points and summarize concepts in your own words. Also, take notes in class.
5. Apply the concepts.	Learning is always easier if you can apply the content to your real-life situation. Think about how you could use the material either now or in the future.
6. Practice critical thinking.	Test the material in the text. Do the concepts make sense? To build critical-thinking skills, answer the questions that accompany the cases at the end of each chapter. Also, many of the exercises in the Building Skills for Career Success require critical thinking.
7. Prepare for exams.	Allow enough time to review the material before exams. Check out the summary and questions at the end of the chapter. Then use the resources on the text website.

Since a text always should be evaluated by the students and instructors who use it, we would welcome and sincerely appreciate your comments and suggestions. Please feel free to contact us by using one of the following e-mail addresses:

Bill Pride: **w-pride@tamu.edu**
Bob Hughes: **bhughes@dcccd.edu**
Jack Kapoor: **kapoorj@cdnet.cod.edu**

Business: A Definition

Business is the organized effort of individuals to produce and sell, for a profit, the goods and services that satisfy society's needs. The general term *business* refers to all such efforts within a society (as in "American business") or within an industry (as in "the steel business"). However, *a business* is a particular organization, such as Kraft Foods, Inc., or Cracker Barrel Old Country Stores. To be successful, a business must perform three activities. It must be organized. It must satisfy needs. And it must earn a profit.

The Organized Effort of Individuals

For a business to be organized, it must combine four kinds of resources: material, human, financial, and informational. *Material* resources include the raw materials used in manufacturing processes, as well as buildings and machinery. For example, Sara Lee Corporation needs flour, sugar, butter, eggs, and other raw materials to produce the food products it sells worldwide. In addition, this Illinois-based company needs human, financial, and informational resources. *Human* resources are the people who furnish their labor and talents to the business in return for wages. The *financial* resource is the money required to pay employees, purchase materials, and generally keep the business operating. And *information* is the resource that tells the managers of the business how effectively the other resources are being combined and used (see Figure 1.1).

Today, businesses usually are organized as one of three specific types. *Manufacturing businesses* process various materials into tangible goods, such as delivery trucks or furniture. Intel, for example, produces computer chips that, in turn, are sold to companies that manufacture computers. *Service businesses* produce services, such as haircuts, legal advice, or tax preparation. And some firms called *marketing intermediaries* buy products from manufacturers and then resell them. Sony Corporation is a manufacturer that produces stereo equipment, among other things. These products may be sold to a marketing intermediary such as Best Buy, which then resells the manufactured goods to consumers in their retail stores.

Satisfying Needs

The ultimate objective of every firm must be to satisfy the needs of its customers. People generally do not buy goods and services simply to own them; they buy products and services to satisfy particular needs. Some of us may feel that the need for transportation is best satisfied by an air-conditioned BMW with stereo compact-disc player, automatic transmission, power seats and windows, and

business the organized effort of individuals to produce and sell, for a profit, the goods and services that satisfy society's needs

FIGURE 1.1: Combining Resources A business must combine all four resources effectively to be successful.

Human resources → BUSINESS ← Informational resources
Material resources → BUSINESS ← Financial resources

remote-control side mirrors. Others may believe that a small Smart car will do just fine. Both products are available to those who want them, along with a wide variety of other products that satisfy the need for transportation.

When firms lose sight of their customers' needs, they are likely to find the going rough. However, when businesses understand their customers' needs and work to satisfy those needs, they are usually successful. Back in 1962, Sam Walton opened his first discount store in Rogers, Arkansas. Although the original store was quite different from the Wal-Mart Superstores you see today, the basic ideas of providing customer service and offering goods that satisfied needs at low prices are part of the reason why this firm has grown to become the largest retailer in the world. Although Wal-Mart has more than 4,100 retail stores in the United States and more than 3,100 retail stores in thirteen different countries, this highly successful discount-store organization continues to open new stores to meet the needs of its customers around the globe.[6]

Business Profit

A business receives money (sales revenue) from its customers in exchange for goods or services. It also must pay out money to cover the expenses involved in doing business. If the firm's sales revenues are greater than its expenses, it has earned a profit. More specifically, as shown in Figure 1.2, **profit** is what remains after all business expenses have been deducted from sales revenue. A negative profit, which results when a firm's expenses are greater than its sales revenue, is called a *loss*. A business cannot continue to operate at a loss for an indefinite period of time. One of the big concerns during the recent economic crisis was the fear that the number of business failures would increase. As the crisis worsened, the fear became a reality as an increasing number of both small and large businesses experienced reduced sales revenues and losses and eventually failed. To avoid failure and improve a firm's chances of success, management and employees must find some way to increase sales revenues and/or reduce expenses in order to return to profitability. If some specific actions aren't taken to eliminate losses, a firm may be forced to file for bankruptcy protection.

In some cases, the pursuit of profits is so important that some corporate executives, including those from such corporations as Enron, WorldCom, and mortgage-lenders Fannie Mae and Freddie Mac have fudged their profit figures to avoid disappointing shareholders, directors, Wall Street analysts, lenders, and other stakeholders. The term **stakeholders** is used to describe all the different people or groups of people who are affected by the decisions made by an organization.

©morgueFile.com

Oil or wind power? To protect the environment as well as to reduce our dependence on foreign nations, many utility companies are developing alternative energy sources such as "wind power." Once developed, these new energy sources may actually be cheaper than using foreign oil. For business firms, reduced energy costs can increase profits. For consumers, reduced energy costs can mean there is more money for spending or investing.

profit what remains after all business expenses have been deducted from sales revenue

stakeholders all the different people or groups of people who are affected by the decisions made by an organization

Concept Check

1. Describe the four resources that must be combined to organize and operate a business.

2. What is the difference between a manufacturing business, a service business, and a marketing intermediary?

3. Explain the relationship among profit, business risk, and the satisfaction of customers' needs.

FIGURE 1.2: The Relationship Between Sales Revenue and Profit Profit is what remains after all business expenses have been deducted from sales revenue.

Sales revenue	
Expenses	Profit

The profit earned by a business becomes the property of its owners. Thus, in one sense, profit is the reward business owners receive for producing goods and services that consumers want. Profit is also the payment that business owners receive for assuming the considerable risks of ownership. One of these is the risk of not being paid. Everyone else—employees, suppliers, and lenders—must be paid before the owners.

A second risk that owners assume is the risk of losing whatever they have invested into the business. A business that cannot earn a profit is very likely to fail, in which case the owners lose whatever money, effort, and time they have invested.

To satisfy society's needs and make a profit, a business must operate within the parameters of a nation's economic system. In the next section, we define economics and describe two different types of economic systems.

LEARNING OBJECTIVE 3

Define economics and describe the two types of economic systems: capitalism and command economy.

Types of Economic Systems

Economics is the study of how wealth is created and distributed. By *wealth*, we mean "anything of value," including the products produced and sold by business. *How wealth is distributed* simply means "who gets what." Experts often use economics to explain the choices we make and how those choices change as we cope with the demands of everyday life. In simple terms, individuals, businesses, governments, and society must make decisions that reflect what is important to each group at a particular time. For example, you want to take a weekend trip to some exotic vacation spot, and you also want to begin an investment program. Because of your financial resources, though, you cannot do both. You must decide what is most important. Business firms, governments, and to some extent society face the same types of decisions. And each group must deal with scarcity when making important decisions. In this case, *scarcity* means "lack of resources"—money, time, natural resources, etc.—that are needed to satisfy a want or need.

Today, experts often study economic problems from two different perspectives: microeconomics and macroeconomics. **Microeconomics** is the study of the decisions made by individuals and businesses. Microeconomics, for example, examines how the prices of homes affect the number of homes built and sold. On the other hand, **macroeconomics** is the study of the national economy and the global economy. Macroeconomics examines the economic effect of taxes, government spending, interest rates, and similar factors on a nation and society. With record home foreclosures, troubled banks on the verge of failure, and stock values dropping on Wall Street, a real application of macroeconomics occurred when the U.S. Congress enacted and President Bush signed the Emergency Economic Stabilization Act of 2008. The **Emergency Economic Stabilization Act** was a $700 billion bailout plan created to stabilize the nation's economy and restore confidence in the banking and financial industries. While the politicians, the president, economists, business leaders, and the general public still debate the merits of a federal rescue plan, one factor became very apparent. Something had to be done to correct what some experts described as the nation's worst economic problems since the Great Depression.

The decisions that individuals, business firms, government, and society make and the way in which people deal with the creation and distribution of wealth determine the kind of economic system, or **economy**, that a nation has.

Over the years, the economic systems of the world have differed in essentially two ways: (1) the ownership of the factors of production and (2) how they answer four basic economic questions that direct a nation's economic activity. **Factors of production** are the resources used to produce goods and services. There are four such factors:

- *Land and natural resources*—elements that can be used in the production process to make appliances, automobiles, and other products. Typical examples include crude oil, forests, minerals, land, water, and even air.
- *Labor*—the time and effort that we use to produce goods and services. It includes human resources such as managers and employees.
- *Capital*—the money, facilities, equipment, and machines used in the operation of organizations. While most people think of capital as just money, it also can

economics the study of how wealth is created and distributed

microeconomics the study of the decisions made by individuals and businesses

macroeconomics the study of the national economy and the global economy

Emergency Economic Stabilization Act a $700 billion bailout plan created to stabilize the nation's economy and restore confidence in the banking and financial industries

economy the way in which people deal with the creation and distribution of wealth

factors of production resources used to produce goods and services

Part 1: The Environment of Business

Land and natural resources can be beautiful. Business firms that operate in any type of economic system must use land and natural resources in order to be successful. And yet, today's business owners and managers are very much aware of the concept of sustainability and protecting our planet.

be the manufacturing equipment in a Coca Cola bottling facility or a computer used in the corporate offices of McDonald's.

- *Entrepreneurship*—the resource that organizes land, labor, and capital. It is the willingness to take risks and the knowledge and ability to use the other factors of production efficiently. An **entrepreneur** is a person who risks his or her time, effort, and money to start and operate a business.

A nation's economic system significantly affects all the economic activities of its citizens. This far-reaching impact becomes more apparent when we consider that a country's economic system determines how the factors of production are used to meet the needs of society. Today, two different economic systems exist: capitalism and command economies. The way each system answers the four basic economic questions below determines a nation's economy.

1. What goods and services—and how much of each—will be produced?
2. How will these goods and services be produced?
3. For whom will these goods and services be produced?
4. Who owns and who controls the major factors of production?

Capitalism

Capitalism is an economic system in which individuals own and operate the majority of businesses that provide goods and services. Capitalism stems from the theories of the eighteenth-century Scottish economist Adam Smith. In his book *Wealth of Nations,* published in 1776, Smith argued that a society's interests are best served when the individuals within that society are allowed to pursue their own self-interest. In other words, people will work hard and invest long hours to produce goods and services only if they can reap the rewards of their labor—more pay or profits in the case of a business owner. According to Smith, when an individual is acting to improve his or her own fortunes, he or she indirectly promotes the good of his or her community and the people in that community. Smith went on to call this concept the "invisible hand." The **invisible hand** is a term created by Adam Smith to describe how an individual's own personal gain benefits others and a nation's economy. For example, the only way a small-business owner who produces shoes can increase personal wealth is to sell shoes to customers. To become even more prosperous, the small-business owner must hire workers to produce even more shoes. According to the invisible hand, people in the small-business owner's community not only would have shoes, but some workers also would have jobs working for the shoemaker. Thus, the success of people in the community and, to some extent, the nation's economy is tied indirectly to the success of the small-business owner.

entrepreneur a person who risks time, effort, and money to start and operate a business

capitalism an economic system in which individuals own and operate the majority of businesses that provide goods and services

invisible hand a term created by Adam Smith to describe how an individual's own personal gain benefits others and a nation's economy

©Getty Images RF

FIGURE 1.3: Basic Assumptions for Adam Smith's Laissez-Faire Capitalism

Laissez-faire capitalism

Right to create wealth

Right to own private property and resources

Right to economic freedom and freedom to compete

Right to limited government intervention

Adam Smith's capitalism is based on the four fundamental issues described below (see Figure 1.3).

1. The creation of wealth is properly the concern of private individuals, not government.
2. Private individuals must own private property and the resources used to create wealth.
3. Economic freedom ensures the existence of competitive markets that allow both sellers and buyers to enter and exit the market as they choose.
4. The role of government should be limited to providing defense against foreign enemies, ensuring internal order, and furnishing public works and education.

market economy an economic system in which businesses and individuals decide what to produce and buy, and the market determines quantities sold and prices

mixed economy an economy that exhibits elements of both capitalism and socialism

One factor that Smith felt was extremely important was the role of government. He believed government should act only as rule maker and umpire. The French term *laissez faire* describes Smith's capitalistic system and implies that there should be no government interference in the economy. Loosely translated, this term means "let them do" (as they see fit).

Adam Smith's laissez faire capitalism is also based on the concept of a market economy. A **market economy** (sometimes referred to as a *free-market economy*) is an economic system in which businesses and individuals decide what to produce and buy, and the market determines prices and quantities sold. The owners of resources should be free to determine how those resources are used and also should be free to enjoy the income, profits, and other benefits derived from ownership of those resources.

Capitalism in the United States

Our economic system is rooted in the laissez-faire capitalism of Adam Smith. However, our real-world economy is not as laissez-faire as Smith would have liked because government participates as more than umpire and rule maker. Our economy is, in fact, a **mixed economy**, one that exhibits elements of both capitalism and socialism.

In a mixed economy, the four basic economic questions discussed at the beginning of this section (what, how, for whom, and who) are answered through the interaction of households, businesses, and governments. The interactions among these three groups are shown in Figure 1.4.

Households Households, made up of individuals, are the consumers of goods and services, as well as owners of some of the factors of production. As *resource owners,* the members of households

A sign of the times! Although there were many problems associated with the recent financial crisis, one that really hit home was a record number of home foreclosures. In the midst of the crisis, approximately 10 percent of American homeowners were either behind on their payments or in foreclosure according to the Mortgage Bankers Association.

Part 1: The Environment of Business

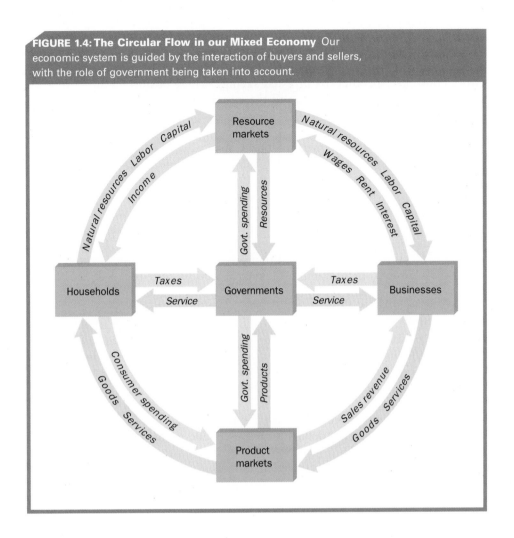

FIGURE 1.4: The Circular Flow in our Mixed Economy Our economic system is guided by the interaction of buyers and sellers, with the role of government being taken into account.

provide businesses with labor, capital, and other resources. In return, businesses pay wages, rent, and dividends and interest, which households receive as income.

As *consumers*, household members use their income to purchase the goods and services produced by business. Today, approximately 70 percent of our nation's total production consists of **consumer products**—goods and services purchased by individuals for personal consumption.[7] This means that consumers, as a group, are the biggest customers of American business.

Businesses Like households, businesses are engaged in two different exchanges. They exchange money for natural resources, labor, and capital and use those resources to produce goods and services. Then they exchange their goods and services for sales revenue. This sales revenue, in turn, is exchanged for additional resources, which are used to produce and sell more goods and services. Thus, the circular flow of Figure 1.4 is continuous.

Along the way, of course, business owners would like to remove something from the circular flow in the form of profits. And households try to retain some income as savings. But are profits and savings really removed from the flow? Usually not! When the economy is running smoothly, households are willing to invest their savings in businesses. They can do so directly by buying stocks in businesses, by purchasing shares in mutual funds that purchase stocks in businesses, or by lending money to businesses. They also can invest indirectly by placing their savings in bank accounts. Banks and other financial institutions then invest these savings as part of their normal business operations.

consumer products goods and services purchased by individuals for personal consumption

When business profits are distributed to business owners, these profits become household income. (Business owners are, after all, members of households.) And, as we saw, household income is retained in the circular flow as either consumer spending or invested savings. Thus, business profits, too, are retained in the business system, and the circular flow is complete. How, then, does government fit in?

Governments The framers of our Constitution desired as little government interference with business as possible. At the same time, the United States Constitution sets forth the responsibility of government to protect and promote the public welfare. Local, state, and federal governments discharge this responsibility through regulation and the provision of services. The numerous government services are important but either (1) would not be produced by private business firms or (2) would be produced only for those who could afford them. Typical services include national defense, police and fire protection, education, and construction of roads and highways. In addition to the typical services citizens expect, the government recently has created a number of stimulus packages in an attempt to improve the nation's sagging economy. These programs, which will cost American taxpayers billions of dollars, are designed to reduce the effects of the economic crisis, move the economy from recession to recovery, improve regulation of financial and insurance firms, and eliminate the problems that caused the nation's economic downturn. To pay for all these services, governments collect a variety of taxes from households (such as personal income taxes and sales taxes) and from businesses (corporate income taxes).

Figure 1.4 shows this exchange of taxes for government services. It also shows government spending of tax dollars for resources and products required to provide those services.

Actually, with government included, our circular flow looks more like a combination of several flows. In reality, it is. The important point is that together the various flows make up a single unit—a complete economic system that effectively provides answers to the basic economic questions. Simply put, the system works.

Command Economies

Before we discuss how to measure a nation's economic performance, we look quickly at another economic system called a *command economy*. A **command economy** is an economic system in which the government decides what goods and services will be produced, how they will be produced, for whom available goods and services will be produced, and who owns and controls the major factors of production. The answers to all four basic economic questions are determined, at least to some degree, through centralized government planning. Today, two types of economic systems— *socialism and communism*—serve as examples of command economies.

Socialism In a socialist economy, the key industries are owned and controlled by the government. Such industries usually include transportation, utilities, communications, banking, and industries producing important materials such as steel. Land, buildings, and raw materials also may be the property of the state in a socialist economy. Depending on the country, private ownership of smaller businesses is permitted to varying degrees. People usually may choose their own occupations, but many work in state-owned industries.

In a socialist economy,

- What to produce and how to produce it are determined in accordance with national goals, which are based on projected needs and the availability of resources.
- The distribution of goods and services—who gets-what—is also controlled by the state to the extent that it controls taxes, rents, and wages.

command economy an economic system in which the government decides what goods and services will be produced, how they will be produced, for whom available goods and services will be produced, and who owns and controls the major factors of production

Among the professed aims of socialist countries are the equitable distribution of income, the elimination of poverty, the distribution of social services (such as medical care) to all who need them, and the elimination of the economic waste that supposedly accompanies capitalistic competition. The disadvantages of socialism include increased taxation and loss of incentive and motivation for both individuals and business owners.

Today, many of the nations that traditionally have been labeled as socialist nations, including France, Sweden, and India, are transitioning to a free-market economy. And currently, many countries that once were thought of as communist countries are now often referred to as socialist countries. Examples of former communist countries often referred to as socialists (or even capitalist) include most of the nations that were formerly part of the Union of Soviet Socialist Republics (USSR), China, and Vietnam.

Communism If Adam Smith was the father of capitalism, Karl Marx was the father of communism. In his writings during the mid-nineteenth century, Marx advocated a classless society whose citizens together owned all economic resources. All workers then would contribute to this *communist* society according to their ability and would receive benefits according to their need.

Since the breakup of the Soviet Union and economic reforms in China and most of the Eastern European countries, the best remaining examples of communism are North Korea and Cuba. Today these so-called communist economies seem to practice a strictly controlled kind of socialism.

Typical conditions in a communist economy include:

- The government owns almost all economic resources.
- The basic economic questions are answered through centralized state plans.
- Emphasis is placed on the production of goods the government needs rather than on the products that consumers might want, so there are frequent shortages of consumer goods.

In a communist country, workers have little choice of jobs, but special skills or talents seem to be rewarded with special privileges. Various groups of professionals (bureaucrats, university professors, and athletes, for example) fare much better than, say, factory workers.

Measuring Economic Performance

Today, it is hard to turn on the radio, watch the news on television, or read the newspaper without hearing or seeing something about the economy. Consider for just a moment the following questions:

- Are U.S. workers as productive as workers in other countries?
- Is the gross domestic product for the United States increasing or decreasing?
- Why is the unemployment rate important?

The information needed to answer these questions, along with the answers to other similar questions, is easily obtainable from many sources. More important, the answers to these and other questions can be used to gauge the economic health of a nation.

The Importance of Productivity in the Global Marketplace

One way to measure a nation's economic performance is to assess its productivity. **Productivity** is the average level of output per worker per hour. An increase in productivity results in economic growth because a larger number of goods and services are produced by a given labor force. Productivity growth in the United States has increased dramatically over the last several years. For example, overall productivity

Concept Check

1. What are the four basic economic questions? How are they answered in a capitalist economy?

2. Describe the four basic assumptions required for a laissez-faire capitalist economy.

3. Why is the American economy called a mixed economy?

4. How does capitalism differ from socialism and communism?

4 LEARNING OBJECTIVE

Identify the ways to measure economic performance.

productivity the average level of output per worker per hour growth averaged 2.5 percent for the period from 1995 through 2008.[8] (*Note:* At the time of publication, 2008 was the last year that complete statistics were available.) This is an extraordinary statistic when compared against historical standards. And yet, before you think that all the nation's productivity problems are solved, consider the following questions:

Question: *How does productivity growth affect the economy?*

Answer: Because of productivity growth, it now takes fewer workers to produce products. As a result, employers have reduced costs, earned more profits, and/or sold their products for less. Finally, productivity growth helps American business to compete more effectively with other nations in a competitive world.

Question: *How does a nation improve productivity?*

Answer: Reducing costs and enabling employees to work more efficiently are at the core of all attempts to improve productivity. Methods used to increase productivity are discussed in detail in Chapter 8.

Question: *Is productivity growth always good?*

Answer: While economists always point to increased efficiency and the ability to produce goods and services for lower costs as a positive factor, fewer workers producing more goods and services can lead to higher unemployment rates. In this case, increased productivity is good for employers but not good for unemployed workers seeking jobs in a very competitive work environment.

Employers in Japan, China, Korea, Taiwan, Germany, and other countries throughout the world are also concerned about productivity. For example, consider the economic growth of China. About 200 years ago, Napoleon returned from China and said, "That is a sleeping dragon. Let him sleep! If he wakes up he will shake the world."[9] Today, China is awake and is shaking the world. Increased productivity has enabled the Chinese to manufacture products that range from trinkets to sophisticated electronic and computer products. And China is just one country. There are many other countries that understand the economic benefits of increased productivity.

Important Economic Indicators That Measure a Nation's Economy

In addition to productivity, a measure called *gross domestic product* can be used to measure the economic well-being of a nation. **Gross domestic product (GDP)** is the total dollar value of all goods and services produced by all people within the boundaries of a country during a one-year period. For example, the value of automobiles produced by employees in both an American-owned Ford plant and a Japanese-owned Toyota plant *in the United States* are both included in the GDP for the United States. The U.S. GDP was $14.3 trillion in 2008.[10] The GDP figure facilitates comparisons between the United States and other countries because it is the standard used in international guidelines for economic accounting. It is also possible to compare the GDP for one nation over several different time periods. This comparison allows observers to determine the extent to which a nation is experiencing economic growth.

To make accurate comparisons of the GDP for different years, we must adjust the dollar amounts for inflation. **Inflation** is a general rise in the level of prices. (The opposite of inflation is deflation.) **Deflation** is a general decrease

gross domestic product (GDP) the total dollar value of all goods and services produced by all people within the boundaries of a country during a one-year period

inflation a general rise in the level of prices

deflation a general decrease in the level of prices

©Diego Cervo/Shutterstock

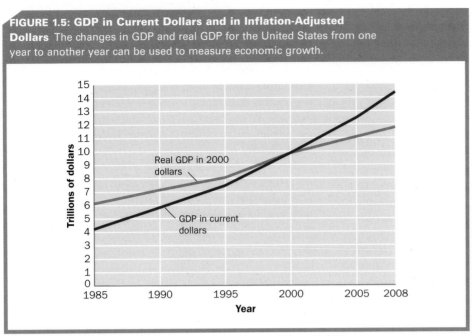

FIGURE 1.5: GDP in Current Dollars and in Inflation-Adjusted Dollars The changes in GDP and real GDP for the United States from one year to another year can be used to measure economic growth.

Source: U.S. Bureau of Economic Analysis website at www.bea.gov, accessed February 27, 2009.

in the level of prices. By using inflation-adjusted figures, we are able to measure the *real* GDP for a nation. In effect, it is now possible to compare the products and services produced by a nation in constant dollars—dollars that will purchase the same amount of goods and services. Figure 1.5 depicts the GDP of the United States in current dollars and the *real* GDP in inflation-adjusted dollars. Note that between 1985 and 2008, America's *real* GDP grew from $6.1 trillion to $11.7 trillion.[11]

TABLE 1.2: Common Measures Used to Evaluate a Nation's Economic Health

Economic Measure	Description
1. Balance of trade	The total value of a nation's exports minus the total value of its imports over a specific period of time.
2. Corporate profits	The total amount of profits made by corporations over selected time periods.
3. Inflation rate	An economic statistic that tracks the increase in prices of goods and services over a period of time. This measure usually is calculated on a monthly or an annual basis.
4. National income	The total income earned by various segments of the population, including employees, self-employed individuals, corporations, and other types of income.
5. New housing starts	The total number of new homes started during a specific time period.
6. Prime interest rate	The lowest interest rate that banks charge their most creditworthy customers.
7. Unemployment rate	The percentage of a nation's labor force that is unemployed at any time.

Concept Check

1. How does an increase in productivity affect business?

2. Define gross domestic product. Why is this economic measure significant?

3. How does inflation affect the prices you pay for goods and services?

4. How is the producer price index related to the consumer price index?

Global Economic Challenges

Cycling through the Business Cycle

How do companies prepare for the ups and downs of the global business cycle? First they need to recognize early warning signs of a significant change in economic activity. An early warning sign for the high-tech industry would be sales of commonly-used components such as memory chips. A downturn in chip sales—more than a momentary blip—suggests the economy is headed into recession; conversely, an upturn in chip sales usually indicates recovery ahead.

During the recent recession, after reporting month after month of lower sales, chip-maker Intel announced that chip sales were slowly but steadily increasing, especially in China and the United States. That's when Hewlett-Packard and other PC makers realized that the economic trough was behind them.

For furniture manufacturers, plumbing supply firms, home improvement retailers, and other businesses that profit from a boom in housing and office construction, the number of building permits is a leading economic indicator. When these businesses note that more permits are being issued in a particular area, they know to prepare for future growth.

However, the business cycle affects different industries in different ways. For example, if steel producers see more building permits being issued, they also have to look at worldwide conditions in the automotive industry before they crank up steel output.

Sources: Carole Vaporean, "Steel Demand Pick Up Seen Sluggish at Best in 2009," *Reuters,* April 29, 2009, www.reuters.com; Kathleen Madigan, "Leading Indicators Continue to Fall," *Wall Street Journal,* April 20, 2009, www.wsj.com; Matt Richtel, "Intel Says PC Sales Have Reached a Bottom and Forecasts Moderate Growth," *New York Times,* April 15, 2009, www.nytimes.com.

In addition to GDP and *real* GDP, other economic measures exist that can be used to evaluate a nation's economy. The **consumer price index (CPI)** is a monthly index that measures the changes in prices of a fixed basket of goods purchased by a typical consumer in an urban area. Goods listed in the CPI include food and beverages, transportation, housing, clothing, medical care, recreation, education and communication, and other goods and services. Economists often use the CPI to determine the effect of inflation on not only the nation's economy but also individual consumers. Another monthly index is the producer's price index. The **producer price index (PPI)** measures prices at the wholesale level. Since changes in the PPI reflect price increases or decreases at the wholesale level, the PPI is an accurate predictor of both changes in the CPI and prices that consumers will pay for many everyday necessities. Some additional terms are described in Table 1.2. Like the measures for GDP, these measures can be used to compare one economic statistic over different periods of time.

consumer price index (CPI) a monthly index that measures the changes in prices of a fixed basket of goods purchased by a typical consumer in an urban area

producer price index (PPI) an index that measures prices at the wholesale level

LEARNING OBJECTIVE 5

Examine the four different phases in the typical business cycle.

The Business Cycle

All industrialized nations of the world seek economic growth, full employment, and price stability. However, a nation's economy fluctuates rather than grows at a steady pace every year. In fact, if you were to graph the economic growth rate for a country such as the United States, it would resemble a roller coaster ride with peaks (high points) and troughs (low points). These fluctuations generally are referred to as the **business cycle**, that is, the recurrence of periods of growth and recession in a nation's economic activity. At the time of publication, the U.S. economy was in a recession caused by a depressed housing market and related problems in the banking and financial industries. Unemployment rates were high, and people were frightened by the prospects of a prolonged downturn in the economy. To help restore confidence in the economy, the Emergency Economic Stabilization Act was passed

business cycle the recurrence of periods of growth and recession in a nation's economic activity

recession two or more consecutive three-month periods of decline in a country's GDP by Congress and signed by president George W. Bush. This $700 billion bailout plan was designed to aid the nation's troubled banks and Wall Street firms and restore confidence in the nation's economy. The bill also contained provisions to help individuals weather the economic storm. It was the hope that the bailout plan along with an economic stimulus package enacted by Congress and signed by president Barack Obama in 2009 would help the nation turn the corner from recession to recovery.

A job search can be frustrating. Often a nation's unemployment rate is a key indicator that can gauge a nation's economy. In this photo, eager job applicants wait in line to interview with New York utility company Con Edison.

The changes that result from either growth or recession affect the amount of products and services that consumers are willing to purchase and, as a result, the amount of products and services produced by business firms. Generally, the business cycle consists of four states: the peak (sometimes called prosperity), recession, the trough, and recovery (sometimes called *expansion*).

During the *peak period*, unemployment is low, and total income is relatively high. As long as the economic outlook remains prosperous, consumers are willing to buy products and services. In fact, businesses often expand and offer new products and services during the peak period in order to take advantage of consumers' increased buying power.

Economists define a **recession** as two or more consecutive three-month periods of decline in a country's GDP. Because unemployment rises during a recession, total buying power declines. The pessimism that accompanies a recession often stifles both consumer and business spending. As buying power decreases, consumers tend to become more value conscious and reluctant to purchase frivolous or unnecessary items. In response to a recession, many businesses focus on the products and services that provide the most value to their customers. Economists define a **depression** as a severe recession that lasts longer than a recession. A depression is characterized by extremely high unemployment rates, low wages, reduced purchasing power, lack of confidence in the economy, and a general decrease in business activity. While many politicians, the president, economists, business leaders, and the general public debate if we are in a recession or a depression, one thing is certain, the economic problems that began in October 2007 have created the worst economic crisis the United States has experienced since the Great Depression.

Economists refer to the third phase of the business cycle as the *trough*. The trough of a recession or depression is the turning point when a nation's output and employment bottom out and reach their lowest levels. To offset the effects of recession and depression, the federal government uses both monetary and fiscal policies. **Monetary policies** are the Federal Reserve's decisions that determine the size of the supply of money in the nation and the level of interest rates. Through **fiscal policy**, the government can influence the amount of savings and expenditures by altering the tax structure and changing the levels of government spending.

Although the federal government collects approximately $2.5 trillion in annual revenues, the government often spends more than it receives, resulting in a **federal deficit**. For example, the government had a federal deficit for each year between 2002 and 2009. The total of all federal deficits is called the

depression a severe recession that lasts longer than a recession

monetary policies Federal Reserve decisions that determine the size of the supply of money in the nation and the level of interest rates

fiscal policy government influence on the amount of savings and expenditures; accomplished by altering the tax structure and by changing the levels of government spending

federal deficit a shortfall created when the federal government spends more in a fiscal year than it receives

Concept Check

1. What are the four steps in the typical business cycle?

2. At the time you are studying the material in this chapter, which phase of the business cycle do you think the U.S. economy in? Justify your answer.

3. How has the government used monetary policy and fiscal policy to reduce the effects of the economic crisis?

national debt. Today, the U.S. national debt is $11 trillion, or approximately $36,500 for every man, woman, and child in the United States.[12]

Some experts believe that effective use of monetary and fiscal policies can speed up recovery and reduce the amount of time the economy is in recession. *Recovery* (or *expansion*) is movement of the economy from recession or depression to prosperity. High unemployment rates decline, income increases, and both the ability and the willingness to buy rise.

Since World War II, business cycles have lasted from three to five years from one peak period to the next peak period. During the same time period, the average length of recessions has been eleven months.[13] While the Federal Reserve has used monetary policy to reduce the effects of a sagging economy and the federal government has implemented economic stimulus programs to increase consumer spending, the nation is still experiencing economic problems.

LEARNING OBJECTIVE 6

Outline the four types of competition.

Types of Competition

Our capitalist system ensures that individuals and businesses make the decisions about what to produce, how to produce it, and what price to charge for the product. Mattel, Inc., for example, can introduce new versions of its famous Barbie doll, license the Barbie name, change the doll's price and method of distribution, and attempt to produce and market Barbie in other countries or over the Internet at **www.mattel.com**. Our system also allows customers the right to choose between Mattel's products and those produced by competitors.

Competition like that between Mattel and other toy manufacturers is a necessary and extremely important by-product of capitalism. Business **competition** is essentially a rivalry among businesses for sales to potential customers. In a capitalistic economy, competition also ensures that a firm will survive only if it serves its customers well by providing products and services that meet needs. Economists recognize four different degrees of competition ranging from ideal, complete competition to no competition at all. These are perfect competition, monopolistic competition, oligopoly, and monopoly. For a quick overview of the different types of competition, including numbers of firms and examples for each type, look at Table 1.3.

Perfect Competition

Perfect (or pure) competition is the market situation in which there are many buyers and sellers of a product, and no single buyer or seller is powerful enough to affect the price of that product. Note that this definition includes several important ideas. First, we are discussing the market for a single product, say, bushels of wheat. Second, all sellers offer essentially the same product for sale. Third, all buyers and sellers know everything there is to know about the market (including, in our example, the prices that all sellers are asking for their wheat). And fourth, the overall market is not affected by the actions of any one buyer or seller.

national debt the total of all federal deficits

competition rivalry among businesses for sales to potential customers

perfect (or pure) competition the market situation in which there are many buyers and sellers of a product, and no single buyer or seller is powerful enough to affect the price of that product

TABLE 1.3: Four Different Types Of Competition The number of firms determines the degree of competition within an industry.

Type of Competition	Number of Business Firms or Suppliers	Real-World Examples
1. Perfect	Many	Corn, wheat, peanuts
2. Monopolistic	Many	Clothing, shoes, furniture
3. Oligopoly	Few	Automobiles, cereals
4. Monopoly	One	Software protected by copyright, local public utilities

When perfect competition exists, every seller should ask the same price that every other seller is asking. Why? Because if one seller wanted 50 cents more per bushel of wheat than all the others, that seller would not be able to sell a single bushel. Buyers could—and would—do better by purchasing wheat from the competition. On the other hand, a firm willing to sell below the going price would sell all its wheat quickly. But that seller would lose sales revenue (and profit) because buyers actually are willing to pay more.

In perfect competition, then, sellers—and buyers as well—must accept the going price. The price of each product is determined by the actions of *all buyers and all sellers together* through the forces of supply and demand.

The Basics of Supply and Demand The **supply** of a particular product is the quantity of the product that producers are willing to sell at each of various prices. Producers are rational people, so we would expect them to offer more of a product for sale at higher prices and to offer less of the product at lower prices, as illustrated by the supply curve in Figure 1.6.

The **demand** for a particular product is the quantity that buyers are willing to purchase at each of various prices. Buyers, too, are usually rational, so we would expect them—as a group—to buy more of a product when its price is low and to buy less of the product when its price is high, as depicted by the demand curve in Figure 1.6.

The Equilibrium, or Market, Price There is always one certain price at which the demanded quantity of a product is exactly equal to the quantity of that product produced. Suppose that producers are willing to *supply* 2 million bushels of wheat at a price of $8 per bushel and that buyers are willing to *purchase* 2 million bushels at a price of $8 per bushel. In other words, supply and demand are in balance, or in equilibrium, at the price of $8. Economists call this price the *market price*. The **market price** of any product is the price at which the quantity demanded is equal to the quantity supplied. If suppliers produce 2 million bushels, then no one who is willing to pay $8 per bushel will have to go without wheat, and no producer who is willing to sell at $8 per bushel will be stuck with unsold wheat.

In theory and in the real world, market prices are affected by anything that affects supply and demand. The *demand* for wheat, for example, might change if

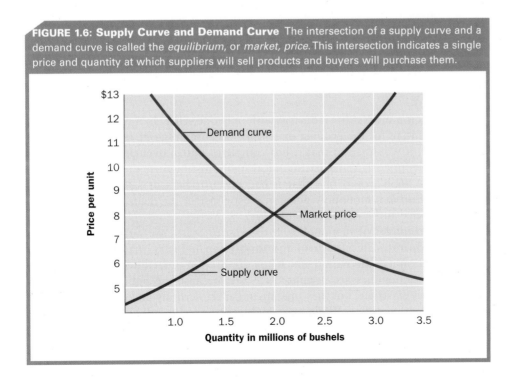

FIGURE 1.6: Supply Curve and Demand Curve The intersection of a supply curve and a demand curve is called the *equilibrium*, or *market, price*. This intersection indicates a single price and quantity at which suppliers will sell products and buyers will purchase them.

supply the quantity of a product that producers are willing to sell at each of various prices

demand the quantity of a product that buyers are willing to purchase at each of various prices

market price the price at which the quantity demanded is exactly equal to the quantity supplied researchers suddenly discovered that it offered a previously unknown health benefit. Then buyers would demand more wheat at every price. Or the *supply* of wheat might change if new technology permitted the production of greater quantities of wheat from the same amount of acreage. Other changes that can affect competitive prices are shifts in buyer tastes, the development of new products, fluctuations in income owing to inflation or recession, or even changes in the weather that affect the production of wheat.

Perfect competition is quite rare in today's world. Many real markets, however, are examples of monopolistic competition.

Monopolistic Competition

Monopolistic competition is a market situation in which there are many buyers along with a relatively large number of sellers. The various products available in a monopolistically competitive market are very similar in nature, and they are all intended to satisfy the same need. However, each seller attempts to make its product different from the others by providing unique product features, an attention-getting brand name, unique packaging, or services such as free delivery or a "lifetime" warranty.

Product differentiation is the process of developing and promoting differences between one's products and all similar products. It is a fact of life for the producers of many consumer goods, from soaps to clothing to furniture to shoes. A furniture manufacturer such as Thomasville sees what looks like a mob of competitors, all trying to chip away at its market. By differentiating each of its products from all similar products produced by competitors, Thomasville obtains some limited control over the market price of its product.

Oligopoly

An **oligopoly** is a market (or industry) situation in which there are few sellers. Generally, these sellers are quite large, and sizable investments are required to enter into their market. Examples of oligopolies are the automobile, airlines, car rental, cereal, and farm implement industries.

Because there are few sellers in an oligopoly, the market actions of each seller can have a strong effect on competitors' sales and prices. If General Motors, for example, reduces its automobile prices, Ford, Chrysler, Toyota, and Nissan usually do the same to retain their market shares. In the absence of much price competition, product differentiation becomes the major competitive weapon. This is very evident in the advertising of the major auto manufacturers. For instance, when General Motors began offering employee-discount pricing, Ford and Chrysler also launched competitive financing deals.

Monopoly

A **monopoly** is a market (or industry) with only one seller. In a monopoly, there is no close substitute for the product or service. Because only one firm is the supplier of a product, it would seem that it has complete control over price. However, no firm can set its price at some astronomical figure just because there is no competition; the firm soon would find that it had no customers or sales revenue either. Instead, the firm in a monopoly position must consider the demand for its product and set the price at the most profitable level.

Classic examples of monopolies in the United States are public utilities. Each utility firm operates in a **natural monopoly**, an industry that requires a huge investment in capital and within which any duplication of facilities would be wasteful. Natural monopolies are permitted to exist because the public interest is best served by their existence, but they operate under the scrutiny and control of various state and federal agencies. While many public utilities are still classified as natural monopolies, there is increased competition in many industries. For example, there have been increased demands for consumer choice when selecting a company that provides electrical service to both homes and businesses.

---

monopolistic competition a market situation in which there are many buyers along with a relatively large number of sellers who differentiate their products from the products of competitors

product differentiation the process of developing and promoting differences between one's products and all similar products

oligopoly a market (or industry) in which there are few sellers

monopoly a market (or industry) with only one seller

natural monopoly an industry requiring huge investments in capital and within which any duplication of facilities would be wasteful and thus not in the public interest

Concept Check

1. Is competition good for business? Is it good for consumers?

2. Compare the four forms of competition.

3. What is the relationship between supply and demand?

4. Explain how the equilibrium, or market, price of a product is determined.

A legal monopoly—sometimes referred to as a *limited monopoly*—is created when the federal government issues a copyright, patent, or trademark. Each of these exists for a specific period of time and can be used to protect the owners of written materials, ideas, or product brands from unauthorized use by competitors that have not shared in the time, effort, and expense required for their development. Because Microsoft owns the copyright on its popular Windows software, it enjoys a limited-monopoly position. Except for natural monopolies and monopolies created by copyrights, patents, and trademarks, federal antitrust laws prohibit both monopolies and attempts to form monopolies.

American Business Today

7 LEARNING OBJECTIVE
Summarize the factors that affect the business environment and the challenges American businesses will encounter in the future.

While our economic system is far from perfect, it provides Americans with a high standard of living compared with people in other countries throughout the world. **Standard of living** is a loose, subjective measure of how well off an individual or a society is mainly in terms of want satisfaction through goods and services. Also, our economic system offers solutions to many of the problems that plague society and provides opportunity for people who are willing to work and to continue learning.

To understand the current business environment and the challenges ahead, it helps to understand how business developed.

Early Business Development

Our American business system has its roots in the knowledge, skills, and values that the earliest settlers brought to this country. Refer to Figure 1.7 for an overall view of our nation's history, the development of our business system, and some major inventions that influenced the nation and our business system.

The first settlers in the New World were concerned mainly with providing themselves with basic necessities—food, clothing, and shelter. Almost all families lived on farms, and the entire family worked at the business of surviving. They used their surplus for trading, mainly by barter, among themselves and with the English trading ships that called at the colonies. **Barter** is a system of exchange in which goods or services are traded directly for other goods and/or services without using money. As this trade increased, small-scale business enterprises began to appear. Some settlers were able to use their skills and their excess time to work under the domestic system of production. The **domestic system** was a method of manufacturing in which an entrepreneur distributed raw materials to various homes, where families would process them into finished goods. The merchant entrepreneur then offered the goods for sale.

Then, in 1789, a young English apprentice mechanic named Samuel Slater decided to sail to America. At this time, British law forbade the export of machinery, technology, and skilled workers. To get around the law, Slater painstakingly memorized the plans for Richard Arkwright's water-powered spinning machine, which had revolutionized the British textile industry, and left England disguised as a farmer. A year later, he set up a textile factory in Pawtucket, Rhode Island, to spin raw cotton into thread. Slater's ingenuity resulted in America's first use of the **factory system** of manufacturing, in which all the materials, machinery, and workers required to manufacture a product are assembled in one place. The Industrial Revolution in America was born. A manufacturing technique called *specialization* was used to improve productivity. **Specialization** is the separation of a manufacturing process into distinct tasks and the assignment of the different tasks to different individuals.

The years from 1820 to 1900 were the golden age of invention and innovation in machinery. Elias Howe's sewing machine became available to convert materials into clothing. The agricultural machinery of John Deere and Cyrus McCormick revolutionized farm production. At the same time, new means of transportation greatly expanded the domestic markets for American products. Many business historians view the period from 1870 to 1900 as the second Industrial Revolution.

standard of living a loose, subjective measure of how well off an individual or a society is mainly in terms of want satisfaction through goods and services

barter a system of exchange in which goods or services are traded directly for other goods and/or services without using money

domestic system a method of manufacturing in which an entrepreneur distributes raw materials to various homes, where families process them into finished goods to be offered for sale by the merchant entrepreneur

factory system a system of manufacturing in which all the materials, machinery, and workers required to manufacture a product are assembled in one place

specialization the separation of a manufacturing process into distinct tasks and the assignment of the different tasks to different individuals

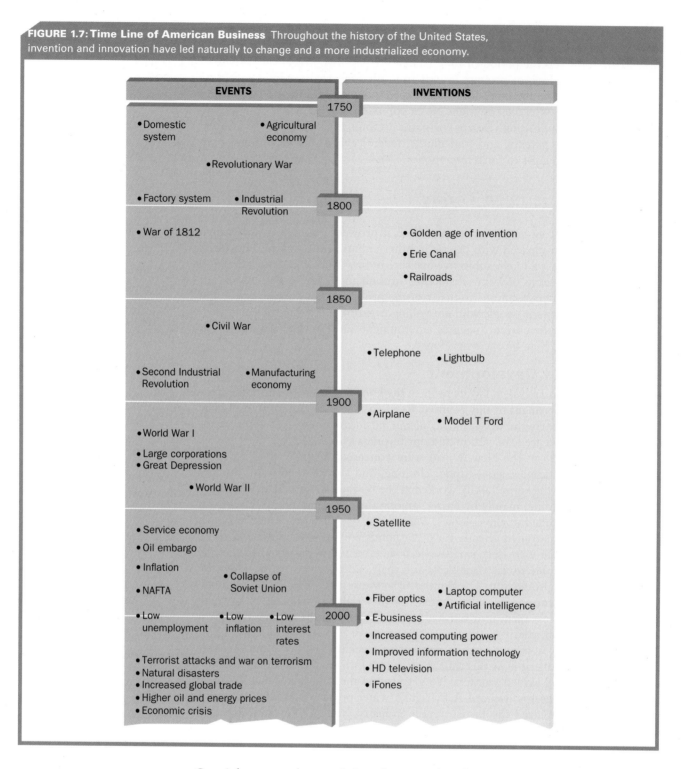

FIGURE 1.7: Time Line of American Business Throughout the history of the United States, invention and innovation have led naturally to change and a more industrialized economy.

EVENTS	INVENTIONS
1750	
• Domestic system • Agricultural economy	
• Revolutionary War	
• Factory system • Industrial Revolution	
1800	
• War of 1812	• Golden age of invention
	• Erie Canal
	• Railroads
1850	
• Civil War	
	• Telephone • Lightbulb
• Second Industrial Revolution • Manufacturing economy	
1900	
	• Airplane • Model T Ford
• World War I	
• Large corporations	
• Great Depression	
• World War II	
1950	
	• Satellite
• Service economy	
• Oil embargo	
• Inflation	
• NAFTA • Collapse of Soviet Union	
	• Fiber optics • Laptop computer
	• Artificial intelligence
• Low unemployment • Low inflation • Low interest rates **2000**	• E-business
	• Increased computing power
• Terrorist attacks and war on terrorism	• Improved information technology
• Natural disasters	• HD television
• Increased global trade	• iFones
• Higher oil and energy prices	
• Economic crisis	

Certainly, many characteristics of our modern business system took form during this time period.

The Twentieth Century

Industrial growth and prosperity continued well into the twentieth century. Henry Ford's moving automotive assembly line, which brought the work to the worker, refined the concept of specialization and helped spur on the mass production of consumer goods. Fundamental changes occurred in business ownership and management as well. No longer were the largest businesses owned by one individual; instead, ownership was in the hands of thousands of corporate shareholders who were willing to invest in—but not to operate—a business.

The Roaring Twenties ended with the sudden crash of the stock market in 1929 and the near collapse of the economy. The Great Depression that followed in the 1930s was a time of misery and human suffering. People lost their faith in business and its ability to satisfy the needs of society without government involvement. After Franklin D. Roosevelt became president in 1933, the federal government devised a number of programs to get the economy moving again. In implementing these programs, the government got deeply involved in business for the first time.

The economy was on the road to recovery when World War II broke out in Europe in 1939. The need for vast quantities of war materials spurred business activity and technological development. This rapid economic pace continued after the war, and the 1950s and 1960s witnessed both increasing production and a rising standard of living.

In the mid-1970s, however, a shortage of crude oil led to a new set of problems for business. As the cost of petroleum products increased, a corresponding price increase took place in the cost of energy and the cost of goods and services. The result was inflation at a rate well over 10 percent per year during the early 1980s. Interest rates also increased dramatically, so both businesses and consumers reduced their borrowing. Business profits fell as the purchasing power of consumers was eroded by inflation and high interest rates.

This is an IBM *typewriter*. In this photo, employees inspect and test IBM typewriters to make sure the machines were examples of the quality products that helped build the company's reputation. Today, IBM is still known for quality, but the product has changed. Now, the company makes all types of computer equipment for both consumers and business customers.

By the early 1990s, unemployment numbers, inflation, and interest—all factors that affect business—were now at record lows. In turn, business took advantage of this economic prosperity to invest in information technology, cut costs, and increase flexibility and efficiency. The Internet became a major force in the economy, with computer hardware, software, and Internet service providers taking advantage of the increased need for information. e-Business—a topic we will continue to explore throughout this text—became an accepted method of conducting business. **e-Business** is the organized effort of individuals to produce and sell *through the Internet*, for a profit, the products and services that satisfy society's needs. As further evidence of the financial health of the new economy, the stock market enjoyed the longest period of sustained economic growth in our history. Unfortunately, by the last part of the twentieth century, a larger number of business failures and declining stock values were initial signs that larger economic problems were on the way.

A New Century: 2000 and Beyond

According to many economic experts, the first few years of the twenty-first century might be characterized as the best of times and the worst of times rolled into one package. On the plus side, technology became available at an affordable price. Both individuals and businesses now could access information with the click of a button. They also could buy and sell merchandise online.

In addition to information technology, the growth of service businesses and increasing opportunities for global trade also changed the way American firms do business in the twenty-first century. Because they employ approximately 85 percent of the American work force, service businesses are a very important component of our economy.[14] As a result, service businesses must find ways to improve productivity and cut costs while at the same time providing jobs for an even larger portion of the work force.

On the negative side, it is hard to watch television, surf the Web, listen to the radio, or read the newspaper without hearing some news about the economy.

e-business the organized effort of individuals to produce and sell *through the Internet*. for a profit, the products and services that satisfy society's needs

©Bettmann/Corbis

Because many of the economic indicators described in Table 1.2 on page 17 indicate troubling economic problems, there is still a certain amount of pessimism surrounding the economy. At the time of publication, many people wonder how much longer the economic crisis will last. Unfortunately, even the experts can't agree on an answer. Unemployment rates are still abnormally high, stock market values are still depressed, and a large number of businesses are experiencing financial problems that may eventually lead to failure—despite the fact that federal government is spending billions of dollars of taxpayer money to fund massive economic stimulus programs. Hopefully, by the time you read this material, our economy will have reached the bottom of the trough and will have begun to recover.

The Current Business Environment

Before reading on, answer the following question:

In today's competitive business world, which of the following environments affects business?

a. The competitive environment
b. The global environment
c. The technological environment
d. The economic environment
e. All of the above

The correct answer is "e." All of the environments listed affect business today. For example, businesses operate in a *competitive environment*. As noted earlier in this chapter, competition is a basic component of capitalism. Every day, business owners must figure out what makes their businesses successful and how their businesses are different from the competition. Often, the answer is contained in the basic definition of business. Just for a moment, review the definition on page 8.

Note the phrase *satisfy society's needs*. Those three words say a lot about how well a successful firm competes with competitors. If you meet customer needs, then you have a better chance at success.

Related to the competitive environment is the *global environment*. Not only do American businesses have to compete with other American businesses, but they also must compete with businesses from all over the globe. According to global experts, China is the fastest-growing economy in the world. And China is not alone. Other countries around the world also compete with U.S. firms. There once was a time when the label "Made in the United States" gave U.S. businesses an inside edge both at home and in the global marketplace. Now, businesses in other countries manufacture and sell goods. According to Richard Haass, president of the Council on Foreign Relations, "There will be winners and losers from globalization. We win every time we go shopping because prices are lower. Choice is greater because of globalization. But there are losers. There are people who will lose their jobs either to foreign competition or [to] technological innovation."[15]

While both foreign competition and technological innovation have changed the way we do business, the *technology environment* for U.S. businesses has never been more challenging. Changes in manufacturing equipment, communication with customers, and distribution of products are all examples of how technology has changed everyday business practices. And the technology will continue to change. New technology will require businesses to spend additional money to keep abreast of an ever-changing technology environment.

In addition to the competitive, global, and technology environments, the *economic environment* always must be considered when making business decisions. While many people believe that business has unlimited resources, the truth is that managers and business owners realize that there is never enough money to fund all the activities a business might want to fund. This fact is especially important when the nation's economy takes a nosedive or an individual firm's sales revenue and profits are declining. For example, both small and large business firms reduced both spending and hiring new employees over the last two to three years because of economic concerns related to the depressed housing, banking, and financial industries.

In addition to economic pressures, today's socially responsible managers and business owners must be concerned about the concept of sustainability. According to the U.S. Environmental Protection Agency, **sustainability** means meeting the needs of the present without compromising the ability of future generations to meet their own needs.[16] A combination of forces including economic factors, growth in population, increased energy use, and concerns for the environment are changing the way individuals live and businesses operate.

When you look back at the original question we asked at the beginning of this section, clearly, each different type of environment affects the way a business does *business*. As a result, there are always opportunities for improvement and challenges that must be considered.

The Challenges Ahead

There it is—the American business system in brief.

When it works well, it provides jobs for those who are willing to work, a standard of living that few countries can match, and many opportunities for personal advancement. However, like every other system devised by humans, it is not perfect. Our business system may give us prosperity, but it also gave us the Great Depression of the 1930s and the economic problems of the 1970s, the 1980s, and the economic crisis that began in late 2007.

Obviously, the system can be improved. Certainly, there are plenty of people who are willing to tell us exactly what *they* think the American economy needs. But often these people provide us only with conflicting opinions. Who is right and who is wrong? Even the experts cannot agree.

The experts do agree, however, that several key issues will challenge our economic system (and our nation) over the next decade. Some of the questions to be resolved include:

- How can we create a more stable economy and create new jobs?
- How can we restore the public's confidence in the banking and financial industries?
- How can we regulate banks, savings and loan associations, credit unions, and other financial institutions to prevent the type of abuses that led to an economic crisis?
- How can we encourage Iraq and Afghanistan to establish a democratic and free society and resolve possible conflict with North Korea and other countries throughout the world?
- How can we meet the challenges of managing culturally diverse work forces to address the needs of a culturally diverse marketplace?
- How can we make American firms more productive and more competitive with foreign firms who have lower labor costs?
- How can we preserve the benefits of competition and small businesses in our American economic system?
- How can we encourage economic growth and at the same time continue to conserve natural resources and sustain our environment?
- How can we meet the needs of two-income families, single parents, older Americans, and the less fortunate who need health care and social programs to exist?

The answers to these questions are anything but simple. In the past, Americans always have been able to solve their economic problems through ingenuity and creativity. Now, as we continue the journey through the twenty-first century, we need that same ingenuity and creativity not only to solve our current problems but also

sustainability meeting the needs of the present without compromising the ability of future generations to meet their own needs

Concept Check

1. How does your standard of living affect the products or services you buy?

2. What is the difference between the domestic system and the factory system?

3. Choose one of the environments that affect business and explain how it affects a small electronics manufacturer located in Portland, Oregon.

4. What do you consider the most important challenge that will face people in the United States in the years ahead?

to compete in the global marketplace. The way we solve these problems will affect our own future, our children's future, and that of our nation. Within the American economic and political system, the answers are ours to provide.

The American business system is not perfect by any means, but it does work reasonably well. We discuss some of its problems in Chapter 2 as we examine the topics of social responsibility and business ethics.

SUMMARY

1 Discuss your future in the world of business.

For many years, people in business—both employees and managers—assumed that prosperity would continue. When faced with both economic problems and increased competition, a large number of these same people then began to ask the question: What do we do now? Although this is a fair question, it is difficult to answer. Certainly, for a college student taking business courses, or an employee just starting a career, or an unemployed worker looking for work, the question is even more difficult to answer. And yet there are still opportunities out there for people who are willing to work hard, continue to learn, and possess the ability to adapt to change. To be sure, employers and our capitalistic economic system are more demanding than ever before. As you begin this course, ask yourself: What can I do that will make employers want to pay me a salary? What skills do I have that employers need? The kind of career you choose ultimately will depend on your own values and what you feel is most important in life. But deciding on the kind of career you want is only a first step. To get a job in your chosen field and to be successful at it, you will have to develop a plan, or road map, that ensures that you have the necessary skills and the knowledge the job requires to become a better employee. By studying business, you may also decide to start your own business and become a better consumer and investor.

2 Define *business* and identify potential risks and rewards.

Business is the organized effort of individuals to produce and sell, for a profit, the goods and services that satisfy society's needs. Four kinds of resources—material, human, financial, and informational—must be combined to start and operate a business. The three general types of businesses are manufacturers, service businesses, and marketing intermediaries. Profit is what remains after all business expenses are deducted from sales revenue. It is the payment that owners receive for assuming the risks of business—primarily the risks of not receiving payment and of losing whatever has been invested in the firm.

3 Define *economics* and describe the two types of economic systems: capitalism and command economy.

Economics is the study of how wealth is created and distributed. An economic system must answer four questions: What goods and services will be produced? How will they be produced? For whom will they be produced? Who owns and who controls the major factors of production? Capitalism (on which our economic system is based) is an economic system in which individuals own and operate the majority of businesses that provide goods and services. Capitalism stems from the theories of Adam Smith. Smith's pure laissez-faire capitalism is an economic system in which the factors of production (land and natural resources, labor, capital, and entrepreneurship) are owned by private entities, and all individuals are free to use their resources as they see fit. Prices are determined by the workings of supply and demand in competitive markets and the economic role of government is limited to rule maker and umpire.

Our economic system today is a mixed economy. In the circular flow that characterizes our business system (see Figure 1.4), households and businesses exchange resources for goods and services, using money as the medium of exchange. In a similar manner, government collects taxes from businesses and households and purchases products and resources with which to provide services.

In a command economy, government, rather than individuals, owns the factors of production and provides the answers to the three other economic questions. Socialist and communist economies are—at least in theory—command economies.

4 Identify the ways to measure economic performance.

One way to evaluate the performance of an economic system is to assess changes in productivity, which is the average level of output per worker per hour. Gross domestic product (GDP) also can be used to measure a nation's economic well-being and is the total dollar value of all goods and services produced by all people within the boundaries of a country during a one-year period. This figure facilitates comparisons between the United States and other countries because it is the standard used in international guidelines for economic accounting. It is also possible to adjust GDP for inflation and thus to measure *real* GDP. In addition to GDP, other economic indicators include a nation's balance of trade, consumer price index (CPI), corporate profits, inflation rate, national income, new housing starts, prime interest rate, producer price index (PPI), and unemployment rate.

5 Examine the four different phases in the typical business cycle.

A nation's economy fluctuates rather than grows at a steady pace every year. These fluctuations generally are referred to as the business cycle. Generally, the business cycle consists of four states: the peak (sometimes referred to as prosperity), recession, the trough, and recovery. Some experts believe that effective use of monetary policy (the Federal Reserve's decisions that determine the size of the supply of money and the level of interest rates) and fiscal policies (the government's influence on the amount of savings and expenditures) can speed up recovery and even eliminate depressions for the business cycle. For example, the Emergency Economic Stabilization Act was enacted in late 2008 to help restore confidence in the economy, help individuals weather the economic crisis, and help the nation turn the corner from recession to recovery. This act, when combined with later stimulus bills passed in 2009, have created a federal deficit—a situation where the government spends more than it receives during one fiscal year. The total of all federal deficits is called the national debt.

6 Outline the four types of competition.

Competition is essentially a rivalry among businesses for sales to potential customers. In a capitalist economy, competition works to ensure the efficient and effective operation of business. Competition also ensures that a firm will survive only if it serves its customers well. Economists recognize four degrees of competition. Ranging from most to least competitive, the four degrees are perfect competition, monopolistic competition, oligopoly, and monopoly. The factors of supply and demand generally influence the price that consumers pay producers for goods and services. The market price for any product is the price at which the quantity demanded is equal to the quantity supplied.

7 Summarize the factors that affect the business environment and the challenges that American businesses will encounter in the future.

From the beginning, through the Industrial Revolution of the early nineteenth century, and to the phenomenal expansion of American industry in the nineteenth and early twentieth centuries, our government maintained an essentially laissez-faire attitude toward business. However, during the Great Depression of the 1930s, the federal government began to provide a number of social services to its citizens. Government's role in business has expanded considerably since that time.

During the 1970s, a shortage of crude oil led to higher prices and inflation. In the 1980s, business profits fell as the consumers' purchasing power was eroded by inflation and high interest rates. By the early 1990s, the U.S. economy began to show signs of improvement and economic growth. Unemployment numbers, inflation, and interest rates—all factors that affect business—were now at record lows. Unfortunately, by the last part of the 1990s, a larger number of business failures and declining stock values were initial signs that more economic problems were on the way.

Now more than ever before, the way a business operates is affected by the competitive environment, global environment, technological environment, and economic environment. As a result, business has a number of opportunities for improvement and challenges for the future.

KEY TERMS

You should now be able to define and give an example relevant to each of the following terms.

free enterprise (3)	entrepreneur (11)	producer price index (PPI) (18)	market price (21)
cultural (or workplace) diversity (5)	capitalism (11)	business cycle (18)	monopolistic competition (22)
business (8)	invisible hand (11)	recession (18)	product differentiation (22)
profit (9)	market economy (12)	depression (19)	oligopoly (22)
stakeholders (9)	mixed economy (12)	monetary policies (19)	monopoly (22)
economics (10)	consumer products (13)	fiscal policy (19)	natural monopoly (22)
microeconomics (10)	command economy (14)	federal deficit (19)	standard of living (23)
macroeconomics (10)	productivity (15)	national debt (20)	barter (23)
Emergency Economic Stabilization Act (10)	gross domestic product (GDP) (16)	competition (20)	domestic system (23)
economy (10)	inflation (16)	perfect (or pure) competition (20)	factory system (23) specialization (23)
factors of production (10)	deflation (16)	supply (21)	e-business (25)
	consumer price index (CPI) (18)	demand (21)	sustainability (27)

DISCUSSION QUESTIONS

1. In what ways have the economic problems caused by the recent crisis in the banking and financial industries affected business firms? In what ways have these problems affected employees and individuals?
2. What factors caused American business to develop into a mixed economic system rather than some other type of economic system?
3. Does an individual consumer really have a voice in answering the basic economic questions?
4. Is gross domestic product a reliable indicator of a nation's economic health? What might be a better indicator?

5. Discuss this statement: "Business competition encourages efficiency of production and leads to improved product quality."
6. In our business system, how is government involved in answering the four basic economic questions? Does government participate in the system or interfere with it?
7. Choose one of the challenges listed on page 27 and describe possible ways that business and society could help to solve or eliminate the problem in the future.

Test Yourself

Matching Questions

1. _____ Materials, machinery, and workers are assembled in one place.

2. _____ The government spends more than it receives.

3. _____ System of exchange.

4. _____ The process of distinguishing Colgate from Crest toothpaste.

5. _____ The average level of output per worker per hour.

6. _____ A study of how wealth is created and distributed.

7. _____ An organized effort to produce and sell goods and services for a profit.

8. _____ A system where individuals own and operate the majority of businesses.

9. _____ A person who takes the risk and invests in a business.

10. _____ Value of all goods and services produced within a country during a one-year period.

   a. capitalism
   b. economics
   c. federal deficit
   d. productivity
   e. product differentiation
   f. business
   g. factory system
   h. entrepreneur
   i. gross domestic product
   j. barter

True False Questions

11. **T F** The majority of small business firms are successful within the first five years.

12. **T F** For a business to be organized, it must combine four categories of resources: workers, natural resources, capital, and ownership.

13. **T F** The equilibrium price means that the supply and demand for a product are in balance.

14. **T F** Under communism, individual consumers determine what will be produced.

15. **T F** Apple Computer and Dell Computer use product differentiation in the marketplace.

16. **T F** If a firm's sales revenues exceed its expenses, the firm has earned a profit.

17. **T F** Fiscal policy determines the level of interest rates.

18. **T F** The main objective of business firms should be to satisfy the needs of their customers.

19. **T F** Adam smith is the father of communism and advocated a classless society.

20. **T F** A business cycle consists of four states: peak, recession, trough, and recovery.

Multiple-Choice Questions

21. _____ Demand is a
   a. relationship between prices and the quantities purchased by buyers.
   b. relationship between prices and the quantities offered by producers.
   c. quantity of goods available for purchase.
   d. price the consumer is willing to pay.
   e. by-product of communism.

22. _____ The process of separating work into distinct tasks is called
   a. bartering.
   b. networking.
   c. specialization.
   d. a factory system.
   e. a domestic system.

23. _____ What term implies that there shall be no government interference in the economy?
   a. market economy.
   b. free-market economy.
   c. command economy.
   d. laissez-faire.
   e. socialism.

24. _____ When the level of prices in an economy rise, it's called
   a. prosperity.
   b. recession
   c. depression.
   d. recovery.
   e. inflation.

Test Yourself

25. _____ The total of all federal deficits is called

    a. depression.

    b. fiscal policy.

    c. gross domestic product.

    d. national debt.

    e. business cycle.

26. _____ The ability to work well with many types of people in the workplace is referred to as

    a. workplace differentiation.

    b. cultural diversity.

    c. economic stability.

    d. career unity.

    e. employee magnification.

27. _____ Best Buy and Wal-Mart are both examples of

    a. production intermediaries.

    b. manufacturing businesses.

    c. service businesses.

    d. marketing intermediaries.

    e. small businesses.

28. _____ The study of the national economy and the global economy is referred to as

    a. factors of the economy.

    b. microeconomics.

    c. macroeconomics.

    d. laissez-faire capitalism.

    e. a command economy.

29. _____ A $700 billion bailout plan created to stabilize the nation's economy is known as the

    a. Economic Retaliation Act.

    b. Tax Recovery and Reduction Act.

    c. National Stabilization Act.

    d. Emergency Economic Stabilization Act.

    e. Global Economic Recovery Act.

30. _____ A monthly index that measures changes in prices that consumers pay for goods is referred to as the

    a. prosperity index.

    b. producer's price index.

    c. prosperity price predictor.

    d. inflation rate index.

    e. consumer price index.

Answers to the "Test Yourself questions appear at the end of the book on page TY-1.

VIDEO CASE

Peet's Coffee & Tea: Building a Community

Alfred Peet had grown up working in his family's coffee business in the Netherlands, so after several years of living and working in the United States, in 1966 he invested in a roaster and decided to open his own shop selling coffee beans and loose tea in California. Peet bought premium coffee beans and roasted them the same way they did in the old country, and thus the gourmet coffee movement in the United States was quietly born.

When customers came into his Berkeley shop, Peet would offer them a fragrant cup of coffee while they waited for their beans to be freshly roasted. Customers enjoying and talking about the coffee created a relaxed community atmosphere that soon proved contagious. Today Peet's Coffee & Tea has more than 120 neighborhood stores, selling and serving a variety of apparently recession-proof coffee and tea products. It also distributes its products online and through more than 8,400 grocery-store partners around the country.

Throughout its history, however, Peet's stores have been the hub of the business, the place where most people sample and discover its unique coffee and tea products for the first time. Peet's employees are enthusiastic about coffee and tea, and they share their passion with store visitors. Educating customers about what makes Peet's different is an important part of their responsibilities.

Peet's also sells coffee and tea through home delivery, which over time has become a significant part of its business. Customers from all over the world can now order Peet's products through the company's call center or website. Because Peet's is able to roast its coffee, pack it, and ship it the same day, it can ensure the freshest possible product reaches customers who don't live near a Peet's store. In 2003, Peet's introduced the highly successfully Peetniks Program, which allows customers to have one or more products shipped to them on a regular basis to ensure a constant supply. Over time, Peet's has expanded this replenishment service to a true customer loyalty program. Peetniks can spend as much or little as they want and still retain membership and a sense of community like that developed in the stores. They use a special phone number to call in their orders and a special place on the website for managing their deliveries, and they enjoy a 15 percent discount on shipping fees and special merchandise. Exclusive special offers and gifts—such as a free Peetnik baseball cap recently sent to all members—also give them a strong sense of belonging, as does the name Peetnik, which is what Peet's calls its employees.

Peet's informs its customers about new products in a number of ways. In addition to encouraging in-store sampling, it trains its call center employees to look at what customers have been ordering, ask them what flavors and qualities they like, and recommend new coffees and teas. Peetniks Program members also receive e-mails announcing new products, describing their flavor and origin, and discussing what makes them special. Peet's discovered that one of the most effective ways to get customers to try new products is through coffee sampler packs. These are promoted through its stores, the call center, the Peetniks Program, and online.

Peet's has built a strong relationship with its customers through education and information. It has successfully bridged the gap between its past and the future. By staying true to its traditions such as hand roasting, and by constantly creating a sense of community with its users, it has developed an international group of satisfied and loyal customers. During the recession of 2008–2009, it posted a 7% revenue increase for one quarter, up to $67.1 million.[17]

For more information about this company, go to www.peets.com.

Questions
1. Is Peet's market monopolistic or an oligopoly?
2. What are some ways that Peet's Coffee & Tea tries to differentiate its product offering?
3. What consumer needs is Peet's satisfying?

BUILDING SKILLS FOR CAREER SUCCESS

1. EXPLORING THE INTERNET
The Internet is a global network of computers that can be accessed by anyone in the world. For example, your school or firm most likely is connected to the Web. You probably have access through a commercial service provider such as AT&T Yahoo! or a host of other smaller Internet service providers.

To familiarize yourself with the wealth of information available through the Internet and its usefulness to business students, this exercise focuses on information services available from a few popular "search engines" used to explore the Web.

To use one of these search engines, enter its *Internet address* in your Web browser. The addresses of some popular search engines are

www.ask.com
www.google.com
www.msn.com
www.yahoo.com

Visit the text website for updates to this exercise.

Assignment
1. Examine the ways in which two search engines present categories of information on their opening screens. Which search engine was better to use in your opinion? Why?
2. Think of a business topic that you would like to know more about, for example, careers, gross domestic product, or another concept introduced in this chapter. Using your preferred search engine, explore a few articles and reports provided on your topic. Briefly summarize your findings.

2. BUILDING TEAM SKILLS
Over the past few years, employees have been expected to function as productive team members instead of working alone. People often believe that they can work effectively in teams, but many people find working with a group of people to be a challenge. Being an effective team member requires skills that encourage other members to participate in the team endeavor.

College classes that function as teams are more interesting and more fun to attend, and students generally learn more about the topics in the course. If your class is to function as a team, it is important to begin building the team early in the semester. One way to begin creating a team is to learn something about each student in the class. This helps team members to feel comfortable with each other and fosters a sense of trust.

Assignment
1. Find a partner, preferably someone you do not know.
2. Each partner has two to three minutes to answer the following questions:
   a. What is your name, and where do you work?
   b. What interesting or unusual thing have you done in your life? (Do not talk about work or college; rather, focus on such things as hobbies, travel, family, and sports.)
   c. Why are you taking this course, and what do you expect to learn? (Satisfying a degree requirement is not an acceptable answer.)
3. Introduce your partner to the class. Use one to two minutes, depending on the size of the class.

3. RESEARCHING DIFFERENT CAREERS
In this chapter, *entrepreneurship* is defined as the willingness to take risks and the knowledge and ability to use the other factors of production efficiently. An *entrepreneur* is a person who risks his or her time, effort, and money to start and operate a business. Often, people believe that these terms apply only to small business operations, but recently, employees with entrepreneurial attitudes have advanced more rapidly in large companies.

Assignment
1. Go to the local library or use the Internet to research how large firms, especially corporations, are rewarding employees who have entrepreneurial skills.
2. Find answers to the following questions:
   a. Why is an entrepreneurial attitude important in corporations today?
   b. What makes an entrepreneurial employee different from other employees?
   c. How are these employees being rewarded, and are the rewards worth the effort?
3. Write a two-page report that summarizes your findings.

Being Ethical and Socially Responsible

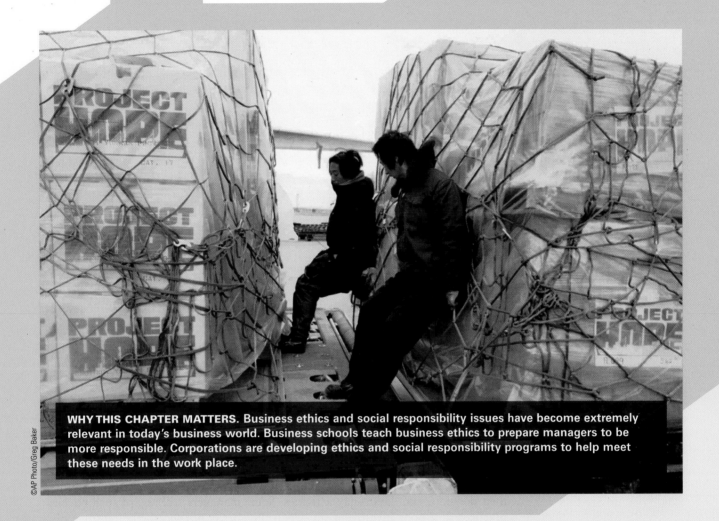

©AP Photo/Greg Baker

WHY THIS CHAPTER MATTERS. Business ethics and social responsibility issues have become extremely relevant in today's business world. Business schools teach business ethics to prepare managers to be more responsible. Corporations are developing ethics and social responsibility programs to help meet these needs in the work place.

LEARNING OBJECTIVES

1 Understand what is meant by *business ethics*.

2 Identify the types of ethical concerns that arise in the business world.

3 Discuss the factors that affect the level of ethical behavior in organizations.

4 Explain how ethical decision making can be encouraged.

5 Describe how our current views on the social responsibility of business have evolved.

6 Explain the two views on the social responsibility of business and understand the arguments for and against increased social responsibility.

7 Discuss the factors that led to the consumer movement and list some of its results.

8 Analyze how present employment practices are being used to counteract past abuses.

9 Describe the major types of pollution, their causes, and their cures.

10 Identify the steps a business must take to implement a program of social responsibility.

FedEx Delivers Corporate Citizenship

FedEx, which made its name through speedy, on-time delivery, has put social responsibility on a fast track. With $38 billion in annual revenue, 290,000 employees, and a global fleet of 670 jets and 80,000 trucks, the company has the money and the muscle to make a real difference. As a good corporate citizen, it donates delivery services for far-flung disaster relief efforts, supports communities and charities worldwide, and does its part to protect the natural environment.

Because FedEx can reach so many people in so many parts of the world, its donated delivery services are a lifeline for victims that need emergency supplies immediately. In any given month, the company may be helping Heart to Heart International fly medical equipment to an earthquake site in China or helping the American Red Cross rush clean water to flood victims in Midwestern states.

As a national supporter of the nonprofit United Way, FedEx contributes both cash and volunteers for community causes such as building playgrounds. In addition, its employees coach students in Junior Achievement programs and work with Safe Kids Worldwide to teach children how to cross streets safely. The company and its employees are also active in many causes, including walking to raise millions of dollars for the March of Dimes every year.

One of FedEx's top priorities is going green. It's racing toward its goal of replacing 30 percent of its truck and jet fuel with biofuel and other gasoline alternatives by 2030. FedEx already operates hundreds of electric-diesel hybrid trucks and is always testing new vehicles as part of its plan to reduce harmful emissions. It uses solar power to run most of its Oakland, California operations and is installing solar panels in other U.S. and European facilities. Considering FedEx's active social responsibility agenda—and its track record of business success—it's no surprise that the firm regularly appears near the top of Fortune magazine's list of the World's Most Admired Companies.[1]

DID YOU KNOW?

By 2030, FedEx aims to replace 30 percent of its truck and jet fuel with biofuel and other gasoline alternatives.

Obviously, organizations like FedEx want to be recognized as responsible corporate citizens. Such companies recognize the need to harmonize their operations with environmental demands and other vital social concerns. Not all firms, however, have taken steps to encourage a consideration of social responsibility and ethics in their decisions and day-to-day activities. Some managers still regard such business practices as a poor investment, in which the cost is not worth the return. Other managers—indeed, most managers—view the cost of these practices as a necessary business expense, similar to wages or rent.

Most managers today, like those at FedEx, are finding ways to balance a growing agenda of socially responsible activities with the drive to generate profits. This also happens to be a good way for a company to demonstrate its values and to attract like-minded employees, customers, and stockholders. In a highly competitive business environment, an increasing number of companies are, like FedEx, seeking to set themselves apart by developing a reputation for ethical and socially responsible behavior.

We begin this chapter by defining *business ethics* and examining ethical issues. Next, we look at the standards of behavior in organizations and how ethical behavior can be encouraged. We then turn to the topic of social responsibility. We compare and contrast two present-day models of social responsibility and present arguments for and against increasing the social responsibility of business. After that, we examine the major elements of the consumer movement. We discuss how social responsibility in business has affected employment practices and environmental concerns. Finally, we consider the commitment, planning, and funding that go into a firm's program of social responsibility.

Business Ethics Defined

1 LEARNING OBJECTIVE

Understand what is meant by *business ethics*.

Ethics is the study of right and wrong and of the morality of the choices individuals make. An ethical decision or action is one that is "right" according to some standard of behavior. **Business ethics** is the application of moral standards to business situations. Recent court cases involving unethical behavior have helped to make business ethics a matter of public concern. In one such case, Copley Pharmaceutical, Inc., pled guilty to federal criminal charges (and paid a $10.65 million fine) for falsifying drug manufacturers' reports to the Food and Drug Administration. In another much-publicized case, lawsuits against tobacco companies have led to $246 billion in settlements, although there has been only one class-action lawsuit filed on behalf of all smokers. That case, *Engle* v. *R. J. Reynolds* could cost tobacco companies an estimated $500 billion. In yet another case, Adelphia Communications Corp., the nation's fifth-largest cable television company agreed to pay $715 million to settle federal investigations stemming from rampant earnings manipulation by its founder John J. Rigas and his son, Timothy J. Rigas. Prosecutors and government regulators charged that the Rigases had misappropriated Adelphia funds for their own use and had failed to pay the corporation for securities they controlled. John J. Rigas was sentenced fifteen years in prison and his son was sentenced to twenty years.[2]

Ethical Issues

2 LEARNING OBJECTIVE

Identify the types of ethical concerns that arise in the business world.

Ethical issues often arise out of a business's relationship with investors, customers, employees, creditors, or competitors. Each of these groups has specific concerns and usually exerts pressure on the organization's managers. For example, investors want management to make sensible financial decisions that will boost sales, profits, and returns on their investments. Customers expect a firm's products to be safe, reliable, and reasonably priced. Employees demand to be treated fairly in hiring, promotion, and compensation decisions. Creditors require accounts to be paid on time and the accounting information furnished by the firm to be accurate. Competitors expect the firm's competitive practices to be fair and honest. Consider TAP Pharmaceutical Products, Inc., whose sales representatives offered every urologist in the United States a big-screen TV, computers, fax machines, and golf vacations if the doctors prescribed TAP's new prostate cancer drug Lupron. Recently, the federal government won an $875 million judgment against TAP.

In late 2006, Hewlett-Packard Co.'s chairman, Patricia Dunn, and general counsel, Ann Baskins, resigned amid allegations that the company used intrusive tactics in observing the personal lives of journalists and company's directors, thus tarnishing Hewlett-Packard's reputation for integrity. According to Congressman John Dingell of Michigan, "We have before us witnesses from Hewlett-Packard to discuss a plunderers' operation that would make (former president) Richard Nixon blush were he still alive."

Or, consider Bernard Madoff, former stockbroker, financial advisor and chairman of NASDAQ stock exchange. In 2009, he was convicted of securities and other frauds including a Ponzi scheme that defrauded clients of $65 billion.

Businesspeople face ethical issues every day, and some of these issues can be difficult to assess. Although some types of issues arise infrequently, others occur regularly. Let's take a closer look at several ethical issues.

Fairness and Honesty

Fairness and honesty in business are two important ethical concerns. Besides obeying all laws and regulations, businesspeople are expected to refrain from knowingly deceiving, misrepresenting, or intimidating others. The consequences of failing to do so can be expensive. Recently, for example, Keith E. Anderson and Wayne Anderson, the leaders of an international tax shelter scheme known as Anderson's Ark and Associates, were sentenced to as many as twenty years in prison. The Andersons,

ethics the study of right and wrong and of the morality of the choices individuals make

business ethics the application of moral standards to business situations

Meet Lehman Brothers Holding Inc. 's chief executive Richard S. Fuld Jr., who earned more than $40 million in 2007. Here, Mr. Fuld is hassled by protesters as he leaves Capitol Hill after testifying before the House Oversight and Government Reform Committee. Just days from becoming the largest bankruptcy in U.S. history. Lehman Brothers gave millions to departing executives even while pleading for a federal bailout plan.

Richard Marks, their chief accounting officer, and Karolyn Grosnickle, the chief administrative officer, were ordered to pay over $200 million in fines and restitution.[3] In yet another case, the accounting firm PricewaterhouseCoopers LLP agreed to pay the U.S. government $42 million to resolve allegations that it made false claims in connection with travel reimbursements it collected for several federal agencies.[4]

Deere & Company requires each employee to deal fairly with its customers, suppliers, competitors, and employees. "No employee should take unfair advantage of anyone through manipulation, concealment, abuse of privileged information, misrepresentation of material facts or any other unfair dealing practice."[5]

Personal data security breaches have become a major threat to personal privacy in the new millennium. Can businesses keep your personal data secure?

Organizational Relationships

A businessperson may be tempted to place his or her personal welfare above the welfare of others or the welfare of the organization. For example, former CEO of Tyco International, Ltd., Leo Dennis Kozlowski was indicted for misappropriating $43 million in corporate funds to make philanthropic contributions in his own name, including $5 million to Seton Hall University, which named its new business-school building Kozlowski Hall. Furthermore, according to Tyco, the former CEO took $61.7 million in interest-free relocation loans without the board's permission. He allegedly used the money to finance many personal luxuries, including a $15 million yacht and a $3.9 million Renoir painting, and to throw a $2 million party for his wife's birthday. Kozlowski was sentenced up to twenty-five years in prison. In a recent letter to *Fortune*, he wrote, "[Prison] is the most difficult of all difficult places to be."[6] Relationships with customers and coworkers often create ethical problems. Unethical behavior in these areas includes taking credit for others' ideas or work, not meeting one's commitments in a mutual agreement, and pressuring others to behave unethically.

Conflict of Interest

Conflict of interest results when a businessperson takes advantage of a situation for his or her own personal interest rather than for the employer's interest. Such conflict

Concept Check

1. What is meant by business ethics?

2. What are the different types of ethical concerns that may arise in the business world?

3. Explain and give an example of how advertising can present ethical questions.

may occur when payments and gifts make their way into business deals. A wise rule to remember is that anything given to a person that might unfairly influence that person's business decision is a bribe, and all bribes are unethical.

For example, Nortel Networks Corporation does not permit its employees, officers, and directors to accept any gifts or to serve as directors or officers of any organization that might supply goods or services to Nortel Networks. However, Nortel employees may work part time with firms that are not competitors, suppliers, or customers. At AT&T, employees are instructed to discuss with their supervisors any investments that may seem improper. Verizon Communications forbids its employees and executives from holding a "significant" financial stake in vendors, suppliers, or customers.

At Procter & Gamble Company (P&G), all employees are obligated to act at all times solely in the best interests of the company. A conflict of interest arises when an employee has a personal relationship or financial or other interest that could interfere with this obligation or when an employee uses his or her position with the company for personal gain. P&G requires employees to disclose all potential conflicts of interest and to take prompt actions to eliminate a conflict when the company asks them to do so. Receiving gifts, entertainment, or other gratuities from people with whom P&G does business generally is not acceptable because doing so could imply an obligation on the part of the company and potentially pose a conflict of interest.

Communications

Business communications, especially advertising, can present ethical questions. False and misleading advertising is illegal and unethical, and it can infuriate customers. Sponsors of advertisements aimed at children must be especially careful to avoid misleading messages. Advertisers of health-related products also must take precautions to guard against deception when using such descriptive terms as *low fat*, *fat free*, and *light*. In fact, the Federal Trade Commission has issued guidelines on the use of these labels.

Is it Ethical?

Who Says?

When consumers don't know who is behind a business communication, is it mysterious or is it misleading? Knowing that customers may tune out traditional advertising, some companies try to reach out in less conventional ways. However, communications that are meant to intrigue may actually backfire instead:

- Sony and Wal-Mart both faced criticism when they set up promotional blogs that appeared to have been written by ordinary people rather than being company-sponsored.
- Questions were raised when one of AT&T's ad agencies had "Bobby Choice"—not his real name—talk up the company's U-verse television service in person and on a special website, arguing for choices beyond cable television.

Although anonymous marketing activities are largely outlawed in the United Kingdom, companies are not always required to disclose their sponsorship of business communications in the United States. In fact, some companies hire specialized agencies to create a buzz by having "brand ambassadors" start conversations about their products. Such initiatives may have to change if the Federal Trade Commission institutes a rule that bloggers and brand ambassadors be held responsible for any false statements they make about a product.

For now, the Word of Mouth Marketing Association has established a three-point ethics code to avoid misunderstandings. It says that brand ambassadors should: (1) say who they're speaking for, (2) say what they believe, and (3) not obscure their identities.

Sources: Michael Bush, "Bloggers Be Warned: FTC May Monitor What You Say," *Advertising Age*, April 13, 2009, www.adage.com; "Sowing the Seeds of Change," *Marketing Week*, May 29, 2008, p. 18; Jonathan Lucas, "Stealth Marketing Hits SoNo Scene," *Stamford Advocate (Stamford, CT)*, June 17, 2007, n.p.; Angelo Fernando, "Transparency Under Attack," *Communication World*, March-April 2007, pp. 9+; womma.org.

Factors Affecting Ethical Behavior

3 LEARNING OBJECTIVE

Discuss the factors that affect the level of ethical behavior in organizations.

Is it possible for an individual with strong moral values to make ethically questionable decisions in a business setting? What factors affect a person's inclination to make either ethical or unethical decisions in a business organization? Although the answers to these questions are not entirely clear, three general sets of factors do appear to influence the standards of behavior in an organization. As shown in Figure 2.1, the sets consist of individual factors, social factors, and opportunity.

FIGURE 2.1: Factors That Affect the Level of Ethical Behavior

LEVEL OF ETHICAL BEHAVIOR

Individual factors

Social factors

Opportunity

Source: Based on O. C. Ferrell and Larry Gresham, "A Contingency Framework for Understanding Ethical Decision Making in Marketing," *Journal of Marketing,* Summer 1985, p. 89.

Individual Factors Affecting Ethics

Several individual factors influence the level of ethical behavior in an organization.

- *Individual knowledge of an issue.* How much an individual knows about an issue is one factor. A decision maker with a greater amount of knowledge regarding a situation may take steps to avoid ethical problems, whereas a less-informed person may take action unknowingly that leads to an ethical quagmire.
- *Personal values.* An individual's moral values and central, value-related attitudes also clearly influence his or her business behavior. Most people join organizations to accomplish personal goals.
- *Personal goals.* The types of personal goals an individual aspires to and the manner in which these goals are pursued have a significant impact on that individual's behavior in an organization. The actions of specific individuals in scandal-plagued companies such as Adelphia, AIG, Fannie Mae, Freddie Mac, Enron, and WorldCom often raise questions about individuals' personal character and integrity.

Social Factors Affecting Ethics

- *Cultural norms.* A person's behavior in the workplace, to some degree, is determined by cultural norms, and these social factors vary from one culture to another. For example, in some countries it is acceptable and ethical for customs agents to receive gratuities for performing ordinary, legal tasks that are a part of their jobs, whereas in other countries these practices would be viewed as unethical and perhaps illegal.
- *Coworkers.* The actions and decisions of coworkers constitute another social factor believed to shape a person's sense of business ethics. For example, if your coworkers make long-distance telephone calls on company time and at company expense, you might view that behavior as acceptable and ethical because everyone does it.
- *Significant others.* The moral values and attitudes of "significant others"—spouses, friends, and relatives, for instance—also can affect an employee's perception of what is ethical and unethical behavior in the workplace.
- *Use of the Internet.* Even the Internet presents new challenges for firms whose employees enjoy easy access to sites through convenient high-speed connections at work. An employee's behavior online can be viewed as offensive to coworkers and possibly lead to lawsuits against the firm if employees engage in unethical behavior on controversial websites not related to their job. Interestingly, one recent survey of employees found that most workers assume that their use of technology at work will be monitored. A large majority of employees approved of most monitoring methods such as monitoring faxes and e-mail, tracking Web use, and even recording telephone calls.

"Opportunity" as a Factor Affecting Ethics

- *Presence of opportunity.* **Opportunity** refers to the amount of freedom an organization gives an employee to behave unethically if he or she makes that choice. In some organizations, certain company policies and procedures reduce the opportunity to be unethical. For example, at some fast-food restaurants, one employee takes your order and receives your payment, and another fills the order. This procedure reduces the opportunity to be unethical because the person handling the money is not dispensing the product, and the person giving out the product is not handling the money.

- *Ethical codes.* The existence of an ethical code and the importance management places on this code are other determinants of opportunity (codes of ethics are discussed in more detail in the next section).
- *Enforcement.* The degree of enforcement of company policies, procedures, and ethical codes is a major force affecting opportunity. When violations are dealt with consistently and firmly, the opportunity to be unethical is reduced.

Do you make personal telephone calls on company time? Many individuals do. Although most employees limit personal calls to a few minutes, some make personal calls in excess of thirty minutes. Whether or not you use company time and equipment to make personal calls is an example of a personal ethical decision.

Now that we have considered some of the factors believed to influence the level of ethical behavior in the workplace, let's explore what can be done to encourage ethical behavior and to discourage unethical behavior.

Concept Check

1. Describe several individual factors that influence the level of ethical behavior in an organization.

2. Explain several social factors that affect ethics in an organization.

3. How does "opportunity" influence the level of ethical behavior in the workplace?

Encouraging Ethical Behavior

4 LEARNING OBJECTIVE

Explain how ethical decision making can be encouraged.

Most authorities agree that there is room for improvement in business ethics. A more problematic question is: Can business be made more ethical in the real world? The majority opinion on this issue suggests that government, trade associations, and individual firms indeed can establish acceptable levels of ethical behavior.

Government's Role in Encouraging Ethics

The government can encourage ethical behavior by legislating more stringent regulations. For example, the landmark **Sarbanes-Oxley Act of 2002** provides sweeping new legal protection for those who report corporate misconduct. At the signing ceremony, President George W. Bush stated, "The act adopts tough new provisions to deter and punish corporate and accounting fraud and corruption, ensure justice for wrongdoers, and protect the interests of workers and shareholders." Among other things, the law deals with corporate responsibility, conflicts of interest, and corporate accountability. However, rules require enforcement, and the unethical businessperson frequently seems to "slip something by" without getting caught. Increased regulation may help, but it surely cannot solve the entire ethics problem.

Trade Associations' Role in Encouraging Ethics

Trade associations can and often do provide ethical guidelines for their members. These organizations, which operate within particular industries, are in an excellent position to exert pressure on members who stoop to questionable business practices. For example, recently, a pharmaceutical trade group adopted a new set of guidelines to halt the extravagant dinners and other gifts sales representatives often give to physicians. However, enforcement and authority vary from association to association. And because trade associations exist for the benefit of their members, harsh measures may be self-defeating.

Individual Companies' Role in Encouraging Ethics

Codes of ethics that companies provide to their employees are perhaps the most effective way to encourage ethical behavior. A **code of ethics** is a written guide to acceptable and ethical behavior as defined by an organization; it outlines uniform policies, standards, and punishments for violations. Because employees know what is expected of them and what will happen if they violate the rules, a code of ethics goes a long way toward encouraging ethical behavior. However, codes cannot possibly cover every situation. Companies also must create an environment in which

Sarbanes-Oxley Act of 2002 provides sweeping new legal protection for employees who report corporate misconduct

code of ethics a guide to acceptable and ethical behavior as defined by the organization

DECEMBER 30, 2002 / JANUARY 6, 2003   SPECIAL DOUBLE ISSUE

PERSONS OF THE YEAR

TIME

The Whistleblowers

CYNTHIA COOPER   COLEEN ROWLEY   SHERRON WATKINS
OF WORLDCOM   OF THE FBI   OF ENRON

www.time.com   AOL Keyword: TIME

employees recognize the importance of complying with the written code. Managers must provide direction by fostering communication, actively modeling and encouraging ethical decision making, and training employees to make ethical decisions.

During the 1980s, an increasing number of organizations created and implemented ethics codes. In a recent survey of *Fortune* 1000 firms, 93 percent of the companies that responded reported having a formal code of ethics. Some companies are now even taking steps to strengthen their codes. For example, to strengthen its accountability, the Healthcare Financial Management Association recently revised its code to designate contact persons who handle reports of ethics violations, to clarify how its board of directors should deal with violations of business ethics, and to guarantee a fair hearing process. S. C. Johnson & Son, makers of Pledge, Drano, Windex, and many other household products, is another firm that recognizes that it must behave in ways the public perceives as ethical; its code includes expectations for employees and its commitment to consumers, the community, and society in general. As shown in Figure 2.2, included in the ethics code of electronics giant Texas Instruments (TI) are issues relating to policies and procedures; laws and regulations; relationships with customers, suppliers, and competitors; conflicts of interest; handling of proprietary information; and code enforcement.

Assigning an ethics officer who coordinates ethical conduct gives employees someone to consult if they are not sure of the right thing to do. An ethics officer meets with employees and top management to provide ethical advice, establishes and maintains an anonymous confidential service to answer questions about ethical issues, and takes action on ethics code violations.

Sometimes even employees who want to act ethically may find it difficult to do so. Unethical practices can become ingrained in an organization. Employees with high personal ethics then may take a controversial step called *whistle-blowing*. **Whistle-blowing** is informing the press or government officials about unethical practices within one's organization.

The year 2002 was labeled as the "Year of the Whistle-blower." Consider Joe Speaker, a 40-year-old acting chief financial officer (CFO) at Rite Aid Corp. in 1999. He discovered that inventories at Rite Aid had been overvalued and that millions in expenses had not been reported properly. Further digging into Rite Aid's books revealed that $541 million in earnings over the previous two years were really $1.6 billion in losses. Mr. Speaker was a main government witness when former Rite Aid Corp. Chairman and CEO Martin L. Grass went on trial. Mr. Speaker is among dozens of corporate managers who have blown the whistle. Enron's Sherron S. Watkins and WorldCom's Cynthia Cooper are now well-known whistle-blowers and *Time* magazine's persons of the year 2002. According to Linda Chatman Thomsen, deputy director for enforcement at the Securities and Exchange Commission, "Whistle-blowers give us an insider's perspective and have advanced our investigation immeasurably."

Whistle-blowing could have averted disaster and prevented needless deaths in the *Challenger* space shuttle disaster, for example. How could employees have known about life-threatening problems and let them pass? Whistle-blowing, on the other hand, can have serious repercussions for employees: Those who "blow whistles" sometimes lose their jobs. However, the Sarbanes-Oxley Act of 2002 protects whistle-blowers who report corporate misconduct. Any executive who retaliates against a whistle-blower can be held criminally liable and imprisoned for up to ten years.

Retaliations do occur, however. For example, in 2005, the U.S. Court of Appeals for the 8th Circuit unanimously upheld the right of Jane Turner, a twenty-five-year veteran FBI agent, to obtain monetary damages and a jury trial against the FBI. The court held that Ms. Turner presented sufficient facts to justify a trial by jury based

whistle-blowing informing the press or government officials about unethical practices within one's organization

TEXAS INSTRUMENTS CODE OF ETHICS

"Integrity is the foundation on which TI is built. There is no other characteristic more essential to a Tler's makeup. It has to be present at all levels. Integrity is expected of managers and individuals when they make commitments. They are expected to stand by their commitments to the best of their ability.

One of TI's greatest strengths is its values and ethics. We had some early leaders who set those values as the standard for how they lived their lives. And it is important that TI grew that way. It's something that we don't want to lose. At the same time, we must move more rapidly. But we don't want to confuse that with the fact that we're ethical and we're moral. We're very responsible, and we live up to what we say."

Tom Engibous, President and CEO
Texas Instruments, 1997

We Respect and Value People By:

Treating others as we want to be treated.

- Exercising the basic virtues of respect, dignity, kindness, courtesy and manners in all work relationships.
- Recognizing and avoiding behaviors that others may find offensive, including the manner in which we speak and relate to one another and the materials we bring into the workplace, both printed and electronically.
- Respecting the right and obligation of every Tler to resolve concerns relating to ethics questions in the course of our duties without retribution and retaliation.
- Giving all Tlers the same opportunity to have their questions, issues and situations fairly considered while understanding that being treated fairly does not always mean that we will all be treated the same.
- Trusting one another to use sound judgment in our use of TI business and information systems.
- Understanding that even though TI has the obligation to monitor its business information systems activity, we will respect privacy by prohibiting random searches of individual Tlers' communications.
- Recognizing that conduct socially and professionally acceptable in one culture and country may be viewed differently in another.

We Are Honest By:

Representing ourselves and our intentions truthfully.

- Offering full disclosure and withdrawing ourselves from discussions and decisions when our business judgment appears to be in conflict with a personal interest.
- Respecting the rights and property of others, including their intellectual property. Accepting confidential or trade secret information only after we clearly understand our obligations as defined in a nondisclosure agreement.
- Competing fairly without collusion or collaboration with competitors to divide markets, set prices, restrict production, allocate customers or otherwise restrain competition.
- Assuring that no payments or favors are offered to influence others to do something wrong.
- Keeping records that are accurate and include all payments and receipts.
- Exercising good judgment in the exchange of business courtesies, meals and entertainment by avoiding activities that could create even the appearance that our decisions could be compromised.
- Refusing to speculate in TI stock through frequent buying and selling or through other forms of speculative trading.

Source: Courtesy of Texas Instruments, **www.ti.com/corp/docs/csr/corpgov/conduct.shtml**, accessed April 29, 2009.

on the FBI's retaliatory transfer of Ms. Turner from her investigatory position in Minot, North Dakota, to a demeaning desk job in Minneapolis. Kris Kolesnik, executive director of the National Whistle Blower Center, said, "Jane Turner is an American hero. She refused to be silent when her co-agents committed misconduct in a child rape case. She refused to be silent when her co-agents stole property from

Ground Zero. She paid the price and lost her job. The 8th Circuit Court did the right thing and insured that justice will take place in her case." In 2008, the U.S. government was ordered to pay $1 million in legal fees to Turner's lawyers.

When firms set up anonymous hotlines to handle ethically questionable situations, employees actually may be more likely to engage in whistle-blowing. When firms instead create an environment that educates employees and nurtures ethical behavior, fewer ethical problems arise, and ultimately, the need for whistle-blowing is greatly reduced.

It is difficult for an organization to develop ethics codes, policies, and procedures to deal with all relationships and every situation. When no company policy or procedures exist or apply, a quick test to determine if a behavior is ethical is to see if others—coworkers, customers, and suppliers—approve of it. Ethical decisions always will withstand scrutiny. Openness and communication about choices often will build trust and strengthen business relationships. Table 2.1 provides some general guidelines for making ethical decisions.

Social Responsibility

Social responsibility is the recognition that business activities have an impact on society and the consideration of that impact in business decision making. In the first few days after Hurricane Katrina hit New Orleans, Wal-Mart delivered $20 million in cash (including $4 million to employees displaced by the storm), 100 truckloads of free merchandise, and food for 100,000 meals. The company also promised a job elsewhere for every one of its workers affected by the catastrophe. Obviously, social responsibility costs money. It is perhaps not so obvious—except in isolated cases— that social responsibility is also good business. Customers eventually find out which firms are acting responsibly and which are not. And just as easily as they cast their dollar votes for a product made by a company that is socially responsible, they can vote against the firm that is not.

Consider the following examples of organizations that are attempting to be socially responsible:

social responsibility the recognition that business activities have an impact on society and the consideration of that impact in business decision making

- Social responsibility can take many forms— including flying lessons. Through Young Eagles, underwritten by S. C. Johnson, Phillips Petroleum, Lockheed Martin, Jaguar, and other corporations, 22,000 volunteer pilots have taken a

TABLE 2.1: Guidelines for Making Ethical Decisions

1. Listen and learn.	Recognize the problem or decision-making opportunity that confronts your company, team, or unit. Don't argue, criticize, or defend yourself—keep listening and reviewing until you are sure that you understand others.
2. Identify the ethical issues.	Examine how coworkers and consumers are affected by the situation or decision at hand. Examine how you feel about the situation, and attempt to understand the viewpoint of those involved in the decision or in the consequences of the decision.
3. Create and analyze options.	Try to put aside strong feelings such as anger or a desire for power and prestige and come up with as many alternatives as possible before developing an analysis. Ask everyone involved for ideas about which options offer the best long-term results for you and the company. Then decide which option will increase your self-respect even if, in the long run, things don't work out the way you hope.
4. Identify the best option from your point of view.	Consider it and test it against some established criteria, such as respect, understanding, caring, fairness, honesty, and openness.
5. Explain your decision and resolve any differences that arise.	This may require neutral arbitration from a trusted manager or taking "time out" to reconsider, consult, or exchange written proposals before a decision is reached.

Source: Tom Rusk with D. Patrick Miller, "Doing the Right Thing," Sky (Delta Airlines), August 1993, pp. 18–22.

half million youngsters on free flights designed to teach flying basics and inspire excitement about flying careers. Young Eagles is just one of the growing number of education projects undertaken by businesses building solid records as good corporate citizens.

- The General Mills Foundation is one of the nation's largest company-sponsored foundations. Since the General Mills Foundation was created, it has awarded over $400 million to its communities. In fiscal 2008, General Mills donated nearly $87 million in grants in the communities it serves.

In the Twin Cities, the foundation provides grants for youth nutrition and fitness, education, arts and culture, social services, and United Way. Beyond financial resources, the foundation also supports organizations with volunteers and mentors who share their expertise and talents. For example, General Mills plays a leadership role in supporting education, arts, and cultural organizations by matching employee and retiree contributions dollar for dollar. At its annual "Report to the Community," Ellen Goldberg Luger, executive director of the General Mills Foundation, said the Foundation hopes to continue its solid support of community activities in fiscal 2009 as the global economic recession deepens.[7]

Spotlight

Recession and Responsibility

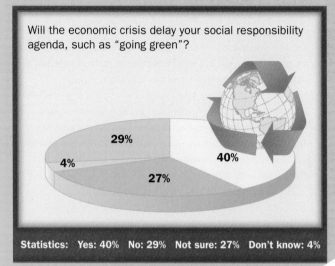

Will the economic crisis delay your social responsibility agenda, such as "going green"?

29% 4% 40% 27%

Statistics: Yes: 40% No: 29% Not sure: 27% Don't know: 4%

Source: Booz & Co. survey of 828 chief executive officers and managers.
Margin of error: 3+/- percentage points.

- As part of Dell's commitment to the community, the Dell Foundation contributes significantly to the quality of life in communities where Dell employees live and work. The foundation supports innovative and effective programs that provide fundamental prerequisites to equip youth to learn and excel in a world driven by the digital economy. The foundation supports a wide range of programs that benefit children from newborn to eighteen years of age in Dell's principal U.S. locations and welcomes proposals from nonprofit organizations that address health and human services, education, and technology access for youth.

Dell's global outreach programs include projects that bring technology to underserved communities around the world. During fiscal year 2008, almost 30,000 Dell employees:

- donated more than 1 million meals to food banks across the United States and Canada.
- volunteered in their communities in Australia, Brazil, India, Ireland, Japan, Malaysia, Panama, South Korea, Spain, and the United States.
- pledged nearly $16 million in the United States and Canada through Dell's Direct Giving campaign, and
- raised more than $500,000 for Dell-sponsored walks including Susan G. Komen Race for the cure, March of Dimes Walk America, Juvenile Diabetes Research Foundation's annual walk, and SafePlace walk.[8]

- Improving public schools around the world continues to be IBM's top social priority. Its efforts are focused on preparing the next generation of leaders and workers. Through Reinventing Education and other strategic efforts, IBM is solving education's toughest problems with solutions that draw on advanced information technologies and the best minds IBM can apply. Its programs are paving the way for reforms in school systems around the world.

IBM launched the World Community Grid in November 2004. It combines excess processing power from thousands of computers into a virtual supercomputer. This grid enables researchers to gather and analyze unprecedented quantities of

Global Economic Challenges

How the Economy Affects Social Responsibility

When the global economy is strong, companies invest in social responsibility programs to do good and because it's good business. But what happens in difficult economic times? During the recent economic downturn, few companies completely abandoned their social responsibility efforts. Many hard-hit firms, such as the insurance giant AIG, continued to give at least some money to causes they regularly support. Others, including Google, fine-tuned their social responsibility investments to more closely connect the causes with their business objectives.

Some companies actually increased their social-responsibility spending. Yum Brands, which operates KFC and other fast-food restaurants, reinforced its social responsibility commitment at the height of the recent recession by pledging more money and more employee volunteer hours to fight world hunger. "Forward thinking corporations are dialing up, not dialing back [social responsibility]," a Yum executive explained. "It's a part of how we do business, and we think it's a smart thing to do."

Travel-related firms saw sales plummet when businesses and industry groups canceled meetings during the recession. In response, the Ritz-Carlton hotel chain put the spotlight on its support of good causes by announcing it would donate to charity 10 percent of the total cost of any conference booked at one of its properties. The program appealed to business customers because, said a spokesperson, it "matches with many companies' growing emphasis on corporate social responsibility."

Sources: "CSR Programs in Good, Bad Times Reap Companies Long-Term Benefits," *PR Week*, April 20, 2009, p. 5; "Full of Hope," *PR Week*, April 20, 2009, n.p.; Vivienne Walt, "Charity Crunch Time," *Time International*, March 30, 2009, p. 43; Roger Vincent, "Corporate Travel: 'AIG' Effect Causes Companies to Cancel $1 Billion in Conferences," *Chicago Tribune*, April 13, 2009, www.chicagotribune.com.

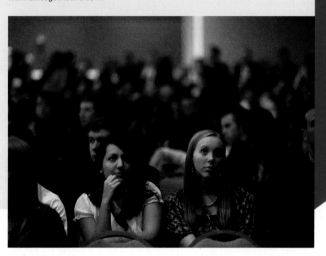

data aimed at advancing research on genomic, diseases, and natural disasters. The first project, the Human Proteome Folding Project, assists in identifying cures for diseases such as malaria and tuberculosis and has registered 85,000 devices around the world to date.

- General Electric Company (GE) has a long history of supporting the communities where its employees work and live through GE's unique combination of resources, equipment, and employees' and retirees' hearts and souls. Today GE's responsibility extends to communities around the world.

  GE applies its long-standing spirit of innovation and unique set of capabilities to take on tough challenges in its communities. In 2007, GE dramatically expanded its signature programs, Developing Health Globally™ and Developing Futures™. Developing Health Globally is an initiative that began in 2004 with a $20-million product donation investment in rural African communities that has since expanded to a five-year, $30-million commitment that includes Latin America. The Developing Futures education program aims to raise standards and increase proficiency in math and science among U.S. students. To these ends, the GE Foundation has made a long-term, $100-million commitment to U.S. students beginning in five school districts (Louisville, Kentucky; Cincinnati, Ohio; Stamford, Connecticut; Erie, Pennsylvania; and Atlanta, Georgia) serving more than 215,000 students. In 2008, GE employees and retirees volunteered about one million hours to improve their communities. The total contributions by the GE family exceeded $237 million in 2008.[9]

- With the help of dedicated Schwab volunteers, Charles Schwab Foundation provides programs and funding to help individuals fill the information gap.

Corporate Social Responsibility may cost money, but it is also good for business.
ConAgra Foods, one of North America's largest packaged food companies, is the national sponsor of Kids Cafe, which provide free meal programs for children at-risk of hunger. Children who participate in Kids Cafe programs report earning better grades in school, having more energy, feeling less fatigued, and having improved concentration.

Here, hungry children in Omaha, Nebraska, are enjoying an early Thanksgiving meal with turkeys donated by ConAgra Foods' Feeding Children Better Foundation and Butterball.

For example, Schwab MoneyWise helps adults teach—and children learn—the basics of financial literacy. Interactive tools are available at **schwabmoneywise. com,** and local workshops cover topics such as getting kids started on a budget. In addition to these efforts, widely distributed publications and news columns by foundation President Carrie Schwab Pomerantz promote financial literacy on a wide range of topics—from savings for a child's education to bridging the health insurance gap for retirees.

Most recently, Schwab employees and board members contributed nearly $3 million to more than 2,200 charitable organizations. About half of employee gifts and matching funds go to education-related charities and over one-fourth of the contributions are for health and human services.[10]

- Improving basic literacy skills in the United States is among the Verizon Foundation's major priorities because of its enormous impact on education, health, and economic development. Here in the United States, more than 30 million American adults have basic or below average literacy skills. Thinkfinity.org is designed to improve education and literacy achievement. This comprehensive free website delivers online resources to advance student achievement. Thinkfinity delivers top-quality K-12 lesson plans, student materials, interactive tools, and connections to educational websites. It gives teachers, instructors, and parents the tools they need to increase student performance.

Domestic violence is the greatest cause of injury to women between the ages of 15 and 44 in the United States—more than muggings, car accidents, and rapes combined. Furthermore, the Verizon Foundation supported domestic violence prevention organizations with $5.4 million in grants. In addition, Verizon Wireless' HopeLine program, which puts wireless technology to work to help victims of domestic violence, collected more than 1 million no-longer-used phones, awarded more than $1.7 million in cash grants to domestic violence agencies, and distributed more than 20,000 phones—with the equivalent of 60 million minutes of service—to be used by victims of domestic violence. For the commitment to end domestic violence, the California State Assembly honored Verizon for "funding innovative initiatives that empower victims to make changes in their lives and in the lives of their loved ones."[11]

- ExxonMobil's commitment to education spans all levels of achievement. One of its corporate primary goals is to support basic education and literacy programs in the developing world. In areas of the world where basic education levels have been met, ExxonMobil supports education programs in science, technology, engineering, and mathematics.

ExxonMobil recognizes the essential role that proficiency in math and science plays not only in the energy business, but also in fostering innovation and facilitating human progress. The company encourages new generations to pursue studies and careers in field involving math and science. Toward that goal, it supports programs focused on laying the foundation for long-term educational improvements, such as the National Math and Science Initiative and the Mickelson ExxonMobil Teachers Academy.

Project NExT, an acronym for "New Experience in Teaching," helps prepare new Ph.D. mathematicians for the challenges of undergraduate teaching. Administered by the Mathematical Association of America, the program gives new teachers access to seasoned professionals and helps acquaint them with a broad array of teaching strategies. This program has benefited more than 1,000 Project NExT fellows at 450 colleges and universities.[12]

- AT&T has built a tradition of supporting education, health and human services, the environment, public policy, and the arts in the communities it serves since Alexander Graham Bell founded the company over a century ago. Since 1984, AT&T has invested more than $600 million in support of education. Currently, more than half the company's contribution dollars, employee volunteer time, and community-service activities is directed toward education. In 1995, AT&T created the AT&T Learning Network, a $150 million corporate commitment to support the education of children in schools across the nation by providing the latest technology and cash grants to schools and communities. Since 1911, AT&T has been a sponsor to the Telephone Pioneers of America, the world's largest industry-based volunteer organization consisting of nearly 750,000 employees and retirees from the telecommunications industry. Each year, the Pioneers volunteer millions of hours and raise millions of dollars for health and human services and the environment. For example, through the AT&T Pioneers, nearly 300,000 AT&T employees and retirees contributed more than 10 million hours of volunteer time, worth more than $195 million, to community outreach activities nationwide in 2008. In schools and neighborhoods, the Pioneers strengthen connections and build communities.

In 2009, responding to President Barack Obama's call to action for all Americans to participate in the annual national day of service, Share Our Strength and AT&T Inc., the Communications Workers of America and the AT&T Pioneers announced two new programs in the fight against childhood hunger. The text-donation program encourages wireless phone users, including AT&T customers, to donate to Share Our Strength via their mobile phones, and a nationwide AT&T employee food drive. Share Our Strength, a national organization dedicated to ending childhood hunger, provides support for hundreds of hunger-relief organizations. Donations are used to help provide food for 12.4 million children at risk of hunger in America.[13]

- At Merck & Co., Inc., the Patient Assistance Program makes the company's medicines available to low-income Americans and their families at no cost. When patients don't have health insurance or a prescription drug plan and are unable to afford the Merck medicines their doctors prescribe, they can work with their physicians to contact the Merck Patient Assistance Program. For nearly fifty years, Merck has provided its medicines completely free of charge to people in need through this program. Patients can get information through **www.merck. com** or by calling a toll-free number, 1-800-727-5400, or from their physician's office. For eligible patients, the medicines are shipped directly to their home or the prescribing physician's office. Each applicant may receive up to one year of medicines, and patients may reapply to the program if their need continues.

    Education programs often link social responsibility with corporate self-interest. For example, Bayer and Merck, two major pharmaceuticals firms, promote science education as a way to enlarge the pool of future employees. Students who visit the Bayer Science Forum in Elkhart, Indiana, work alongside scientists conducting a variety of experiments. And workshops created by the Merck Institute for Science Education show teachers how to put scientific principles into action through hands-on experiments.

    These are just a few illustrations from the long list of companies big and small that attempt to behave in socially responsible ways. In general, people are more likely to want to work for and buy from such organizations.

The Evolution of Social Responsibility in Business

Business is far from perfect in many respects, but its record of social responsibility today is much better than in past decades. In fact, present demands for social responsibility have their roots in outraged reactions to the abusive business practices of the early 1900s.

Historical Evolution of Business Social Responsibility

During the first quarter of the twentieth century, businesses were free to operate pretty much as they chose. Government protection of workers and consumers was minimal. As a result, people either accepted what business had to offer or they did without. Working conditions often were deplorable by today's standards. The average work week in most industries exceeded sixty hours, no minimum-wage law existed, and employee benefits were almost nonexistent. Work areas were crowded and unsafe, and industrial accidents were the rule rather than the exception. To improve working conditions, employees organized and joined labor unions. During the early 1900s, however, businesses—with the help of government—were able to use court orders, brute force, and even the few existing antitrust laws to defeat union attempts to improve working conditions.

During this period, consumers generally were subject to the doctrine of **caveat emptor**, a Latin phrase meaning "let the buyer beware." In other words, "what you see is what you get," and if it is not what you expected, too bad. Although victims of unscrupulous business practices could take legal action, going to court was very expensive, and consumers rarely won their cases. Moreover, no consumer groups or government agencies existed to publicize their consumers' grievances or to hold sellers accountable for their actions.

Prior to the 1930s, most people believed that competition and the action of the marketplace would, in time, correct abuses. Government therefore became involved in day-to-day business activities only in cases of obvious abuse of the free-market system. Six of the more important business-related federal laws passed between 1887 and 1914 are described in Table 2.2. As you can see, these laws were aimed more at encouraging competition than at correcting abuses, although two of them did deal with the purity of food and drug products.

Concept Check

1. How can the government encourage the ethical behavior of organizations?

2. What is trade association's role in encouraging ethics?

3. What is whistle-blowing? Who protects the whistle blowers?

4. What is social responsibility? How can businesses be socially responsible?

5 LEARNING OBJECTIVE

Describe how our current views on the social responsibility of business have evolved.

caveat emptor a Latin phrase meaning "let the buyer beware"

TABLE 2.2: Early Government Regulations That Affected American Business

Government Regulation	Major Provisions
Interstate Commerce Act (1887)	First federal act to regulate business practices; provided regulation of railroads and shipping rates
Sherman Antitrust Act (1890)	Prevented monopolies or mergers where competition was endangered
Pure Food and Drug Act (1906)	Established limited supervision of interstate sale of food and drugs
Meat Inspection Act (1906)	Provided for limited supervision of interstate sale of meat and meat products
Federal Trade Commission Act (1914)	Created the Federal Trade Commission to investigate illegal trade practices
Clayton Antitrust Act (1914)	Eliminated many forms of price discrimination that gave large businesses a competitive advantage over smaller firms

The collapse of the stock market on October 29, 1929, triggered the Great Depression and years of dire economic problems for the United States. Factory production fell by almost one-half, and up to 25 percent of the nation's work-force was unemployed. Before long, public pressure mounted for government to "do something" about the economy and about worsening social conditions.

Soon after Franklin D. Roosevelt was inaugurated as president in 1933, he instituted programs to restore the economy and improve social conditions. Laws were passed to correct what many viewed as the monopolistic abuses of big business, and various social services were provided for individuals. These massive federal programs became the foundation for increased government involvement in the dealings between business and society.

As government involvement has increased, so has everyone's awareness of the social responsibility of business. Today's business owners are concerned about the return on their investment, but at the same time most of them demand ethical behavior from employees. In addition, employees demand better working conditions, and consumers want safe, reliable products. Various advocacy groups echo these concerns and also call for careful consideration of our earth's delicate ecological balance. Managers therefore must operate in a complex business environment—one in which they are just as responsible for their managerial actions as for their actions as individual citizens. Interestingly, today's high-tech and Internet-based firms fare relatively well when it comes to environmental issues, worker conditions, the representation of minorities and women in upper management, animal testing, and charitable donations.

Concept Check

1. Outline the historical evolution of business social responsibility.

2. What is the doctrine of caveat emptor?

3. What are the six important business-related federal laws passed between 1887 and 1914?

LEARNING OBJECTIVE 6

Explain the two views on the social responsibility of business and understand the arguments for and against increased social responsibility.

economic model of social responsibility the view that society will benefit most when business is left alone to produce and market profitable products that society needs

Two Views of Social Responsibility

Government regulation and public awareness are *external* forces that have increased the social responsibility of business. But business decisions are made *within* the firm—and there, social responsibility begins with the attitude of management. Two contrasting philosophies, or models, define the range of management attitudes toward social responsibility.

The Economic Model

According to the traditional concept of business, a firm exists to produce quality goods and services, earn a reasonable profit, and provide jobs. In line with this concept, the **economic model of social responsibility** holds that society will benefit most when business is left alone to produce and market profitable products that society needs. The economic model has its origins in the eighteenth century, when businesses were owned primarily by entrepreneurs or owner-managers. Competition was vigorous among small firms, and short-run profits and survival were the primary concerns.

To the manager who adopts this traditional attitude, social responsibility is someone else's job. After all, stockholders invest in a corporation to earn a return on their investment, not because the firm is socially responsible, and the firm is legally obligated to act in the economic interest of its stockholders. Moreover, profitable firms pay federal, state, and local taxes that are used to meet the needs of society. Thus, managers who concentrate on profit believe that they fulfill their social responsibility indirectly through the taxes paid by their firms. As a result, social responsibility becomes the problem of government, various environmental groups, charitable foundations, and similar organizations.

The Socioeconomic Model

In contrast, some managers believe that they have a responsibility not only to stockholders but also to customers, employees, suppliers, and the general public. This broader view is referred to as the **socioeconomic model of social responsibility**, which places emphasis not only on profits but also on the impact of business decisions on society.

socioeconomic model of social responsibility the concept that business should emphasize not only profits but also the impact of its decisions on society

Recently, increasing numbers of managers and firms have adopted the socioeconomic model, and they have done so for at least three reasons. First, business is dominated by the corporate form of ownership, and the corporation is a creation of society. If a corporation does not perform as a good citizen, society can and will demand changes. Second, many firms have begun to take pride in their social responsibility records, among them Starbucks Coffee, Hewlett-Packard, Colgate-Palmolive, and Coca-Cola. Each of these companies is a winner of a Corporate Conscience Award in the areas of environmental concern, responsiveness to employees, equal opportunity, and community involvement. And of course, many other corporations are much more socially responsible today than they were ten years ago. Third, many businesspeople believe that it is in their best interest to take the initiative in this area. The alternative may be legal action brought against the firm by some special-interest group; in such a situation, the firm may lose control of its activities.

The Pros and Cons of Social Responsibility

Business owners, managers, customers, and government officials have debated the pros and cons of the economic and socioeconomic models for years. Each side seems to have four major arguments to reinforce its viewpoint.

Arguments for Increased Social Responsibility Proponents of the socioeconomic model maintain that a business must do more than simply seek profits. To support their position, they offer the following arguments:

1. Because business is a part of our society, it cannot ignore social issues.
2. Business has the technical, financial, and managerial resources needed to tackle today's complex social issues.

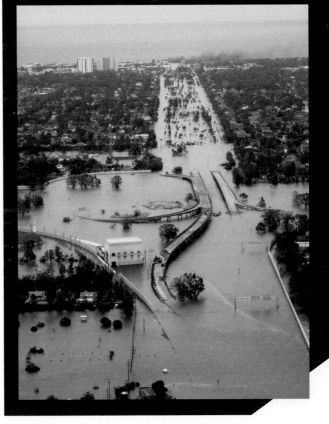

Studies show that global warming is occurring and we are causing it by burning fossil fuels (coal, oil and natural gas) and cutting forests. The U.S. National Academy of Sciences states, "It is vital that all nations identify cost-effective steps that they can take now, to contribute to substantial and long-term reduction in net global greenhouse gas emissions." Global warming is feared to cause the world's glaciers to melt and increase the frequency and intensity of many kinds of extreme weather, such as Hurricane Katrina.

©AP Photo/US Coast Guard, Petty Officer 2nd class Kyle Niemi

3. By helping resolve social issues, business can create a more stable environment for long-term profitability.
4. Socially responsible decision making by firms can prevent increased government intervention, which would force businesses to do what they fail to do voluntarily.

These arguments are based on the assumption that a business has a responsibility not only to its stockholders but also to its customers, employees, suppliers, and the general public.

Arguments Against Increased Social Responsibility Opponents of the socioeconomic model argue that business should do what it does best: earn a profit by manufacturing and marketing products that people want. Those who support this position argue as follows:

1. Business managers are responsible primarily to stockholders, so management must be concerned with providing a return on owners' investments.
2. Corporate time, money, and talent should be used to maximize profits, not to solve society's problems.
3. Social problems affect society in general, so individual businesses should not be expected to solve these problems.
4. Social issues are the responsibility of government officials who are elected for that purpose and who are accountable to the voters for their decisions.

These arguments obviously are based on the assumption that the primary objective of business is to earn profits and that government and social institutions should deal with social problems.

Table 2.3 compares the economic and socioeconomic viewpoints in terms of business emphasis. Today, few firms are either purely economic or purely socioeconomic in outlook; most have chosen some middle ground between the two extremes. However, our society generally seems to want—and even to expect—some degree of social responsibility from business. Thus, within this middle ground, businesses are leaning toward the socioeconomic view. In the next several sections, we look at some results of this movement in four specific areas: consumerism, employment practices, concern for the environment, and implementation of social responsibility programs.

Concept Check

1. Explain the two views on the social responsibility of business.

2. What are the arguments for increased social responsibility?

3. What are the arguments against increased social responsibility?

TABLE 2.3: A Comparison of the Economic and Socioeconomic Models of Social Responsibility as Implemented in Business

Economic Model Primary Emphasis		Socioeconomic Model Primary Emphasis
1. Production		1. Quality of life
2. Exploitation of natural resources		2. Conservation of natural resources
3. Internal, market-based decisions	Middle ground	3. Market-based decisions, with some community controls
4. Economic return (profit)		4. Balance of economic return and social return
5. Firm's or manager's interest		5. Firm's and community's interests
6. Minor role for government		6. Active government

Source: Adapted from Keith Davis, William C. Frederick, and Robert L. Blomstron, *Business and Society: Concepts and Policy Issues* (New York: McGraw-Hill, 1980), p. 9. Used by permission of McGraw-Hill Book Company.

Consumerism

7 LEARNING OBJECTIVE

Discuss the factors that led to the consumer movement and list some of its results.

Consumerism consists of all activities undertaken to protect the rights of consumers. The fundamental issues pursued by the consumer movement fall into three categories: environmental protection, product performance and safety, and information disclosure. Although consumerism has been with us to some extent since the early nineteenth century, the consumer movement became stronger in the 1960s. It was then that President John F. Kennedy declared that the consumer was entitled to a new "bill of rights."

The Six Basic Rights of Consumers

President Kennedy's consumer bill of rights asserted that consumers have a right to safety, to be informed, to choose, and to be heard. Two additional rights added since 1975 are the right to consumer education and the right to courteous service. These six rights are the basis of much of the consumer-oriented legislation passed during the last forty years. These rights also provide an effective outline of the objectives and accomplishments of the consumer movement.

The Right to Safety The consumers' right to safety means that the products they purchase must be safe for their intended use, must include thorough and explicit directions for proper use, and must be tested by the manufacturer to ensure product quality and reliability. There are several reasons why American business firms must be concerned about product safety.

Corrective Actions Can Be Expensive. Federal agencies such as the Food and Drug Administration and the Consumer Product Safety Commission have the power to force businesses that make or sell defective products to take corrective actions. Such actions include offering refunds, recalling defective products, issuing public warnings, and reimbursing consumers—all of which can be expensive.

Increasing Number of Lawsuits. Business firms also should be aware that consumers and the government have been winning an increasing number of product-liability lawsuits against sellers of defective products. Moreover, the amount of the awards in these suits has been increasing steadily. Fearing the outcome of numerous lawsuits filed around the nation, tobacco giants Philip Morris and R. J. Reynolds, which for decades had denied that cigarettes cause illness, began negotiating in 1997 with state attorneys general, plaintiffs' lawyers, and anti-smoking activists. The tobacco giants proposed sweeping curbs on their sales and advertising practices and the payment of hundreds of billions of dollars in compensation.

Consumer Demand. Yet another major reason for improving product safety is consumers' demand for safe products. People simply will stop buying a product they believe is unsafe or unreliable.

The Right to Be Informed The right to be informed means that consumers must have access to complete information about a product before they buy it. Detailed information about ingredients and nutrition must be provided on food containers, information about fabrics and laundering methods must be attached to clothing, and lenders must disclose the true cost of borrowing the money they make available to customers who purchase merchandise on credit.

In addition, manufacturers must inform consumers about the potential dangers of using their products. Manufacturers that fail to provide such information can be held responsible for

consumerism all activities undertaken to protect the rights of consumers

The right to be informed. The Consumer Bill of Rights asserts consumers' basic rights. The right to be informed and the right to choose mean that consumers must have complete information about a product and a choice of products.

©Monkey Business Images/Shutterstock

personal injuries suffered because of their products. For example, Maytag provides customers with a lengthy booklet that describes how they should use an automatic clothes washer. Sometimes such warnings seem excessive, but they are necessary if user injuries (and resulting lawsuits) are to be avoided.

The Right to Choose The right to choose means that consumers must have a choice of products, offered by different manufacturers and sellers, to satisfy a particular need. The government has done its part by encouraging competition through antitrust legislation. The greater the competition, the greater is the choice available to consumers.

Competition and the resulting freedom of choice provide additional benefits for customers by reducing prices. For example, when personal computers were introduced, they cost over $5,000. Thanks to intense competition and technological advancements, personal computers today can be purchased for less than $500.

The Right to Be Heard This fourth right means that someone will listen and take appropriate action when customers complain. Actually, management began to listen to consumers after World War II, when competition between businesses that manufactured and sold consumer goods increased. One way that firms got a competitive edge was to listen to consumers and provide the products they said they wanted and needed. Today, businesses are listening even more attentively, and many larger firms have consumer relations departments that can be contacted easily via toll-free phone numbers. Other groups listen, too. Most large cities and some states have consumer affairs offices to act on citizens' complaints.

Additional Consumer Rights In 1975, President Gerald Ford added to the consumer bill of rights the right to consumer education, which entitles people to be fully informed about their rights as consumers. In 1994, President Bill Clinton added a sixth right, the right to service, which entitles consumers to convenience, courtesy, and responsiveness from manufacturers and sellers of consumer products.

Major Consumerism Forces

The major forces in consumerism are individual consumer advocates and organizations, consumer education programs, and consumer laws. Consumer advocates, such as Ralph Nader, take it on themselves to protect the rights of consumers. They band together into consumer organizations, either independently or under government sponsorship. Some organizations, such as the National Consumers' League and the Consumer Federation of America, operate nationally, whereas others are active at state and local levels. They inform and organize other consumers, raise issues, help businesses to develop consumer-oriented programs, and pressure lawmakers to enact consumer protection laws. Some consumer advocates and organizations encourage consumers to boycott products and businesses to which they have objections. Today, the consumer movement has adopted corporate-style marketing and addresses a broad range of issues. Current campaigns include efforts (1) to curtail the use of animals for testing purposes, (2) to reduce liquor and cigarette billboard advertising in low-income, inner-city neighborhoods, and (3) to encourage recycling.

Educating consumers to make wiser purchasing decisions is perhaps one of the most far-reaching aspects of consumerism. Increasingly, consumer education is becoming a part of high school and college curricula and adult-education programs. These programs cover many topics—for instance, what major factors should be considered when buying specific products, such as insurance, real estate, automobiles, appliances and furniture, clothes, and food; the provisions of certain consumer-protection laws; and the sources of information that can help individuals become knowledgeable consumers.

Major advances in consumerism have come through federal legislation. Some laws enacted in the last fifty years to protect your rights as a consumer are listed and described in Table 2.4. Most businesspeople now realize that they ignore consumer

Concept Check

1. Describe the six basic rights of consumers.

2. What are the major forces in consumerism today?

3. What are some of the federal laws enacted in the last fifty years to protect your rights as a consumer?

TABLE 2.4: Major Federal Legislation Protecting Consumers Since 1960

Legislation	Major Provisions
Federal Hazardous Substances Labeling Act (1960)	Required warning labels on household chemicals if they are highly toxic
Kefauver-Harris Drug Amendments (1962)	Established testing practices for drugs and required manufacturers to label drugs with generic names in addition to trade names
Cigarette Labeling Act (1965)	Required manufacturers to place standard warning labels on all cigarette packages and advertising
Fair Packaging and Labeling Act (1966)	Called for all products sold across state lines to be labeled with net weight, ingredients, and manufacturer's name and address
Motor Vehicle Safety Act (1966)	Established standards for safer cars
Wholesome Meat Act (1967)	Required states to inspect meat (but not poultry) sold within the state
Flammable Fabrics Act (1967)	Extended flammability standards for clothing to include children's sleepwear in sizes 0 to 6X
Truth in Lending Act (1968)	Required lenders and credit merchants to disclose the full cost of finance charges in both dollars and annual percentage rates
Child Protection and Toy Act (1969)	Banned toys with mechanical or electrical defects from interstate commerce
Credit Card Liability Act (1970)	Limited credit-card holder's liability to $50 per card and stopped credit-card companies from issuing unsolicited cards
Fair Credit Reporting Act (1971)	Required credit bureaus to provide credit reports to consumers regarding their own credit files; also provided for correction of incorrect information
Consumer Product Safety Commission Act (1972)	Established an abbreviated procedure for registering certain generic drugs
Trade Regulation Rule (1972)	Established a "cooling off" period of 72 hours for door-to-door sales
Fair Credit Billing Act (1974)	Amended the Truth in Lending Act to enable consumers to challenge billing errors
Equal Credit Opportunity Act (1974)	Provided equal credit opportunities for males and females and for married and single individuals
Magnuson-Moss Warranty-Federal Trade Commission Act (1975)	Provided for minimum disclosure standards for written consumer-product warranties for products that cost more than $15
Amendments to the Equal Credit Opportunity Act (1976, 1994)	Prevented discrimination based on race, creed, color, religion, age, and income when granting credit
Fair Debt Collection Practices Act (1977)	Outlawed abusive collection practices by third parties
Drug Price Competition and Patent Restoration Act (1984)	Established the Consumer Product Safety Commission
Orphan Drug Act (1985)	Amended the original 1983 Orphan Drug Act and extended tax incentives to encourage the development of drugs for rare diseases
Nutrition Labeling and Education Act (1990)	Required the Food and Drug Administration to review current food labeling and packaging focusing on nutrition label content, label format, ingredient labeling, food descriptors and standards, and health messages
Telephone Consumer Protection Act (1991)	Prohibited the use of automated dialing and prerecorded-voice calling equipment to make calls or deliver messages
Consumer Credit Reporting Reform Act (1997)	Placed more responsibility for accurate credit data on credit issuers; required creditors to verify that disputed data are accurate and to notify a consumer before reinstating the data
Children's Online Privacy Protection Act (2000)	Placed parents in control over what information is collected online from their children under age 13; required commercial website operators to maintain the confidentiality, security, and integrity of personal information collected from children
Do Not Call Implementation Act (2003)	Directed the FCC and the FTC to coordinate so that their rules are consistent regarding telemarketing call practices including the Do Not Call Registry and other lists, as well as call abandonment

issues only at their own peril. Managers know that improper handling of consumer complaints can result in lost sales, bad publicity, and lawsuits.

LEARNING
OBJECTIVE **8**

Analyze how present
employment practices
are being used to counteract
past abuses.

Employment Practices

Managers who subscribe to the socioeconomic view of a business's social responsibility, together with significant government legislation enacted to protect the buying public, have broadened the rights of consumers. The last five decades have seen similar progress in affirming the rights of employees to equal treatment in the workplace.

Everyone should have the opportunity to land a job for which he or she is qualified and to be rewarded on the basis of ability and performance. This is an important issue for society, and it also makes good business sense. Yet, over the years, this opportunity has been denied to members of various minority groups. A **minority** is a racial, religious, political, national, or other group regarded as different from the larger group of which it is a part and that is often singled out for unfavorable treatment.

The federal government responded to the outcry of minority groups during the 1960s and 1970s by passing a number of laws forbidding discrimination in the workplace. (These laws are discussed in Chapter 9 in the context of human resources management.) Now, forty-six years after passage of the first of these (the Civil Rights Act of 1964), abuses still exist. An example is the disparity in income levels for whites, blacks, Hispanics, and Asians, as illustrated in Figure 2.3. Lower incomes and higher unemployment rates also characterize Native Americans, handicapped persons, and women. Responsible managers have instituted a number of programs to counteract the results of discrimination.

minority a racial, religious, political, national, or other group regarded as different from the larger group of which it is a part and that is often singled out for unfavorable treatment

affirmative action program a plan designed to increase the number of minority employees at all levels within an organization

Affirmative Action Programs

An **affirmative action program** is a plan designed to increase the number of minority employees at all levels within an organization. Employers with federal contracts of more than $50,000 per year must have written affirmative action plans. The objective of such programs is to ensure that minorities are represented within the organization in approximately the same proportion as in the surrounding community. If 25 percent of the electricians in a geographic area in which a company is located are black, then approximately 25 percent of the electricians it employs also should be black. Affirmative action plans encompass all areas of human resources management: recruiting, hiring, training, promotion, and pay.

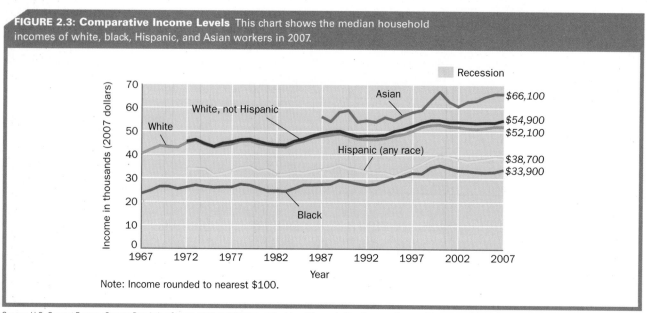

FIGURE 2.3: Comparative Income Levels This chart shows the median household incomes of white, black, Hispanic, and Asian workers in 2007.

Note: Income rounded to nearest $100.

Source: U.S. Census Bureau, Current Population Survey, 1968 to 2008 Annual Social and Economic Supplements, *Income, Poverty, and Health Insurance Coverage in the United States: 2007*, issued August 2008, U.S. Census Bureau, U.S. Department of Commerce, p. 6, **www.census.gov/prod/2008pubs/p60-235.pdf**, accessed May 1, 2009.

Unfortunately, affirmative action programs have been plagued by two problems. The first involves quotas. In the beginning, many firms pledged to recruit and hire a certain number of minority members by a specific date. To achieve this goal, they were forced to consider only minority applicants for job openings; if they hired non-minority workers, they would be defeating their own purpose. However, the courts have ruled that such quotas are unconstitutional even though their purpose is commendable. They are, in fact, a form of discrimination called *reverse discrimination*.

The second problem is that although most such programs have been reasonably successful, not all businesspeople are in favor of affirmative action programs. Managers not committed to these programs can "play the game" and still discriminate against workers. To help solve this problem, Congress created (and later strengthened) the **Equal Employment Opportunity Commission (EEOC)**, a government agency with the power to investigate complaints of employment discrimination and sue firms that practice it.

The threat of legal action has persuaded some corporations to amend their hiring and promotional policies, but the discrepancy between men's and women's salaries still exists, as illustrated in Figure 2.4. For more than fifty years, women have consistently earned only about 78 cents for each dollar earned by men.

Strong opinions about affirmative action. Affirmative action programs ensure that minorities are represented within the organization in approximately the same proportion as in the surrounding community. Here, in the Winston-Salem Police Department, of the 30 recruits in the Basic Law Enforcement Training classes, 24 are white men, two are Hispanic men, two are black women, one is a white woman and one is an American Indian man.

Equal Employment Opportunity Commission (EEOC) a government agency with power to investigate complaints of employment discrimination and power to sue firms that practice it

hard-core unemployed workers with little education or vocational training and a long history of unemployment

Training Programs for the Hard-Core Unemployed

For some firms, social responsibility extends far beyond placing a help-wanted ad in the local newspaper. These firms have assumed the task of helping the **hard-core unemployed**, workers with little education or vocational training and a long history of unemployment. For example, a few years ago, General Mills helped establish

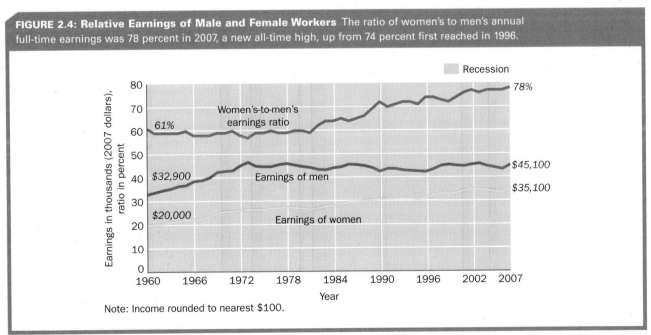

FIGURE 2.4: Relative Earnings of Male and Female Workers The ratio of women's to men's annual full-time earnings was 78 percent in 2007, a new all-time high, up from 74 percent first reached in 1996.

Note: Income rounded to nearest $100.

Source: U.S. Census Bureau, Current Population Survey, 1968 to 2008 Annual Social and Economic Supplements, *Income, Poverty, and Health Insurance Coverage in the United States: 2007*, issued August 2008, U.S. Census Bureau, U.S. Department of Commerce, p. 11, **www.census.gov/prod/2008pubs/p60-235.pdf**, accessed May 1, 2009.

Concept Check

1. What is an affirmative action program? What is its purpose?

2. Why did Congress create (and later strengthened) the Equal Employment Opportunity Commission?

3. What is the National Alliance of Business?

Siyeza, a frozen soul-food processing plant in North Minneapolis. Through the years, Siyeza has provided stable, high-quality full-time jobs for a permanent core of eighty unemployed or underemployed minority inner-city residents. In addition, groups of up to a hundred temporary employees are called in when needed. In the past, such workers often were turned down routinely by personnel managers, even for the most menial jobs.

Obviously, such workers require training; just as obviously, this training can be expensive and time consuming. To share the costs, business and community leaders have joined together in a number of cooperative programs. One particularly successful partnership is the **National Alliance of Business (NAB)**, a joint business-government program to train the hard-core unemployed. The alliance's 5,000 members include companies of all sizes and industries, their CEOs and senior executives, as well as educators and community leaders. NAB, founded in 1968 by President Lyndon Johnson and Henry Ford II, is a major national business organization focusing on education and workforce issues.

LEARNING OBJECTIVE 9

Describe the major types of pollution, their causes, and their cures.

Concern for the Environment

The social consciousness of responsible business managers, the encouragement of a concerned government, and an increasing concern on the part of the public have led to a major effort to reduce environmental pollution, conserve natural resources, and reverse some of the worst effects of past negligence in this area. **Pollution** is the contamination of water, air, or land through the actions of people in an industrialized society. For several decades, environmentalists have been warning us about the dangers of industrial pollution. Unfortunately, business and government leaders either ignored the problem or were not concerned about it until pollution became a threat to life and health in America. Today, Americans expect business and government leaders to take swift action to clean up our environment—and to keep it clean.

Effects of Environmental Legislation

As in other areas of concern to our society, legislation and regulations play a crucial role in pollution control. The laws outlined in Table 2.5 reflect the scope of current environmental legislation: laws to promote clean air, clean water, and even quiet work and living environments. Of major importance was the creation of the Environmental Protection Agency (EPA), the federal agency charged with enforcing laws designed to protect the environment.

When they are aware of a pollution problem, many firms respond to it rather than wait to be cited by the EPA. Other owners and managers, however, take the position that environmental standards are too strict. (Loosely translated, this means that compliance with present standards is too expensive.) Consequently, it often has been necessary for the EPA to take legal action to force firms to install antipollution equipment and to clean up waste storage areas.

Experience has shown that the combination of environmental legislation, voluntary compliance, and EPA action can succeed in cleaning up the environment and keeping it clean. However, much still remains to be done.

Water Pollution The Clean Water Act has been credited with greatly improving the condition of the waters in the United States. This success comes largely from the control of pollutant discharges from industrial and wastewater treatment plants. Although the quality of our nation's rivers, lakes, and streams has improved significantly in recent years, many of these surface waters remain severely polluted. Currently, one of the most serious water-quality problems results from the high level of toxic pollutants found in these waters.

Among the serious threats to people posed by water pollutants are respiratory irritation, cancer, kidney and liver damage, anemia, and heart failure. Toxic

National Alliance of Business (NAB) a joint business-government program to train the hard-core unemployed

pollution the contamination of water, air, or land through the actions of people in an industrialized society

TABLE 2.5: Summary of Major Environmental Laws

Legislation	Major Provisions
National Environmental Policy Act (1970)	Established the Environmental Protection Agency (EPA) to enforce federal laws that involve the environment
Clean Air Amendment (1970)	Provided stringent automotive, aircraft, and factory emission standards
Water Quality Improvement Act (1970)	Strengthened existing water pollution regulations and provided for large monetary fines against violators
Resource Recovery Act (1970)	Enlarged the solid-waste disposal program and provided for enforcement by the EPA
Water Pollution Control Act Amendment (1972)	Established standards for cleaning navigable streams and lakes and eliminating all harmful waste disposal by 1985
Noise Control Act (1972)	Established standards for major sources of noise and required the EPA to advise the Federal Aviation Administration on standards for airplanes
Clean Air Act Amendment (1977)	Established new deadlines for cleaning up polluted areas; also required review of existing air-quality standards
Resource Conservation and Recovery Act (1984)	Amended the original 1976 act and required federal regulation of potentially dangerous solid-waste disposal
Clean Air Act Amendment (1987)	Established a national air-quality standard for ozone
Oil Pollution Act (1990)	Expanded the nation's oil-spill prevention and response activities; also established the Oil Spill Liability Trust Fund
Clean Air Act Amendments (1990)	Required that motor vehicles be equipped with onboard systems to control about 90 percent of refueling vapors
Food Quality Protection Act (1996)	Amended the Federal Insecticide, Fungicide and Rodenticide Act and the Federal Food Drug and Cosmetic Act; the requirements included a new safety standard—reasonable certainty of no harm—that must be applied to all pesticides used on foods

pollutants also damage fish and other forms of wildlife. In fish, they cause tumors or reproductive problems; shellfish and wildlife living in or drinking from toxin-laden waters also have suffered genetic defects. Recently, the Pollution Control Board of Kerala in India ordered Coca-Cola to close its major bottling plant. For years, villagers in the nearby areas had accused Coke of depleting local ground-water and producing other local pollution. The village council president said, "We are happy that the government is finally giving justice to the people who are affected by the plant."

The task of water cleanup has proved to be extremely complicated and costly because of pollution runoff and toxic contamination. And yet improved water quality is not only necessary; it is also achievable. Consider Cleveland's Cuyahoga River. A few years ago, the river was so contaminated by industrial wastes that it burst into flames one hot summer day! Now, after a sustained community cleanup effort, the river is pure enough for fish to thrive in.

Another serious issue is acid rain, which is contributing significantly to the deterioration of coastal waters, lakes, and marine life in the eastern United States. Acid rain forms when sulfur emitted by smokestacks in industrialized areas combines with moisture in the atmosphere to form acids that are spread by winds. The acids eventually fall to the earth in rain, which finds its way into streams, rivers, and lakes. The acid-rain problem has spread rapidly in recent years, and experts fear that the situation will worsen if the nation begins to burn more coal to generate electricity. To solve the problem, investigators first must determine where the sulfur is being emitted. The costs of this vital investigation and cleanup are going to be high. The human costs of having ignored the problem so long may be higher still.

Air Pollution Aviation emissions are a potentially significant and growing percentage of greenhouse gases that contribute to global warming. Aircraft emissions are significant for several reasons. First, jet aircraft are the main source of human emissions deposited directly into the upper atmosphere, where they may have a greater warming effect than if they were released at the earth's surface. Second, carbon dioxide—the primary aircraft emission—is the main focus of international concern. For example, it survives in the atmosphere for nearly one hundred years and contributes to global warming, according to the Intergovernmental Panel on Climate Change. The carbon dioxide emissions from worldwide aviation roughly equal those of some industrialized countries. Third, carbon dioxide emissions, combined with other gases and particles emitted by jet aircraft, could have two to four times as great an effect on the atmosphere as carbon dioxide alone. Fourth, the Intergovernmental Panel recently concluded that the rise in aviation emissions owing to the growing demand for air travel would not be fully offset by reductions in emissions achieved solely through technological improvements.

Usually, two or three factors combine to form air pollution in any given location. The first factor is large amounts of carbon monoxide and hydrocarbons emitted by motor vehicles concentrated in a relatively small area. The second is the smoke and other pollutants emitted by manufacturing facilities. These two factors can be eliminated in part through pollution control devices on cars, trucks, and smokestacks.

A third factor that contributes to air pollution—one that cannot be changed—is the combination of weather and geography. The Los Angeles Basin, for example, combines just the right weather and geographic conditions for creating dense smog. Los Angeles has strict regulations regarding air pollution. Even so, Los Angeles still struggles with air pollution problems because of uncontrollable conditions.

How effective is air pollution control? The EPA estimates that the Clean Air Act and its amendments eventually will result in the removal of 56 billion pounds of pollution from the air each year, thus measurably reducing lung disease, cancer, and other serious health problems caused by air pollution. Other authorities note that we have already seen improvement in air quality. A number of cities have cleaner air today than they did thirty years ago. Even in southern California, bad air quality days have dropped to less than forty days a year, about 60 percent lower than just a decade ago. Numerous chemical companies have recognized that they must take responsibility for operating their plants in an environmentally safe manner; some now devote considerable capital to purchasing antipollution devices. For example, 3M's pioneering Pollution Prevention Pays (3P) program, designed to find ways to avoid the generation of pollutants, marked its thirtieth anniversary in 2005. Since 1975, more than 5,600 employee-driven 3P projects have prevented the generation of more than 2.2 billion pounds of pollutants and produced first-year savings of nearly $1 billion.

Land Pollution Air and water quality may be improving, but land pollution is still a serious problem in many areas. The fundamental issues are (1) how to restore damaged or contaminated land at a reasonable cost and (2) how to protect unpolluted land from future damage.

The land pollution problem has been worsening over the past few years because modern technology has continued to produce increasing amounts of chemical and radioactive waste. U.S. manufacturers produce an estimated 40 to 60 million tons of contaminated oil, solvents, acids, and sludges each year. Service businesses, utility companies, hospitals, and other industries also dump vast amounts of wastes into the environment.

Individuals in the United States contribute to the waste-disposal problem, too. A shortage of landfills, owing to stricter regulations, makes garbage disposal a serious problem in some areas. Incinerators help to solve the landfill-shortage problem, but they bring with them their own problems. They reduce the amount of garbage but also leave tons of ash to be buried—ash that often has a higher concentration of toxicity than the original garbage. Other causes of land pollution include strip-mining of coal, nonselective cutting of forests, and the development of agricultural land for housing and industry.

To help pay the enormous costs of cleaning up land polluted with chemicals and toxic wastes, Congress created a $1.6 billion Superfund in 1980. Originally, money was to flow into the Superfund from a tax paid by 800 oil and chemical companies that produce toxic waste. The EPA was to use the money in the Superfund to finance the cleanup of hazardous waste sites across the nation. To replenish the Superfund, the EPA had two options: It could sue companies guilty of dumping chemicals at specific waste sites, or it could negotiate with guilty companies and thus completely avoid the legal system. During the 1980s, officials at the EPA came under fire because they preferred negotiated settlements. Critics referred to these settlements as "sweetheart deals" with industry. They felt that the EPA should be much more aggressive in reducing land pollution. Of course, most corporate executives believe that cleanup efficiency and quality might be improved if companies were more involved in the process. Many firms, including Delphi Automotive Systems Corporation and 3M, have modified or halted the production and sale of products that have a negative impact on the environment. For example, after tests showed that ScotchGuard does not decompose in the environment, 3M announced a voluntary end to production of the forty-year-old product, which had generated $300 million in sales.

Noise Pollution Excessive noise caused by traffic, aircraft, and machinery can do physical harm to human beings. Research has shown that people who are exposed to loud noises for long periods of time can suffer permanent hearing loss. The Noise Control Act of 1972 established noise emission standards for aircraft and airports, railroads, and interstate motor carriers. The act also provided funding for noise research at state and local levels.

Noise levels can be reduced by two methods. The source of noise pollution can be isolated as much as possible. (Thus, many metropolitan airports are located outside the cities.) And engineers can modify machinery and equipment to reduce noise levels. If it is impossible to reduce industrial noise to acceptable levels, workers should be required to wear earplugs to guard against permanent hearing damage.

Who Should Pay for a Clean Environment?

Governments and businesses are spending billions of dollars annually to reduce pollution—over $45 billion to control air pollution, $33 billion to control water pollution, and $12 billion to treat hazardous wastes. To make matters worse, much of the money required to purify the environment is supposed to come from already depressed industries, such as the chemical industry. And a few firms have discovered that it is cheaper to pay a fine than to install expensive equipment for pollution control.

Who, then, will pay for the environmental cleanup? Many business leaders offer one answer—tax money should be used to clean up the environment and to keep it clean. They reason that business is not the only source of pollution, so business should not be forced to absorb the entire cost of the cleanup. Environmentalists disagree. They believe that the cost of proper treatment and disposal of industrial wastes is an expense of doing business. In either case, consumers probably will pay a large part of the cost—either as taxes or in the form of higher prices for goods and services.

Concept Check

1. Describe the major types of pollution? What are their causes, and their cures?

2. Summarize major provisions of federal environmental laws enacted since 1970.

3. Who should pay for a clean environment?

Implementing a Program of Social Responsibility

10 LEARNING OBJECTIVE

Identify the steps a business must take to implement a program of social responsibility.

A firm's decision to be socially responsible is a step in the right direction—but only the first step. The firm then must develop and implement a program to reach this goal. The program will be affected by the firm's size, financial resources, past record in the area of social responsibility, and competition. Above all, however, the program must have the firm's total commitment or it will fail.

Developing a Program of Social Responsibility

An effective program for social responsibility takes time, money, and organization. In most cases, developing and implementing such a program will require four steps: securing the commitment of top executives, planning, appointing a director, and preparing a social audit.

Commitment of Top Executives

Without the support of top executives, any program will soon falter and become ineffective. For example, the Boeing Company's Ethics and Business Conduct Committee is responsible for the ethics program. The committee is appointed by the Boeing board of directors, and its members include the company chairman and CEO, the president and chief operating officer, the presidents of the operating groups, and senior vice presidents. As evidence of their commitment to social responsibility, top managers should develop a policy statement that outlines key areas of concern. This statement sets a tone of positive support and later will serve as a guide for other employees as they become involved in the program.

Planning

Next, a committee of managers should be appointed to plan the program. Whatever form their plan takes, it should deal with each of the issues described in the top managers' policy statement. If necessary, outside consultants can be hired to help develop the plan.

Appointment of a Director

After the social responsibility plan is established, a top-level executive should be appointed to implement the organization's plan. This individual should be charged with recommending specific policies and helping individual departments to understand and live up to the social responsibilities the firm has assumed. Depending on the size of the firm, the director may require a staff to handle the program on a day-to-day basis. For example, at the Boeing Company, the director of ethics and business conduct administers the ethics and business conduct program.

The Social Audit

At specified intervals, the program director should prepare a social audit for the firm. A **social audit** is a comprehensive report of what an organization has done and is doing with regard to social issues that affect it. This document provides the information the firm needs to evaluate and revise its social responsibility program. Typical subject areas include human resources, community involvement, the quality and safety of products, business practices, and efforts to reduce pollution and improve the environment. The information included in a social audit should be as accurate and as quantitative as possible, and the audit should reveal both positive and negative aspects of the program.

Today, many companies listen to concerned individuals within and outside the company. For example, the Boeing Ethics Line listens to and acts on concerns expressed by employees and others about possible violations of company policies, laws, or regulations, such as improper or unethical business practices, as well as health, safety, and environmental issues. Employees are encouraged to communicate their concerns, as well as ask questions about ethical issues. The Ethics Line is available to all Boeing employees, including Boeing subsidiaries. It is also available to concerned individuals outside the company.

Funding the Program

We have noted that social responsibility costs money. Thus, just like any other corporate undertaking, a program to improve social responsibility must be funded. Funding can come from three sources:

1. Management can pass the cost on to consumers in the form of higher prices.
2. The corporation may be forced to absorb the cost of the program if, for example, the competitive situation does not permit a price increase. In this case, the cost is treated as a business expense, and profit is reduced.
3. The federal government may pay for all or part of the cost through tax reductions or other incentives.

social audit a comprehensive report of what an organization has done and is doing with regard to social issues that affect it

Concept Check

1. What steps a business must take to implement a program of social responsibility?

2. What is the social audit? Who should prepare a social audit for the firm?

3. What are the three sources of funding the social responsibility program?

SUMMARY

1 Understand what is meant by *business* ethics.

Ethics is the study of right and wrong and of the morality of choices. Business ethics is the application of moral standards to business situations.

2 Identify the types of ethical concerns that arise in the business world.

Ethical issues arise often in business situations out of relationships with investors, customers, employees, creditors, or competitors. Businesspeople should make every effort to be fair, to consider the welfare of customers and others within the firm, to avoid conflicts of interest, and to communicate honestly.

3 Discuss the factors that affect the level of ethical behavior in organizations.

Individual, social, and opportunity factors all affect the level of ethical behavior in an organization. Individual factors include knowledge level, moral values and attitudes, and personal goals. Social factors include cultural norms and the actions and values of coworkers and significant others. Opportunity factors refer to the amount of leeway that exists in an organization for employees to behave unethically if they so choose.

4 Explain how ethical decision making can be encouraged.

Governments, trade associations, and individual firms all can establish guidelines for defining ethical behavior. Governments can pass stricter regulations. Trade associations provide ethical guidelines for their members. Companies provide codes of ethics—written guides to acceptable and ethical behavior as defined by an organization—and create an atmosphere in which ethical behavior is encouraged. An ethical employee working in an unethical environment may resort to whistle-blowing to bring a questionable practice to light.

5 Describe how our current views on the social responsibility of business have evolved.

In a socially responsible business, management realizes that its activities have an impact on society and considers that impact in the decision-making process. Before the 1930s, workers, consumers, and government had very little influence on business activities; as a result, business leaders gave little thought to social responsibility. All this changed with the Great Depression. Government regulations, employee demands, and consumer awareness combined to create a demand that businesses act in socially responsible ways.

6 Explain the two views on the social responsibility of business and understand the arguments for and against increased social responsibility.

The basic premise of the economic model of social responsibility is that society benefits most when business is left alone to produce profitable goods and services. According to the socioeconomic model, business has as much responsibility to society as it has to its owners. Most managers adopt a viewpoint somewhere between these two extremes.

7 Discuss the factors that led to the consumer movement and list some of its results.

Consumerism consists of all activities undertaken to protect the rights of consumers. The consumer movement generally has demanded—and received—attention from business in the areas of product safety, product information, product choices through competition, and the resolution of complaints about products and business practices. Although concerns over consumer rights have been around to some extent since the early nineteenth century, the movement became more powerful in the 1960s when President John F. Kennedy initiated the consumer "bill of rights." The six basic rights of consumers include the right to safety, the right to be informed, the right to choose, the right to be heard, and the rights to consumer education and courteous service.

8 Analyze how present employment practices are being used to counteract past abuses.

Legislation and public demand have prompted some businesses to correct past abuses in employment practices—mainly with regard to minority groups. Affirmative action and training of the hard-core unemployed are two types of programs that have been used successfully.

9 Describe the major types of pollution, their causes, and their cures.

Industry has contributed to the noise pollution and the pollution of our land and water through the dumping of wastes and to air pollution through vehicle and smokestack emissions. This contamination can be cleaned up and controlled, but the big question is: Who will pay? Present cleanup efforts are funded partly by government tax revenues, partly by business, and in the long run by consumers.

10 Identify the steps a business must take to implement a program of social responsibility.

A program to implement social responsibility in a business begins with total commitment by top management. The program should be planned carefully, and a capable director should be appointed to implement it. Social audits should be prepared periodically as a means of evaluating and revising the program. Programs may be funded through price increases, reduction of profit, or federal incentives.

KEY TERMS

You should now be able to define and give an example relevant to each of the following terms:

ethics (35)
business ethics (35)
Sarbanes-Oxley Act of 2002 (39)
code of ethics (39)
whistle-blowing (40)

social responsibility (42)
caveat emptor (47)
economic model of social responsibility (48)
socioeconomic model of social responsibility (49)

consumerism (51)
minority (54)
affirmative action program (54)
Equal Employment Opportunity Commission (EEOC) (55)

hard-core unemployed (55)
National Alliance of Business (NAB) (56)
pollution (56)
social audit (60)

DISCUSSION QUESTIONS

1. When a company acts in an ethically questionable manner, what types of problems are caused for the organization and its customers?
2. How can an employee take an ethical stand regarding a business decision when his or her superior already has taken a different position?
3. Overall, would it be more profitable for a business to follow the economic model or the socioeconomic model of social responsibility?
4. Why should business take on the task of training the hard-core unemployed?
5. To what extent should the blame for vehicular air pollution be shared by manufacturers, consumers, and government?
6. Why is there so much government regulation involving social responsibility issues? Should there be less?

Get Flash Cards, Quizzes, Games, Crosswords and more @ www.cengage.com/introbusiness/pride

Test Yourself

Matching Questions

1. _____ An application of moral standards to business situations.
2. _____ Provides legal protection for employees who report corporate misconduct.
3. _____ A guide to acceptable and ethical behavior as defined by the organization.
4. _____ All activities undertaken to protect the rights of consumers.
5. _____ Informing the press or government officials about unethical practices within one's organization.
6. _____ A Latin phrase meaning "let the buyer beware."
7. _____ A racial, religious, political, national, or other group regarded as different from the larger group of which it is a part.
8. _____ A plan designed to increase the number of minority employees at all levels within an organization.
9. _____ A joint business-government program to train the hard-core unemployed.
10. _____ The contamination of water, air, or land.

a. whistle-blowing
b. pollution
c. social audit
d. minority
e. code of ethics
f. National Alliance of Business (NAB)
g. Sarbanes-Oxley Act of 2002
h. economic model of social responsibility
i. affirmative action program
j. business ethics
k. consumerism
l. caveat emptor

True False Questions

11. **T F** The field of business ethics applies moral standards to business situations.
12. **T F** Business ethics rarely involves the application of moral standards to the business activity of a normal company.
13. **T F** The economic model of social responsibility emphasizes the effect of business decisions on society.

Test Yourself

14. **T F** Consumerism consists of all activities undertaken to protect the rights of consumers.

15. **T F** Manufacturers are not required by law to inform consumers about the potential dangers of using their products.

16. **T F** Affirmative-action plans encompass all areas of human resources management, including recruiting, hiring, training, promotion, and pay.

17. **T F** A successful program for training hard-core unemployed people is the National Alliance of Business.

18. **T F** The EPA was created by the government to develop new improved ways to clean and improve the environment.

19. **T F** Consumers will probably pay in large part for cleaning up our environment through increased taxes or increased product cost.

20. **T F** A key step in developing and implementing a social responsibility program is the environmental audit.

Multiple-Choice Questions

21. _____ Business ethics
    a. is laws and regulations that govern business.
    b. is the application of moral standards to business situations.
    c. do not vary from one person to another.
    d. is most important for advertising agencies.
    e. is well-defined rules for appropriate business behavior.

22. _____ Customers expect a firm's products to
    a. boost sales.
    b. be profitable.
    c. earn a reasonable return on investment
    d. be available everywhere.
    e. be safe, reliable, and reasonably priced.

23. _____ Some AIG executives were aware of the financial problems the company was facing and yet failed to reveal this information to the public. These actions taken by AIG executives were
    a. moral.
    b. normal.
    c. in the best interests of shareholders.
    d. unethical.
    e. in the best interests of the employees.

24. _____ Bribes are
    a. unethical.
    b. ethical only under certain circumstances.
    c. uncommon in many foreign countries.

    d. economic returns.
    e. ethical.

25. _____ What are three sets of factors that influence the standards of behavior in an organization?
    a. Organizational norms, circumstances, morals
    b. Peer pressure, attitudes, social factors
    c. Historical factors, management attitudes, opportunity
    d. Opportunity, individual factors, social factors
    e. Financial factors, opportunity, morals

26. _____ Informing the press or government officials about unethical practices within one's organization is called
    a. unethical behavior.
    b. whistling.
    c. whistle-blowing
    d. trumpeting.
    e. a company violation.

27. _____ Social responsibility
    a. has little or no associated costs.
    b. can be extremely expensive and provides very little benefit to a company.
    c. has become less important as businesses become more competitive.
    d. is generally a crafty scheme to put competitors out of business.
    e. is costly but provides tremendous benefits to society and the business.

28. _____ *Caveat emptor*
    a. is a French term that implies laissez faire.
    b. implies disagreements over peer evaluations.
    c. is a Latin phrase meaning "let the buyer beware."
    d. is a Latin phrase meaning "let the seller beware."
    e. is a Latin phrase meaning "the cave is empty."

29. _____ Where does social responsibility of business have to begin?
    a. Government
    b. Management
    c. Consumers
    d. Consumer protection groups
    e. Society

30. _____ Primary emphasis in the economic model of social responsibility is on
    a. quality of life.
    b. conservation of resources.
    c. market-based decisions.
    d. production.
    e. firm's and community's interests.

Answers on p. TY-1

VIDEO CASE

At New Belgium Brewing, Greater Efficiency Is Blowing in the Wind

New Belgium Brewing (NBB), America's first wind-powered brewery, aims to make both a better beer and a better society. Founded by husband-and-wife entrepreneurs Jeff Lebesch and Kim Jordan, the company offers European-style beers under intriguing brands such as Fat Tire and Sunshine Wheat. Lebesch hatched the idea for brewing his own beers after sipping local beers while touring Belgium on bicycle. Returning home with a special yeast strain, Lebesch experimented in his basement and came up with a beer he dubbed Fat Tire Amber Ale in honor of his bicycle trip.

By 1991, he and his wife were bottling and delivering five Belgian-style beers to liquor stores and other retailers in and around their hometown of Fort Collins, Colorado. Within a few years, sales had grown so rapidly that NBB needed much more space. Lebesch and Jordan moved the operation into a former railroad depot and then moved again into a new state-of-the-art brewery.

Not only is the 80,000-square-foot facility highly automated for efficiency, but it is also designed with the environment in mind. For example, sun tubes bring daylight to areas that lack windows, which reduces the brewery's energy requirements. As another energy-saving example, the brewery's kettles have steam condensers to capture and reuse hot water again and again. The biggest energy-conservation measure is a special cooling device that reduces the need for air conditioning in warm weather. In the office section, NBB employees reuse and recycle paper and as many other supplies as possible.

Soon after opening the new brewery, the entire staff voted to convert it to wind power, which is kinder to the environment because it does not pollute or require scarce fossil fuels. In addition to saving energy and natural resources, NBB is actually transforming the methane from its waste stream into energy through the process of cogeneration. It also has found ways to cut carbon dioxide emissions and reuse brewing by-products as cattle feed. Going further, NBB donates $1 to charitable causes for every barrel of beer it sells—which translates into more than $200,000 per year. Moreover, it donates the proceeds of its annual Tour de Fat biking event to nonprofit bicycling organizations.

Employee involvement is a key element of NBB's success. Lebesch and Jordan have unleashed the entrepreneurial spirit of the workforce through employee ownership. Employees share in decisions, serve as taste testers, and receive detailed information about NBB's financial performance, including costs and profits. Being empowered as part owners not only motivates employees, but it also gives them a great sense of pride in their work. And reminiscent of the bicycle trip that prompted Lebesch to brew his own beers, all employees receive a cruising bicycle on their first anniversary of joining the company.

Still, customers are most concerned with the taste of NBB's beers, which have won numerous awards and have attracted a large, loyal customer base in twelve states. In the last five years, Fat Tire's annual sales have grown from 0.9 million cases to 2.6 million cases. Many people become customers after hearing about the beer from long-time fans, and as its popularity grows, the word spreads even further. NBB does some advertising, but its budget is tiny compared with deep-pocketed rivals such as Anheuser-Busch and Miller Brewing. Instead of glitzy commercials on national television, NBB uses a low-key approach to show customers that the company is comprised of "real people making real beer."

Today, the company employs 140 people and is the sixth largest company selling draft beer in America. Clearly, sales and profits are vital ingredients in NBB's long-term recipe, but they are not the only important elements. Jordan stresses that the company is not just about making beer—it is about creating what she calls "magic." Reflecting on her continued involvement in NBB, she says: "How do you support a community of people? How do you show up in the larger community? How do you strive to be a business role model? That's the part that keeps me really engaged here."

In fact, NBB has integrated social responsibility into its operations so successfully that it recently received an award from *Business Ethics* magazine. The award cited the company's "dedication to environmental excellence in every part of its innovative brewing process." Jordan, Lebesch, and all the NBB employee-owners can take pride in their efforts to build a better society as well as a better beer.[14]

For more information about this company, go to **www.newbelgium.com.**

Questions

1. What do you think Kim Jordan means when she talks about how New Belgium Brewing strives to be a "business role model," not just a beer maker?

2. Given New Belgium Brewing's emphasis on social responsibility, what would you suggest the company look at when preparing a social audit?

3. Should businesses charge more for products that are produced using more costly but environmentally friendly methods such as wind power? Should consumers pay more for products that are *not* produced using environmentally friendly methods because of the potential for costly environmental damage? Explain your answers.

BUILDING SKILLS FOR CAREER SUCCESS

1. EXPLORING THE INTERNET

Socially responsible business behavior can be as simple as donating unneeded older computers to schools, mentoring interested learners in good business practices, or supplying public speakers to talk about career opportunities. Students, as part of the public at large, perceive a great deal of information about a company, its employees, and its owners by the positive social actions taken and perhaps even more by actions not taken. Microsoft donates millions of dollars of computers and software to educational institutions every year. Some people consider this level of corporate giving to be insufficient given the scale of the wealth of the corporation. Others believe that firms have no obligation to give back any more than they wish and that recipients should be grateful. Visit the text website for updates to this exercise.

Assignment

1. Select any firm involved in high technology and the Internet such as Microsoft or IBM. Examine its website and report its corporate position on social responsibility and giving as it has stated it. What activities is it involved in? What programs does it support, and how does it support them?
2. Search the Internet for commentary on business social responsibility, form your own opinions, and then evaluate the social effort demonstrated by the firm you have selected. What more could the firm have done?

2. BUILDING TEAM SKILLS

A firm's code of ethics outlines the kinds of behaviors expected within the organization and serves as a guideline for encouraging ethical behavior in the workplace. It reflects the rights of the firm's workers, shareholders, and consumers.

Assignment

1. Working in a team of four, find a code of ethics for a business firm. Start the search by asking firms in your community for a copy of their codes, by visiting the library, or by searching and downloading information from the Internet.

2. Analyze the code of ethics you have chosen, and answer the following questions:
   a. What does the company's code of ethics say about the rights of its workers, shareholders, consumers, and suppliers? How does the code reflect the company's attitude toward competitors?
   b. How does this code of ethics resemble the information discussed in this chapter? How does it differ?
   c. As an employee of this company, how would you personally interpret the code of ethics? How might the code influence your behavior within the workplace? Give several examples.

3. RESEARCHING DIFFERENT CAREERS

Business ethics has been at the heart of many discussions over the years and continues to trouble employees and shareholders. Stories about dishonesty and wrongful behavior in the workplace appear on a regular basis in newspapers and on the national news.

Assignment

Prepare a written report on the following:

1. Why can it be so difficult for people to do what is right?
2. What is your personal code of ethics? Prepare a code outlining what you believe is morally right. The document should include guidelines for your personal behavior.
3. How will your code of ethics affect your decisions about:
   a. The types of questions you should ask in a job interview?
   b. Selecting a company in which to work?

3 Exploring Global Business

©Lourraine Swanson/Shutterstock

WHY THIS CHAPTER MATTERS. Free trade—are you for or against it? Most economists support free-trade policies, but public support can be lukewarm, and certain groups are adamantly opposed, alleging that "trade harms large segments of U.S. workers," "degrades the environment," and "exploits poor countries."

LEARNING OBJECTIVES

1 Explain the economic basis for international business.

2 Discuss the restrictions nations place on international trade, the objectives of these restrictions, and their results.

3 Outline the extent of international trade and identify the organizations working to foster it.

4 Define the methods by which a firm can organize for and enter into international markets.

5 Describe the various sources of export assistance.

6 Identify the institutions that help firms and nations finance international business.

Global Growth Tops the McDonald's Menu

Every day, 58 million fast-food fans enjoy a breakfast, lunch, dinner, or midnight snack with a dash of local flavor at McDonald's 32,000 restaurants worldwide. Whether it's Big Macs in Pittsburgh, Deluxe Brekkie Rolls in Preston, Australia, or Chicken Bacon Onion sandwiches in Prague, McDonald's offers a menu item for every palate and every budget. In fact, during the recent economic downturn, when many businesses struggled, the company's emphasis on value pushed yearly revenues beyond $23 billion.

One reason for McDonald's global success is its ability to adapt to local tastes and cultural differences. For example, in India, where customers eat neither beef nor pork, McDonald's offers the Chicken Maharaja Mac sandwich and the McVeggie burger. In France, the company builds on the popularity of traditional favorites with adaptations such as the Croque McDo, a ham-and-cheese sandwich. In Hong Kong, it caters to kids with breakfast specials such as Sausage and Egg Twisty Pasta. In the United States, health-conscious customers can choose low-calorie McDonald's Snack Wraps, while meat lovers can order Double Quarter Pounder hamburgers.

Another reason that McDonald's has done so well on every continent is its careful attention to every detail of the dining experience. All McDonald's restaurants are welcoming, clean, and bright. New menu boards and packaging worldwide echo the familiar "I'm Loving It" advertising tagline and highlight food quality. Although individual menu items may vary from area to area—some featuring organic or locally-grown ingredients—the red-and-yellow McDonald's brand looks the same everywhere.

Now McDonald's has turned up the competitive heat in many global markets with its introduction of the McCafé line of gourmet coffee drinks. The idea is to attract customers who enjoy mochas and lattes but don't want to pay upscale coffee-house prices. Some McDonald's are also competing by offering the option to have orders delivered to home or office. Watch for more innovations as McDonald's continues to gobble up market share and expand aggressively around the world.[1]

DID YOU KNOW?

Every day, McDonald's serves 58 million customers worldwide; every year, it rings up $23 billion in annual sales.

McDonald's is just one of a growing number of foreign companies, large and small, that are doing business in other countries. Some companies, such as Coca-Cola, sell to firms in other countries; others, such as Pier 1 Imports, buy goods around the world to import into the United States. Whether they buy or sell products across national borders, these companies are all contributing to the volume of international trade that is fueling the global economy.

Theoretically, international trade is every bit as logical and worthwhile as interstate trade between, say, California and Washington. Yet nations tend to restrict the import of certain goods for a variety of reasons. For example, in the early 2000s, the United States restricted the import of Mexican fresh tomatoes because they were undercutting price levels of domestic fresh tomatoes.

Despite such restrictions, international trade has increased almost steadily since World War II. Many of the industrialized nations have signed trade agreements intended to eliminate problems in international business and to help less-developed nations participate in world trade. Individual firms around the world have seized the opportunity to compete in foreign markets by exporting products and increasing foreign production, as well as by other means.

Signing the Trade Act of 2002, President George W. Bush remarked, "Trade is an important source of good jobs for our workers and a source of higher growth for our economy. Free trade is also a proven strategy for building global prosperity and adding to the momentum of political freedom. Trade is an engine of economic growth. In our lifetime, trade has helped lift millions of people and whole nations out of poverty and put them on the path of prosperity.[2] In his national best-seller, *The World is Flat*, Thomas L. Friedman states, *"The flattening of the world has presented us with new opportunities, new challenges, new partners but, also, alas new dangers, particularly as Americans it is imperative that we be the best global citizens that we can be— because in a flat world, if you don't visit a bad neighborhood, it might visit you."*

We describe international trade in this chapter in terms of modern specialization, whereby each country trades the surplus goods and services it produces most efficiently for products in short supply. We also explain the restrictions nations place on products and services from other countries and present some of the possible advantages and disadvantages of these restrictions. We then describe the extent of international trade and identify the organizations working to foster it. We describe several methods of entering international markets and the various sources of export assistance available from the federal government. Finally, we identify some of the institutions that provide the complex financing necessary for modern international trade.

LEARNING OBJECTIVE 1

Explain the economic basis for international business.

The Basis for International Business

International business encompasses all business activities that involve exchanges across national boundaries. Thus, a firm is engaged in international business when it buys some portion of its input from or sells some portion of its output to an organization located in a foreign country. (A small retail store may sell goods produced in some other country. However, because it purchases these goods from American distributors, it is not engaged in international trade.)

Absolute and Comparative Advantage

Some countries are better equipped than others to produce particular goods or services. The reason may be a country's natural resources, its labor supply, or even customs or a historical accident. Such a country would be best off if it could *specialize* in the production of such products because it can produce them most efficiently. The country could use what it needed of these products and then trade the surplus for products it could not produce efficiently on its own.

Saudi Arabia thus has specialized in the production of crude oil and petroleum products; South Africa, in diamonds; and Australia, in wool. Each of these countries is said to have an absolute advantage with regard to a particular product. An **absolute advantage** is the ability to produce a specific product more efficiently than any other nation.

One country may have an absolute advantage with regard to several products, whereas another country may have no absolute advantage at all. Yet it is still worthwhile for these two countries to specialize and trade with each other. To see why this is so, imagine that you are the president of a successful manufacturing firm and that you can accurately type ninety words per minute. Your assistant can type eighty words per minute but would run the business poorly. Thus, you have an absolute advantage over your assistant in both typing and managing. However, you cannot afford to type your own letters because your time is better spent in managing the business. That is, you have a **comparative advantage** in managing. A comparative advantage is the ability to produce a specific product more efficiently than any other product.

Your assistant, on the other hand, has a comparative advantage in typing because he or she can do that better than managing the business. Thus, you spend your time managing, and you leave the typing to your assistant. Overall, the business is run as efficiently as possible because you are each working in accordance with your own comparative advantage.

international business all business activities that involve exchanges across national boundaries

absolute advantage the ability to produce a specific product more efficiently than any other nation

comparative advantage the ability to produce a specific product more efficiently than any other product

The same is true for nations. Goods and services are produced more efficiently when each country specializes in the products for which it has a comparative advantage. Moreover, by definition, every country has a comparative advantage in *some* product. The United States has many comparative advantages—in research and development, high-technology industries, and identifying new markets, for instance.

Exporting and Importing

Suppose that the United States specializes in producing corn. It then will produce a surplus of corn, but perhaps it will have a shortage of wine. France, on the other hand, specializes in producing wine but experiences a shortage of corn. To satisfy both needs—for corn and for wine—the two countries should trade with each other. The United States should export corn and import wine. France should export wine and import corn.

Exporting is selling and shipping raw materials or products to other nations. The Boeing Company, for example, exports its airplanes to a number of countries for use by their airlines. Figure 3.1 shows the top ten merchandise-exporting states in this country.

Importing is purchasing raw materials or products in other nations and bringing them into one's own country. Thus buyers for Macy's department stores may purchase rugs in India or raincoats in England and have them shipped back to the United States for resale.

Importing and exporting are the principal activities in international trade. They give rise to an important concept called the *balance of trade*. A nation's

Exploiting absolute advantage. Saudi Arabia and Siberia have long specialized in the production of crude oil and petroleum products. Because of their natural oil resources, Siberia, Saudi Arabia and other countries in the Middle East enjoy an absolute advantage—their ability to produce petroleum products more efficiently than in any other area of the world.

©George Spade/Shutterstock

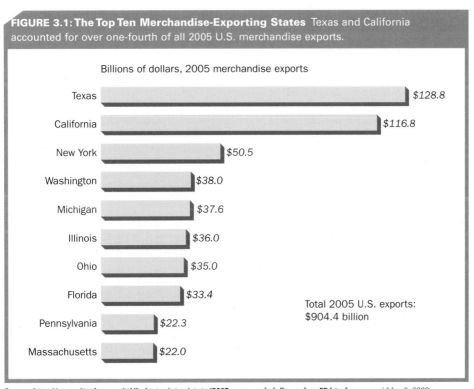

FIGURE 3.1: The Top Ten Merchandise-Exporting States Texas and California accounted for over one-fourth of all 2005 U.S. merchandise exports.

Billions of dollars, 2005 merchandise exports

State	Exports
Texas	$128.8
California	$116.8
New York	$50.5
Washington	$38.0
Michigan	$37.6
Illinois	$36.0
Ohio	$35.0
Florida	$33.4
Pennsylvania	$22.3
Massachusetts	$22.0

Total 2005 U.S. exports: $904.4 billion

exporting selling and shipping raw materials or products to other nations

importing purchasing raw materials or products in other nations and bringing them into one's own country

Source: **http://www.ita.doc.gov/td/industry/otea/state/2005_year_end_dollar_value_05.html**, accessed May 2, 2009.

Concept Check

1. Why do firms engage in international trade?

2. What is the difference between an absolute advantage and a comparative advantage?

3. What is the difference between balance of trade and balance of payments?

balance of trade is the total value of its exports *minus* the total value of its imports over some period of time. If a country imports more than it exports, its balance of trade is negative and is said to be *unfavorable*. (A negative balance of trade is unfavorable because the country must export money to pay for its excess imports.)

In 2008, the United States imported $2,517 billion worth of goods and services and exported $1,836 billion worth. It thus had a trade deficit of $681 billion. A **trade deficit** is a negative balance of trade (see Figure 3.2). However, the United States has consistently enjoyed a large and rapidly growing surplus in services. For example, in 2008, the United States imported $405 billion worth and exported $544 billion worth of services, thus creating a favorable balance of $139 billion.[3]

Question: Are trade deficits bad?

Answer: In testimony before the Senate Finance Committee, Daniel T. Griswold, associate director of the Center for Trade Policy at the Cato Institute, remarked,

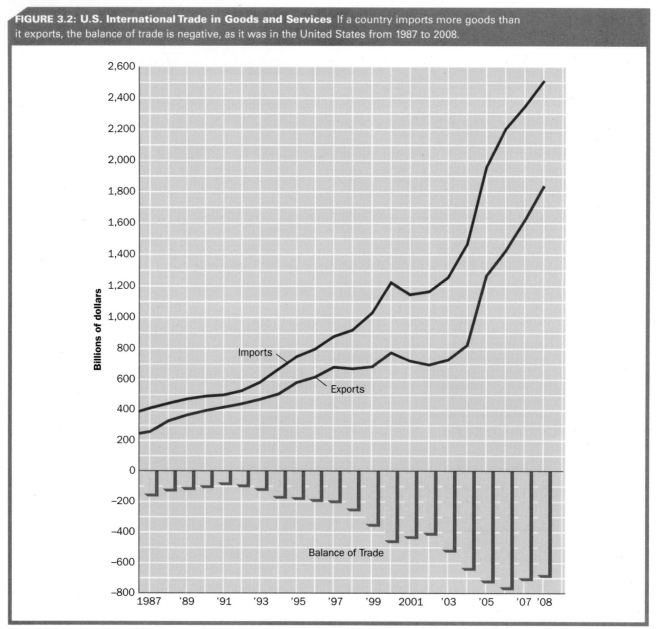

FIGURE 3.2: U.S. International Trade in Goods and Services If a country imports more goods than it exports, the balance of trade is negative, as it was in the United States from 1987 to 2008.

Source: U.S. Department of Commerce, International Trade Administration, U.S. Bureau of Economic Analysis, **http://bea.gov/international/bp_web/action.cfm**, accessed April 16, 2009.

"The trade deficit is not a sign of economic distress, but of rising domestic demand and investment. Imposing new trade barriers will only make Americans worse off while leaving the **trade deficit** virtually unchanged."

On the other hand, when a country exports more than it imports, it is said to have a *favorable* balance of trade. This has consistently been the case for Japan over the last two decades or so.

A nation's **balance of payments** is the total flow of money into a country *minus* the total flow of money out of that country over some period of time. Balance of payments therefore is a much broader concept than balance of trade. It includes imports and exports, of course. But it also includes investments, money spent by foreign tourists, payments by foreign governments, aid to foreign governments, and all other receipts and payments.

A continual deficit in a nation's balance of payments (a negative balance) can cause other nations to lose confidence in that nation's economy. A continual surplus may indicate that the country encourages exports but limits imports by imposing trade restrictions.

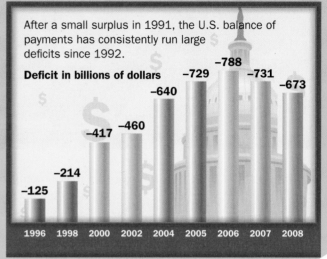

Spotlight
The Growing Deficit

After a small surplus in 1991, the U.S. balance of payments has consistently run large deficits since 1992.

Deficit in billions of dollars

-125 (1996) -214 (1998) -417 (2000) -460 (2002) -640 (2004) -729 (2005) -788 (2006) -731 (2007) -673 (2008)

Source: U.S. Department of Commerce, Bureau of Economic Analysis, http://www.bea.gov/international/index.htm#bop, accessed May 1, 2009.

Restrictions to International Business

2 LEARNING OBJECTIVE

Discuss the restrictions nations place on international trade, the objectives of these restrictions, and their results.

Specialization and international trade can result in the efficient production of want-satisfying goods and services on a worldwide basis. As we have noted, international business generally is increasing. Yet the nations of the world continue to erect barriers to free trade. They do so for reasons ranging from internal political and economic pressures to simple mistrust of other nations. We examine first the types of restrictions that are applied and then the arguments for and against trade restrictions.

Types of Trade Restrictions

Nations generally are eager to export their products. They want to provide markets for their industries and to develop a favorable balance of trade. Hence, most trade restrictions are applied to imports from other nations.

Tariffs Perhaps the most commonly applied trade restriction is the customs (or import) duty. An **import duty** (also called a **tariff**) is a tax levied on a particular foreign product entering a country. For example, the United States imposes a 2.2 percent import duty on fresh Chilean tomatoes, an 8.7 percent duty if tomatoes are dried and packaged, and nearly 12 percent if tomatoes are made into ketchup or salsa. The two types of tariffs are revenue tariffs and protective tariffs; both have the effect of raising the price of the product in the importing nations, but for different reasons. *Revenue tariffs* are imposed solely to generate income for the government. For example, the United States imposes a duty on Scotch whiskey solely for revenue purposes. *Protective tariffs*, on the other hand, are imposed to protect a domestic industry from competition by keeping the price of competing imports level with or higher than the price of similar domestic products. Because fewer units of the product will be sold at the increased price, fewer units will be imported. The French and Japanese agricultural sectors would both shrink drastically if their nations abolished the protective tariffs that keep the price of imported farm products high. Today, U.S. tariffs are the lowest in history, with average tariff rates on all imports of under 3 percent.

Some countries rationalize their protection-ist policies as a way of offsetting an international trade practice called *dumping*. **Dumping** is the exportation of large

balance of trade the total value of a nation's exports minus the total value of its imports over some period of time

trade deficit a negative balance of trade

balance of payments the total flow of money into a country minus the total flow of money out of that country over some period of time

import duty (tariff) a tax levied on a particular foreign product entering a country

dumping exportation of large quantities of a product at a price lower than that of the same product in the home market quantities of a product at a price lower than that of the product in the home market.

Thus, dumping drives down the price of the domestic item. Recently, for example, the Pencil Makers Association, which represents eight U.S. pencil manufacturers, charged that low-priced pencils from Thailand and the People's Republic of China were being sold in the United States at less than fair value prices. Unable to compete with these inexpensive imports, several domestic manufacturers had to shut down. To protect themselves, domestic manufacturers can obtain an antidumping duty through the government to offset the advantage of the foreign product. In 2009, for example, the U.S. Department of Commerce imposed antidumping duties of up to 101 percent on a variety of steel products imported from China. Similarly, in 2009, the European Union imposed antidumping duties on imports of biodiesel from the United States.

Nontariff Barriers A **nontariff barrier** is a nontax measure imposed by a government to favor domestic over foreign suppliers. Nontariff barriers create obstacles to the marketing of foreign goods in a country and increase costs for exporters. The following are a few examples of government-imposed nontariff barriers:

- An **import quota** is a limit on the amount of a particular good that may be imported into a country during a given period of time. The limit may be set in terms of either quantity (so many pounds of beef) or value (so many dollars' worth of shoes). Quotas also may be set on individual products imported from specific countries. Once an import quota has been reached, imports are halted until the specified time has elapsed.
- An **embargo** is a complete halt to trading with a particular nation or in a particular product. The embargo is used most often as a political weapon. At present, the United States has import embargoes against Iran and North Korea—both as a result of extremely poor political relations.
- A **foreign-exchange control** is a restriction on the amount of a particular foreign currency that can be purchased or sold. By limiting the amount of foreign currency importers can obtain, a government limits the amount of goods importers can purchase with that currency. This has the effect of limiting imports from the country whose foreign exchange is being controlled.
- A nation can increase or decrease the value of its money relative to the currency of other nations. **Currency devaluation** is the reduction of the value of a nation's currency relative to the currencies of other countries.

Devaluation increases the cost of foreign goods while it decreases the cost of domestic goods to foreign firms. For example, suppose that the British pound is worth $2. Then an American-made $2,000 computer can be purchased for £1,000. However, if the United Kingdom devalues the pound so that it is worth only $1, that same computer will cost £2,000. The increased cost, in pounds, will reduce the import of American computers—and all foreign goods—into England.

On the other hand, before devaluation, a £500 set of English bone china will cost an American $1,000. After the devaluation, the set of china will cost only $500. The decreased cost will make the china—and all English goods—much more attractive to U.S. purchasers. Bureaucratic red tape is more subtle than the other forms of nontariff barriers. Yet it can be the most frustrating trade barrier of all. A few

nontariff barrier a nontax measure imposed by a government to favor domestic over foreign suppliers

import quota a limit on the amount of a particular good that may be imported into a country during a given period of time

embargo a complete halt to trading with a particular nation or in a particular product

foreign-exchange control a restriction on the amount of a particular foreign currency that can be purchased or sold

currency devaluation the reduction of the value of a nation's currency relative to the currencies of other countries

Many countries, including South Korea, banned imports of U.S. beef products in 2003, soon after one case of mad cow disease was found in the United States. South Korea lifted the ban in 2008, and other Asian nations, such as Japan, Taiwan, and China may follow South Korea's lead. Here, in Seoul, South Korea, protestors march to the Presidential House during a protest against U.S. imported beef.

examples are unnecessarily restrictive application of standards and complex requirements related to product testing, labeling, and certification.

Another type of nontariff barrier is related to cultural attitudes. Cultural barriers can impede acceptance of products in foreign countries. For example, illustrations of feet are regarded as despicable in Thailand. When customers are unfamiliar with particular products from another country, their general perceptions of the country itself affect their attitude toward the product and help to determine whether they will buy it. Because Mexican cars have not been viewed by the world as being quality products, Volkswagen, for example, may not want to advertise that some of its models sold in the United States are made in Mexico. Many retailers on the Internet have yet to come to grips with the task of designing an online shopping site that is attractive and functional for all global customers.

Reasons for Trade Restrictions

Various reasons are advanced for trade restrictions either on the import of specific products or on trade with particular countries. We have noted that political considerations usually are involved in trade embargoes. Other frequently cited reasons for restricting trade include the following:

- *To equalize a nation's balance of payments.* This may be considered necessary to restore confidence in the country's monetary system and in its ability to repay its debts.
- *To protect new or weak industries.* A new, or *infant*, industry may not be strong enough to withstand foreign competition. Temporary trade restrictions may be used to give it a chance to grow and become self-sufficient. The problem is that once an industry is protected from foreign competition, it may refuse to grow, and "temporary" trade restrictions will become permanent. For example, a recent report by the General Accounting Office (GAO), the congressional investigative agency, has accused the federal government of routinely imposing

quotas on foreign textiles without "demonstrating the threat of serious damage" to U.S. industry. The GAO said that the Committee for the Implementation of Textile Agreements sometimes applies quotas even though it cannot prove the textile industry's claims that American companies have been hurt or jobs eliminated.

- *To protect national security.* Restrictions in this category generally apply to technological products that must be kept out of the hands of potential enemies. For example, strategic and defense-related goods cannot be exported to unfriendly nations.
- *To protect the health of citizens.* Products may be embargoed because they are dangerous or unhealthy (e.g., farm products contaminated with insecticides).
- *To retaliate for another nation's trade restrictions.* A country whose exports are taxed by another country may respond by imposing tariffs on imports from that country.
- *To protect domestic jobs.* By restricting imports, a nation can protect jobs in domestic industries. However, protecting these jobs can be expensive. For example, to protect 9,000 jobs in the U.S. carbon-steel industry costs $6.8 billion, or $750,000 per job. In addition, Gary Hufbauer and Ben Goodrich, economists at the Institute for International Economics, estimate that the tariffs could temporarily save 3,500 jobs in the steel industry, but at an annual cost to steel users of $2 billion, or $584,000 per job saved. Yet recently the United States imposed tariffs of up to 616 percent on steel pipes imported from China, South Korea, and Mexico.

Reasons against Trade Restrictions

Trade restrictions have immediate and long-term economic consequences—both within the restricting nation and in world trade patterns. These include

- *Higher prices for consumers.* Higher prices may result from the imposition of tariffs or the elimination of foreign competition, as described earlier. For example, imposing quota restrictions and import protections adds $25 billion annually to U.S. consumers' apparel costs by directly increasing costs for imported apparel.
- *Restriction of consumers' choices.* Again, this is a direct result of the elimination of some foreign products from the marketplace and of the artificially high prices that importers must charge for products that still *are* imported.
- *Misallocation of international resources.* The protection of weak industries results in the inefficient use of limited resources. The economies of both the restricting nation and other nations eventually suffer because of this waste.
- *Loss of jobs.* The restriction of imports by one nation must lead to cutbacks—and the loss of jobs—in the export-oriented industries of other nations. Furthermore, trade protection has a significant effect on the composition of employment. U.S. trade restrictions—whether on textiles, apparel, steel, or automobiles—benefit only a few industries while harming many others. The gains in employment accrue to the protected industries and their primary suppliers, and the losses are spread across all other industries. A few states gain employment, but many other states lose employment.

Concept Check

1. List and briefly describe the principal restrictions that may be applied to a nation's imports.

2. What reasons are generally given for imposing trade restrictions?

3. What are the general effects of import restrictions on trade?

LEARNING OBJECTIVE 3

Outline the extent of international trade and identify the organizations working to foster it.

The Extent of International Business

Restrictions or not, international business is growing. Although the worldwide recessions of 1991, 2001–2002, and 2008–2009 slowed the rate of growth, globalization is a reality of our time. In the United States, international trade now accounts for over one-fourth of GDP. As trade barriers decrease, new competitors enter the global marketplace, creating more choices for consumers and new opportunities for job seekers. International business will grow along with the expansion of commercial use of the Internet.

The World Economic Outlook for Trade

While the global economy continued to grow robustly until 2007 for the fourth consecutive year, economic performance has not been equal: growth in the advanced economies slowed, while emerging and developing economies continued to grow rapidly. Looking ahead, the International Monetary Fund (IMF), an international bank with 185 member nations, expected growth to decline in 2009 and 2010 in both advanced and emerging developing economies.[4]

While the U.S. economy had been growing steadily since 2000 and recorded the longest peacetime expansion in the nation's history, the worldwide recession which began in December 2007, has slowed the rate of growth. The IMF estimated that the U.S. economy grew by only 1.1 percent in 2008 and, due to subprime mortgage lending and other financial problems, declined 1.6 percent in 2009. International experts expected global gross domestic product (GDP) to fall to at least 1/2 percent in 2009, which would be the first annual decline in world GDP in 60 years.

Canada and Western Europe Our leading export partner, Canada, is projected to show the decline of 1.2 percent in 2009 and a growth rate of 1.6 percent in 2010. The Euro area grew by 1.0 percent in 2008, and is expected to decline 2 percent in 2009. The United Kingdom and smaller European countries, such as Austria, the Netherlands, Sweden, and Switzerland will experience a deep recession.

Mexico and Latin America Our second largest export customer, Mexico, suffered its sharpest recession ever in 1995 but its growth rate in 2008 was just over 1.8 percent. In general, however, the Latin American economies grew 4.6 percent in 2008, the region's best four-year performance since the 1970s. Growth in the region was projected at 1.1 percent in 2009 and 3 percent in 2010.

Japan Japan's economy is regaining momentum. Stronger consumer demand and business investment make Japan less reliant on exports for growth. The IMF estimated the growth for Japan at –2.6 percent in 2009 and 0.6 percent in 2010.

Asia The economic growth in Developing Asia remained strong in 2007. Growth was led by China, where its economy expanded by 11.4 percent in the second half of 2007, but it was estimated at 9 percent in 2008 and 6.7 percent in 2009. Growth in India slowed modestly to 7.3 percent in 2008 and 5.1 percent in 2009. A strong consumer demand supported economic growth in Indonesia, Malaysia, Hong Kong, the Philippines, and Singapore. The growth in emerging Asia remained at 7.8 percent in 2008 and 5.5 percent in 2009.

U.S. beef processors and beef cattle ranchers lose billions of dollars in exports annually because of animal health and food safety restrictions in other countries. Here, in a Tokyo supermarket, a salesperson arranges U.S. beef as Japan resumes sales. According to the U.S. International Trade Commission, animal health and food safety restrictions in importing countries reduced beef exports by $2.5 billion to $3.1 billion per year.

©AP Photo/Itsuo Inouye

Is it Ethical?

WHO vs. Tobacco

NO SMOKING

Limit smoking and tobacco advertising—that's the World Health Organization's formula for saving a billion lives during the 21st century. Despite on-pack warnings and advertising restrictions, smoking is on the rise in developing nations. For example, China is home to 30 percent of the world's smokers. In fact, its smoking population of 350 million people is larger than the entire U.S. population.

The Chinese government owns the country's largest tobacco companies, and a package of cigarettes is far cheaper in China than anywhere else in the world, two factors that complicate efforts to curb smoking. Still, China recently began requiring prominent health warnings on cigarette packs and banned smoking in Beijing's museums and other public buildings.

In India, the world's second-largest market for cigarettes, tobacco companies are not allowed to advertise their products. For years, they got around restrictions through "surrogate advertising," promoting different products with the same brand as their cigarettes. When India tightened regulation of surrogate advertising, many cigarette companies turned to sponsorship of sports and fashion events. Now cigarette packaging in India must carry a pictorial warning of the dangers of smoking, which will bring the message to people who can't read the written health notice.

To save lives, the World Health Organization wants governments to ban all tobacco marketing and outlaw smoking in all workplaces. What's next for the global cigarette business?

Sources: Bobby Ramakant, "Pictorial Health Warnings on Tobacco Products from 30th May 2009," *Op-Ed News,* April 27, 2009, http://www.opednews.com/articles/Pictorial-health-warnings-by-Bobby-Ramakant-090417-589.html; "China Tobacco Merger to Form Industry Leader: Report," *Reuters,* August 26, 2008, www.reuters.com; Mark Magnier, "Smoke-Free Olympics," *Houston Chronicle,* May 11, 2008, p. 23; Niraj Sheth, "India Liquor, Tobacco Firms Shift Tack," *Wall Street Journal,* May 6, 2008, p. B8; Bill Marsh, "A Growing Cloud Over the Planet," *New York Times,* February 24, 2008, p. WK-4; "How to Save a Billion Lives," *The Economist,* February 9, 2008, p. 66.

China's emergence as a global economic power has been among the most dramatic economic developments of recent decades. From 1980 to 2004, China's economy averaged a real GDP growth rate of 9.5 percent and became the world's sixth-largest economy. China's total share in world trade expanded from 1 percent in 1980 to almost 6 percent in 2003. By 2004, China had become the third-largest trading nation in dollar terms, behind the United States and Germany and just ahead of Japan.[5]

Central and Eastern Europe Economic growth in this region was 3.2 percent in 2008. Hungary, Turkey, Estonia, and Latvia experienced a slower growth. Nonetheless, 2008 marked the seventh consecutive year during which emerging Europe grew much faster than western Europe. The 2010 growth for the region was expected to be 2.5 percent.

Commonwealth of Independent States The growth was expected to be 2.2 percent in 2010. Moderate growth was expected to continue in Azerbaijan and Armenia, while it will remain stable in Moldova, Tajikistan, and Uzbekistan.

After World War II, trade between the United States and the communist nations of central and Eastern Europe was minimal. The United States maintained high tariff barriers on imports from most of these countries and also restricted its exports. However, since the disintegration of the Soviet Union and the collapse of communism, trade between the United States and central and Eastern Europe has expanded substantially.

The countries that made the transition from communist to market economies quickly have recorded positive growth for several years—those that did not continue to struggle. Among the nations that have enjoyed several years of positive economic growth are the member countries of the Central European Free Trade Association (CEFTA): Hungary, the Czech Republic, Poland, Slovenia, and the Republic of Slovakia.

U.S. exports to central and Eastern Europe and Russia will increase, as will U.S. investment in these countries, as demand for capital goods and technology opens new markets for U.S. products. There already has been a substantial expansion in trade between the United States and the Czech Republic, the Republic of Slovakia, Hungary, and Poland. Table 3.1 shows the growth rates from 2007 to 2010 for most regions of the world.

Exports and the U.S. Economy Globalization represents a huge opportunity for all countries—rich or poor. The fifteen-fold increase in trade volume over the past fifty-five years has been one of the most important factors in the rise of living standards around the world. During this time, exports have become increasingly important to the U.S. economy. Exports as a percentage of U.S. GDP have increased steadily since 1985, except in the 2001 recession. And our exports to developing and newly industrialized countries are on the rise. Table 3.2 shows the value of U.S. merchandise exports to and imports from each of the nation's ten

TABLE 3.1: Global Growth Remains Sluggish Growth has been led by developing countries and emerging markets

	2007	2008	Projected 2009	Projected 2010
		(annual percent change)		
World	5.2	3.4	0.5	3.0
United States	2.0	1.1	−1.6	1.6
Euro area	2.6	1.0	−2.0	0.2
United Kingdom	3.0	0.7	−2.8	0.2
Japan	2.4	−0.3	−2.6	0.6
Canada	2.7	0.6	−1.2	1.6
Other advanced economies	4.6	1.9	−2.4	2.2
Newly industrialized Asian economies	5.6	2.1	−3.9	3.1
Developing countries and emerging markets	8.3	6.3	3.3	5.0
Africa	6.2	5.2	3.4	4.9
Developing Asia	10.6	7.8	5.5	6.9
CIS	8.6	6.0	−0.4	2.2
Middle East	6.4	6.1	3.9	4.7
Western Hemisphere	5.7	4.6	1.1	3.0

Source: *International Monetary Fund: World Economic Outlook* by International Monetary Fund. Copyright 2009 by International Monetary Fund. Reproduced with permission of International Monetary Fund via Copyright Clearance Center.

major trading partners. Note that Canada and Mexico are our best partners for our exports; China and Canada, for imports.

Figure 3.3 shows the U.S. goods export and import shares in 2008. Major U.S. exports and imports are manufactured goods, agricultural products, and mineral fuels.

TABLE 3.2: Value of U.S. Merchandise Exports and Imports, 2008

Rank/Trading Partner	Exports ($ billions)	Rank/Trading Partner	Imports ($ billions)
1 Canada	261.4	1 China	337.8
2 Mexico	151.5	2 Canada	335.6
3 China	71.5	3 Mexico	215.9
4 Japan	66.6	4 Japan	139.2
5 Germany	54.7	5 Germany	97.6
6 United Kingdom	53.8	6 United Kingdom	58.6
7 Netherlands	40.2	7 Saudi Arabia	54.8
8 South Korea	34.8	8 Venezuela	51.4
9 Brazil	32.9	9 South Korea	48.1
10 France	29.2	10 France	44.0

Source: U.S. Department of Commerce, International Trade Administration, **http://www.ita.doc.gov/td/industry/otea/ttp/Top_Trade_Partners.pdf**, accessed May 1, 2009.

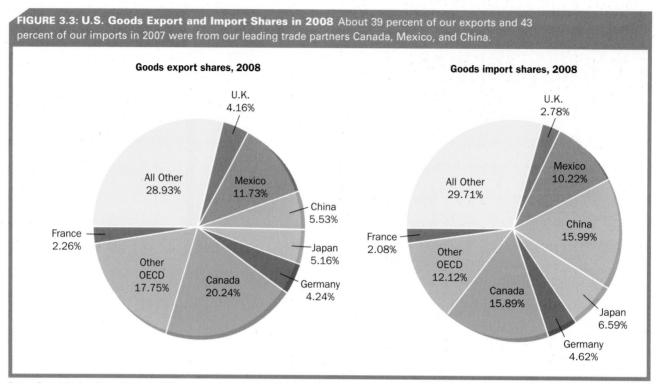

FIGURE 3.3: U.S. Goods Export and Import Shares in 2008 About 39 percent of our exports and 43 percent of our imports in 2007 were from our leading trade partners Canada, Mexico, and China.

Goods export shares, 2008

- U.K. 4.16%
- All Other 28.93%
- Mexico 11.73%
- China 5.53%
- France 2.26%
- Japan 5.16%
- Other OECD 17.75%
- Canada 20.24%
- Germany 4.24%

Goods import shares, 2008

- U.K. 2.78%
- Mexico 10.22%
- All Other 29.71%
- China 15.99%
- France 2.08%
- Other OECD 12.12%
- Canada 15.89%
- Japan 6.59%
- Germany 4.62%

Source: Federal Reserve Bank of St. Louis, *National Economic Trends*, May 2009, p. 18, **http://researchstlouisfed.org/publications/net/20090501/netpub.pdf**, accessed May 1, 2009.

International Trade Agreements

The General Agreement on Tariffs and Trade and the World Trade Organization

At the end of World War II, the United States and twenty-two other nations organized the body that came to be known as *GATT*. The **General Agreement on Tariffs and Trade (GATT)** was an international organization of 153 nations dedicated to reducing or eliminating tariffs and other barriers to world trade. These 153 nations accounted for 90 percent of the world's merchandise trade. GATT, headquartered in Geneva, Switzerland, provided a forum for tariff negotiations and a means for settling international trade disputes and problems. *Most-favored-nation status* (MFN) was the famous principle of GATT. It meant that each GATT member nation was to be treated equally by all contracting nations. MFN therefore ensured that any tariff reductions or other trade concessions were extended automatically to all GATT members. From 1947 to 1994, the body sponsored eight rounds of negotiations to reduce trade restrictions. Three of the most fruitful were the Kennedy Round, the Tokyo Round, and the Uruguay Round.

The Kennedy Round (1964–1967) In 1962, the U.S. Congress passed the Trade Expansion Act. This law gave President John F. Kennedy the authority to negotiate reciprocal trade agreements that could reduce U.S. tariffs by as much as 50 percent. Armed with this authority, which was granted for a period of five years, President Kennedy called for a round of negotiations through GATT.

These negotiations, which began in 1964, have since become known as the *Kennedy Round*. They were aimed at reducing tariffs and other barriers to trade in both industrial and agricultural products. The participants succeeded in reducing tariffs on these products by an average of more than 35 percent. They were less successful in removing other types of trade barriers.

The Tokyo Round (1973–1979) In 1973, representatives of approximately one hundred nations gathered in Tokyo for another round of GATT negotiations.

General Agreement on Tariffs and Trade (GATT) was an international organization of 153 nations dedicated to reducing or eliminating tariffs and other barriers to world trade.

The *Tokyo Round* was completed in 1979. The participants negotiated tariff cuts of 30 to 35 percent, which were to be implemented over an eight-year period. In addition, they were able to remove or ease such nontariff barriers as import quotas, unrealistic quality standards for imports, and unnecessary red tape in customs procedures.

The Uruguay Round (1986–1993) In 1986, the *Uruguay Round* was launched to extend trade liberalization and widen the GATT treaty to include textiles, agricultural products, business services, and intellectual-property rights. This most ambitious and comprehensive global commercial agreement in history concluded overall negotiations on December 15, 1993, with delegations on hand from 109 nations. The agreement included provisions to lower tariffs by greater than one-third, to reform trade in agricultural goods, to write new rules of trade for intellectual property and services, and to strengthen the dispute-settlement process. These reforms were expected to expand the world economy by an estimated $200 billion annually.

The Uruguay Round also created the **World Trade Organization (WTO)** on January 1, 1995. The WTO was established by GATT to oversee the provisions of the Uruguay Round and resolve any resulting trade disputes. Membership in the WTO obliges 148 member nations to observe GATT rules. The WTO has judicial powers to mediate among members disputing the new rules. It incorporates trade in goods, services, and ideas and exerts more binding authority than GATT.

The Doha Round (2001) On November 14, 2001, in Doha, Qatar, the WTO members agreed to further reduce trade barriers through multilateral trade negotiations over the next three years. This new round of negotiations focuses on industrial tariffs and nontariff barriers, agriculture, services, and easing trade rules. U.S. exporters of industrial and agricultural goods and services should have improved access to overseas markets. The Doha Round has set the stage for WTO members to take an important step toward significant new multilateral trade liberalization. It is a difficult task, but the rewards—lower tariffs, more choices for consumers, and further integration of developing countries into the world trading system—are sure to be worth the effort. Some experts suggest that U.S. exporters of industrial and agricultural goods and services should have improved access to overseas markets, whereas others disagree.

International Economic Organizations Working to Foster Trade

The primary objective of the WTO is to remove barriers to trade on a worldwide basis. On a smaller scale, an **economic community** is an organization of nations formed to promote the free movement of resources and products among its members and to create common economic policies. A number of economic communities now exist.

- The *European Union* (EU), also known as the *European Economic Community* and the *Common Market*, was formed in 1957 by six countries—France, the Federal Republic of Germany, Italy, Belgium, the Netherlands, and Luxembourg. Its objective was freely conducted commerce among these nations and others that might later join. As shown in Figure 3.4, many more nations have joined the EU since then.
- On January 1, 2007, the twenty-five nations of the EU became the EU27 as Bulgaria and Romania became new members. The EU is now an economic force with a collective economy larger than much of the United States or Japan.

In celebrating the EU's fiftieth anniversary in 2007, the president of the European Commission, Jose Manuel Durao Baroso, declared, "Let us first recognize fifty years of achievement. Peace, liberty, and prosperity, beyond the dreams of even the most optimistic founding fathers of Europe. In 1957, fifteen of our twenty-seven members were either under dictatorship or were not allowed to exist as independent countries.

World Trade Organization (WTO) powerful successor to GATT that incorporates trade in goods, services, and ideas

economic community an organization of nations formed to promote the free movement of resources and products among its members and to create common economic policies

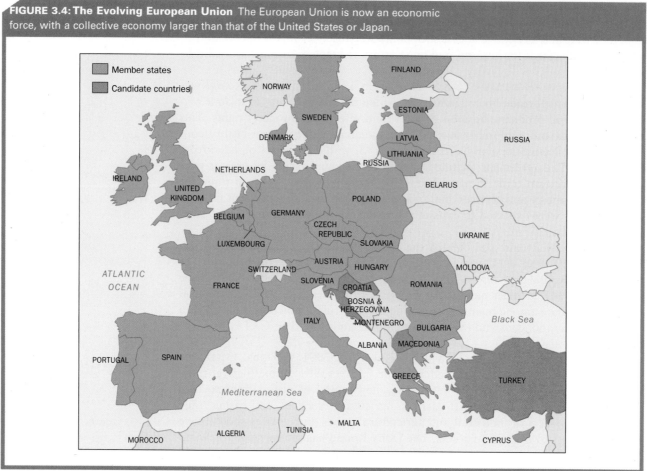

Source: **http://europa.eu/abc/european_countries/index_en.htm**, accessed May 2, 2009.

Now we are all prospering democracies. The EU of today is around fifty times more prosperous and with three times the population of the EU of 1957."

Since January 2002, sixteen member nations of the EU are participating in the new common currency, the euro. The euro is the single currency of the European Monetary Union nations. But three EU members, Denmark, the United Kingdom, and Sweden, still keep their own currencies.

- A second community in Europe, the *European Economic Area* (EEA), became effective in January 1994. This pact consists of Iceland, Norway, Liechtenstein, and the twenty-seven member nations of the EU. The EEA, encompassing an area inhabited by more than 500 million people, allows for the free movement of goods throughout all thirty countries.

- The *North American Free Trade Agreement* (NAFTA) joined the United States with its first- and second-largest export trading partners, Canada and Mexico. Implementation of NAFTA on January 1, 1994, created a market of over 450 million people. This market consists of Canada (population 34 million), the United States (306 million), and Mexico (110 million). According to the Office of the U.S. Trade Representative, after 14 years, NAFTA has achieved its core goals of expanding trade and investment between the United States, Canada, and Mexico. For example, from 1993 to 2007, trade among the NAFTA nations more than tripled, from $297 billion to $930 billion. Business investment in the Untied States has risen by 117 percent since 1993, compared to a 45 percent increase between 1979 and 1993. During the same period, the U.S. employment rose from 110.8 million people in 1993 to 137.6 million in 2007, an increase of 24 percent. The average unemployment rate was 5.1 percent in the period 1994–2007, compared to 7.1 percent during the period 1980–1993.[6]

NAFTA is built on the Canadian Free Trade Agreement (FTA), signed by the United States and Canada in 1989, and on the substantial trade and investment reforms undertaken by Mexico since the mid-1980s. Initiated by the Mexican government, formal negotiations on NAFTA began in June 1991 among the three governments. The support of NAFTA by President Bill Clinton, past U.S. Presidents Ronald Reagan and Jimmy Carter, and Nobel Prize–winning economists provided the impetus for U.S. congressional ratification of NAFTA in November 1993. NAFTA will gradually eliminate all tariffs on goods produced and traded among Canada, Mexico, and the United States to provide for a totally free-trade area by 2009. Chile is expected to become the fourth member of NAFTA, but political forces may delay its entry into the agreement for several years.

Celebrating the 18th Anniversary. The MERCOSUR alliance represents over 267 million consumers—67 percent of South America's population making it the third-largest trading block. Here, Paraguayan President Fernando Lugo speaks during a ceremony celebrating the 18th anniversary of the creation of the MERCOSUR trade block.

- The *Central American Free Trade Agreement* (CAFTA) was created in 2003 by the United States and four Central American countries—El Salvador, Guatemala, Honduras, and Nicaragua. The CAFTA became CAFTA-DR when the Dominican Republic joined the group in 2007. The volume of trade between the United States and its CAFTA partners has increased by 17 percent since 2005, rising from $27.9 billion in 2005 to $32.6 billion in 2007.[7]

- The *Association of Southeast Asian Nations* (ASEAN), with headquarters in Jakarta, Indonesia, was established in 1967 to promote political, economic, and social cooperation among its seven member countries: Indonesia, Malaysia, Philippines, Singapore, Thailand, Brunei, and Vietnam. With the three new members, Cambodia, Laos, and Myanmar, this region is already our fifth largest trading partner. The 10-member region, with a population of 580 million has $2.8 trillion in gross domestic product and accounts for over $169 million worth of trade with the United States.[8]

- The *Pacific Rim,* referring to countries and economies bordering the Pacific Ocean, is an informal, flexible term generally regarded as a reference to East Asia, Canada, and the United States. At a minimum, the Pacific Rim includes Canada, Japan, China, Taiwan, and the United States.

- The *Commonwealth of Independent States* (CIS) was established in December 1991 by the newly independent states (NIS) as an association of eleven republics of the former Soviet Union.

- The *Caribbean Basin Initiative* (CBI) is an inter-American program led by the United States to give economic assistance and trade preferences to Caribbean and Central American countries. CBI provides duty-free access to the U.S. market for most products from the region and promotes private-sector development in member nations.

- The *Common Market of the Southern Cone* (MERCOSUR) was established in 1991 under the Treaty of Asuncion to unite Argentina, Brazil, Paraguay, and Uruguay as a free-trade alliance; Colombia, Ecuador, Peru, Bolivia, and Chile joined later as associates. The alliance represents over 267 million consumers—67 percent of South America's population, making it the third-largest trading bloc behind NAFTA and the EU. Like NAFTA, MERCOSUR promotes "the free circulation of goods, services and production factors among the countries" and established a common external tariff and commercial policy.

©Jorge Adorno/Reuters/Landov

Concept Check

1. Define and describe the major objectives of the World Trade Organization (WTO) and the international economic communities.

2. Which nations are the principal trading partners of the United States? What are the major U.S. imports and exports?

3. What is the importance of exports to the U.S. economy?

- The *Organization of Petroleum Exporting Countries* (OPEC) was founded in 1960 in response to reductions in the prices that oil companies were willing to pay for crude oil. The organization was conceived as a collective-bargaining unit to provide oil-producing nations with some control over oil prices.
- The *Organization for Economic Cooperation and Development* (OECD) is a group of thirty industrialized market-economy countries of North America, Europe, the Far East, and the South Pacific. OECD, headquartered in Paris, was established in 1961 to promote economic development and international trade.

LEARNING OBJECTIVE 4

Define the methods by which a firm can organize for and enter into international markets.

Methods of Entering International Business

A firm that has decided to enter international markets can do so in several ways. We will discuss several different methods. These different approaches require varying degrees of involvement in international business. Typically, a firm begins its international operations at the simplest level. Then, depending on its goals, it may progress to higher levels of involvement.

Licensing

Licensing is a contractual agreement in which one firm permits another to produce and market its product and use its brand name in return for a royalty or other compensation. For example, Yoplait yogurt is a French yogurt licensed for production in the United States. The Yoplait brand maintains an appealing French image, and in return, the U.S. producer pays the French firm a percentage of its income from sales of the product.

Licensing is especially advantageous for small manufacturers wanting to launch a well-known domestic brand internationally. For example, all Spalding sporting products are licensed worldwide. The licensor, the Questor Corporation, owns the Spalding name but produces no goods itself. Licensing thus provides a simple method for expanding into a foreign market with virtually no investment. On the other hand, if the licensee does not maintain the licensor's product standards, the product's image may be damaged. Another possible disadvantage is that a licensing arrangement may not provide the original producer with any foreign marketing experience.

Exporting

A firm also may manufacture its products in its home country and export them for sale in foreign markets. As with licensing, exporting can be a relatively low-risk method of entering foreign markets. Unlike licensing, however, it is not a simple method; it opens up several levels of involvement to the exporting firm.

At the most basic level, the exporting firm may sell its products outright to an *export-import merchant*, which is essentially a merchant wholesaler. The merchant assumes all the risks of product ownership, distribution, and sale. It may even purchase the goods in the producer's home country and assume responsibility for exporting the goods. An important and practical issue for domestic firms dealing with foreign customers is securing payment. This is a two-sided issue that reflects the mutual concern rightly felt by both parties to the trade deal: The exporter would like to be paid before shipping the merchandise, whereas the importer obviously would prefer to know that it has received the shipment before releasing any funds. Neither side wants to take the risk of fulfilling its part of the deal only later to discover that the other side has not. The result would lead to legal costs and complex, lengthy dealings wasteful of everyone's resources. This mutual level of mistrust is in fact good business sense and has been around since the beginning of trade centuries ago. The solution then was as it still is today—for both parties to use a mutually trusted go-between who can ensure that the payment is held until the merchandise is in fact delivered according to the terms of the trade contract. The go-between representatives employed by the importer and exporter are still, as they were in the past, the local domestic banks involved in international business.

licensing a contractual agreement in which one firm permits another to produce and market its product and use its brand name in return for a royalty or other compensation

Globally, international trade of goods amounts to about $14 trillion annually, and, according to the World Trade Organization (WTO), 90 percent of these transactions involve trade financing. Trade-related credit is primarily issued by banks via letters of credit, whose purpose is to secure payment for the exporter. Letters of credit prove that an importer is able to pay and allow exporters to load cargo for shipments with the assurance of being paid.

Here is a simplified version of how it works. After signing contracts detailing the merchandise sold and terms for its delivery, an importer will ask its local bank to issue a **letter of credit** for the amount of money needed to pay for the merchandise. The letter of credit is issued "in favor of the exporter," meaning that the funds are tied specifically to the trade contract involved. The importer's bank forwards the letter of credit to the exporter's bank, which also normally deals in international transactions. The exporter's bank then notifies the exporter that a letter of credit has been received in its name, and the exporter can go ahead with the shipment. The carrier transporting the merchandise provides the exporter with evidence of the shipment in a document called a **bill of lading**. The exporter signs over title to the merchandise (now in transit) to its bank by delivering signed copies of the bill of lading and the letter of credit.

In exchange, the exporter issues a **draft** from the bank, which orders the importer's bank to pay for the merchandise. The draft, bill of lading, and letter of credit are sent from the exporter's bank to the importer's bank. Acceptance by the importer's bank leads to return of the draft and its sale by the exporter to its bank, meaning that the exporter receives cash and the bank assumes the risk of collecting the funds from the foreign bank. The importer is obliged to pay its bank on delivery of the merchandise, and the deal is complete.

In most cases, the letter of credit is part of a lending arrangement between the importer and its bank, and of course, both banks earn fees for issuing letters of credit and drafts and for handling the import-export services for their clients. Furthermore, the process incorporates the fact that both importer and exporter will have different local currencies and might even negotiate their trade in a third currency. The banks look after all the necessary exchanges. For example, the vast majority of international business is negotiated in U.S. dollars, even though the trade may be between countries other than the United States. Thus, although the importer may end up paying for the merchandise in its local currency and the exporter may receive payment in another local currency, the banks involved will exchange all necessary foreign funds in order to allow the deal to take place.

The exporting firm instead may ship its products to an *export-import agent*, which for a commission or fee arranges the sale of the products to foreign intermediaries. The agent is an independent firm—like other agents—that sells and may perform other marketing functions for the exporter. The exporter, however, retains title to the products during shipment and until they are sold.

An exporting firm also may establish its own *sales offices*, or *branches*, in foreign countries. These installations are international extensions of the firm's distribution system. They represent a deeper involvement in international business than the other exporting techniques we have discussed—and thus they carry a greater risk. The exporting firm maintains control over sales, and it gains both experience in and knowledge of foreign markets. Eventually, the firm also may develop its own sales force to operate in conjunction with foreign sales offices.

Joint Ventures

A *joint venture* is a partnership formed to achieve a specific goal or to operate for a specific period of time. A joint venture with an established firm in a foreign country provides immediate market knowledge and access, reduced risk, and control over product attributes. However, joint-venture agreements established across national borders can become extremely complex. As a result, joint-venture agreements generally require a very high level of commitment from all the parties involved.

letter of credit issued by a bank on request of an importer stating that the bank will pay an amount of money to a stated beneficiary

bill of lading document issued by a transport carrier to an exporter to prove that merchandise has been shipped

draft issued by the exporter's bank, ordering the importer's bank to pay for the merchandise, thus guaranteeing payment once accepted by the importer's bank

Chrysler-Fiat alliance. In early 2009, Bob Nardelli, chairman and CEO of Chrysler announced that Chrysler-Fiat alliance "enables us to better serve our customers and dealers with broader and more competitive line-up of environmentally friendly, fuel-efficient higher quality vehicles. Benefits to the new company include access to exciting products that complement our current portfolio, technology cooperation and stronger global distribution." Here, a Fiat car is parked in front of a Chrysler dealer in Milan, Italy.

A joint venture may be used to produce and market an existing product in a foreign nation or to develop an entirely new product. Recently, for example, Archer Daniels Midland Company (ADM), one of the world's leading food processors, entered into a joint venture with Gruma SA, Mexico's largest corn flour and tortilla company. Besides a 22 percent stake in Gruma, ADM also received stakes in other joint ventures operated by Gruma. One of them will combine both companies' U.S. corn flour operations, which account for about 25 percent of the U.S. market. ADM also has a 40 percent stake in a Mexican wheat flour mill. ADM's joint venture increased its participation in the growing Mexican economy, where ADM already produces corn syrup, fructose, starch, and wheat flour.

Totally Owned Facilities

At a still deeper level of involvement in international business, a firm may develop *totally owned facilities,* that is, its own production and marketing facilities in one or more foreign nations. This *direct investment* provides complete control over operations, but it carries a greater risk than the joint venture. The firm is really establishing a subsidiary in a foreign country. Most firms do so only after they have acquired some knowledge of the host country's markets.

Direct investment may take either of two forms:

Form A. In the first, the firm builds or purchases manufacturing and other facilities in the foreign country. It uses these facilities to produce its own established products and to market them in that country and perhaps in neighboring countries. Firms such as General Motors, Union Carbide, and Colgate-Palmolive are multinational companies with worldwide manufacturing facilities. Colgate-Palmolive factories are becoming *Eurofactories,* supplying neighboring countries as well as their own local markets.

Form B. A second form of direct investment in international business is the purchase of an existing firm in a foreign country under an arrangement that allows it to operate independently of the parent company. When Sony Corporation (a Japanese firm) decided to enter the motion-picture business in the United States, it chose to purchase Columbia Pictures Entertainment, Inc., rather than start a new motion-picture studio from scratch.

Strategic Alliances

A **strategic alliance,** the newest form of international business structure, is a partnership formed to create competitive advantage on a worldwide basis. Strategic alliances are very similar to joint ventures. The number of strategic alliances is growing at an estimated rate of about 20 percent per year. In fact, in the automobile and computer industries, strategic alliances are becoming the predominant means of competing. International competition is so fierce and the costs of competing on a global basis are so high that few firms have all the resources needed to do it alone. Thus, individual firms that lack the internal resources essential for international success may seek to collaborate with other companies.

An example of such an alliance is the New United Motor Manufacturing, Inc. (NUMMI), formed by Toyota and General Motors to make automobiles of both firms. This enterprise united the quality engineering of Japanese cars with the marketing expertise and market access of General Motors.[9]

strategic alliances a partnership formed to create competitive advantage on a worldwide basis

Trading Companies

A **trading company** provides a link between buyers and sellers in different countries. A trading company, as its name implies, is not involved in manufacturing or owning assets related to manufacturing. It buys products in one country at the lowest price consistent with quality and sells to buyers in another country. An important function of trading companies is taking title to products and performing all the activities necessary to move the products from the domestic country to a foreign country. For example, large grain-trading companies operating out of home offices both in the United States and overseas control a major portion of the world's trade in basic food commodities. These trading companies sell homogeneous agricultural commodities that can be stored and moved rapidly in response to market conditions.

Countertrade

In the early 1990s, many developing nations had major restrictions on converting domestic currency into foreign currency. Exporters therefore had to resort to barter agreements with importers. **Countertrade** is essentially an international barter transaction in which goods and services are exchanged for different goods and services. Examples include Saudi Arabia's purchase of ten 747 jets from Boeing with payment in crude oil and Philip Morris's sale of cigarettes to Russia in return for chemicals used to make fertilizers.

Multinational Firms

A **multinational enterprise** is a firm that operates on a worldwide scale without ties to any specific nation or region. The multinational firm represents the highest level of involvement in international business. It is equally "at home" in most countries of the world. In fact, as far as the operations of the multinational enterprise are concerned, national boundaries exist only on maps. It is, however, organized under the laws of its home country.

Table 3.3 shows the ten largest foreign and U.S. public multinational companies; the ranking is based on a composite score reflecting each company's best three out of four rankings for sales, profits, assets, and market value. Table 3.4 describes steps in entering international markets.

According to the chairman of the board of Dow Chemical Company, a multinational firm of U.S. origin, "The emergence of a world economy and of the multinational corporation has been accomplished hand in hand." He sees multinational

TABLE 3.3: The Ten Largest Foreign and U.S. Multinational Corporations

2008 Rank	Company	Business	Country	Revenue ($millions)
1	Royal Dutch/Shell Group	Energy	Netherlands/ United Kingdom	458,361
2	ExxonMobil	Energy	United States	442,851
3	Wal-Mart Stores	General merchandise	United States	405,607
4	BP	Energy	United Kingdom	367,053
5	Chevron	Energy	United States	263,159
6	Total	Energy	France	234,674
7	ConocoPhillips	Energy	United States	230,764
8	ING Group	Financial Services	Netherlands	226,577
9	Sinopec	Energy	China	207,814
10	Toyota Motor	Automobiles	Japan	204,352

Source: **http://money.cnn.com/magazines/fortune/global500/2009/snapshots/6350.html**, accessed July 17, 2009.

trading company provides a link between buyers and sellers in different countries

countertrade an international barter transaction

multinational enterprise a firm that operates on a worldwide scale without ties to any specific nation or region

TABLE 3.4: Steps in Entering International Markets

Step	Activity	Marketing Tasks
1	Identify exportable products	Identify key selling features Identify needs that they satisfy Identify the selling constraints that are imposed
2	Identify key foreign markets for the products	Determine who the customers are Pinpoint what and when they will buy Do market research Establish priority, or "target," countries
3	Analyze how to sell in each priority market (methods will be affected by product characteristics and unique features of country/market)	Locate available government and private-sector resources Determine service and backup sales requirements
4	Set export prices and payment terms, methods, and techniques	Establish methods of export pricing Establish sales terms, quotations, invoices, and conditions of sale Determine methods of international payments, secured and unsecured
5	Estimate resource requirements and returns	Estimate financial requirements Estimate human resources requirements (full- or part-time export department or operation?) Estimate plant production capacity Determine necessary product adaptations
6	Establish overseas distribution network	Determine distribution agreement and other key marketing decisions (price, repair policies, returns, territory, performance, and termination) Know your customer (use U.S. Department of Commerce international marketing services)
7	Determine shipping, traffic, and documentation procedures and requirements	Determine methods of shipment (air or ocean freight, truck, rail) Finalize containerization Obtain validated export license Follow export-administration documentation procedures
8	Promote, sell, and be paid	Use international media, communications, advertising, trade shows, and exhibitions Determine the need for overseas travel (when, where, and how often?) Initiate customer follow-up procedures
9	Continuously analyze current marketing, economic, and political situations	Recognize changing factors influencing marketing strategies Constantly reevaluate

Source: U.S. Department of Commerce, International Trade Administration, Washington, D.C.

Concept Check

1. Two methods of engaging in the international business may be categorized as either direct or indirect. How would you classify each of the methods described in this chapter? Why?

2. What is a letter of credit? A bill of lading? A draft?

3. In what ways is a multinational enterprise different from a large corporation that does business in several countries?

4. What are the steps in entering international markets?

Part 1: The Environment of Business

enterprises moving toward what he calls the "anational company," a firm that has no nationality but belongs to all countries. In recognition of this movement, there already have been international conferences devoted to the question of how such enterprises would be controlled.

Sources of Export Assistance

5 LEARNING OBJECTIVE

Describe the various sources of export assistance.

In September 1993, President Bill Clinton announced the *National Export Strategy* (NES) to revitalize U.S. exports. Under the NES, the *Trade Promotion Coordinating Committee* (TPCC) assists U.S. firms in developing export-promotion programs. The export services and programs of the nineteen TPCC agencies can help American firms to compete in foreign markets and create new jobs in the United States. Table 3.5 provides an overview of selected export assistance programs.

These and other sources of export information enhance the business opportunities of U.S. firms seeking to enter expanding foreign markets. Another vital energy factor is financing.

TABLE 3.5: U.S. Government Export Assistance Programs

1	U.S. Export Assistance Centers, www.sba.gov/oit/export/useac.html	Provides assistance in export marketing and trade finance.
2	International Trade Administration, www.ita.doc.gov/	Offers assistance and information to exporters through its domestic and overseas commercial officers.
3	U.S. and Foreign Commercial Services, www.export.gov/	Helps U.S. firms compete more effectively in the global marketplace and provides information on foreign markets.
4	Advocacy Center, www.ita.doc.gov/advocacy	Facilitates advocacy to assist U.S. firms competing for major projects and procurements worldwide.
5	Trade Information Center, www.export.gov.	Provides U.S. companies information on federal programs and activities that support U.S. exports.
6	STAT-USA/Internet, www.stat-usa.gov/	Offers a comprehensive collection of business, economic, and trade information on the Web.
7	Small Business Administration, www.sba.gov/oit/	Publishes many helpful guides to assist small and medium-sized companies.
8	National Trade Data Bank, www.stat-usa.gov/tradtest.nsf	Provides international economic and export promotion information supplied by over twenty U.S. agencies.

Concept Check

1. How does the Trade Promotion Coordinating Committee (TPCC) assist the U.S. firms?

2. List some key sources of export assistance. How can these sources be useful to small business firms?

Financing International Business

6 LEARNING OBJECTIVE

Describe the Identify the institutions that help firms and nations finance international business. sources of export assistance.

According to the International Monetary Fund, world trade volumes are expected to decline for the first time since 1982, mostly as a result of a near collapse of import demand from developed countries. As trade finance conditions tighten as a result of the global financial crisis, governments and multilateral institutions are stepping in to provide export financing where the private sector is no longer willing

The Entrepreneurial Spirit

Building a Business Around Expatriates

Many entrepreneurs are building successful businesses by catering to the needs of expatriates, people who live and work far from their home countries. For example, specialty-food businesses in and around major cities import products to attract expatriates who crave a taste of home. When Oscar Espinosa teamed up with a partner to open De Mi Pueblo in Springfield, Virginia, they originally focused on cheeses from Central America. Today they import hundreds of thousands of pounds of cheese, beans, crackers, and other foods every month from Nicaragua and surrounding nations.

Sonni Kohli opened Kohli's Indian Emporium in Pittsburgh to sell authentic ingredients such as atta flour and prepared foods such as rose, mango, and saffron-pistachio ice cream. In addition to serving expatriates, Kohli's also attracts local customers who are interested in Indian food.

Graciela and Inocente Hernandez started their first Mexican foods grocery store in Milwaukee in 2002. Sales were so strong that the couple decided to open a second store six years later. Despite the serious economic downturn, the Hernandezes were able to create a solid business plan and find financing to open the store with the help of the Latino Entrepreneurial Network of Southeastern Wisconsin.

Patricia Cruz, originally from Mexico City, makes and sells tacos at Washington D.C.'s weekly Mi Tierra outdoor food and craft market. She and the other entrepreneurs who operate booths at the market also attend management and accounting classes offered by a local nonprofit organization. Cruz's goal: To open a restaurant and build her business by attracting expatriates and others who love good Mexican food.

Sources: Eliza Barclay, "Home Is Where the Tacos Are," *Washington Post*, April 1, 2009, p. F1; Tannette Johnson-Elie, "Network Pairs Hispanic Entrepreneurs with Resources," *Journal Sentinel Online (Milwaukee)*, September 16, 2008, www.jsonline.com; Marcela Sanchez, "Turning a Taste for Home into a Win-Win for Trade," *Washington Post.com*, September 5, 2008, www.washingtonpost.com; Cecilia Kang, "Ethnic Grocers Losing Their Niche," *Washington Post*, September 3, 2007, p. D1.

to extend credit. In the words of WTO President Pascal Lamy, "the world economy is slowing and trade is decreasing. If trade finance is not tackled, we run the risk of further exacerbating this downward spiral."

International trade compounds the concerns of financial managers. Currency exchange rates, tariffs and foreign-exchange controls, and the tax structures of host nations all affect international operations and the flow of cash. In addition, financial managers must be concerned both with the financing of their international operations and with the means available to their customers to finance purchases.

Fortunately, along with business in general, a number of large banks have become international in scope. Many have established branches in major cities around the world. Thus, like firms in other industries, they are able to provide their services where and when they are needed. In addition, financial assistance is available from U.S. government and international sources.

Several of today's international financial organizations were founded many years ago to facilitate free trade and the exchange of currencies among nations. Some, such as the Inter-American Development Bank, are supported internationally and focus on developing countries. Others, such as the Export-Import Bank, are operated by one country but provide international financing.

The Export-Import Bank of the United States

The **Export-Import Bank of the United States**, created in 1934, is an independent agency of the U.S. government whose function it is to assist in financing the exports of American firms. *Eximbank*, as it is commonly called, extends and guarantees credit to overseas buyers of American goods and services and guarantees short-term financing for exports. For example, in November 2008, the Ex-Im Bank announced that it would provide up to $2.9 billion in credit insurance for Korean financial institutions. In fiscal year 2008 Ex-Im Bank authorized $14.4 billion in loans, guarantees, and credit insurance worldwide, which were estimated to support $19.6 billion of U.S. exports.[10] It also cooperates with commercial banks in helping American exporters to offer credit to their overseas customers.

Export-Import Bank of the United States an independent agency of the U.S. government whose function it is to assist in financing the exports of American firms

Multilateral Development Banks

A **multilateral development bank (MDB)** is an internationally supported bank that provides loans to developing countries to help them grow. The most familiar is the World Bank, which operates worldwide. The World Bank, established in 1944, and headquartered in Washington, D.C., is owned by 185 countries. It is a vital source of financial and technical assistance to developing countries around the world. The Bank's two institutions—the International Bank for Reconstruction and Development (IBRD) and the International Development Association (IDA)—provide low-interest loans, interest-free credits and grants to developing countries for education, health, public administration, agriculture, environmental and natural resource management. Four other MDBs operate primarily in Central and South America, Asia, Africa, and Eastern and Central Europe. All five are supported by the industrialized nations, including the United States.

The *Inter-American Development Bank* (IDB), the oldest and largest regional bank, was created in 1959 by nineteen Latin American countries and the United States. The bank, which is headquartered in Washington, D.C., makes loans and provides technical advice and assistance to countries. Today, the IDB is owned by forty-eight member states and has offices in all 26 countries of Latin America and the Caribbean.

With sixty-seven member nations, the *Asian Development Bank* (ADB), created in 1966 and headquartered in the Philippines, promotes economic and social progress in Asian and Pacific regions. The U.S. government is the second-largest contributor to the ADB's capital, after Japan.

The *African Development Bank* (AFDB), also known as *Banque Africaines de Development*, was established in 1964 with headquarters in Abidjan, Ivory Coast. Its members include fifty-three African and twenty-four non-African countries from the Americas, Europe, and Asia. The AFDB's goal is to foster the economic and social development of its African members. The bank pursues this goal through loans, research, technical assistance, and the development of trade programs.

Established in 1991 to encourage reconstruction and development in the Eastern and Central European countries, the London-based *European Bank for Reconstruction and Development* (EBRD) is owned by sixty-one countries and two intergovernmental institutions. Its loans are geared toward developing market-oriented economies and promoting private enterprise.

The International Monetary Fund

Courtesy Warwick Mills

The **International Monetary Fund (IMF)** is an international bank with 185 member nations that makes short-term loans to developing countries experiencing balance-of-payment deficits. This financing is contributed by member nations, and it must be repaid with interest. Loans are provided primarily to fund international trade.

multilateral development bank (MDB) an internationally supported bank that provides loans to developing countries to help them grow

International Monetary Fund (IMF) an international bank with 185 member nations that makes short-term loans to developing countries experiencing balance-of-payment deficits

Concept Check

1. What is the Export-Import Bank of the United States? How does it assist U.S. exporters?

2. What is a multilateral development bank (MDB)? Who supports these banks?

3. What is the International Monetary Fund? What types of loans does the IMF provide?

SUMMARY

1 Explain the economic basis for international business.

International business encompasses all business activities that involve exchanges across national boundaries. International trade is based on specialization, whereby each country produces the goods and services that it can produce more efficiently than any other goods and services. A nation is said to have a comparative advantage relative to these goods. International trade develops when each nation trades its surplus products for those in short supply.

A nation's balance of trade is the difference between the value of its exports and the value of its imports. Its balance of payments is the difference between the flow of money into and out of the nation. Generally, a negative balance of trade is considered unfavorable.

2 Discuss the restrictions nations place on international trade, the objectives of these restrictions, and their results.

Despite the benefits of world trade, nations tend to use tariffs and nontariff barriers (import quotas, embargoes, and other restrictions) to limit trade. These restrictions typically are justified as being needed to protect a nation's economy, industries, citizens, or security. They can result in the loss of jobs, higher prices, fewer choices in the marketplace, and the misallocation of resources.

3 Outline the extent of international trade and identify the organizations working to foster it.

World trade is generally increasing. Trade between the United States and other nations is increasing in dollar value but decreasing in terms of our share of the world market. The General Agreement on Tariffs and Trade (GATT) was formed to dismantle trade barriers and provide an environment in which international business can grow. Today, the World Trade Organization (WTO) and various economic communities carry on that mission.

4 Define the methods by which a firm can organize for and enter into international markets.

A firm can enter international markets in several ways. It may license a foreign firm to produce and market its products. It may export its products and sell them through foreign intermediaries or its own sales organization abroad. Or it may sell its exports outright to an export-import merchant. It may enter into a joint venture with a foreign firm. It may establish its own foreign subsidiaries. Or it may develop into a multinational enterprise.

Generally, each of these methods represents an increasingly deeper level of involvement in international business, with licensing being the simplest and the development of a multinational corporation the most involved.

5 Describe the various sources of export assistance.

Many government and international agencies provide export assistance to U.S. and foreign firms. The export services and programs of the nineteen agencies of the U.S. Trade Promotion Coordinating Committee (TPCC) can help U.S. firms to compete in foreign markets and create new jobs in the United States. Sources of export assistance include U.S. Export Assistance Centers, the International Trade Administration, U.S. and Foreign Commercial Services, Export Legal Assistance Network, Advocacy Center, National Trade Data Bank, and other government and international agencies.

6 Identify the institutions that help firms and nations finance international business.

The financing of international trade is more complex than that of domestic trade. Institutions such as the Ex-Im bank and the International Monetary Fund have been established to provide financing and ultimately to increase world trade for American and international firms.

KEY TERMS

You should now be able to define and give an example relevant to each of the following terms:

international business (68)	dumping (71)	World Trade Organization (WTO) (79)	countertrade (85)
absolute advantage (68)	nontariff barrier (72)	economic community (79)	multinational enterprise (85)
comparative advantage (68)	import quota (72)	licensing (82)	Export-Import Bank of the United States (88)
exporting (69)	embargo (72)	letter of credit (83)	multilateral development bank (MDB) (89)
importing (69)	foreign-exchange control (72)	bill of lading (83)	International Monetary Fund (IMF) (89)
balance of trade (71)	currency devaluation (72)	draft (83)	
trade deficit (71)	General Agreement on Tariffs and Trade (GATT) (78)	strategic alliance (84)	
balance of payments (71)		trading company (85)	
import duty (tariff) (71)			

DISCUSSION QUESTIONS

1. The United States restricts imports but, at the same time, supports the WTO and international banks whose objective is to enhance world trade. As a member of Congress, how would you justify this contradiction to your constituents?

2. What effects might the devaluation of a nation's currency have on its business firms? On its consumers? On the debts it owes to other nations?

3. Should imports to the United States be curtailed by, say, 20 percent to eliminate our trade deficit? What might happen if this were done?

4. When should a firm consider expanding from strictly domestic trade to international trade? When should it consider becoming further involved in international trade? What factors might affect the firm's decisions in each case?

5. How can a firm obtain the expertise needed to produce and market its products in, for example, the EU?

Get Flash Cards, Quizzes, Games, Crosswords and more @ www.cengage.com/introbusiness/ pride

Test Yourself

Matching Questions

1. _____ The total value of a nation's exports minus the total value of its imports over some period of time.

2. _____ The ability to produce a specific product more efficiently than any other nation.

3. _____ Selling and shipping raw materials or products to other nations.

4. _____ The ability to produce a specific product more efficiently than any other product.

5. _____ All business activities that involve exchanges across national boundaries.

6. _____ The total flow of money into a country minus the total flow of money out of that country over same period of time.

7. _____ A tax levied on a particular foreign product entering a country.

8. _____ A complete halt to trading with a particular nation or in a particular product.

9. _____ An international barter transaction.

10. _____ An internationally supported bank that provides loans to developing countries to help them grow.

  a. countertrade
  b. foreign exchange control
  c. multilateral development bank (MDB)
  d. absolute advantage
  e. import duty
  f. embargo
  g. exporting
  h. international business
  i. balance of trade
  j. comparative advantage
  k. Export-Import Bank of the United States
  l. balance of payments

True False Questions

11. **T F** The United States has enjoyed a trade surplus during the last two decades.

12. **T F** Tariff is a tax levied on a particular foreign product entering a country.

13. **T F** Quotas may be set on worldwide imports or on imports from a specific country.

14. **T F** The participants in the Kennedy Round have succeeded in reducing tariffs by less than 20 percent.

15. **T F** Licensing and exporting can be considered relatively low-risk methods of entering foreign markets.

16. **T F** A letter of credit is issued in favor of the importer.

17. **T F** A letter of credit is issued by the transport carrier to the exporter to prove that merchandise has been shipped.

18. **T F** Strategic alliances are partnerships formed to create competitive advantage on a worldwide basis.

19. **T F** A firm that has no ties to a specific nation or region and operates on a worldwide scale is called a national enterprise.

20. **T F** The International Monetary Fund (IMF) makes short-term loans to developing countries experiencing balance-of-payment deficits.

Test Yourself

Multiple-Choice Questions

21. _____ By definition, every country has a(n) _____ advantage in some product.
    a. relative
    b. absolute
    c. comparative
    d. superior
    e. inferior

22. _____ Purchasing products or materials in other nations and bringing them into one's own country is
    a. trading.
    b. balancing.
    c. exporting.
    d. importing.
    e. dumping.

23. _____ General Motors and Ford products produced in the United States are found around the world. The United States is _____ these automobiles.
    a. tariffing
    b. importing
    c. exporting
    d. releasing
    e. dumping

24. _____ _____ is the exportation of large quantities of a product at a price lower than that of the same product in the home market.
    a. Embargo
    b. Duty
    c. Dumping
    d. Export quota
    e. Dropping

25. _____ A complete halt to trading with a particular nation or in a particular product is called a(n)
    a. embargo.
    b. stoppage.
    c. stay.
    d. closure.
    e. barricade.

26. _____ Because it has not been around long enough to establish itself, the Russian automobile industry could be classified as a(n)
    a. hopeless industry.
    b. soft industry.
    c. infant industry.
    d. protected industry.
    e. toddler industry.

27. _____ The World Trade Organization was created by the
    a. Kennedy Round.
    b. United Nations.
    c. League of Nations.
    d. Tokyo Round.
    e. Uruguay Round.

28. _____ CAFTA, NAFTA, OECD, and OPEC are all examples of
    a. political organizations.
    b. peace treaties.
    c. international economic communities.
    d. World Trade Organization members.
    e. democratic organizations.

29. _____ Foreign licensing is similar to
    a. starting from scratch.
    b. franchising.
    c. wholesaling.
    d. establishing a subsidiary in another country.
    e. establishing a sales office in a foreign country.

30. _____ The World Bank is an example of a(n) _____, owned by 185 nations, including the United States.
    a. Ex-Im bank
    b. IMF
    c. MDB
    d. EFTA
    e. LAFTA

Answers on p. TY-1

VIDEO CASE

Fossil: Keeping Watch on a Global Business

Since its founding in 1984, Fossil has grown into a global company and a world class brand in the fashion accessory industry. The core of the company is its watch division, which sells more than 500 styles in its line. They boast they have a watch for every wrist. Fossil also manufactures and markets sunglasses, belts, purses, and other related leather goods. The key to Fossil's success is its emphasis on fashion-forward design, creative packaging, and a distinctive marketing campaign that depicts the nostalgia of 1950s America. Every watch comes in a free collectible tin box reminiscent of that period.

Its products are not retro, but their brand image is. This image is the heartbeat of the company, and Fossil believes its brand image gives it a differential advantage versus competitors such as Guess and Swatch.

Fossil has become the number one fashion watch line in almost every department store in the United States. The company has done this through value pricing, making it easy for customers to find their watches in stores, designing their products so they are easily identifiable, and by always being in the forefront of design and style. In short, Fossil tries to make the purchase of its products easy, quick, fun, and trendy.

Ten years ago, the company went international when it entered the German market. In the last five years, Fossil has concentrated on becoming a global company, and today its products are manufactured and sold in more than 70 countries around the world. The company's global expansion has been the result of a multifaceted strategic plan that consists of (1) working closely with international retailers to ensure that they have the right product for the market, (2) developing marketing programs that are uniform and cohesive worldwide, (3) ensuring they have the infrastructure to deliver their products and marketing programs to the proper channels, and (4) selecting the right partners to help them execute their plans. Partners include offshore manufacturers, distributors, sales representative companies, and of course, retailers. The company also has wholly owned subsidiaries in several countries.

Some of Fossil's strongest manufacturing and distribution partners are in Hong Kong. This is because the company believes that Hong Kong has the infrastructure and systems in place to manufacture and assemble products and deliver them in a timely manner, at an acceptable cost, anywhere in the world.

As a global company, Fossil keeps a watchful eye on an ever-changing worldwide political and economic environment. Currencies can literally devaluate 30 percent in one day and then bounce back 50 percent the next day. This kind of volatility can have a significant effect on the company's costs, revenues, and profitability. In order to deal with this changing environment, Fossil constantly monitors its business drivers. They talk to their distributors weekly, sometimes daily, to ensure they have enough product in the pipeline. Fossil's principals meet once a week to minimize the company's downside risk in the event a financial crisis occurs somewhere in the world. They do this by adjusting inventory, evaluating their purchasing needs, analyzing the sales of every watch style, and identifying business trends. This attention to detail has played an important role in the company's past success. With sales on the rise, new designs and products on the horizon, and a strong stable of international partners, Fossil is well on its way to achieving its number one goal: "To be the major fashion accessory brand in the world."[10]

Questions

1. What comparative advantage, if any, does Fossil have over its competitors?
2. If Brazil devaluated its currency by 50 percent, what effect would it have on Fossil?
3. Given that Fossil is not marketed in every country in the world, would you recommend that the company license its products to expand its presence in additional countries where it is not currently represented?

BUILDING SKILLS FOR CAREER SUCCESS

1. EXPLORING THE INTERNET

A popular question debated among firms actively involved on the Internet is whether or not there exists a truly global Internet-based customer, irrespective of any individual culture, linguistic, or nationality issues. Does this Internet-based universal customer see the Internet and products sold there in pretty much the same way? If so, then one model might fit all customers. For example, although Yahoo.com translates its Web pages so that they are understood around the world, the pages look pretty much the same regardless of which international site you use. Is this good strategy, or should the sites reflect local customers differently? Visit the text website for updates to this exercise.

Assignment

1. Examine a website such as Yahoo's (**www.yahoo.com**) and its various international versions that operate in other languages around the world. Compare their similarities and differences as best you can, even if you do not understand the individual languages.
2. After making your comparison, do you now agree that there are indeed universal Internet products and customers? Explain your decision.

2. BUILDING TEAM SKILLS

The North American Trade Agreement among the United States, Mexico, and Canada went into effect on January 1, 1994. It has made a difference in trade among the countries and has affected the lives of many people.

Assignment

1. Working in teams and using the resources of your library, investigate NAFTA. Answer the following questions:
   a. What are NAFTA's objectives?
   b. What are its benefits?
   c. What impact has NAFTA had on trade, jobs, and travel?
   d. Some Americans were opposed to the implementation of NAFTA. What were their objections? Have any of these objections been justified?
   e. Has NAFTA influenced your life? How?
2. Summarize your answers in a written report. Your team also should be prepared to give a class presentation.

3. RESEARCHING DIFFERENT CAREERS

Today, firms around the world need employees with special skills. In some countries, such employees are not always available, and firms then must search abroad for qualified applicants. One way they can do this is through global workforce databases. As business and trade operations continue to grow globally, you may one day find yourself working in a foreign country, perhaps for an American company doing business there or for a foreign company. In what foreign country would you like to work? What problems might you face?

Assignment

1. Choose a country in which you might like to work.
2. Research the country. The National Trade Data Bank (NTDA) is a good place to start. Find answers to the following questions:
   a. What language is spoken in this country? Are you proficient in it? What would you need to do if you are not proficient?
   b. What are the economic, social, and legal systems like in this nation?
   c. What is its history?
   d. What are its culture and social traditions like? How might they affect your work or your living arrangements?
3. Describe what you have found out about this country in a written report. Include an assessment of whether you would want to work there and the problems you might face if you did.

The Rise of Finagle A Bagel

Would bagels sell in Hong Kong? Laura Beth Trust and Alan Litchman planned to find out. Trust was in Hong Kong working in the garment manufacturing industry, and Litchman was in real estate, but they were eager to start their own business. They were particularly interested in running a business where they would have direct customer contact and be able to get first-hand feedback about their products and services. And no matter what kind of business they started, it would be a family undertaking: The two entrepreneurs recently had decided to get married.

Looking around Hong Kong, Litchman and Trust noticed numerous Western-style food chains such as McDonald's, Pizza Hut, KFC, and Starbucks but no bagel places. Yet they believed that Hong Kong's sophisticated, multicultural population would welcome authentic New York–style bagels. Although both the entrepreneurs had MBA degrees from the Sloan School of Management, neither had any restaurant experience or knew how to make a bagel. Still, because they sensed a profitable opportunity and possessed solid business skills, Trust and Litchman decided to move ahead. The two incorporated a company, found a partner, and then returned to the United States to investigate the bagel business. As part of their research, they approached two knowledgeable experts for advice.

One of the bagel experts was Larry Smith, who in 1982 had cofounded a tiny cheesecake store in Boston's historic Quincy Market. When business was slow, the store began selling bagels topped with leftover cream cheese. By the late 1980s, this sideline was doing so well that Smith and his partners changed their focus from cheesecakes to bagels and changed the store's name from Julian's Cheesecakes to Finagle A Bagel. They relocated the store from a cramped 63-square-foot storefront into a more spacious 922-square-foot space in the same busy market complex. Soon, so many customers were lining up for bagels that the owners began opening additional Finagle A Bagel stores around downtown Boston.

New Ownership, New Growth

By the time Trust and Litchman met Smith, he was operating six successful bagel stores, was ringing up $10 million in annual sales, and was looking for a source of capital to open more stores. Therefore, instead of helping the entrepreneurs launch a business in Hong Kong, Smith suggested that they stay and become involved in Finagle A Bagel. Because Litchman and Trust had roots in the Boston area, the opportunity to join a local bagel business was appealing both personally and professionally. Late in 1998, they bought a majority stake in Finagle A Bagel from Smith. The three owners agreed on how to divide management responsibilities and collaborated on plans for more aggressive expansion. Within a few years, Trust and Litchman completed a deal to

buy the rest of the business and became the sole owners and copresidents.

The business has grown every year since the conversion to bagels. Today, Finagle A Bagel operates twenty stores in downtown Boston and the surrounding suburbs. Because Finagle A Bagel outgrew its original production facilities, the owners recently purchased a new corporate headquarters and production center in Newton, Massachusetts. This is where tens of thousands of bagels are prepared every day, along with enough cream cheese and cookies to supply a much larger network of stores.

Branding the Bagel

Over time, the owners have introduced a wide range of bagels, sandwiches, salads, and soups linked to the core bagel product. Bagels are baked fresh every day, and the stores receive daily deliveries of fresh salad fixings and other ingredients. Employees make each menu item to order while the customer watches. Some of the most popular offerings include a breakfast bagel pizza, salads with bagel-chip croutons, and BLT (bacon-lettuce-tomato) bagel sandwiches.

Finagle A Bagel is also boosting revenues by wholesaling its bagels to thousands of universities, hospitals, and corporate cafeterias. In addition, it sells several varieties of bagels under the Finagle A Bagel brand to the Shaw's Market grocery chain. Shaw's has been expanding in New England through mergers and acquisitions, opening new opportunities for its bagel supplier. "As they grow, we grow with them," comments Litchman. "More importantly, it gets our name into markets where we're not. And we can track the sales and see how we're doing." If a particular Shaw's supermarket registers unusually strong bagel sales, the copresidents will consider opening a store in or near that community.

The Bagel Economy

Although Finagle A Bagel competes with other bagel chains in and around Boston, its competition goes well beyond restaurants in that category. "You compete with a person selling a cup of coffee; you compete with a grocery store selling a salad," Litchman notes. "People only have so many 'dining dollars' and you need to convince them to spend those dining dollars in your store." Finagle A Bagel's competitive advantages are high-quality, fresh products, courteous and competent employees, and clean, attractive, and inviting restaurants.

During a recent economic recession, Boston's tourist traffic slumped temporarily, and corporate customers cut back on catering orders from Finagle A Bagel. After the company's sales revenues remained flat for about a year, they began inching up as the economy moved toward recovery. Now the business sells more than $20 million worth of bagels, soups, sandwiches, and salads every year.

©Barbara Helgason

Social Responsibility Through Bagels

Social responsibility is an integral part of Finagle A Bagel's operations. Rather than simply throw away unsold bagels at the end of the day, the owners donate the bagels to schools, shelters, and other nonprofit organizations. When local non-profit groups hold fund-raising events, the copresidents contribute bagels to feed the volunteers. Over the years, Finagle A Bagel has provided bagels to bicyclists raising money for St. Jude Children's Research Hospital, to swimmers raising money for breast cancer research, and to people building community playgrounds. Also, the copresidents are strongly committed to being fair to their customers by offering good value and a good experience. "Something that we need to remember and instill in our people all the time," Trust emphasizes, "is that customers are coming in, and your responsibility is to give them the best that you can give them."

Even with 320-plus employees, the copresidents find that owning a business is a nonstop proposition. "Our typical day never ends," says Trust. They are constantly visiting stores, dealing with suppliers, reviewing financial results, and planning for the future. Despite all these responsibilities, this husband-and-wife entrepreneurial team enjoys applying their educational background and business experience to build a company that satisfies thousands of customers every day.

Questions

1. How has the business cycle affected Finagle A Bagel?
2. What is Finagle A Bagel doing to differentiate itself from competitors that want a share of customers' dining dollars?
3. Why would Finagle A Bagel donate bagels to local charities rather than give them away to customers or employees?
4. If you wanted to open a bagel restaurant in Hong Kong, would you license the Finagle A Bagel brand? Why or why not?

A *business plan* is a carefully constructed guide for a person starting a business. The purpose of a well-prepared business plan is to show how practical and attainable the entrepreneur's goals are. It also serves as a concise document that potential investors can examine to see if they would like to invest or assist in financing a new venture. A business plan should include the following twelve components:

- Introduction
- Executive summary
- Benefits to the community
- Company and industry
- Management team
- Manufacturing and operations plan
- Labor force
- Marketing plan
- Financial plan
- Exit strategy
- Critical risks and assumptions
- Appendix

A brief description of each of these sections is provided in Chapter 5 (see also Table 5.4 on page 147).

This is the first of seven exercises that appear at the ends of each of the seven major parts in this textbook. The goal of these exercises is to help you work through the preceding components to create your own business plan. For example, in the exercise for this part, you will make decisions and complete the research that will help you to develop the introduction for your business plan and the benefits to the community that your business will provide. In the exercises for Parts 2 through 6, you will add more components to your plan and eventually build a plan that actually could be used to start a business. The flowchart shown in Figure 3.5 gives an overview of the steps you will be taking to prepare your business plan.

THE FIRST STEP: CHOOSING YOUR BUSINESS

One of the first steps for starting your own business is to decide what type of business you want to start. Take some time to think about this decision. Before proceeding, answer the following questions:

- Why did you choose this type of business?
- Why do you think this business will be successful?
- Would you enjoy owning and operating this type of business?

Warning: Don't rush this step. This step often requires much thought, but it is well worth the time and effort. As an added bonus, you are more likely to develop a quality business plan if you really want to open this type of business.

Now that you have decided on a specific type of business, it is time to begin the planning process. The goal for this part is to complete the introduction and benefits-to-the-community components of your business plan.

Before you begin, it is important to note that the business plan is not a document that is written and then set aside. It is a living document that an entrepreneur should refer to continuously in order to ensure that plans are being carried through appropriately. As the entrepreneur begins to execute the plan, he or she should monitor the business environment continuously and make changes to the plan to address any challenges or opportunities that were not foreseen originally.

Throughout this course, you will, of course, be building your knowledge about business. Therefore, it will be appropriate for you to continually revisit parts of the plan that you have already written in order to refine them based on your more comprehensive knowledge. You will find that writing your plan is not a simple matter of starting at the beginning and moving chronologically through to the end. Instead, you probably will find yourself jumping around the various components, making refinements as you go. In fact, the second component—the executive summary—should be written last, but because of its comprehensive nature and its importance to potential investors, it appears after the introduction in the final business plan. By the end of this course, you should be able to put the finishing touches on your plan, making sure that all the parts create a comprehensive and sound whole so that you can present it for evaluation.

THE INTRODUCTION COMPONENT

1.1. Start with the cover page. Provide the business name, street address, telephone number, Web address (if any), name(s) of owner(s) of the business, and the date the plan is issued.
1.2. Next, provide background information on the company and include the general nature of the business: retailing, manufacturing, or service; what your product or service is; what is unique about it; and why you believe that your business will be successful.
1.3. Then include a summary statement of the business's financial needs, if any. You probably will need to revise your financial needs summary after you complete a detailed financial plan later in Part 6.
1.4. Finally, include a statement of confidentiality to keep important information away from potential competitors.

THE BENEFITS-TO-THE-COMMUNITY COMPONENT

In this section, describe the potential benefits to the community that your business could provide. Chapter 2 in your

FIGURE 3.5: Business Plan

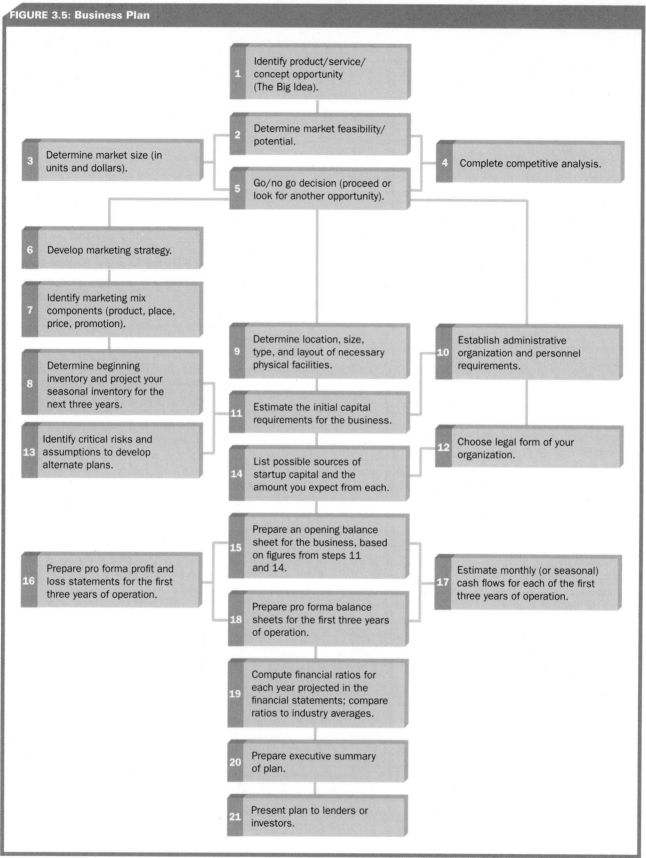

1. Identify product/service/concept opportunity (The Big Idea).
2. Determine market feasibility/potential.
3. Determine market size (in units and dollars).
4. Complete competitive analysis.
5. Go/no go decision (proceed or look for another opportunity).
6. Develop marketing strategy.
7. Identify marketing mix components (product, place, price, promotion).
8. Determine beginning inventory and project your seasonal inventory for the next three years.
9. Determine location, size, type, and layout of necessary physical facilities.
10. Establish administrative organization and personnel requirements.
11. Estimate the initial capital requirements for the business.
12. Choose legal form of your organization.
13. Identify critical risks and assumptions to develop alternate plans.
14. List possible sources of startup capital and the amount you expect from each.
15. Prepare an opening balance sheet for the business, based on figures from steps 11 and 14.
16. Prepare pro forma profit and loss statements for the first three years of operation.
17. Estimate monthly (or seasonal) cash flows for each of the first three years of operation.
18. Prepare pro forma balance sheets for the first three years of operation.
19. Compute financial ratios for each year projected in the financial statements; compare ratios to industry averages.
20. Prepare executive summary of plan.
21. Present plan to lenders or investors.

Source: Hatten, Timothy, *Small Business Management*, Fourth Edition. Copyright © 2009 by Houghton Mifflin Company. Reprinted with permission.

textbook, "Being Ethical and Socially Responsible," can help you in answering some of these questions. At the very least, address the following issues:

1.5. Describe the number of skilled and nonskilled jobs the business will create, and indicate how purchases of supplies and other materials can help local businesses.

1.6. Next, describe how providing needed goods or services will improve the community and its standard of living.

1.7. Finally, state how your business can develop new technical, management, or leadership skills; offer attractive wages; and provide other types of individual growth.

REVIEW OF BUSINESS PLAN ACTIVITIES

Read over the information that you have gathered. Because the Building a Business Plan exercises at the end of Parts 2 through 6 are built on the work you do in Part 1, make sure that any weaknesses or problem areas are resolved before continuing. Finally, write a brief statement that summarizes all the information for this part of the business plan.

The information contained in "Building a Business Plan" will also assist you in completing the online *Interactive Business Plan.*

Choosing a Form of Business Ownership

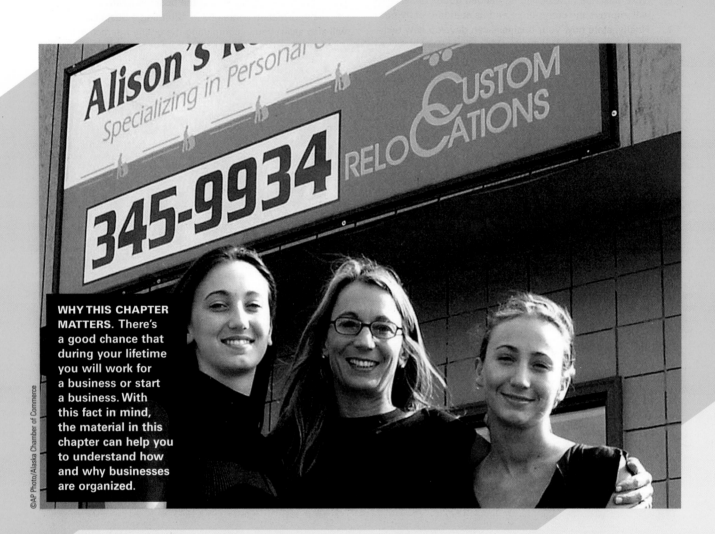

WHY THIS CHAPTER MATTERS. There's a good chance that during your lifetime you will work for a business or start a business. With this fact in mind, the material in this chapter can help you to understand how and why businesses are organized.

©AP Photo/Alaska Chamber of Commerce

LEARNING OBJECTIVES

1 Describe the advantages and disadvantages of sole proprietorships.

2 Explain the different types of partners and the importance of partnership agreements.

3 Describe the advantages and disadvantages of partnerships.

4 Summarize how a corporation is formed.

5 Describe the advantages and disadvantages of a corporation.

6 Examine special types of corporations, including S-corporations, limited-liability companies, and not-for-profit corporations.

7 Discuss the purpose of a cooperative, joint venture, and syndicate.

8 Explain how growth from within and growth through mergers can enable a business to expand.

Get Flash Cards, Quizzes, Games, Crosswords and more @ www.cengage.com/introbusiness/pride

Entertainment Giants Tune Into Hulu

Move over, YouTube: Hulu is here, and it's changing the world of online video. NBC Universal and News Corp. started Hulu as a joint venture to build a new website for streaming videos, with brief ads embedded, over the Internet. Both companies have a library of hit television shows and movies, NBC through its ownership of the NBC network and Universal Studios and News Corp. through its ownership of the Fox network and 20th Century Fox Studios.

The two equity partners envisioned Hulu as an online destination for viewing professionally-produced entertainment, distinct from the free videos—many created by consumers—on the wildly popular YouTube site. From the start, Hulu negotiated to include movies and television episodes from other networks and studios and offered advertising deals to companies seeking a large online audience.

Hulu was organized as a limited-liability company to give the partners more flexibility in managing the joint venture. As it turned out, this worked well because new equity partners have joined the venture over the years. Soon after Hulu was formed, Providence Equity Partners invested $100 million to become a part-owner. Hulu later attracted another key partner, Walt Disney, which invested millions in Hulu and added its ABC television programs to the site's fast-growing lineup of video offerings.

Today, Hulu offers premium entertainment content from many sources beyond its joint-venture partners, including MTV, PBS, Sony Pictures, Comedy Central, MGM, National Geographic, and Warner Brothers. Among the advertisers that air commercials during Hulu videos and display banner ads on the Hulu site are Best Buy, McDonald's, Visa, Nissan, Cisco, Johnson & Johnson, and Procter & Gamble. Hulu's rapid rise in viewership demonstrates that people are willing to sit through brief ads to watch their favorite shows streamed online, on demand. Can Hulu pass YouTube to become the most-viewed video site on the Internet? Can Hulu earn enough profit to reward the firms that own this joint venture? Tune in tomorrow.[1]

DID YOU KNOW?

Hulu is a joint-venture online entertainment destination where visitors view more than 300 million videos every month.

Many people dream of opening a business, and one of the first decisions they must make is what form of ownership to choose. We begin this chapter by describing the three common forms of business ownership: sole proprietorships, partnerships, and corporations. We discuss how these types of businesses are formed and note the advantages and disadvantages of each. Next, we consider several types of business ownership usually chosen for special purposes, including S-corporations, limited-liability companies, not-for-profit corporations, cooperatives, joint ventures, and syndicates. We conclude the chapter with a discussion of how businesses can grow through internal expansion or through mergers with other companies.

Sole Proprietorships

1 LEARNING OBJECTIVE

Describe the advantages and disadvantages of sole proprietorships.

A **sole proprietorship** is a business that is owned (and usually operated) by one person. Although a few sole proprietorships are large and have many employees, most are small. Sole proprietorship is the simplest form of business ownership and the easiest to start. Some of today's largest corporations, including Ford Motor Company, H.J. Heinz Company, and Procter & Gamble Company, started out as tiny—and in many cases, struggling—sole proprietorships.

As you can see in Figure 4.1, there are more than 21.5 million sole proprietorships in the United States. They account for 72 percent of the country's business firms. Although the most popular form of ownership when compared with

sole proprietorship a business that is owned (and usually operated) by one person

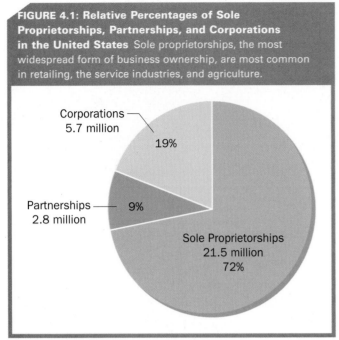

FIGURE 4.1: Relative Percentages of Sole Proprietorships, Partnerships, and Corporations in the United States Sole proprietorships, the most widespread form of business ownership, are most common in retailing, the service industries, and agriculture.

Corporations
5.7 million

19%

Partnerships
2.8 million

9%

Sole Proprietorships
21.5 million
72%

Source: U.S. Bureau of the Census, *Statistical Abstract of the United States*, Washington, D.C., 2009, p. 483 (**www.census.gov**).

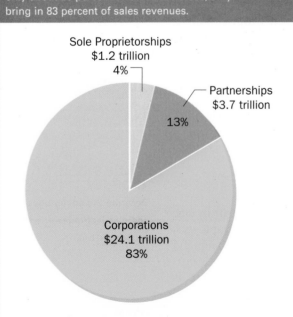

FIGURE 4.2: Total Sales Receipts of American Businesses Although corporations account for only about 20 percent of U.S. businesses, they bring in 83 percent of sales revenues.

Sole Proprietorships
$1.2 trillion
4%

Partnerships
$3.7 trillion

13%

Corporations
$24.1 trillion
83%

Source: U.S. Bureau of the Census, *Statistical Abstract of the United States*, Washington, D.C., 2009, p. 483 (**www.census.gov**).

partnerships and corporations, they rank last in total sales revenues. As shown in Figure 4.2, sole proprietorships account for $1.2 trillion, or about 4 percent, of total sales.

Sole proprietorships are most common in retailing, service, and agriculture. Thus, the clothing boutique, television-repair shop down the street, and small, independent farmers are likely to be sole proprietorships.

Advantages of Sole Proprietorships

Most of the advantages of sole proprietorships arise from the two main characteristics of this form of ownership: simplicity and individual control.

Ease of Start-Up and Closure Sole proprietorship is the simplest and cheapest way to start a business. Often, start-up requires no contracts, agreements, or other legal documents. Thus, a sole proprietorship can be, and most often is, established without the services of an attorney. The legal requirements often are limited to registering the name of the business and obtaining any necessary licenses or permits.

If a sole proprietorship does not succeed, the firm can be closed as easily as it was opened. Creditors must be paid, of course, but generally, the owner does not have to go through any legal procedure before hanging up an "Out of Business" sign.

Pride of Ownership A successful sole proprietor is often very proud of her or his accomplishments—and rightfully so. In almost every case, the owner deserves a great deal of credit for assuming the risks and solving the day-to-day problems associated with operating sole proprietorships. Unfortunately, the reverse is also true. When the business fails, it is often the sole proprietor who is to blame.

Retention of All Profits Because all profits become the personal earnings of the owner, the owner has a strong incentive to succeed. This direct financial reward attracts many entrepreneurs to the sole proprietorship form of business and, if the business succeeds, is a source of great satisfaction.

Flexibility of Being Your Own Boss A sole proprietor is completely free to make decisions about the firm's operations. Without asking or waiting for anyone's approval, a sole proprietor can switch from retailing to wholesaling, move a shop's location, open a new store, or close an old one. Suppose that the sole proprietor of an appliance store finds that many customers now prefer to shop on Sunday afternoons. He or she can make an immediate change in business hours to take advantage of this information. The manager of a store in a large corporate chain such as Best Buy Company may have to seek the approval of numerous managers and company officials before making such a change.

No Special Taxes Profits earned by a sole proprietorship are taxed as the personal income of the

Why are these people smiling? When an entrepreneur starts a restaurant or any other type of business, it takes more than just a dream or idea to be successful. In fact, *quality* employees that produce *quality* products or provide *quality* services are critical for any type of business—sole proprietorship, partnership, corporation, or one of the specialized forms of business ownership discussed in the last part of this chapter—to be successful.

owner. As a result, sole proprietors must report certain financial information on their personal income tax returns and make estimated quarterly tax payments to the federal government. Thus, a sole proprietorship does not pay the special state and federal income taxes that corporations pay.

Disadvantages of Sole Proprietorships

The disadvantages of a sole proprietorship stem from the fact that these businesses are owned by one person. Some capable sole proprietors experience no problems. Individuals who start out with few management skills and little money are most at risk for failure.

Unlimited Liability **Unlimited liability** is a legal concept that holds a business owner personally responsible for all the debts of the business. There is legally no difference between the debts of the business and the debts of the proprietor. If the business fails, or if the business is involved in a lawsuit and loses, the owner's personal property—including savings and other assets—can be seized (and sold if necessary) to pay creditors.

Unlimited liability is perhaps the major factor that tends to discourage would-be entrepreneurs with substantial personal wealth from using this form of business organization.

Lack of Continuity Legally, the sole proprietor *is* the business. If the owner retires, dies, or is declared legally incompetent, the business essentially ceases to exist. In many cases, however—especially when the business is a profitable enterprise—the owner's heirs take it over and either sell it or continue to operate it. The business also can suffer if the sole proprietor becomes ill and cannot work for an extended period of time. An illness can be devastating if the sole proprietor's personal skills are what determine if the business is a success or a failure.

Lack of Money Banks, suppliers, and other lenders usually are unwilling to lend large sums of money to sole proprietorships. Only one person—the sole proprietor—can be held responsible for repaying such loans, and the assets of most sole

unlimited liability a legal concept that holds a business owner personally responsible for all the debts of the business

©Creatas Images/Jupiter Images

proprietors usually are limited. Moreover, these assets may have been used already as the basis for personal borrowing (a home mortgage or car loan) or for short-term credit from suppliers. Lenders also worry about the lack of continuity of sole proprietorships: Who will repay a loan if the sole proprietor dies? Finally, many lenders are concerned about the large number of sole proprietorships that fail—a topic discussed in Chapter 5.

The limited ability to borrow money can prevent a sole proprietorship from growing. It is the main reason that many business owners, when in need of relatively large amounts of capital, change from a sole proprietorship to a partnership or corporate form of ownership.

Limited Management Skills The sole proprietor is often the sole manager—in addition to being the only salesperson, buyer, accountant, and on occasion, janitor. Even the most experienced business owner is unlikely to have expertise in all these areas. Unless he or she obtains the necessary expertise by hiring employees, assistants, or consultants, the business can suffer in the areas in which the owner is less knowledgeable. For the many sole proprietors who cannot afford to hire the help they need, there just are not enough hours in the day to do everything that needs to be done.

Difficulty in Hiring Employees The sole proprietor may find it hard to attract and keep competent help. Potential employees may feel that there is no room for advancement in a firm whose owner assumes all managerial responsibilities. And when those who *are* hired are ready to take on added responsibility, they may find that the only way to do so is to quit the sole proprietorship and go to work for a larger firm or start up their own businesses. The lure of higher salaries and increased benefits (especially health insurance) also may cause existing employees to change jobs.

Beyond the Sole Proprietorship

Like many others, you may decide that the major disadvantage of a sole proprietorship is the limited amount that one person can do in a workday. One way to reduce the effect of this disadvantage (and retain many of the advantages) is to have more than one owner.

Concept Check

1. What is a sole proprietorship?

2. What are the advantages of a sole proprietorship?

3. What are the disadvantages of a sole proprietorship?

LEARNING OBJECTIVE 2

Explain the different types of partners and the importance of partnership agreements.

Partnerships

A person who would not think of starting and running a business alone may enthusiastically seize the opportunity to enter into a business partnership. The U.S. Uniform Partnership Act defines a **partnership** as a voluntary association of two or more persons to act as co-owners of a business for profit. For example, in 1990, two young African-American entrepreneurs named Janet Smith and Gary Smith started Ivy Planning Group—a company that provides strategic planning and performance measurement for clients. Today, 20 years later, the company has evolved into a multimillion-dollar company that has hired a diverse staff of employees and provides cultural diversity training for *Fortune* 1000 firms, large not-for-profit organizations, and government agencies. In recognition of its efforts, Ivy Planning Group has been honored by DiversityBusiness.com as one of the top 50 minority-owned companies and by *Black Enterprise* and *Working Mother* magazines. And both Janet Smith and Gary Smith—Ivy Planning Group's founders—have been named "1 of 50 Most Influential Minorities in Business" by Minority Business and Professionals Network.[2]

As shown in Figures 4.1 and 4.2, there are approximately 2.8 million partnerships in the United States, and this type of ownership accounts for about $3.7 trillion in sales receipts each year. Note, however, that this form of ownership is much less common than the sole proprietorship or the corporation. In fact, as Figure 4.1 shows, partnerships represent only about 9 percent of all American businesses.

partnership a voluntary association of two or more persons to act as co-owners of a business for profit

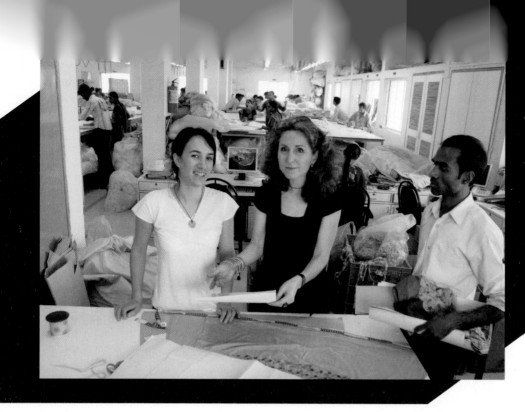

Two heads are better than one. When Rachel Liu and Antoinette Giorgi began their organic clothing business, they made a decision to choose the partnership form of business ownership. For these two entrepreneurs, it was the right choice because their firm now produces and sells more than 300,000 organic garments each year.

Although there is no legal maximum on the number of partners a partnership may have, most have only two. Large accounting, law, and advertising partnerships, however, are likely to have multiple partners. Regardless of the number of people involved, a partnership often represents a pooling of special managerial skills and talents; at other times, it is the result of a sole proprietor's taking on a partner for the purpose of obtaining more capital.

Types of Partners

All partners are not necessarily equal. Some may be active in running the business, whereas others may have a limited role.

General Partners A **general partner** is a person who assumes full or shared responsibility for operating a business. General partners are active in day-to-day business operations, and each partner can enter into contracts on behalf of the other partners. He or she also assumes unlimited liability for all debts, including debts incurred by any other general partner without his or her knowledge or consent. A *general partnership* is a business co-owned by two or more general partners who are liable for everything the business does. To avoid future liability, a general partner who withdraws from the partnership must give notice to creditors, customers, and suppliers.

Limited Partners A **limited partner** is a person who invests money in a business but who has no management responsibility or liability for losses beyond his or her investment in the partnership. A *limited partnership* is a business co-owned by one or more general partners who manage the business and limited partners who invest money in it. Limited partnerships may be formed to finance real estate, oil and gas, motion-picture, and other business ventures. Typically, the general partner or partners collect management fees and receive a percentage of profits. Limited partners receive a portion of profits and tax benefits.

Because of potential liability problems, special rules apply to limited partnerships. These rules are intended to protect customers and creditors who deal with limited partnerships. For example, prospective partners in a limited partnership must file a formal declaration, usually with the secretary of state or at their county

general partner a person who assumes full or shared responsibility for operating a business

limited partner a person who contributes capital to a business but has no management responsibility or liability for losses beyond the amount he or she invested in the partnership courthouse, that describes the essential details of the partnership and the liability status of each partner involved in the business. At least one general partner must be responsible for the debts of the limited partnership. Also, some states prohibit the use of the limited partner's name in the partnership's name.

A special type of limited partnership is referred to as a *master limited partnership*. A **master limited partnership (MLP)** (sometimes referred to as a *publicly traded partnership*, or PTP) is a business partnership that is owned and managed like a corporation but often taxed like a partnership. This special ownership arrangement has a major advantage: Units of ownership in MLPs can be sold to investors to raise capital and often are traded on organized security exchanges. Because MLP units can be traded on an exchange, investors can sell their units of ownership at any time, hopefully for a profit. For more information on MLPs, visit the National Association of Publicly Traded Partnerships website at **www. naptp.org.**

Originally, there were tax advantages to forming an MLP. Today, the Internal Revenue Service has limited many of the tax advantages of MLPs. While there are exceptions, most MLPs typically are in natural resources, energy, or real-estate-related businesses.[3]

master limited partnership (MLP) a business partnership that is owned and managed like a corporation but often taxed like a partnership

FIGURE 4.3: Articles of Partnership Articles of partnership are a written or oral agreement that lists and explains the terms of a partnership.

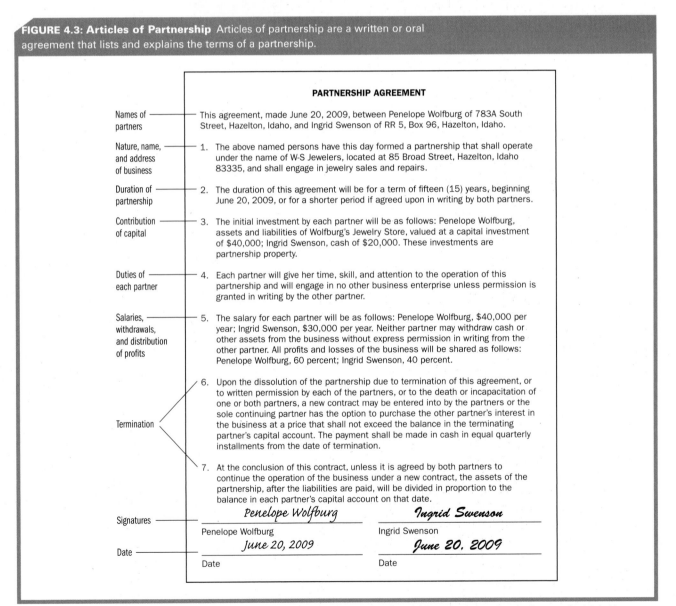

Source: Adapted from Goldman and Sigismond, *Business Law*, 7th edition. Boston: Houghton Mifflin, 2007. Copyright © 2007 by Cengage Learning Company. Reprinted with permission.

The Partnership Agreement

Articles of partnership are an agreement listing and explaining the terms of the partnership. Although both oral and written partnership agreements are legal and can be enforced in the courts, a written agreement has an obvious advantage: It is not subject to lapses of memory.

Figure 4.3 shows a typical partnership agreement. The partnership agreement should state:

- Who will make the final decisions
- What each partner's duties will be
- The investment each partner will make
- How much profit or loss each partner receives or is responsible for
- What happens if a partner wants to dissolve the partnership or dies

Although the people involved in a partnership can draft their own agreement, most experts recommend consulting an attorney.

When entering into a partnership agreement, partners would be wise to let a neutral third party—a consultant, an accountant, a lawyer, or a mutual friend—assist with any disputes that might arise.

Advantages of Partnerships

Partnerships have many advantages. The most important are described below.

Ease of Start-Up Partnerships are relatively easy to form. As with a sole proprietorship, the legal requirements often are limited to registering the name of the business and obtaining any necessary licenses or permits. It may not even be necessary to prepare written articles of partnership, although doing so is generally a good idea.

Availability of Capital and Credit Because partners can pool their funds, a partnership usually has more capital available than a sole proprietorship does. This additional capital, coupled with the general partners' unlimited liability, can form the basis for a better credit rating. Banks and suppliers may be more willing to extend credit or approve larger loans to such a partnership than to a sole proprietor. This does not mean that partnerships can borrow all the money they need. Many partnerships have found it hard to get long-term financing simply because lenders worry about the possibility of management disagreements and lack of continuity.

Personal Interest General partners are very concerned with the operation of the firm—perhaps even more so than sole proprietors. After all, they are responsible for the actions of all other general partners, as well as for their own. The pride of ownership from solving the day-to-day problems of operating a business—with the help of another person(s)—is a strong motivating force and often makes all the people involved in the partnership work harder to become more successful.

Combined Business Skills and Knowledge Partners often have complementary skills. The weakness of one partner—in manufacturing, for example—may be offset by another partner's strength in that area. Moreover, the ability to discuss important decisions with another concerned individual often relieves some pressure and leads to more effective decision making.

Retention of Profits As in a sole proprietorship, all profits belong to the owners of the partnership. The partners share directly in the financial rewards and therefore are highly motivated to do their best to make the firm succeed. As noted, the partnership agreement should state how much profit or loss each partner receives or is responsible for.

Concept Check

1. How does a sole proprietorship differ from a partnership?

2. Explain the difference between a general partner and a limited partner?

3. What is a master limited partnership?

4. Describe the issues that should be included in a partnership agreement?

3 LEARNING OBJECTIVE

Describe the advantages and disadvantages of partnerships.

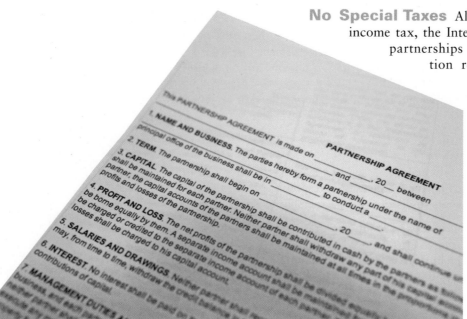

No Special Taxes Although a partnership pays no income tax, the Internal Revenue Service requires partnerships to file an annual information return that states the names and addresses of all partners involved in the business. The return also must provide information about income and expenses and distributions made to each partner. Then each partner is required to report his or her share of profit (or loss) from the partnership business on his or her individual tax return and is taxed on his or her share of the profit—in the same way a sole proprietor is taxed.

Disadvantages of Partnerships

Although partnerships have many advantages when compared with sole proprietorships and corporations, they also have some disadvantages, which anyone thinking of forming a partnership should consider.

Unlimited Liability As we have noted, each *general* partner has unlimited liability for all debts of the business. Each partner is legally and personally responsible for the debts and actions of any other partner conducting partnership business, even if that partner did not incur those debts or do anything wrong. General partners thus run the risk of having to use their personal assets to pay creditors. *Limited* partners, however, risk only their original investment.

Today, many states allow partners to form a *limited-liability partnership* (LLP), in which a partner may have limited-liability protection from legal action resulting from the malpractice or negligence of the other partners. Most states that allow LLPs restrict this type of ownership to certain types of professionals such as accountants, architects, attorneys, and similar professionals. (Note the difference between a limited partnership and a limited-liability partnership. A limited partnership must have at least one general partner that has unlimited liability. On the other hand, all partners in a limited-liability partnership may have limited liability *for the malpractice of the other partners*.)

Management Disagreements What happens to a partnership if one of the partners brings a spouse or a relative into the business? What happens if a partner wants to withdraw more money from the business? Notice that each of the preceding situations—and for that matter, most of the other problems that can develop in a partnership—involves one partner doing something that disturbs the other partner(s). This human factor is especially important because business partners—with egos, ambitions, and money on the line—are especially susceptible to friction. When partners begin to disagree about decisions, policies, or ethics, distrust may build and get worse as time passes—often to the point where it is impossible to operate the business successfully.

Lack of Continuity Partnerships are terminated if any one of the general partners dies, withdraws, or is declared legally incompetent. However, the remaining partners can purchase that partner's ownership share. For example, the partnership agreement may permit surviving partners to continue the business after buying a deceased partner's interest from his or her estate. However, if the partnership loses an owner whose specific management or technical skills cannot be replaced, it is not likely to survive.

Frozen Investment It is easy to invest money in a partnership, but it is sometimes quite difficult to get it out. This is the case, for example, when remaining partners are unwilling to buy the share of the business that belongs to a partner who retires or wants to relocate to another city. To avoid such difficulties, the partnership agreement should include some procedure for buying out a partner.

In some cases, a partner must find someone outside the firm to buy his or her share. How easy or difficult it is to find an outsider depends on how successful the business is and how willing existing partners are to accept a new partner.

Beyond the Partnership

The main advantages of a partnership over a sole proprietorship are the added capital and management expertise of the partners. However, some of the basic disadvantages of the sole proprietorship also plague the general partnership. One disadvantage in particular—unlimited liability—can cause problems. A third form of business ownership, the corporation, overcomes this disadvantage.

Concept Check

1. What are the advantages of a partnership?

2. What are the disadvantages of a partnership?

Corporations

4 LEARNING OBJECTIVE

Summarize how a corporation is formed.

Back in 1837, William Procter and James Gamble—two sole proprietors—formed a partnership called Procter & Gamble and set out to compete with fourteen other soap and candle makers in Cincinnati, Ohio. Then, in 1890, Procter & Gamble incorporated to raise additional capital for expansion that eventually allowed the company to become a global giant. Today, Procter & Gamble brands touch the lives of consumers in 180 countries around the globe.[4] While not all sole proprietorships and partnerships become corporations, there are reasons why business owners choose the corporate form of ownership. Let's begin with a definition of a corporation. Perhaps the best definition of a corporation was given by Chief Justice John Marshall in a famous Supreme Court decision in 1819. A corporation, he said, "is an artificial person, invisible, intangible, and existing only in contemplation of the law." In other words, a **corporation** (sometimes referred to as a *regular* or *C-corporation*) is an artificial person created by law, with most of the legal rights of a real person. These include:

- The right to start and operate a business
- The right to buy or sell property
- The right to borrow money
- The right to sue or be sued
- The right to enter into binding contracts

Unlike a real person, however, a corporation exists only on paper. There are 5.7 million corporations in the United States. They comprise only about 19 percent of all businesses, but they account for 83 percent of sales revenues (see Figures 4.1 and 4.2). Table 4.1 lists the seven largest U.S. industrial corporations, ranked according to sales.

Corporate Ownership

The shares of ownership of a corporation are called **stock**. The people who own a corporation's stock—and thus own part of the corporation—are called **stockholders** or sometimes *shareholders*. Once a corporation has been formed, it may sell its stock to individuals or other companies that want to invest in the corporation. It also may issue stock as a reward to key employees in return for certain services or as a return to investors (in place of cash payments).

corporation an artificial person created by law with most of the legal rights of a real person, including the rights to start and operate a business, to buy or sell property, to borrow money, to sue or be sued, and to enter into binding contracts

stock the shares of ownership of a corporation

stockholder a person who owns a corporation's stock

TABLE 4.1: The Seven Largest U.S. Industrial Corporations, Ranked by Sales Revenues

Rank	Company	Revenues ($ millions)	Profits ($ millions)
1	Wal-Mart Stores	378,799.0	12,731.0
2	Exxon Mobil	372,824.0	40,610.0
3	Chevron	210,783.0	18,688.0
4	General Motors	182,347.0	−38,732.0
5	ConocoPhillips	178,558.0	11,891.0
6	General Electric	176,656.0	22,208.0
7	Ford Motor	172,468.0	−2,723.0

Source: *Fortune* website at **www.fortune.com**, accessed April 6, 2009.

closed corporation a corporation whose stock is owned by relatively few people and is not sold to the general public

open corporation a corporation whose stock can be bought and sold by any individual

A **closed corporation** is a corporation whose stock is owned by relatively few people and is not sold to the general public. As an example, DeWitt and Lila Wallace owned virtually all the stock of Reader's Digest Association, making it one of the largest corporations of this kind. A person who wishes to sell the stock of a closed corporation generally arranges to sell it *privately* to another stockholder or a close acquaintance.

Although founded in 1922 as a closed corporation, the Reader's Digest Association became an open corporation when it sold stock to investors for the first time in 1990. An **open corporation** is one whose stock can be bought and sold by any individual. Examples of open corporations include General Electric, Microsoft, and Johnson & Johnson.

Forming a Corporation

Although you may think that incorporating a business guarantees success, it does not. There is no special magic about placing the word *Incorporated* or the abbreviation *Inc.* after the name of a business. Unfortunately, like sole proprietorships or partnerships, incorporated businesses can go broke. The decision to incorporate a business therefore should be made only after carefully considering whether the corporate form of ownership suits your needs better than the sole proprietorship or partnership forms.

If you decide that the corporate form is the best form of organization for you, most experts recommend that you begin the incorporation process by consulting a lawyer to be sure that all legal requirements are met. While it may be possible to incorporate a business without a lawyer, it is well to keep in mind the old saying, "A man who acts as his own attorney has a fool for a client." Table 4.2 lists some aspects of starting and running a business that may require legal help.

Where to Incorporate A business is allowed to incorporate in any state that it chooses. The decision

An entrepreneur and a cartoon character that led to a very successful corporation. Some would say that Walt Disney and an animated cartoon character—Mickey Mouse—were partners. To be sure, the "partners" both became famous. More importantly, this partnership led to one of the most successful corporations in the entertainment industry.

©Hulton Archives/Getty Images

TABLE 4.2: Ten Aspects of Business That May Require Legal Help

1. Choosing either the sole proprietorship, partnership, or corporate form of ownership	6. Filing for licenses or permits at the local, state, and federal levels
2. Constructing a partnership agreement	7. Purchasing an existing business or real estate
3. Incorporating a business	8. Creating valid contracts
4. Registering a corporation's stock	9. Hiring employees and independent contractors
5. Obtaining a trademark, patent, or copyright	10. Extending credit and collecting debts

on where to incorporate usually is based on two factors: (1) the cost of incorporating in one state compared with the cost in another state and (2) the advantages and disadvantages of each state's corporate laws and tax structure. Most small and medium-sized businesses are incorporated in the state where they do the most business. The founders of larger corporations or of those that will do business nationwide often compare the benefits that various states provide to corporations. Some states are more hospitable than others, and some offer fewer restrictions, lower taxes, and other benefits to attract new firms. Delaware and Nevada are often chosen by corporations that do business in more than one state because of their corporation friendly laws.[5]

An incorporated business is called a **domestic corporation** in the state in which it is incorporated. In all other states where it does business, it is called a **foreign corporation**. Sears Holdings Corporation, the parent company of Sears and Kmart, is incorporated in Delaware, where it is a domestic corporation. In the remaining forty-nine states, Sears is a foreign corporation. Sears must register in all states where it does business and also pay taxes and annual fees to each state. A corporation chartered by a foreign government and conducting business in the United States is an **alien corporation**. Volkswagen AG, Sony Corporation, and the Royal Dutch/Shell Group are examples of alien corporations.

The Corporate Charter Once a home state has been chosen, the incorporator(s) submits *articles of incorporation* to the secretary of state. When the articles of incorporation are approved, they become a contract between a corporation and the state in which the state recognizes the formation of the artificial person that is the corporation. Usually, the articles of incorporation include the following information:

- The firm's name and address
- The incorporators' names and addresses
- The purpose of the corporation
- The maximum amount of stock and types of stock to be issued
- The rights and privileges of stockholders
- The length of time the corporation is to exist

To help you to decide if the corporate form of organization is the right choice, you may want to review the material available on the Yahoo! Small Business website (**http://smallbusiness.yahoo.com**). Once at the site, click on News & Resources. In addition, before making a decision to organize your business as a corporation, you may want to consider two additional areas: stockholders' rights and the importance of the organizational meeting.

Stockholders' Rights There are two basic types of stock. Owners of **common stock** may vote on corporate matters. Generally, an owner of common stock has one vote for each share owned. However, any claims of common stock owners on profits and assets of the corporation are subordinate to the claims of others. The owners of **preferred stock** usually have no voting rights, but their claims on dividends are paid before those of common stock owners. While large corporations may

domestic corporation a corporation in the state in which it is incorporated

foreign corporation a corporation in any state in which it does business except the one in which it is incorporated

alien corporation a corporation chartered by a foreign government and conducting business in the United States

common stock stock owned by individuals or firms who may vote on corporate matters but whose claims on profit and assets are subordinate to the claims of others

preferred stock stock owned by individuals or firms who usually do not have voting rights but whose claims on dividends are paid before those of common stock owners

Spotlight

Corporate Dividends Paid to Stockholders

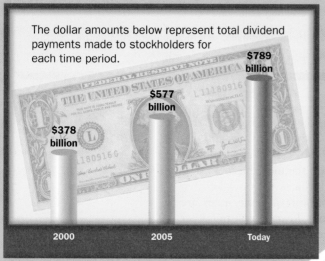

The dollar amounts below represent total dividend payments made to stockholders for each time period.

$378 billion — 2000
$577 billion — 2005
$789 billion — Today

Source: U.S. Department of Commerce, Bureay of Economic Analysis website at www.bea.gov, access April 13, 2009.

dividend a distribution of earnings to the stockholders of a corporation

proxy a legal form listing issues to be decided at a stockholders' meeting and enabling stockholders to transfer their voting rights to some other individual or individuals

board of directors the top governing body of a corporation, the members of which are elected by the stockholders

Concept Check

1. Explain the difference between an open corporation and a closed corporation.

2. How is a domestic corporation different from a foreign corporation and an alien corporation?

3. Outline the incorporation process, and describe the basic corporate structure.

4. What rights do stockholders have?

issue both common and preferred stock, generally small corporations issue only common stock.

Perhaps the most important right of owners of both common and preferred stock is to share in the profit earned by the corporation through the payment of dividends. A **dividend** is a distribution of earnings to the stockholders of a corporation. Other rights include receiving information about the corporation, voting on changes to the corporate charter, and attending the corporation's annual stockholders' meeting, where they may exercise their right to vote.

Because common stockholders usually live all over the nation, very few actually may attend a corporation's annual meeting. Instead, they vote by proxy. A **proxy** is a legal form listing issues to be decided at a stockholders' meeting and enabling stockholders to transfer their voting rights to some other individual or individuals. The stockholder can register a vote and transfer voting rights simply by signing and returning the form. Today, most corporations also allow stockholders to exercise their right to vote by proxy by accessing the Internet or using a toll-free phone number.

Organizational Meeting As the last step in forming a corporation, the incorporators and original stockholders meet to adopt corporate by-laws and elect their first board of directors. (Later, directors will be elected or reelected at the corporation's annual meetings.) The board members are directly responsible to the stockholders for the way they operate the firm.

Corporate Structure

The organizational structure of most corporations is more complicated than that of a sole proprietorship or partnership. This is especially true as the corporation begins to grow and expand. In a corporation, both the board of directors and the corporate officers are involved in management.

Board of Directors As an artificial person, a corporation can act only through its directors, who represent the corporation's stockholders. The **board of directors** is the top governing body of a corporation and is elected by the stockholders. Board members can be chosen from within the corporation or from outside it. *Note:* For a small corporation, only one director is required in many states although you can choose to have more.

Directors who are elected from within the corporation are usually its top managers—the president and executive vice presidents, for example. Those elected from outside the corporation generally are experienced managers or entrepreneurs with proven leadership ability and/or specific talents the organization seems to need. In smaller corporations, majority stockholders usually serve as board members.

The major responsibilities of the board of directors are to set company goals and develop general plans (or strategies) for meeting those goals. The board also is responsible for the firm's overall operation.

Corporate Officers **Corporate officers** are appointed by the board of directors. The chairman of the board, president, executive vice presidents, corporate secretary, and treasurer are all corporate officers. They help the board to make plans, carry out strategies established by the board, hire employees, and manage day-to-day business activities. Periodically (usually each month), they report to the board of directors. And at the annual meeting, the directors report to the stockholders.

Stockholders (owners) → *Elect* → Board of directors → *Appoints* → Officers → *Hire* → Employees

In theory, then, the stockholders are able to control the activities of the entire corporation through its directors because they are the group that elects the board of directors (see Figure 4.4).

Advantages of Corporations

Back in October 2000, Manny Ruiz decided that it was time to start his own company. With the help of a team of media specialists, he founded Hispanic PR Wire. In a business where hype is the name of the game, Hispanic PR Wire is the real thing and has established itself as the nation's premier news distribution service reaching U.S. Hispanic media and opinion leaders. Today, the business continues to build on its early success.[6] Mr. Ruiz chose to incorporate this business because it provided a number of advantages that other forms of business ownership did not offer. Typical advantages include limited liability, ease of raising capital, ease of transfer of ownership, perpetual life, and specialized management.

Limited Liability One of the most attractive features of corporate ownership is **limited liability**. With few exceptions, each owner's financial liability is limited to the amount of money he or she has paid for the corporation's stock. This feature arises from the fact that the corporation is itself a legal person, separate from its owners. If a corporation fails, creditors have a claim only on the corporation's assets, not on the owners' (stockholders') personal assets. Because it overcomes the problem of unlimited liability connected with sole proprietorships and general partnerships, limited liability is one of the chief reasons why entrepreneurs often choose the corporate form of organization.

Ease of Raising Capital The corporation is by far the most effective form of business ownership for raising capital. Like sole proprietorships and partnerships, corporations can borrow from lending institutions. However, they also can raise additional sums of money by selling stock. Individuals are more willing to invest in corporations than in other forms of business because of limited liability, and they can sell their stock easily—hopefully for a profit.

Ease of Transfer of Ownership Accessing a brokerage firm website or a telephone call to a stockbroker is all that is required to put stock up for sale. Willing buyers are available for most stocks at the market price. Ownership is transferred when the sale is made, and practically no restrictions apply to the sale and purchase of stock issued by an open corporation.

Perpetual Life Since it is essentially a legal "person," a corporation exists independently of its owners and survives them. The withdrawal, death, or incompetence of a key executive or owner does not cause the corporation to be terminated. Sears, Roebuck incorporated in 1893 and is one of the nation's largest retailing corporations, even though its original owners, Richard Sears and Alvah Roebuck, have been dead for decades.

Specialized Management Typically, corporations are able to recruit more skilled, knowledgeable, and talented managers than proprietorships and partnerships. This is so because they pay bigger salaries, offer excellent fringe benefits,

5 LEARNING OBJECTIVE

Describe the advantages and disadvantages of a corporation.

corporate officers the chairman of the board, president, executive vice presidents, corporate secretary, treasurer, and any other top executive appointed by the board of directors

limited liability a feature of corporate ownership that limits each owner's financial liability to the amount of money that he or she has paid for the corporation's stock

Who is the boss? While Claus-Dietrich Lahrs is the new chief executive officer (CEO) of German fashion concern Hugo Boss, he was appointed by the board of directors. In a corporation, the stockholders elect the members of the board of directors. Then the board appoints the CEO, president, executive vice presidents, and other corporate officers.

and are large enough to offer considerable opportunity for advancement. Within the corporate structure, administration, human resources, finance, marketing, and operations are placed in the charge of experts in these fields.

Disadvantages of Corporations

Like its advantages, many of a corporation's disadvantages stem from its legal definition as an artificial person or legal entity. The most serious disadvantages are described below. (See Table 4.3 for a comparison of some of the advantages and disadvantages of a sole proprietorship, general partnership, and corporation.)

Difficulty and Expense of Formation Forming a corporation can be a relatively complex and costly process. The use of an attorney usually is necessary to complete the legal forms that are submitted to the secretary of state. Application fees, attorney's fees, registration costs associated with selling stock, and other organizational costs can amount to thousands of dollars for even a medium-sized corporation. The costs of incorporating, in terms of both time and money, discourage many owners of smaller businesses from forming corporations.

TABLE 4.3: Some Advantages and Disadvantages of a Sole Proprietorship, Partnership, and Corporation

	Sole Proprietorship	General Partnership	Regular (C) Corporation
Protecting against liability for debts	Difficult	Difficult	Easy
Raising money	Difficult	Difficult	Easy
Ownership transfer	Difficult	Difficult	Easy
Preserving continuity	Difficult	Difficult	Easy
Government regulations	Few	Few	Many
Formation	Easy	Easy	Difficult
Income taxation	Once	Once	Twice

Government Regulation and Increased Paperwork A corporation must meet various government standards before it can sell its stock to the public. Then it must file many reports on its business operations and finances with local, state, and federal governments. In addition, the corporation must make periodic reports to its stockholders about various aspects of the business. To prepare all the necessary reports, even small corporations often need the help of an attorney, certified public accountant, and other professionals on a regular basis. In addition, a corporation's activities are restricted by law to those spelled out in its charter.

Conflict Within the Corporation Because a large corporation may employ thousands of employees, some conflict is inevitable. For example, the pressure to increase sales revenue, reduce expenses, and increase profits often leads to increased stress and tension for both managers and employees. This is especially true when a corporation operates in a competitive industry, attempts to develop and market new products, or must downsize the workforce to reduce employee salary expense.

Double Taxation Corporations must pay a tax on their profits. In addition, stockholders must pay a personal income tax on profits received as dividends. Corporate profits thus are taxed twice—once as corporate income and a second time as the personal income of stockholders. *Note:* Both the S-corporation and the limited-liability company discussed in the next section are taxed like a partnership but still provide limited liability for the personal assets of the owners.

Lack of Secrecy Because open corporations are required to submit detailed reports to government agencies and to stockholders, they cannot keep their operations confidential. Competitors can study these corporate reports and then use the information to compete more effectively. In effect, every public corporation has to share some of its secrets with its competitors.

Special Types of Business Ownership

In addition to the sole proprietorship, partnership, and the regular corporate form of organization, some entrepreneurs choose other forms of organization that meet their special needs. Additional organizational options include S-corporations, limited-liability companies, and not-for-profit corporations.

S-Corporations

If a corporation meets certain requirements, its directors may apply to the Internal Revenue Service for status as an S-corporation. An **S-corporation** is a corporation that is taxed as though it were a partnership. In other words, the corporation's income is taxed only as the personal income of its stockholders. Corporate profits or losses "pass through" the business and are reported on the owners' personal income tax returns.

Becoming an S-corporation can be an effective way to avoid double taxation while retaining the corporation's legal benefit of limited liability. To qualify for the special status of an S-corporation, a firm must meet the following criteria:[7]

1. No more than 100 stockholders are allowed.
2. Stockholders must be individuals, estates, or exempt organizations.
3. There can be only one class of outstanding stock.
4. The firm must be a domestic corporation eligible to file for S-corporation status.
5. There can be no nonresident-alien stockholders.
6. All stockholders must agree to the decision to form an S-corporation.

Limited-Liability Companies

A new form of ownership called a *limited-liability company* has been approved in all fifty states—although each state's laws may differ. A **limited-liability company (LLC)** is a form of business ownership that combines the benefits of a corporation

6 LEARNING OBJECTIVE

Examine special types of corporations, including S-corporations, limited-liability companies, and not-for-profit corporations.

S-corporation a corporation that is taxed as though it were a partnership

limited-liability company (LLC) a form of business ownership that combines the benefits of a corporation and a partnership while avoiding some of the restrictions and disadvantages of those forms of ownership

CONSERVATION

FUND

SEAWORLD® & BUSCH GARDENS®

and a partnership while avoiding some of the restrictions and disadvantages of those forms of ownership. Chief advantages of an LLC are as follows:

1. LLCs with at least two members are taxed like a partnership and thus avoid the double taxation imposed on most corporations. LLCs with just one member are taxed like a sole proprietorship.
2. Like a corporation, it provides limited-liability protection. An LLC thus extends the concept of personal-asset protection to small business owners.
3. The LLC type of organization provides more management flexibility when compared with corporations. LLCs, for example, are not required to hold annual meetings and record meeting minutes.

Although many experts believe that the LLC is nothing more than a variation of the S-corporation, there is a difference. An LLC is not restricted to 100 stockholders—a common drawback of the S-corporation. LLCs are also less restricted than S-corporations in terms of who can become an owner. Although the owners of an LLC must file articles of organization with their state's secretary of state, they are not hampered by lots of Internal Revenue Service rules and government regulations that apply to corporations. As a result, experts are predicting that LLCs may become one of the most popular forms of business ownership available. For help in understanding the differences between a regular corporation, S-corporation, and limited-liability company, see Table 4.4.

Not-for-Profit Corporations

A **not-for-profit corporation** (sometimes referred to as *nonprofit*) is a corporation organized to provide a social, educational, religious, or other service rather than to earn a profit. Various charities, museums, private schools, and colleges are organized in this way, primarily to ensure limited liability. Habitat for Humanity is a not-for-profit corporation and was formed to provide homes for qualified low-income people who could not afford housing. Even though this corporation may receive more money than it spends, any surplus funds are "reinvested" in building activities to provide low-cost housing. It is a not-for-profit corporation because its primary purpose is to provide a social service. Other examples include the Public Broadcasting System (PBS), the Girl Scouts, and the Bill and Melinda Gates Foundation.

not-for-profit corporation a corporation organized to provide a social, educational, religious, or other service rather than to earn a profit

Concept Check

1. Explain the difference between an S-corporation and a limited liability company.

2. How does a regular (C) corporation differ from a not-for-profit corporation?

TABLE 4.4: Some Advantages and Disadvantages of a Regular Corporation, S-Corporation, and Limited-Liability Company

	Regular (C) Corporation	S-Corporation	Limited-Liability Company
Double taxation	Yes	No	No
Limited liability and personal-asset protection	Yes	Yes	Yes
Management and ownership flexibility	No	No	Yes
Restrictions on the number of owners/stockholders	No	Yes	No
Internal Revenue Service tax regulations	Many	Many	Fewer

Cooperatives, Joint Ventures, and Syndicates

7 LEARNING OBJECTIVE

Discuss the purpose of a cooperative, joint venture, and syndicate.

Today, three additional types of business organizations—cooperatives, joint ventures, and syndicates—are used for special purposes. Each of these forms of organization is unique when compared with more traditional forms of business ownership.

Cooperatives

A **cooperative** is an association of individuals or firms whose purpose is to perform some business function for its members. The cooperative can perform its function more effectively than any member could by acting alone. For example, cooperatives purchase goods in bulk and distribute them to members; thus the unit cost is lower than it would be if each member bought the goods in a much smaller quantity.

Although cooperatives are found in all segments of our economy, they are most prevalent in agriculture. Farmers use cooperatives to purchase supplies, to buy services such as trucking and storage, and to process and market their products. Ocean Spray Cranberries, Inc., for example, is a cooperative of some 600 cranberry growers and more than 50 citrus growers spread throughout the country.[8]

Joint Ventures

A **joint venture** is an agreement between two or more groups to form a business entity in order to achieve a specific goal or to operate for a specific period of time. Both the scope of the joint venture and the liabilities of the people or businesses involved usually are limited to one project. Once the goal is reached, the period of time elapses, or the project is completed, the joint venture is dissolved.

Corporations, as well as individuals, may enter into joint ventures. Major oil producers often have formed a number of joint ventures to share the extremely high cost of exploring for offshore petroleum deposits. And many U.S. companies are forming joint ventures with foreign firms in order to enter new markets around the globe. For example, Wal-Mart has joined forces with India's Bharti Enterprises to begin selling merchandise and capture a share of India's $350 billion retail market. Together, the two firms will set up 15 wholesale cash-and-carry stores over the next seven years.[9] Finally, Japanese consumer electronics manufacturer Sony and Swedish telecom giant Ericsson have formed a joint venture to manufacture and market mobile communications equipment.[10]

Syndicates

A **syndicate** is a temporary association of individuals or firms organized to perform a specific task that requires a large amount of capital. The syndicate is formed because no one person or firm is willing to put up the entire amount required for the undertaking. Like a joint venture, a syndicate is dissolved as soon as its purpose has been accomplished.

Syndicates are used most commonly to underwrite large insurance policies, loans, and investments. To share the risk of default, banks have formed syndicates to provide loans to developing countries. Stock brokerage firms usually join together in the same way to market a new issue of stock. For example, Goldman Sachs, JP Morgan Chase, and other Wall Street firms formed a syndicate to sell shares of stock in Visa. The initial public offering (IPO) is the largest in U.S. history—too large for Goldman Sachs and JP Morgan Chase to handle without help from other Wall Street firms.[11] (An *initial public offering* is the term used to describe the first time a corporation sells stock to the general public.)

cooperative an association of individuals or firms whose purpose is to perform some business function for its members

joint venture an agreement between two or more groups to form a business entity in order to achieve a specific goal or to operate for a specific period of time

syndicate a temporary association of individuals or firms organized to perform a specific task that requires a large amount of capital

Concept Check

1. Why are cooperatives formed? Explain how they operate.

2. In what ways are joint ventures and syndicates alike? In what ways do they differ?

Corporate Growth

8 LEARNING OBJECTIVE

Explain how growth from within and growth through mergers can enable a business to expand

Growth seems to be a basic characteristic of business. One reason for seeking growth has to do with profit: A larger firm generally has greater sales revenue and thus greater profit. Another reason is that in a growing economy, a business that does not grow is actually shrinking relative to the economy.

Is it Ethical?

Yogurt Responsibility

Can yogurt make the world a better place? Bangladesh's Grameen Bank and France's Danone think so. The two have teamed up in a joint venture called Grameen Danone Foods to fight malnutrition and raise the standard of living in northern Bangladesh.

Danone provided the start-up capital and designed the first factory, an environmentally friendly facility that runs partly on solar power. It also developed a recipe for specially fortified yogurt that could be sold for less than ten cents per biodegradable container. Grameen Bank lent local farmers money to buy cows and helped arrange centralized locations for milk collection. In addition, Grameen recruited "Grameen Ladies" who go door to door in and around the city of Bogra and earn about a penny for each cup of yogurt they sell.

Open since 2007, the factory now produces more than 10,000 cups of extra-nutritious, affordable yogurt every day. Counting the dairy farmers, factory workers, and Grameen Ladies, the joint venture provides much-needed income for more than 1,500 local residents. Just as important, the company is not a charity but will soon be self supporting. "The strength is that it is a business, and if it is a business, it is sustainable," says Danone's CEO.

Sources: Carol Matlack, "Danone Innovates to Help Feed the Poor," *Business Week*, April 28, 2008, www.businessweek.com; Sheridan Prasso, "Saving the World with a Cup of Yogurt," *Fortune*, March 15, 2007, http://money.cnn.com/magazines/fortune/fortune_archive/2007/02/05/8399198/index.htm; www.danonecommunities.com.

Growth poses new problems and requires additional resources that first must be available and then must be used effectively. The main ingredient in growth is capital—and as we have noted, capital is most readily available to corporations. Thus, to a great extent, business growth means corporate growth.

Growth from Within

Most corporations grow by expanding their present operations. Some introduce and sell new but related products. Others expand the sale of present products to new geographic markets or to new groups of consumers in geographic markets already served. Currently, Wal-Mart has more than 4,100 stores in the United States and over 3,100 stores in thirteen different countries and has long-range plans for expanding into additional international markets.[12]

Growth from within, especially when carefully planned and controlled, can have relatively little adverse effect on a firm. For the most part, the firm continues to do what it has been doing, but on a larger scale. For instance, Larry Ellison, cofounder and CEO of Oracle Corporation of Redwood Shores, California, built the firm's annual revenues up from a mere $282 million in 1988 to approximately $24 billion today.[13] Much of this growth has taken place since 1994 as Oracle capitalized on its global leadership in information management software.

Growth through Mergers and Acquisitions

Another way a firm can grow is by purchasing another company. The purchase of one corporation by another is called a **merger.** An *acquisition* is essentially the same thing as a merger, but the term usually is used in reference to a large corporation's purchases of other corporations. Although most mergers and acquisitions are friendly, hostile takeovers also occur. A **hostile takeover** is a situation in which the management and board of directors of a firm targeted for acquisition disapprove of the merger.

When a merger or acquisition becomes hostile, a corporate raider—another company or a wealthy investor—may make a tender offer or start a proxy fight to gain control of the target company. A **tender offer** is an offer to purchase the stock of a firm targeted for acquisition at a price just high enough to tempt stockholders to sell their shares. Corporate raiders also may initiate a proxy fight. A **proxy fight** is a technique used to gather enough stockholder votes to control a targeted company.

If the corporate raider is successful and takes over the targeted company, existing management usually is replaced. Faced with this probability, existing management may take specific actions sometimes referred to as "poison pills," "shark repellents," or "porcupine provisions" to maintain control of the firm and avoid the hostile takeover. Whether mergers are friendly or hostile, they are generally classified as *horizontal, vertical,* or *conglomerate* (see Figure 4.5).

merger the purchase of one corporation by another

hostile takeover a situation in which the management and board of directors of a firm targeted for acquisition disapprove of the merger

tender offer an offer to purchase the stock of a firm targeted for acquisition at a price just high enough to tempt stockholders to sell their shares

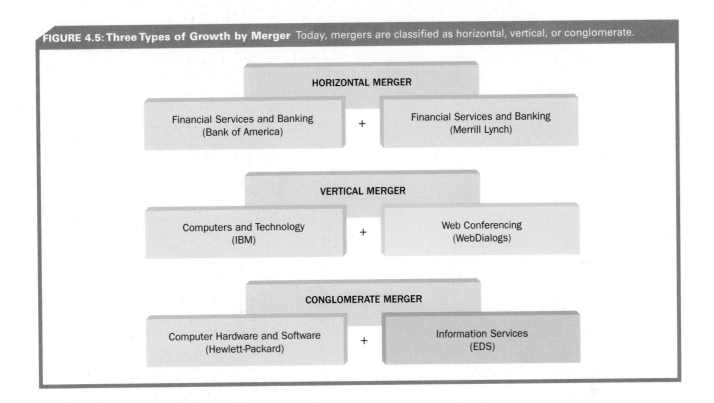

FIGURE 4.5: Three Types of Growth by Merger Today, mergers are classified as horizontal, vertical, or conglomerate.

HORIZONTAL MERGER

Financial Services and Banking (Bank of America) + Financial Services and Banking (Merrill Lynch)

VERTICAL MERGER

Computers and Technology (IBM) + Web Conferencing (WebDialogs)

CONGLOMERATE MERGER

Computer Hardware and Software (Hewlett-Packard) + Information Services (EDS)

Horizontal Mergers A *horizontal merger* is a merger between firms that make and sell similar products or services in similar markets. The merger between Bank of America and Merrill Lynch is an example of a horizontal merger because both firms are in the financial services and banking industry. This type of merger tends to reduce the number of firms in an industry—and thus may reduce competition. While this merger was approved because of problems in the economy at the time of the merger, most mergers are reviewed carefully by federal agencies before they are approved.

Vertical Mergers A *vertical merger* is a merger between firms that operate at different but related levels in the production and marketing of a product. Generally, one of the merging firms is either a supplier or a customer of the other. A vertical merger occurred when IBM acquired WebDialogs. At the time of the merger, WebDialogs, a privately held company, was a leading provider of Web conferencing services. At the same time, IBM needed this type of technology to enable companies of any size to use Web conferencing services. Rather than develop its own Web conferencing services, IBM simply purchased the WebDialogs company.[14]

Conglomerate Mergers A *conglomerate merger* takes place between firms in completely different industries. One of the largest conglomerate mergers in recent history occurred when Hewlett-Packard (computer hardware and software) merged with EDS (information services). While both companies were recognized as successful companies that have a history of increasing sales revenues and profits, they operate in different industries. The Hewlett-Packard–EDS merger was friendly because it was beneficial for both firms.

Current Merger Trends

Economists, financial analysts, corporate managers, and stockholders still hotly debate whether takeovers are good for the economy—or for individual companies—in the long run. One thing is clear, however: There are two sides to the takeover question. Takeover advocates argue that for companies that have been taken over,

proxy fight a technique used to gather enough stockholder votes to control a targeted company

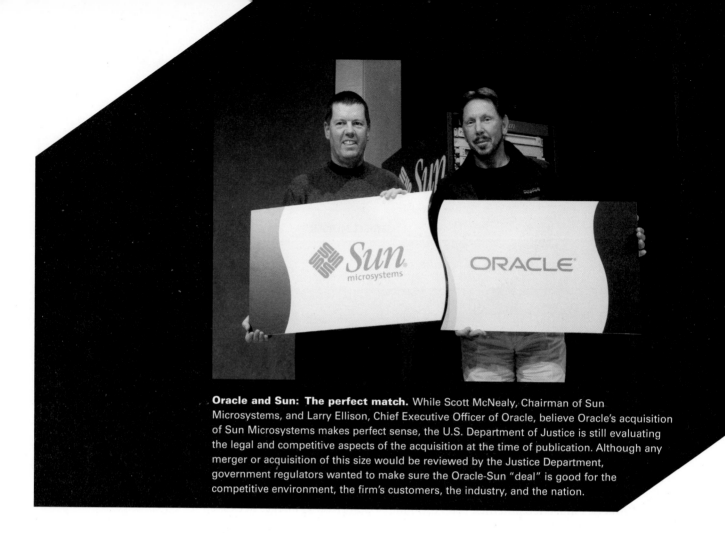

Oracle and Sun: The perfect match. While Scott McNealy, Chairman of Sun Microsystems, and Larry Ellison, Chief Executive Officer of Oracle, believe Oracle's acquisition of Sun Microsystems makes perfect sense, the U.S. Department of Justice is still evaluating the legal and competitive aspects of the acquisition at the time of publication. Although any merger or acquisition of this size would be reviewed by the Justice Department, government regulators wanted to make sure the Oracle-Sun "deal" is good for the competitive environment, the firm's customers, the industry, and the nation.

leveraged buyout (LBO) a purchase arrangement that allows a firm's managers and employees or a group of investors to purchase the company

Concept Check

1. What happens when a firm makes a decision to grow from within?

2. What is a hostile takeover? How is it related to a tender offer and a proxy fight?

3. Explain the three types of mergers.

4. Describe current merger trends and how they affect the businesses involved and their stockholders.

the purchasers have been able to make the company more profitable and productive by installing a new top-management team, by reducing expenses, and by forcing the company to concentrate on one main business.

Takeover opponents argue that takeovers do nothing to enhance corporate profitability or productivity. These critics argue that threats of takeovers have forced managers to devote valuable time to defending their companies from takeover, thus robbing time from new-product development and other vital business activities. This, they believe, is why U.S. companies may be less competitive with companies in such countries as Japan, Germany, and South Korea, where takeovers occur only rarely. Finally, the opposition argues that the only people who benefit from take-overs are investment bankers, brokerage firms, and takeover "artists," who receive financial rewards by manipulating U.S. corporations rather than by producing tangible products or services.

Most experts now predict that mergers and acquisitions during the first part of the twenty-first century will be the result of cash-rich companies looking to acquire businesses that will enhance their position in the marketplace. Analysts also anticipate more mergers that involve companies or investors from other countries. Regardless of the companies involved or where the companies are from, future mergers and acquisitions will be driven by solid business logic and the desire to compete in the international marketplace.

Finally, experts predict more leveraged buyouts in the future. A **leveraged buyout (LBO)** is a purchase arrangement that allows a firm's managers and employees or a group of investors to purchase the company. (LBO activity is sometimes referred to as *taking a firm private*.) To gain control of a company, LBOs usually rely on borrowed money to purchase stock from existing stockholders. The borrowed money is later repaid through the company's earnings, sale of assets, or money obtained from selling more stock.

Global Economic Challenges

The Economics of Multinational Mergers

A major multinational seeking to grow through a merger faces special challenges in getting permission from all the countries where the combined firm will operate. For example, China is particularly concerned about mergers that might upset the competitive balance in a particular product category. Chinese officials cited such anti-trust considerations when they prevented Atlanta's Coca-Cola from acquiring China's Huiyuan Juice Group Ltd. not long ago. Instead of pursuing another merger with a local firm, Coca-Cola invested in new factories to build its business in the fast-growing Chinese economy.

The Chinese government even had a say when InBev, which is based in Belgium, acquired Anheuser-Busch, which is headquartered in St. Louis, Missouri. Regulators insisted that the combined company not increase its equity stake in the company that owns Tsingtao, one of China's best-known beers. Anheuser-Busch Inbev soon sold most of its stake in Tsingtao but retained its ownership of 20 smaller Chinese beer brands.

On the other hand, when Chrysler's precarious financial position forced it into bankruptcy during the recent economic crisis, the U.S. government actively encouraged the Detroit automaker's merger with Italy's Fiat. Although Chrysler first slimmed down by shedding thousands of jobs and hundreds of dealerships, the multinational merger saved the jobs of many U.S. employees and kept orders flowing to many of Chrysler's U.S. suppliers.

Sources: Shaun Rein, "Why Most M&A Deals End Up Badly," *Forbes*, June 16, 2009, www.forbes.com; David Kiley and David Welch, "Chrysler, Fiat Drive Off the Lot," *BusinessWeek*, June 10, 2009, www.businessweek.com; John W. Miller, "Anheuser-Busch Pares Stake in China Brewer," *Wall Street Journal*, January 24, 2009, www.wsj.com.

Whether they are sole proprietorships, partnerships, corporations, or some other form of business ownership, most U.S. businesses are small. In the next chapter, we focus on these small businesses. We examine, among other things, the meaning of the word *small* as it applies to business and the place of small business in the American economy.

SUMMARY

1 Describe the advantages and disadvantages of sole proprietorships.

In a sole proprietorship, all business profits become the property of the owner, but the owner is also personally responsible for all business debts. A successful sole proprietorship can be a great source of pride for the owner. When comparing different types of business ownership, the sole proprietorship is the simplest form of business to enter, control, and leave. It also pays no special taxes. Perhaps for these reasons, 72 percent of all American business firms are sole proprietorships. Sole proprietorships nevertheless have disadvantages, such as unlimited liability and limits on one person's ability to borrow or to be an expert in all fields. As a result, this form of ownership accounts for only 4 percent of total revenues when compared with partnerships and corporations.

2 Explain the different types of partners and the importance of partnership agreements.

Like sole proprietors, general partners are responsible for running the business and for all business debts. Limited partners receive a share of the profit in return for investing in the business. However, they are not responsible for business debts beyond the amount they have invested. It is also possible to form a master limited partnership (MLP) and sell units of ownership to raise capital. Regardless of the type of partnership, it is always a good idea to have a written agreement (or articles of partnership) setting forth the terms of a partnership.

3 Describe the advantages and disadvantages of partnerships.

Although partnership eliminates some of the disadvantages of sole proprietorship, it is the least popular of the major forms of business ownership. The major advantages of a partnership include ease of start-up, availability of capital and credit, personal interest, combined skills and knowledge, retention of profits, and no special taxes. The effects of management disagreements are one of the major disadvantages of a partnership. Other disadvantages include unlimited liability (in a general partnership), lack of continuity, and frozen investment. By forming a limited partnership, the disadvantage of unlimited liability may be eliminated for the limited partner(s). This same disadvantage may be eliminated for partners that form a limited-liability partnership. Of course, special requirements must be met if partners form either the limited partnership or the limited-liability partnership.

4 Summarize how a corporation is formed.

A corporation is an artificial person created by law, with most of the legal rights of a real person, including the right to start and operate a business, to own property, to borrow money, to be sued or sue, and to enter into contracts. With the corporate form of ownership, stock can be sold to individuals to raise capital. The people who own a corporation's stock—and thus own part of the corporation—are called stockholders or sometimes shareholders. Generally, corporations are classified as closed corporations (few stockholders) or open corporations (many stockholders).

The process of forming a corporation is called incorporation. Most experts believe that the services of a lawyer are necessary when making decisions about where to incorporate and about obtaining a corporate charter, issuing stock, holding an organizational meeting, and all other legal details involved in incorporation. In theory, stockholders are able to control the activities of the corporation because they elect the board of directors who appoint the corporate officers.

5 Describe the advantages and disadvantages of a corporation.

Perhaps the major advantage of the corporate form is limited liability—stockholders are not liable for the corporation's debts beyond the amount they paid for its stock. Other important advantages include ease of raising capital, ease of transfer of ownership, perpetual life, and specialized management. A major disadvantage of a large corporation is double taxation: All profits are taxed once as corporate income and again as personal income because stockholders must pay a personal income tax on the profits they receive as dividends. Other disadvantages include difficulty and expense of formation, government regulation, conflict within the corporation, and lack of secrecy.

6 Examine special types of corporations, including S-corporations, limited-liability companies, and not-for-profit corporations.

S-corporations are corporations that are taxed as though they were partnerships but that enjoy the benefit of limited liability. To qualify as an S-corporation, a number of criteria must be met. A limited-liability company (LLC) is a form of business ownership that provides limited liability and has fewer government restrictions. LLCs with at least two members are taxed like a partnership and thus avoid the double taxation imposed on most corporations. LLCs with just one member are taxed like a sole proprietorship. When compared with a regular corporation or an S-corporation, an LLC is more flexible. Not-for-profit corporations are formed to provide social services rather than to earn profits.

7 Discuss the purpose of a cooperative, joint venture, and syndicate.

Three additional forms of business ownership—the cooperative, joint venture, and syndicate—are used by their owners to meet special needs. A cooperative is an association of individuals or firms whose purpose is to perform some business function for its members. A joint venture is formed when two or more groups form a business entity in order to achieve a specific goal or to operate for a specific period of time. Once the goal is reached, the time period elapses, or the project is completed, the joint venture is dissolved. A syndicate is a temporary association of individuals or firms organized to perform a specific task that requires large amounts of capital. Like a joint venture, a syndicate is dissolved as soon as its purpose has been accomplished.

8 Explain how growth from within and growth through mergers can enable a business to expand.

A corporation may grow by expanding its present operations or through a merger or an acquisition. Although most mergers are friendly, hostile takeovers also occur. A hostile takeover is a situation in which the management and board of directors of a firm targeted for acquisition disapprove of the merger. Mergers generally are classified as horizontal, vertical, or conglomerate.

While economists, financial analysts, corporate managers, and stockholders debate the merits of mergers, some trends should be noted. First, experts predict that future mergers will be the result of cash-rich companies looking to acquire businesses that will enhance their position in the marketplace. Second, more mergers are likely to involve foreign companies or investors. Third, mergers will be driven by business logic and the desire to compete in the international marketplace. Finally, more leveraged buyouts are expected.

KEY TERMS

You should now be able to define and give an example relevant to each of the following terms:

sole proprietorship (101)
unlimited liability (103)
partnership (104)
general partner (105)
limited partner (105)
master limited partnership (MLP) (106)
corporation (109)
stock (109)

stockholder (109)
closed corporation (110)
open corporation (110)
domestic corporation (111)
foreign corporation (111)
alien corporation (111)
common stock (111)
preferred stock (111)
dividend (112)

proxy (112)
board of directors (112)
corporate officers (113)
limited liability (113)
S-corporation (115)
limited-liability company (LLC) (115)
not-for-profit corporation (116)
cooperative (117)

joint venture (117)
syndicate (117)
merger (118)
hostile takeover (118)
tender offer (118)
proxy fight (119)
leveraged buyout (LBO) (120)

1. If you were to start a business, which ownership form would you choose? What factors might affect your choice?
2. Why might an investor choose to become a limited partner instead of purchasing the stock of an open corporation?
3. Many entrepreneurs incorporate their businesses in an attempt to protect their personal assets. How does the incorporation process provide liability protection for these entrepreneurs?
4. Discuss the following statement: "Corporations are not really run by their owners."
5. Is growth a good thing for all firms? How does management know when a firm is ready to grow?
6. Assume that a corporate raider wants to purchase your firm, dismantle it, and sell the individual pieces. What could you do to avoid this hostile takeover?

Get Flash Cards, Quizzes, Games, Crosswords and more @ www.cengage.com/introbusiness/pride

Test Yourself

Matching Questions

1. _____ It is an association of two or more business owners.

2. _____ A distribution of earnings to the stockholders of a corporation.

3. _____ This type of ownership is the easiest type of business to start.

4. _____ A person who invests only capital in a partnership.

5. _____ The concept of being personally responsible for all debts of a business.

6. _____ A business entity or artificial being with most of the legal rights of a person.

7. _____ A legal document that describes the purpose of the corporation.

8. _____ An offer to purchase the stock of a firm targeted for acquisition.

9. _____ A temporary association of individuals or firms organized to perform a specific task.

10. _____ A company chartered in a foreign country doing business in the United States.

   a. alien corporation
   b. corporate charter
   c. syndicate
   d. tender offer
   e. vertical venture
   f. limited partner
   g. voluntary association
   h. corporation
   i. dividend
   j. partnership
   k. sole proprietorship
   l. unlimited liability

True False Questions

11. **T F** Unlimited liability is an advantage of a sole proprietorship.

12. **T F** Preferred stockholders elect the board of directors that manage the day-to-day business activities of a corporation.

13. **T F** Cooperatives are owned by their members.

14. **T F** A limited partner is responsible for any debts of the partnership, regardless of whether he or she was directly involved in the transaction that created the debt.

15. **T F** The articles of partnership is a written contract describing the terms of a partnership.

16. **T F** Compared to a corporation, a partnership is more difficult and expensive to establish.

17. **T F** The S-corporation form of organization allows a corporation to avoid double taxation.

18. **T F** A corporation chartered in Mexico and doing business in the United States is known as a foreign corporation in the United States.

19. **T F** The board of directors is directly responsible to the stockholders.

20. **T F** The amount paid for stock is the most a shareholder can lose in the corporate form of ownership.

Test Yourself

21. _____ During college, Elyssa Wood earned extra money by using her culinary skills to cater special parties. After graduation, she decided to turn her part-time job into a full-time business that she plans to expand in the future. In the meantime, she wants to maintain complete control of the business. She will most likely organize the business as a

    a. master limited partnership.
    b. corporation.
    c. general partnership.
    d. sole proprietorship.
    e. cooperative.

22. _____ Which of the following is not an advantage of a corporate form of ownership?

    a. It is easier to raise capital.
    b. Ownership can be transferred easily and quickly.
    c. The death of an owner does not terminate the corporation.
    d. Profits are taxed twice.
    e. The liability of the owners is limited.

23. _____ A corporation incorporated in Texas doing business in New York is known in

    a. New York as a domestic corporation.
    b. Texas as a foreign corporation.
    c. Texas as a domestic corporation.
    d. New York as an alien corporation.
    e. The firm cannot do business in New York.

24. _____ PepsiCo acquired Pizza Hut. What type of merger was this?

    a. Limited
    b. Syndicated
    c. Joint venture
    d. Horizontal
    e. Vertical

25. _____ J. R. Imax, a financial investor, wants to control the Simex Company. So far he has been unsuccessful in purchasing enough stock to give him control. To reach his goal, which technique should he use to gather enough stockholder votes to control the company?

    a. Stock offer
    b. Liability takeover

    c. Merger
    d. Acquisition
    e. Proxy fight

26. _____ A corporation whose stock is owned by relative few people is called a(n)

    a. limited corporation.
    b. open corporation.
    c. closed corporation.
    d. domestic corporation.
    e. friendly corporation.

27. _____ When two business firms need large sums of money to finance a major project, they are likely to establish a

    a. closed corporation.
    b. syndicate.
    c. new sole proprietorship business.
    d. legal tender corporation.
    e. conglomerate venture.

28. _____ The ability to combine skills and knowledge is an advantage of a

    a. partnership.
    b. sole proprietorship.
    c. limited venture.
    d. an enterprise venture.
    e. a horizontal business.

29. _____ A _____ merger takes place between firms in completely different industries.

    a. vertical
    b. horizontal
    c. diagonal
    d. conglomerate
    e. unrestricted

30. _____ Unlimited liability means

    a. there is no limit on the amount an owner can borrow.
    b. creditors will absorb any loss from nonpayment of debt.
    c. the business can borrow money for any type of purchase.
    d. the owner is responsible for all business debts.
    e. stockholders can borrow money from the business.

Answers on p. TY-1

VIDEO CASE

Having Fun Is Serious Business at Jordan's Furniture

Jordan's Furniture is a unique retail chain. In fact, every one of its stores in New England is unique—and highly profitable. And that's what caught the eye of Warren Buffett, the head of conglomerate Berkshire Hathaway, who is famous for his astute investments. Buffet bought Jordan's Furniture in 1999 and has left the founding family in charge to continue the retailer's winning ways.

The company's history stretches back to 1918, when Samuel Tatelman opened a small furniture store in Waltham, Massachusetts. His son Edward became involved in the family business during the 1930s. By the 1950s, Edward's children, Barry and Eliot, were learning about furniture retailing first-hand as they helped out during busy periods. In the early 1970s, the two brothers jointly assumed responsibility for running the store, which then had eight employees.

The brothers then made two key decisions that dramatically altered the future course of the business. First, they decided to gear their merchandise and store decor to 18- to 34-year-olds because people in this age group need furniture when they settle down and start families. Second, they resolved to make the business fun for themselves, their customers, and their employees by adding a large element of entertainment to the shopping experience.

For example, the 110,000-square-foot store in Natick, Massachusetts, evokes the spirit of Bourbon Street in New Orleans, complete with steamboat and Mardi Gras festivities. One section of the store holds a 262-seat IMAX 3D theater, popcorn and all. The Reading, Massachusetts, store is home to Beantown, a series of jelly-bean creations depicting Boston landmarks, such as the leftfield wall in Fenway Park, home of the Red Sox. Just as the Reading store is more than twice as large as the Natick store, its IMAX theater is also larger, roomy enough for an audience of 500 people.

The two-story Avon, Massachusetts, branch is home to the twenty-minute M.O.M., better known as the Motion Odyssey 3D Movie Ride, which draws children of all ages. Continuing the fun theme, visitors to the Nashua, New Hampshire, store are invited to munch on free fresh-baked chocolate chip cookies and sip coffee in the snack bar. And by the way, every one of the four stores also features a huge inventory of furniture for all tastes.

Ordinarily, customers shop for furniture only to fill a particular need. By making its stores exciting destinations for the entire family, Jordan's Furniture is out to change that behavior. When their children ask to visit the in-store IMAX theater, for instance, the parents may spot an entertainment unit or a chair they want to buy. "People come in here for fun," observes Eliot Tatelman. "They wind up having fun but also buying."

After Warren Buffett bought Jordan's Furniture, the brothers remained in charge to direct the chain's expansion. They also added a spiffy website and continued writing the funny television commercials for which the company was known throughout the Boston area. Eventually, they closed the original Waltham site to concentrate on the four stores built with entertainment in mind. By the time Barry left in 2006 to pursue a career as a Broadway producer, Eliot's two sons had followed family tradition and joined the company.

And that's how a small business founded as a sole proprietor-ship wound up as a corporation merged into a large conglomerate. Today, Jordan's Furniture is an established, profitable retail operation employing more than 1,200 people. It serves thousands of shoppers every day, and its sales average of $950 per square foot is considerably higher than that of the typical furniture store. But then, Jordan's Furniture is hardly a typical store, as its slogan suggests: "Not just a store, an experience!"[15]

For more information about this company, go to **www. jordans.com**

Questions

1. Warren Buffett's Berkshire Hathaway owns three other furniture retailers in addition to Jordan's. Why do you think the conglomerate left the Tatelman family in charge of Jordan's after the merger?
2. What do you think Berkshire Hathaway and Jordan's have each gained from the merger?
3. How much influence are Berkshire Hathaway's stockholders likely to have (or want) over Jordan's management? Explain your answer.

BUILDING SKILLS FOR CAREER SUCCESS

1. EXPLORING THE INTERNET

Arguments about mergers and acquisitions often come down to an evaluation of who benefits and by how much. Sometimes the benefits include access to new products, talented management, new customers, or new sources of capital. Often, the debate is complicated by the involvement of firms based in different countries.

The Internet is a fertile environment for information and discussion about mergers. The firms involved will provide their view about who will benefit and why it is either a good thing or not. Journalists will report facts and offer commentary as to how they see the future result of any merger, and of course, chat rooms located on the websites of many journals promote discussion about the issues. Visit the text website for updates to this exercise.

Assignment

1. Using an Internet search engine such as Google or Yahoo!, locate two or three sites providing information about a recent merger (use a keyword such as *merger*).
2. After examining these sites and reading journal articles, report information about the merger, such as the dollar value, the reasons behind the merger, and so forth.

3. Based on your assessment of the information you have read, do you think the merger is a good idea or not for the firms involved, the employees, the investors, the industry, and society as a whole? Explain your reasoning.

2. BUILDING TEAM SKILLS

Suppose that you have decided to quit your job as an insurance adjuster and open a bakery. Your business is now growing, and you have decided to add a full line of catering services. This means more work and responsibility. You will need someone to help you, but you are undecided about what to do. Should you hire an employee or find a partner? If you add a partner, what type of decisions should be made to create a partnership agreement?

Assignment

1. In a group, discuss the following questions:
   a. What are the advantages and disadvantages of adding a partner versus hiring an employee?
   b. Assume that you have decided to form a partnership. What articles should be included in a partnership agreement?
   c. How would you go about finding a partner?
2. Summarize your group's answers to these questions, and present them to your class.
3. As a group, prepare an articles-of-partnership agreement. Be prepared to discuss the pros and cons of your group's agreement with other groups from your class, as well as to examine their agreements.

3. RESEARCHING DIFFERENT CAREERS

Many people spend their entire lives working in jobs that they do not enjoy. Why is this so? Often, it is because they have taken the first job they were offered without giving it much thought. How can you avoid having this happen to you? First, you should determine your "personal profile" by identifying and analyzing your own strengths, weaknesses, things you enjoy, and things you dislike. Second, you should identify the types of jobs that fit your profile. Third, you should identify and research the companies that offer those jobs.

Assignment

1. Take two sheets of paper and draw a line down the middle of each sheet, forming two columns on each page. Label column 1 "Things I Enjoy or Like to Do," column 2 "Things I Do Not Like Doing," column 3 "My Strengths," and column 4 "My Weaknesses."
2. Record data in each column over a period of at least one week. You may find it helpful to have a relative or friend give you input.
3. Summarize the data, and write a profile of yourself.
4. Take your profile to a career counselor at your college or to the public library and ask for help in identifying jobs that fit your profile. Your college may offer testing to assess your skills and personality. The Internet is another resource.
5. Research the companies that offer the types of jobs that fit your profile.
6. Write a report on your findings.

Small Business, Entrepreneurship, and Franchises

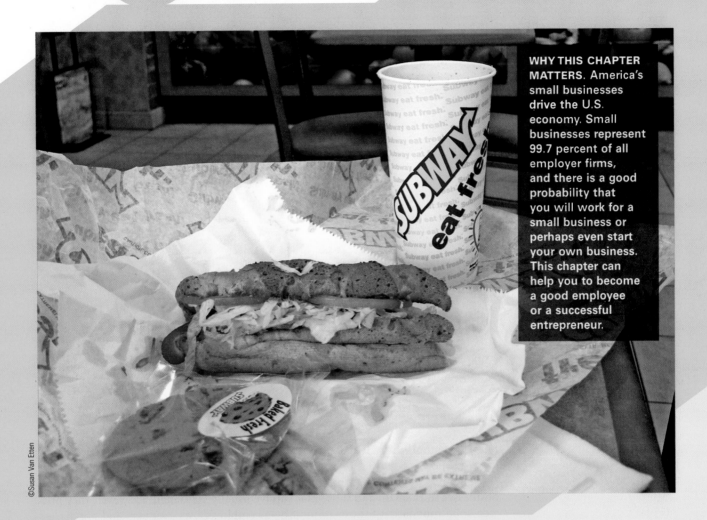

©Susan Van Etten

WHY THIS CHAPTER MATTERS. America's small businesses drive the U.S. economy. Small businesses represent 99.7 percent of all employer firms, and there is a good probability that you will work for a small business or perhaps even start your own business. This chapter can help you to become a good employee or a successful entrepreneur.

LEARNING OBJECTIVES

1 Define what a small business is and recognize the fields in which small businesses are concentrated.

2 Identify the people who start small businesses and the reasons why some succeed and many fail.

3 Assess the contributions of small businesses to our economy.

4 Judge the advantages and disadvantages of operating a small business.

5 Explain how the Small Business Administration helps small businesses.

6 Appraise the concept and types of franchising.

7 Analyze the growth of franchising and franchising's advantages and disadvantages.

Calling All App Entrepreneurs

How did Ethan Nicholas make $35,000 in a day? By selling thousands of downloads of a game he developed for the Apple iPhone. Nicholas is not the only entrepreneur making money selling "apps," downloadable software applications designed for use on cell phones and other mobile digital devices. Kostas Eleftheriou and two friends, developers of the iSteam app, earned $100,000 in just three months. Steve Demeter, a software developer for a bank, made more than $200,000 in two months with his Trism game for the iPhone.

Although these apps were runaway hits, most sell much more modestly. Still, the app opportunity is increasingly attractive to tech-savvy entrepreneurs. Ethan Nicholas worked for Sun Microsystems when he started programming his iShoot game for the iPhone. Within six weeks he was ready to submit the finished product to Apple for its approval, which he quickly received. Nicholas priced his game at $4.99 per download, and Apple listed it on its App Store. (For every game sold, Apple receives 30 percent of the selling price.)

The game drew some buyers, but Nicholas believed even more people would buy if they could play before they paid. After he submitted a stripped-down version of the game as a free download, 2 million people downloaded it. Did customers enjoy the game so much that they were willing to pay $2.99 for the full-featured version? Yes—more than 10,000 downloaded the game in a single day, putting $35,000 in Nicholas's pocket. The experience convinced him to quit his day job and become a full-time app developer.

To date, users have downloaded more than 1 billion apps from Apple's App Store. Now Nokia, Microsoft, and other firms are cashing in on the trend by opening their own online app stores. The overall market for apps is expected to be worth more than $25 billion by 2014. No wonder venture-capital firms are offering millions of dollars to fund app entrepreneurs with clever new ideas.[1]

DID YOU KNOW?

The global market for mobile applications, software designed to run on cell phones and other digital devices, will reach $25 billion by 2014.

Entrepreneurial spirit, as demonstrated by Ethan Nicholas, Kostas Eleftheriou and Steve Demeter, is alive and well. Although these entrepreneurs are experiencing considerable growth, this kind of growth is unusual. Most entrepreneurs and small businesses start small, and those that survive usually stay small. However, they provide solid foundation for our economy—as employers, as suppliers and purchasers of goods and services, and taxpayers.

In this chapter, we do not take small businesses and entrepreneurs for granted. Instead, we look closely at this important business sector—beginning with a definition of small business, a description of industries that often attract small businesses, and a profile of some of the people who start small businesses. Next, we consider the importance of small businesses in our economy. We also present the advantages and disadvantages of smallness in business. We then describe services provided by the Small Business Administration, a government agency formed to assist owners and managers of small businesses. We conclude the chapter with a discussion of the pros and cons of franchising, an approach to small-business ownership that has become very popular in the last forty years.

small business one that is independently owned and operated for profit and is not dominant in its field

LEARNING OBJECTIVE 1

Define what a small business is and recognize the fields in which small businesses are concentrated.

Small Business: A Profile

The Small Business Administration (SBA) defines a **small business** as "one which is independently owned and operated for profit and is not dominant in its field." How small must a firm be not to dominate its field? That depends on the particular industry it is in. The SBA has developed the following specific "smallness" guidelines for the various industries, as shown in Table 5.1.[2] The SBA periodically revises and simplifies its small-business size regulations.

Annual sales in the millions of dollars may not seem very small. However, for many firms, profit is only a small percentage of total sales. Thus, a firm may earn only $40,000 or $50,000 on yearly sales of $1 million—and that *is* small in comparison with the profits earned by most medium-sized and large firms. Moreover, most small firms have annual sales well below the maximum limits in the SBA guidelines.

The Small-Business Sector

In the United States, it typically takes four days and $210 to establish a business as a legal entity. The steps include registering the name of the business, applying for tax IDs, and setting up unemployment and workers' compensation insurance. In Japan, however, a typical entrepreneur spends more than $3,500 and thirty-one days to follow eleven different procedures (see Table 5.2).

A surprising number of Americans take advantage of their freedom to start a business. There are, in fact, about 27.2 million businesses in this country. Only just over 17,000 of these employ more than 500 workers—enough to be considered large.

Interest in owning or starting a small business has never been greater than it is today. During the last decade, the number of small businesses in the United States has increased 49 percent, and for the last few years, new-business formation in the United States has broken successive records, except during the 2001–2002 recession. Recently, nearly 637,000 new businesses were incorporated. Furthermore, part-time entrepreneurs have increased fivefold in recent years; they now account for one-third of all small businesses.[3]

According to a recent study, two-thirds of new businesses survive at least two years, 44 percent survive at least four years, and 31 percent survive at least seven years.[4] The primary reason for these failures is mismanagement resulting from a lack of business know-how. The makeup of the small-business sector thus is constantly changing. Despite the high failure rate, many small businesses succeed modestly. Some, like Apple Computer, Inc., are extremely successful—to the point where they can no longer be considered small. Taken

TABLE 5.1: Industry Group-Size Standards Small-business size standards are usually stated in number of employees or average annual sales. In the United States, 99.7 percent of all businesses are considered small

Industry Group	Size Standard
Manufacturing	500 employees
Wholesale trade	100 employees
Agriculture	$750,000
Retail trade	$7 million
General & heavy construction (except dredging)	$33.5 million
Dredging	$20 million
Special trade contractors	$14 million
Travel agencies	$3.5 million (commissions & other income)
Business and personal services except	$7 million
• Architectural, engineering, surveying, and mapping services	$4.5 million
• Dry cleaning and carpet cleaning services	$4.5 million

Source: **http://www.sba.gov/services/contractingopportunities/owners/basics/GC_SMALL_BUSINESS.html**, accessed May 4, 2009.

TABLE 5.2: Establishing a Business Around the World The entrepreneurial spirit provides the spark that enriches the U.S. economy. The growth will continue if lawmakers resist the urge to overregulate entrepreneurs and provide policies that foster free enterprise

	Number of Procedures	Time (days)	Cost (US$)	Minimum Capital (% per capita income)
Australia	2	2	402	0
Belgium	7	56	2,633	75.1
Canada	2	3	127	0
Denmark	4	4	0	52.3
France	10	53	663	32.1
Germany	9	45	1,341	103.8
Greece	16	45	8,115	145.3
Ireland	3	12	2,473	0
Italy	9	23	4,565	49.6
Japan	11	31	3,518	71.3
Netherlands	7	11	3,276	70.7
New Zealand	3	3	28	0
Norway	4	24	1,460	33.1
Portugal	11	95	1,360	43.4
Spain	11	115	2,366	19.6
Sweden	3	16	190	41.4
Switzerland	6	20	3,228	33.8
United Kingdom	6	18	264	0
United States	5	4	210	0

Source: World Bank (2004); as found in *Inside the Vault*, Federal Reserve Bank of St. Louis, Fall 2004, p. 1.

together, small businesses are also responsible for providing a high percentage of the jobs in the United States. According to some estimates, the figure is well over 50 percent.

Industries That Attract Small Businesses

Some industries, such as auto manufacturing, require huge investments in machinery and equipment. Businesses in such industries are big from the day they are started—if an entrepreneur or group of entrepreneurs can gather the capital required to start one.

By contrast, a number of other industries require only a low initial investment and some special skills or knowledge. It is these industries that tend to attract new businesses. Growing industries, such as outpatient-care facilities, are attractive because of their profit potential. However, knowledgeable entrepreneurs choose areas with which they are familiar, and these are most often the more established industries.

Small enterprise spans the gamut from corner newspaper vending to the development of optical fibers. The owners of small businesses sell gasoline, flowers, and coffee to go. They publish magazines, haul freight, teach languages, and program computers. They make wines, movies, and high-fashion clothes. They build new homes and restore old ones. They fix appliances, recycle metals, and sell used cars.

Going Green

Local Businesses Build on Slow Food

Fast food may be big business, but Slow Food is helping local businesses grow and prosper. The Slow Food movement began in Italy during the 1980s as a reaction to the rapid growth of giant fast-food restaurant chains. Not only does the movement promote the idea of savoring meals cooked slowly from scratch, it also encourages cooks to get fresh, quality ingredients from small farms and other local businesses.

Shipping fruits, vegetables, and other foods by train, plane, or truck to commercial kitchens thousands of miles away takes time and consumes a lot of energy. The Slow Food movement wants to reduce energy use and pollution by encouraging restaurants and other companies to buy fresh from local growers.

Now big businesses are jumping on the Slow Food bandwagon. The food-services firm Sodexo buys produce from hundreds of small farmers in the communities where it does business. Chipotle Mexican Grill buys some of its produce from small growers near its 730 restaurants. And local honey producers, herb growers, and other small businesses are seeing sales go up as Slow Food catches on.

A growing number of colleges and universities are adopting Slow Food principles and buying from local sources. For example, twice-monthly Slow Food dinners at College of the Holy Cross in Worcester, Massachusetts, feature dairy products from a Vermont creamery, seasonal fruits and vegetables from nearby farms, and meats from local producers. Students slow down and savor each bite—no cell phones or digital devices allowed.

Sources: Tracy Jan, "Slow-Food Meal Gives Holy Cross Students a Break from Hectic Pace," *Boston Globe*, May 3, 2009. www.boston.com; "Revolutionaries by the Bay," *The Economist*, September 11, 2008, www.economist.com; Bobby White, "The Challenges of Eating 'Slow,'" *Wall Street Journal*, September 2, 2008, www. wsj.com; Jane Black, "As Food Becomes a Cause, Meeting Puts Issues on the Table," *Washington Post*, August 30, 2008, p. A1.

They drive cabs and fly planes. They make us well when we are ill, and they sell us the products of corporate giants. In fact, 74 percent of real estate, rental, and leasing industries; 61 percent of the businesses in the leisure and hospitality services; and 86 percent of the construction industries are dominated by small businesses.[5] The various kinds of businesses generally fall into three broad categories of industry: distribution, service, and production.

Distribution Industries This category includes retailing, wholesaling, transportation, and communications—industries concerned with the movement of goods from producers to consumers. Distribution industries account for approximately 33 percent of all small businesses. Of these, almost three-quarters are involved in retailing, that is, the sale of goods directly to consumers. Clothing and jewelry stores, pet shops, bookstores, and grocery stores, for example, are all retailing firms. Slightly less than one-quarter of the small distribution firms are wholesalers. Wholesalers purchase products in quantity from manufacturers and then resell them to retailers.

Service Industries This category accounts for over 48 percent of all small businesses. Of these, about three-quarters provide such nonfinancial services as medical and dental care; watch, shoe, and TV repairs; haircutting and styling; restaurant meals; and dry cleaning. About 8 percent of the small service firms offer financial services, such as accounting, insurance, real estate, and investment counseling. An increasing number of self-employed Americans are running service businesses from home.

Production Industries This last category includes the construction, mining, and manufacturing industries. Only about 19 percent of all small businesses are in this group, mainly because these industries require relatively large initial investments. Small firms that do venture into production generally make parts and subassemblies for larger manufacturing firms or supply special skills to larger construction firms.

Concept Check

1. What information would you need to determine whether a particular business is small according to SBA guidelines?

2. Which two areas of business generally attract the most small business? Why are these areas attractive to small businesses?

3. Distinguish among service industries, distribution industries, and production industries.

LEARNING OBJECTIVE **2**

Identify the people who start small businesses and the reasons why some succeed and many fail.

The People in Small Businesses: The Entrepreneurs

The entrepreneurial spirit is alive and well in the United States. A recent study revealed that the U.S. population is quite entrepreneurial when compared with those of other countries. More than 70 percent of Americans would prefer being an entrepreneur to working for someone else. This compares with 46 percent of adults in Western Europe and 58 percent of adults in Canada. Another recent study on entrepreneurial activity found that of thirty-six countries studied, the United States was in the top third in entrepreneurial activity and was the leader when compared with Japan, Canada, and Western Europe.[6]

Small businesses typically are managed by the people who started and own them. Most of these people have held jobs with other firms and still could be so employed if they wanted. Yet owners of small businesses would rather take the risk of starting and operating their own firms, even if the money they make is less than the salaries they otherwise might earn.

Researchers have suggested a variety of personal factors as reasons why people go into business for themselves. These are discussed below.

Characteristics of Entrepreneurs

Entrepreneurial spirit is the desire to create a new business. For example, Nikki Olyai always knew that she wanted to create and develop her own business. Her father, a successful businessman in Iran, was her role model. She came to the United States at the age of seventeen and lived with a host family in Salem, Oregon, attending high school there. Undergraduate and graduate degrees in computer science led her to start Innovision Technologies while she held two other jobs to keep the business going and took care of her four-year-old son. Recently, Nikki Olyai's business was honored by the Women's Business Enterprise National Council's "Salute to Women's Business Enterprises" as one of eleven top successful firms. For three consecutive years, her firm was selected as a "Future 50 of Greater Detroit Company."

Other Personal Factors

Other personal factors in small-business success include

- Independence
- A desire to determine one's own destiny
- A willingness to find and accept a challenge
- Family background (In particular, researchers think that people whose families have been in business, successfully or not, are most apt to start and run their own businesses.)
- Age (Those who start their own businesses also tend to cluster around certain ages—more than 70 percent are between 24 and 44 years of age; see Figure 5.1.)

Motivation

There must be some motivation to start a business. A person may decide that he or she simply has "had enough" of working and earning a profit for someone else. Another may lose his or her job for some reason and decide to start the business he or she has always wanted rather than to seek another job. Still another person may have an idea for a new product or a new way to sell an existing product. Or the opportunity to go into business may arise suddenly, perhaps as a result of a hobby. For example, Cheryl Strand started baking and decorating cakes from her home while working full time as a word processor at Clemson University. Her cakes became so popular that she soon found herself working through her lunch breaks and late into the night to meet customer demand.

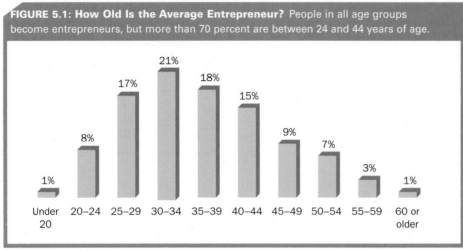

FIGURE 5.1: How Old Is the Average Entrepreneur? People in all age groups become entrepreneurs, but more than 70 percent are between 24 and 44 years of age.

1%	8%	17%	21%	18%	15%	9%	7%	3%	1%
Under 20	20–24	25–29	30–34	35–39	40–44	45–49	50–54	55–59	60 or older

Source: Data developed and provided by the National Federation of Independent Business Foundation and sponsored by the American Express Travel Related Services Company, Inc.

Women as Small-Business Owners

- Women are 51 percent of the U.S. population, and according to the SBA, they owned at least 50 percent of all small businesses in 2008.
- Women already own 66 percent of the home-based businesses in this country, and the number of men in home-based businesses is growing rapidly.
- According to the SBA, 10.4 million women-owned businesses in the United States provide almost 13 million jobs and generate $2 trillion in sales.
- Women-owned businesses in the United States have proven that they are more successful; over 40 percent have been in business for twelve years or more.
- According to Dun and Bradstreet, women-owned businesses are financially sound and creditworthy, and their risk of failure is lower than average.
- Compared to other working women, self-employed women are older, better educated, and have more managerial experience.
- Women are about 57 percent less likely than men to start a business.
- Women with more advanced degrees are more likely to start a business, especially in the financial industries, education and health sectors, and other service categories.
- Just over one-half of small businesses are home-based, and 91 percent have no employees. About 60 percent of home-based businesses are in service industries, 16 percent in construction, 14 percent in retail trade, and the rest in manufacturing, finance, transportation, communications, wholesaling, and other industries.[7]

Teenagers as Small-Business Owners

High-tech teen entrepreneurship is definitely exploding. "There's not a period in history where we've seen such a plethora of young entrepreneurs," comments Nancy F. Koehn, associate professor of business administration at Harvard Business School. Still, teen entrepreneurs face unique pressures in juggling their schoolwork, their social life, and their high-tech workload. Some ultimately quit school, whereas others quit or cut back on their business activities. Consider Brian Hendricks at Winston Churchill High School in Potomac, Maryland. He is the founder of StartUpPc and VB Solutions, Inc. StartUpPc, founded in 2001, sells custom-built computers and computer services for

Winning in a male-dominated world. Meet Heidi Smith Price, president, Spartan Constructors, LLC, of Sugar Hill, Georgia. Recently, Spartan and Heidi Smith Price, has been recognized as one of the fastest growing women owned companies by Womenentrepreneur.com.

home users, home offices, small businesses, and students. Brian's services include design, installation of systems, training, networking, and on-site technical support. In October 2002, Brian founded VB Solutions, Inc., which develops and customizes websites and message boards. The firm sets up advertising contracts and counsels website owners on site improvements. The company has designed corporate ID kits, logos, and websites for clients from all over the world. Brian learned at a very young age that working for yourself is one of the best jobs available. According to Brian, a young entrepreneur must possess "the five P's of entrepreneurship"—planning, persistence, patience, people, and profit. Brian knows what it takes to be a successful entrepreneur. His accolades include Junior Achievement's "National Youth Entrepreneur of the Year" and SBA's 2005 "Young Entrepreneur of the Year" awards.[8]

In some people, the motivation to start a business develops slowly as they gain the knowledge and ability required for success as a business owner. Knowledge and ability—especially management ability—are probably the most important factors involved. A new firm is very much built around the entrepreneur. The owner must be able to manage the firm's finances, its personnel (if there are any employees), and its day-to-day operations. He or she must handle sales, advertising, purchasing, pricing, and a variety of other business functions. The knowledge and ability to do so are acquired most often through experience working for other firms in the same area of business.

Why Some Entrepreneurs and Small Businesses Fail

Small businesses are prone to failure. Capital, management, and planning are the key ingredients in the survival of a small business, as well as the most common reasons for failure. Businesses can experience a number of money-related problems. It may take several years before a business begins to show a profit. Entrepreneurs need to have not only the capital to open a business but also the money to operate it in its possibly lengthy start-up phase. One cash-flow obstacle often leads to others. And a series of cash-flow predicaments usually ends in a business failure. This scenario is played out all too often by small and not-so-small start-up Internet firms that fail to meet their financial backers' expectations and so are denied a second wave of investment dollars to continue their drive to establish a profitable online firm. According to Maureen Borzacchiello, co-owner of Creative Display Solutions, a trade show products company, "Big businesses such as Bear Stearns, Fannie Mae, Freddie Mac and AIG can get bailouts, but small-business owners are on their own when times are tough and credit is tight."

Many entrepreneurs lack the management skills required to run a business. Money, time, personnel, and inventory all need to be managed effectively if a small business is to succeed. Starting a small business requires much more than optimism and a good idea.

Success and expansion sometimes lead to problems. Frequently, entrepreneurs with successful small businesses make the mistake of overexpansion. Fast growth often results in dramatic changes in a business. Thus, the entrepreneur must plan carefully and adjust competently to new and potentially disruptive situations.

Every day, and in every part of the country, people open new businesses. For example, recently, 637,100 new businesses opened their doors, but at the same time, 560,300 businesses closed their business and 28,322 businesses declared bankruptcy. (See Table 5.3.)[9] Although many fail, others represent well-conceived ideas developed by entrepreneurs who have the expertise, resources, and determination to make their businesses succeed. As these well-prepared entrepreneurs pursue their individual goals, our society benefits in many ways from their work and creativity. Such billion-dollar companies as Apple Computer, McDonald's Corporation, and Procter & Gamble are all examples of small businesses that expanded into industry giants.

TABLE 5.3: U.S. Business Start-ups, Closures, and Bankruptcies

	New	Closures	Bankruptcies
2008	N.A.	N.A.	43,500
2007	637,100e	560,300e	28,322
2006	640,800e	587,800e	19,695
2005	644,122	565,745	39,201
2004	628,917	541,047	34,317
2003	612,296	540,658	35,037

e = Advocacy estimate. For a discussion of methodology, see Brian Headd, 2005 (**www.sba.gov/advo/research/rs258tot.pdf**).
N.A. = Not available

Source: U.S. Department of Commerce, Bureau of the Census; Administrative Office of the U.S. Courts; U.S. Department of Labor, Employment and Training Administration, Small Business Administration, Office of Advocacy, *Frequently Asked Questions*, September 2008, www.sba.gov/advo, accessed October 4, 2008, **http://web.sba.gov/faqs/faqIndexAll.cfm?areaid=24**; and SBA *Quarterly Indicators*, First Quarter 2009, released May 8, 2009, p. 1.

The Importance of Small Businesses in Our Economy

3 LEARNING OBJECTIVE

Assess the contributions of small businesses to our economy.

This country's economic history abounds with stories of ambitious men and women who turned their ideas into business dynasties. The Ford Motor Company started as a one-man operation with an innovative method for industrial production. L.L. Bean, Inc., can trace its beginnings to a basement shop in Freeport, Maine. Both Xerox and Polaroid began as small firms with a better way to do a job.

Providing Technical Innovation

Invention and innovation are part of the foundations of our economy. The increases in productivity that have characterized the past 200 years of our history are all rooted in one principal source: new ways to do a job with less effort for less money. Studies show that the incidence of innovation among small-business workers is significantly higher than among workers in large businesses. Small firms produce two and a half times as many innovations as large firms relative to the number of persons employed. In fact, small firms employ 40 percent of all high-tech workers such as scientists, engineers, and computer specialists. No wonder small firms produce thirteen to fourteen times more patents per employee than large patenting firms.[10]

According to the U.S. Office of Management and Budget, more than half the major technological advances of the twentieth century originated with individual inventors and small companies. Even just a sampling of those innovations is remarkable:

- Air conditioning
- Airplane
- Automatic transmission
- FM radio
- Heart valve
- Helicopter
- Instant camera
- Insulin
- Jet engine
- Penicillin
- Personal computer
- Power steering

Concept Check

1. What kinds of factors encourage certain people to start new businesses?

2. What are the major causes of small-business failure? Do these causes also apply to larger businesses?

Lifetime Achievement Award. Meet Al Gross, shown here with the world's first handheld walkie-talkie he built in 1938. Gross invented other wireless devices such as the pager and the cordless telephone. He is the winner of the Lemelson-MIT Lifetime Achievement award for Invention and Innovation. The award recognizes outstanding achievement in invention and innovation by living American inventors and innovators.

Perhaps even more remarkable—and important—is that many of these inventions sparked major new U.S. industries or contributed to an established industry by adding some valuable service.

Providing Employment

Small firms traditionally have added more than their proportional share of new jobs to the economy. Small businesses creating the most new jobs recently included educational and health services. Small firms hire a larger proportion of employees who are younger workers, older workers, women, or workers who prefer to work part time. Furthermore, small businesses provide 67 percent of workers with their first jobs and initial on-the-job training in basic skills. According to the SBA, small businesses represent 99.7 percent of all employers, employ about 50 percent of the private workforce, and provide about two-thirds of the net new jobs added to our economy. Small businesses thus contribute significantly to solving unemployment problems. Note, however, that due to the global economic recession, the U.S. economy lost 2.1 million jobs in the first 3 months of 2009 and a total of 5.7 million between December 2007 and April 2009. The American Recovery and Reinvestment Act of 2009 provides tax incentives and financing opportunities that will help small businesses create more jobs.[11]

Providing Competition

Small businesses challenge larger, established firms in many ways, causing them to become more efficient and more responsive to consumer needs. A small business cannot, of course, compete with a large firm in all respects. But a number of small firms, each competing in its own particular area and its own particular way, together have the desired competitive effect. Thus, several small janitorial companies together add up to reasonable competition for the no-longer-small ServiceMaster.

Filling Needs of Society and Other Businesses

Small firms also provide a variety of goods and services to each other and to much larger firms. Sears, Roebuck purchases merchandise from approximately 12,000 suppliers—and most of them are small businesses. Large firms generally buy parts and assemblies from smaller firms for one very good reason: It is less expensive than manufacturing the parts in their own factories. This lower cost eventually is reflected in the price that consumers pay for their products.

It is clear that small businesses are a vital part of our economy and that, as consumers and as members of the labor force, we all benefit enormously from their existence. Now let us look at the situation from the viewpoint of the owners of small businesses.

Concept Check

1. Briefly describe four contributions of small business to the American economy.

2. Give examples of how small businesses fill needs of society and other businesses.

LEARNING OBJECTIVE 4

Judge the advantages and disadvantages of operating a small business.

The Pros and Cons of Smallness

Do most owners of small businesses dream that their firms will grow into giant corporations—managed by professionals—while they serve only on the board of directors? Or would they rather stay small, in a firm where they have the opportunity (and the responsibility) to do everything that needs to be done? The answers depend on the personal characteristics and motivations of the individual owners. For many, the advantages of remaining small far outweigh the disadvantages.

Advantages of Small Business

Small-business owners with limited resources often must struggle to enter competitive new markets. They also have to deal with increasing international competition. However, they enjoy several unique advantages.

Personal Relationships with Customers and Employees For those who like dealing with people, small business is the place to be. The owners of retail shops get to know many of their customers by name and deal with them on a personal basis. Through such relationships, small-business owners often become involved in the social, cultural, and political life of the community.

Relationships between owner-managers and employees also tend to be closer in smaller businesses. In many cases, the owner is a friend and counselor as well as the boss.

These personal relationships provide an important business advantage. The personal service small businesses offer to customers is a major competitive weapon—one that larger firms try to match but often cannot. In addition, close relationships with employees often help the small-business owner to keep effective workers who might earn more with a larger firm.

Ability to Adapt to Change Being his or her own boss, the owner-manager of a small business does not need anyone's permission to adapt to change. An owner may add or discontinue merchandise or services, change store hours, and experiment with various price strategies in response to changes in market conditions. And through personal relationships with customers, the owners of small businesses quickly become aware of changes in people's needs and interests, as well as in the activities of competing firms.

Simplified Record Keeping Many small firms need only a simple set of records. Record keeping might consist of a checkbook, a cash-receipts journal in which to record all sales, and a cash-disbursements journal in which to record all amounts paid out. Obviously, enough records must be kept to allow for producing and filing accurate tax returns.

Independence Small-business owners do not have to punch in and out, bid for vacation times, take orders from superiors, or worry about being fired or laid off. They are the masters of their own destinies—at least with regard to employment. For many people, this is the prime advantage of owning a small business.

Other Advantages According to the SBA, the most profitable companies in the United States are small firms that have been in business for more than ten years and employ fewer than twenty people. Small-business owners also enjoy all the advantages of sole proprietorships, which were discussed in Chapter 4. These

The Entrepreneurial Sprit

Artsy Etsy

Artists and craftspeople are clicking with customers at the online marketplace Etsy, "your place to buy and sell all things handmade." Founded in 2005, the website hosts more than 250,000 small businesses and lists nearly 2 million artsy items for sale at any one time.

Because Etsy is as much an online community as a retail site, jewelry designers, furniture makers, glassblowers, quilters, potters, and other artisans can really connect with the people who buy their work. "We really want to have that personal interaction in what would normally be an impersonal transaction," an Etsy official explains. "We're trying to reverse the way that business can be done." Just as important, personal interaction via the Internet allows small businesspeople to sell to customers across the continent as easily as they can sell to customers across town.

Artisans pay nothing to set up an online Etsy "shop." They pay Etsy 20 cents per item for a four-month listing and, when the item sells, they pay Etsy a commission of 3.5 percent of the purchase price. Because buying and selling can be done with a few clicks, Artsy Etsy has become a hit with both customers and artisans. As one Etsy artisan says: "My favorite thing about Etsy is that I make a living at it."

Sources: Geoffrey A. Fowler, "How #etsyday Grew on Twitter," *Wall Street Journal*, April 24, 2009, www.wsj.com; Shara Tibken, "Beyond Fair Trade: The Web Has Given Artists an Easier Way to Pursue Their Passions," *Wall Street Journal*, June 16, 2008, p. R9; Thomas Pack, "Web Users Are Getting Crafty," *Information Today*, March 2008, pp. 36–37; Jim Cota, "At Etsy.com, Buyers Meet Their Creative Makers," *Indianapolis Business Journal*, July 7, 2008, p. 38A.

Spotlight

Small-Business Owners' Priorities

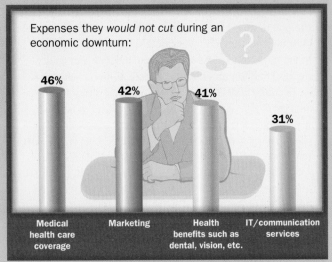

Expenses they *would not cut* during an economic downturn:

- **46%** Medical health care coverage
- **42%** Marketing
- **41%** Health benefits such as dental, vision, etc.
- **31%** IT/communication services

Source: DYMO survey of 187 small-business owners with 100 or fewer employees. By Jae Yang and Alejandro Gonzalez, *USA Today*, January 22, 2009.
Note: Multiple responses allowed.

include being able to keep all profits, the ease and low cost of going into business and (if necessary) going out of business, and being able to keep business information secret.

Disadvantages of Small Business

Personal contacts with customers, closer relationships with employees, being one's own boss, less cumbersome record-keeping chores, and independence are the bright side of small business. In contrast, the dark side reflects problems unique to these firms.

Risk of Failure As we have noted, small businesses (especially new ones) run a heavy risk of going out of business—about two out of three close their doors within the first six years. Older, well-established small firms can be hit hard by a business recession mainly because they do not have the financial resources to weather an extended difficult period.

Limited Potential Small businesses that survive do so with varying degrees of success. Many are simply the means of making a living for the owner and his or her family. The owner may have some technical skill—as a hair stylist or electrician, for example—and may have started a business to put this skill to work. Such a business is unlikely to grow into big business. Also, employees' potential for advancement is limited.

Limited Ability to Raise Capital Small businesses typically have a limited ability to obtain capital. Figure 5.2 shows that most small-business financing

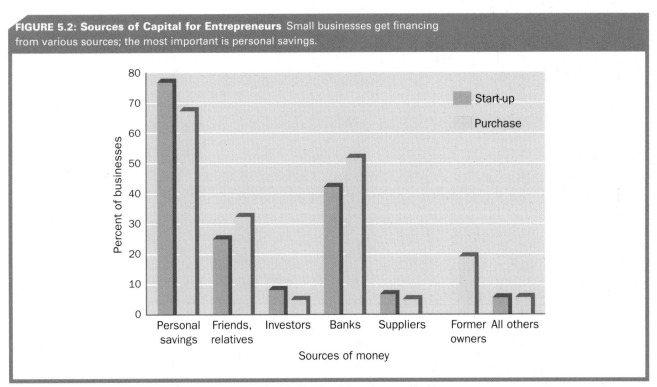

FIGURE 5.2: Sources of Capital for Entrepreneurs Small businesses get financing from various sources; the most important is personal savings.

Source: Data developed and provided by the National Federation of Independent Business Foundation and sponsored by the American Express Travel Related Services Company, Inc.

Getting personal. For those who like dealing with people, small business is the place to be. Here, a business-owner-manager provides personal service with a smile to a happy customer.

comes out of the owner's pocket. Personal loans from lending institutions provide only about one-fourth of the capital required by small businesses. About 50 percent of all new firms begin with less than $30,000 in total capital, according to Census Bureau and Federal Reserve surveys. In fact, almost 36 percent of new firms begin with less than $20,000, usually provided by the owner or family members and friends.[12]

Although every person who considers starting a small business should be aware of the hazards and pitfalls we have noted, a well-conceived business plan may help to avoid the risk of failure. The U.S. government is also dedicated to helping small businesses make it. It expresses this aim most actively through the SBA.

Developing a Business Plan

Lack of planning can be as deadly as lack of money to a new small business. Planning is important to any business, large or small, and never should be overlooked or taken lightly. A **business plan** is a carefully constructed guide for the person starting a business. Consider it as a tool with three basic purposes: communication, management, and planning. As a communication tool, a business plan serves as a concise document that potential investors can examine to see if they would like to invest or assist in financing a new venture. It shows whether a business has the potential to make a profit. As a management tool, the business plan helps to track, monitor, and evaluate the progress. The business plan is a living document; it is modified as the entrepreneur gains knowledge and experience. It also serves to establish timelines and milestones and allows comparison of growth projections against actual accomplishments. Finally, as a planning tool, the business plan guides a businessperson through the various phases of business. For example, the plan helps to identify obstacles to avoid and to establish alternatives. According to Robert Krummer, Jr., chairman of First Business Bank in Los Angeles, "The business plan is a necessity.

business plan a carefully constructed guide for the person starting a business

If the person who wants to start a small business can't put a business plan together, he or she is in trouble."

Components of a Business Plan

Table 5.4 shows the twelve sections that a business plan should include. Each section is further explained at the end of each of the seven major parts in the text. The goal of each end-of-the part exercise is to help a businessperson create his or her own business plan. When constructing a business plan, the businessperson should strive to keep it easy to read, uncluttered, and complete. Like other busy executives, officials of financial institutions do not have the time to wade through pages of extraneous data. The business plan should answer the four questions banking officials and investors are most interested in: (1) What exactly is the nature and mission of the new venture? (2) Why is this new enterprise a good idea? (3) What are the businessperson's goals? (4) How much will the new venture cost?

The great amount of time and consideration that should go into creating a business plan probably will end up saving time later. For example, Sharon Burch, who was running a computer software business while earning a degree in business administration, had to write a business plan as part of one of her courses. Burch has said, "I wish I'd taken the class before I started my business. I see a lot of things I could have done differently. But it has helped me since because I've been using the business plan as a guide for my business." Table 5.5 provides a business plan checklist. Accuracy and realistic expectations are crucial to an effective business plan. It is unethical to deceive loan officers, and it is unwise to deceive yourself.

Concept Check

1. What are the major advantages and disadvantages of smallness in business?

2. What are the major components of a business plan? Why should an individual develop a business plan?

TABLE 5.4: Components of a Business Plan

1. *Introduction.* Basic information such as the name, address, and phone number of the business; the date the plan was issued; and a statement of confidentiality to keep important information away from potential competitors.

2. *Executive Summary.* A one- to two-page overview of the entire business plan, including a justification why the business will succeed.

3. *Benefits to the Community.* Information on how the business will have an impact on economic development, community development, and human development.

4. *Company and Industry.* The background of the company, choice of the legal business form, information on the products or services to be offered, and examination of the potential customers, current competitors, and the business's future.

5. *Management Team.* Discussion of skills, talents, and job descriptions of management team, managerial compensation, management training needs, and professional assistance requirements.

6. *Manufacturing and Operations Plan.* Discussion of facilities needed, space requirements, capital equipment, labor force, inventory control, and purchasing requirement.

7. *Labor Force.* Discussion of the quality of skilled workers available and the training, compensation, and motivation of workers.

8. *Marketing Plan.* Discussion of markets, market trends, competition, market share, pricing, promotion, distribution, and service policy.

9. *Financial Plan.* Summary of the investment needed, sales and cash-flow forecasts, breakeven analysis, and sources of funding.

10. *Exit Strategy.* Discussion of a succession plan or going public. Who will take over the business?

11. *Critical Risks and Assumptions.* Evaluation of the weaknesses of the business and how the company plans to deal with these and other business problems.

12. *Appendix.* Supplementary information crucial to the plan, such as résumés of owners and principal managers, advertising samples, organization chart, and any related information.

Source: Adapted from Timothy S. Hatten, *Small Business Management: Entrepreneurship and Beyond,* 4th ed. Copyright © 2009 by Houghton Mifflin Company, pp. 93–118. Reprinted with permission.

TABLE 5.5: Business Plan Checklist

1. Does the executive summary grab the reader's attention and highlight the major points of the business plan?

2. Does the business-concept section clearly describe the purpose of the business, the customers, the value proposition, and the distribution channel and convey a compelling story?

3. Do the industry and market analyses support acceptance and demand for the business concept in the marketplace and define a first customer in depth?

4. Does the management-team plan persuade the reader that the team could implement the business concept successfully? Does it assure the reader that an effective infrastructure is in place to facilitate the goals and operations of the company?

5. Does the product/service plan clearly provide details on the status of the product, the timeline for completion, and the intellectual property that will be acquired?

6. Does the operations plan prove that the product or service could be produced and distributed efficiently and effectively?

7. Does the marketing plan successfully demonstrate how the company will create customer awareness in the target market and deliver the benefit to the customer?

8. Does the financial plan convince the reader that the business model is sustainable—that it will provide a superior return on investment for the investor and sufficient cash flow to repay loans to potential lenders?

9. Does the growth plan convince the reader that the company has long-term growth potential and spin-off products and services?

10. Does the contingency and exit-strategy plan convince the reader that the risk associated with this venture can be mediated? Is there an exit strategy in place for investors?

Source: Kathleen R. Allen, *Launching New Ventures: An Entrepreneurial Approach*, 5th ed. Copyright © 2009 by Houghton Mifflin Company, p.225. Reprinted with permission.

The Small Business Administration

5 LEARNING OBJECTIVE

Explain how the Small Business Administration helps small businesses.

The **Small Business Administration (SBA)** created by Congress in 1953, is a governmental agency that assists, counsels, and protects the interests of small businesses in the United States. It helps people get into business and stay in business. The agency provides assistance to owners and managers of prospective, new, and established small businesses. Through more than 1,000 offices and resource centers throughout the nation, the SBA provides both financial assistance and management counseling. Recently, the SBA provided training, technical assistance, and education to over 3 million small businesses. It helps small firms to bid for and obtain government contracts, and it helps them to prepare to enter foreign markets.

SBA Management Assistance

Statistics show that most failures in small business are related to poor management. For this reason, the SBA places special emphasis on improving the management ability of the owners and managers of small businesses. The SBA's Management Assistance Program is extensive and diversified. It includes free individual counseling, courses, conferences, workshops, and a wide range of publications. Recently, the SBA provided management and technical assistance to over 1 million small businesses through its 1,100 Small Business Development Centers and 11,200 volunteers from the Service Corps of Retired Executives.[13]

Management Courses and Workshops The management courses offered by the SBA cover all the functions, duties, and roles of managers. Instructors may be teachers from local colleges and universities or other professionals, such as management consultants, bankers, lawyers, and accountants. Fees for these courses are quite low. The most popular such course is a general survey of eight to ten different areas of business management. In follow-up studies, businesspeople may concentrate in-depth on one or more of these areas depending on their particular

Small Business Administration (SBA) a governmental agency that assists, counsels, and protects the interests of small businesses in the United States strengths and weaknesses. The SBA occasionally offers one-day conferences. These conferences are aimed at keeping owner-managers up to date on new management developments, tax laws, and the like. The Small Business Training Network (SBTN) is an online training network consisting of eighty-three SBA-run courses, workshops, and resources. Recently, more than 240,000 small-business owners benefited from SBA's free online business courses.

SCORE Formerly known as the **Service Corps of Retired Executives, SCORE** was created in 1964. Today it's a group of more than 11,200 businesspeople, including over 2,000 women, who volunteer their services to help small businesses. The collective experience of SCORE volunteers, some retired and some still active in business, spans the full range of American enterprise. These volunteers have worked for such notable companies as Eastman Kodak, General Electric, IBM, and Procter & Gamble. Experts in areas of accounting, finance, marketing, engineering, and retailing provide counseling and mentoring to entrepreneurs.

A small-business owner who has a particular problem can request free counseling from a local SCORE office. A counselor sits down with the entrepreneur and together they analyze the situation. If the problem is particularly complex, the counselor may call on other volunteer experts to assist. Finally, the counselor helps the entrepreneur develop a plan to resolve the problem and is available for follow-up assistance and mentoring throughout the process.

Consider the plight of Elizabeth Halvorsen, a mystery writer from Minneapolis. Her husband had built up the family advertising and graphic arts firm for seventeen years when he was called to serve in the Persian Gulf War. The only one left behind who could run the business was Mrs. Halvorsen, who admittedly had no business experience. Enter SCORE. With a SCORE management expert at her side, she kept the business on track. In 2008, SCORE volunteers served 358,000 small-businesspeople like Mrs. Halvorsen and offered over 42,000 online workshops.[14]

Service Corps of Retired Executives (SCORE) a group of businesspeople who volunteer their services to small businesses through the SBA

Help for Minority-Owned Small Businesses

Americans who are members of minority groups have had difficulty entering the nation's economic mainstream. Raising money is a nagging problem for minority business owners, who also may lack adequate training. Members of minority groups are, of course, eligible for all SBA programs, but the SBA makes a special effort to assist those who want to start small businesses or expand existing ones. For example, the Minority Business Development Agency awards grants to develop and increase business opportunities for members of racial and ethnic minorities.

Helping women become entrepreneurs is also a special goal of the SBA. Emily Harrington, one of nine children, was born in Manila, the Philippines. She arrived in the United States in 1972 as a foreign-exchange student. Convinced that there was a market for hard-working, dedicated minorities and women, she launched Qualified Resources International. *Inc.* magazine selected her firm as one of "America's Fastest Growing Private Companies" just six years later. Harrington credits the SBA with giving her the technical support that made her first loan possible.

Nailing down a successful business. Hanh Nguyen is one of a growing number of minority women who are small business owners. Hanh is an entrepreneur from Saigon, Vietnam, who wants her manicure business in Memphis, Tennessee, to succeed. She is determined to adjust to a new lifestyle in America and to learn a new language and the "American Way" of doing business. She even named her business "Kathy's Nails," after her newly adopted first name.

©Tan Kian Khoon/Shutterstock

Finding a SCORE counselor who worked directly with her, she refined her business plan until she got a bank loan. Before contacting the SBA, Harrington was turned down for business loans "by all the banks I approached," even though she worked as a manager of loan credit and collection for a bank. Later, Emily Harrington was SBA's winner of the local, regional, and national Small Business Entrepreneurial Success Award for Rhode Island, the New England region, and the nation! For several years in a row, Qualified Resources, Inc., was named one of the fastest-growing private companies in Rhode Island. Now with over 100 Women's Business Centers, entrepreneurs like Harrington can receive training and technical assistance, access to credit and capital, federal contracts, and international markets. In fiscal 2008, Women's Business Centers counseled or trained more than 145,000 women.[15]

Small-Business Institutes **Small-business institutes (SBIs)** created in 1972, are groups of senior and graduate students in business administration who provide management counseling to small businesses. SBIs have been set up on over 520 college campuses as another way to help business owners. The students work in small groups guided by faculty advisers and SBA management-assistance experts. Like SCORE volunteers, they analyze and help solve the problems of small-business owners at their business establishments.

Small-Business Development Centers **Small-business development centers (SBDCs)** are university-based groups that provide individual counseling and practical training to owners of small businesses. SBDCs draw from the resources of local, state, and federal governments, private businesses, and universities. These groups can provide managerial and technical help, data from research studies, and other types of specialized assistance of value to small businesses. In 2009, there were over 1,100 SBDC locations, primarily at colleges and universities, assisting people such as Kathleen DuBois. After scribbling a list of her abilities and the names of potential clients on a napkin in a local restaurant, Kathleen DuBois decided to start her own marketing firm. Beth Thornton launched her engineering firm after a discussion with a colleague in the ladies room of the Marriott. When Richard Shell was laid off after twenty years of service with Nisource (Columbia Gas), he searched the Internet tirelessly before finding the right franchise option. Introduced by mutual friends, Jim Bostic and Denver McMillion quickly connected, built a high level of trust, and combined their diverse professional backgrounds to form a manufacturing company. Although these entrepreneurs took different routes in starting their new businesses in West Virginia, all of them turned to the West Virginia Small Business Development Center for the technical assistance to make their dreams become a reality. In Fiscal 2008, Small Business Development Centers served more than 600,000 entrepreneurs nationwide.[16]

SBA Publications The SBA issues management, marketing, and technical publications dealing with hundreds of topics of interest to present and prospective managers of small firms. Most of these publications are available from the SBA free of charge. Others can be obtained for a small fee from the U.S. Government Printing Office.

SBA Financial Assistance

Small businesses seem to be constantly in need of money. An owner may have enough capital to start and operate the business. But then he or she may require more money to finance increased operations during peak selling seasons, to pay for required pollution control equipment, to finance an expansion, or to mop up after a natural disaster such as a flood or a terrorist attack. For

small-business institutes (SBIs) groups of senior and graduate students in business administration who provide management counseling to small businesses

small-business development centers (SBDCs) university-based groups that provide individual counseling and practical training to owners of small businesses

venture capital money that is invested in small (and sometimes struggling) firms that have the potential to become very successful

small-business investment companies (SBICs) privately owned firms that provide venture capital to small enterprises that meet their investment standards

franchise a license to operate an individually owned business as though it were part of a chain of outlets or stores

Concept Check

1. Identify six ways in which the SBA provides management assistance to small businesses.

2. Identify two ways in which the SBA provides financial assistance to small businesses.

3. Why does the SBA concentrate on providing management and financial assistance to small business?

4. What is venture capital? How does the SBA help small businesses to obtain it?

LEARNING OBJECTIVE 6

Appraise the concept and types of franchising.

franchising the actual granting of a franchise

franchisor an individual or organization granting a franchise

franchisee a person or organization purchasing a franchise

example, the Supplemental Terrorist Activity Relief (STAR) program has made $3.7 billion in loans to 8,202 small businesses harmed or disrupted by the September 11 terrorist attacks. In October 2005, the SBA guaranteed loans of up to $150,000 to small businesses affected by Hurricanes Katrina and Rita. Since the 2005 hurricanes, SBA has made more than $4.9 billion in disaster loans to 102,903 homeowners and renters in the Gulf region. Businesses in the area received 16,828 business disaster loans with disbursements worth $1.5 billion.[17] The SBA offers special financial-assistance programs that cover all these situations. However, its primary financial function is to guarantee loans to eligible businesses.

Regular Business Loans Most of the SBA's business loans are actually made by private lenders such as banks, but repayment is partially guaranteed by the agency. That is, the SBA may guarantee that it will repay the lender up to 90 percent of the loan if the borrowing firm cannot repay it. Guaranteed loans approved on or after October 1, 2002, may be as large as $1.5 million (this loan limit may be increased in the future). The average size of an SBA-guaranteed business loan is about $300,000, and its average duration is about eight years.

Small-Business Investment Companies Venture capital is money that is invested in small (and sometimes struggling) firms that have the potential to become very successful. In many cases, only a lack of capital keeps these firms from rapid and solid growth. The people who invest in such firms expect that their investments will grow with the firms and become quite profitable.

The popularity of these investments has increased over the past thirty years, but most small firms still have difficulty obtaining venture capital. To help such businesses, the SBA licenses, regulates, and provides financial assistance to **small-business investment companies (SBICs)**.

An SBIC is a privately owned firm that provides venture capital to small enterprises that meet its investment standards. Such small firms as America Online, Apple Computer, Federal Express, Compaq Computer, Intel Corporation, Outback Steakhouse, and Staples, Inc., all were financed through SBICs during their initial growth period. SBICs are intended to be profit-making organizations. The aid the SBA offers allows them to invest in small businesses that otherwise would not attract venture capital. Since Congress created the program in 1958, SBICs have financed over 102,000 small businesses for a total of over $50.6 billion.[18]

We have discussed the importance of the small-business segment of our economy. We have weighed the advantages and drawbacks of operating a small business as compared with a large one. But is there a way to achieve the best of both worlds? Can one preserve one's independence as a business owner and still enjoy some of the benefits of "bigness"? Let's take a close look at franchising.

Franchising

A **franchise** is a license to operate an individually owned business as if it were part of a chain of outlets or stores. Often, the business itself is also called a *franchise*. Among the most familiar franchises are McDonald's, H & R Block, AAMCO Transmissions, GNC (General Nutrition Centers), and Dairy Queen. Many other franchises carry familiar names; this method of doing business has become very popular in the last thirty years or so. It is an attractive means of starting and operating a small business.

What Is Franchising?

Franchising is the actual granting of a franchise. A **franchisor** is an individual or organization granting a franchise. A **franchisee** is a person or organization purchasing a franchise. The franchisor supplies a known and advertised business name, management skills, the required training and materials, and a method of doing business. The franchisee supplies labor and capital, operates the franchised business, and agrees to abide by the provisions of the franchise agreement. Table 5.6 lists the basic franchisee rights and obligations that would be covered in a typical franchise agreement.

Types of Franchising

Franchising arrangements fall into three general categories. In the first approach, a manufacturer authorizes a number of retail stores to sell a certain brand-name item. This type of franchising arrangement, one of the oldest, is prevalent in sales of passenger cars and trucks, farm equipment, shoes, paint, earth-moving equipment, and petroleum. About 90 percent of all gasoline is sold through franchised, independent retail service stations, and franchised dealers handle virtually all sales of new cars and trucks. In the second type of franchising arrangement, a producer licenses distributors to sell a given product to retailers. This

©Susan Van Etten

The growth of franchising. Franchising is designed to provide a tested formula for success, along with ongoing advice and training. The franchiser, such as Starbucks, supplies a known and advertised business name, management skills, the required training and materials and a method of doing business. Franchising, however, is not a guarantee of success for either franchisees or fanchisors.

TABLE 5.6: Basic Rights and Obligations Delineated in a Franchise Agreement

Franchisee obligations include:	Franchisee rights include:
1. to carry on the business franchised and no other business upon the approved and nominated premises.	1. use of trademarks, trade names and patents of the franchisor.
2. to observe certain minimum operating hours.	2. use of the brand image and the design and decor of the premises developed by the franchisor.
3. to pay a franchise fee.	3. use of the franchisor's secret methods.
4. to follow the accounting system laid down by the franchisor.	4. use of the franchisor's copyright materials.
5. not to advertise without prior approval of the advertisements by the franchisor.	5. use of recipes, formulae, specifications, processes, and methods of manufacture developed by the franchisor.
6. to use and display such point of sale advertising materials as the franchisor stipulates.	6. conducting the franchised business upon or from the agreed premises strictly in accordance with the franchisor's methods and subject to the franchisor's directions.
7. to maintain the premises in good, clean and sanitary condition and to redecorate when required to do so by the franchisor.	7. guidelines established by the franchisor regarding exclusive territorial rights.
8. to maintain the widest possible insurance coverage.	8. rights to obtain suppliers from nominated suppliers at special prices.
9. to permit the franchisor's staff to enter the premises to inspect and see if the franchisor's standards are being maintained.	
10. to purchase goods or products from the franchisor or his designated suppliers.	
11. to train your staff in the franchisor's methods to ensure that they are neatly and appropriately clothed.	
12. not to assign the franchise contract without the franchisor's consent.	

Source: Excerpted from the SBA's "Is Franchising for Me?" accessed on January 5, 2009 from **http://www.sba.gov**.

Concept Check

1. Explain the relationships among a franchise, the franchisor, and the franchisee.

2. Describe the three general categories of franchising arrangements.

arrangement is common in the soft-drink industry. Most national manufacturers of soft-drink syrups—The Coca-Cola Company, Dr. Pepper/Seven-Up Companies, PepsiCo, Royal Crown Companies, Inc.—franchise independent bottlers who then serve retailers. In a third form of franchising, a franchisor supplies brand names, techniques, or other services instead of a complete product. Although the franchisor may provide certain production and distribution services, its primary role is the careful development and control of marketing strategies. This approach to franchising, which is the most typical today, is used by Holiday Inns, Howard Johnson Company, AAMCO Transmissions, McDonald's, Dairy Queen, Avis, Hertz Corporation, KFC (Kentucky Fried Chicken), and SUBWAY, to name but a few.

LEARNING OBJECTIVE 7

Analyze the growth of franchising and franchising's advantages and disadvantages.

The Growth of Franchising

Franchising, which began in the United States around the time of the Civil War, was used originally by large firms, such as the Singer Sewing Company, to distribute their products. Franchising has been increasing steadily in popularity since the early 1900s, primarily for filling stations and car dealerships; however, this retailing strategy has experienced enormous growth since the mid-1970s. The franchise proliferation generally has paralleled the expansion of the fast-food industry. As Table 5.7 shows, five of *Entrepreneur* magazine's top-rated franchises for 2009 were in this category.

TABLE 5.7: Entrepreneur's Top Ten Franchises in 2009

Rank	Franchise	Total Investment	Franchise Fee	Royalty Fee	Net-Worth Requirement	Cash Requirement	Comments
1.	SUBWAY	$78,600–$238,300	$15,000	8%	$30,000–$90,000	$80,000–$310,000	20-year renewable term
2.	McDonald's	$950,200–$1,800,000	$45,000	12.5%+		$300,000	20-year renewable
3.	Liberty Tax Service	$56,800–$69,900	$40,000	Varies		$50,000	Perpetual, renewable
4.	Sonic Drive In Restaurants	$1,200,000–$3,200,000	$45,000	2–5%	$1,000,000	$500,000	20-year renewable
5.	Inter-Continental Hotels Group	Varies	Varies	5%			10-year (average), renewable
6.	Ace Hardware Corp.	$400,000–$1,100,000	$5,000		$400,000	$250,000	Term of Agreement, not renewable
7.	Pizza Hut Inc.	$638,000–$2,970,000	$25,000	6.5%	$1,000,000	$360,000	Term of Agreement, not renewable
8.	UPS Store, The Mail Boxes Etc.	$171,200–$280,000	$29,950	5%	$150,000	$60,000–$100,000	10-year, renewable
9.	Circle K	$161,000–$1,400,000	$15,000	4%			10-year, renewable
10.	Papa John's Int'l. Inc.	$135,800–$491,600	$25,000	5%	$250,000		10-year, renewable

Of course, franchising is not limited to fast foods. Hair salons, tanning parlors, and dentists and lawyers are expected to participate in franchising arrangements in growing numbers. Franchised health clubs, pest exterminators, and campgrounds are already widespread, as are franchised tax preparers and travel agencies. The real estate industry also has experienced a rapid increase in franchising.

Also, franchising is attracting more women and minority business owners in the United States than ever before. One reason is that special outreach programs designed to encourage franchisee diversity have developed. Consider Angela Trammel, a young mother of two. She had been laid off from her job at the Marriott after 9/11. Since she was a member of a Curves Fitness Center and liked the concept of empowering women to become physically fit, she began researching the cost of purchasing a Curves franchise and ways to finance the business. "I was online looking for financing, and I linked to Enterprise Development Group in Washington, D.C. I knew that they had diverse clients." The cost for the franchise was $19,500, but it took $60,000 to open the doors to her fitness center. "Applying for a loan to start the business was much harder than buying a house," said Trammel. Just three years later, Angela and her husband, Ernest, own three Curves Fitness Centers with twelve employees. Recently, giving birth to her third child, she has found the financial freedom and flexibility needed to care for her busy family. In fact, within a three-year period, the Trammel's grew their annual household income from $80,000 to $250,000.[19] Franchisors such as Wendy's, McDonald's, Burger King, and Church's Chicken all have special corporate programs to attract minority and women franchisees. Just as important, successful women and minority franchisees are willing to get involved by offering advice and guidance to new franchisees.

Herman Petty, the first black McDonald's franchisee, remembers that the company provided a great deal of help while he worked to establish his first units. In turn, Petty traveled to help other black franchisees, and he invited new franchisees to gain hands-on experience in his Chicago restaurants before starting their own establishments. Petty also organized a support group, the National Black McDonald's Operators Association, to help black franchisees in other areas. Today, this support group has thirty-three local chapters and more than 330 members across the country. "We are really concentrating on helping our operators to be successful both operationally and financially," says Craig Welburn, the McDonald's franchisee who leads the group.

Dual-branded franchises, in which two franchisors offer their products together, are a new small-business trend. For example, in 1993, pleased with the success of its first cobranded restaurant with Texaco in Beebe, Arkansas, McDonald's now has over 400 cobranded restaurants in the United States. Also, an agreement between franchisors Doctor's Associates, Inc., and TCBY Enterprises, Inc., now allows franchisees to sell SUBWAY sandwiches and TCBY yogurt in the same establishment.

Are Franchises Successful?

Franchising is designed to provide a tested formula for success, along with ongoing advice and training. The success rate for businesses owned and operated by franchisees is significantly higher than the success rate for other independently owned small businesses. In a recent nationwide Gallup poll of 944 franchise owners, 94 percent of franchisees indicated that they were very or somewhat successful, only 5 percent believed that they were very unsuccessful or somewhat unsuccessful, and 1 percent did not know. Despite these impressive statistics, franchising is not a guarantee of success for either franchisees or franchisors. Too rapid expansion, inadequate capital or management skills, and a host of other problems can cause failure for both franchisee and franchisor. Thus, for example, the Dizzy Dean's Beef and Burger franchise is no longer in business. Timothy Bates, a Wayne State University economist, warns, "Despite the hype that franchising is the safest way to go when starting a new business, the research just doesn't bear that out." Just consider Boston Chicken, which once had more than 1,200 restaurants before declaring bankruptcy in 1998.

Brand marriage made in heaven. According to Chuck Rawley, president and chief operating officer of Kentucky Fried Chicken, "KFC/A&W brands merge well. Both have a strong signature product: KFC's fried chicken and A&W's root beer floats. There is a lot of similarities with both established brands that are old yet contemporary."

Advantages of Franchising

Franchising plays a vital role in our economy and soon may become the dominant form of retailing. Why? Because franchising offers advantages to both the franchisor and the franchisee.

To the Franchisor The franchisor gains fast and well-controlled distribution of its products without incurring the high cost of constructing and operating its own outlets. The franchisor thus has more capital available to expand production and to use for advertising. At the same time, it can ensure, through the franchise agreement, that outlets are maintained and operated according to its own standards.

The franchisor also benefits from the fact that the franchisee—a sole proprietor in most cases—is likely to be very highly motivated to succeed. The success of the franchise means more sales, which translate into higher royalties for the franchisor.

To the Franchisee The franchisee gets the opportunity to start a business with limited capital and to make use of the business experience of others. Moreover, an outlet with a nationally advertised name, such as Radio Shack, McDonald's, or Century 21 Real Estate, has guaranteed customers as soon as it opens.

If business problems arise, the franchisor gives the franchisee guidance and advice. This counseling is primarily responsible for the very high degree of success enjoyed by franchises. In most cases, the franchisee does not pay for such help.

The franchisee also receives materials to use in local advertising and can take part in national promotional campaigns sponsored by the franchisor. McDonald's and its franchisees, for example, constitute one of the nation's top twenty purchasers of advertising. Finally, the franchisee may be able to minimize the cost of advertising, supplies, and various business necessities by purchasing them in cooperation with other franchisees.

Disadvantages of Franchising

The main disadvantage of franchising affects the franchisee, and it arises because the franchisor retains a great deal of control. The franchisor's contract can dictate every aspect of the business: decor, design of employee uniforms, types of signs, and all the details of business operations. All Burger King French fries taste the same because all Burger King franchisees have to make them the same way.

Contract disputes are the cause of many lawsuits. For example, Rekha Gabhawala, a Dunkin' Donuts franchisee in Milwaukee, alleged that the franchisor was forcing her out of business so that the company could profit by reselling the downtown franchise to someone else; the company, on the other hand, alleged that Gabhawala breached the contract by not running the business according to company standards. In another case, Dunkin' Donuts sued Chris Romanias, its franchisee in Pennsylvania, alleging that Romanias intentionally underreported gross sales to the company. Romanias, on the other hand, alleged that Dunkin' Donuts, Inc., breached the contract because it failed to provide assistance in operating the franchise. Other franchisees claim that contracts are unfairly tilted toward the franchisors. Yet others have charged that they lost their franchise and investment because their franchisor would not approve the sale of the business when they found a buyer.

To arbitrate disputes between franchisors and franchisees, the National Franchise Mediation Program was established in 1993 by thirty member firms, including Burger King Corporation, McDonald's Corporation, and Wendy's International, Inc. Negotiators have since resolved numerous cases through mediation. Recently, Carl's Jr. brought in one of its largest franchisees to help set its system straight, making most franchisees happy for the first time in years. The program also helped PepsiCo settle a long-term contract dispute and renegotiate its franchise agreements.

Because disagreements between franchisors and franchisees have increased in recent years, many franchisees have been demanding government regulation of franchising. In 1997, to avoid government regulation, some of the largest franchisors proposed a new self-policing plan to the Federal Trade Commission.

Franchise holders pay for their security, usually with a one-time franchise fee and continuing royalty and advertising fees, collected as a percentage of sales. As Table 5.7 shows, a McDonald's franchisee pays an initial franchise fee of $45,000, and an annual royalty fee of 12.5+ percent of gross sales. In Table 5.7, you can see how much money a franchisee needs to start a new franchise for selected organizations. In some fields, franchise agreements are not uniform. One franchisee may pay more than another for the same services.

Even success can cause problems. Sometimes a franchise is so successful that the franchisor opens its own outlet nearby, in direct competition—although franchisees may fight back. For example, a court recently ruled that Burger King could not enter into direct competition with the franchisee because the contract was not specific on the issue. A spokesperson for one franchisor contends that the company "gives no geographical protection" to its franchise holders and thus is free to move in on them. Franchise operators work hard. They often put in ten- and twelve-hour days, six days a week. The International Franchise Association advises prospective franchise purchasers to investigate before investing and to approach buying a franchise cautiously. Franchises vary widely in approach as well as in products. Some, such as Dunkin' Donuts and Baskin-Robbins, demand long hours. Others, such as Great Clips hair salons and Albert's Family Restaurants, are more appropriate for those who do not want to spend many hours at their stores.

Global Perspectives in Small Business

For small American businesses, the world is becoming smaller. National and international economies are growing more and more interdependent as political leadership and national economic directions change and trade barriers diminish or disappear. Globalization and instant worldwide communications are rapidly shrinking distances at the same time that they are expanding business opportunities. According to a recent study, the Internet is increasingly important to small-business strategic thinking, with more than 50 percent of those surveyed indicating that the Internet represented their most favored strategy for growth. This was more than double the next-favored choice, strategic alliances reflecting the opportunity to reach both global and domestic customers. The Internet and online payment systems enable even very small businesses to serve international customers. In fact, technology now gives small businesses the leverage and power to reach markets that were once limited solely to large corporations. No wonder the number of businesses exporting their goods and services has tripled since 1990, with two-thirds of that boom coming from companies with fewer than twenty employees.[20]

The SBA offers help to the nation's small-business owners who want to enter the world markets. The SBA's efforts include counseling small firms on how and where to market overseas, matching U.S. small-business executives with potential overseas customers, and helping exporters to secure financing. The agency brings small U.S. firms into direct contact with potential overseas buyers and partners. The SBA International Trade Loan program provides guarantees of up to $1.75 million in loans to small-business owners. These loans help small firms in expanding or developing new export markets. The U.S. Commercial Service, a Commerce Department division, aids small and medium-sized businesses in selling overseas. The division's global network includes over 109 offices in the United States and 151 others in eighty-three countries around the world.[21]

International trade will become more important to small-business owners as they face unique challenges in the new century. Small businesses, which are expected to remain the dominant form of organization in this country, must be prepared to adapt to significant demographic and economic changes in the world marketplace.

This chapter ends our discussion of American business today. From here on, we shall be looking closely at various aspects of business operations. We begin, in the next chapter, with a discussion of management—what management is, what managers do, and how they work to coordinate the basic economic resources within a business organization.

Concept Check

1. What does the franchisor receive in a franchising agreement? What does the franchisee receive? What does each provide?

2. Cite one major benefit of franchising for the franchisor. Cite one major benefit of franchising for the franchisee.

3. How does the SBA help small business-owners who want to enter the world markets?

SUMMARY

1 Define what a small business is and recognize the fields in which small businesses are concentrated.

A small business is one that is independently owned and operated for profit and is not dominant in its field. There are about 23 million businesses in this country, and more than 90 percent of them are small businesses. Small businesses employ more than half the nation's workforce, even though about 70 percent of new businesses can be expected to fail within five years. More than half of all small businesses are in retailing and services.

2 Identify the people who start small businesses and the reasons why some succeed and many fail.

Such personal characteristics as independence, desire to create a new enterprise, and willingness to accept a challenge may encourage individuals to start small businesses. Various external circumstances, such as special expertise or even the loss of a job, also can supply the motivation to strike out on one's own. Poor planning and lack of capital and management experience are the major causes of small-business failures.

3 Assess the contributions of small businesses to our economy.

Small businesses have been responsible for a wide variety of inventions and innovations, some of which have given rise to new industries. Historically, small businesses have created the bulk of the nation's new jobs. Further, they have mounted effective competition to larger firms. They provide things that society needs, act as suppliers to larger firms, and serve as customers of other businesses, both large and small.

4 Judge the advantages and disadvantages of operating a small business.

The advantages of smallness in business include the opportunity to establish personal relationships with customers and employees, the ability to adapt to changes quickly, independence, and simplified record keeping. The major disadvantages are the high risk of failure, the limited potential for growth, and the limited ability to raise capital.

5 Explain how the Small Business Administration helps small businesses.

The Small Business Administration (SBA) was created in 1953 to assist and counsel the nation's millions of small-business owners. The SBA offers management courses and workshops; managerial help, including one-to-one counseling through SCORE; various publications; and financial assistance through guaranteed loans and SBICs. It places special emphasis on aid to minority-owned businesses, including those owned by women.

6 Appraise the concept and types of franchising.

A franchise is a license to operate an individually owned business as though it were part of a chain. The franchisor provides a known business name, management skills, a method of doing business, and the training and required materials. The franchisee contributes labor and capital, operates the franchised business, and agrees to abide by the provisions of the franchise agreement. There are three major categories of franchise agreements.

7 Analyze the growth of franchising and franchising's advantages and disadvantages.

Franchising has grown tremendously since the mid-1970s. The franchisor's major advantage in franchising is fast and well-controlled distribution of products with minimal capital outlay.

In return, the franchisee has the opportunity to open a business with limited capital, to make use of the business experience of others, and to sell to an existing clientele. For this, the franchisee usually must pay both an initial franchise fee and a continuing royalty based on sales. He or she also must follow the dictates of the franchise with regard to operation of the business.

Worldwide business opportunities are expanding for small businesses. The SBA assists small-business owners in penetrating foreign markets. The next century will present unique challenges and opportunities for small-business owners.

KEY TERMS

You should now be able to define and give an example relevant to each of the following terms:

small business (128)
business plan (139)
Small Business Administration (SBA) (141)

Service Corps of Retired Executives (SCORE) (142)
small-business institutes (SBIs) (143)

small-business development centers (SBDCs) (143)
venture capital (144)
small-business investment companies (SBICs) (144)

franchise (144)
franchising (144)
franchisor (144)
franchisee (144)

DISCUSSION QUESTIONS

1. Most people who start small businesses are aware of the high failure rate and the reasons for it. Why, then, do some take no steps to protect their firms from failure? What steps should they take?
2. Are the so-called advantages of small business really advantages? Wouldn't every small-business owner like his or her business to grow into a large firm?
3. Do average citizens benefit from the activities of the SBA, or is the SBA just another way to spend our tax money?
4. Would you rather own your own business independently or become a franchisee? Why?

Get Flash Cards, Quizzes, Games, Crosswords and more @ www.cengage.com/introbusiness/pride

Test Yourself

Matching Questions

1. _____ A carefully constructed guide for the person starting a business.
2. _____ A group of business people who volunteer their services to small businesses through the SBA.
3. _____ A government agency that assists, counsels, and protects the interests of small businesses in the United States.
4. _____ Money that is invested in small (and sometimes struggling) firms that have the potential to become very successful.
5. _____ Group of senior and graduate students in business administration who provide management counseling to small businesses.
6. _____ A business that is independently owned and operated for profit and is not dominant in its field.
7. _____ A person or organization purchasing a franchise.
8. _____ A license to operate an individually owned business as though it were a part of a chain of outlets or stores.
9. _____ The actual granting of a franchise.

Test Yourself

10. _____ An individual or organization granting a franchise.

  a. venture capital
  b. franchisee
  c. joint venture
  d. Small Business Institutes (SBIs)
  e. SCORE
  f. small business
  g. franchise
  h. strategic alliance
  i. business plan
  j. franchising
  k. S.B.A.
  l. franchisor

True False Questions

11. **T F** The SBA has defined a small business as one independently owned, operated for profit, and not dominant in its field.

12. **T F** The various types of businesses attracting small business are generally grouped into service industries, distribution industries, and financial industries.

13. **T F** Small businesses are generally managed by professional managers.

14. **T F** Small firms have traditionally added more than their proportional share of new jobs to the economy.

15. **T F** Economically, the U.S. government is not concerned with whether or not small businesses make it.

16. **T F** SCORE is a group of business executives offering their services to small businesses for a fee.

17. **T F** A small-business investment company (SBIC) is a government agency that provides venture capital to small enterprises.

18. **T F** The purchaser of a franchise is called the franchisor.

19. **T F** An agreement between two franchisees in which the two franchisees offer their products together is called double franchising.

20. **T F** International trade will become more important to small-business owners in the new century.

Multiple-Choice Questions

21. _____ What is the primary reason that so many new businesses fail?

  a. Owner does not work hard enough
  b. Mismanagement resulting from lack of business know-how
  c. Low employee quality for new businesses
  d. Lack of brand-name recognition
  e. Inability to compete with well-established brand names

22. _____ Businesses such as flower shops, restaurants, bed and breakfasts, and automobile repair are good candidates for entrepreneurs because they

  a. do not require any skills.
  b. are the most likely to succeed.
  c. can obtain financing easily.
  d. require no special equipment.
  e. have a relatively low initial investment.

23. _____ An individual's desire to create a new business is referred to as

  a. the entrepreneurial spirit.
  b. the desire for ownership.
  c. self-determination.
  d. self-evaluation.
  e. the laissez-faire spirit.

24. _____ What is a common mistake that small-business owners make when their businesses begin growing?

  a. They sell more goods and services.
  b. They put too much money in advertising.
  c. They move beyond their local area.
  d. They overexpand without proper planning.
  e. They invest too much of their own money.

25. _____ The fact that insulin and power steering both originated with individual inventors and small companies is testimony to the power of small businesses as providers of

  a. employment.
  b. competition.
  c. technical innovation.
  d. capital.
  e. quality products.

26. _____ In her small retail shop, Jocelyn knows most of her best customers by name and knows their preferences in clothing and shoes. This demonstrates which advantage of a small business?

  a. Ability to adapt to change
  b. Independence from customer's desires
  c. Simplified record keeping
  d. Personal relationships with customers
  e. Small customer base

Test Yourself

27. _____ Your friend, Shonta, started a graphic design firm about a year ago. The business has done well, but it needs a lot more equipment, computers, and employees to continue expanding. Shonta does not see any problem because she thinks she can easily get all the money she will need from her local bank. What advice might you give to her?

   a. She is right—the bank is likely to lend her as much as she needs because banks primarily focus on supporting small businesses.
   b. She is crazy—banks do not lend money to small businesses but only to well-known, well-established organizations.
   c. She should sell her business immediately before it fails because most small businesses fail during the first five years.
   d. She should not accept any new clients so that she can end the need to add additional equipment and employees.
   e. She should consider alternative sources of financing because banks provide only about one-fourth of the total capital to small businesses.

28. _____ Volunteers for SCORE are

   a. mostly university business professors.
   b. active franchisors from large corporations.
   c. generally either lawyers or accountants.
   d. graduate business students working on projects.
   e. businesspeople from different industries.

29. _____ An individual or organization granting a license to operate an individually owned business as though it were part of a chain of outlets or stores is a(n)

   a. franchise.
   b. franchisor.
   c. franchisee.
   d. venture capitalist.
   e. entrepreneur.

30. _____ Manju Iyer asks for your advice in opening a new business. She plans to provide tax-related services to individuals and small-business owners in her community. Of course, she wants an attractive means of starting and operating her business with a reasonable hope of succeeding in it. What will be your advice?

   a. Start your own independent business.
   b. Form a partnership with a CPA.
   c. Consider purchasing a franchise.
   d. Forget about opening the business because it is too risky.
   e. First secure a loan from the Small Business Administration.

Answers on p. TY-1.

VIDEO CASE

No Funny Business at Newbury Comics

The two college students who started Newbury Comics have become serious business owners. Mike Dreese and John Brusger started Newbury Comics in 1978 with $2,000 and a valuable comic book collection. Their first store was actually a tiny apartment on Boston's popular Newbury Street, which they rented for $260 per month. Three decades later, the company operates twenty-six stores in Massachusetts, Maine, New Hampshire, and Rhode Island. It still does business on Newbury Street—in a spacious storefront that rents for $23,000 per month.

How did Newbury Comics grow into a multimillion-dollar business? First, the owners identified a need that they could fill. They understood what kind of comic books collectors were interested in buying, and they enjoyed dealing with these customers. They also realized that customer needs can change, which is why they have tested hundreds of new items over the years.

Second, Dreese and Brusger thought of their business as a business. As much as they liked comics, they recognized the profit potential of carrying other products. Over time, they started stocking music and added movies, novelty items, and clothing accessories. They were among the first U.S. stores to import recordings by European groups such as U2. Today, comic books account for only a fraction of Newbury Comics' revenue, whereas CDs and DVDs account for about 70 percent of the revenue.

Third, the entrepreneurs didn't do everything themselves—they knew when to delegate to others. As Newbury Comics expanded beyond comics and opened new stores, the owners hired professionals to negotiate leases, make buying decisions, and select the exact merchandise assortment for each store. They also hired technology experts to design systems for tracking what was in stock, what had been sold, how much the company was spending, and how much each store was contributing to total sales. Now, if a new CD or DVD is selling particularly well, the buyer will know within three minutes—in plenty of time to reorder and satisfy customer demand.

Fourth, Dreese and Brusger have paid close attention to Newbury Comics' financial situation. They're careful to pay suppliers on time, and in exchange, they can get fast-selling products even when supplies are limited. Consider what happened during the Pokemon fad. Newbury Comics originally ordered a small quantity of cards, which quickly sold out. Every time it placed another order, it sent the supplier a check by express delivery. By the height of the fad, when demand was so high that the supplier could not fill every retailer's order, Newbury Comics still got its shipment. By the time the fad faded, the company had sold $4 million worth of Pokemon cards and made more than $2 million in profits.

Newbury Comics remains profitable, although Dreese notes that sales growth has slowed during the past few years. As a result, he says, "We have all had to grow up a little" and improve the way Newbury Comics operates. The company has formalized its store payroll budgets, assigned employees to check the quality of customer service at each store, and begun offering more products for sale online.

Despite the company's success, Dreese does not expect to expand beyond New England. A new superstore has opened in nearby Norwood, but he knows that a key strength is being able to restock quickly—and that means locating stores within a half-day's drive of the distribution center in Brighton, Massachusetts. Because Newbury Comics owns six trucks, it can resupply every store at least three times a week. Many competitors are far bigger, but no competitor knows its customers and its products better than the team at Newbury Comics.[22]

For more information about this company, go to www.newburycomics.com.

Questions

1. This chapter cites five advantages of small business. Which of these seems to apply to the owners' experience with Newbury Comics?
2. This chapter cites three disadvantages of small business. Based on what you know of Newbury Comics, which of these is likely to be the biggest problem in the coming years?
3. Newbury Comics was started without a formal business plan. If you were writing its plan today, what critical risks and assumptions would you examine—and why?

BUILDING SKILLS FOR CAREER SUCCESS

1. EXPLORING THE INTERNET

Perhaps the most challenging difficulty for small businesses is operating with scarce resources, especially people and money. To provide information and point small-business operators in the right direction, many Internet sites offer helpful products and services. Although most are sponsored by advertising and may be free of charge, some charge a fee, and others are a combination of both. The SBA within the U.S. Department of Commerce provides a wide array of free information and resources. You can find your way to the SBA through www.sbaonline.sba.gov or www.sba.gov. Visit the text website for updates to this exercise.

Assignment
1. Describe the various services provided by the SBA site.
2. What sources of funding are there?
3. What service would you like to see improved? How?

2. BUILDING TEAM SKILLS

A business plan is a written statement that documents the nature of a business and how that business intends to achieve its goals. Although entrepreneurs should prepare a business plan *before* starting a business, the plan also serves as an effective guide later on. The plan should concisely describe the business's mission, the amount of capital it requires, its target market, competition, resources, production plan, marketing plan, organizational plan, assessment of risk, and financial plan.

Assignment
1. Working in a team of four students, identify a company in your community that would benefit from using a business plan, or create a scenario in which a hypothetical entrepreneur wants to start a business.

2. Using the resources of the library or the Internet and/or interviews with business owners, write a business plan incorporating the information in Table 5.4.
3. Present your business plan to the class.

3. RESEARCHING DIFFERENT CAREERS

Many people dream of opening and operating their own businesses. Are you one of them? To be successful, entrepreneurs must have certain characteristics; their profiles generally differ from those of people who work for someone else. Do you know which personal characteristics make some entrepreneurs succeed and others fail? Do you fit the successful entrepreneur's profile? What is your potential for opening and operating a successful small business?

Assignment
1. Use the resources of the library or the Internet to establish what a successful entrepreneur's profile is and to determine whether your personal characteristics fit that profile. Internet addresses that can help you are www.smartbiz.com/sbs/arts/ieb1.html and www.sba.gov (see "Start your Business" and "FAQ"). These sites have quizzes online that can help you to assess your personal characteristics. The SBA also has helpful brochures.
2. Interview several small-business owners. Ask them to describe the characteristics they think are necessary for being a successful entrepreneur.
3. Using your findings, write a report that includes the following:
   a. A profile of a successful small-business owner
   b. A comparison of your personal characteristics with the profile of the successful entrepreneur
   c. A discussion of your potential as a successful small-business owner

Finagle A Bagel, a fast-growing small business co-owned by Alan Litchman and Laura Trust, is at the forefront of one of the freshest concepts in the food-service business: fresh food. Each of the twenty stores bakes a new batch of bagels every hour, and each receives new deliveries of cheeses, vegetables, fruits, and other ingredients every day. Rather than prepackage menu items, store employees make everything to order so that they can satisfy the specific needs of each *guest* (Finagle A Bagel's term for a customer). As a result, customers get fresh food prepared to their exact preferences—whether it's extra cheese on a bagel pizza or no onions in a salad—along with prompt, friendly service.

"Every sandwich, every salad is built to order, so there's a lot of communication between the customers and the cashiers, the customers and the sandwich makers, the customers and the managers," explains Trust. This allows Finagle A Bagel's store employees ample opportunity to build customer relationships and encourage repeat business. Many, like Mirna Hernandez of the Tremont Street store in downtown Boston, are so familiar with what certain customers order that they spring into action when regulars enter the store. "We know what they want, and we just ring it in and take care of them," she says. Some employees even know their customers by name and make conversation as they create a sandwich or fill a coffee container.

Buying and Building the Business and Brand

The combination of a strong local following and favorable brand image is what attracted the entrepreneurs to Finagle A Bagel. Looking back, Litchman says that he and his wife recognized that building a small business would require more than good business sense. "It has a lot to do with having a great brand and having great food and reinforcing the brand every day," he remembers. "That's one of the key things that we brought."

To further reinforce the brand and reward customer loyalty, Finagle A Bagel created the Frequent Finagler card. Cardholders receive one point for every dollar spent in a Finagle A Bagel store and can redeem accumulated points for coffee, juice, sandwiches, or other rewards. To join, customers visit the company's website (www.finagleabagel.com) and complete a registration form asking for name, address, and other demographics. Once the account is set up, says Litchman, "It's a web-based program where customers can log on, check their points, and receive free gifts by mail. The Frequent Finagler is our big push right now to use technology as a means of generating store traffic."

Bagels Online?

Soon Litchman plans to expand the website so that customers can order food and catering services directly online. Although some competitors already invite online orders, Finagle A Bagel has a more extensive menu, and its fresh-food concept is not as easily adapted to e-commerce. "In our stores, all the food is prepared fresh, and it is very customized," Litchman notes. "This entails a fair amount of interaction between employees and customers: 'What kind of croutons do you want? What kind of dressing? What kind of mustard?' When we're ready to go in that direction, it is going to be a fairly sizable technology venture for us to undertake."

Finagle A Bagel occasionally receives Web or phone orders from customers hundreds or thousands of miles away. Still, the copresidents have no immediate plans to expand outside the Boston metropolitan area. Pointing to regional food-service firms that have profited by opening more stores in a wider geographic domain, Trust says, "We see that the most successful companies have really dominated their area first. Cheesecake Factory is an example of a company that's wildly successful right now, but they were a concept in California for decades before they moved beyond that area. In-and-Out Burger is an outstanding example of a food-service company in the west that's done what we're trying to do. They had seventeen stores at one time, and now they have hundreds of stores. They're very successful, but they never left their backyard. That's kind of why we're staying where we are."

Financing a Small Business

Some small businesses achieve rapid growth through franchising. The entrepreneurs running Finagle A Bagel resisted franchising for a long time. "When you franchise, you gain a large influx of capital," says Trust, "but you begin to lose control over the people, the place, and the product." Since the beginning, the owners and their senior managers routinely popped into different Finagle A Bagel stores every day to check quality and service. Now the company says that it will begin granting franchises in the near future and institute a stringent quality-control regimen to maintain the highest standards wherever the brand name appears.

As a corporation, Finagle a Bagel could, as some other small businesses do, raise money for growth through an initial public offering (IPO) of corporate stock. The copresidents prefer not to transform their company into an open corporation at this time. "Going public is very tricky in the food-service business," Trust observes. "Some people have done it very successfully; others have not."

The copresidents want to maintain total control over the pace and direction of growth rather than feeling pressured to meet the growth expectations of securities analysts and shareholders. Running a fast-growing small business is their major challenge for now.

Questions

1. Why would Finagle A Bagel maintain a business-to-customer (B2C) website even though it is not yet set up to process online orders from individuals?
2. Do you agree with Finagle A Bagel's plan to franchise its fresh-food concept and brand name? Support your answer.
3. Although opening new stores is costly, the copresidents have chosen not to raise money through an IPO. Do you agree with this decision? Discuss the advantages and disadvantages.
4. If you were writing the executive summary of Finagle A Bagel's business plan to show to lenders, what key points would you stress?

After reading Part 2, "Trends in Business Today," you should be ready to tackle the company and industry component of your business plan. In this section, you will provide information about the background of the company, choice of the legal business form, information on the product or services to be offered, and descriptions of potential customers, current competitors, and the business's future. Chapter 4 in your textbook, "Choosing a Form of Business Ownership," and Chapter 5, "Small Business, Entrepreneurship, and Franchises," can help you to answer some of the questions in this part of the business plan.

THE COMPANY AND INDUSTRY COMPONENT

The company and industry analysis should include the answers to at least the following questions:

2.1. What is the legal form of your business? Is your business a sole proprietorship, a partnership, or a corporation?

2.2. What licenses or permits will you need, if any?

2.3. Is your business a new independent business, a take-over, an expansion, or a franchise?

2.4. If you are dealing with an existing business, how did your company get to the point where it is today?

2.5. What does your business do, and how does it satisfy customers' needs?

2.6. How did you choose and develop the products or services to be sold, and how are they different from those currently on the market?

2.7. What industry do you operate in, and what are the industry-wide trends?

2.8. Who are the major competitors in your industry?

2.9. Have any businesses recently entered or exited? Why did they leave?

2.10. Why will your business be profitable, and what are your growth opportunities?

2.11. Does any part of your business involve e-business?

REVIEW OF BUSINESS PLAN ACTIVITIES

Make sure to check the information you have collected, make any changes, and correct any weaknesses before beginning Part 3. *Reminder:* Review the answers to questions in the preceding part to make sure that all your answers are consistent throughout the business plan. Finally, write a summary statement that incorporates all the information for this part of the business plan.

The information contained in "Building a Business Plan" will also assist you in completing the online *Interactive Business Plan.*

Understanding the Management Process

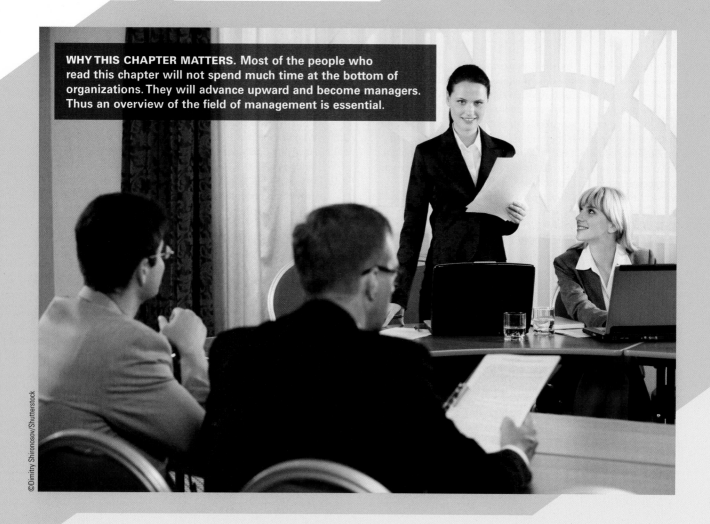

WHY THIS CHAPTER MATTERS. Most of the people who read this chapter will not spend much time at the bottom of organizations. They will advance upward and become managers. Thus an overview of the field of management is essential.

©Dimitry Shironosov/Shutterstock

LEARNING OBJECTIVES

1 Define what management is.

2 Describe the four basic management functions: planning, organizing, leading and motivating, and controlling.

3 Distinguish among the various kinds of managers in terms of both level and area of management.

4 Identify the key management skills and the managerial roles.

5 Explain the different types of leadership.

6 Discuss the steps in the managerial decision-making process.

7 Describe how organizations benefit from total quality management.

8 Summarize what it takes to become a successful manager today.

Xerox: Managing for the Future

Xerox invented the photocopying industry in 1949 with the introduction of its Model A copier. By 2000, the company was losing money and momentum while higher-tech and lower-cost competitors captured market share. Then a new team of senior managers drafted a strategic plan to return the company to profitability.

Under this new leadership, Xerox sold off peripheral business units, changed the way its divisions and activities were organized, reinvigorated employee motivation, and tightened control over operations. Managers at all levels faced difficult decisions about personnel, products, and priorities—decisions that would determine whether Xerox would survive, let alone thrive. In the process of preparing Xerox for a profitable future, "we also learned a lot about identifying failure quickly," the CEO remembers.

The turnaround plan succeeded. Today the company, once again profitable, generates more than $17 billion in annual sales and employs 57,000 people worldwide. Now deeply rooted in digital technology, Xerox offers a wide array of powerful document imaging, storage, and printing systems. One of its fastest-growing divisions, Xerox Global Services, helps major corporations streamline back-office operations for paperless document handling.

Around the world, every Xerox division is working on ways to help managers develop the skills and experience they need to meet tomorrow's challenges. In some departments, managers use software to assess their skill levels and sharpen their technical and conceptual skills. Managers at all levels are periodically shifted to different assignments and departments to hone their decision-making skills by learning to solve new problems in new business situations.

Every year, Xerox offers a handful of managers the opportunity to take a sabbatical and volunteer to lend their expertise at a nonprofit organization of their choosing. For example, one Xerox marketing manager used his twelve-month sabbatical to revamp a Chicago nonprofit's fundraising efforts. Participants receive full pay and benefits from Xerox while they volunteer. When their sabbaticals end, they either resume their previous job duties or receive new management assignments, better prepared for the challenges of shaping the Xerox of tomorrow.[1]

DID YOU KNOW?

As Xerox's managers returned the company to profitability, they "learned a lot about identifying failure quickly," says the CEO.

The leadership employed at Xerox illustrates that management can be one of the most exciting and rewarding professions available today. Depending on its size, a firm may employ a number of specialized managers who are responsible for particular areas of management, such as marketing, finance, and operations. That same organization also includes managers at several levels within the firm. In this chapter, we define *management* and describe the four basic management functions of planning, organizing, leading and motivating, and controlling. Then we focus on the types of managers with respect to levels of responsibility and areas of expertise. Next, we focus on the skills of effective managers and the different roles managers must play. We examine several styles of leadership and explore the process by which managers make decisions. We also describe how total quality management can improve customer satisfaction. We conclude the chapter with a discussion of what it takes to be a successful manager today.

What Is Management?

1 LEARNING OBJECTIVE

Define what management is.

Management is the process of coordinating people and other resources to achieve the goals of an organization. As we saw in Chapter 1, most organizations make use of four kinds of resources: material, human, financial, and informational (see Figure 6.1).

Material resources are the tangible, physical resources an organization uses. For example, Ford uses steel, glass, and fiberglass to produce cars and trucks

management the process of coordinating people and other resources to achieve the goals of an organization on complex machine-driven assembly lines. A college or university uses books, classroom buildings, desks, and computers to educate students. And the Mayo Clinic uses beds, operating room equipment, and diagnostic machines to provide health care.

Perhaps the most important resources of any organization are its *human resources*—people. In fact, some firms live by the philosophy that their employees are their most important assets. One such firm is Southwest Airlines. Southwest treats its employees with the same respect and attention it gives its passengers. Southwest selectively seeks employees with upbeat attitudes and promotes from within 80 percent of the time. In decision making, everyone who will be affected is encouraged to get involved in the process. In an industry in which deregulation, extreme price competition, and fluctuating fuel costs have eliminated several major competitors, Southwest keeps growing and making a profit because of its employees. Many experts would agree with Southwest's emphasis on employees. Some managers believe that the way employees are developed and managed may have more impact on an organization than other vital components such as marketing, sound financial decisions about large expenditures, production, or use of technology.

Financial resources are the funds an organization uses to meet its obligations to investors and creditors. A 7-Eleven convenience store obtains money from customers at the check-out counters and uses a portion of that money to pay its suppliers. Citicorp, a large New York bank, borrows and lends money. Your college obtains money in the form of tuition, income from its endowments, and state and federal grants. It uses the money to pay utility bills, insurance premiums, and professors' salaries.

Finally, many organizations increasingly find that they cannot afford to ignore *information*. External environmental conditions—including the economy, consumer markets, technology, politics, and cultural forces—are all changing so rapidly that a business that does not adapt probably will not survive. And to adapt to change, the business must know what is changing and how it is changing. Most companies gather information about their competitors to increase their knowledge about changes in their industry and to learn from other companies' failures and successes.

It is important to realize that the four types of resources described earlier are only general categories of resources. Within each category are hundreds or thousands of more specific resources. It is this complex mix of specific resources—and not simply "some of each" of the four general categories—that managers must coordinate to produce goods and services.

Another interesting way to look at management is in terms of the different functions managers perform. These functions have been identified as planning, organizing, leading and motivating employees, and controlling. We look at each of these management functions in the next section.

Concept Check

1. What is management?

2. What are the four kinds of resources?

©AP Photo/Paul Sancya

Basic Management Functions

2 LEARNING OBJECTIVE

Describe the four basic management functions: planning, organizing, leading and motivating, and controlling.

Management functions such as those just described do not occur according to some rigid, preset timetable. Managers do not plan in January, organize in February, lead and motivate in March, and control in April. At any given time, managers may engage in a number of functions simultaneously. However, each function tends to lead naturally to others. Figure 6.2 provides a visual framework for a more detailed discussion of the four basic management functions. How well managers perform these key functions determines whether a business is successful.

Planning

Planning, in its simplest form, is establishing organizational goals and deciding how to accomplish them. It is often referred to as the "first" management function because all other management functions depend on planning. Organizations such as Nissan, Houston Community Colleges, and the U.S. Secret Service begin the planning process by developing a mission statement.

An organization's **mission** is a statement of the basic purpose that makes that organization different from others. Google's mission statement is "to organize the world's information and make it universally accessible and useful."[2] Houston Community College System's mission is to provide an education for local citizens. The mission of the Secret Service is to protect the life of the President. Once an organization's mission has been described in a mission statement, the next step is to develop organizational goals and objectives, usually through strategic planning. **Strategic planning** is the process of establishing an organization's major goals and objectives and allocating the resources to achieve them.

Establishing Goals and Objectives A **goal** is an end result that an organization is expected to achieve over a one- to ten-year period. An **objective** is a specific statement detailing what the organization intends to accomplish over a shorter period of time.

Goals and objectives can deal with a variety of factors, such as sales, company growth, costs, customer satisfaction, and employee morale. Whereas a small manufacturer may focus primarily on sales objectives for the next six months, a large firm may be more interested in goals for several years ahead. Under the leadership of CEO Will Manzer, Eastern Mountain Sports (EMS) has a goal to return to its roots as a hardcore sports gear provider. Over years of declining profits, EMS has blurred its image by shifting to "soft" merchandise that appeals to a broader market. The company's managers know that goals take time to achieve, and they are willing to invest to reach their goal of becoming the edgy outfitter they once were. They are taking action with objectives such as dropping all their "soft" merchandise, hiring hardcore sporting enthusiasts, and stocking gear for even the most fringe sports out there (e.g., kite skiing, ice climbing, and high-speed sledding).[3] Finally, goals are set at every level of an organization. Every member of an organization—the president of the company, the head of a department, and

planning establishing organizational goals and deciding how to accomplish them

mission a statement of the basic purpose that makes an organization different from others

strategic planning the process of establishing an organization's major goals and objectives and allocating the resources to achieve them

goal an end result that an organization is expected to achieve over a one- to ten-year period

objective a specific statement detailing what an organization intends to accomplish over a shorter period of time

FIGURE 6.2: The Management Process Note that management is not a step-by-step procedure but a process with a feedback loop that represents a flow.

Planning → Organizing → Leading and motivating → Controlling

Review and modify

Mission statement. The mission statement of Microsoft is "We work to help people and businesses throughout the world realize their full potential."

an operating employee at the lowest level—has a set of goals that he or she hopes to achieve.

The goals developed for these different levels must be consistent. However, it is likely that some conflict will arise. A production department, for example, may have a goal of minimizing costs. One way to do this is to produce only one type of product and offer "no frills." Marketing may have a goal of maximizing sales. One way to implement this goal is to offer customers a wide range of products and options. As part of goal setting, the manager who is responsible for *both* departments must achieve some sort of balance between conflicting goals. This balancing process is called *optimization.*

The optimization of conflicting goals requires insight and ability. Faced with the marketing-versus-production conflict just described, most managers probably would not adopt either viewpoint completely. Instead, they might decide on a reasonably diverse product line offering only the most widely sought-after options. Such a compromise would seem to be best for the whole organization.

plan an outline of the actions by which an organization intends to accomplish its goals and objectives

strategic plan an organization's broadest plan, developed as a guide for major policy setting and decision making

Establishing Plans to Accomplish Goals and Objectives Once goals and objectives have been set for the organization, managers must develop plans for achieving them. A **plan** is an outline of the actions by which an organization intends to accomplish its goals and objectives. Just as it has different goals and objectives, the organization also develops several types of plans, as shown in Figure 6.3.

Resulting from the strategic planning process, an organization's **strategic plan** is its broadest plan, developed as a guide for major policy setting and decision

©AP Photo/Ted S. Warren

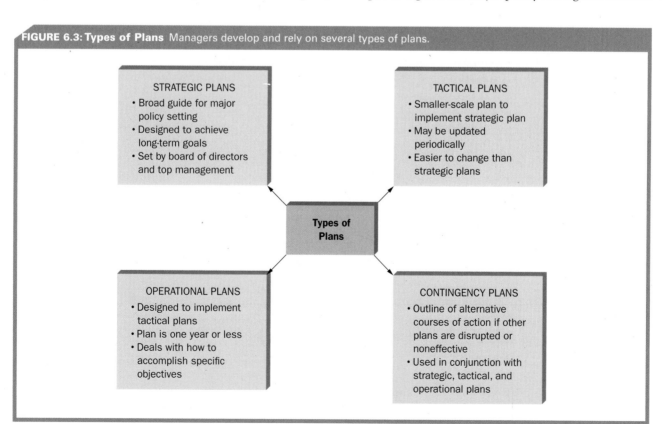

FIGURE 6.3: Types of Plans Managers develop and rely on several types of plans.

STRATEGIC PLANS
- Broad guide for major policy setting
- Designed to achieve long-term goals
- Set by board of directors and top management

TACTICAL PLANS
- Smaller-scale plan to implement strategic plan
- May be updated periodically
- Easier to change than strategic plans

Types of Plans

OPERATIONAL PLANS
- Designed to implement tactical plans
- Plan is one year or less
- Deals with how to accomplish specific objectives

CONTINGENCY PLANS
- Outline of alternative courses of action if other plans are disrupted or noneffective
- Used in conjunction with strategic, tactical, and operational plans

making. Strategic plans are set by the board of directors and top management and generally are designed to achieve the long-term goals of the organization. Thus, a firm's strategic plan defines what business the company is in or wants to be in and the kind of company it is or wants to be. When top management at one of the world's biggest consumer products companies, Procter & Gamble, decided to expand and to diversify its three main business units, they created separate executive teams for the global personal care products, global hair care products, and global prestige products. This long-term strategy has been adopted to more effectively compete globally and to better serve customers in numerous global markets.[4]

The Internet has challenged traditional strategic thinking. For example, reluctant to move from a face-to-face sales approach to a less personal website approach, Allstate has created an Internet presence to support its established sales force.

In addition to strategic plans, most organizations also employ several narrower kinds of plans. A **tactical plan** is a smaller-scale plan developed to implement a strategy. Most tactical plans cover a one- to three-year period. If a strategic plan will take five years to complete, the firm may develop five tactical plans, one covering each year. Tactical plans may be updated periodically as dictated by conditions and experience. Their more limited scope permits them to be changed more easily than strategies. In an attempt to fulfill its diversification strategy, Procter & Gamble purchased NIOXIN Research Laboratories, Inc., a leader in the scalp care part of the professional hair care product category. NIOXIN offers a range of innovative products that focus on problems associated with thinning hair and are distributed through salons and salon stores in more than 40 countries. This acquisition was in line with Procter & Gamble's strategy of focusing on faster growing, higher margin businesses and a tactical plan used for achieving its long-term goals.[5]

An **operational plan** is a type of plan designed to implement tactical plans. Operational plans usually are established for one year or less and deal with how to accomplish the organization's specific objectives. Procter & Gamble has adopted the *Go-to-Market plan* in order to speed up the availability of products to retailers and thus to consumers. The strategic and tactical plans have been kept in mind in order to achieve this plan. It includes making significant changes in the way that Procter & Gamble distributes its products.[6]

Regardless of how hard managers try, sometimes business activities do not go as planned. Today, most corporations also develop contingency plans along with strategies, tactical plans, and operational plans. A **contingency plan** is a plan that outlines alternative courses of action that may be taken if an organization's other plans are disrupted or become ineffective.

Organizing the Enterprise

After goal setting and planning, the second major function of the manager is organization. **Organizing** is the grouping of resources and activities to accomplish some end result in an efficient and effective manner. Consider the case of an inventor who creates a new product and goes into business to sell it. At first, the inventor will do everything on his or her own—purchase raw materials, make the product, advertise it, sell it, and keep business records. Eventually, as business grows, the inventor will need help. To begin with, he or she might hire a professional sales representative and a part-time bookkeeper. Later, it also might be necessary to hire sales staff, people to assist with production, and an accountant. As the inventor hires new personnel, he or she must decide what each person will do, to whom each person will report, and how each person can best take part in the organization's activities. We discuss these and other facets of the organizing function in much more detail in Chapter 7.

Leading and Motivating

The leading and motivating function is concerned with the human resources within an organization. Specifically, **leading** is the process of influencing people to work

tactical plan a smaller-scale plan developed to implement a strategy

operational plan a type of plan designed to implement tactical plans

contingency plan a plan that outlines alternative courses of action that may be taken if an organization's other plans are disrupted or become ineffective

organizing the grouping of resources and activities to accomplish some end result in an efficient and effective manner

leading the process of influencing people to work toward a common goal

Creating a satisfying work environment can be challenging. Designers of the work environment at Google spent considerable time talking with approximately 350 employees regarding what they wanted in their offices and work areas.

toward a common goal. **Motivating** is the process of providing reasons for people to work in the best interests of an organization. Together, leading and motivating are often referred to as **directing**.

We have already noted the importance of an organization's human resources. Because of this importance, leading and motivating are critical activities. Obviously, different people do things for different reasons—that is, they have different *motivations*. Some are interested primarily in earning as much money as they can. Others may be spurred on by opportunities to get promoted. Part of a manager's job, then, is to determine what factors motivate workers and to try to provide those incentives to encourage effective performance. Jeffrey R. Immelt, GE's chairman and CEO has worked to transform GE into a leader in essential themes tied to world development, such as emerging markets, environmental solutions, demographics, and digital connections. He believes in giving freedom to his teams and wants them to come up with their own solutions. However, he does not hesitate to intervene if the situation demands. He believes that a leader's primary role is to teach, and he makes people feel that he is willing to share what he has learned. Mr. Immelt also laid the vision for GE's ambitious "ecomagination initiative" and has been named one of the "World's Best CEOs" three times by *Barron's*.[7] A lot of research has been done on both motivation and leadership. As you will see in Chapter 10, research on motivation has yielded very useful information. Research on leadership has been less successful. Despite decades of study, no one has discovered a general set of personal traits or characteristics that makes a good leader. Later in this chapter, we discuss leadership in more detail.

Controlling Ongoing Activities

Controlling is the process of evaluating and regulating ongoing activities to ensure that goals are achieved. To see how controlling works, consider a rocket launched by NASA to place a satellite in orbit. Do NASA personnel simply fire the rocket and then check back in a few days to find out whether the satellite is in place? Of course not. The rocket is monitored constantly, and its course is regulated and adjusted as needed to get the satellite to its destination.

The control function includes three steps (see Figure 6.4). The first is *setting standards* with which performance can be compared. The second is *measuring actual performance* and comparing it with the standard. And the third is *taking corrective action* as necessary. Notice that the control function is circular in nature. The steps in the control function must be repeated periodically until the goal is achieved. For example, suppose that Southwest Airlines establishes a goal of increasing profits by 12 percent. To ensure that this goal is reached, Southwest's management might monitor its profit on a monthly basis. After three months, if profit has increased by 3 percent, management might be able to assume that plans are going according to schedule. Probably no action will be taken. However, if profit has increased by only 1 percent after three months, some corrective action would be needed to get the firm on track. The particular action that is required depends on the reason for the small increase in profit.

motivating the process of providing reasons for people to work in the best interests of an organization

directing the combined processes of leading and motivating

controlling the process of evaluating and regulating ongoing activities to ensure that goals are achieved

FIGURE 6.4: The Control Function The control function includes three steps: setting standards, measuring actual performance, and taking corrective action.

1 Setting standards

2 Measuring actual performance

3 Taking corrective action

Concept Check

1. Why is planning sometimes referred to as the "first" management function?

2. What is a plan? Differentiate between the major types of plans.

3. What kind of motivations do different employees have?

4. What are the three steps of controlling?

Kinds of Managers

3 LEARNING OBJECTIVE

Distinguish among the various kinds of managers in terms of both level and area of management.

Managers can be classified in two ways: according to their level within an organization and according to their area of management. In this section, we use both perspectives to explore the various types of managers.

Levels of Management

For the moment, think of an organization as a three-story structure (as illustrated in Figure 6.5). Each story corresponds to one of the three general levels of management: top managers, middle managers, and first-line managers.

Top Managers A **top manager** is an upper-level executive who guides and controls the overall fortunes of an organization. Top managers constitute a small group. In terms of planning, they are generally responsible for developing the organization's mission. They also determine the firm's strategy. It takes years of hard work, long hours, and perseverance, as well as talent and no small share of good luck, to reach the ranks of top management in large companies. Common job titles associated with top managers are president, vice president, chief executive officer (CEO), and chief operating officer (COO).

Middle Managers Middle managers probably make up the largest group of managers in most organizations. A **middle manager** is a manager who implements the strategy and major policies developed by top management. Middle managers develop tactical plans and operational plans, and they coordinate and supervise the activities of first-line managers. Titles at the middle-management level include division manager, department head, plant manager, and operations manager.

First-Line Managers A **first-line manager** is a manager who coordinates and supervises the activities of operating employees. First-line managers spend most of their time working with and motivating their employees, answering questions, and solving day-to-day problems. Most first-line managers are former operating employees who, owing to their hard work and potential, were promoted into management. Many of today's middle and top managers began their careers on this first management level. Common titles for first-line managers include office manager, supervisor, and foreman.

top manager an upper-level executive who guides and controls the overall fortunes of an organization

middle manager a manager who implements the strategy and major policies developed by top management

first-line manager a manager who coordinates and supervises the activities of operating employees

FIGURE 6.5: Management Levels Found in Most Companies The coordinated effort of all three levels of managers is required to implement the goals of any company.

Top management

Middle management

First-line management

Going Green

Ford's Green Future

Henry Ford revolutionized the car industry with his Model T. More than 100 years later, his great-grandson, William Clay Ford, Jr., is leading a green revolution inside the Ford Motor Company. When he was first named to the board of directors, he was told to "stop associating with any known or suspected environmentalists," he remembers. "And I said: 'No, of course I have no intention of stopping.'"

Now, as executive chairman, Ford has used his leadership position to move environmental initiatives into the fast lane at the company his family founded. For example, he led the $2 billion effort to revamp the firm's Rouge River factory in Dearborn, Michigan, into a model of green manufacturing. Much of the plant's power comes from renewable sources such as solar panels and fuel cells. The redesigned facility is cleaner and leaner, using less water and power. And the site is literally green with sustainable landscaping and wildlife habitats.

Today Ford and his management team are expanding worldwide production of environmentally-friendly vehicles that run on electric batteries or hybrid gas-electric motors. "Our vision for Ford is green, global, and high tech," Ford says. The executive chairman is also using his influence to encourage other business leaders to see green. "We need to do our part as an industry, but we are only one piece of a much bigger puzzle," he adds.

Sources: Ben Rooney, "Ford Plant Dumps SUVs, Goes Small," *Fortune,* May 6, 2009, http://money.cnn.com/2009/05/06/autos/ford_focus_plant/index.htm; "Ford Seeks Loan Guarantees for Green Tech," *Associated Press,* September 5, 2008, www.cnnmoney.com; Maria Bartiromo, "Bill Ford on Tipping Points and Thinking Small," *BusinessWeek,* August 11, 2008, p. 18; Jennette Smith, "Ford Calls for Greater R&D, Integrated Energy Policy," *Crain's Detroit Business,* June 4, 2007, p. M66; www.ford.com.

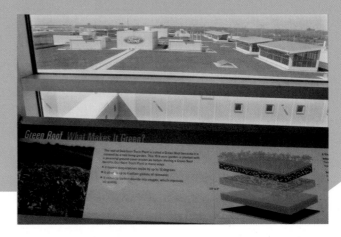

Areas of Management Specialization

Organizational structure also can be divided into areas of management specialization (see Figure 6.6). The most common areas are finance, operations, marketing, human resources, and administration. Depending on its mission, goals, and objectives, an organization may include other areas as well—research and development (R&D), for example.

Financial Managers A **financial manager** is primarily responsible for an organization's financial resources. Accounting and investment are specialized areas within financial management. Because financing affects the operation of the entire firm, many of the CEOs and presidents of this country's largest companies are people who got their "basic training" as financial managers.

Operations Managers An **operations manager** manages the systems that convert resources into goods and services. Traditionally, operations management has been equated with manufacturing—the production of goods. However, in recent years, many of the techniques and procedures of operations management have been applied to the production of services and to a variety of nonbusiness activities. As with financial management, operations management has produced a large percentage of today's company CEOs and presidents.

financial manager a manager who is primarily responsible for an organization's financial resources

operations manager a manager who manages the systems that convert resources into goods and services

FIGURE 6.6: Areas of Management Specialization Other areas may have to be added, depending on the nature of the firm and the industry.

Finance	Operations	Marketing	Human resources	Administration	Other (e.g., research and development)

Managing Your Career

Moving Into First-Line Management

Congratulations on being promoted into the ranks of first-line management. Now you'll be supervising employees who just days ago were your peers. Some former peers may resent your promotion. Others may fear their friendly relationship with you will never be the same. You may feel awkward supervising people you once worked with as equals. What can you do to smooth your transition into management?

- *Start the conversation.* Meet with each member of your team to discuss individual goals and concerns. Also hold group meetings to discuss specific transition issues. Listen closely, express your expectations, invite new ideas, and emphasize the positive.

- *Champion your group.* Remind your employees that you can be a strong champion for the group because you are so familiar with its strengths and capabilities. You should also be a champion for change to improve your group's performance.

- *Be professional.* Any hint of favoritism will derail your transition. Use this opportunity to establish a professional, objective working relationship with all your employees.

- *Be a role model for change.* Acknowledge that change can be a challenge—and be a leader in embracing the many changes that will come with your new promotion.

Sources: Megan K. Scott, "At Work, Be Leader, Be Positive," *Journal Gazette (Fort Wayne, IN),* May 11, 2009, www.journalgazette.net/article/20090511/FEAT/305119933/1162; Ron Brown, "Showing Them Who's Boss," *Condé Nast Portfolio,* September 23, 2008, www.portfolio.com; "Dear Jeremy: Problems at Work," *The Guardian (UK),* March 15, 2008, pl. 4; Joanne Murray, "From Colleague to Boss: How to Navigate the Transition," *Monster Career Advice,* n.d., www.career-advice.monster.com.

Marketing Managers A **marketing manager** is responsible for facilitating the exchange of products between an organization and its customers or clients. Specific areas within marketing are marketing research, product management, advertising, promotion, sales, and distribution. A sizable number of today's company presidents have risen from the ranks of marketing management.

Human Resources Managers A **human resources manager** is charged with managing an organization's human resources programs. He or she engages in human resources planning; designs systems for hiring, training, and evaluating the performance of employees; and ensures that the organization follows government regulations concerning employment practices. Some human resources managers are making effective use of technology. For example, over 1 million job openings are posted on Monster.com, which attracts about 20 million visitors monthly.[8]

Administrative Managers An **administrative manager** (also called a *general manager*) is not associated with any specific functional area but provides overall administrative guidance and leadership. A hospital administrator is an example of an administrative manager. He or she does not specialize in operations, finance, marketing, or human resources management but instead coordinates the activities of specialized managers in all these areas. In many respects, most top managers are really administrative managers.

Whatever their level in the organization and whatever area they specialize in, successful managers generally exhibit certain key skills and are able to play certain managerial roles. However, as we shall see, some skills are likely to be more critical at one level of management than at another.

What Makes Effective Managers?

In general, effective managers are those who (1) possess certain important skills and (2) are able to use those skills in a number of managerial roles. Probably no manager is called on to use any particular skill *constantly* or to play a particular role *all the time*. However, these skills and abilities must be available when they are needed.

marketing manager a manager who is responsible for facilitating the exchange of products between an organization and its customers or clients

human resources manager a person charged with managing an organization's human resources programs

administrative manager a manager who is not associated with any specific functional area but who provides overall administrative guidance and leadership

Concept Check

1. Describe the three levels of management.

2. Identify the various areas of management specialization, and describe the responsibilities of each.

4 LEARNING OBJECTIVE

Identify the key management skills and the managerial roles.

Human resources managers. Human resource managers are responsible for numerous HR activities including performance evaluations.

Key Management Skills

The skills that typify effective managers fall into three general categories: technical, conceptual, and interpersonal.

Technical Skills A **technical skill** is a specific skill needed to accomplish a specialized activity. For example, the skills engineers and machinists need to do their jobs are technical skills. First-line managers (and, to a lesser extent, middle managers) need the technical skills relevant to the activities they manage. Although these managers may not perform the technical tasks themselves, they must be able to train subordinates, answer questions, and otherwise provide guidance and direction. A first-line manager in the accounting department of the Hyatt Corporation, for example, must be able to perform computerized accounting transactions and help employees complete the same accounting task. In general, top managers do not rely on technical skills as heavily as managers at other levels. Still, understanding the technical side of a business is an aid to effective management at every level.

Conceptual Skills **Conceptual skill** is the ability to think in abstract terms. Conceptual skill allows a manager to see the "big picture" and understand how the various parts of an organization or idea can fit together. These skills are useful in a wide range of situations, including the optimization of goals described earlier. They are usually more useful for top managers than for middle or first-line managers.

Interpersonal Skills An **interpersonal skill** is the ability to deal effectively with other people, both inside and outside an organization. Examples of interpersonal skills are the ability to relate to people, understand their needs and motives, and show genuine compassion. One reason why Mary Kay Ash, founder of Mary Kay Cosmetics, has been so successful is her ability to motivate her employees and to inspire their loyalty to her vision for the firm. And although it is obvious that a CEO such as Mary Kay Ash must be able to work with employees throughout the organization, what is not so obvious is that middle and first-line managers also must possess interpersonal skills. For example, a first-line manager on an assembly line at Procter & Gamble must rely on employees to manufacture Tide detergent. The better the manager's interpersonal skills, the more likely the manager will be able to lead and motivate those employees. When all other things are equal, the manager able to exhibit these skills will be more successful than the arrogant and brash manager who does not care about others.

Managerial Roles

Research suggests that managers must, from time to time, act in ten different roles if they are to be successful.[9] (By *role*, we mean a set of expectations that one must fulfill.) These ten roles can be grouped into three broad categories: decisional, interpersonal, and informational.

Decisional Roles A **decisional role** involves various aspects of management decision making. The decisional role can be subdivided into four specific managerial roles. In the role of *entrepreneur,* the manager is the voluntary initiator of change. For example, the CEO of DuPont decided to put more financial resources into

technical skill a specific skill needed to accomplish a specialized activity

conceptual skill the ability to think in abstract terms

interpersonal skill the ability to deal effectively with other people

decisional role a role that involves various aspects of management decision making its Experimental Station, a large R&D center, to increase new products. This entrepreneurial emphasis on R&D led to the creation of Sorona, a synthetic fiber that could be used for clothing, car upholstery, and carpeting. DuPont hopes that these decisions will pay great dividends in the long run.[10] A second role is that of *disturbance handler*. A manager who settles a strike is handling a disturbance. Third, the manager also occasionally plays the role of *resource allocator*. In this role, the manager might have to decide which departmental budgets to cut and which expenditure requests to approve. The fourth role is that of *negotiator*. Being a negotiator might involve settling a dispute between a manager and a worker assigned to the manager's work group.

Interpersonal Roles Dealing with people is an integral part of the manager's job. An **interpersonal role** is a role in which the manager deals with people. Like the decisional role, the interpersonal role can be broken down according to three managerial functions. The manager may be called on to serve as a *figurehead,* perhaps by attending a ribbon-cutting ceremony or taking an important client to dinner. The manager also may have to play the role of *liaison* by serving as a go-between for two different groups. As a liaison, a manager might represent his or her firm at meetings of an industry-wide trade organization. Finally, the manager often has to serve as a *leader.* Playing the role of leader includes being an example for others in the organization as well as developing the skills, abilities, and motivation of employees.

Informational Roles An **informational role** is one in which the manager either gathers or provides information. The informational role can be subdivided as follows: In the role of *monitor,* the manager actively seeks information that may be of value to the organization. For example, a manager who hears about a good business opportunity is engaging in the role of monitor. The second informational role is that of *disseminator*. In this role, the manager transmits key information to those who can use it. As a disseminator, the manager who heard about a good business opportunity would tell the appropriate marketing manager about it. The third informational role is that of *spokesperson*. In this role, the manager provides information to people outside the organization, such as the press, television reporters, and the public.

Leadership

Leadership has been defined broadly as the ability to influence others. A leader has power and can use it to affect the behavior of others. Leadership is different from management in that a leader strives for voluntary cooperation, whereas a manager may have to depend on coercion to change employee behavior.

Formal and Informal Leadership

Some experts make distinctions between formal leadership and informal leadership. Formal leaders have legitimate power of position. They have *authority* within an organization to influence others to work for the organization's objectives. Informal leaders usually have no such authority and may or may not exert their influence in support of the organization. Both formal and informal leaders make use of several

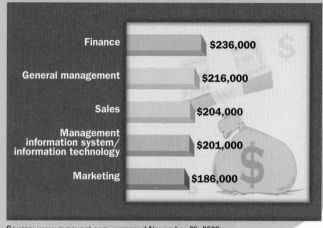

Spotlight

How Much Do Executives in Selected Business Areas Earn Yearly?

Business Area	Yearly Earnings
Finance	$236,000
General management	$216,000
Sales	$204,000
Management information system/ information technology	$201,000
Marketing	$186,000

Source: www.execunet.com, accessed November 25, 2008.

Concept Check

Which of the three managerial roles would you be using if you needed to (a) give a press conference, (b) develop a budget, or (c) motivate employees?

5 LEARNING OBJECTIVE

Explain the different types of leadership.

interpersonal role a role in which the manager deals with people

informational role a role in which the manager either gathers or provides information

leadership the ability to influence others

Leadership style. Apple CEO, Steve Jobs, has a leadership style that helps to create an environment that nurtures and enhances the creation of technology-based products, many of which become highly successful.

kinds of power, including the ability to grant rewards or impose punishments, the possession of expert knowledge, and personal attraction or charisma. Informal leaders who identify with the organization's goals are a valuable asset to any organization. However, a business can be brought to its knees by informal leaders who turn work groups against management.

Styles of Leadership

For many years, leadership was viewed as a combination of personality traits, such as self-confidence, concern for people, intelligence, and dependability. Achieving a consensus on which traits were most important was difficult, however, and attention turned to styles of leadership behavior. In the last few decades, several styles of leadership have been identified: authoritarian, laissez-faire, and democratic. The **authoritarian leader** holds all authority and responsibility, with communication usually moving from top to bottom. This leader assigns workers to specific tasks and expects orderly, precise results. The leaders at UPS employ authoritarian leadership. At the other extreme is the **laissez-faire leader**, who gives authority to employees. With the laissez-faire style, subordinates are allowed to work as they choose with a minimum of interference. Communication flows horizontally among group members. Leaders at Apple Computer employ a laissez-faire leadership style to give employees as much freedom as possible to develop new products. The **democratic leader** holds final responsibility but also delegates authority to others, who determine work assignments. In this leadership style, communication is active upward and downward. Employee commitment is high because of participation in the decision-making process. Managers for both Wal-Mart and Saturn have used democratic leadership to encourage employees to become more than just rank-and-file workers.

Which Managerial Leadership Style Is Best?

Today, most management experts agree that no "best" managerial leadership style exists. Each of the styles described—authoritarian, laissez-faire, and democratic—has advantages and disadvantages. Democratic leadership can motivate employees to work effectively because they are implementing *their own* decisions. However, the decision making process in democratic leadership takes time that subordinates could be devoting to the work itself.

Although hundreds of research studies have been conducted to prove which leadership style is best, there are no definite conclusions. The "best" leadership seems to occur when the leader's style matches the situation. Each of the leadership styles can be effective in the right situation. The *most* effective style depends on interaction among employees, characteristics of the work situation, and the manager's personality.

authoritarian leader one who holds all authority and responsibility, with communication usually moving from top to bottom

Concept Check

1. Describe the major leadership styles.

2. Which one is best?

LEARNING OBJECTIVE 6

Discuss the steps in the managerial decision-making process.

Managerial Decision Making

Decision making is the act of choosing one alternative from a set of alternatives.[11] In ordinary situations, decisions are made casually and informally. We encounter a problem, mull it over, settle on a solution, and go on. Managers, however, require a more systematic method for solving complex problems. As shown in Figure 6.7,

FIGURE 6.7: Major Steps in the Managerial Decision-Making Process Managers require a systematic method for solving problems in a variety of situations.

managerial decision making involves four steps: (1) identifying the problem or opportunity, (2) generating alternatives, (3) selecting an alternative, and (4) implementing and evaluating the solution.

Identifying the Problem or Opportunity

A **problem** is the discrepancy between an actual condition and a desired condition—the difference between what is occurring and what one wishes would occur. For example, a marketing manager at Campbell Soup Company has a problem if sales revenues for Campbell's Hungry Man frozen dinners are declining (the actual condition). To solve this problem, the marketing manager must take steps to increase sales revenues (desired condition). Most people consider a problem to be "negative;" however, a problem also can be "positive." A positive problem should be viewed as an "opportunity."

Although accurate identification of a problem is essential before it can be solved or turned into an opportunity, this stage of decision making creates many difficulties for managers. Sometimes managers' preconceptions of the problem prevent them from seeing the actual situation. They produce an answer before the proper question has been asked. In other cases, managers overlook truly significant issues by focusing on unimportant matters. Also, managers may mistakenly analyze problems in terms of symptoms rather than underlying causes.

Effective managers learn to look ahead so that they are prepared when decisions must be made. They clarify situations and examine the causes of problems, asking whether the presence or absence of certain variables alters a situation. Finally, they consider how individual behaviors and values affect the way problems or opportunities are defined.

Generating Alternatives

After a problem has been defined, the next task is to generate alternatives. The more important the decision, the more attention is devoted to this stage. Managers should be open to fresh, innovative ideas as well as obvious answers.

Certain techniques can aid in the generation of creative alternatives. Brainstorming, commonly used in group discussions, encourages participants to produce many new ideas. Other group members are not permitted to criticize or ridicule. Another approach, developed by the U.S. Navy, is called "Blast! Then Refine." Group members tackle a recurring problem by erasing all previous solutions and procedures. The group then re-evaluates its original objectives, modifies them if necessary, and devises new solutions. Other techniques—including trial and error—are also useful in this stage of decision making.

Selecting an Alternative

Final decisions are influenced by a number of considerations, including financial constraints, human and informational resources, time limits, legal obstacles, and political factors. Managers must select the alternative that will be most effective and practical.

laissez-faire leader one who gives authority to employees and allows subordinates to work as they choose with a minimum of interference; communication flows horizontally among group members

democratic leader one who holds final responsibility but also delegates authority to others, who help to determine work assignments; communication is active upward and downward

decision making the act of choosing one alternative from a set of alternatives

problem the discrepancy between an actual condition and a desired condition

At times, two or more alternatives or some combination of alternatives will be equally appropriate. Managers may choose solutions to problems on several levels. The coined word "satisfice" describes solutions that are only adequate and not ideal. When lacking time or information, managers often make decisions that "satisfice." Whenever possible, managers should try to investigate alternatives carefully and select the ideal solution.

Implementing and Evaluating the Solution

Implementation of a decision requires time, planning, preparation of personnel, and evaluation of results. Managers usually deal with unforeseen consequences even when they have carefully considered the alternatives.

The final step in managerial decision making entails evaluating the effectiveness of a decision. If the alternative that was chosen removes the difference between the actual condition and the desired condition, the decision is judged effective. If the problem still exists, managers may select one of the following choices:

- Decide to give the chosen alternative more time to work.
- Adopt a different alternative.
- Start the problem identification process all over again.

Concept Check

1. Describe the major steps in the managerial decision-making process.

2. Why does a manager need to evaluate the solution and look for problems after a solution has been implemented?

LEARNING OBJECTIVE 7

Describe how organizations benefit from total quality management.

Managing Total Quality

The management of quality is a high priority in some organizations today. Major reasons for a greater focus on quality include foreign competition, more demanding customers, and poor financial performance resulting from reduced market shares and higher costs. Over the last few years, several U.S. firms have lost the dominant competitive positions they had held for decades.

Total quality management is a much broader concept than just controlling the quality of the product itself (which is discussed in Chapter 9). **Total quality management (TQM)** is the coordination of efforts directed at improving customer satisfaction, increasing employee participation, strengthening supplier partnerships, and facilitating an organizational atmosphere of continuous quality improvement. For TQM programs to be effective, management must address each of the following components:

- *Customer satisfaction.* Ways to improve include producing higher-quality products, providing better customer service, and showing customers that the company cares.
- *Employee participation.* This can be increased by allowing employees to contribute to decisions, develop self-managed work teams, and assume responsibility for improving the quality of their work.
- *Strengthening supplier partnerships.* Developing good working relationships with suppliers can ensure that the right supplies and materials will be delivered on time at lower costs.
- *Continuous quality improvement.* This should not be viewed as achievable through one single program that has a target objective. A program based on continuous improvement has proven to be the most effective long-term approach.

Although many factors influence the effectiveness of a TQM program, two issues are crucial. First, top management must make a strong commitment to a TQM program by treating quality improvement as a top priority and giving it frequent attention. Firms that establish a TQM program but then focus on other priorities will find that their quality-improvement initiatives will fail. Second, management must coordinate the specific elements of a TQM program so that they work in harmony with each other.

total quality management (TQM) the coordination of efforts directed at improving customer satisfaction, increasing employee participation, strengthening supplier partnerships, and facilitating an organizational atmosphere of continuous quality improvement

Concept Check

1. Why does top management need to be strongly committed to TQM programs?

2. Describe the major components of a TQM program.

Although not all U.S. companies have TQM programs, these programs provide many benefits. Overall financial benefits include lower operating costs, higher return on sales and on investments, and an improved ability to use premium pricing rather than competitive pricing.

What It Takes to Become a Successful Manager Today

8 LEARNING OBJECTIVE

Summarize what it takes to become a successful manager today.

Everyone hears stories about the corporate elite who make salaries in excess of $1 million a year, travel to and from work in chauffeur-driven limousines, and enjoy lucrative pension plans that provide for a luxurious lifestyle after they retire. Although management obviously can be a rewarding career, what is not so obvious is the amount of time and hard work needed to achieve the impressive salaries and perks.

A Day in the Life of a Manager

Organizations pay managers for performance. As already pointed out, managers coordinate an organization's resources. They also perform the four basic management functions: planning, organizing, leading and motivating, and controlling. And managers make decisions and then implement and evaluate those decisions. This heavy workload requires that managers work long hours, and most do not get paid overtime. Typically, the number of hours increases as a manager advances.

Today's managers have demanding jobs. Managers spend a great deal of time talking with people on an individual basis. The purpose of these conversations is usually to obtain information or to resolve problems. In addition, a manager often spends time in meetings with other managers and employees. In most cases, the purpose of the meetings—some brief and some lengthy—is to resolve problems. And if the work is not completed by the end of the day, the manager usually packs his or her unfinished tasks in a briefcase.

Skills Required for Success

To be successful in today's competitive business environment, you must possess a number of skills. Some of these skills—technical, conceptual, and interpersonal skills—were discussed earlier in this chapter. However, you also need "personal" skills. Oral and written communication skills, computer skills, and critical-thinking skills may give you the edge in getting an entry-level management position.

- *Oral communication skills.* Because a large part of a manager's day is spent conversing with others, the ability to speak *and* listen is critical. Oral communication skills are used when a manager makes sales presentations, conducts interviews, and holds press conferences.
- *Written communication skills.* A manager's ability to prepare letters, e-mails, memos, sales reports, and other written documents may spell the difference between success and failure.
- *Computer skills.* Most employers do not expect you to be an expert computer programmer, but they do expect that you should know how to use

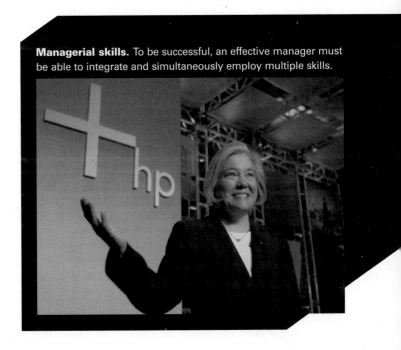

Managerial skills. To be successful, an effective manager must be able to integrate and simultaneously employ multiple skills.

©Getty Images

a computer to prepare written and statistical reports and to communicate with other managers and employees.

- *Critical-thinking skills.* Employers expect managers to use the steps for effective managerial decision making. They also expect managers to use critical-thinking skills to identify problems correctly, generate reasonable alternatives, and select the "best" alternatives to solve problems.

The Importance of Education and Experience

Although most experts agree that management skills must be learned on the job, the concepts that you learn in business courses lay the foundation for a successful career. In addition, successful completion of college courses or obtaining a degree can open doors to job interviews and career advancement.

There are methods you can use to "beef up" your résumé and to capitalize on your work experience. First, obtain summer jobs that provide opportunities to learn about the field that interests you. Chosen carefully, part-time jobs can provide work experience that other job applicants may not have. Some colleges and universities sponsor cooperative work/school programs that give students college credit for job experience. Even with solid academics and work experience, many would-be managers find it difficult to land the "right" job. Often they start in an entry-level position to gain more experience.

In the next chapter we examine the organizing function of managers in some detail. We look specifically at various organizational forms that today's successful businesses use. As with many factors in management, how a business is organized depends on its goals, strategies, and personnel.

Concept Check

1. What types of skills are needed to be an effective manager?

2. Why is education and experience necessary?

SUMMARY

1 Define what management is.

Management is the process of coordinating people and other resources to achieve the goals of an organization. Managers are concerned with four types of resources—material, human, financial, and informational.

2 Describe the four basic management functions: planning, organizing, leading and motivating, and controlling.

Managers perform four basic functions. Management functions do not occur according to some rigid, preset timetable, though. At any time, managers may engage in a number of functions simultaneously. However, each function tends to lead naturally to others. First, managers engage in planning—determining where the firm should be going and how best to get there. Three types of plans, from the broadest to the most specific, are strategic plans, tactical plans, and operational plans. Managers also organize resources and activities to accomplish results in an efficient and effective manner, and they lead and motivate others to work in the best interests of the organization. In addition, managers control ongoing activities to keep the organization on course. There are three steps in the control function: setting standards, measuring actual performance, and taking corrective action.

3 Distinguish among the various kinds of managers in terms of both level and area of management.

Managers—or management positions—may be classified from two different perspectives. From the perspective of level within the organization, there are top managers, who control the fortunes of the organization; middle managers, who implement strategies and major policies; and first-line managers, who supervise the activities of operating employees. From the viewpoint of area of management, managers most often deal with the areas of finance, operations, marketing, human resources, and administration.

4 Identify the key management skills and the managerial roles.

Effective managers tend to possess a specific set of skills and to fill three basic managerial roles. Technical, conceptual, and interpersonal skills are all important, although the relative importance of each varies with the level of management within the organization. The primary managerial roles can be classified as decisional, interpersonal, or informational.

5 Explain the different types of leadership.

Managers' effectiveness often depends on their styles of leadership—that is, their ability to influence others, either formally or informally. Leadership styles include the authoritarian "do-it-my-way" style, the laissez-faire "do-it-your-way" style, and the democratic "let's-do-it-together" style.

6 Discuss the steps in the managerial decision-making process.

Decision making, an integral part of a manager's work, is the process of developing a set of possible alternative solutions to a problem and choosing one alternative from among the set. Managerial decision making involves four steps: Managers must accurately identify problems, generate several possible solutions, choose the solution that will be most effective under the circumstances, and implement and evaluate the chosen course of action.

7 Describe how organizations benefit from total quality management.

Total quality management (TQM) is the coordination of efforts directed at improving customer satisfaction, increasing employee participation, strengthening supplier partnerships, and facilitating an organizational atmosphere of continuous quality improvement. To have an effective TQM program, top management must make a strong, sustained commitment to the effort and must be able to coordinate all the program's elements so that they work in harmony. Overall financial benefits of TQM include lower operating costs, higher return on sales and on investment, and an improved ability to use premium pricing rather than competitive pricing.

8 Summarize what it takes to become a successful manager today.

Organizations pay managers for their performance. Managers coordinate resources. They also plan, organize, lead, motivate, and control. They make decisions that can spell the difference between an organization's success and failure. To complete their tasks, managers work long hours at a hectic pace. To be successful, they need personal skills (oral and written communication skills, computer skills, and critical-thinking skills), an academic background that provides a foundation for a management career, and practical work experience.

KEY TERMS

You should now be able to define and give an example relevant to each of the following terms:

management (159)
planning (161)
mission (161)
strategic planning (161)
goal (161)
objective (161)
plan (162)
strategic plan (162)
tactical plan (163)
operational plan (163)

contingency plan (163)
organizing (163)
leading (163)
motivating (164)
directing (164)
controlling (164)
top manager (165)
middle manager (165)
first-line manager (165)
financial manager (166)

operations manager (166)
marketing manager (167)
human resources manager (167)
administrative manager (167)
technical skill (168)
conceptual skill (168)
interpersonal skill (168)
decisional role (168)

interpersonal role (169)
informational role (169)
leadership (169)
authoritarian leader (170)
laissez-faire leader (171)
democratic leader (171)
decision making (171)
problem (171)
total quality management (TQM) (172)

DISCUSSION QUESTIONS

1. What is the mission of a neighborhood restaurant? Of the Salvation Army? What might be reasonable objectives for these organizations?
2. How do a strategic plan, a tactical plan, and an operational plan differ? What do they all have in common?
3. Why are leadership and motivation necessary in a business in which people are paid for their work?
4. In what ways are management skills related to the roles managers play? Provide a specific example to support your answer.
5. Compare and contrast the major styles of leadership.
6. Discuss what happens during each of the four steps of the managerial decision-making process.
7. What are the major benefits of a total quality management program?

8. Does a healthy firm (one that is doing well) have to worry about effective management? Explain.
9. Which of the management functions, skills, and roles do not apply to the owner-operator of a sole proprietorship?
10. Which leadership style might be best suited to each of the three general levels of management within an organization?
11. According to this chapter, the leadership style that is *most* effective depends on interaction among the employees, characteristics of the work situation, and the manager's personality. Do you agree or disagree? Explain your answer.
12. Do you think that people are really as important to an organization as this chapter seems to indicate?

Get Flash Cards, Quizzes,
Games, Crosswords and more
@ www.cengage.com/introbusiness/
pride

Test Yourself

Matching Questions

1. _____ It is the process of accomplishing objectives through people.

2. _____ Its purpose is to implement a strategy.

3. _____ It is a process of establishing an organization's goals and objectives.

4. _____ The ability to influence others is what it is about.

5. _____ A combination of leading and motivating is the essence of this process.

6. _____ It is a process of influencing people to work.

7. _____ This person delegates authority.

8. _____ A distribution handler settles a strike is an example.

9. _____ A vast amount of time is spent motivating employees.

10. _____ It is needed to work a computer.

    a. decisional role
    b. directing
    c. first-line manager
    d. total quality management (TQM)
    e. laissez-faire leader
    f. leadership
    g. leading
    h. management
    i. strategic planning
    j. contingency plan
    k. tactical plan
    l. technical skill

True False Questions

11. **T F** Developing self-managed work teams is a way to increase employee participation and to improve quality in the workplace.

12. **T F** As managers carry out their functions, the first step is to control, the second to organize, and the third to plan.

13. **T F** Operational plans aimed at increasing sales would include specific advertising activities.

14. **T F** Measuring actual performance is the first step in the control process.

15. **T F** Optimization is the process for balancing conflicting goals.

16. **T F** An organization's mission is the means by which it fulfills its purpose.

17. **T F** A democratic leader makes all the decisions and tells subordinates what to do.

18. **T F** Top managers rely on technical skills more than managers at other levels.

19. **T F** Brainstorming is a common technique used to generate alternatives in solving problems.

20. **T F** Implementation of a decision requires time, planning, preparation of personnel, and evaluation of results.

Multiple-Choice Questions

21. _____ The process of developing a set of goals and committing an organization to them is called

    a. organizing.
    b. planning.
    c. optimizing.
    d. controlling.
    e. directing.

22. _____ Who is responsible for developing a firm's mission?

    a. Top managers
    b. First-level managers
    c. Operations managers
    d. Middle managers
    e. Supervisors

23. _____ Acme Houseware established a goal to increase its sales by 20 percent in the next year. To ensure that the firm reaches its goal, the sales reports are monitored on a weekly basis. When sales show a slight decline, the sales manager takes actions to correct the problem. Which management function is the manager using?

    a. Leading
    b. Controlling
    c. Directing
    d. Organizing
    e. Planning

Test Yourself

24. _____ The chief executive officer of Southwest Airlines provides the company with leadership and overall guidance and is responsible for developing its mission and establishing its goals. Which area of management is being used?

    a. Human resources
    b. Operations
    c. Financial
    d. Administrative
    e. Marketing

25. _____ Establishing a structure to carry out plans is called

    a. organizing.
    b. directing.
    c. leading.
    d. planning.
    e. influencing.

26. _____ This manager is responsible for facilitating the exchange of products between an organization and its customers or clients.

    a. Human resources manager
    b. Marketing manager
    c. Materials manager
    d. Financial manager
    e. Facilitating manager

27. _____ These types of skills allow a manager to see the "big picture" and understand how the various parts of an organization or idea can fit together:

    a. Interpersonal skills
    b. Conceptual skills
    c. Technical skills
    d. Management skills
    e. Decisional skills

28. _____ Effective managers do not engage in which of the following behaviors?

    a. They believe in themselves.
    b. They are constantly studying the competition when solving a problem.
    c. They clarify situations and examine the causes of problems, asking whether the presence or absence of certain variables alters a situation.
    d. They are moral and ethical.
    e. They are fair with almost all employees.

29. _____ Which one of the following statements is correct about TQM?

    a. Top management must make a strong commitment to a TQM program by treating quality improvement as a top priority.
    b. Employees should be aware of TQM movement, not necessarily involved in it.
    c. Managers need to ask for input occasionally in order to practice TQM.
    d. The top administration should appear to be interested in TQM.
    e. In order for TQM to function effectively, you need a lot of resources.

30. _____ Because a large part of a manager's day is spent conversing with others, it is important for the manager to have

    a. written skills.
    b. people skills.
    c. idea skills.
    d. oral communication skills.
    e. interpersonal skills.

Answers on p. TY-1

VIDEO CASE

The Leadership Advantage at Student Advantage

Student Advantage LLC, based in Boston, provides college students at over a thousand U.S. campuses with credit cards that give them discounts in shops and restaurants nationwide and with companies like Alamo Rental Cars, AT&T, Amtrak, Barnes & Noble, Dick's Sporting Goods, Foot Locker, Toshiba, Greyhound, Target Stores, and Verizon Wireless.

Student Advantage started as a small entrepreneurial company and experienced explosive growth. The challenge for Ray Sozzi, the company's founder and CEO, was to keep the spirit and culture that made the company an initial success while bringing in needed new processes (and the bureaucracies that came with them) as the company grew. His approach was to tie empowerment to accountability—

that is, to make sure his managers take ownership for their decisions.

Sozzi does not create plans and direct the organization to execute them. Rather, he lets his managers develop plans and then empowers them to execute them. Sozzi believes one of the most powerful management strategies is to let people tell him what they want to do and then let them do it. His managers know that if they mess up either side of that equation, they're going to fail.

Another way in which Sozzi empowers his managers is to give them a different perspective on what they want to do. Middle managers often have so many day-to-day tasks to confront and people reporting to them that they have difficulty finding time to step back and look at the bigger picture. That's where Ray Sozzi plays an important role as a sounding board or devil's advocate. As CEO he also has a different perspective from his managers. He's more aware of what is happening in the competitive environment, he is better acquainted with the needs and preferences of company shareholders, and he understands the need to balance investing in the company with providing shareholder value. Thus he helps his managers either firm up the position they're taking or step back and rethink it.

Responsibility, delegation, and accountability are central to the company's management style, and these principles have become even more important as Student Advantage has grown to over 400 employees. The company is organized into a number of teams, including Business Development, Marketing, Finance, and Human Resources. It is each team manager's responsibility to make that team's plans work.

Communication is key in delegation. All team members need to understand what the team wants to accomplish and each person's role in making it happen. It's hard sometimes for a manager to give up control, and it requires a certain amount of trust to give other people responsibility. Yet it's critical for an effective organization. As one Student Advantage manager put it, "if you don't delegate, you die!"

The chain of command from CEO to COO to Department Head to Assistant Manager is pretty clear, but how does an effective organization work laterally, as opposed to vertically? Within Student Advantage's marketing department, the marketing project manager is responsible for acquiring new members (that is, students) and communicating with them. This person works with the account manager, who supports the partner companies that pay for the member discounts. These employees don't have rigidly defined roles; rather they help each other serve their respective members and partners, brainstorming together and using the resources they need to accomplish the department's common goals. The lines between the various job functions in marketing (as well as in the other teams) are very soft. Decisions are never made by just one department within marketing; everyone discusses everything with everyone else. This lateral way of working leads to better decisions and also allows each person to get experience beyond his or her job title and responsibility.

Student Advantage is still a relatively small company so its employees wear many hats. With flexible job descriptions, teamwork, and staff empowerment, it appears poised to continue its strong growth in a very challenging marketplace.[12]

Questions

1. How would you describe Ray Sozzi's leadership style?
2. In terms of the management process (shown in Figure 6.2), how does Ray Sozzi control the planning function?
3. What are some advantages and disadvantages of the management practices at Student Advantage?

BUILDING SKILLS FOR CAREER SUCCESS

1. EXPLORING THE INTERNET

Most large companies call on a management consulting firm for a variety of services, including employee training, help in the selection of an expensive purchase such as a computer system, recruitment of employees, and direction in reorganization and strategic planning.

Large consulting firms generally operate globally and provide information to companies considering entry into foreign countries or business alliances with foreign firms. They use their websites, along with magazine-style articles, to celebrate achievements and present their credentials to clients. Business students can acquire an enormous amount of up-to-date information in the field of management by perusing these sites.

Assignment

1. Explore each of the following websites:
   Accenture: www.accenture.com
   BearingPoint (formerly KPMG Consulting):
   www.bearingpoint.com
   Cap Gemini Ernst & Young: www.capgemini.com
   Visit the text website for updates to this exercise.
2. Judging from the articles and notices posted, what are the current areas of activities of one of these firms?
3. Explore one of these areas in more detail by comparing postings from each firm's site. For instance, if "global business opportunities" appears to be a popular area of management consulting, how has each firm distinguished itself in this area? Who would you call first for advice?

4. Given that consulting firms are always trying to fill positions for their clients and to meet their own recruitment needs, it is little wonder that employment postings are a popular area on their sites. Examine these in detail. Based on your examination of the site and the registration format, what sort of recruit are they interested in?

2. BUILDING TEAM SKILLS

Over the past few years, an increasing number of employees, stockholders, and customers have been demanding to know what their companies are about. As a result, more companies have been taking the time to analyze their operations and to prepare mission statements that focus on the purpose of the company. The mission statement is becoming a critical planning tool for successful companies. To make effective decisions, employees must understand the purpose of their company.

Assignment

1. Divide into teams and write a mission statement for one of the following types of businesses:
   Food service, restaurant
   Banking
   Airline
   Auto repair
   Cabinet manufacturing
2. Discuss your mission statement with other teams. How did the other teams interpret the purpose of your company? What is the mission statement saying about the company?
3. Write a one-page report on what you learned about developing mission statements.

3. RESEARCHING DIFFERENT CAREERS

A successful career requires planning. Without a plan, or roadmap, you will find it very difficult, if not impossible, to reach your desired career destination. The first step in planning is to establish what your career goal is. You then must set objectives and develop plans for accomplishing those objectives. This kind of planning takes time, but it will pay off later.

Assignment

Complete the following statements:

1. My career goal is to

   _____

   _____

   This statement should encapsulate what you want to accomplish over the long run. It may include the type of job you want and the type of business or industry you want to work in. Examples include the following:

   - My career goal is to work as a top manager in the food industry.
   - My career goal is to supervise aircraft mechanics.
   - My career goal is to win the top achievement award in the advertising industry.

2. My career objectives are to

   _____

   _____

   Objectives are benchmarks along the route to a career destination. They are more specific than a career goal. A statement about a career objective should specify what you want to accomplish, when you will complete it, and any other details that will serve as criteria against which you can measure your progress. Examples include the following:

   - My objective is to be promoted to supervisor by January 1, 20xx.
   - My objective is to enroll in a management course at Main College in the spring semester 20xx.
   - My objective is to earn an A in the management course at Main College in the spring semester 20xx.
   - My objective is to prepare a status report by September 30 covering the last quarter's activities by asking Charlie in Quality Control to teach me the procedures.

3. Exchange your goal and objectives statements with another class member. Can your partner interpret your objectives correctly? Are the objectives concise and complete? Do they include criteria against which you can measure your progress? If not, discuss the problem and rewrite the objective.

7 Creating a Flexible Organization

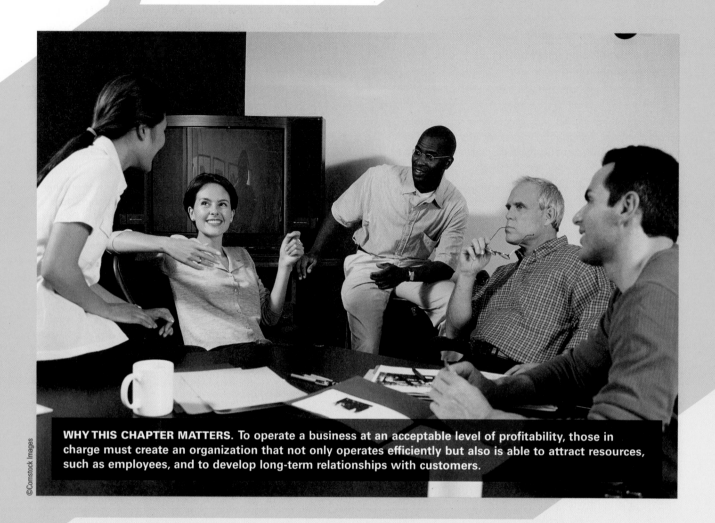

©Comstock Images

WHY THIS CHAPTER MATTERS. To operate a business at an acceptable level of profitability, those in charge must create an organization that not only operates efficiently but also is able to attract resources, such as employees, and to develop long-term relationships with customers.

LEARNING OBJECTIVES

1 Understand what an organization is and identify its characteristics.

2 Explain why job specialization is important.

3 Identify the various bases for departmentalization.

4 Explain how decentralization follows from delegation.

5 Understand how the span of management describes an organization.

6 Understand how the chain of command is established by using line and staff management.

7 Describe the four basic forms of organizational structure: bureaucratic, matrix, cluster, and network.

8 Summarize the use of corporate culture, intrapreneurship, committees, coordination techniques, informal groups, and the grapevine.

Creating the Future at Hewlett-Packard

Founded in a Silicon Valley garage in 1939, Hewlett-Packard's first product was an audio oscillator to test sound levels, and its first customer was Walt Disney. Today the company has 320,000 employees, rings up $118 billion in annual sales, and spends $3.5 billion on research and development every year to stay ahead of its high-tech competition.

Hewlett-Packard is organized by product into three divisions: The Personal Systems Group, which makes PCs and mobile computing devices; the Imaging and Printing Group, which makes printers and printing supplies; and the Technology Solutions Group, which offers data storage and networking equipment, software, and technical consulting services. All three divisions depend on HP Labs, the company's advanced research arm, for scientific breakthroughs that will lay the foundation for future goods and services.

Guided by the motto "creating the future," 600 scientists work in HP Labs located in California, India, China, England, Israel, Russia, and Japan. In the past, the labs pursued as many as 150 projects at any given time, investigating promising theories and materials without knowing where their discoveries might lead. Although some research projects led to innovative new products such as the inkjet printer, many ultimately had little or no potential for adding to Hewlett-Packard's bottom line.

Now, after a top-down reordering of priorities, HP Labs has narrowed its focus to 40 key projects with practical long-term applications for the three divisions. For example, its scientists are exploring how to bring 3D multimedia technology into the home and how to improve the cost-efficiency and quality of print-on-demand publishing. The scientists don't just stay in their labs conducting research—they get out and talk with customers, and they develop business plans for bringing their discoveries to market. To get a head-start on the products of tomorrow, HP Labs is also collaborating on research projects with 35 universities worldwide. "Unless we continue to innovate, we won't have a leadership position in the future," says the director.[1]

DID YOU KNOW?

With 320,000 employees and $118 billion in annual sales, Hewlett-Packard spends $3.5 billion on research and development every year to stay ahead of the competition.

To survive and to grow, companies such as Hewlett-Packard must constantly look for ways to improve their methods of doing business. Managers at Hewlett-Packard, like those at many other organizations, deliberately reorganized the company to achieve its goals and to create satisfying products that foster long-term customer relationships.

When firms are organized, or reorganized, the focus is sometimes on achieving low operating costs. Other firms, such as Nike, emphasize providing high-quality products to ensure customer satisfaction. A firm's organization influences its performance. Thus, the issue of organization is important.

We begin this chapter by examining the business organization—what it is and how it functions in today's business environment. Next, we focus one by one on five characteristics that shape an organization's structure. We discuss job specialization within a company, the grouping of jobs into manageable units or departments, the delegation of power from management to workers, the span of management, and establishment of a chain of command. Then we step back for an overall view of four approaches to organizational structure: the bureaucratic structure, the matrix structure, the cluster structure, and the network structure. Finally, we look at the network of social interactions—the informal organization—that operates within the formal business structure.

organization a group of two or more people working together to achieve a common set of goals

What Is an Organization?

We used the term *organization* throughout Chapter 6 without really defining it mainly because its everyday meaning is close to its business meaning. Here, however, let us agree that an **organization** is a group of two or more people work-

1 LEARNING OBJECTIVE

Understand what an organization is and identify its characteristics.

Job specialization. These workers have jobs with a considerable amount of specialization. In this factory, umbrellas will be completed after more than 80 different processes.

AP Photo/Wang guohong/Imaginechina

ing together to achieve a common set of goals. A neighborhood dry cleaner owned and operated by a husband-and-wife team is an organization. IBM and Home Depot, which employ thousands of workers worldwide, are also organizations in the same sense. Although each corporation's organizational structure is more complex than the dry-cleaning establishment, all must be organized to achieve their goals.

An inventor who goes into business to produce and market a new invention hires people, decides what each will do, determines who will report to whom, and so on. These activities are the essence of organizing, or creating, the organization. One way to create this "picture" is to create an organization chart.

Developing Organization Charts

An **organization chart** is a diagram that represents the positions and relationships within an organization. An example of an organization chart is shown in Figure 7.1.

FIGURE 7.1: A Typical Corporate Organization Chart A company's organization chart represents the positions and relationships within the organization and shows the managerial chains of command.

KEY:

— Chain of command
--- Staff

Vice president, operations

Plant manager

Plant manager

Department manager

Department manager

Department manager

Department manager

Supervisor

Supervisor

Supervisor

Supervisor

Supervisor

Supervisor

Supervisor

Supervisor

Part 3: Management and Organization

Each rectangle represents a particular position or person in the organization. At the top is the president; at the next level are the vice presidents. The solid vertical lines connecting the vice presidents to the president indicate that the vice presidents are in the chain of command. The **chain of command** is the line of authority that extends from the highest to the lowest levels of the organization. Moreover, each vice president reports directly to the president. Similarly, the plant managers, regional sales managers, and accounting department manager report to the vice presidents. The chain of command can be short or long. For example, at Royer's Roundtop Café, an independent restaurant in Roundtop, Texas, the chain of command is very short. Bud Royer, the owner, is responsible only to himself and can alter his hours or change his menu quickly. On the other hand, the chain of command at McDonald's is long. Before making certain types of changes, a McDonald's franchisee seeks permission from regional management, which, in turn, seeks approval from corporate headquarters.

In the chart, the connections to the directors of legal services, public affairs, and human resources are shown as broken lines; these people are not part of the direct chain of command. Instead, they hold *advisory,* or *staff,* positions. This difference will be examined later in this chapter when we discuss line and staff positions.

Most smaller organizations find organization charts useful. They clarify positions and reporting relationships for everyone in the organization, and they help

organization chart a diagram that represents the positions and relationships within an organization

chain of command the line of authority that extends from the highest to the lowest levels of an organization

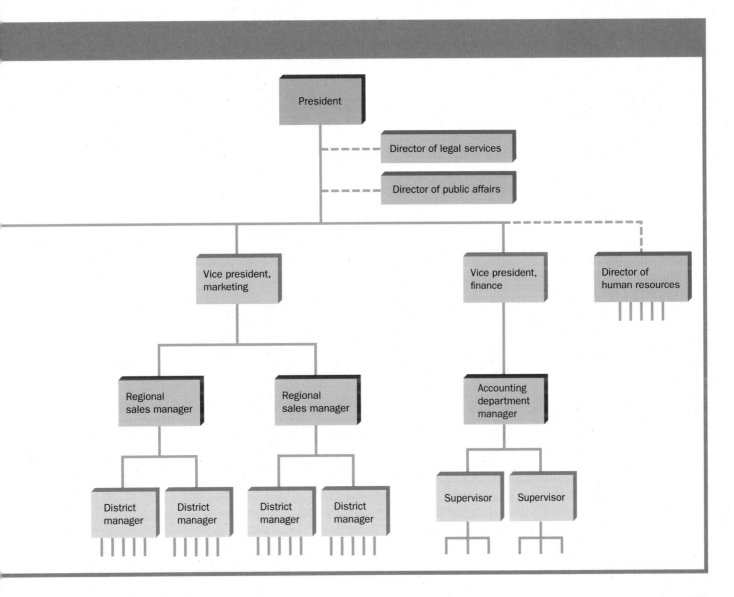

managers to track growth and change in the organizational structure. For two reasons, however, many large organizations, such as ExxonMobil, Kellogg's, and Procter & Gamble, do not maintain complete, detailed charts. First, it is difficult to chart even a few dozen positions accurately, much less the thousands that characterize larger firms. And second, larger organizations are almost always changing parts of their structure. An organization chart would be outdated before it was completed. However, organization must exist even without a chart in order for a business to be successful. Technology is helping large companies implement up-to-date organization charts. Workstream, Inc., is a provider of enterprise workforce management software and has signed big-name clients. Carol Caruso, an organizational design specialist at Mercedes-Benz USA, reported that the software saves time and effort in communicating organizational structure. Aside from providing organization charts, the software also will support human resources processes such as workflow approval and succession planning.[2]

Five Steps for Organizing a Business

When a firm is started, management must decide how to organize the firm. These decisions are all part of five major steps that sum up the organizing process. The five steps are as follows:

1. *Job design.* Divide the work that is to be done by the entire organization into separate parts, and assign those parts to positions within the organization.
2. *Departmentalization.* Group the various positions into manageable units or departments.
3. *Delegation.* Distribute responsibility and authority within the organization.
4. *Span of management.* Determine the number of subordinates who will report to each manager.
5. *Chain of command.* Establish the organization's chain of command by designating the positions with direct authority and those that are support positions.

In the next several sections, we discuss major issues associated with these steps.

Concept Check

1. How do large and small organizations use organization charts differently?

2. Identify and describe the five steps for organizing a business.

LEARNING OBJECTIVE 2

Explain why job specialization is important.

Job Design

In Chapter 1, we defined *specialization* as the separation of a manufacturing process into distinct tasks and the assignment of different tasks to different people. Here we are extending that concept to *all* the activities performed within an organization.

Job Specialization

Job specialization is the separation of all organizational activities into distinct tasks and the assignment of different tasks to different people. Adam Smith, the eighteenth-century economist whose theories gave rise to capitalism, was the first to emphasize the power of specialization in his book, *The Wealth of Nations*. According to Smith, the various tasks in a particular pin factory were arranged so that one worker drew the wire for the pins, another straightened the wire, a third cut it, a fourth ground the point, and a fifth attached the head. Smith claimed that ten men were able to produce 48,000 pins per day. Before specialization, they could produce only 200 pins per day because each worker had to perform all five tasks!

The Rationale for Specialization

For a number of reasons, some job specialization is necessary in every organization because the "job" of most organizations is too large for one person to handle. In a firm such as Ford, thousands of people are needed to manufacture automobiles. Others are needed to sell the cars, control the firm's finances, and so on.

Second, when a worker has to learn one specific, highly specialized task, that individual should be able to learn it very efficiently. Third, a worker repeating the

job specialization the separation of all organizational activities into distinct tasks and the assignment of different tasks to different people same job does not lose time changing from operations, as the pin workers did when producing complete pins. Fourth, the more specialized the job, the easier it is to design specialized equipment. And finally, the more specialized the job, the easier is the job training.

Alternatives to Job Specialization

Unfortunately, specialization can have negative consequences as well. The most significant drawback is the boredom and dissatisfaction employees may feel when repeating the same job. Bored employees may be absent from work frequently, may not put much effort into their work, and may even sabotage the company's efforts to produce quality products.

To combat these problems, managers often turn to job rotation. **Job rotation** is the systematic shifting of employees from one job to another. For example, a worker may be assigned a different job every week for a four-week period and then return to the first job in the fifth week. Job rotation provides a variety of tasks so that workers are less likely to become bored and dissatisfied.

Two other approaches—job enlargement and job enrichment—also can provide solutions to the problems caused by job specialization. These topics, along with other methods used to motivate employees, are discussed in Chapter 10.

Departmentalization

After jobs are designed, they must be grouped together into "working units," or departments. This process is called *departmentalization*. More specifically, **departmentalization** is the process of grouping jobs into manageable units. Several departmentalization bases are used commonly. In fact, most firms use more than one. Today, the most common bases for organizing a business into effective departments are by function, by product, by location, and by customer.

By Function

Departmentalization by function groups jobs that relate to the same organizational activity. Under this scheme, all marketing personnel are grouped together in the marketing department, all production personnel in the production department, and so on.

Most smaller and newer organizations departmentalize by function. Supervision is simplified because everyone is involved in the same activities, and coordination is easy. The disadvantages of this method of grouping jobs are that it can lead to slow decision making and that it tends to emphasize the department over the whole organization.

By Product

Departmentalization by product groups activities related to a particular good or service. This approach is used often by older and larger firms that produce and sell a variety of products. Each department handles its own marketing, production, financial management, and human resources activities.

Departmentalization by product makes decision making easier and provides for the integration of all activities associated with each product. However, it causes some duplication of specialized activities—such as finance—from department to department. And the emphasis is placed on the product rather than on the whole organization.

By Location

Departmentalization by location groups activities according to the defined geographic area in which they are performed. Departmental areas may range from whole countries (for international firms) to regions within countries (for national firms) to areas of several city blocks (for police departments organized into precincts). Departmentalization by location allows the organization to respond readily to the unique demands or requirements of different locations. Nevertheless, a large

3 LEARNING OBJECTIVE

Identify the various bases for departmentalization.

job rotation the systematic shifting of employees from one job to another

departmentalization the process of grouping jobs into manageable units

departmentalization by function grouping jobs that relate to the same organizational activity

departmentalization by product grouping activities related to a particular product or service

departmentalization by location grouping activities according to the defined geographic area in which they are performed

departmentalization by customer grouping activities according to the needs of various customer populations

delegation assigning part of a manager's work and power to other workers

Concept Check

1. What are the four most common bases for departmentalization?

2. Give an example of each.

LEARNING OBJECTIVE 4

Explain how decentralization follows from delegation.

responsibility the duty to do a job or perform a task

authority the power, within an organization, to accomplish an assigned job or task

accountability the obligation of a worker to accomplish an assigned job or task

administrative staff and an elaborate control system may be needed to coordinate operations in many locations.

By Customer

Departmentalization by customer groups activities according to the needs of various customer populations. A local Honda dealership, for example, may have one sales staff to deal with individual consumers and a different sales staff to work with customers who bring their cars in for service. The obvious advantage of this approach is that it allows the firm to deal efficiently with unique customers or customer groups. The biggest drawback is that a larger-than-usual administrative staff is needed.

Combinations of Bases

Many organizations use more than one of these departmentalization bases.

Take a moment to examine Figure 7.2. Notice that departmentalization by customer is used to organize New-Wave Fashions, Inc., into three major divisions: men's, women's, and children's clothing. Then functional departmentalization is used to distinguish the firm's production and marketing activities. Finally, location is used to organize the firm's marketing efforts.

Delegation, Decentralization, and Centralization

The third major step in the organizing process is to distribute power in the organization. **Delegation** assigns part of a manager's work and power to other workers. The degree of centralization or decentralization of authority is determined by the overall pattern of delegation within the organization.

Delegation of Authority

Because no manager can do everything, delegation is vital to completion of a manager's work. Delegation is also important in developing the skills and abilities of subordinates. It allows those who are being groomed for higher-level positions to play increasingly important roles in decision making.

Steps in Delegation The delegation process generally involves three steps (see Figure 7.3). First, the manager must *assign responsibility*. **Responsibility** is the

FIGURE 7.2: Multibase Departmentalization for New-Wave Fashions, Inc. Most firms use more than one basis for departmentalization to improve efficiency and to avoid overlapping positions.

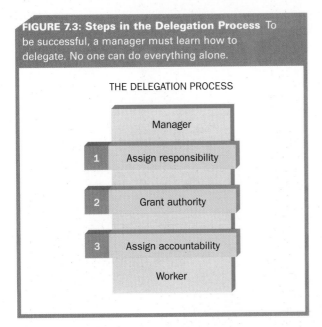

FIGURE 7.3: Steps in the Delegation Process To be successful, a manager must learn how to delegate. No one can do everything alone.

THE DELEGATION PROCESS

Manager

1 Assign responsibility

2 Grant authority

3 Assign accountability

Worker

duty to do a job or perform a task. In most job settings, a manager simply gives the worker a job to do. Typical job assignments might range from having a worker prepare a report on the status of a new quality control program to placing the person in charge of a task force. Second, the manager must *grant authority*. **Authority** is the power, within the organization, to accomplish an assigned job or task. This might include the power to obtain specific information, order supplies, authorize relevant expenditures, or make certain decisions. Finally, the manager must *create accountability*. **Accountability** is the obligation of a worker to accomplish an assigned job or task.

Note that accountability is created, but it cannot be delegated. Suppose that you are an operations manager for Target and are responsible for performing a specific task. You, in turn, delegate this task to someone else. You nonetheless remain accountable to your immediate supervisor for getting the task done properly. If the other person fails to complete the assignment, you—not the person to whom you delegated the task—will be held accountable.

Barriers to Delegation For several reasons, managers may be unwilling to delegate work. Many managers are reluctant to delegate because they want to be sure that the work gets done. Another reason for reluctance stems from the opposite situation. The manager fears that the worker will do the work well and attract the approving notice of higher-level managers. Finally, some managers do not delegate because they are so disorganized that they simply are not able to plan and assign work effectively.

Decentralization of Authority

The pattern of delegation throughout an organization determines the extent to which that organization is decentralized or centralized. In a **decentralized organization,**

Is it Ethical?

Is an Employee Just a Number?

With 385,000 employees worldwide and $103 billion in annual revenue, IBM is always looking for better ways to organize and manage its workforce. It's not surprising that IBM would use its technical expertise to be sure the right people are doing the right things. But is IBM taking job specialization too far by reducing employees' knowledge, skills, activities, and internal connections to numbers that can be mathematically manipulated for maximum efficiency?

The company already collects and analyzes lots of employee information. Although confidential files are excluded, IBM tracks nearly everything else about its technical consultants. It examines their work experience, educational background, and compensation level. It looks at their computerized calendars to see where they are, who they meet, and what they do, hour by hour. And it monitors their online activities, cell-phone usage, and e-mail patterns.

IBM's goal is to use the data to improve the way it defines organizational tasks and relationships. Through sophisticated computer modeling, the company will soon be able to determine the exact role a specific employee might play in a project and calculate the financial impact of having a different employee in that role. It is also opening Analytics Solution Centers around the world and hiring thousands of analytics experts to offer such modeling services to its business clients. Despite the bottom-line possibilities, should IBM pay more attention to human elements rather than approaching job specialization in terms of numbers?

Sources: "IBM to Open Global Network of Advanced Analytics Centers," *Reuters*, April 28, 2009, www.reuters.com; Eddie Evans, "Mathematicians Are New Masters of the Universe," *Reuters*, September 12, 2008, www.reuters.com; Stephen Baker, "Management by the Numbers," *BusinessWeek*, September 8, 2008, pp. 32–38.

decentralized organization an organization in which management consciously attempts to spread authority widely across various organization levels

Delegation. At this auto production plant in North Carolina, a manager delegates tasks necessary for this product to move to the next stage of production.

©AP Photo/The News & Observer, Jill Leonard

centralized organization an organization that systematically works to concentrate authority at the upper levels of the organization

span of management (or **span of control**) the number of workers who report directly to one manager

Concept Check

1. Identify and describe the three steps in the delegation process.

2. Differentiate decentralized organization and centralized organization.

LEARNING OBJECTIVE 5

Understand how the span of management describes an organization.

management consciously attempts to spread authority widely across various organization levels. A **centralized organization**, on the other hand, systematically works to concentrate authority at the upper levels. For example, many publishers of college-level textbooks are centralized organizations, with authority concentrated at the top. Large organizations may have characteristics of both decentralized and centralized organizations.

A number of factors can influence the extent to which a firm is decentralized. One is the external environment in which the firm operates. The more complex and unpredictable this environment, the more likely it is that top management will let lower-level managers make important decisions. After all, lower-level managers are closer to the problems. Another factor is the nature of the decision itself. The riskier or more important the decision, the greater is the tendency to centralize decision making. A third factor is the abilities of lower-level managers. If these managers do not have strong decision-making skills, top managers will be reluctant to decentralize. And, in contrast, strong lower-level decision-making skills encourage decentralization. Finally, a firm that traditionally has practiced centralization or decentralization is likely to maintain that posture in the future.

In principle, neither decentralization nor centralization is right or wrong. What works for one organization may or may not work for another. Kmart Corporation and McDonald's are very successful—and both practice centralization. But decentralization has worked very well for General Electric and Sears. Every organization must assess its own situation and then choose the level of centralization or decentralization that will work best.

The Span of Management

The fourth major step in organizing a business is establishing the **span of management** (or **span of control**), which is the number of workers who report directly to one manager. For hundreds of years, theorists have searched for an ideal span of management. When it became apparent that there is no perfect number of subordinates for a manager to supervise, they turned their attention to the general issue of whether the span should be wide or narrow. This issue is complicated because the span of management may change by department within the same organization. For example, the span of management at FedEx varies within the company. Departments in which workers do the same tasks on a regular basis—customer service agents, handlers, sorters, and couriers—usually have a span of management of fifteen to twenty employees per manager. Groups performing multiple and different tasks are more likely to have smaller spans of management consisting of five or six employees.[3] Thus, FedEx uses a wide span of control in some departments and a narrower one in others.

Wide and Narrow Spans of Control

A *wide* span of management exists when a manager has a larger number of subordinates. A *narrow* span exists when the manager has only a few subordinates. Several factors determine the span that is better for a particular manager (see Figure 7.4). Generally, the span of control may be wide when (1) the manager and the subordinates are very competent, (2) the organization has a well-established set of standard operating procedures, and (3) few new problems are expected to arise. The span should be narrow when (1) workers are physically located far from one another, (2) the manager has much work to do in addition to supervising workers, (3) a great deal of interaction is required between supervisor and workers, and (4) new problems arise frequently.

Organizational Height

The span of management has an obvious impact on relations between managers and workers. It has a more subtle but equally important impact on the height of the organization. **Organizational height** is the number of layers, or levels, of management in a firm. The span of management plays a direct role in determining the height of the organization, as shown in Figure 7.4. If spans of management are wider, fewer levels are needed, and the organization is *flat*. If spans of management generally are narrow, more levels are needed, and the resulting organization is *tall*.

In a taller organization, administrative costs are higher because more managers are needed. Communication among levels may become distorted because information has to pass up and down through more people. When companies are cutting costs, one option is to decrease organizational height in order to reduce related administrative expenses. Although flat organizations avoid these problems, their managers may perform more administrative duties simply because there are fewer managers. Wide spans of management also may require managers to spend considerably more time supervising and working with subordinates.

organizational height the number of layers, or levels, of management in a firm

Concept Check

1. Describe the two spans of control.

2. What are problems associated with each one?

FIGURE 7.4: The Span of Management Several criteria determine whether a firm uses a wide span of management, in which a number of workers report to one manager, or a narrow span, in which a manager supervises only a few workers.

WIDE SPAN
- High level of competence in managers and workers
- Standard operating procedures
- Few new problems

Flat organization

NARROW SPAN
- Physical dispersion of subordinates
- Manager has additional tasks
- High level of interaction required between manager and workers
- High frequency of new problems

Tall organization

LEARNING OBJECTIVE 6

Understand how the chain of command is established by using line and staff management.

Chain of Command: Line and Staff Management

Establishing the chain of command is another step in organizing a business. It reaches from the highest to the lowest levels of management. A **line management position** is part of the chain of command; it is a position in which a person makes decisions and gives orders to subordinates to achieve the goals of the organization. A **staff management position**, by contrast, is a position created to provide support, advice, and expertise to someone in the chain of command. Staff managers are not part of the chain of command but do have authority over their assistants (see Figure 7.5).

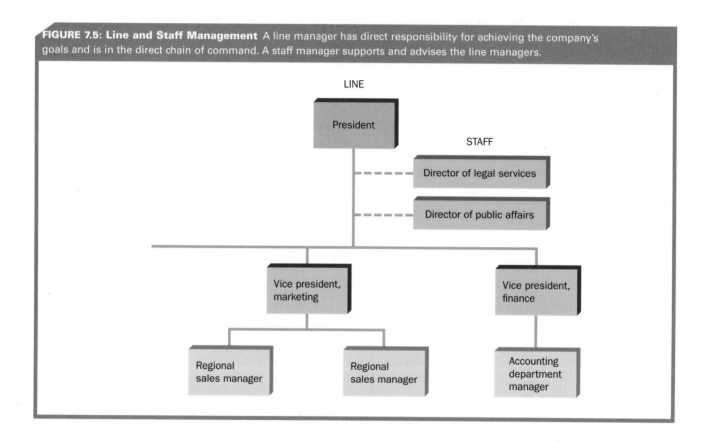

FIGURE 7.5: Line and Staff Management A line manager has direct responsibility for achieving the company's goals and is in the direct chain of command. A staff manager supports and advises the line managers.

Line and Staff Positions Compared

Both line and staff managers are needed for effective management, but the two positions differ in important ways. The basic difference is in terms of authority. Line managers have *line authority*, which means that they can make decisions and issue directives relating to the organization's goals.

Staff managers seldom have this kind of authority. Instead, they usually have either advisory authority or functional authority. *Advisory authority* is the expectation that line managers will consult the appropriate staff manager when making decisions. Functional authority is stronger. *Functional authority* is the authority of staff managers to make decisions and issue directives about their areas of expertise. For example, a legal adviser for Nike can decide whether to retain a particular clause in a contract but not product pricing.

Line-Staff Conflict

For a variety of reasons, conflict between line managers and staff managers is fairly common in businesses. Staff managers often have more formal education

line management position a part of the chain of command; it is a position in which a person makes decisions and gives orders to subordinates to achieve the goals of the organization

staff management position a position created to provide support, advice, and expertise within an organization and sometimes are younger (and perhaps more ambitious) than line managers. Line managers may perceive staff managers as a threat to their own authority and thus may resent them. For their part, staff managers may become annoyed or angry if their expert recommendations—in public relations or human resources management, for example—are not adopted by line management.

Fortunately, there are several ways to minimize the likelihood of such conflict. One way is to integrate line and staff managers into one team. Another is to ensure that the areas of responsibility of line and staff managers are clearly defined. Finally, line and staff managers both can be held accountable for the results of their activities.

Before studying the next topic—forms of organizational structure—you may want to review the five organization-shaping characteristics that we have just discussed. See Table 7.1 for a summary.

Line and staff positions. Ronald McDonald occupies a staff position and does not have direct authority over other employees at McDonald's. The other individuals shown here occupy line positions and do have direct authority over some of the other McDonald's employees.

TABLE 7.1: Five Characteristics of Organizational Structure

Dimension	Purpose
Job design	To divide the work performed by an organization into parts and assign each part a position within the organization.
Departmentalization	To group various positions in an organization into manageable units. Departmentalization may be based on function, product, location, customer, or a combination of these bases.
Delegation	To distribute part of a manager's work and power to other workers. A deliberate concentration of authority at the upper levels of the organization creates a centralized structure. A wide distribution of authority across various levels of the organization creates a decentralized structure.
Span of management	To set the number of workers who report directly to one manager. A narrow span has only a few workers reporting to one manager. A wide span has a large number of workers reporting to one manager.
Line and staff management	To distinguish between those positions that are part of the chain of command and those that provide support, advice, or expertise to those in the chain of command.

Concept Check

1. Compare and contrast line and staff positions.

2. What are the common reasons for line-staff conflict?

Forms of Organizational Structure

7 LEARNING OBJECTIVE

Describe the four basic forms of organizational structure: bureaucratic, matrix, cluster, and network.

Up to this point, we have focused our attention on the major characteristics of organizational structure. In many ways, this is like discussing the parts of a jigsaw puzzle one by one. It is time to put the puzzle together. In particular, we discuss four basic forms of organizational structure: bureaucratic, matrix, cluster, and network.

The Bureaucratic Structure

The term *bureaucracy* is used often in an unfavorable context to suggest rigidity and red tape. This image may be negative, but it does capture some of the essence of the bureaucratic structure.

A **bureaucratic structure** is a management system based on a formal framework of authority that is outlined carefully and followed precisely. A bureaucracy is likely to have the following characteristics:

1. A high level of job specialization
2. Departmentalization by function
3. Formal patterns of delegation
4. A high degree of centralization
5. Narrow spans of management, resulting in a tall organization
6. Clearly defined line and staff positions with formal relationships between the two

Perhaps the best examples of contemporary bureaucracies are government agencies, colleges, and universities. Consider the very rigid college entrance and registration procedures. The reason for such procedures is to ensure that the organization is able to deal with large numbers of people in an equitable and fair manner. We may not enjoy them, but regulations and standard operating procedures guarantee uniform treatment.

Another example of a bureaucratic structure is the U.S. Postal Service. Like colleges and universities, the Postal Service relies on procedures and rules to accomplish the organization's goals. However, the Postal Service has streamlined some of its procedures and initiated new services in order to compete with FedEx, UPS, and other delivery services. As a result, customer satisfaction has begun to improve.

The biggest drawback to the bureaucratic structure is lack of flexibility. A bureaucracy has trouble adjusting to change and coping with the unexpected. Because today's business environment is dynamic and complex, many firms have found that the bureaucratic structure is not an appropriate organizational structure.

The Matrix Structure

When the matrix structure is used, individuals report to more than one superior at the same time. The **matrix structure** combines vertical and horizontal lines of authority. The matrix structure occurs when product departmentalization is superimposed on a functionally departmentalized organization. In a matrix organization, authority flows both down and across.

To understand the structure of a matrix organization, consider the usual functional arrangement, with people working in departments such as engineering, finance, and marketing. Now suppose that we assign people from these departments to a special group that is working on a new project as a team—a cross-functional team. A **cross-functional team** consists of individuals with varying specialties, expertise, and skills that are brought together to achieve a common task. Frequently, cross-functional teams are charged with the responsibility of developing new products. For example, Ford Motor Company assembled a special project team to design and manufacture its global cars. The manager in charge of a team is usually called a *project manager*. Any individual who is working with the team reports to *both* the project manager and the individual's superior in the functional department (see Figure 7.6).

Cross-functional team projects may be temporary, in which case the team is disbanded once the mission is accomplished, or they may be permanent. These teams often are empowered to make major decisions. When a cross-functional team is employed, prospective team members may receive special training because effective teamwork can require different skills. For cross-functional teams to be successful, team members must be given specific information on the job each performs. The team also must develop a sense of cohesiveness and maintain good communications among its members.

Matrix structures offer advantages over other organizational forms. Added flexibility is probably the most obvious advantage. The matrix structure also can increase productivity, raise morale, and nurture creativity and innovation. In addition, employees experience personal development through doing a variety of jobs.

The matrix structure also has disadvantages. Having employees report to more than one supervisor can cause confusion about who is in charge. Like committees, teams may take longer to resolve problems and issues than individuals working alone. Other difficulties include personality clashes, poor communication, undefined individual roles, unclear responsibilities, and finding ways to reward individual and

bureaucratic structure a management system based on a formal framework of authority that is outlined carefully and followed precisely

matrix structure an organizational structure that combines vertical and horizontal lines of authority, usually by superimposing product departmentalization on a functionally departmentalized organization

cross-functional team a team of individuals with varying specialties, expertise, and skills that are brought together to achieve a common task

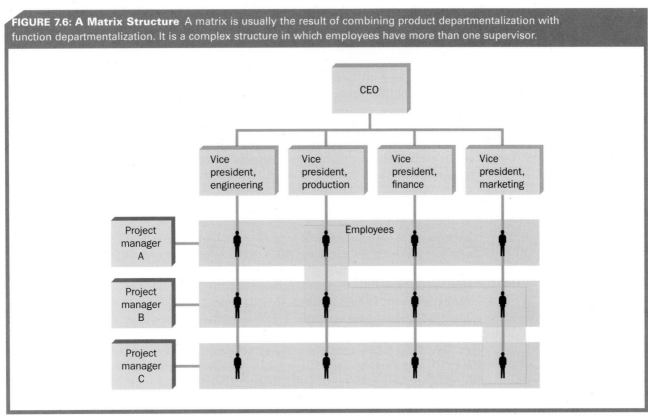

Source: Ricky W. Griffin, *Management*, 9th ed. Copyright © 2008 by Houghton Mifflin Company. Adapted with permission.

team performance simultaneously. Because more managers and support staff may be needed, a matrix structure may be more expensive to maintain.

The Cluster Structure

A **cluster structure** is a type of business that consists primarily of teams with no or very few underlying departments. This type of structure is also called *team* or

cluster structure an organization that consists primarily of teams with no or very few underlying departments

Bureaucratic structure. The U.S. Postal Service is a bureaucracy with numerous rules, requirements, and specified procedures.

©AP Photo/Salt Lake Tribune

collaborative. In this type of organization, team members work together on a project until it is finished, and then the team may remain intact and be assigned another project, or team members may be reassigned to different teams, depending on their skills and the needs of the organization. In a cluster organization, the operating unit is the team, and it remains relatively small. If a team becomes too large, it can be split into multiple teams, or individuals can be assigned to other existing teams.

The cluster organizational structure has both strengths and weaknesses. Keeping the teams small provides the organization with the flexibility necessary to change directions quickly, to try new techniques, and to explore new ideas. Some employees in these types of organizations express concerns regarding job security and the increased amount of stress that arises owing to the fact that changes occur rapidly.[4]

The Network Structure

In a **network structure** (sometimes called a *virtual organization*), administration is the primary function performed, and other functions such as engineering, production, marketing, and finance are contracted out to other organizations. Frequently, a network organization does not manufacture the products it sells. This type of organization has a few permanent employees consisting of top management and hourly clerical workers. Leased facilities and equipment, as well as temporary workers, are increased or decreased as the needs of the organization change. Thus, there is rather limited formal structure associated with a network organization.

An obvious strength of a network structure is flexibility that allows the organization to adjust quickly to changes. Some of the challenges faced by managers in network-structured organizations include controlling the quality of work performed by other organizations, low morale and high turnover among hourly workers, and the vulnerability associated with relying on outside contractors.

Additional Factors That Influence an Organization

As you might expect, other factors in addition to those already covered in this chapter affect the way a large corporation operates on a day-to-day basis. To get a "true picture" of the organizational structure of a huge corporation such as Marriott, for example, which employs over 146,000 people,[5] you need to consider the topics discussed in this section.

Corporate Culture

Most managers function within a corporate culture. A **corporate culture** is generally defined as the inner rites, rituals, heroes, and values of a firm. An organization's culture has a powerful influence on how employees think and act. It also can determine public perception of the organization.

Corporate culture generally is thought to have a very strong influence on a firm's performance over time. Hence, it is useful to be able to assess a firm's corporate culture. Common indicators include the physical setting (building, office layouts), what the company says about its corporate culture (in advertising and news releases), how the company greets guests (does it have formal or informal reception areas?), and how employees spend their time (working alone in an office or working with others).

Goffee and Jones have identified four distinct types of corporate cultures (see Figure 7.7). One is called the *networked culture,* characterized by a base of trust and friendship among employees, a strong commitment to the organization, and an informal environment. The *mercenary culture* embodies the feelings of passion, energy, sense of purpose, and excitement for one's work. The term *mercenary* does not imply that employees are motivated to work only for the money, but this is part of it. In this culture, employees are very intense, focused, and determined to win. In the *fragmented culture,* employees do not become friends, and they work "at" the organization, not "for" it. Employees have a high degree of autonomy, flexibility, and equality. The *communal culture* combines the positive

network structure an organization in which administration is the primary function, and most other functions are contracted out to other firms

corporate culture the inner rites, rituals, heroes, and values of a firm

High		
Networked Culture	**Communal Culture**	
• Extrovert energized by relationships • Tolerant of ambiguities and have low needs for structure • Can spot politics and act to stop "negative" politics • Consider yourself easygoing, affable, and loyal to others	• You consider yourself passionate • Strong need to identify with something bigger than yourself • You enjoy being in teams • Prepared to make sacrifices for the greater good	
Fragmented Culture	**Mercenary Culture**	
• Are a reflective and self-contained introvert • Have a high autonomy drive and strong desire to work independently • Have a strong sense of self	• Goal-oriented and have an obsessive desire to complete tasks • Thrive on competitive energy • Keep "relationships" out of work—develop them	

Sociability

Source: "Types of Corporate Culture," in Rob Goffee and Gareth Jones, *The Character of a Corporation* (New York: HarperCollins, 1998). Copyright © 1998 by Rob Goffee and Gareth Jones. Permission granted by Rob Goffee and Gareth Jones by arrangement with The Helen Rees Literary Agency.

traits of the networked culture and the mercenary culture—those of friendship, commitment, high focus on performance, and high energy. People's lives revolve around the product in this culture, and success by anyone in the organization is celebrated by all.[6]

Some experts believe that cultural change is needed when a company's environment changes, when the industry becomes more competitive, the company's performance is mediocre, and when the company is growing or is about to become a truly large organization. For example, top executives at Dell Computer allocated considerable time and resources to develop a strong, positive corporate culture aimed at increasing employee loyalty and the success of the company. Organizations in the future will look quite different. Experts predict that tomorrow's businesses

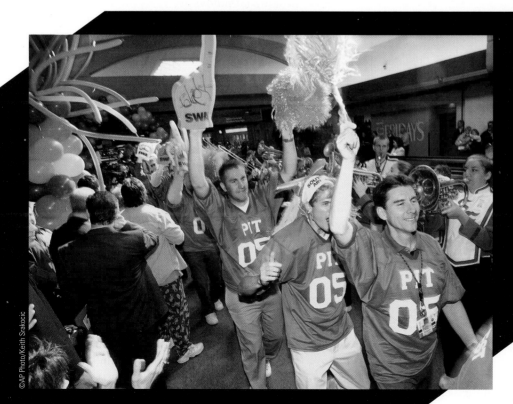

©AP Photo/Keith Srakocic

Corporate culture—let the good times roll (and fly)! Southwest Airlines employees celebrate a new Southwest Airlines route. Southwest Airlines' corporate culture values altruism, humor, hard work, and fun.

The Entrepreneurial Spirit

Intrapreneurship: An Inside Job

Do you have what it takes to be an intrapreneur? For a start, you'll need:

- *Ideas.* You don't have to be a top-level executive to have good ideas. "Creative ideas can come from anywhere," says the CEO of software giant Adobe, which actively solicits employees' ideas for new products and projects.
- *Perspective.* Put your idea into perspective. What will it do for customers and the company? "There is no more powerful way to communicate why your idea is an improvement than to use the words of a customer or employee who is clamoring for it," notes Alicia Ledlie, a store manager who was on the team that launched Wal-Mart into the business of in-store health clinics.
- *Vision.* How will your idea help your company succeed in the future? Steve Kietz believed that his employer, Citigroup, would profit from offering innovative banking services delivered via cell phone. His vision—which the company supported—was "to develop a new business and create value where there was none before."
- *Persistence.* "Pursuing innovation at today's companies is like running a marathon at a sprint— it's incredibly hard work that seems to go on forever," says Kathy Hollenhorst of Caribou Coffee. She spent more than a year researching and fine-tuning her idea to test a customer loyalty reward program. Hollenhorst's persistence paid off: The test went so well that her program has now been implemented throughout the company.

Sources: Maria Bruno-Britz, "Catering to Customers," *Bank Systems + Technology,* October 1, 2008, p. 43; Shreya Biswas, "India Inc Bets on 'Intrapreneurs,'" *The Economic Times,* September 10, 2008, www.economictimes.indiatimes.com; Georgia Flight, "How They Did It: Seven Intrapreneur Success Stories," *BNet Business Network,* n,d., www.bnet.com/2403-13070_23-196890.html; Georgia Flight, "Rules of Innovation from a Wal-Mart Pro," *Bnet Business Network,* n.d., www.bnet.com/2403-13070_23-196887.html.

will be comprised of small, task-oriented work groups, each with control over its own activities. These small groups will be coordinated through an elaborate computer network and held together by a strong corporate culture. Businesses operating in fast-changing industries will require leadership that supports trust and risk taking. Creating a culture of trust in an organization can lead to increases in growth, profit, productivity, and job satisfaction. A culture of trust can retain the best people, inspire customer loyalty, develop new markets, and increase creativity.

Another area where corporate culture plays a vital role is the integration of two or more companies. Business leaders often cite the role of corporate cultures in the integration process as one of the primary factors affecting the success of a merger or acquisition. Experts note that corporate culture is a way of conducting business both within the company and externally. If two merging companies do not address differences in corporate culture, they are setting themselves up for missed expectations and possibly failure.

Intrapreneurship

Since innovations and new-product development are important to companies, and since entrepreneurs are innovative people, it seems almost natural that an entrepreneurial character would surface prominently in many of today's larger organizations. An **intrapreneur** is an employee who takes responsibility for pushing an innovative idea, product, or process through an organization.[7] An intrapreneur possesses the confidence and drive of an entrepreneur but is allowed to use organizational resources for idea development. For example, Art Fry, inventor of the colorful Post-it Notes that Americans can't live without, is a devoted advocate of intrapreneurship. Nurturing his notepad idea at Minnesota Mining and Manufacturing (3M) for years, Fry speaks highly of the intrapreneurial commitment at 3M. Fry indicates that an *intrapreneur* is an individual who does not have all the skills to get the job done and thus has to work within an organization, making use of its skills and attributes.

Committees

Today, business firms use several types of committees that affect organizational structure. An **ad hoc committee** is created for a specific short-term purpose, such as reviewing the firm's employee benefits plan. Once its work is finished, the ad hoc committee disbands. A **standing committee** is a relatively permanent committee charged with performing a recurring task. A firm might establish a budget review committee, for example, to review departmental budget requests on an

intrapreneur an employee who pushes an innovative idea, product, or process through an organization

ad hoc committee a committee created for a specific short-term purpose

standing committee a relatively permanent committee charged with performing some recurring task

©Hintau Aliaksei/Shutterstock

ongoing basis. Finally, a **task force** is a committee established to investigate a major problem or pending decision. A firm contemplating a merger with another company might form a task force to assess the pros and cons of the merger.

Committees offer some advantages over individual action. Their several members are able to bring information and knowledge to the task at hand. Furthermore, committees tend to make more accurate decisions and to transmit their results through the organization more effectively. However, committee deliberations take longer than individual actions. In addition, unnecessary compromise may take place within the committee. Or the opposite may occur, as one person dominates (and thus negates) the committee process.

Coordination Techniques

A large organization is forced to coordinate organizational resources to minimize duplication and to maximize effectiveness. One technique is simply to make use of the **managerial hierarchy**, which is the arrangement that provides increasing authority at higher levels of management. One manager is placed in charge of all the resources being coordinated. That person is able to coordinate them by virtue of the authority accompanying his or her position.

Resources also can be coordinated through rules and procedures. For example, a rule can govern how a firm's travel budget is allocated. This particular resource, then, would be coordinated in terms of that rule.

In complex situations, more sophisticated coordination techniques may be called for. One approach is to establish a liaison. A *liaison* is a go-between—a person who coordinates the activities of two groups. Suppose that Ford is negotiating a complicated contract with a supplier of steering wheels. The supplier might appoint a liaison whose primary responsibility is to coordinate the contract negotiations. Finally, for *very* complex coordination needs, a committee could be established. Suppose that Ford is in the process of purchasing the steering wheel supplier. In this case, a committee might be appointed to integrate the new firm into Ford's larger organizational structure.

The Informal Organization

So far, we have discussed the organization as a formal structure consisting of interrelated positions. This is the organization that is shown on an organization chart. There is another kind of organization, however, that does not show up on any chart. We define this **informal organization** as the pattern of behavior and interaction that stems from personal rather than official relationships. Firmly embedded within every informal organization are informal groups and the notorious grapevine.

Informal Groups An **informal group** is created by the group members themselves to accomplish goals that may or may not be relevant to the organization. Workers may create an informal group to go bowling, form a union, get a particular

task force a committee established to investigate a major problem or pending decision

managerial hierarchy the arrangement that provides increasing authority at higher levels of management

informal organization the pattern of behavior and interaction that stems from personal rather than official relationships

Informal Groups. Informal groups, can be a source of information and camaradere for participants. These groups can create both challenges and benefits for an organizations.

manager fired or transferred, or for lunch. The group may last for several years or a few hours.

Informal groups can be powerful forces in organizations. They can restrict output, or they can help managers through tight spots. They can cause disagreement and conflict, or they can help to boost morale and job satisfaction. They can show new people how to contribute to the organization, or they can help people to get away with substandard performance. Clearly, managers should be aware of these informal groups. Those who make the mistake of fighting the informal organization have a major obstacle to overcome.

The Grapevine The **grapevine** is the informal communications network within an organization. It is completely separate from—and sometimes much faster than—the organization's formal channels of communication. Formal communications usually follow a path that parallels the organizational chain of command. Information can be transmitted through the grapevine in any direction—up, down, diagonally, or horizontally across the organizational structure. Subordinates may pass information to their bosses, an executive may relay something to a maintenance worker, or there may be an exchange of information between people who work in totally unrelated departments. Grapevine information may be concerned with topics ranging from the latest management decisions to gossip.

How should managers treat the grapevine? Certainly, it would be a mistake to try to eliminate it. People working together, day in and day out, are going to communicate. A more rational approach is to recognize its existence. For example, managers should respond promptly and aggressively to inaccurate grapevine information to minimize the damage that such misinformation might do. Moreover, the grapevine can come in handy when managers are on the receiving end of important communications from the informal organization.

In the next chapter, we apply these and other management concepts to an extremely important business function: the production of goods and services.

---

informal group a group created by the members themselves to accomplish goals that may or may not be relevant to an organization

grapevine the informal communications network within an organization

Concept Check

1. Explain the four types of corporate cultures.

2. How do intrapreneurship, committees, and managerial hierarchy influence the organization of a firm?

3. How do informal organizational structures differ from formal ones?

SUMMARY

1 Understand what an organization is and identify its characteristics.

An organization is a group of two or more people working together to achieve a common set of goals. The relationships among positions within an organization can be illustrated by means of an organization chart. Five specific characteristics—job design, departmentalization, delegation, span of management, and chain of command—help to determine what an organization chart and the organization itself look like.

2 Explain why job specialization is important.

Job specialization is the separation of all the activities within an organization into smaller components and the assignment of those different components to different people. Several factors combine to make specialization a useful technique for designing jobs, but high levels of specialization may cause employee dissatisfaction and boredom. One technique for overcoming these problems is job rotation.

3 Identify the various bases for departmentalization.

Departmentalization is the grouping of jobs into manageable units. Typical bases for departmentalization are by function, product, location, or customer. Because each of these bases provides particular advantages, most firms—especially larger ones—use a combination of different bases in different organizational situations.

4 Explain how decentralization follows from delegation.

Delegation is the assigning of part of a manager's work to other workers. It involves the following three steps: (a) assigning responsibility, (b) granting authority, and (c) creating accountability. A decentralized firm is one that delegates as much power as possible to people in the lower management levels. In a centralized firm, on the other hand, power is systematically retained at the upper levels.

5 Understand how the span of management describes an organization.

The span of management is the number of workers who report directly to a manager. Spans generally are characterized as wide (many workers per manager) or narrow (few workers per manager). Wide spans generally result in flat organizations (few layers of management); narrow spans generally result in tall organizations (many layers of management).

6 Understand how the chain of command is established by using line and staff management.

A line position is one that is in the organization's chain of command or line of authority. A manager in a line position makes decisions and gives orders to workers to achieve the goals of the organization. On the other hand, a manager in a staff position provides support, advice, and expertise to someone in the chain of command. Staff positions may carry some authority, but it usually applies only within staff areas of expertise.

7 Describe the four basic forms of organizational structure: bureaucratic, matrix, cluster, and network.

There are four basic forms of organizational structure. The bureaucratic structure is characterized by formality and rigidity. With the bureaucratic structure, rules and procedures are used to ensure uniformity. The matrix structure may be visualized as product departmentalization superimposed on functional departmentalization. With the matrix structure, an employee on a cross-functional team reports to both the project manager and the individual's supervisor in a functional department. A cluster structure is an organization that consists primarily of teams with very few underlying functional departments. In an organization with a network structure, the primary function performed internally is administration, and other functions are contracted out to other firms.

8 Summarize the use of corporate culture, intrapreneurship, committees, coordination techniques, informal groups, and the grapevine.

Corporate culture—the inner rites, rituals, heroes, and values of a firm—is thought to have a very strong influence on a firm's performance over time. An intrapreneur is an employee in an organizational environment who takes responsibility for pushing an innovative idea, product, or process through the organization. Additional elements that influence an organization include the use of committees and the development of techniques for achieving coordination among various groups within the organization. Finally, both informal groups created by group members and an informal communication network called the grapevine may affect an organization and its performance.

KEY TERMS

You should now be able to define and give an example relevant to each of the following terms:

organization (181)
organization chart (183)
chain of command (183)
job specialization (184)
job rotation (185)
departmentalization (185)
departmentalization by function (185)
departmentalization by product (185)
departmentalization by location (185)

departmentalization by customer (186)
delegation (186)
responsibility (186)
authority (186)
accountability (186)
decentralized organization (187)
centralized organization (188)
span of management (or span of control) (188)
organizational height (189)

line management position (190)
staff management position (190)
bureaucratic structure (192)
matrix structure (192)
cross-functional team (192)
cluster structure (193)
network structure (194)
corporate culture (194)
intrapreneur (196)
ad hoc committee (196)

standing committee (196)
task force (197)
managerial hierarchy (197)
informal organization (197)
informal group (198)
grapevine (198)

DISCUSSION QUESTIONS

1. In what way do organization charts create a picture of an organization?
2. Describe how job rotation can be used to combat the problems caused by job specialization.
3. Why do most firms employ a combination of departmentalization bases?
4. What three steps are involved in delegation? Explain each.
5. How is organizational height related to the span of management?
6. What are the key differences between line and staff positions?
7. Contrast the bureaucratic and matrix forms of organizational structure.
8. What are the differences between the cluster structure and the network structure?
9. How may the managerial hierarchy be used to coordinate the organization's resources?
10. How do decisions concerning span of management, the use of committees, and coordination techniques affect organizational structure?

Get Flash Cards, Quizzes,
Games, Crosswords and more
@ www.cengage.com/introbusiness/
pride

Test Yourself

Matching Questions

1. _____ Two or more people working toward a common goal.

2. _____ The line of authority from highest to lowest levels.

3. _____ It investigates problems.

4. _____ Line and staff positions are clearly defined.

5. _____ The process of grouping similar things together.

6. _____ The process of giving authority to subordinates.

7. _____ The duty to do a job or perform a task.

8. _____ The power to do an assigned task.

9. _____ One who works within a firm to develop ideas.

10. _____ An informal communications network.

    a. authority
    b. matrix structure
    c. bureaucratic structure
    d. chain of command
    e. delegation
    f. departmentalization
    g. grapevine
    h. cross-functional team
    i. intrapreneur
    j. organization
    k. responsibility
    l. task force

True False Questions

11. **T F** A benefit of specialization is improved efficiency and increased productivity.

12. **T F** Job rotation involves assigning an employee more tasks and greater control.

13. **T F** Accountability is created, not delegated.

14. **T F** Many firms find that by using matrix organization, the motivation level is lowered, and personal growth of employees is limited.

15. **T F** The power to make decisions is granted through authority.

16. **T F** Line positions support staff positions in decision making.

17. **T F** Ad hoc committees can be used effectively to review a firm's employee benefits plan.

18. **T F** The span of management should be wide when a great deal of interaction is required between the supervisor and worker.

19. **T F** Functional authority is being practiced when staff managers exercise the authority to make decisions and issue directives.

20. **T F** A cluster structure is also called team or collaborative.

Multiple-Choice Questions

21. _____ A committee is organized to review applications for scholarships. The group will award two scholarships to recent high school graduates. What type of committee would work best?

    a. Ad hoc committee
    b. Task force
    c. Liaison committee
    d. Standing committee
    e. Self-managed team

22. _____ ABC Distributors is reorganizing to better control costs. The company decided to group hospitals, schools, and churches together into one department. Which departmentalization base is the company using?

    a. Location
    b. Function
    c. Basis
    d. Product
    e. Customer

23. _____ A supervisor assigned to Wendy, the most proficient employee in the accounting department, a project on cost control that was due in three weeks. For Wendy to be accountable for the project, what must Wendy be given?

    a. Responsibility
    b. Power
    c. Authority
    d. Training
    e. Control

24. _____ A narrow span of control works best when

    a. subordinates are located close together.
    b. the manager has few responsibilities outside of supervision.

c. little interaction is required between the manager and the worker.

d. new problems arise frequently.

e. few problems arise on a daily basis.

25. _____ The process of dividing work to be done by an entire organization into separate parts and assigning the parts to positions within the organization is called

a. departmentalization.

b. delegation.

c. job design.

d. specialization.

e. organizing.

26. _____ Many larger organizations do not maintain complete, detailed organizational charts. One of the reasons for this is that

a. most organizations are not very clear about the chain of command.

b. organizations typically do not follow organization charts.

c. it is difficult to plot the thousands of positions that characterize a large organization.

d. organizations find it expensive to make these charts.

e. organizations find plotting the charts is a waste of time.

27. _____ Who was the first to recognize the power of specialization?

a. Karl Marx

b. Max Weber

c. John Kenneth Galbraith

d. Adam Smith

e. Thomas Friedman

28. _____ Older and larger firms that produce and sell a variety of products organize by

a. location.

b. process.

c. customer.

d. function.

e. executive decisions.

29. _____ Many managers are reluctant to delegate. Which one of the following is *not* one of the reasons they are reluctant to do so?

a. They want to be sure that the work gets done.

b. They fear that workers will do the work well and attract the approving notice of higher-level managers.

c. They are so disorganized that they simply are not able to plan and assign work.

d. Most managers are workaholics.

e. Most subordinates are reluctant to accept delegated tasks.

30. _____ A relatively permanent committee charged with performing some recurring task is called

a. an ad hoc committee.

b. a standing committee.

c. a task force.

d. a managerial committee.

e. a permanent committee.

Answers on p. TY-1

VIDEO CASE

Organizing for Success at Green Mountain Coffee Roasters

Even with a workforce of 600, Green Mountain Coffee Roasters, based in Waterbury, Vermont, stays as entrepreneurial as when Bob Stiller founded the company in 1981 with one coffee shop and a handful of employees. The original plan was to open a series of coffee shops throughout New England. By the time Green Mountain Coffee had grown to twelve shops, profitability was faltering, so Stiller switched to importing, roasting, and wholesaling high-quality coffee beans for stores, food-service professionals, and restaurants around the country. Today, his company brews up profits of about $137 million in annual sales to Aramark Food Service, McDonald's New England outlets, Wild Oats Market groceries, Publix supermarkets, and 7,000 other businesses.

Jobs at Green Mountain Coffee are departmentalized into six functions: sales and marketing, operations, human resources, finance, information systems, and social respon-

sibility. The organization chart shows how specialized jobs are linked by a distinct chain of command leading to CEO Bob Stiller at the top. What the chart doesn't show, however, is how collaboration and communication among all levels—rather than strict hierarchy—give the company a decision-making edge.

This is a flat organization, with only four levels between a corporate salesperson and the CEO. In line with the company's collaborative culture, decisions are made by inviting employees from different functions and different levels to offer their input. Decisions may take a little more time under this system, but they're more informed and usually yield a better solution to the problem than if handled by a single manager or a tiny group.

For a particularly challenging decision, Green Mountain Coffee relies on a "constellation" of communication to collect ideas from around the organization. Managers frequently post decision data on the corporate computer system and ask coworkers for comments. They also exchange a blizzard of e-mail messages and call cross-functional meetings, when necessary, to share information and opinions. Ultimately, the manager closest to the situation is responsible for evaluating all the data and making the decision, guided by the company's values.

Green Mountain Coffee's values are revealed in its mission statement: "We create the ultimate coffee experience in every life we touch from tree to cup—transforming the way the world understands business." Because the company buys from hundreds of coffee growers and sells to thousands of businesses as well as thousands of consumers who order by mail or online, it touches many lives. Social responsibility ranks high on Green Mountain Coffee's corporate agenda. It is known for donating considerable cash, coffee, and volunteer time to the communities it serves in the United States and in coffee-producing nations.

Every year the company flies dozens of employees to Central America to see how coffee beans are grown, meet the growers, and learn about the farming communities. "The effect is profound," says Stephen Sabol, vice president of development. "The knowledge of the care that goes into the coffee is important, but when [employees] see the social part of it, and how dependent these growers are on us being a quality partner, it hits right home—the obligation we have to do well." After one of these "Coffee Source Trips," employees come back to work with renewed energy and dedication.

Green Mountain Coffee Roasters has not only been cited as one of the fastest-growing companies in the United States, but it also has been named among the most socially responsible. The CEO recognizes that his company must do well in order to do good. "To help the world, we have to be successful," Stiller says. "If we help the world and go out of business, we're not going to help anybody."[8]

For more information about this company, visit its Website at www.greenmountaincoffee.com.

Questions

1. How is Green Mountain Coffee's "constellation" of communication likely to affect the informal organization?
2. Does Green Mountain Coffee appear to have a networked, communal, mercenary, or fragmented culture? Support your answer.
3. Is Green Mountain Coffee a centralized or decentralized organization? How do you know?

BUILDING SKILLS FOR CAREER SUCCESS

1. EXPLORING THE INTERNET

After studying the various organizational structures described in this chapter and the reasons for employing them, you may be interested in learning about the organizational structures in place at large firms. As noted in the chapter, departmentalization typically is based on function, product, location, and customer. Many large firms use a combination of these organizational structures successfully. You can gain a good sense of which organizational theme prevails in an industry by looking at several corporate sites.

Assignment

1. Explore the website of any large firm that you believe is representative of its industry, and find its organization chart or a description of its organization. Create a brief organization chart from the information you have found.
2. Describe the bases on which this firm is departmentalized.

2. BUILDING TEAM SKILLS

An organization chart is a diagram showing how employees and tasks are grouped and how the lines of communication and authority flow within an organization. These charts can look very different depending on a number of factors, including the nature and size of the business, the way it is departmentalized, its patterns of delegating authority, and its span of management.

Assignment

1. Working in a team, use the following information to draw an organization chart: The KDS Design Center works closely with two home-construction companies, Amex and Highmass. KDS's role is to help customers select materials for their new homes and to ensure that their selections are communicated accurately to the builders. The company is also a retailer of wallpaper, blinds, and drapery. The retail department, the Amex accounts, and the Highmass accounts make up KDS's three departments. The company has the following positions:

   President
   Executive vice president
   Managers, 2
   Appointment coordinators, 2
   Amex coordinators, 2
   Highmass coordinators, 2
   Consultants/designers for the Amex and Highmass accounts, 15
   Retail positions, 4
   Payroll and billing personnel, 1

2. After your team has drawn the organization chart, discuss the following:
   a. What type of organizational structure does your chart depict? Is it a bureaucratic, matrix, cluster, or network structure? Why?
   b. How does KDS use departmentalization?
   c. To what extent is authority in the company centralized or decentralized?
   d. What is the span of management within KDS?
   e. Which positions are line positions and which are staff? Why?
3. Prepare a three-page report summarizing what the chart revealed about relationships and tasks at the KDS Design Center and what your team learned about the value of organization charts. Include your chart in your report.

3. RESEARCHING DIFFERENT CAREERS

In the past, company loyalty and ability to assume increasing job responsibility usually ensured advancement within an organization. While the reasons for seeking advancement (the desire for a better-paying position, more prestige, and job satisfaction) have not changed, the qualifications for career advancement have. In today's business environment, climbing the corporate ladder requires packaging and marketing yourself. To be promoted within your company or to be considered for employment with another company, it is wise to improve your skills continually. By taking workshops and seminars or enrolling in community college courses, you can keep up with the changing technology in your industry. Networking with people in your business or community can help you to find a new job. Most jobs are filled through personal contacts. Who you know can be important.

A list of your accomplishments on the job can reveal your strengths and weaknesses. Setting goals for improvement helps to increase your self-confidence.

Be sure to recognize the signs of job dissatisfaction. It may be time to move to another position or company.

Assignment

Are you prepared to climb the corporate ladder? Do a self-assessment by analyzing the following areas, and summarize the results in a two-page report.

1. Skills
   - What are your most valuable skills?
   - What skills do you lack?
   - Describe your plan for acquiring new skills and improving your skills.
2. Networking
   - How effective are you at using a mentor?
   - Are you a member of a professional organization?
   - In which community, civic, or church groups are you participating?
   - Whom have you added to your contact list in the last six weeks?
3. Accomplishments
   - What achievements have you reached in your job?
   - What would you like to accomplish? What will it take for you to reach your goal?
4. Promotion or new job
   - What is your likelihood for getting a promotion?
   - Are you ready for a change? What are you doing or willing to do to find another job?

Producing Quality Goods and Services

WHY THIS CHAPTER MATTERS. Think for a moment about the products and services you bought in the past week. If it weren't for the production activities described in this chapter, those products and services would not be available.

©Susan Van Etten

LEARNING OBJECTIVES

1 Explain the nature of production.

2 Outline how the conversion process transforms raw materials, labor, and other resources into finished products or services.

3 Describe how research and development lead to new products and services.

4 Discuss the components involved in planning the production process.

5 Explain how purchasing, inventory control, scheduling, and quality control affect production.

6 Summarize how productivity and technology are related.

Award-Winning Quality at Cargill Corn Milling

Cargill Corn Milling (CCM) is putting a high-tech cloak of quality around food, feed, and fuel products made from one of the nation's oldest crops—corn. Its food products include corn syrup, corn oil, corn starch, and corn meal; its animal feed products include corn gluten feed; and its fuel product is ethanol. The company, a division of the food and agricultural giant Cargill, serves 3,000 customers, rings up more than $1 billion in annual revenue, and employs 2,400 people.

CCM relies on cutting-edge quality systems to control the complexities of manufacturing and moving all its corn-based products through nine production plants and eleven distribution facilities in fourteen states. For example, the central control room of its processing plant in Wahpeton, North Dakota, is outfitted with 14 computer monitors that flash the current status of every major production system. Operations technicians can respond right away if a monitor shows that the temperature in the refining room has changed or the flow of corn into the milling area has slowed.

The Wahpeton plant is organized into a series of teams that are responsible for specific aspects of the operation, including employee safety, energy conservation, plant leadership, and plant innovation. Every team uses CCM's Best Practice Model to evaluate the productivity and cost-efficiency of existing plant processes and innovations undergoing testing. When a team proves it can get significantly better results from a new process, it documents the improvement and shares the details with the rest of the CCM plants. In fact, the Wahpeton plant has achieved an error-free delivery rate of 99.9 percent and twice been honored as one of Cargill's best plants.

For its organization-wide success in attaining top-notch quality, improving productivity, and satisfying customers, CCM was recently honored with the prestigious Malcolm Baldrige National Quality Award. U.S. companies must meet rigorous quality standards to qualify for the Baldrige Award. Another Cargill company, Cargill Kitchen Solutions, won the award two times in six years. Will CCM become a repeat Baldrige winner, as well?[1]

DID YOU KNOW?

Cargill Corn Milling was recently honored with the Malcolm Baldrige National Quality Award for its achievements in top-notch quality, productivity improvements, and customer satisfaction.

Question: What do quality, teams, and corn have in common? Answer: Each factor has helped Cargill Corn Milling, the company profiled in the Inside Business opening case, to become a successful and profitable company that serves its customers well while employing 2,400 people. As a result of the company's desire to be the best, the company was awarded the Malcolm Baldrige National Quality Award by the President of the United States. The fact is that Cargill Corn Milling is an excellent example of what this chapter's content—the production of quality goods and services—is all about.

We begin this chapter with an overview of operations management—the activities required to produce goods and services that meet the needs of customers. In this section, we also discuss competition in the global marketplace and careers in operations management. Next, we describe the conversion process that makes production possible and also note the growing role of services in our economy. Then we examine more closely three important aspects of operations management: developing ideas for new products, planning for production, and effectively controlling operations after production has begun. We close the chapter with a look at productivity trends and ways that productivity can be improved through the use of technology.

What Is Production?

Have you ever wondered where a new pair of Levi jeans comes from? Or a new Mitsubishi flat panel television, Izod pullover sweater, or Uniroyal tire for your car? Even factory service on a Hewlett-Packard notebook computer or a Maytag clothes

1 LEARNING OBJECTIVE

Explain the nature of production.

dryer would be impossible if it weren't for the activities described in this chapter. In fact, these products and services and millions of others like them would not exist if it weren't for production activities.

Let's begin this chapter by reviewing what an operating manager does. In Chapter 6, we described an *operations manager* as a person who manages the systems that convert resources into goods and services. This area of management is usually referred to as **operations management**, which consists of all the activities managers engage in to produce goods and services.

To produce a product or service successfully, a business must perform a number of specific activities. For example, suppose that an organization such as Lexus has an idea for a new aerodynamic, convertible automobile that will cost approximately $50,000. Marketing research must determine not only if customers are willing to pay the price for this product but also what special features they want. Then operations managers for Lexus must turn the concept into reality.

Lexus' managers cannot just push the "start button" and immediately begin producing the new automobile. Production must be planned. As you will see, planning takes place both *before* anything is produced and *during* the production process.

Managers also must concern themselves with the control of operations to ensure that the organization's goals are achieved. For a product such as the Lexus convertible, control of operations involves a number of important issues, including product quality, performance standards, the amount of inventory of both raw materials and finished products, and production costs.

We discuss each of the major activities of operations management later in this chapter. First, however, let's take a closer look at American manufacturers and how they compete in the global marketplace.

operations management all activities managers engage in to produce goods and services

Competition in the Global Marketplace

After World War II, the United States became the most productive country in the world. For almost thirty years, until the late 1970s, its leadership was never threatened. By then, however, manufacturers in Japan, Germany, Great Britain, Taiwan, Korea, Sweden, and other industrialized nations were offering U.S. firms increasing competition. And now the Chinese are manufacturing everything from sophisticated electronic equipment and automobiles to less expensive everyday items—often for lower cost than the same goods can be manufactured in other countries. As a result, the goods Americans purchase may have been manufactured in the United States *or* in other countries around the globe and shipped to the United States. Competition has never been fiercer, and in some ways the world has never been smaller.

In an attempt to regain a competitive edge on foreign manufacturers, U.S. firms have taken another look at the importance of improving quality and meeting the needs of their customers. The most successful U.S. firms also have focused on the following:

1. Motivating employees to cooperate with management and improve productivity
2. Reducing costs by selecting suppliers that offer higher-quality raw materials and components at reasonable prices
3. Replacing outdated equipment with state-of-the-art manufacturing equipment

Where did these blue toy rabbits come from? Answer: China. In today's competitive global marketplace, many products like these stuffed animals are manufactured in China and then shipped to nations around the globe. Today, people in all nations want to sell the products and services they produce to customers in their own nation *and* to customers in the global marketplace. In fact, the experts say the world has become a smaller place because of increased global trade.

4. Using computer-aided and flexible manufacturing systems that allow a higher degree of customization
5. Improving control procedures to help ensure lower manufacturing costs
6. Building new manufacturing facilities in foreign countries where labor costs are lower

Although competing in the global economy is a major challenge, it is a worthwhile pursuit. For most firms, competing in the global marketplace is not only profitable, but it is also an essential activity that requires the cooperation of everyone within the organization.

Careers in Operations Management

Although it is hard to provide information about specific career opportunities in operations management, some generalizations do apply to this management area. First, you must appreciate the manufacturing process and the steps required to produce a product or service. A basic understanding of mass production and the difference between an analytical process and a synthetic process is essential. **Mass production** is a manufacturing process that lowers the cost required to produce a large number of identical or similar products over a long period of time. An **analytical process** breaks raw materials into different component parts. For example, a barrel of crude oil refined by Marathon Oil Corporation—a Texas-based oil and chemical refiner—can be broken down into gasoline, oil and lubricants, and many other petroleum by-products. A **synthetic process** is just the opposite of the analytical one; it combines raw materials or components to create a finished product. Black & Decker uses a synthetic process when it combines plastic, steel, rechargeable batteries, and other components to produce a cordless drill.

Once you understand that operations managers are responsible for producing tangible products or services that customers want, you must determine how you fit into the production process. Today's successful operations managers must

1. be able to motivate and lead people.
2. understand how technology can make a manufacturer more productive and efficient.
3. appreciate the control processes that help lower production costs and improve product quality.
4. understand the relationship between the customer, the marketing of a product, and the production of a product.

If operations management seems like an area you might be interested in, why not do more career exploration? You could take an operations management course if your college or university offers one, or you could obtain a part-time job during the school year or a summer job in a manufacturing company.

The Conversion Process

2 LEARNING OBJECTIVE

To have something to sell, a business must convert ideas and resources into goods and services. The resources are materials, finances, people, and information—the same resources discussed in Chapters 1 and 6. The goods and services are varied, ranging from consumer products to heavy manufacturing equipment to fast food. The purpose of this conversion of resources into goods and services is to provide utility to customers. **Utility** is the ability of a good or service to satisfy a human need. Although there are four types of utility—form, place, time, and possession—operations management focuses primarily on form utility. **Form utility** is created by people converting raw materials, finances, and information into finished products. The other types of utility—place, time, and possession—are discussed in Chapter 11.

But how does the conversion take place? How does Kellogg's convert grain, sugar, salt, and other ingredients; money from previous sales and stockholders'

mass production a manufacturing process that lowers the cost required to produce a large number of identical or similar products over a long period of time

analytical process a process in operations management in which raw materials are broken into different component parts

synthetic process a process in operations management in which raw materials or components are combined to create a finished product

Concept Check

1. List all the activities in operations management.

2. What steps have U.S. firms taken to regain a competitive edge in the global marketplace?

3. What is the difference between an analytical and a synthetic manufacturing process? Give an example of each type of process.

Outline how the conversion process transforms raw materials, labor, and other resources into finished products or services.

utility the ability of a good or service to satisfy a human need

form utility utility created by people converting raw materials, finances, and information into finished products

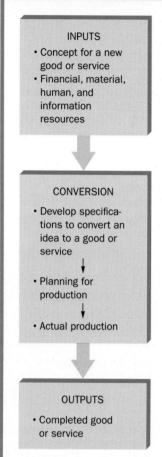
investments; production workers and managers; and economic and marketing forecasts into Frosted Flakes cereal products? How does New York Life Insurance convert office buildings, insurance premiums, actuaries, and mortality tables into life insurance policies? They do so through the use of a conversion process like the one illustrated in Figure 8.1. As indicated by our New York Life Insurance example, the conversion process is not limited to manufacturing products. The conversion process also can be used to produce services.

Manufacturing Using a Conversion Process

The conversion of resources into products and services can be described in several ways. We limit our discussion here to three: the focus or major resource used in the conversion process, its magnitude of change, and the number of production processes employed.

Focus By the *focus* of a conversion process, we mean the resource or resources that make up the major or most important *input*. For a bank such as Citibank, financial resources are the major resource. A chemical and energy company such as Chevron concentrates on material resources. Your college or university is concerned primarily with information. And temporary employment services focus on the use of human resources.

Magnitude of Change The *magnitude* of a conversion process is the degree to which the resources are physically changed. At one extreme lie such processes as the one by which the Glad Products Company produces Glad Cling Wrap. Various chemicals in liquid or powder form are combined to produce long, thin sheets of plastic Glad Cling Wrap. Here, the original resources are totally unrecognizable in the finished product. At the other extreme, Southwest Airlines produces *no* physical change in its original resources. The airline simply provides a service and transports people from one place to another.

Number of Production Processes A single firm may employ one production process or many. In general, larger firms that make a variety of products use multiple production processes. For example, General Electric manufactures some of its own products, buys other merchandise from suppliers, and operates multiple divisions including a credit division, an insurance division, an entertainment division, and a medical equipment division. Smaller firms, by contrast, may use one production process. For example, Texas-based Advanced Cast Stone, Inc., manufactures one basic product: building materials made from concrete.

Operations Management in the Service Industry

The application of the basic principles of operations management to the production of services has coincided with a dramatic growth in the number and diversity of service businesses. In 1900, only 28 percent of American workers were employed in service firms. By 1950, this figure had grown to 40 percent, and by 2009, it had risen to 85 percent.[2] In fact, the American economy is now characterized as a **service economy** (see Figure 8.2). A service economy is one in which more effort is devoted to the production of services than to the production of goods.

Today, the managers of restaurants, laundries, real estate agencies, banks, movie theaters, airlines, travel bureaus, and other service firms have realized that they can benefit from the experience of manufacturers. And yet the production of services is very different from the production of manufactured goods in the following four ways:

1. Services are consumed immediately and, unlike manufactured goods, cannot be stored. For example, a hair stylist cannot store completed haircuts.
2. Services are provided when and where the customer desires the service. In many cases, customers will not travel as far to obtain a service.

service economy an economy in which more effort is devoted to the production of services than to the production of goods

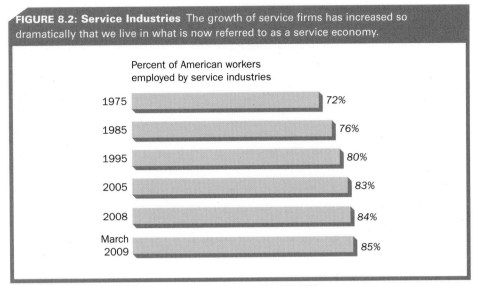

FIGURE 8.2: Service Industries The growth of service firms has increased so dramatically that we live in what is now referred to as a service economy.

Percent of American workers
employed by service industries

Year	Percent
1975	72%
1985	76%
1995	80%
2005	83%
2008	84%
March 2009	85%

Source: U.S. Bureau of Labor Statistics website, **www.bls.gov**, accessed April 21, 2009.

3. Services are usually labor-intensive because the human resource is often the most important resource used in the production of services.
4. Services are intangible, and it is therefore more difficult to evaluate customer satisfaction.[3]

Although it is often more difficult to measure customer satisfaction, today's successful service firms work hard at providing the services customers want. Compared

Concept Check

1. Explain how utility is related to form utility?

2. In terms of focus, magnitude, and number, characterize the production processes used by a local pizza parlor, a dry-cleaning establishment, and an auto repair shop.

3. How is the production of services similar to the production of manufactured goods?

4 How is production of services different from the production of manufactured goods?

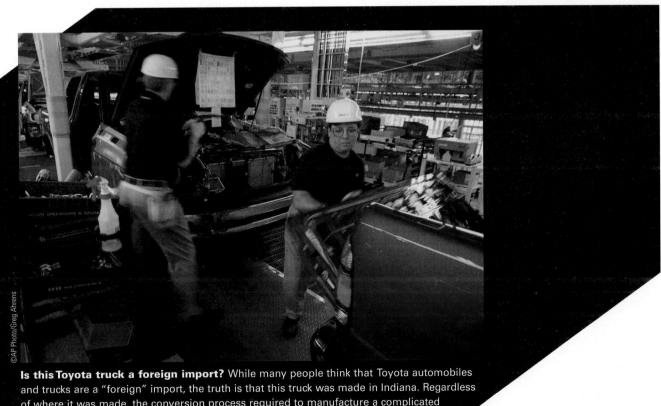

©AP Photo/Greg Ahrens

Is this Toyota truck a foreign import? While many people think that Toyota automobiles and trucks are a "foreign" import, the truth is that this truck was made in Indiana. Regardless of where it was made, the conversion process required to manufacture a complicated product like a truck still requires a number of steps to convert an idea into an actual product that will meet customer needs.

with manufacturers, service firms often listen more carefully to customers and respond more quickly to the market's changing needs.

Now that we understand something about the production process that is used to transform resources into goods and services, we can consider three major activities involved in operations management. These are product development, planning for production, and operations control.

LEARNING OBJECTIVE 3

Describe how research and development lead to new products and services.

Where Do New Products and Services Come From?

No firm can produce a product or service until it has an idea. In other words, someone first must come up with a new way to satisfy a need—a new product or an improvement in an existing product. Apple's iPod and San Disk's Flash Drive began as an idea. While no one can predict with 100 percent accuracy what types of products will be available in the next five years, it is safe to say that companies will continue to introduce new products that will change the way we take care of ourselves, interact with others, and find the information and services we need.

Research and Development

research and development (R&D) a set of activities intended to identify new ideas that have the potential to result in new goods and services

How did we get laptop computers and HD televisions? We got them the same way we got light bulbs and automobile tires—from people working with new ideas.

Thomas Edison created the first light bulb, and Charles Goodyear discovered the vulcanization process that led to tires. In the same way, scientists and researchers working in businesses and universities have produced many of the newer products we already take for granted.

These activities generally are referred to as *research and development*. For our purposes, **research and development (R&D)** are a set of activities intended to identify new ideas that have the potential to result in new goods and services.

Today, business firms use three general types of R&D activities. *Basic research* consists of activities aimed at uncovering new knowledge. The goal of basic research is scientific advancement, without regard for its potential use in the development of goods and services. *Applied research*, in contrast, consists of activities geared toward discovering new knowledge with some potential use. *Development and implementation* are research activities undertaken specifically to put new or existing knowledge to use in producing goods and services. The 3M Company has always been known for its development and implementation research activities. As a result of its R&D efforts, the company has developed more than 55,000 products designed to make people's lives easier. Does a company like 3M quit innovating because it has developed successful products? No, not at all! Currently, the company employs more than 7,000 researchers worldwide and has invested more than $6.7 billion over the last five years to develop new products designed to make people's lives easier and safer. Just recently, the 3M Company used development and implementation to create a new, state-of-the-art passport scanner that can be used to facilitate the check-in process for frequent travelers.[4]

Product Extension and Refinement

When a brand-new product is first marketed, its sales are zero and slowly increase from that point. If the product is

Disney's magical express! Like magic, guests and their baggage are whisked from the Orlando International Airport to the Walt Disney World Resort. Complementary round-trip shuttle service to one of 22 hotels in the Orlando, Florida, area is just one of the many services Disney provides to make a guest's stay more enjoyable.

PR NewsFoto/Walt Disney Resort

Going Green

Peterbilt Trucks Go Green

Peterbilt trucks are getting greener, thanks to parent company PACCAR's multimillion-dollar investments in research and development. Based in Bellevue, Washington, PACCAR has developed a number of new truck motors and braking systems that reduce engine emissions and increase fuel efficiency. One fuel-saving innovation is the ability to store up energy when the truck brakes and then release it to power acceleration. In addition, many of the new Peterbilt trucks are quieter and can go longer between service visits. Corporate customers such as Coca-Cola have placed large orders for these Peterbilt trucks because they're cost-efficient as well as eco-friendly.

Greener truck technology takes shape at PACCAR's leading-edge manufacturing center in Mississippi, where engineers and designers collaborate on research and development. After testing prototypes under laboratory conditions, the company creates road-ready versions for extensive field testing. For example, the company is currently testing new trucks that run on diesel-electric hybrid engines and new tractors that run on liquid natural gas.

The Peterbilt production facilities are also going green. Both the Texas and Tennessee plants have received ISO 14001 environmental certification and have programs in high gear to cut waste and conserve natural resources. In today's high-pressure economy, such conservation efforts are a good way to save the planet and save money at the same time.

Sources: Steve Wilhelm, "Paccar CEO Optimistic About Economic Recovery," *Puget Sound Business Journal,* April 28, 2009, www.bizjournals.com/seattle/stories/2009/04/27/daily21.html; Seth Skydel, "Developing Technologies: Pete Hybrids," *Fleet Equipment,* February 2008, p. 6; "Future Focus," *Fleet Owner,* May 1, 2008, n.p.; "PACCAR Breaks Ground for Engine Plant," *Mississippi Business Journal,* July 30, 2007, p. 15; www.peterbilt.com.

©Luca Flor/Shutterstock

successful, annual sales increase more and more rapidly until they reach some peak. Then, as time passes, annual sales begin to decline, and they continue to decline until it is no longer profitable to manufacture the product. (This rise-and-decline pattern, called the *product life cycle,* is discussed in more detail in Chapter 12.)

If a firm sells only one product, when that product reaches the end of its life cycle, the firm will die, too. To stay in business, the firm must, at the very least, find ways to refine or extend the want-satisfying capability of its product. Consider television sets. Since they were introduced in the late 1930s, television sets have been constantly *refined* so that they now provide clearer, sharper pictures with less dial adjusting. During the same time, television sets also were *extended.* There are color sets, television-only sets, and others that include DVD players. There are even television sets that allow their owners to access the Internet. And the latest development—high-definition (HD) television—is already the standard for television receivers.

Each refinement or extension results in an essentially "new" product whose sales make up for the declining sales of a product that was introduced earlier. When consumers discovered that the original five varieties of Campbell's Soup were of the highest quality, as well as inexpensive, the soups were an instant success. Although one of the most successful companies at the beginning of the 1900s, Campbell's had to continue to innovate, refine, and extend its product line. For example, many consumers in the United States live in what is called an on-the-go society. To meet this need, Campbell's Soup has developed ready-to-serve products that can be popped into a microwave at work or school.[5]

Concept Check

1. Describe how research and development lead to new products.

2. What is the difference between basic research, applied research, and development and implementation?

3. Explain why product extension and refinement are important.

How Do Managers Plan Production?

4 LEARNING OBJECTIVE

Discuss the components involved in planning the production process.

Only a few of the many ideas for new products, refinements, and extensions ever reach the production stage. For those ideas that do, however, the next step is planning for production. Once a new product idea has been identified, planning for

McDonald's has gone fishing. For McDonald's Holding Company, the Japanese subsidiary of U.S.–based McDonald's Corporation, Fish McDippers are a logical product extension of McDonald's popular fish sandwiches. Similar to the fast-food giant's Chicken McNuggets, McDonald's Japanese unit added more fish items to its menus in order to combat consumer concerns about mad cow disease and the spread of bird flu in Japan.

production involves three major phases: design planning, site selection and facilities planning, and operational planning (see Figure 8.3).

Design Planning

When the R&D staff at Hewlett-Packard recommended to top management that the firm produce and market an affordable netbook computer, the company could not simply swing into production the next day. Instead, a great deal of time and energy had to be invested in determining what the new computer would look like, where and how it would be produced, and what options would be included. These decisions are a part of design planning. **Design planning** is the development of a plan for converting a product idea into an actual product or service. The major decisions involved in design planning deal with product line, required capacity, and use of technology.

Product Line A **product line** is a group of similar products that differ only in relatively minor characteristics. During the design-planning stage, a computer manufacturer such as Hewlett-Packard needs to determine how many different netbook models to produce and what major options to offer. A restaurant chain such as Pizza Hut must decide how many menu items to offer.

An important issue in deciding on the product line is to balance customer preferences and production requirements. For this reason, marketing managers play an important role in making product-line decisions. Typically, marketing personnel want a "long" product line that offers customers many options. Because a long product line with more options gives customers greater choice, it is easier to sell products that meet the needs of individual customers. On the other hand, production personnel generally want a "short" product line because products are easier to produce. With a short product line, the production process is less complex because there are fewer options, and most products are produced using the same basic steps. In many cases, the actual choice between a long and short product line involves balancing customer preferences with the cost and problems associated with a more complex production process.

Once the product line has been determined, each distinct product within the product line must be designed. **Product design** is the process of creating a set of specifications from which a product can be produced. When designing a new product,

design planning the development of a plan for converting a product idea into an actual product or service

product line a group of similar products that differ only in relatively minor characteristics

product design the process of creating a set of specifications from which a product can be produced

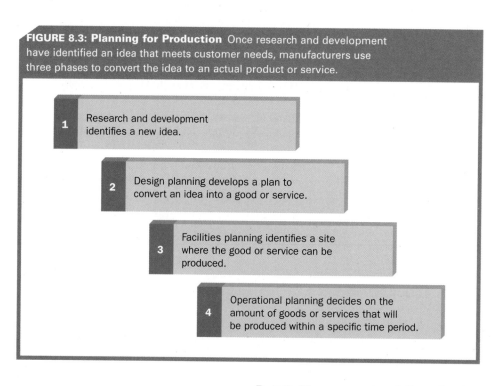

FIGURE 8.3: Planning for Production Once research and development have identified an idea that meets customer needs, manufacturers use three phases to convert the idea to an actual product or service.

1. Research and development identifies a new idea.

2. Design planning develops a plan to convert an idea into a good or service.

3. Facilities planning identifies a site where the good or service can be produced.

4. Operational planning decides on the amount of goods or services that will be produced within a specific time period.

specifications are extremely important. For example, product engineers for Whirlpool Corporation must make sure that a new frost-free refrigerator keeps food frozen in the freezer compartment. At the same time, they must make sure that lettuce and tomatoes do not freeze in the crisper section of the refrigerator. The need for a complete product design is fairly obvious; products that work cannot be manufactured without it. But services should be designed carefully as well—and *for the same reason.*

Required Production Capacity

Capacity is the amount of products or services that an organization can produce in a given period of time. (For example, the capacity of a Saab automobile assembly plant might be 80,000 cars per year.) Operations managers—again working with the firm's marketing managers—must determine the required capacity. This, in turn, determines the size of the production facility. If the facility is built with too much capacity, valuable resources (plant, equipment, and money) will lie idle. If the facility offers insufficient capacity, additional capacity may have to be added later when it is much more expensive than in the initial building stage.

Capacity means about the same thing to service businesses. For example, the capacity of a restaurant such as the Hard Rock Cafe in Nashville, Tennessee, is the number of customers it can serve at one time. As with the manufacturing facility described earlier, if the restaurant is built with too much capacity—too many tables and chairs—valuable resources will be wasted. If the restaurant is too small, customers may have to wait for service; if the wait is too long, they may leave and choose another restaurant.

Use of Technology During the design-planning stage, management must determine the degree to which *automation* will be used to produce a product or service. Here, there is a tradeoff between high initial costs and low operating costs (for automation) and low initial costs and high operating costs (for human labor). Ultimately, management must choose between a labor-intensive technology and a capital-intensive technology. A **labor-intensive technology** is a process in which people must do most of the work. Housecleaning services and the New York Yankees baseball team, for example, are labor intensive. A **capital-intensive technology** is a process in which machines and equipment do most of the work. A Motorola automated assembly plant is capital intensive.

Site Selection and Facilities Planning

Once initial decisions have been made about a new product line, required capacity, and the use of technology, it is time to determine where the products or services are going to be produced. Generally, a business will choose to produce a new product in an existing factory as long as (1) the existing factory has enough capacity to handle customer demand for both the new product and established products and (2) the cost of refurbishing an existing factory is less than the cost of building a new one.

After exploring the capacity of existing factories, management may decide to build a new production facility. Once again, a number of decisions must be made. Should all the organization's production capacity be placed in one or two large facilities? Or should it be divided among several smaller facilities? In general, firms that market a wide variety of products find it more economical to have a number of smaller facilities. Firms that produce only a small number of products tend to have fewer but larger facilities.

capacity the amount of products or services that an organization can produce in a given time

labor-intensive technology a process in which people must do most of the work

capital-intensive technology a process in which machines and equipment do most of the work

Automated assembly lines: The key to increasing both quality and productivity. The hot, dirty job of welding, which is key to many manufacturing and construction tasks, is changing. Today, welders are becoming operators of robots that can do welding quicker and with more precision. To help companies plan for the future, Lincoln Electric, the company that produces this robotic rapid arc welder, has just opened a 100,000-square foot automation center where potential customers can see the latest in manufacturing technology.

In determining where to locate production facilities, management must consider a number of variables, including the following:

- Locations of major customers and suppliers
- Availability and cost of skilled and unskilled labor
- Quality of life for employees and management in the proposed location
- The cost of both land and construction required to build a new facility
- Local and state taxes, environmental regulations, and zoning laws
- The amount of financial support, if any, offered by local and state governments
- Special requirements, such as great amounts of energy or water used in the production process

The choice of a location often involves balancing the most important variables for each production facility. Before making a final decision about where a proposed plant will be located and how it will be organized, two other factors—human resources and plant layout—should be examined.

Human Resources Several issues involved in facilities planning and site selection fall within the province of the human resources manager. Thus, at this stage, human resources and operations managers work closely together. For example, suppose that a U.S. firm such as Reebok International wants to lower labor costs by constructing a sophisticated production plant in China. The human resources manager will have to recruit managers and employees with the appropriate skills who are willing to relocate to a foreign country or develop training programs for local Chinese workers or both.

Plant Layout Plant layout is the arrangement of machinery, equipment, and personnel within a production facility. Three general types of plant layout are used (see Figure 8.4).

The *process layout* is used when different operations are required for creating small batches of different products or working on different parts of a product. The plant is arranged so that each operation is performed in its own particular area. An auto repair facility at a local automobile dealership provides an example of a process layout. The various operations may be engine and transmission repair, body work, wheel alignment, and safety inspection. Each operation is performed in a different area. If you take your Lincoln Navigator for a wheel alignment, your car "visits" only the area where alignments are performed.

A *product layout* (sometimes referred to as an *assembly line*) is used when all products undergo the same operations in the same sequence. Workstations are arranged to match the sequence of operations, and work flows from station to station. An assembly line is the best example of a product layout. For example, California-based Maxim Integrated Products, Inc., uses a product layout to manufacture components for consumer and business electronic products.

A *fixed-position layout* is used when a very large product is produced. Aircraft manufacturers and shipbuilders apply this method because of the difficulty of moving a large product such as an airliner or a ship. The product remains stationary,

plant layout the arrangement of machinery, equipment, and personnel within a production facility

FIGURE 8.4: Facilities Planning The process layout is used when small batches of different products are created or when working on different parts of a product. The product layout (assembly line) is used when all products undergo the same operations in the same sequence. The fixed-position layout is used in producing a product too large to move.

PROCESS LAYOUT

Lincoln repair shop

Car in need of repairs → [Wheel alignment] [Body work] [Safety inspection] [Engine repair] → Repaired car

PRODUCT LAYOUT

Maxim Integrated Products assembly line

Electronic components → Workstation → Workstation → Workstation → Finished circuit boards

FIXED-POSITION LAYOUT

Boeing assembly site for a 787 Dreamliner jet aircraft

Resources and components → [Workstation] [Workstation] [Workstation] [Workstation] [Workstation] → Finished plane

and people and machines are moved as needed to assemble the product. Boeing, for example, uses the fixed-position layout to build 787 Dreamliner jet aircraft at its Everett, Washington, manufacturing facility.

Operational Planning

Once the product has been designed and a decision has been made to use an existing production facility or build a new one, operational plans must be developed. The objective of operational planning is to decide on the amount of products or services each facility will produce during a specific period of time. Four steps are required.

Step 1: Selecting a Planning Horizon A **planning horizon** is simply the time period during which an operational plan will be in effect. A common planning horizon for production plans is one year. Then, before each year is up, management must plan for the next.

A planning horizon of one year generally is long enough to average out seasonal increases and decreases in sales. At the same time, it is short enough for planners to

planning horizon the period during which an operational plan will be in effect adjust production to accommodate long-range sales trends. Firms that operate in a rapidly changing business environment with many competitors may find it best to select a shorter planning horizon to keep their production planning current.

Step 2: Estimating Market Demand The *market demand* for a product is the quantity that customers will purchase at the going price. This quantity must be estimated for the time period covered by the planning horizon. Sales projections developed by marketing managers are the basis for market-demand estimates.

Step 3: Comparing Market Demand with Capacity The third step in operational planning is to compare the estimated market demand with the facility's capacity to satisfy that demand. (Remember that capacity is the amount of products or services that an organization can produce in a given time period.) One of three outcomes may result: Demand may exceed capacity, capacity may exceed demand, or capacity and demand may be equal. If they are equal, the facility should be operated at full capacity. However, if market demand and capacity are not equal, adjustments may be necessary.

Step 4: Adjusting Products or Services to Meet Demand The biggest reason for changes to a firm's production schedule is changes in the amount of products or services that a company sells to its customers. For example, Indiana-based Berry Plastics uses an injection-molded manufacturing process to produce all kinds of plastic products. One particularly successful product line for Berry Plastics is drink cups that can be screen-printed to promote a company or the company's products or services.[6] If Berry Plastics obtains a large contract to provide promotional mugs to a large fast-food chain such as Whataburger or McDonald's, the company may need to work three shifts a day, seven days a week until the contract is fulfilled. Unfortunately, the reverse is also true. If the company's sales force does not generate new sales, there may be only enough work for the employees on one shift.

When market demand exceeds capacity, several options are available to a firm. Production of products or services may be increased by operating the facility overtime with existing personnel or by starting a second or third work shift. For manufacturers, another response is to subcontract or outsource a portion of the work to other manufacturers. If the excess demand is likely to be permanent, the firm may expand the current facility or build another facility.

What happens when capacity exceeds market demand? Again, there are several options. To reduce output temporarily, workers may be laid off and part of the facility shut down. Or the facility may be operated on a shorter-than-normal work week for as long as the excess capacity persists. To adjust to a permanently decreased demand, management may shift the excess capacity of a manufacturing facility to the production of other goods or services. The most radical adjustment is to eliminate the excess capacity by selling unused manufacturing facilities.

Concept Check

1. What are the major elements of design planning?

2. Define capacity. Why is it important for a manufacturing business or a service business?

3. What factors should be considered when selecting a site for a new manufacturing facility?

4. What is the objective of operational planning? What four steps are used to accomplish this objective?

LEARNING OBJECTIVE 5

Explain how purchasing, inventory control, scheduling, and quality control affect production.

Operations Control

We have discussed the development of an idea for a product or service and the planning that translates that idea into the reality. Now we are ready to push the "start button" to begin the production process. In this section, we examine four important areas of operations control: purchasing, inventory control, scheduling, and quality control (see Figure 8.5).

Purchasing

purchasing all the activities involved in obtaining required materials, supplies, components, and parts from other firms

Purchasing consists of all the activities involved in obtaining required materials, supplies, components (or subassemblies), and parts from other firms. Levi Strauss must purchase denim cloth, thread, and zippers before it can produce a single pair

FIGURE 8.5: Four Aspects of Operations Implementing the operations control system in any business requires the effective use of purchasing, inventory control, scheduling, and quality control.

of jeans. Similarly, Nike, Inc., must purchase leather, rubber, cloth for linings, and laces before manufacturing a pair of athletic shoes. For all firms, the purchasing function is far from routine, and its importance should not be underestimated. For some products, purchased materials make up more than 50 percent of their whole-sale costs.

The objective of purchasing is to ensure that required materials are available when they are needed, in the proper amounts, and at minimum cost. Generally, the company with purchasing needs and suppliers must develop a working relationship built on trust. In addition to a working relationship built on trust, many companies believe that purchasing is one area where they can promote diversity. For example, AT&T has developed a Supplier Diversity Program that includes minorities, women, and disabled veteran business enterprises. Goals for the AT&T program include purchasing a total of 21.5 percent of all products and services from these three groups. As a result of its Supplier Diversity Program, the company is now recognized as one of the nation's leading companies in supplier diversity.[7]

Purchasing personnel should be on the lookout constantly for new or backup suppliers, even when their needs are being met by their present suppliers, because problems such as strikes and equipment breakdowns can cut off the flow of purchased materials from a primary supplier at any time.

The choice of suppliers should result from careful analysis of a number of factors. The following are especially critical:

- *Price.* Comparing prices offered by different suppliers is always an essential part of selecting a supplier. Even tiny differences in price add up to enormous sums when large quantities are purchased.
- *Quality.* Purchasing specialists always try to buy materials at a level of quality in keeping with the type of product being manufactured. The minimum acceptable quality is usually specified by product designers.
- *Reliability.* An agreement to purchase high-quality materials at a low price is the purchaser's dream. But the dream becomes a nightmare if the supplier does not deliver.
- *Credit terms.* Purchasing specialists should determine if the supplier demands immediate payment or will extend credit. Also, does the supplier offer a cash discount or reduction in price for prompt payment?
- *Shipping costs.* Low prices and favorable credit terms offered by a supplier can be wiped out when the buyer must pay the shipping costs. Above all, the question of who pays the shipping costs should be answered before any supplier is chosen.

Inventory Control

Can you imagine what would happen if a Coca-Cola manufacturing plant ran out of the company's familiar red and white aluminum cans? It would be impossible to complete the manufacturing process and ship the cases of Coke to retailers. Management would be forced to shut the assembly line down until the next shipment of cans arrived from a supplier. In reality, operations managers for Coca-Cola realize the disasters that a shortage of needed materials can cause and will avoid this type of problem if at all possible. The simple fact is that shutdowns are expensive because costs such as rent, wages, and insurance still must be paid.

Operations managers are concerned with three types of inventories. A *raw-materials inventory* consists of materials that will become part of the product during the production process. The *work-in-process inventory* consists of partially completed products. The *finished-goods inventory* consists of completed goods. Associated with each type of inventory are a *holding cost,* or storage cost, and a *stock-out cost,* the cost of running out of inventory. **Inventory control** is the process of managing inventories in such a way as to minimize inventory costs, including both holding costs and potential stock-out costs.

Today, computer systems are being used to keep track of inventories, provide periodic inventory reports, and alert managers to impending stock-outs. One of the most sophisticated methods of inventory control used today is materials requirements planning. **Materials requirements planning (MRP)** is a computerized system that integrates production planning and inventory control. One of the great advantages of an MRP system is its ability to juggle delivery schedules and lead times effectively. For a complex product such as an automobile or airplane, it is virtually impossible for individual managers to oversee the hundreds of parts that go into the finished product. However, a manager using an MRP system can arrange both order and delivery schedules so that materials, parts, and supplies arrive when they are needed.

Because large firms can incur huge inventory costs, much attention has been devoted to inventory control. The just-in-time system being used by some businesses is one result of all this attention. A **just-in-time inventory system** is designed to ensure that materials or supplies arrive at a facility just when they are needed so that storage and holding costs are minimized. The customer must specify what will be needed, when, and in what amounts. The supplier must be sure that the right supplies arrive at the agreed-on time and location. For example, managers using a just-in-time inventory system at a Toyota assembly plant determine the number of automobiles that will be assembled in a specified time period. Then Toyota purchasing personnel order *just* the parts needed to produce those automobiles. In turn, suppliers deliver the parts *in time* or when they are needed on the assembly line.

Without proper inventory control, it is impossible for operations managers to schedule the work required to produce goods that can be sold to customers.

Scheduling

Scheduling is the process of ensuring that materials and other resources are at the right place at the right time. The materials and resources may be moved from a warehouse to the workstations, they may move from station to station along an assembly line, or they may arrive at workstations "just in time" to be made part of the work in process there.

As our definition implies, both place and time are important to scheduling. The *routing* of materials is the sequence of workstations that the materials will follow. Assume that Drexel-Heritage—one of America's largest and oldest furniture manufacturers—is scheduling production of an oval coffee table made from cherry wood. Operations managers would route the needed materials (wood, screws, packaging materials, and so on) through a series of individual workstations along an assembly line. At each workstation, a specific task would be performed, and then the partially finished coffee table would move to the next workstation. When routing materials,

inventory control the process of managing inventories in such a way as to minimize inventory costs, including both holding costs and potential stock-out costs

materials requirements planning (MRP) a computerized system that integrates production planning and inventory control

just-in-time inventory system a system designed to ensure that materials or supplies arrive at a facility just when they are needed so that storage and holding costs are minimized

scheduling the process of ensuring that materials and other resources are at the right place at the right time

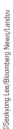

©Seokyong Lee/Bloomberg News/Landov

operations managers are especially concerned with the sequence of each step of the production process. For the coffee table, the top and legs must be cut to specifications before the wood is finished. (If the wood were finished before being cut, the finish would be ruined, and the coffee table would have to be stained again.)

When scheduling production, managers also are concerned with timing. The *timing* function specifies when the materials will arrive at each station and how long they will remain there. For the cherry coffee table, it may take workers thirty minutes to cut the table top and legs and another thirty minutes to drill the holes and assemble the table. Before packaging the coffee table for shipment, it must be finished with cherry stain and allowed to dry. This last step may take as long as three days depending on weather conditions and humidity.

Whether or not the finished product requires a simple or complex production process, operations managers are responsible for monitoring schedules—called *follow-up*—to ensure that the work flows according to a timetable.

Quality Control

As mentioned earlier in this chapter, American business firms that compete in the very competitive global marketplace have taken another look at the importance of improving quality. Today, there is even a national quality award. The **Malcolm Baldrige National Quality Award** is given by the President of the United States to organizations that apply and are judged to be outstanding in specific managerial tasks that lead to improved quality for both products and services. Winners include Ritz-Carlton Hotels, Boeing Aerospace Support Group, Motorola, 3M Dental Products Division, Richland Communtiy College (part of the Dallas Community College District), and many others. For many organizations, using the Baldrige criteria results in

- better employee relations,
- higher productivity,
- greater customer satisfaction,
- increased market share, and
- improved profitability.[8]

While winning the "Baldrige" can mean prestige and lots of free media coverage, the winners all have one factor in common: They use quality control to improve their firm's products or services.

Quality control is the process of ensuring that goods and services are produced in accordance with design specifications. The major objective of quality control is to see that the organization lives up to the standards it has set for itself on quality. Some firms, such as Mercedes-Benz and Neiman Marcus, have built their reputations on quality. Customers pay more for their products in return for assurances of high quality. Other firms adopt a strategy of emphasizing lower prices along with reasonable (but not particularly high) quality.

Is it Ethical?

Keeping Buyers Free from Influence

If you were a professional buyer, would a free lunch or T-shirt influence you to choose one supplier over another? Companies worry that purchasing personnel may be swayed if a supplier offers them something for free. In fact, two buyers who used to work for Home Depot recently pleaded guilty to taking money from suppliers in exchange for preferential treatment.

To keep employees out of ethically-questionable situations, many firms spell out exactly what buyers can and cannot accept. For example, Wal-Mart's code of ethics states that purchasing personnel are not allowed to receive any type of free goods, services, or entertainment from current or would-be suppliers. Buyers are advised to avoid "even the appearance of a conflict between personal interests and professional responsibility."

Costco, one of Wal-Mart's main competitors, also has a strict code of ethics that bars buyers from accepting supplier gifts. At the same time, Costco's code reflects the company's emphasis on mutual respect, requiring buyers to "treat all suppliers and their representatives as you would expect to be treated if visiting their places of business."

Intel, which makes computer chips, specifies in its code of ethics that buyers "not seek favors directly or indirectly, such as gifts, entertainment, sponsorships, or contributions from organizations doing business or seeking to do business with Intel." The high-tech firm even provides supplier ethics training (in several languages) so everybody knows the rules.

Sources: Jeff Chu and Kate Rockwood, "CEO Interview: Costco's Jim Sinegal," *Fast Company*, November 2008, www.fastcompany.com; David Armstrong, "At CVS Golf Gala, Suppliers Pay for Access to Executives," *Wall Street Journal*, September 24, 2008, www.wsj.com; James Bandler and Gary McWilliams, "Wal-Mart Chief Bought Ring from Firm's Vendor," *Wall Street Journal*, May 30, 2007, p. A4; www.walmart.com; www.intel.com; www.costco.com.

Malcolm Baldrige National Quality Award an award given by the President of the United States to organizations that apply and are judged to be outstanding in specific managerial tasks that lead to improved quality for both products and services

quality control the process of ensuring that goods and services are produced in accordance with design specifications

Inspections Increased effort is also being devoted to **inspection**, which is the examination of the quality of work in process. Inspections are performed at various times during production. Purchased materials may be inspected when they arrive at the production facility. Subassemblies and manufactured parts may be inspected before they become part of a finished product. And finished goods may be inspected before they are shipped to customers. Items that are within design specifications continue on their way. Those that are not within design specifications are removed from production.

Improving Quality Through Employee Participation Over the years, more and more managers have realized that quality is an essential "ingredient" of the good or service being provided. This view of quality provides several benefits. The number of defects decreases, which causes profits to increase. Making products right the first time reduces many of the rejects and much of the rework. And making employees responsible for quality often eliminates the need for inspection. An employee is encouraged to accept full responsibility for the quality of his or her work.

The use of a **quality circle**, a team of employees who meet on company time to solve problems of product quality, is another way manufacturers are achieving better quality at the operations level. Quality circles have been used successfully in such companies as IBM, Northrop Grumman Corporation, and Compaq Computers.

Because of increased global competition, many American manufacturers have also adopted a goal that calls for better quality in their products. As noted in Chapter 6, a *total quality management* (TQM) program coordinates the efforts directed at improving customer satisfaction, increasing employee participation, strengthening supplier partnerships, and facilitating an organizational atmosphere of continuous quality improvement. Firms such as American Express, AT&T, Motorola, and Hewlett Packard all have used TQM to improve product quality and, ultimately, customer satisfaction.

Another technique that businesses may use to improve not only quality but also overall performance is Six Sigma. **Six Sigma** is a disciplined approach that relies on statistical data and improved methods to eliminate defects for a firm's products and services. While many experts agree that Six Sigma is similar to TQM, Six Sigma often has more top-level support, much more teamwork, and a new corporate attitude or culture. The companies that developed, refined, and have the most experience with Six Sigma are Motorola, General Electric, Allied Signal, and Honeywell. While each of these companies is a corporate giant, the underlying principles of Six Sigma can be used by all firms regardless of size. For more information about Six Sigma, go to **www.isixsigma.com**.[9]

Concept Check

1. Why is selecting a supplier important? What factors should be considered when selecting a supplier?

2. What costs must be balanced and minimized through inventory control?

3. Explain in what sense scheduling is a control function of operations managers.

4. How can a business firm improve the quality of its products or services?

LEARNING OBJECTIVE 6

Summarize how productivity and technology are related.

inspection the examination of the quality of work in process

quality circle a team of employees who meet on company time to solve problems of product quality

Six Sigma a disciplined approach that relies on statistical data and improved methods to eliminate defects for a firm's products and services

Management of Productivity and Technology

No coverage of production and operations management would be complete without a discussion of productivity. Productivity concerns all managers, but it is especially important to operations managers, the people who must oversee the creation of a firm's goods or services. In Chapter 1, we defined *productivity* as the average level of output per worker per hour. Hence, if each worker at plant A produces seventy-five units per day and each worker at plant B produces only seventy units per day, the workers at plant A are more productive. If one bank teller serves twenty-five customers per hour and another serves twenty-eight per hour, the second teller is more productive.

Productivity Trends

Overall productivity growth for the business sector averaged 4.0 percent for the period 1979–2007.[10] More specifically, productivity in 2008 increased 2.7 percent.[11]

It's a real plus to have help when solving problems. At Google's European headquarters in Dublin, Ireland, employee participation helps to improve the quality of the services that the world's number one search engine provides to Internet users around the globe.

(*Note:* At the time of publication, 2008 was the last year that complete statistics were available.) Using comparable data for the latest year available, our productivity growth rate ranked fourth among the 17 countries that the U.S. Bureau of Labor Statistics tracks. Our productivity growth rate is lagging behind the productivity growth rates of such countries as Korea, Taiwan, and Germany.[12] While many people think of productivity growth rate as just another economic statistic, it is a very important statistic because it is a main determinant of changes in our standard of living. (Remember, *standard of living* was defined in Chapter 1 as a loose, subjective measure of how well off an individual or a society is mainly in terms of want satisfaction through goods and services.)

Improving Productivity Growth Rates

Several techniques and strategies have been suggested to improve current productivity growth rates. For example:

- Government policies that may be hindering productivity growth could be eliminated or at least modified.
- Increased cooperation between labor and management could be fostered to improve productivity.
- Increased employee motivation and participation can enhance productivity.
- Changing the incentives for work and altering the reward system so that people are paid for what they contribute rather than for the time they put in may motivate employees to produce at higher levels.
- Investing more money in facilities, equipment, technology, and employee training could improve productivity.

The Impact of Computers and Robotics on Production

Automation is the total or near-total use of machines to do work. The rapid increase in automated procedures has been made possible by the microprocessor, a silicon chip that led to the production of desktop computers for businesses, homes, and schools. In factories, microprocessors are used in robotics and in computer manufacturing systems.

automation the total or near-total use of machines to do work

Robotics **Robotics** is the use of programmable machines to perform a variety of tasks by manipulating materials and tools. Robots work quickly, accurately, and steadily. For example, Illumina, Inc., a San Diego company, uses robots to screen blood samples and identify DNA quirks that cause diseases. The information then is sold to some of the world's largest pharmaceutical companies, where it is used to alter existing prescription drugs, develop new drug therapies, and customize diagnoses and treatments for all kinds of serious diseases. As an added bonus, Illumina's robots can work 24 hours a day at much lower costs than if human lab workers performed the same tests.[13]

Robots are especially effective in tedious, repetitive assembly-line jobs, as well as in handling hazardous materials. They are also useful as artificial "eyes" that can check the quality of products as they are being processed on the assembly lines. To date, the automotive industry has made the most extensive use of robotics, but robots also have been used to mine coal, inspect the inner surfaces of pipes, assemble computer components, provide certain kinds of patient care in hospitals, and clean and guard buildings at night.

Computer Manufacturing Systems People are quick to point out how computers have changed their everyday lives, but most people do not realize the impact computers have had on manufacturing. For most manufacturers, the changeover began with the use of computer-aided design and computer-aided manufacturing. **Computer-aided design (CAD)** is the use of computers to aid in the development of products. Using CAD, Ford speeds up car design, Canon designs new photocopiers, and American Greetings creates new birthday cards. **Computer-aided manufacturing (CAM)** is the use of computers to plan and control manufacturing processes. A well-designed CAM system allows manufacturers to become much more productive. Not only are a greater number of products produced, but speed and quality also increase. Toyota, Hasbro, Oneida, and Apple Computer all have used CAM to increase productivity.

If you are thinking that the next logical step is to combine the CAD and CAM computer systems, you are right. Today, the most successful manufacturers use CAD and CAM together to form a computer-integrated manufacturing system. Specifically, **computer-integrated manufacturing (CIM)** is a computer system that not only helps to design products but also controls the machinery needed to produce the finished product. For example, Liz Claiborne, Inc., uses CIM to design clothing, to establish patterns for new fashions, and then to cut the cloth needed to produce the finished product. Other advantages of using CIM include improved flexibility, more efficient scheduling, and higher product quality—all factors that make a production facility more competitive in today's global economy.

Flexible Manufacturing Systems Manufacturers have known for a number of years that the old-style, traditional assembly lines used to manufacture products present a number of problems. For example, although traditional assembly lines turn out extremely large numbers of identical products economically, the system requires expensive, time-consuming retooling of equipment whenever a new product is to be manufactured. This type of manufacturing is often referred to as a continuous process. **Continuous process** is a manufacturing process in which a firm produces the same product(s) over a long period of time. Now it is possible to use flexible manufacturing systems to solve such problems. A **flexible manufacturing system (FMS)** combines robotics and computer-integrated manufacturing in a single production system. Instead of having to spend vast amounts of time and effort to retool the traditional mechanical equipment on an assembly line for each new product, an FMS is rearranged simply by reprogramming electronic machines. Because FMSs require less time and expense to reprogram, manufacturers can produce smaller batches of a variety of products without raising the production cost.

robotics the use of programmable machines to perform a variety of tasks by manipulating materials and tools

computer-aided design (CAD) the use of computers to aid in the development of products

computer-aided manufacturing (CAM) the use of computers to plan and control manufacturing processes

computer-integrated manufacturing (CIM) a computer system that not only helps to design products but also controls the machinery needed to produce the finished product

continuous process a manufacturing process in which a firm produces the same product(s) over a long period of time

flexible manufacturing system (FMS) a single production system that combines robotics and computer-integrated manufacturing

Flexible manufacturing is sometimes referred to as an intermittent process. An **intermittent process** is a manufacturing process in which a firm's manufacturing machines and equipment are changed to produce different products. When compared with the continuous process (longer production runs), an intermittent process has a shorter production run.

For most manufacturers, the driving force behind flexible manufacturing systems is the customer. In fact, the term *customer-driven production* is often used by operations managers to describe a manufacturing system that is driven by customer needs and what customers want to buy. For example, advanced software and a flexible manufacturing system have enabled Dell Computer to change to a more customer-driven manufacturing process. The process starts when a customer phones a sales representative on a toll-free line or accesses Dell's website. Then the representative or the customer enters the specifications for the new product directly into a computer. The order then is sent to a nearby plant. Once the order is received, a team of employees with the help of a reprogrammable assembly line can build the product just the way the customer wants it. Products include desktop computers, laptop computers, and other Dell equipment.[14] Although the costs of designing and installing an FMS such as this are high, the electronic equipment is used more frequently and efficiently than the machinery on a traditional assembly line.

Technological Displacement Automation is increasing productivity by cutting manufacturing time, reducing error, and simplifying retooling procedures. Many of the robots being developed for use in manufacturing will not replace human employees. Rather, these robots will work with employees in making their jobs easier and help to prevent accidents. No one knows, however, what the effect will be on the workforce. Some experts estimate that automation will bring new changes to more than half of all jobs within the next ten years. Total unemployment may not increase, but many workers will be faced with the choice of retraining for new jobs or seeking jobs in other sectors of the economy. Government, business, and education will have to cooperate to prepare workers for new roles in an automated workplace.

The next chapter discusses many of the issues caused by technological displacement. In addition, a number of major components of human resources management are described, and we see how managers use various reward systems to boost motivation, productivity, and morale.

intermittent process a manufacturing process in which a firm's manufacturing machines and equipment are changed to produce different products

Concept Check

1. How might productivity be measured in a restaurant? In a department store? In a public school system?

2. How can robotics, computer manufacturing systems, and flexible manufacturing systems help a manufacturer to produce products?

SUMMARY

1 Explain the nature of production.

Operations management consists of all the activities that managers engage in to create goods and services. Operations are as relevant to service organizations as to manufacturing firms. Generally, three major activities are involved in producing goods or services: product development, planning for production, and operations control. Today, U.S. manufacturers are forced to compete in an ever-smaller world to meet the needs of more demanding customers. In an attempt to regain a competitive edge, they have taken another look at the importance of improving quality and meeting the needs of their customers. They also have used new techniques to motivate employees, reduced costs, replaced outdated equipment, used computer-aided and flexible manufacturing systems, improved

control procedures, and built new manufacturing facilities in foreign countries where labor costs are lower. Competing in the global economy is not only profitable, but it is also an essential activity that requires the cooperation of everyone within an organization.

2 Outline how the conversion process transforms raw materials, labor, and other resources into finished products or services.

A business transforms resources into goods and services in order to provide utility to customers. Utility is the ability of a good or service to satisfy a human need. Form utility is created by people converting raw materials, finances, and information into finished products. Conversion processes vary in terms of the major resources used to produce goods and services (focus), the degree to which resources are changed (magnitude of change), and the number of production processes that a business uses. The application of the basic principles of operations management to the production of services has coincided with the growth and importance of service businesses in the United States.

3 Describe how research and development lead to new products and services.

Operations management often begins with product research and development (R&D). The results of R&D may be entirely new products or extensions and refinements of existing products. R&D activities are classified as basic research (aimed at uncovering new knowledge), applied research (discovering new knowledge with some potential use), and development and implementation (using new or existing knowledge to produce goods and services). If a firm sells only one product, when that product reaches the end of its life cycle, the firm will die, too. To stay in business, the firm must, at the very least, find ways to refine or extend the want-satisfying capability of its product.

4 Discuss the components involved in planning the production process.

Planning for production involves three major phases: design planning, site selection and facilities planning, and operational planning. First, design planning is undertaken to address questions related to the product line, required production capacity, and the use of technology. Production facilities, site selection, human resources, and plant layout, then must be considered. Operational planning focuses on the use of production facilities and resources. The steps for operational planning include (a) selecting a planning horizon, (b) estimating market demand, (c) comparing market demand with capacity, and (d) adjusting production of products or services to meet demand.

5 Explain how purchasing, inventory control, scheduling, and quality control affect production.

The major areas of operations control are purchasing, inventory control, scheduling, and quality control.

Purchasing involves selecting suppliers. The choice of suppliers should result from careful analysis of a number of factors, including price, quality, reliability, credit terms, and shipping costs. Inventory control is the management of stocks of raw materials, work in process, and finished goods to minimize the total inventory cost. Today, most firms use a computerized system to maintain inventory records. In addition, many firms use a just-in-time inventory system, in which materials or supplies arrive at a facility just when they are needed so that storage and holding costs are minimized. Scheduling ensures that materials and other resources are at the right place at the right time. Quality control guarantees that products meet the design specifications for those products. The major objective of quality control is to see that the organization lives up to the standards it has set for itself on quality.

6 Summarize how productivity and technology are related.

The productivity growth rate in the United States has fallen behind the pace of growth in some of the other industrialized nations in recent years. Possible solutions to increase productivity include less government regulation, increased cooperation between management and labor, increased employee motivation and participation, new incentives for work, and additional investment by business to fund new or renovated facilities, equipment, employee training, and the use of technology.

Automation, the total or near-total use of machines to do work, has for some years been changing the way work is done in factories. A growing number of industries are using programmable machines called robots to perform tasks that are tedious or hazardous to human beings. Computer-aided design, computer-aided manufacturing, and computer-integrated manufacturing use computers to help design and manufacture products. The flexible manufacturing system combines robotics and computer-integrated manufacturing to produce smaller batches of products more efficiently than on the traditional assembly line. Instead of having to spend vast amounts of time and effort to retool the traditional mechanical equipment on an assembly line for each new product, an FMS is rearranged simply by reprogramming electronic machines.

KEY TERMS

You should now be able to define and give an example relevant to each of the following terms:

operations management (206)
mass production (207)
analytical process (207)
synthetic process (207)
utility (207)
form utility (207)
service economy (208)
research and development (R&D) (210)
design planning (212)
product line (212)

product design (212)
capacity (213)
labor-intensive technology (213)
capital-intensive technology (213)
plant layout (214)
planning horizon (215)
purchasing (216)
inventory control (218)
materials requirements planning (MRP) (218)

just-in-time inventory system (218)
scheduling (218)
Malcolm Baldrige National Quality Award (219)
quality control (219)
inspection (220)
quality circle (220)
Six Sigma (220)
automation (221)
robotics (222)

computer-aided design (CAD) (222)
computer-aided manufacturing (CAM) (222)
computer-integrated manufacturing (CIM) (222)
continuous process (222)
flexible manufacturing system (FMS) (222)
intermittent process (223)

1. Why would Rubbermaid—a successful U.S. company—need to expand and sell its products to customers in foreign countries?
2. Do certain kinds of firms need to stress particular areas of operations management? Explain.
3. Is it really necessary for service firms to engage in research and development? In planning for production and operations control?
4. How are the four areas of operations control interrelated?
5. In what ways can employees help to improve the quality of a firm's products?
6. Is operations management relevant to nonbusiness organizations such as colleges and hospitals? Why or why not?

Get Flash Cards, Quizzes, Games, Crosswords and more @ www.cengage.com/introbusiness/pride

Test Yourself

Matching Questions

1. _____ It is a plan for converting a product idea into an actual product.
2. _____ Raw materials are broken into different components.
3. _____ Its focus is minimizing holding costs and potential stock-out costs.
4. _____ It is created by people converting materials, finances and information into finished goods.
5. _____ A manufacturing process in which a firm's manufacturing machines and equipment are changed to produce different products.
6. _____ Work is accomplished mostly by equipment.
7. _____ Input from workers is used to improve the workplace.
8. _____ The average level of output per worker per hour.
9. _____ Computers are the main tool used in the development of products.
10. _____ The time period during which an operational plan will be in effect.

   a. analytical process
   b. capital-intensive technology
   c. product line
   d. computer-aided design
   e. design planning
   f. form utility
   g. inventory control
   h. plant layout
   i. planning horizon
   j. productivity
   k. quality circle
   l. intermittent process

True False Questions

11. **T F** Capacity is the degree to which input resources are physically changed by the conversion process.
12. **T F** The rise-and-decline pattern of sales for an existing product is called the product life cycle.
13. **T F** Operations management is the process of creating a set of specifications from which the product can be produced.
14. **T F** A purchasing agent need not worry about a tiny difference in price when a large quantity is being bought.
15. **T F** A synthetic process combines raw materials or components to create a finished product.
16. **T F** When work stations are arranged to match the sequence of operations, a process layout is being used.
17. **T F** Work-in-process inventories are raw materials and supplies waiting to be processed.
18. **T F** The purpose of research and development is to identify new ideas that have the potential to result in new goods and services.
19. **T F** For a food-processing plant such as Kraft Foods, capacity refers to the number of employees working on an assembly line.
20. **T F** Labor-intensive technology is accompanied by low initial costs and high operating costs.

Test Yourself

Multiple-Choice Questions

21. _____ One worker in Department A produces forty-five units of work per day on a computer, whereas a coworker produces only forty units of work per day on a computer. Since the first worker produces more units, that worker has a

    a. lower capacity to use technology.
    b. higher productivity rate.
    c. desire to help the coworker.
    d. computer-integrated system.
    e. computer-aided system

22. _____ Services differ from the production of manufactured goods in all ways except that services

    a. are consumed immediately and cannot be stored.
    b. aren't as important as manufactured products to the U.S. economy.
    c. are provided when and where the customer desires the service.
    d. are usually labor-intensive.
    e. are intangible, and it's more difficult to evaluate customer service.

23. _____ The goal of basic research is to

    a. uncover new knowledge without regard for its potential use.
    b. discover new knowledge with regard for potential use in development.
    c. discover knowledge for potential use.
    d. put new or existing knowledge to use.
    e. combine ideas.

24. _____ Two important components of scheduling are

    a. lead time and planning.
    b. designing and arranging.
    c. monitoring and controlling.
    d. place and time.
    e. logistics and flow.

25. _____ A common planning horizon for production activities is

    a. one day.
    b. a week.
    c. a month.
    d. six months.
    e. one year.

26. _____ A _____ manufacturing system combines robotics and computer-integrated manufacturing in a single-production system.

    a. continuous
    b. analytic
    c. synthetic
    d. flexible
    e. automation

27. _____ The process of acquiring materials, supplies, components, and parts from other firms is known as

    a. acquisition.
    b. planning.
    c. purchasing.
    d. inventory requisition.
    e. materials requirements planning.

28. _____ Procter & Gamble uses _____ production to produce household products.

    a. efficient order
    b. demand
    c. supply order
    d. mass
    e. effective

29. _____ If a good or service satisfies a human need, it has

    a. form.
    b. value.
    c. focus.
    d. magnitude
    e. utility.

30. _____ The American economy is now characterized as a(n) _____ economy.

    a. civilized
    b. stagnant
    c. service
    d. bureaucratic
    e. industrialized

Answers on p. TY-1

VIDEO CASE

Washburn Guitars: Signature Model Quality

Washburn Guitars produces a wide variety of acoustic and electric guitars, selling about 50,000 instruments a year for $40 million in total revenues. An Illinois-based company in business for over 125 years, Washburn maintains a workforce of people who love music, play music, and value the craft and design of each guitar.

The production process at Washburn starts when its designers give the engineer an idea for a new product . The engineer uses CAD (computer-aided-design) software to design a computer mock-up of the new instrument so the production people can check the quality of technical details like string alignment and string angle. Once the drawing has been approved, the wood boards—of mahogany, alder, poplar, or swamp ash—are selected, cut, and reduced to the desired size and thickness. (The wood's degree of porosity is what gives a guitar its unique tone.) The boards are then sent to CNC machines, computer-assisted manufacturing devices that cut out the various parts of the guitar to the specifications provided by the CAD software. Anything the software can draw, the machines can automatically cut.

The guitar parts next go to various departments for body sanding, neck assembly, and painting. After two weeks in "the dry room," the wood is leveled and buffed. The guitar then goes to a subassembly bench where the strings are put on and tuned, and finally the finished instrument is played to make sure it meets Washburn's quality standards. If it does, the guitar gets a quality tag signed by all the department heads.

The keys to quality for a guitar are form, fit, and function. You can have the best-looking guitar on the market, but if it doesn't play well and sound good, guitar enthusiasts will not be interested in purchasing it, and word will quickly travel throughout the music industry.

Two major changes have improved Washburn guitar quality substantially in recent years. First, the company hired a new production manager. Gil Vasquez had been at Baker Guitars on the West Coast, manufacturing low-volume, high-end guitars for top musicians. At Washburn he undertook a relentless pursuit of quality improvements. The second change came when Washburn acquired Parker Guitar, a company founded by an aviation engineer that also caters to high-end customers. Parker's production approach injected new quality standards into Washburn's processes, and Washburn's production approach added volume efficiencies to Parker's processes. Thus, the acquisition improved both companies.

A production model guitar has no variations. If twelve pieces are made in a run, all the guitars are going to be of the same wood, be the same color, and have the same features. So Washburn also has a custom shop, where it makes more expensive specialty guitars for high-profile musicians and performers who request specific colors, special woods, unique components, and the highest-grade accessories. The custom shop's production has risen from 60 to 300 guitars in just two years, while its staff has grown from 8 people to 65.

A signature model increases the appeal of a guitar among aficionados. It makes a statement about the guitar's quality, and it strengthens Washburn's relationship with rock stars such as Dan Donegan (lead guitarist for the rock band Disturbed) and his millions of fans. Such stars want an instrument unique to them that doesn't look like every other guitar in music stores around the country. In fact, Donegan helped design the Maya Pro DD75, which includes a range of features and high-end components that fit his specific needs. This signature model requires additional hand crafting and care, which can be challenging to a production facility like Washburn's.

Once the design of a signature model has been finalized, the production process is similar to the one described above except that Washburn's craftspeople are especially motivated to do their best for a high-profile guitarist like Donegan. Washburn knows that to be considered a quality producer, it has to be associated with quality users of its products.[15]

For more information about this company, go to **www.washburn.com**.

Questions

1. Using the concepts of focus, magnitude of change, and number of production processes, discuss Washburn's manufacturing conversion process.
2. How would you describe Dan Donegan's role in the production process that produced his signature guitar?
3. What form of plant layout does Washburn appear to employ in the manufacture of its guitars?

BUILDING SKILLS FOR CAREER SUCCESS

1. EXPLORING THE INTERNET

Improvements in the quality of products and services is an ever-popular theme in business management. Besides the obvious increase to profitability to be gained by such improvements, a company's demonstration of its continuous search for ways to improve operations can be a powerful statement to customers, suppliers, and investors. Two of the larger schools of thought in this field are Six Sigma and Total Quality Management. Visit the text website for updates to this exercise.

Assignment

1. Use Internet search engines to find more information about each of these topics.
2. From the information on the Internet, can you tell whether there is any real difference between these two approaches?
3. Describe one success story of a firm that realized improvement by adopting either approach.

2. BUILDING TEAM SKILLS

Suppose that you are planning to build a house in the country. It will be a brick, one-story structure of approximately 2,000 square feet, centrally heated and cooled. It will have three bedrooms, two bathrooms, a family room, a dining room, a kitchen with a breakfast nook, a study, a utility room, an entry foyer, a two-car garage, a covered patio, and a fireplace. Appliances will operate on electricity and propane fuel. You have received approval and can be connected to the cooperative water system at any time. Public sewerage services are not available; therefore, you must rely on a septic system. You want to know how long it will take to build the house.

Assignment

1. Identify the major activities involved in the project and sequence them in the proper order.
2. Estimate the time required for each activity.
3. Present your list of activities to the class and ask for comments and suggestions.

3. RESEARCHING DIFFERENT CAREERS

Because service businesses are now such a dominant part of our economy, job seekers sometimes overlook the employment opportunities available in production plants. Two positions often found in these plants are quality control inspector and purchasing agent.

Assignment

1. Using the *Occupational Outlook Handbook* at your local library or on the Internet (http://stats.bls.gov/oco/), find the following information for the jobs of quality control inspector and purchasing agent: Nature of work, including main activities and responsibilities, Job Outlook, Earnings, Training, and Qualifications.

2. Look for other production jobs that may interest you and compile the same sort of information about them.

3. Summarize in a two-page report the key things you learned about jobs in production plants.

Finagle A Bagel's Management, Organization, and Production Finesse

"We don't have a traditional corporate organizational chart," states Heather Robertson, Finagle A Bagel's director of marketing, human resources, and research and development. When she hires new employees, Robertson draws the usual type of organization chart showing the copresidents on the top and the store employees on the bottom. Then she turns it upside down, explaining: "The most important people in our stores are the crew members, and the store manager's role is to support those crew members. Middle management's role is to support the store managers. And the copresidents' responsibility is to support us," referring to herself and her middle-management colleagues.

In short, the copresidents and all the people in corporate headquarters work as a team to help the general managers (who run the stores) and their crew members. Every store strives to achieve preset sales goals within budget guidelines. Higher-level managers are available to help any general manager whose store's performance falls outside the expected ranges. Moreover, each general manager is empowered to make decisions that will boost sales and make the most of opportunities to build positive relationships with local businesses and community organizations. "We want our general managers to view the store as their business," copresident Laura Trust emphasizes. "If a general manager wants to do something that will alleviate a store problem or increase sales, we give him [or her] the leeway to do it."

Many Bagels, One Factory

Although the copresidents decentralized authority for many store-level decisions, they achieved more efficiency by centralizing the authority and responsibility for food procurement and preparation. For example, headquarters handles payroll, invoices, and many other time-consuming activities on behalf of all the stores. This reduces the paperwork burden on general managers and frees them to concentrate on managing store-level food service to satisfy customers.

Finagle A Bagel also decided to centralize production and supply functions in its recently opened Newton facility, where the factory has enough capacity to supply up to 100 stores. "We outgrew our old facility, and we wanted to find some place we could expand our operations," copresident Laura Trust explains. Production employees prepare and shape dough for 100,000 bagels and mix 2,000 pounds of flavored cream cheese spreads every day. In addition, they slice 1,500 pounds of fruit every week. Then they gather whatever each store needs—raw dough, salad fixings, packages of condiments, or plastic bowls—and load it on the truck for daily delivery.

Baking Bagels and More

Once the raw dough reaches a store, crew members follow the traditional New York–style method of boiling and baking bagels in various varieties, ranging from year-round favorites such as sesame to seasonal offerings such as pumpkin raisin. In line with Finagle A Bagel's fresh-food concept, the stores bake bagels every hour and tumble them into a line of bins near the front counter. Each store has a unique piece of equipment, dubbed the "bagel buzz saw," to slice and move bagels to the sandwich counter after customers have placed their orders. This equipment not only helps to prevent employee accidents and speeds food preparation, but it also entertains customers as they wait for their sandwiches.

Finagle A Bagel is constantly introducing new menu items to bring customers back throughout the day. One item the company has perfected is the bagel pizza. Earlier bagel pizzas turned out soggy, but the newest breakfast pizzas are both crunchy and tasty. The central production facility starts by mixing egg bagel dough, forms it into individual flat breads, grills the rounds, and ships them to the stores. There, a crew member tops each round with the customer's choice of ingredients, heats it, and serves it toasty fresh.

Managing a Bagel Restaurant

Finagle A Bagel's general managers stay busy from the early morning, when they open the store and help crew members to get ready for customers, to the time they close the store at night after one last look to see whether everything is in order for the next day. General managers such as Paulo Pereira, who runs the Harvard Square Finagle A Bagel in Cambridge, must have the technical skills required to run a fast-paced food-service operation.

General managers also need good conceptual skills so that they can look beyond each individual employee and task to see how everything should fit together. One way Pereira does this is by putting himself in the customer's shoes. He is constantly evaluating how customers would judge the in-store experience, from courteous, attentive counter service to the availability of fresh foods, clean tables, and well-stocked condiment containers.

Just as important, Pereira—like other Finagle A Bagel general managers—must have excellent interpersonal skills to work effectively with customers, crew members, colleagues, and higher-level managers. Pereira knows that he can't be successful without being able to work well with other people, especially those he supervises. "You need to have a good crew behind you to help you every single hour of the day," he says. "Every employee needs to feel special and appreciated. I try to treat employees as fairly as possible, and I try to accommodate their needs."

©Barbara Helgason

Questions

1. What does Finagle A Bagel's upside-down organization chart suggest about the delegation of authority and coordination techniques within the company?

2. Is Finagle A Bagel a tall or flat organization? How do you know?

3. What values seem to permeate Finagle A Bagel's corporate culture?

4. Why would Finagle A Bagel build a dough factory that has more capacity than the company needs to supply its stores and its wholesale customers?

Now you should be ready to provide evidence that you have a management team with the necessary skills and experience to execute your business plan successfully. Only a competent management team can transform your vision into a successful business. You also should be able to describe your manufacturing and operations plans. The three chapters in Part 3 of your textbook, "Understanding the Management Process," "Creating a Flexible Organization," and "Producing Quality Goods and Services," should help you in answering some of the questions in this part of the business plan.

THE MANAGEMENT TEAM COMPONENT

The management team component should include the answers to at least the following questions:

3.1.   How is your team balanced in technical, conceptual, interpersonal, and other special skills needed in your business?
3.2.   What will be your style of leadership?
3.3.   How will your company be structured? Include a statement of the philosophy of management and company culture.
3.4.   What are the key management positions, compensation, and key policies?
3.5.   Include a job description for each management position, and specify who will fill that position. *Note:* Prepare an organization chart and provide the résumé of each key manager for the appendix.
3.6.   What other professionals, such as a lawyer, an insurance agent, a banker, and a certified public accountant, will you need for assistance?

THE MANUFACTURING AND OPERATIONS PLANS COMPONENT

If you are in a manufacturing business, now is a good time to describe your manufacturing and operations plans, space requirements, equipment, labor force, inventory control, and purchasing requirements. Even if you are in a service-oriented business, many of these questions still may apply.

The manufacturing and operations plan component should include the answers to at least the following questions:

3.7.   What are the advantages and disadvantages of your planned location in terms of

- Wage rates
- Unionization
- Labor pool
- Proximity to customers and suppliers
- Types of transportation available
- Tax rates
- Utility costs
- Zoning requirements

3.8.   What facilities does your business require? Prepare a floor plan for the appendix. Will you rent, lease, or purchase the facilities?
3.9.   Will you make or purchase component parts to be assembled into the finished product? Make sure to justify your "make-or-buy decision."
3.10.   Who are your potential subcontractors and suppliers?
3.11.   How will you control quality, inventory, and production? How will you measure your progress?
3.12.   Is there a sufficient quantity of adequately skilled people in the local labor force to meet your needs?

REVIEW OF BUSINESS PLAN ACTIVITIES

Be sure to go over the information you have gathered. Check for any weaknesses, and resolve them before beginning Part 4. Also review all the answers to the questions in Parts 1, 2, and 3 to be certain that all answers are consistent throughout the entire business plan. Finally, write a brief statement that summarizes all the information for this part of the business plan.

The information contained in "Building a Business Plan" will also assist you in completing the online *Interactive Business Plan*.

Attracting and Retaining the Best Employees

©Yuri Arcurs/Shutterstock

WHY THIS CHAPTER MATTERS. Being able to understand how to attract and keep the right people is crucial. Also, you can better understand about your own interactions with your coworkers.

LEARNING OBJECTIVES

1 Describe the major components of human resources management.

2 Identify the steps in human resources planning.

3 Describe cultural diversity and understand some of the challenges and opportunities associated with it.

4 Explain the objectives and uses of job analysis.

5 Describe the processes of recruiting, employee selection, and orientation.

6 Discuss the primary elements of employee compensation and benefits.

7 Explain the purposes and techniques of employee training, development, and performance appraisal.

8 Outline the major legislation affecting human resources management.

How Google Grows

Google is not only the world's most popular search engine—it's also one of the best U.S. companies to work for, according to *Fortune* magazine. It offers challenging work, generous salaries and benefits, and numerous paid vacation days and holidays. Its larger facilities boast free extras such as gourmet meals, ping-pong tables, yoga classes, volleyball courts, even laundry facilities and car washes. Engineers are encouraged to follow their dreams by spending 20 percent of their time on projects of their own choosing. No wonder 777,000 people apply for jobs at Google every year.

Competition for open positions is fierce, and Google is choosy about which new graduates and experienced employees it hires. The company's sizable staff of professional recruiters invites résumés and inquiries through the corporate website, through a special Google Student channel on YouTube (which Google owns), and through an on-campus presence at top universities. Google also pays employees a bonus for referring qualified applicants who are ultimately hired.

Applicants who have the credentials and experience for a particular position are pre-screened during a 30-minute phone interview before any in-person interviews are scheduled. When candidates do sit down with Google managers and peers, they can expect to spend several hours answering questions about their technical abilities and demonstrating creative thinking by working out the solution to a job-related problem. All Google personnel who interview the candidates for a particular opening have a say in the final hiring decision.

For the first ten years of its corporate life, Google was expanding so rapidly that it never stopped recruiting. In fact, from 2006 to 2008, as the company approached $21 billion in annual revenue, it doubled the size of its workforce by recruiting 10,000 employees. Although the recent economic crisis slowed Google's growth and its recruiting, the company remains one of the most desirable employers in America—a place where talented employees can challenge themselves, polish their skills, make a difference, and be rewarded for outstanding performance.[1]

DID YOU KNOW?

Google doubled the size of its workforce from 2006 to 2008 by recruiting 10,000 employees, and it still attracts 777,000 job applications every year.

Google spends considerable resources to hire highly talented employees. A number of companies focus on hiring a diverse mix of employees to serve a diverse customer base. For many companies, these are important factors to consider when attracting, motivating, and retaining the appropriate mix of human resources.

We begin our study of human resources management (HRM) with an overview of how businesses acquire, maintain, and develop their human resources. After listing the steps by which firms match their human resources needs with the supply available, we explore several dimensions of cultural diversity. Then we examine the concept of job analysis. Next, we focus on a firm's recruiting, selection, and orientation procedures as the means of acquiring employees. We also describe forms of employee compensation that motivate employees to remain with a firm and to work effectively. Then we discuss methods of employee training, management development, and performance appraisal. Finally, we consider legislation that affects HRM practices.

Human Resources Management: An Overview

1 LEARNING OBJECTIVE

Describe the major components of human resources management.

The human resource is not only unique and valuable, but it is also an organization's most important resource. It seems logical that an organization would expend a great deal of effort to acquire and make full use of such a resource. This effort is known as *human resources management* (HRM). It also has been called *staffing* and *personnel management*.

Human resources management (HRM) consists of all the activities involved in acquiring, maintaining, and developing an organization's human resources. As the definition implies, HRM begins with acquisition—getting people to work for the organization. Next, steps must be taken to keep these valuable resources. (After all, they are the only business resources that can leave an organization.) Finally, the human resources should be developed to their full capacity.

HRM Activities

Each of the three phases of HRM—acquiring, maintaining, and developing human resources—consists of a number of related activities. Acquisition, for example, includes planning, as well as the various activities that lead to hiring new personnel. Altogether this phase of HRM includes five separate activities. They are as follows:

- *Human resources planning*—determining the firm's future human resources needs
- *Job analysis*—determining the exact nature of the positions
- *Recruiting*—attracting people to apply for positions
- *Selection*—choosing and hiring the most qualified applicants
- *Orientation*—acquainting new employees with the firm

Maintaining human resources consists primarily of encouraging employees to remain with the firm and to work effectively by using a variety of HRM programs, including the following:

- *Employee relations*—increasing employee job satisfaction through satisfaction surveys, employee communication programs, exit interviews, and fair treatment
- *Compensation*—rewarding employee effort through monetary payments
- *Benefits*—providing rewards to ensure employee well-being

The development phase of HRM is concerned with improving employees' skills and expanding their capabilities. The two important activities within this phase are

- *Training and development*—teaching employees new skills, new jobs, and more effective ways of doing their present jobs
- *Performance appraisal*—assessing employees' current and potential performance levels

These activities are discussed in more detail shortly, when we have completed this overview of HRM.

Responsibility for HRM

In general, HRM is a shared responsibility of line managers and staff HRM specialists. In very small organizations, the owner handles all or most HRM activities. As a firm grows in size, a human resources manager is hired to take over staff responsibilities. In firms as large as Disney, HRM activities tend to be very highly specialized. There are separate groups to deal with compensation, benefits, training and development, and other staff activities.

Specific HRM activities are assigned to those who are in the best position to perform them. Human resources planning and job analysis usually are done by staff specialists, with input from line managers. Similarly, recruiting and selection are handled by staff experts, although line managers are involved in hiring decisions. Orientation programs are devised by staff specialists and carried out by both staff specialists and line managers. Compensation systems (including benefits) most often are developed and administered by the HRM staff. However, line managers recommend pay increases and promotions. Training and development activities are the joint responsibility of staff and line managers. Performance appraisal is the job of the line manager, although HRM personnel design the firm's appraisal system in many organizations.

human resources management (HRM) all the activities involved in acquiring, maintaining, and developing an organization's human resources

Concept Check

1. What are the three phases of human resources management?

2. Identify the activities associated with each phase.

3. How does the responsibility of HRM change with the size of a firm?

Human Resources Planning

Human resources planning is the development of strategies to meet a firm's future human resources needs. The starting point is the organization's overall strategic plan. From this, human resources planners can forecast future demand for human resources. Next, the planners must determine whether the needed human resources will be available. Finally, they have to take steps to match supply with demand.

Forecasting Human Resources Demand

Planners should base forecasts of the demand for human resources on as much relevant information as available. The firm's overall strategic plan will provide information about future business ventures, new products, and projected expansions or contractions of specific product lines. Information on past staffing levels, evolving technologies, industry staffing practices, and projected economic trends also can be helpful.

HRM staff use this information to determine both the number of employees required and their qualifications. Planners use a wide range of methods to forecast specific personnel needs. For example, with one simple method, personnel requirements are projected to increase or decrease in the same proportion as sales revenue. Thus, if a 30 percent increase in sales volume is projected over the next two years, then up to a 30 percent increase in personnel requirements may be expected for the same period. (This method can be applied to specific positions as well as to the work-force in general. It is not, however, a very precise forecasting method.) At the other extreme are elaborate, computer-based personnel planning models used by some large firms such as ExxonMobil Corporation.

Forecasting Human Resources Supply

The forecast of the supply of human resources must take into account both the present workforce and any changes that may occur within it. For example, suppose that planners project that in five years a firm that currently employs 100 engineers will need to employ a total of 200 engineers. Planners simply cannot assume that they will have to hire 100 engineers; during that period, some of the firm's present engineers are likely to be promoted, leave the firm, or move to other jobs within the firm. Thus, planners may project the supply of engineers in five years at 87, which means that the firm will have to hire a total of 113 new engineers. When forecasting supply, planners should analyze the organization's existing employees to determine who can be retrained to perform the required tasks.

Two useful techniques for forecasting human resources supply are the replacement chart and the skills inventory. A **replacement chart** is a list of key personnel and their possible replacements within a firm. The chart is maintained to ensure that top-management positions can be filled fairly quickly in the event of an unexpected death, resignation, or retirement. Some firms also provide additional training for employees who might eventually replace top managers.

A **skills inventory** is a computerized data bank containing information on the skills and experience of all present employees. It is used to search for candidates to fill available positions. For a special project, a manager may be seeking a current employee with specific information technology skills, at least six years of experience, and fluency in French. The skills inventory can quickly identify employees who possess such qualifications. Skill-assessment tests can be administered inside an organization, or they can

human resources planning the development of strategies to meet a firm's future human resources needs

replacement chart a list of key personnel and their possible replacements within a firm

skills inventory a computerized data bank containing information on the skills and experience of all present employees

Human resources. Hospitals need to consider the organizational factors impacting the demand and supply for hospital staff, including hospital laboratory personnel.

©Supri Sharjoto/Shutterstock

be provided by outside vendors. For example, SkillView Technologies, Inc., and Bookman Testing Services TeckChek are third-party information technology skill-assessment providers.

Matching Supply with Demand

Once they have forecasted the supply and demand for personnel, planners can devise a course of action for matching the two. When demand is predicted to be greater than supply, plans must be made to recruit new employees. The timing of these actions depends on the types of positions to be filled. Suppose that we expect to open another plant in five years. Along with other employees, a plant manager and twenty-five maintenance workers will be needed. We probably can wait quite a while before we begin to recruit maintenance personnel. However, because the job of plant manager is so critical, we may start searching for the right person for that position immediately.

When supply is predicted to be greater than demand, the firm must take steps to reduce the size of its workforce. When the oversupply is expected to be temporary, some employees may be *laid off*—dismissed from the workforce until they are needed again.

Perhaps the most humane method for making personnel cutbacks is through attrition. *Attrition* is the normal reduction in the workforce that occurs when employees leave a firm. In the past few years, as much as 15 percent of Ford Motor Company's white collar workers in North America have left the company through a combination of involuntary layoffs and normal attrition. This, along with debt reduction and deals with the UAW, gave the company smaller-than-expected losses in 2009, despite a $7 billion reduction in revenue in 2008.[2]

Early retirement is another option. Under early retirement, people who are within a few years of retirement are permitted to retire early with full benefits. Depending on the age makeup of the workforce, this may or may not reduce the staff enough.

As a last resort, unneeded employees are sometimes simply *fired*. However, because of its negative impact, this method generally is used only when absolutely necessary.

Cultural Diversity in Human Resources

Today's workforce is made up of many types of people. Firms can no longer assume that every employee has similar beliefs or expectations. Whereas North American white males may believe in challenging authority, Asians tend to respect and defer to it. In Hispanic cultures, people often bring music, food, and family members to work, a custom that U.S. businesses traditionally have not allowed. A job applicant who will not make eye contact during an interview may be rejected for being unapproachable, when, according to his or her culture, he or she was just being polite.

Since a larger number of women, minorities, and immigrants have entered the U.S. workforce, the workplace is more diverse. It is estimated that women make up about 47 percent of the U.S. workforce; African Americans and Hispanics each make up about 11 and 14 percent of U.S. workers, respectively.[3]

Cultural (or **workplace**) **diversity** refers to the differences among people in a workforce owing to race, ethnicity, and gender. Increasing cultural diversity is forcing managers to learn to supervise and motivate people with a broader range of value systems. The high proportion of women in the work force, combined with a new emphasis on participative parenting by men, has brought many family-related issues to the workplace. Today's more educated employees also want greater independence and flexibility. In return for their efforts, they want both compensation and a better quality of life.

Although cultural diversity presents a challenge, managers should view it as an opportunity rather than a limitation. When managed properly, cultural diversity

cultural (workplace) diversity differences among people in a workforce owing to race, ethnicity, and gender

The value of cultural diversity. Organizations that are dedicated to diversity, such as American Airlines, gain significant benefits from their efforts. American Airlines received one of the 40 Best Companies for Diversity awards presented by Black Enterprise magazine.

can provide competitive advantages for an organization. Table 9.1 shows several benefits that creative management of cultural diversity can offer. A firm that manages diversity properly can develop cost advantages over other firms. Moreover, organizations that manage diversity creatively are in a much better position to

TABLE 9.1: Competitive Advantages of Cultural Diversity	
Cost	As organizations become more diverse, the cost of doing a poor job of integrating workers will increase. Companies that handle this well thus can create cost advantages over those that do a poor job. In addition, companies also experience cost savings by hiring people with knowledge of various cultures as opposed to having to train Americans, for example, about how German people do business.
Resource acquisition	Companies develop reputations as being favorable or unfavorable prospective employers for women and ethnic minorities. Those with the best reputations for managing diversity will win the competition for the best personnel.
Marketing edge	For multinational organizations, the insight and cultural sensitivity that members with roots in other countries bring to marketing efforts should improve these efforts in important ways. The same rationale applies to marketing subpopulations domestically.
Flexibility	Culturally diverse employees often are open to a wider array of positions within a company and are more likely to move up the corporate ladder more rapidly, given excellent performance.
Creativity	Diversity of perspectives and less emphasis on conformity to norms of the past should improve the level of creativity.
Problem solving	Differences within decision-making and problem-solving groups potentially produce better decisions through a wider range of perspectives and more thorough critical analysis of issues.
Bilingual skills	Cultural diversity in the workplace brings with it bilingual and bicultural skills, which are very advantageous to the ever-growing global marketplace. Employees with knowledge about how other cultures work not only can speak to them in their language but also can prevent their company from making embarrassing moves owing to a lack of cultural sophistication. Thus, companies seek job applicants with perhaps a background in cultures in which the company does business.

Sources: Taylor H. Cox and Stacy Blake, "Managing Cultural Diversity: Implications for Organizational Competitiveness," *Academy of Management Executive* 5(3):46, 1991; Graciela Kenig, "Yo Soy Ingeniero: The Advantages of Being Bilingual in Technical Professions," *Diversity Monthly*, February 28, 1999, p. 13; and "Dialogue Skills in the Multicultural Workplace," *North American Post*, March 19, 1999, p. 2.

attract the best personnel. A culturally diverse organization may gain a marketing edge because it understands different cultural groups. Proper guidance and management of diversity in an organization also can improve the level of creativity. Culturally diverse people frequently are more flexible in the types of positions they will accept.

Because cultural diversity creates challenges along with advantages, it is important for an organization's employees to understand it. To accomplish this goal, numerous U.S. firms have trained their managers to respect and manage diversity. Diversity training programs may include recruiting minorities, training minorities to be managers, training managers to view diversity positively, teaching English as a second language, and facilitating support groups for immigrants. Many companies are realizing the necessity of having diversity training spanning beyond just racial issues. For example, Kroger is among a growing number of companies in Virginia that include diversity training as a regular part of employee training. These companies recognize the need to meld a cohesive workforce from a labor pool that reflects Virginia's rapidly changing demographics.[4]

A diversity program will be successful only if it is systematic, is ongoing, and has a strong, sustained commitment from top leadership. Cultural diversity is here to stay. Its impact on organizations is widespread and will continue to grow within corporations. Management must learn to overcome the obstacles and capitalize on the advantages associated with culturally diverse human resources.

Concept Check

1. What is cultural diversity in an organization?

2. What are some of the benefits and challenges of cultural diversity in an organization?

LEARNING OBJECTIVE 4

Explain the objectives and uses of job analysis.

Job Analysis

There is no sense in hiring people unless we know what we are hiring them for. In other words, we need to know the nature of a job before we can find the right person to do it.

Job analysis is a systematic procedure for studying jobs to determine their various elements and requirements. Consider the position of clerk, for example. In a large corporation, there may be fifty kinds of clerk positions. They all may be called "clerks," but each position may differ from the others in the activities to be performed, the level of proficiency required for each activity, and the particular set of qualifications that the position demands. These distinctions are the focus of job analysis. Some companies, such as HR.BLR.COM, help employers with preparing the material for job analysis and keeping them updated about state and federal HR employment laws. They provide employers with easy-to-use online service for the resources needed for HR success.[5]

The job analysis for a particular position typically consists of two parts—a job description and a job specification. A **job description** is a list of the elements that make up a particular job. It includes the duties to be performed, the working conditions, the responsibilities, and the tools and equipment that must be used on the job (see Figure 9.1).

A **job specification** is a list of the qualifications required to perform a particular job. Included are the skills, abilities, education, and experience the jobholder must have. When attempting to hire a financial analyst, Bank of America might use the following job specification: "Requires 8–10 years of financial experience, a broad-based financial background, strong customer focus, the ability to work confidently with the client's management team, strong analytical skills. Must have strong Excel and Word skills. Personal characteristics should include strong desire to succeed, impact performer (individually and as a member of a team), positive attitude, high energy level and ability to influence others."

The job analysis is not only the basis for recruiting and selecting new employees; it is also used in other areas of HRM, including evaluation and the determination of equitable compensation levels.

job analysis a systematic procedure for studying jobs to determine their various elements and requirements

job description a list of the elements that make up a particular job

job specification a list of the qualifications required to perform a particular job

Concept Check

1. What is job analysis?

2. What is job specification? How can it be used to hire the right person for the job?

SOUTH-WESTERN
JOB DESCRIPTION

TITLE:	Georgia Sales Coordinator	**DATE:**	3/25/09
DEPARTMENT:	College, Sales	**GRADE:**	12
REPORTS TO:	Regional Manager	**EXEMPT/NON-EXEMPT:**	Exempt

BRIEF SUMMARY:

Supervise one other Georgia-based sales representative to gain supervisory experience. Captain the 4 members of the outside sales rep team that are assigned to territories consisting of colleges and universities in Georgia. Oversee, coordinate, advise, and make decisions regarding Georgia sales activities. Based upon broad contact with customers across the state and communication with administrators of schools, the person will make recommendations regarding issues specific to the needs of higher education in the state of Georgia such as distance learning, conversion to the semester system, potential statewide adoptions, and faculty training.

PRINCIPLE ACCOUNTABILITIES:

1. Supervises/manages/trains one other Atlanta-based sales rep.
2. Advises two other sales reps regarding the Georgia schools in their territories.
3. Increases overall sales in Georgia as well as individual sales territory.
4. Assists regional manager in planning and coordinating regional meetings and Atlanta conferences.
5. Initiates a dialogue with campus administrators, particularly in the areas of the semester conversion, distance learning, and faculty development.

DIMENSIONS:

This position will have one direct report in addition to the leadership role played within the region. Revenue most directly impacted will be within the individually assigned territory, the supervised territory, and the overall sales for the state of Georgia.

KNOWLEDGE AND SKILLS:

Must have displayed a history of consistently outstanding sales in personal territory. Must demonstrate clear teamwork and leadership skills and be willing to extend beyond the individual territory goals. Should have a clear understanding of the company's systems and product offerings in order to train and lead other sales representatives. Must have the communication skills and presence to communicate articulately with higher education administrators and to serve as a bridge between the company and higher education in the state.

Recruiting, Selection, and Orientation

In an organization with jobs waiting to be filled, HRM personnel need to (1) find candidates for those jobs and (2) match the right candidate with each job. Three activities are involved: recruiting, selection, and new employee orientation.

Recruiting

Recruiting is the process of attracting qualified job applicants. Because it is a vital link in a costly process (the cost of hiring an employee can be several thousand dollars), recruiting needs to be a systematic process. One goal of recruiters is to attract the "right number" of applicants. The right number is enough to allow a good match between applicants and open positions but not so many that matching them requires too much time and effort. For example, if there are five open positions and five applicants, the firm essentially has no choice. It must hire those five applicants (qualified or not), or the positions will remain open. At the other

recruiting the process of attracting qualified job applicants

The Entrepreneurial Spirit

How Small Businesses Attract Top Talent

How can small businesses attract talented employees to keep growing? This is one of the most pressing problems any entrepreneur faces, according to the National Federation of Independent Business. Yet few small businesses have the budget to match the generous compensation and benefits that deep-pocketed corporations can offer.

Even without a big payroll budget, entrepreneurs can play up several important advantages when recruiting job candidates. First, a new hire will have many opportunities to work closely with top management and to get involved in the key decisions that make a real difference in a small business. This is rarely the case in big corporations.

Second, employees often play several roles in a small workplace, which allows them to expand their knowledge, skills, and experience in a short time. In fact, ambitious new hires who learn quickly and prove their value can expect to move up to bigger things in a small business.

Finally, employees who prefer a flexible work environment will probably feel more at home in a small business than in a big one. In their quest for top talent, entrepreneurs are usually very willing to tailor responsibilities, schedules, training, or almost any other aspect of the job for the right candidate.

Sources: Deb Koen, "Promote Strengths to Woo Employees to New, Small Firm," *Rochester Democrat and Chronicle* (Rochester, NY), October 5, 2008, www.democratandchronicle.com; "Surveys Agree: It's Still Hard to Find Skills," *WFC Resources Newsbrief,* November 2007, p. 4; Karen E. Klein, "Hiring Advantages for Small Business," *BusinessWeek Online,* July 24, 2007, www.businessweek.com.

extreme, if several hundred job seekers apply for the five positions, HRM personnel will have to spend weeks processing their applications.

Recruiters may seek applicants outside the firm, within the firm, or both. The source used depends on the nature of the position, the situation within the firm, and sometimes the firm's established or traditional recruitment policies.

External Recruiting **External recruiting** is the attempt to attract job applicants from outside an organization. External recruiting may include newspaper advertising, employment agencies, recruiting on college campuses, soliciting recommendations from present employees, conducting "open houses," and online employment organizations. The biggest of the online job-search sites is Monster.com, which has almost all of the *Fortune* 500 companies, as well as small and midsized businesses, as clients. In addition, many people simply apply at a firm's employment office.

Clearly, it is best to match the recruiting means with the kind of applicant being sought. For example, private employment agencies most often handle professional people, whereas public employment agencies (operated by state or local governments) are more concerned with operations personnel. We might approach a private agency when looking for a vice president but contact a public agency to hire a machinist. Procter & Gamble hires graduates directly out of college. It picks the best and brightest—those not "tainted" by another company's culture. It promotes its own "inside" people. This policy makes sure that the company retains the best and brightest and trains new recruits. Procter & Gamble pays competitively and offers positions in many countries. Employee turnover is very low.[6]

The primary advantage of external recruiting is that it brings in people with new perspectives and varied business backgrounds. A disadvantage of external recruiting is that it is often expensive, especially if private employment agencies must be used. External recruiting also may provoke resentment among present employees.

Internal Recruiting **Internal recruiting** means considering present employees as applicants for available positions. Generally, current employees are considered for *promotion* to higher-level positions. However, employees may be considered for *transfer* from one position to another at the same level. Among leading companies, 85 percent of CEOs are promoted from within. In the companies that hire CEOs from outside, 40 percent of the CEOs are gone after eighteen months.[7]

Promoting from within provides strong motivation for current employees and helps the firm to retain quality personnel. General Electric, ExxonMobil, and Eastman Kodak are companies dedicated to promoting from within. The practice of *job posting,* or informing current employees of upcoming openings, may be a company policy or required by union contract. The primary disadvantage of internal recruiting is that promoting a current employee leaves another position to be filled. Not only does the firm still incur recruiting and selection costs, but it also must train two employees instead of one.

external recruiting the attempt to attract job applicants from outside an organization

internal recruiting considering present employees as applicants for available positions

In many situations it may be impossible to recruit internally. For example, a new position may be such that no current employee is qualified. Or the firm may be growing so rapidly that there is no time to reassign positions that promotion or transfer requires.

Selection

Selection is the process of gathering information about applicants for a position and then using that information to choose the most appropriate applicant. Note the use of the word *appropriate*. In selection, the idea is not to hire the person with the *most* qualifications but rather the applicant who is *most appropriate*. The selection of an applicant is made by line managers responsible for the position. However, HRM personnel usually help by developing a pool of applicants and by expediting the assessment of these applicants. Common means of obtaining information about applicants' qualifications are employment applications, interviews, references, and assessment centers.

Employment Applications An employment application is useful in collecting factual information on a candidate's education, work experience, and personal history (see Figure 9.2). The data obtained from applications usually are used for two purposes: to identify applicants who are worthy of further scrutiny and to familiarize interviewers with their backgrounds.

Many job candidates submit résumés, and some firms require them. A *résumé* is a one- or two-page summary of the candidate's background and qualifications. It may include a description of the type of job the applicant is seeking. A résumé may be sent to a firm to request consideration for available jobs, or it may be submitted along with an employment application.

To improve the usefulness of information, HRM specialists ask current employees about factors in their backgrounds most related to their current jobs. Then these factors are included on the applications and may be weighted more heavily when evaluating new applicants' qualifications.

Employment Tests Tests administered to job candidates usually focus on aptitudes, skills, abilities, or knowledge relevant to the job. Such tests (basic computer skills tests, for example) indicate how well the applicant will do the job. Occasionally, companies use general intelligence or personality tests, but these are seldom helpful in predicting specific job performance. However, *Fortune* 500 companies, as well as an increasing number of medium- and small-sized companies, are using predictive behavior personality tests as administration costs decrease.

At one time, a number of companies were criticized for using tests that were biased against certain minority groups—in particular, African Americans. The test results were, to a great extent, unrelated to job performance. Today, a firm must be able to prove that a test is not discriminatory by demonstrating that it accurately measures one's ability to perform. Applicants who believe that they have been discriminated against through an invalid test may file a complaint with the Equal Employment Opportunity Commission (EEOC).

Interviews The interview is perhaps the most widely used selection technique. Job candidates are interviewed by at least one member of the HRM staff and by the person for whom they will be working. Candidates for higher-level jobs may meet with a department head or vice president over several interviews.

Interviews provide an opportunity for applicants and the firm to learn more about each other. Interviewers can pose problems to test the candidate's abilities, probe employment history, and learn something about the candidate's attitudes and motivation. The candidate has a chance to find out more about the job and potential coworkers.

Photo courtesy of Susan Van Etten

selection the process of gathering information about applicants for a position and then using that information to choose the most appropriate applicant

Source: Courtesy of 3M.

Concept Check

1. What are the differences between internal and external recruiting?

2. Under what conditions are each one of these used?

3. Identify and briefly describe the types of practices and tools that are used in the selection process.

Unfortunately, interviewing may be the stage at which discrimination begins. For example, suppose that a female applicant mentions that she is the mother of small children. Her interviewer may assume that she would not be available for job related travel. In addition, interviewers may be unduly influenced by such factors as appearance. Or they may ask different questions of different applicants so that it becomes impossible to compare candidates' qualifications.

Some of these problems can be solved through better interviewer training and use of structured interviews. In a *structured interview*, the interviewer asks only a prepared set of job-related questions. The firm also may consider using several different interviewers for each applicant, but this is likely to be costly.

References A job candidate generally is asked to furnish the names of references—people who can verify background information and provide personal evaluations. Naturally, applicants tend to list only references who are likely to say good things. Thus, personal evaluations obtained from references may not be of much value. However, references are often contacted to verify such information as previous job responsibilities and the reason an applicant left a former job.

Assessment Centers An assessment center is used primarily to select current employees for promotion to higher-level positions. Typically, a group of employees is sent to the center a few days. While there, they participate in activities designed to simulate the management environment and to predict managerial effectiveness. Trained observers make recommendations regarding promotion possibilities. Although this technique is gaining popularity, the expense involved limits its use.

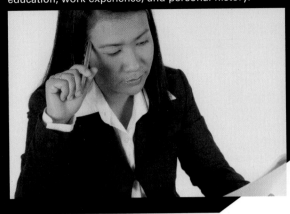

Applying for a job. An employment application is useful in collecting factual information on a candidate's education, work experience, and personal history.

Orientation

Once all information about job candidates has been collected and analyzed, a job offer is extended. If it is accepted, the candidate becomes an employee.

Soon after a candidate joins a firm, he or she goes through the firm's orientation program. **Orientation** is the process of acquainting new employees with an organization. Orientation topics range from the location of the company cafeteria to career paths within the firm. The orientation itself may consist of a half-hour informal presentation by a human resources manager. Or it may be an elaborate program involving dozens of people and lasting several days or weeks.

Compensation and Benefits

6 LEARNING OBJECTIVE

Discuss the primary elements of employee compensation and benefits.

An effective employee reward system must (1) enable employees to satisfy basic needs, (2) provide rewards comparable with those offered by other firms, (3) be distributed fairly within the organization, and (4) recognize that different people have different needs.

A firm's compensation system can be structured to meet the first three of these requirements. The fourth is more difficult because it must account for many variables. Most firms offer a number of benefits that, taken together, generally help to provide for employees' varying needs.

Compensation Decisions

Compensation is the payment employees receive in return for their labor. Its importance to employees is obvious. And because compensation may account for up to 80 percent of a firm's operating costs, it is equally important to management. The firm's **compensation system**, the policies and strategies that determine employee compensation, therefore must be designed carefully to provide for employee needs while keeping labor costs within reasonable limits. For most firms, designing an effective compensation system requires three separate management decisions—wage level, wage structure, and individual wages.

Wage Level Management first must position the firm's general pay level relative to pay levels of comparable firms. Most firms choose a pay level near the industry average. A firm that is not in good financial shape may pay less than average, and large, prosperous organizations may pay more than average.

To determine what the average is, the firm may use wage surveys. A **wage survey** is a collection of data on prevailing wage rates within an industry or a geographic area. Such surveys are compiled by industry associations, local governments, personnel associations, and (occasionally) individual firms.

Wage Structure Next, management must decide on relative pay levels for all the positions within the firm. Will managers be paid more than secretaries? Will

orientation the process of acquainting new employees with an organization

compensation the payment employees receive in return for their labor

compensation system the policies and strategies that determine employee compensation

wage survey a collection of data on prevailing wage rates within an industry or a geographic area

©Lorely Medina/Shutterstock

Employee benefits. Companies vary among themselves on the types of employee benefits provided. Some provide child care.

secretaries be paid more than custodians? The result of this set of decisions is often called the firm's *wage structure.*

The wage structure almost always is developed on the basis of a job evaluation. **Job evaluation** is the process of determining the relative worth of the various jobs within a firm. Most observers probably would agree that a secretary should make more money than a custodian, but how much more? Job evaluation should provide the answer to this question.

A number of techniques may be used to evaluate jobs. The simplest is to rank all the jobs within the firm according to value. A more frequently used method is based on the job analysis. Points are allocated to each job for each of its elements and requirements. For example, "college degree required" might be worth fifty points, whereas the need for a high school education might count for only twenty-five points. The more points a job is allocated, the more important it is presumed to be (and the higher its level in the firm's wage structure).

Individual Wages Finally, the specific payments individual employees will receive must be determined. Consider the case of two secretaries working side by side. Job evaluation has been used to determine the relative level of secretarial pay within the firm's wage structure. However, suppose that one secretary has fifteen years of experience and can type eighty words per minute accurately. The other has two years of experience and can type only fifty-five words per minute. In most firms these two people would not receive the same pay. Instead, a wage range would be established for the secretarial position. In this case, the range might be $8.50 to $12.50 per hour. The more experienced and proficient secretary then would be paid an amount near the top of the range (say, $12.25 per hour); the less experienced secretary would receive an amount that is lower but still within the range (say, $8.75 per hour).

Two wage decisions come into play here. First, the employee's initial rate must be established. It is based on experience, other qualifications, and expected performance. Later, the employee may be given pay increases based on seniority and performance.

Comparable Worth

One reason women in the workforce are paid less may be that a proportion of women occupy female-dominated jobs—nurses, secretaries, and medical records analysts, for example—that require education, skills, and training equal to higher-paid positions but are undervalued. **Comparable worth** is a concept that seeks equal compensation for jobs that require about the same level of education, training, and skills. Several states have enacted laws requiring equal pay for comparable work in government positions. Critics of comparable worth argue that the market has determined the worth of jobs and laws should not tamper with the pricing mechanism of the market. The Equal Pay Act, discussed later in this chapter, does not address the issue of comparable worth. Critics also argue that artificially inflating salaries for female-dominated occupations encourages women to keep these jobs rather than seek out higher-paying jobs.

Types of Compensation

Compensation can be paid in a variety of forms. Most forms of compensation fall into the following categories: hourly wage, weekly or monthly salary, commissions, incentive payments, lump-sum salary increases, and profit sharing.

Hourly Wage An **hourly wage** is a specific amount of money paid for each hour of work. People who earn wages are paid their hourly wage for the first

job evaluation the process of determining the relative worth of the various jobs within a firm

comparable worth a concept that seeks equal compensation for jobs requiring about the same level of education, training, and skills

hourly wage a specific amount of money paid for each hour of work forty hours worked in any week. They are then paid one and one-half times their hourly wage for time worked in excess of forty hours. (That is, they are paid "time and a half" for overtime.) Workers in retailing and fast-food chains, on assembly lines, and in clerical positions usually are paid an hourly wage.

Weekly or Monthly Salary A **salary** is a specific amount of money paid for an employee's work during a set calendar period, regardless of the actual number of hours worked. Salaried employees receive no overtime pay, but they do not lose pay when they are absent from work. Most professional and managerial positions are salaried.

Commissions A **commission** is a payment that is a percentage of sales revenue. Sales representatives and sales managers often are paid entirely through commissions or through a combination of commissions and salary.

Incentive Payments An **incentive payment** is a payment in addition to wages, salary, or commissions. Incentive payments are really extra rewards for outstanding job performance. They may be distributed to all employees or only to certain employees. Some firms distribute incentive payments to all employees annually. The size of the payment depends on the firm's earnings and, at times, on the particular employee's length of service with the firm. Firms sometimes offer incentives to employees who exceed specific sales or production goals, a practice called *gain sharing*.

To avoid yearly across-the-board salary increases, some organizations reward outstanding workers individually through *merit pay*. This pay-for-performance approach allows management to control labor costs while encouraging employees to work more efficiently. An employee's merit pay depends on his or her achievements relative to those of others.

Lump-Sum Salary Increases In traditional reward systems, an employee who receives an annual pay increase is given part of the increase in each pay period. For example, suppose that an employee on a monthly salary gets a 10 percent annual pay hike. He or she actually receives 10 percent of the former monthly salary added to each month's paycheck for a year. Companies that offer a **lump-sum salary increase** give the employee the option of taking the entire pay raise in one lump sum. The employee then draws his or her "regular" pay for the rest of the year. The lump-sum payment typically is treated as an interest-free loan that must be repaid if the employee leaves the firm during the year.

Profit Sharing **Profit sharing** is the distribution of a percentage of a firm's profit among its employees. The idea is to motivate employees to work effectively by giving them a stake in the company's financial success. Some firms—including Sears, Roebuck—have linked their profit-sharing plans to employee retirement programs; that is, employees receive their profit-sharing distributions, with interest, when they retire.

Employee Benefits

An **employee benefit** is a reward in addition to regular compensation that is provided indirectly to employees. Employee benefits consist mainly of services (such as

Spotlight
Are Women Paid Less?

Among workers 25 or older who worked full time, women made an average of 77 cents for every dollar earned by men.

$46,788

$35,759

Women   Men

Median earnings

Source: Census Bureau, January 2009.

salary a specific amount of money paid for an employee's work during a set calendar period, regardless of the actual number of hours worked

commission a payment that is a percentage of sales revenue

incentive payment a payment in addition to wages, salary, or commissions

lump-sum salary increase an entire pay raise taken in one lump sum

profit sharing the distribution of a percentage of a firm's profit among its employees

employee benefit a reward in addition to regular compensation that is provided indirectly to employees insurance) that are paid for partially or totally by employers and employee expenses (such as college tuition) that are reimbursed by employers. Currently, the average cost of these benefits is 29.4 percent of an employee's total compensation, which includes wages plus benefits.[8] Thus a person who received total compensation (including benefits) of $50,000 a year earned $35,300 in wages and received an additional $14,700 in benefits.

Types of Benefits Employee benefits take a variety of forms. *Pay for time not worked* covers such absences as vacation time, holidays, and sick leave. *Insurance packages* may include health, life, and dental insurance for employees and their families. Some firms pay the entire cost of the insurance package, and others share the cost with the employee. The costs of *pension and retirement programs* also may be borne entirely by the firm or shared with the employee.

Some benefits are required by law. For example, employers must maintain *workers' compensation insurance,* which pays medical bills for injuries that occur on the job and provides income for employees who are disabled by job-related injuries. Employers also must pay for *unemployment insurance* and contribute to each employee's federal *Social Security* account.

Other benefits provided by employers include tuition-reimbursement plans, credit unions, child care, company cafeterias, exercise rooms, and broad stock-option plans available to all employees. Some companies offer special benefits to U.S. military reservists who are called up for active duty.

Some companies offer unusual benefits in order to attract and retain employees. Compuware Corporation, a software company, makes cheap meals available to workers to take home after a workout in the company gym. NetApp, which is ranked number one in *Fortune* magazine's "Top 100 Companies to Work For," allows employees to take five paid days off for community service. Employees at Recreational Equipment get a 30% discount on trips booked with the company's travel agency. Recreational Equipment also offers a Challenge Grant, which provides funds for recreational goals of selected employees, such as a 50-mile bike ride to Mt. Everest. Google gives employees a free lunch and dinner every day. Other fun activities at Google include football, volleyball, video games, pool, ping pong, and even roller hockey twice a week in the parking lot. However, Google has had to cut some frills, such as afternoon tea and an annual ski trip, due to the economy. Seattle law firm Perkins Coie is known for its unusual perks, like Happiness Committees that consist of teams of employees who roam the offices and drop surprise gifts on the desks of their colleagues. Every quarter, Perkins Coie holds random drawings and gives away six pairs of round-trip airline tickets to lucky winners. This company even has an in-house rock band.[9]

Flexible Benefit Plans Through a **flexible benefit plan**, an employee receives a predetermined amount of benefit dollars and may allocate those dollars to various categories of benefits in the mix that best fits his or her needs. Some flexible benefit plans offer a broad array of benefit options, including health care, dental care, life insurance, accidental death and dismemberment coverage for both the worker and dependents, long-term disability coverage, vacation benefits, retirement savings, and dependent-care benefits. Other firms offer limited options, primarily in health and life insurance and retirement plans.

Although the cost of administering flexible plans is high, a number of organizations, including Quaker Oats and Coca-Cola, have implemented this option for several reasons. Because employees' needs are so diverse, flexible plans help firms to offer benefit packages that more specifically meet their employees' needs. Flexible plans can, in the long run, help a company to contain costs because a

flexible benefit plan compensation plan whereby an employee receives a predetermined amount of benefit dollars to spend on a package of benefits he or she has selected to meet individual needs

Concept Check

1. Identify the major compensation decisions that HRM managers make.

2. What are the different forms of compensation?

3. What are the major types of employee benefits?

4. How do flexible benefit plans work?

©Vadim Kozlovsky/Shutterstock

Part 4: Human Resources

specified amount is allocated to cover the benefits of each employee. Furthermore, organizations that offer flexible plans with many choices may be perceived as being employee friendly. Thus, they are in a better position to attract and retain qualified employees.

Training and Development

7 LEARNING OBJECTIVE

Explain the purposes and techniques of employee training, development, and performance appraisal.

Training and development are extremely important at the Container Store. Because great customer service is so important, every first-year full-time salesperson receives about 185 hours of formal training as opposed to the industry standard, which is approximately seven hours. Training and development continue throughout a person's career. Each store has a full-time trainer called the *super sales trainer* (SST). This trainer provides product training, sales training, and employee development training. A number of top managers believe that the financial and human resources invested in training and development are well worth it.

Both training and development are aimed at improving employees' skills and abilities. However, the two are usually differentiated as either employee training or management development. **Employee training** is the process of teaching operations and technical employees how to do their present jobs more effectively and efficiently. **Management development** is the process of preparing managers and other professionals to assume increased responsibility in both present and future positions. Thus, training and development differ in who is being taught and the purpose of the teaching. Both are necessary for personal and organizational growth. Companies that hope to stay competitive typically make huge commitments to employee training and development. Internet-based e-learning is growing. Driven by cost, travel, and time savings, online learning alone (and in conjunction with face-to-face situations) is a strong alternative strategy. Development of a training program usually has three components: analysis of needs, determination of training and development methods, and creation of an evaluation system to assess the program's effectiveness.

Analysis of Training Needs

When thinking about developing a training program, managers first must determine if training is needed and, if so, what types of training needs exist. At times, what at first appears to be a need for training is actually, on assessment, a need for motivation. Training needs can vary considerably. For example, some employees may need training to improve their technical skills, or they may need training about organizational procedures. Training also may focus on business ethics, product information, or customer service. Because training is expensive, it is critical that the correct training needs be identified.

Training and Development Methods

A number of methods are available for employee training and management development. Some of these methods may be more suitable for one or the other, but most can be applied to both training and management development.

- *On-the-job methods.* The trainee learns by doing the work under the supervision of an experienced employee.
- *Simulations.* The work situation is simulated in a separate area so that learning takes place away from the day-to-day pressures of work.
- *Classroom teaching and lectures.* You probably already know these methods quite well.
- *Conferences and seminars.* Experts and learners meet to discuss problems and exchange ideas.
- *Role playing.* Participants act out the roles of others in the organization for better understanding of those roles (primarily a management development tool).

employee training the process of teaching operations and technical employees how to do their present jobs more effectively and efficiently

management development the process of preparing managers and other professionals to assume increased responsibility in both present and future positions

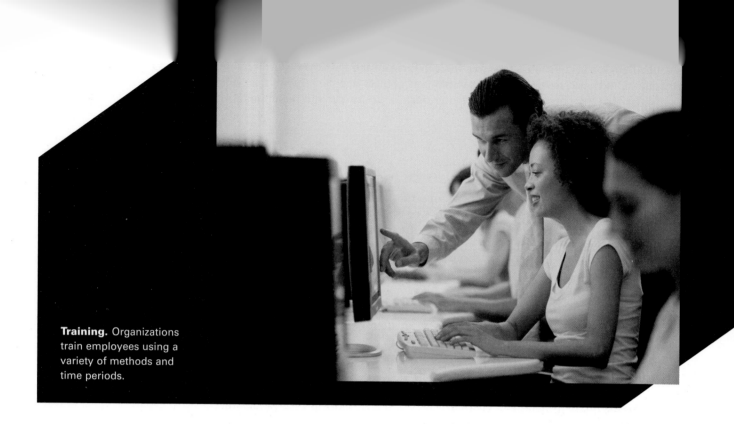

Training. Organizations train employees using a variety of methods and time periods.

Evaluation of Training and Development

Training and development are very expensive. The training itself costs quite a bit, and employees are usually not working—or are working at a reduced load and pace—during training sessions. To ensure that training and development are cost-effective, the managers responsible should evaluate the company's efforts periodically.

The starting point for this evaluation is a set of verifiable objectives that are developed *before* the training is undertaken. Suppose that a training program is expected to improve the skills of machinists. The objective of the program might be stated as follows: "At the end of the training period, each machinist should be able to process thirty parts per hour with no more than one defective part per ninety parts completed." This objective clearly specifies what is expected and how training results may be measured or verified. Evaluation then consists of measuring machinists' output and the ratio of defective parts produced after the training.

The results of training evaluations should be made known to all those involved in the program—including trainees and upper management. For trainees, the results of evaluations can enhance motivation and learning. For upper management, the results may be the basis for making decisions about the training program itself.

Performance Appraisal

performance appraisal the evaluation of employees' current and potential levels of performance to allow managers to make objective human resources decisions

Performance appraisal is the evaluation of employees' current and potential levels of performance to allow managers to make objective human resources decisions. The process has three main objectives. First, managers use performance appraisals to let workers know how well they are doing and how they can do better in the future. Second, a performance appraisal provides an effective basis for distributing rewards, such as pay raises and promotions. Third, performance appraisal helps the organization monitor its employee selection, training, and development activities. If large numbers of employees continually perform below expectations, the firm may need to revise its selection process or strengthen its training and development activities.

Managing Your Career

Off to a Fast Start

Congratulations! You've found a new job—now how do you get off to a fast start? Experts offer these tips:

- *Introduce yourself.* Reach out, rather than waiting for colleagues to notice you. "Try to meet at least three new people every single day," advises an Atlanta career coach. "Tell them you recently started, along with your title and department, and ask them what they do."
- *Go for early wins.* Learn your department's goals and find ways to demonstrate your value right away. "Look for small, quick wins that you can accomplish," says a public relations executive.
- *Join the team.* Observe how things get done in your company and make the most of opportunities to get involved. For example, when coworkers or managers need information or assistance with a rush project, offer your help.
- *Ask for early feedback.* Request early feedback on your performance so you can do an even better job as time goes on. "In most circumstances, your boss will agree to meet with you weekly and give you feedback," explains an experienced recruiter.

Sources: Susan Kreimer, "Key Early Days for New Hires," *Washington Post,* August 24, 2008, p. K1; Marshall Goldsmith, "Tough Career Advice for Tough Times," *BusinessWeek Online,* August 13, 2008, www.businessweek.com; Guido Sacchi, "Career Advice: Dealing with 'Clueless' New Hires," *ComputerWorld,* October 7, 2008, www.computerworld.com.

Common Evaluation Techniques

The various techniques and methods for appraising employee performance are either objective or judgmental in nature.

Objective Methods Objective appraisal methods use some measurable quantity as the basis for assessing performance. Units of output, dollar volume of sales, number of defective products, and number of insurance claims processed are all objective, measurable quantities. Thus, an employee who processes an average of twenty-six insurance claims per week is given a higher evaluation than one whose average is nineteen claims per week.

Such objective measures may require some adjustment for the work environment. Suppose that the first of our insurance-claims processors works in New York City, and the second works in rural Iowa. Both must visit each client because they are processing homeowners' insurance claims. The difference in their average weekly output may be due entirely to the long distances the Iowan must travel to visit clients. In this case, the two workers may very well be equally competent and motivated. Thus, a manager must take into account circumstances that may be hidden by a purely statistical measurement.

Judgmental Methods Judgmental appraisal methods are used much more frequently than objective methods. They require that the manager judge or estimate the employee's performance level. However, judgmental methods are not capricious. These methods are based on employee ranking or rating scales. When ranking is used, the manager ranks subordinates from best to worst. This approach has a number of drawbacks, including the lack of any absolute standard. Rating scales are the most popular judgmental appraisal technique. A *rating scale* consists of a number of statements; each employee is rated on the degree to which the statement applies (see Figure 9.3). For example, one statement might be, "This employee always does high-quality work." The supervisor would give the employee a rating, from 5 down to 1, corresponding to gradations ranging from "strongly agree" to "strongly disagree." The ratings on all the statements are added to obtain the employee's total evaluation.

Avoiding Appraisal Errors Managers must be cautious if they are to avoid making mistakes when appraising employees. It is common to overuse one portion of an evaluation instrument, thus overemphasizing some issues and underemphasizing others. A manager must guard against allowing an employee's

3M **Contribution and Development Summary**
FORM 37450 - B

Employee Name	Employee Number	Job Title
Department		Location
Coach/Supervisor(s) Name(s)		Review Period
		From :

Major Job Responsibilities

Goals/Expectations — **Contributions/**

Contribution (To be completed by coach/supervisor)

☐ Good Level of Contribution for this year   ☐ Exceptional

☐ Unsatisfactory Level of Contribution for this year

Development Summary

Areas of Strength	Development Priorities

Career Interests

Next job	Longer Range

Current Mobility

☐ **0** - Currently Unable to Relocate   ☐ **3** - Position Within O.U.S. Area (ex: Europe, Asia)

☐ **1** - Position In Home Country Only (Use if Home Country is Outside U.S.)   ☐ **4** - Position In U.S.

☐ **2** - Position Within O.U.S. Region (e: Nordic, SEA...)   ☐ **5** - Position Anywhere In The World

Development

☐ **W** - Well placed. Development plans achievable in current role for at least the next year   ☐ **X** - Not well placed. Action required to resolve placement issues.

☐ **C** - Ready now for a move to a different job for career broadening experience   **Comments on Development**

☐ **I** - Ready now for a move to a different job involving increased responsibility

Employee Comments

Coach/Supervisor Comments   **Other Supervisor (if applicable) and/or Reviewer**

Signatures

Coach/Supervisor	Date	Other Coach/Supervisor or Reviewer	Date
Employee			Date

page 4

Source: Courtesy of 3M.

poor performance on one activity to influence his or her judgment of that subordinate's work on other activities. Similarly, putting too much weight on recent performance distorts an employee's evaluation. For example, if the employee is being rated on performance over the last year, a manager should not permit last month's disappointing performance to overshadow the quality of the work done in the first eleven months of the year. Finally, a manager must guard against discrimination on the basis of race, age, gender, religion, national origin, or sexual orientation.

Performance Feedback

No matter which appraisal technique is used, the results should be discussed with the employee soon after the evaluation is completed. The manager should explain the basis for present rewards and should let the employee know what he or she can do to be recognized as a better performer in the future. The information provided to an employee in such discussions is called a *performance feedback,* and the process is known as a *performance feedback interview.*

There are three major approaches to performance feedback interviews: tell and sell, tell and listen, and problem solving. In a *tell-and-sell* feedback interview, the superior tells the employee how good or bad the employee's performance has been and then attempts to persuade the employee to accept this evaluation. Since the employee has no input into the evaluation, the tell-and-sell interview can lead to defensiveness, resentment, and frustration on the part of the subordinate. The employee may not accept the results of the interview and may not be committed to achieving the goals that are set.

With the *tell-and-listen* approach, the supervisor tells the employee what has been right and wrong with the employee's performance and then gives the employee a chance to respond. The subordinate simply may be given an opportunity to react to the supervisor's statements or may be permitted to offer a full self-appraisal, challenging the supervisor's assessment.

In the *problem-solving* approach, employees evaluate their own performance and set their own goals for future performance. The supervisor is more a colleague than a judge and offers comments and advice in a noncritical manner. An active and open dialogue ensues in which goals for improvement are established mutually. The problem-solving interview is more likely to result in the employee's commitment to the established goals.

To avoid some of the problems associated with the tell-and-sell interview, a mixed approach sometimes is used. The mixed interview uses the tell-and-sell approach to communicate administrative decisions and the problem-solving approach to discuss employee-development issues and future performance goals.[10]

An appraisal approach that has become popular is called a *360-degree evaluation.* A 360-degree evaluation collects anonymous reviews about an employee from his or her peers, subordinates, and supervisors and then compiles these reviews into a feedback report that is given to the employee. Companies that invest significant resources in employee-development efforts are especially

Concept Check

1. What are the main objectives of performance appraisal?

2. What methods are used?

3. Describe the three approaches to performance feedback interviews.

likely to use 360-degree evaluations. An employee should not be given a feedback report without first having a one-on-one meeting with his or her supervisor. The most appropriate way to introduce a 360-degree evaluation system in a company is to begin with upper-level management. Then managers should be trained on how to interpret feedback reports so that they can coach their employees on how to use the feedback to achieve higher-level job-related skills and behaviors.[11]

Finally, we should note that many managers find it difficult to discuss the negative aspects of an appraisal. Unfortunately, they may ignore performance feedback altogether or provide it in a very weak and ineffectual manner. In truth, though, most employees have strengths that can be emphasized to soften the discussion of their weaknesses. An employee may not even be aware of weaknesses and their consequences. If such weaknesses are not pointed out through performance feedback, they cannot possibly be eliminated. Only through tactful, honest communication can the results of an appraisal be fully utilized.

LEARNING OBJECTIVE 8

Outline the major legislation affecting human resources management.

The Legal Environment of HRM

Legislation regarding HRM practices has been passed mainly to protect the rights of employees, to promote job safety, and to eliminate discrimination in the work place. The major federal laws affecting HRM are described in Table 9.2.

National Labor Relations Act and Labor-Management Relations Act

These laws are concerned with dealings between business firms and labor unions. This general area is, in concept, a part of HRM. However, because of its importance, it is often treated as a separate set of activities.

Fair Labor Standards Act

This act, passed in 1938 and amended many times since, applies primarily to wages. It established minimum wages and overtime pay rates. Many managers and other professionals, however, are exempt from this law. Managers, for example, seldom get paid overtime when they work more than forty hours a week.

Equal Pay Act

Passed in 1963, this law overlaps somewhat with Title VII of the Civil Rights Act (see below). The Equal Pay Act specifies that men and women who are doing equal jobs must be paid the same wage. Equal jobs are jobs that demand equal effort, skill, and responsibility and that are performed under the same conditions. Differences in pay are legal if they can be attributed to differences in seniority, qualifications, or performance. However, women cannot be paid less (or more) for the same work solely because they are women.

Civil Rights Acts

Title VII of the Civil Rights Act of 1964 applies directly to selection and promotion. It forbids organizations with fifteen or more employees to discriminate in those areas on the basis of sex, race, color, religion, or national origin. The purpose of Title VII is to ensure that employers make personnel decisions on the basis of employee qualifications only. As a result of this act, discrimination in employment (especially against African Americans) has been reduced in this country.

The Equal Employment Opportunity Commission (EEOC) is charged with enforcing Title VII. A person who believes that he or she has been discriminated against can file a complaint with the EEOC. The EEOC investigates the complaint, and if it finds that the person has, in fact, been the victim of discrimination, the commission can take legal action on his or her behalf.

The Civil Rights Act of 1991 facilitates an employee's suing and collecting punitive damages for sexual discrimination. Discriminatory promotion and termination

TABLE 9.2: Federal Legislation Affecting Human Resources Management

Law	Purpose
National Labor Relations Act (1935)	Established a collective-bargaining process in labor–management relations as well as the National Labor Relations Board (NLRB)
Fair Labor Standards Act (1938)	Established a minimum wage and an overtime pay rate for employees working more than forty hours per week
Labor-Management Relations Act (1947)	Provided a balance between union power and management power; also known as the Taft-Hartley Act
Equal Pay Act (1963)	Specified that men and women who do equal jobs must be paid the same wage
Title VII of the Civil Rights Act (1964)	Outlawed discrimination in employment practices based on sex, race, color, religion, or national origin
Age Discrimination in Employment Act (1967–1986)	Outlawed personnel practices that discriminate against people aged 40 and older; the 1986 amendment eliminated a mandatory retirement age
Occupational Safety and Health Act (1970)	Regulated the degree to which employees can be exposed to hazardous substances and specified the safety equipment that the employer must provide
Employment Retirement Income Security Act (1974)	Regulated company retirement programs and provided a federal insurance program for retirement plans that go bankrupt
Worker Adjustment and Retraining Notification (WARN) Act (1988)	Required employers to give employees sixty days notice regarding plant closure or layoff of fifty or more employees
Americans with Disabilities Act (1990)	Prohibited discrimination against qualified individuals with disabilities in all employment practices, including job-application procedures, hiring, firing, advancement, compensation, training, and other terms, conditions, and privileges of employment
Civil Rights Act (1991)	Facilitated employees' suing employers for sexual discrimination and collecting punitive damages
Family and Medical Leave Act (1993)	Required an organization with fifty or more employees to provide up to twelve weeks of leave without pay on the birth (or adoption) of an employee's child or if an employee or his or her spouse, child, or parent is seriously ill

decisions as well as on-the-job issues, such as sexual harassment, are covered by this act.

Age Discrimination in Employment Act

The general purpose of this act, which was passed in 1967 and amended in 1986, is the same as that of Title VII—to eliminate discrimination. However, as the name implies, the Age Discrimination in Employment Act is concerned only with discrimination based on age. It applies to companies with twenty or more employees. In particular, it outlaws personnel practices that discriminate against people aged 40 or older. (No federal law forbids discrimination against people younger than age 40, but several states have adopted age discrimination laws that apply to a variety of age groups.) Also outlawed are company policies that specify a mandatory retirement age. Employers must base employment decisions on ability and not on a number.

Occupational Safety and Health Act

Passed in 1970, this act is concerned mainly with issues of employee health and safety. For example, the act regulates the degree to which employees can be exposed to hazardous substances. It also specifies the safety equipment that the employer must provide.

The Occupational Safety and Health Administration (OSHA) was created to enforce this act. Inspectors from OSHA investigate employee complaints regarding unsafe working conditions. They also make spot checks on companies operating in particularly hazardous industries, such as chemicals and mining, to ensure compliance with the law. A firm found to be in violation of federal standards can be heavily fined or shut down. Many people feel that issuing OSHA violations is not enough to protect workers from harm.

Employee Retirement Income Security Act

This act was passed in 1974 to protect the retirement benefits of employees. It does not require that firms provide a retirement plan. However, it does specify that *if* a retirement plan is provided, it must be managed in such a way that the interests of employees are protected. It also provides federal insurance for retirement plans that go bankrupt.

Affirmative Action

Affirmative action is not one act but a series of executive orders issued by the President of the United States. These orders established the requirement for affirmative action in personnel practices. This stipulation applies to all employers with fifty or more employees holding federal contracts in excess of $50,000. It prescribes that such employers (1) actively encourage job applications from members of minority groups and (2) hire qualified employees from minority groups not fully represented in their organizations. Many firms that do not hold government contracts voluntarily take part in this affirmative action program.

Americans with Disabilities Act

The Americans with Disabilities Act (ADA) prohibits discrimination against qualified individuals with disabilities in all employment practices—including job-application procedures, hiring, firing, advancement, compensation, training, and other terms and conditions of employment. All private employers and government agencies with fifteen or more employees are covered by the ADA. Defining who is a qualified individual with a disability is, of course, difficult. Depending on how *qualified individual with a disability* is interpreted, up to 43 million Americans can be included under this law. This law also mandates that all businesses that serve the public must make their facilities accessible to people with disabilities.

Not only are individuals with obvious physical disabilities protected under the ADA, but also safeguarded are those with less visible conditions such as heart disease, diabetes, epilepsy, cancer, AIDS, and mental illnesses. Because of this law, many organizations no longer require job applicants to pass physical examinations as a condition of employment.

Employers are required to provide disabled employees with reasonable accommodation. *Reasonable accommodation* is any modification or adjustment to a job or work environment that will enable a qualified employee with a disability to perform a central job function. Examples of reasonable accommodation include making existing facilities readily accessible to and usable by an individual confined to a wheelchair. Reasonable accommodation also might mean restructuring a job, modifying work schedules, acquiring or modifying equipment, providing qualified readers or interpreters, or changing training programs.

Concept Check

1. How is the National Labor Relations Act different from the Fair Labor Standards Act?

2. How does the Civil Rights Act influence the selection and promotion of employees?

3. What is the Occupational Safety and Health Act?

4. What is the purpose of the Americans with Disabilities Act?

SUMMARY

1 Describe the major components of human resources management.

Human resources management (HRM) is the set of activities involved in acquiring, maintaining, and developing an organization's human resources. Responsibility for HRM is shared by specialized staff and line managers. HRM activities include human resources planning, job analysis, recruiting, selection, orientation, compensation, benefits, training and development, and performance appraisal.

2 Identify the steps in human resources planning.

Human resources planning consists of forecasting the human resources that a firm will need and those that it will have available and then planning a course of action to match supply with demand. Layoffs, attrition, early retirement, and (as a last resort) firing are ways to reduce the size of the workforce. Supply is increased through hiring.

3 Describe cultural diversity and understand some of the challenges and opportunities associated with it.

Cultural diversity refers to the differences among people in a workforce owing to race, ethnicity, and gender. With an increasing number of women, minorities, and immigrants entering the U.S. workforce, management is faced with both challenges and competitive advantages. Some organizations are implementing diversity-related training programs and working to make the most of cultural diversity. With the proper guidance and management, a culturally diverse organization can prove beneficial to all involved.

4 Explain the objectives and uses of job analysis.

Job analysis provides a job description and a job specification for each position within a firm. A job description is a list of the elements that make up a particular job. A job specification is a list of qualifications required to perform a particular job. Job analysis is used in evaluation and in determining compensation levels and serves as the basis for recruiting and selecting new employees.

5 Describe the processes of recruiting, employee selection, and orientation.

Recruiting is the process of attracting qualified job applicants. Candidates for open positions may be recruited from within or outside a firm. In the selection process, information about candidates is obtained from applications, résu-

més, tests, interviews, references, or assessment centers. This information then is used to select the most appropriate candidate for the job. Newly hired employees then will go through a formal or informal orientation program to acquaint them with the firm.

6 Discuss the primary elements of employee compensation and benefits.

Compensation is the payment employees receive in return for their labor. In developing a system for paying employees, management must decide on the firm's general wage level (relative to other firms), the wage structure within the firm, and individual wages. Wage surveys and job analyses are useful in making these decisions. Employees may be paid hourly wages, salaries, or commissions. They also may receive incentive payments, lump-sum salary increases, and profit-sharing payments. Employee benefits, which are nonmonetary rewards to employees, add about 28 percent to the cost of compensation.

7 Explain the purposes and techniques of employee training, development, and performance appraisal.

Employee training and management-development programs enhance the ability of employees to contribute to a firm. When developing a training program, training needs should be analyzed. Then training methods should be selected. Because training is expensive, an organization should evaluate the effectiveness of its training programs periodically.

Performance appraisal, or evaluation, is used to provide employees with performance feedback, to serve as a basis for distributing rewards, and to monitor selection and training activities. Both objective and judgmental appraisal techniques are used. Their results are communicated to employees through three performance feedback approaches: tell and sell, tell and listen, and problem solving.

8 Outline the major legislation affecting human resources management.

A number of laws have been passed that affect HRM practices and that protect the rights and safety of employees. Some of these are the National Labor Relations Act of 1935, the Labor-Management Relations Act of 1947, the Fair Labor Standards Act of 1938, the Equal Pay Act of 1963, Title VII of the Civil Rights Act of 1964, the Age Discrimination in Employment Acts of 1967 and 1986, the Occupational Safety and Health Act of 1970, the Employment Retirement Income Security Act of 1974, the Worker Adjustment and Retraining Notification Act of 1988, the Americans with Disabilities Act of 1990, the Civil Rights Act of 1991, and the Family and Medical Leave Act of 1993.

KEY TERMS

You should now be able to define and give an example relevant to each of the following terms:

human resources
   management (HRM) (234)
human resources planning
   (235)
replacement chart (235)
skills inventory (235)
cultural (workplace) diversity
   (236)
job analysis (238)

job description (238)
job specification (238)
recruiting (239)
external recruiting (240)
internal recruiting (240)
selection (241)
orientation (243)
compensation (243)
compensation system (243)

wage survey (243)
job evaluation (244)
comparable worth (244)
hourly wage (244)
salary (245)
commission (245)
incentive payment (245)
lump-sum salary increase
   (245)

profit sharing (245)
employee benefit (245)
flexible benefit plan (246)
employee training (247)
management development
   (247)
performance appraisal (248)

DISCUSSION QUESTIONS

1. In general, on what basis is responsibility for HRM divided between line and staff managers?
2. How is a forecast of human resources demand related to a firm's organizational planning?
3. How do human resources managers go about matching a firm's supply of workers with its demand for workers?
4. What are the major challenges and benefits associated with a culturally diverse workforce?
5. What are the advantages and disadvantages of external recruiting? Of internal recruiting?
6. How is a job analysis used in the process of job evaluation?
7. Suppose that you have just opened a new Ford sales showroom and repair shop. Which of your employees

would be paid wages, which would receive salaries, and which would receive commissions?
8. Why is it so important to provide feedback after a performance appraisal?
9. How accurately can managers plan for future human resources needs?
10. Are employee benefits really necessary? Why?
11. As a manager, what actions would you take if an operations employee with six years of experience on the job refused ongoing training and ignored performance feedback?
12. Why are there so many laws relating to HRM practices? Which are the most important laws, in your opinion?

Get Flash Cards, Quizzes, Games, Crosswords and more @ www.cengage.com/introbusiness/pride

Test Yourself

Matching Questions

1. _____ Jobs are studied to determine specific tasks.
2. _____ People are acquired, maintained, and developed for the firm.
3. _____ Personal qualifications required in a job are described.
4. _____ Potential applicants are made aware of available positions.
5. _____ The reward employees receive for their labor.
6. _____ The process for teaching employees to do their jobs more efficiently.
7. _____ An employee's work performance is evaluated.
8. _____ Gain sharing is an example.

9. _____ It seeks equal compensation for similar jobs.
10. _____ Employees may choose from a wide array of benefit options.

a. comparable worth
b. compensation
c. employee training
d. flexible benefit plan
e. human resources management
f. incentive payment
g. wage survey
h. job analysis
i. job specification
j. performance appraisal
k. recruiting
l. profit sharing

Test Yourself

True False Questions

11. **T F** Recruiting is an activity of human resources acquisition.

12. **T F** Transfers involve moving employees into higher-level positions.

13. **T F** In a structured interview, the interviewer uses a prepared set of questions.

14. **T F** The most widely used selection technique is the employment test.

15. **T F** Staffing, personnel management, and human resources management are synonymous terms.

16. **T F** Attrition is the process of acquiring information on applicants.

17. **T F** The selection process matches the right candidate with each job.

18. **T F** Employee benefits such as vacation and sick leave are required by law.

19. **T F** The purpose of Title VII is to ensure that employers make personnel decisions on the basis of employee qualifications.

20. **T F** The Employee Retirement Income Security Act requires firms to provide a retirement plan for their employees.

Multiple-Choice Questions

21. _____ Required retirement before age 70 was outlawed in the
    a. Age Discrimination in Employment Act.
    b. Equal Pay Act.
    c. Fair Labor Standards Act.
    d. Employee Retirement Income Security Act.
    e. Civil Rights Act.

22. _____ A one-page summary of an applicant's qualifications is known as a(n)
    a. application form.
    b. data sheet.
    c. summary sheet.
    d. résumé.
    e. qualification sheet.

23. _____ Melinda walked into the First National Bank to pick up an application for an administrative assistant position. When she asked about the duties and working conditions, the busy receptionist handed her a job
    a. description.
    b. inventory.
    c. analysis.

d. orientation.
e. specification.

24. _____ Human resources planning requires the following steps *except*
    a. using the firm's strategic plan.
    b. forecasting the firm's future demand.
    c. determining availability of human resources.
    d. acquiring funds for implementation.
    e. matching supply with demand.

25. _____ Larry was hurt while playing football in his senior year in high school. Since then, he has been confined to a wheel chair. After receiving his college diploma, he applied for a supervision job in a local warehouse. Under ADA, the employer must provide *reasonable accommodation* for disabled employees. Which activity will not legally cover Larry?
    a. Providing adequate home medical care
    b. Making existing facilities accessible
    c. Modifying work schedules
    d. Providing qualified readers
    e. Changing examinations

26. _____ Which of the following is the best way to describe "employee relations"?
    a. Attracting the best people to apply for positions
    b. Using satisfaction surveys and employee communication programs
    c. Recruiting experienced employees from other firms
    d. Providing rewards to ensure employee well-being
    e. Improving employees' skills and expanding their capabilities

27. _____ Which of the following is *least likely* to be the responsibility of a line manager?
    a. Developing a compensation system
    b. Implementing an orientation program
    c. Job analysis
    d. Recommending a promotion
    e. Hiring employees

28. _____ Companies develop reputations as being favorable or unfavorable prospective employers for women and ethnic minorities. Based on this understanding or company reputation, what advantage do companies that have a good record for managing diversity have over others?
    a. Resource acquisition
    b. Flexibility

Test Yourself

c. Bilingual skills

d. Cost saving

e. Creativity

29. _____ Which of the following is the term used to describe a process of "recruiting minorities, training minorities to be managers, training managers to view diversity positively, and teaching English as a second language"?

a. Problem solving

b. Flexibility

c. Resource acquisition

d. Diversity training

e. Acquiring bilingual skills

30. _____ Which of the following is a good example of the "judgmental method" of evaluation?

a. Each employee is rated on the degree to which the statement applies.

b. The number of insurance claims processed is evaluated.

c. The units of output per employee are calculated.

d. An employee's dollar volume of sales per week is assessed.

e. The number of defective products an employee produces, on average, is counted.

Answers on p. TY-1

VIDEO CASE

The New England Aquarium Casts a Wide Recruitment Net

From seals and sea turtles to porpoises and penguins, the nonprofit New England Aquarium in Boston houses an incredibly diverse array of the world's sea life. The aquarium's official mission statement is "to present, promote, and protect the world of water." It also wants to appeal to a broad audience and build a work force of paid and unpaid staff that reflects Boston's diversity.

Volunteers are a major resource for the New England Aquarium. Its staff of 1,000 volunteers contributes 100,000 hours of service yearly. Many high school and college student volunteers try out possible career choices. Adults with and without specialized college degrees (in fields such as marine biology and environmental affairs) volunteer their time as well. And the New England Aquarium's internships offer college students and recent graduates hands-on experience in veterinary services, communications, and other key areas.

The aquarium's director of volunteer programs is a champion for workplace diversity. Most organizations "are good at putting diversity in their mission statements and talking about it, but not actually accomplishing it," she observes. She and her colleagues reach out to recruit volunteers, interns, and employees of different races, ethnicities, socioeconomic levels, physical abilities, and ages. In addition, they welcome people of diverse educational backgrounds, personalities, and viewpoints because of the new resources these differences can bring to meeting the organization's opportunities and challenges.

One reason the New England Aquarium needs to constantly recruit and train new volunteers (and employees) is that it attracts more visitors every year as it expands its exhibit space and educational activities. Like most nonprofits, it also has a very limited budget and must manage its payroll carefully. Therefore, the organization is always looking for volunteers to assist paid staff in various departments, including education, administration, and animal rescue.

The New England Aquarium must plan for employees, volunteers, or interns to handle certain tasks whenever the facility is open. For example, it needs cashiers to collect admission fees during daytime, evening, and weekend hours. Volunteers are often available to work during weekend hours, but filling daytime positions can be difficult. This is another reason aquarium managers attend community meetings and find creative ways to encourage volunteerism.

The Internet is an important and cost-effective recruiting tool for the aquarium. Prospective volunteers can browse its website to find open positions, read job descriptions and specifications, and download an application form to complete and submit. Aquarium managers read all the applications and ask those who seem most qualified to come in for a personal interview. Once the final selections are made, volunteers are notified about their assignments and working hours. They receive training in the organization's procedures and learn their specific duties before they start their jobs.

Candidates for internships must send a letter expressing interest in working as an intern and include a résumé plus two academic or professional references. As an option, candidates can send a letter of reference and a college transcript to support the application letter. The New England Aquarium's internship coordinators interview the most promising candidates and make the final selections. Interns, like volunteers, gain valuable experience and can list their positions on their résumés when looking for future employment.

Paid employees receive a full package of valuable benefits, including paid holidays and sick days, insurance, and tuition reimbursement. Just as important, employees gain an opportunity to make a difference. When hired, they become part of an organization that protects the underwater environment, educates the public, and improves and saves the lives of whales and other marine life.[12]

For more information about this organization, go to **www.neaq.org**.

1. Why would the New England Aquarium require people to apply in writing for unpaid volunteer and internship positions?
2. In addition to using the web and attending community meetings, what other external recruiting techniques would you suggest the aquarium use to attract volunteers? Why?
3. Do you think that the New England Aquarium should evaluate the performance of its volunteers periodically? Support your answer.

BUILDING SKILLS FOR CAREER SUCCESS

1. EXPLORING THE INTERNET

Although you may believe that your formal learning will end when you graduate and enter the working world, it won't. Companies both large and small spend billions of dollars annually in training employees and updating their knowledge and skills. Besides supporting employees who attend accredited continuing-education programs, companies also may provide more specialized in-house course work on new technologies, products, and markets for strategic planning. The Internet is an excellent search tool to find out about course work offered by private training organizations, as well as by traditional academic institutions. Learning online is a fast-growing alternative, especially for busy employees requiring updates to skills in the information technology (IT) field, where software knowledge must be refreshed continuously. Visit the text website for updates to this exercise.

Assignment

1. Visit the websites of several academic institutions and examine their course work offerings. Also examine the offerings of some of the following private consulting firms:
   Learning Tree International: **www.learningtree.com**
   Accenture: **www.accenture.com**
   KPMG: **www.kpmg.com**
   Ernst & Young: **www.ey.com/global**
2. What professional continuing-education training and services are provided by one of the academic institutions whose site you visited?
3. What sort of training is offered by one of the preceding consulting firms?
4. From the company's point of view, what is the total real cost of a day's worth of employee training? What is the money value of one day of study for a full-time college student? Can you explain why firms are willing to pay higher starting salaries for employees with higher levels of education?
5. The American Society for Training & Development (**www.astd.org/**) and the Society for Human Resource Management (**www.shrm.org/**) are two good sources for information about online training programs. Describe what you found out at these and other sites providing online learning solutions.

2. BUILDING TEAM SKILLS

The New Therapy Company is soliciting a contract to provide five nursing homes with physical, occupational, speech, and respiratory therapy. The therapists will float among the five nursing homes. The therapists have not yet been hired, but the nursing homes expect them to be fully trained and ready to go to work in three months. The previous therapy company lost its contract because of high staff turnover owing to "burnout" (a common problem in this type of work), high costs, and low-quality care. The nursing homes want a plan specifying how the New Therapy Company will meet staffing needs, keep costs low, and provide high-quality care.

Assignment

1. Working in a group, discuss how the New Therapy Company can meet the three-month deadline and still ensure that the care its therapists provide is of high quality. Also discuss the following:
   a. How many of each type of therapist will the company need?
   b. How will it prevent therapists from "burning out"?
   c. How can it retain experienced staff and still limit costs?
   d. Are promotions available for any of the staff? What is the career ladder?
   e. How will the company manage therapists at five different locations? How will it keep in touch with them (computer, voice mail, monthly meetings)? Would it make more sense to have therapists work permanently at each location rather than rotate among them?
   f. How will the company justify the travel costs? What other expenses might it expect?
2. Prepare a plan for the New Therapy Company to present to the nursing homes.

3. RESEARCHING DIFFERENT CAREERS

A résumé provides a summary of your skills, abilities, and achievements. It also may include a description of the type of job you want. A well-prepared résumé indicates that you know what your career objectives are, shows that you have given serious thought to your career, and tells a potential employer what you are qualified to do. The way a résumé is prepared can make a difference in whether you are considered for a job.

Assignment

1. Prepare a résumé for a job that you want using the information in Appendix A (see text website).
   a. First, determine what your skills are and decide which skills are needed to do this particular job.
   b. Decide which type of format—chronological or functional—would be most effective in presenting your skills and experience.
   c. Keep the résumé to one page, if possible (definitely no more than two pages). (Note that portfolio items may be attached for certain types of jobs, such as artwork.)
2. Have several people review the résumé for accuracy.
3. Ask your instructor to comment on your résumé.

10

Motivating and Satisfying Employees and Teams

WHY THIS CHAPTER MATTERS. As you move up into management positions or operate your own business, you will need to understand what motivates others in an organization.

©Michael Newman/PhotoEdit

LEARNING OBJECTIVES

1 Explain what motivation is.

2 Understand some major historical perspectives on motivation.

3 Describe three contemporary views of motivation: equity theory, expectancy theory, and goal-setting theory.

4 Explain several techniques for increasing employee motivation.

5 Understand the types, development, and uses of teams.

SAS Zigs When Competitors Zag

For more than 30 years, SAS has been developing sophisticated software to serve corporate customers such as Kraft, Expedia, General Electric, and Monsanto. Its 11,000 employees worldwide create and customize programs to help businesses improve e-commerce sales, manage parts and suppliers, analyze customer buying patterns, and make better management decisions. In 1976, the year SAS was founded, its revenue was $138,000. Today, the company remains profitable and privately held, with annual revenue topping $2.2 billion.

SAS's top managers have always taken great care to nurture their workforce, saying that "satisfied employees create satisfied customers." Even during the worst of the recent economic woes, when other firms were slimming down, emptying offices, and laying off workers, SAS resisted the downsizing trend. Instead, it continued its growth strategy of introducing new products, opening sizeable new facilities, and hiring the best and the brightest.

From the beginning, SAS has encouraged employees to find an appropriate balance between professional and personal responsibilities. Its spurs employees on to top performance through a combination of challenging assignments and advanced professional training. Some of its 400 offices offer alternatives to the usual 9-to-5 workday such as working flexible hours, telecommuting, and working part-time through job-sharing. SAS's headquarters complex in Cary, North Carolina and several of its regional offices provide on-site child-care services, health services, fitness and recreation facilities, and other amenities that make a difference in employees' lives. Weekly snack traditions such as fresh fruit on Mondays, M&Ms on Wednesdays, and breakfast goodies on Friday keep the mood upbeat even when the pressure is on.

SAS's employees are so happy in their jobs that in any given year, only 3 percent leave. Competition to join SAS's workforce is particularly fierce: It receives more than 1,000 applications for every open position. No wonder that, for the past 12 years, its satisfied workforce has voted SAS onto *Fortune* magazine's annual list of "100 Best Companies to Work For."[1]

To achieve its goals, any organization—whether it's SAS, FedEx, or a local convenience store—must be sure that its employees have more than the right raw materials, adequate facilities, and equipment that works. The organization also must ensure that its employees are *motivated*. To some extent, a high level of employee motivation derives from effective management practices.

In this chapter, after first explaining what motivation is, we present several views of motivation that have influenced management practices over the years: Taylor's ideas of scientific management, Mayo's Hawthorne Studies, Maslow's hierarchy of needs, Herzberg's motivation-hygiene theory, McGregor's Theory X and Theory Y, Ouchi's Theory Z, and reinforcement theory. Then, turning our attention to contemporary ideas, we examine equity theory, expectancy theory, and goal-setting theory. Finally, we discuss specific techniques managers can use to foster employee motivation and satisfaction.

motivation the individual internal process that energizes, directs, and sustains behavior; the personal "force" that causes you or me to behave in a particular way

What Is Motivation?

1 LEARNING OBJECTIVE

Explain what motivation is.

A *motive* is something that causes a person to act. A successful athlete is said to be "highly motivated." A student who avoids work is said to be "unmotivated." We define **motivation** as the individual internal process that energizes, directs, and sustains behavior. It is the personal "force" that causes you or me to act in a particular way. For example, job rotation may increase your job satisfaction and your enthusiasm for your work so that you devote more energy to it, but perhaps job rotation would not have the same impact on me.

Morale is an employee's attitude or feelings about the job, about superiors, and about the firm itself. To achieve organizational goals effectively, employees need more than the right raw materials, adequate facilities, and equipment that works. High morale results mainly from the satisfaction of needs on the job or as a result of the job. One need that might be satisfied on the job is the need *to be recognized* as an important contributor to the organization. A need satisfied as a result of the job is the need for *financial security*. High morale, in turn, leads to dedication and loyalty, as well as to the desire to do the job well. Low morale can lead to shoddy work, absenteeism, and high turnover rates as employees leave to seek more satisfying jobs with other firms. A study conducted by the Society for Human Resource Management (SHRM) showed that 75 percent of all employees are actively or passively seeking new employment opportunities. To offset this turnover trend, companies are creating retention plans focused on employee morale. Sometimes creative solutions are needed to motivate people and boost morale. This is especially true where barriers to change are deeply rooted in cultural stereotypes of the job and in the industry.

Motivation, morale, and the satisfaction of employees' needs are thus intertwined. Along with productivity, they have been the subject of much study since the end of the nineteenth century. We continue our discussion of motivation by outlining some landmarks of that early research.

Concept Check

1. What is motivation?

2. Why is understanding motivation important?

LEARNING OBJECTIVE 2

Understand some major historical perspectives on motivation.

Historical Perspectives on Motivation

Researchers often begin a study with a fairly narrow goal in mind. After they develop an understanding of their subject, however, they realize that both their goal and their research should be broadened. This is exactly what happened when early research into productivity blossomed into the more modern study of employee motivation.

Scientific Management

Toward the end of the nineteenth century, Frederick W. Taylor became interested in improving the efficiency of individual workers. This interest stemmed from his own experiences in manufacturing plants. It eventually led to **scientific management**, the application of scientific principles to management of work and workers.

One of Taylor's first jobs was with the Midvale Steel Company in Philadelphia, where he developed a strong distaste for waste and inefficiency. He also observed a practice he called "soldiering." Workers "soldiered," or worked slowly, because they feared that if they worked faster, they would run out of work and lose their jobs. Taylor realized that managers were not aware of this practice because they had no idea what the workers' productivity levels *should* be.

Taylor later left Midvale and spent several years at Bethlehem Steel. It was there that he made his most significant contribution. In particular, he suggested that each job should be broken down into separate tasks. Then management should determine (1) the best way to perform these tasks and (2) the job output to expect when the tasks were performed properly. Next, management should carefully choose the best person for each job and train that person to do the job properly. Finally, management should cooperate with workers to ensure that jobs were performed as planned.

Taylor also developed the idea that most people work only to earn money. He therefore reasoned that pay should be tied directly to output. The more a person produced, the more he or she should be paid. This gave rise to the **piece-rate system**, under which employees are paid a certain amount for each unit of output they produce. Under Taylor's piece-rate system, each employee was assigned an output quota. Those exceeding the quota were paid a higher per-unit rate for *all* units they produced (see Figure 10.1). Today, the piece-rate system is still used by some manufacturers and by farmers who grow crops that are harvested by farm laborers.

morale an employee's feelings about his or her job, superiors, and the firm itself

scientific management the application of scientific principles to management of work and workers

piece-rate system a compensation system under which employees are paid a certain amount for each unit of output they produce

FIGURE 10.1: Taylor's Piece-Rate System Workers who exceeded their quota were rewarded by being paid at a higher rate per piece for all the pieces they produced.

WORKER A

Quota
60 pieces
per hour

Output — 60 pieces

Pay: 10¢ each — $6.00 per hour

WORKER B

Quota

Output — 85

Pay: 12¢ each — $10.20 per hour

When Taylor's system was put into practice at Bethlehem Steel, the results were dramatic. Average earnings per day for steel handlers rose from $1.15 to $1.88. (Don't let the low wages that prevailed at the time obscure the fact that this was an increase of better than 60 percent!) The average amount of steel handled per day increased from sixteen to fifty-seven tons.

Taylor's revolutionary ideas had a profound impact on management practice. However, his view of motivation soon was recognized as overly simplistic and narrow. It is true that most people expect to be paid for their work, but it is also true that people work for a variety of reasons other than pay. Simply increasing a person's pay may not increase that person's motivation or productivity.

The Hawthorne Studies

Between 1927 and 1932, Elton Mayo conducted two experiments at the Hawthorne plant of the Western Electric Company in Chicago. The original objective of these

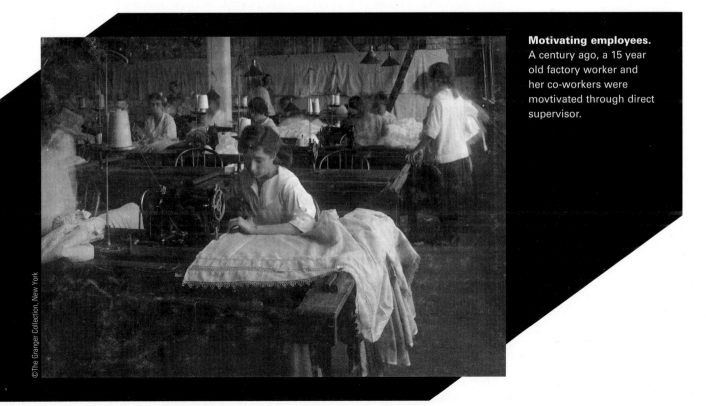

Motivating employees. A century ago, a 15 year old factory worker and her co-workers were movtivated through direct supervisor.

studies, now referred to as the *Hawthorne Studies,* was to determine the effects of the work environment on employee productivity.

In the first set of experiments, lighting in the workplace was varied for one group of workers but not for a second group. Then the productivity of both groups was measured to determine the effect of the light. To the amazement of the researchers, productivity increased for *both* groups. And for the group whose lighting was varied, productivity remained high until the light was reduced to the level of moonlight!

The second set of experiments focused on the effectiveness of the piece-rate system in increasing the output of *groups* of workers. Researchers expected that output would increase because faster workers would put pressure on slower workers to produce more. Again, the results were not as expected. Output remained constant no matter what "standard" rates management set.

The researchers came to the conclusion that *human factors* were responsible for the results of the two experiments. In the lighting experiments, researchers had given both groups of workers a *sense of involvement* in their jobs merely by asking them to participate in the research. These workers—perhaps for the first time—felt as though they were an important part of the organization. In the piece-rate experiments, each group of workers informally set the acceptable rate of output for the group. To gain or retain the *social acceptance* of the group, each worker had to produce at that rate. Slower or faster workers were pressured to maintain the group's pace.

The Hawthorne Studies showed that such human factors are at least as important to motivation as pay rates. From these and other studies, the *human relations movement* in management was born. Its premise was simple: Employees who are happy and satisfied with their work are motivated to perform better. Hence management would do best to provide a work environment that maximizes employee satisfaction.

Maslow's Hierarchy of Needs

Abraham Maslow, an American psychologist whose best-known works were published in the 1960s and 1970s, developed a theory of motivation based on a hierarchy of needs. A **need** is a personal requirement. Maslow assumed that humans are "wanting" beings who seek to fulfill a variety of needs. He observed that these needs can be arranged according to their importance in a sequence now known as **Maslow's hierarchy of needs** (see Figure 10.2).

At the most basic level are **physiological needs**, the things we require to survive. They include food and water, clothing, shelter, and sleep. In the employment context, these needs usually are satisfied through adequate wages.

need a personal requirement

Maslow's hierarchy of needs a sequence of human needs in the order of their importance

physiological needs the things we require for survival

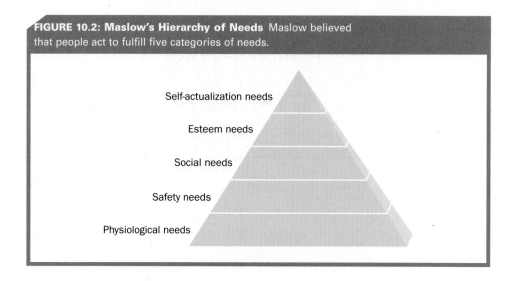

FIGURE 10.2: Maslow's Hierarchy of Needs Maslow believed that people act to fulfill five categories of needs.

- Self-actualization needs
- Esteem needs
- Social needs
- Safety needs
- Physiological needs

At the next level are **safety needs**, the things we require for physical and emotional security. Safety needs may be satisfied through job security, health insurance, pension plans, and safe working conditions. During a time of falling corporate profits, many companies are facing increasing insurance premiums for employee health care. Both General Electric (GE) and Hershey recently endured strikes centered on the issue of increased health care costs. Reduced health care coverage is a threat to employees' need for safety. Some companies are trying to find unique solutions. For example, SAS, a software company, maintains its own health care center that offers free physical examinations, emergency treatment, immunizations, and care for chronic illnesses.[2]

Next are the **social needs**, the human requirements for love and affection and a sense of belonging. To an extent, these needs can be satisfied through relationships in the work environment and the informal organization. However, social networks beyond the workplace—with family and friends, for example—usually are needed, too. Casino operator Isle of Capri Casinos, Inc., uses unique methods to help employees meet their social needs. The company holds an annual retreat for managers that is fun and exciting. The latest retreat was called "Isle Survive" and featured a *Survivor*-like game where employees were teamed up and given money and other resources and sent on a sort of scavenger hunt. This is just one of the ways Isle of Capri motivates its workers, and the company seems to be successful in meeting its employees' needs, as evidenced by the lowest employee turnover in the industry.

At the level of **esteem needs**, we require respect and recognition from others and a sense of our own accomplishment and worth (self-esteem). These needs may be satisfied through personal accomplishment, promotion to more responsible jobs, various honors and awards, and other forms of recognition.

At the top of the hierarchy are our **self-actualization needs**, the need to grow, develop, and become all that we are capable of being. These are the most difficult needs to satisfy, and the means of satisfying them tend to vary with the individual. For some people, learning a new skill, starting a new career after retirement, or becoming "the best there is" at some endeavor may be the way to realize self-actualization.

Maslow suggested that people work to satisfy their physiological needs first, then their safety needs, and so on, up the "needs ladder." In general, they are motivated by the needs at the lowest level that remain unsatisfied. However, needs at one level do not have to be satisfied completely before needs at the next-higher level come into play. If the majority of a person's physiological and safety needs are satisfied, that person will be motivated primarily by social needs. But any physiological and safety needs that remain unsatisfied also will be important.

Maslow's hierarchy of needs provides a useful way of viewing employee motivation, as well as a guide for management. By and large, American business has been able to satisfy workers' basic needs, but the higher-order needs present more of a challenge. These needs are not satisfied in a simple manner, and the means of satisfaction vary from one employee to another.

Herzberg's Motivation-Hygiene Theory

In the late 1950s, Frederick Herzberg interviewed approximately two hundred accountants and engineers in Pittsburgh. During the interviews, he asked them to think of a time when they had felt especially good about their jobs and their work. Then he asked them to describe the factor or factors that had caused them to feel that way. Next, he did the same regarding a time

safety needs the things we require for physical and emotional security

social needs the human requirements for love, affection, and a sense of belonging

esteem needs our need for respect, recognition, and a sense of our own accomplishment and worth

self-actualization needs the need to grow and develop and to become all that we are capable of being

Esteem needs. Employee recognition helps to satisfy esteem needs. Recognition of this type shows respect for an individual and his or her accomplishments.

when they had felt especially bad about their work. He was surprised to find that feeling good and feeling bad resulted from entirely different sets of factors; that is, low pay may have made a particular person feel bad, but it was not high pay that had made that person feel good. Instead, it was some completely different factor.

Satisfaction and Dissatisfaction

Before Herzberg's interviews, the general assumption was that employee satisfaction and dissatisfaction lay at opposite ends of the same scale. People felt satisfied, dissatisfied, or somewhere in between. But Herzberg's interviews convinced him that satisfaction and dissatisfaction may be different dimensions altogether. One dimension might range from satisfaction to no satisfaction, and the other might range from dissatisfaction to no dissatisfaction. In other words, the opposite of satisfaction is not dissatisfaction. The idea that satisfaction and dissatisfaction are separate and distinct dimensions is referred to as the **motivation-hygiene theory** (see Figure 10.3).

The job factors that Herzberg found most frequently associated with satisfaction are achievement, recognition, responsibility, advancement, growth, and the work itself. These factors generally are referred to as **motivation factors** because their presence increases motivation. However, their absence does not necessarily result in feelings of dissatisfaction. When motivation factors are present, they act as *satisfiers*.

Job factors cited as causing dissatisfaction are supervision, working conditions, interpersonal relationships, pay, job security, company policies, and administration. These factors, called **hygiene factors**, reduce dissatisfaction when they are present to an acceptable degree. However, they do not necessarily result in high levels of motivation. When hygiene factors are absent, they act as *dissatisfiers*.

Using Herzberg's Motivation-Hygiene Theory

Herzberg provides explicit guidelines for using the motivation-hygiene theory of employee motivation. He suggests that the hygiene factors must be present to ensure that a worker can function comfortably. He warns, however, that a state of *no dissatisfaction* never exists. In any situation, people always will be dissatisfied with something.

According to Herzberg, managers should make hygiene as positive as possible but then should expect only short-term, not long-term, improvement in motivation. Managers must focus instead on providing those motivation factors that presumably *will* enhance motivation and long-term effort.

We should note that employee pay has more effect than Herzberg's theory indicates. He suggests that pay provides only short-term change and not true motivation. Yet, in many organizations, pay constitutes a form of recognition and reward for achievement—and recognition and achievement are both motivation factors. The effect of pay may depend on how it is distributed. If a pay increase does not

motivation-hygiene theory the idea that satisfaction and dissatisfaction are separate and distinct dimensions

motivation factors job factors that increase motivation but whose absence does not necessarily result in dissatisfaction

hygiene factors job factors that reduce dissatisfaction when present to an acceptable degree but that do not necessarily result in high levels of motivation

FIGURE 10.3: Herzberg's Motivation-Hygiene Theory Herzberg's theory takes into account that there are different dimensions to job satisfaction and dissatisfaction and that these factors do not overlap.

MOTIVATION FACTORS
- Achievement
- Recognition
- Responsibility
- Advancement
- Growth
- The work itself

Satisfaction — No satisfaction

HYGIENE FACTORS
- Supervision
- Working conditions
- Interpersonal relationships
- Pay
- Job security
- Company policies and administration

Dissatisfaction — No dissatisfaction

depend on performance (as in across-the-board or cost-of-living raises), it may not motivate people. However, if pay is increased as a form of recognition (as in bonuses or incentives), it may play a powerful role in motivating employees to higher performance.

Theory X and Theory Y

The concepts of Theory X and Theory Y were advanced by Douglas McGregor in his book *The Human Side of Enterprise*. They are, in essence, sets of assumptions that underlie management's attitudes and beliefs regarding worker behavior.[3]

Theory X is a concept of employee motivation generally consistent with Taylor's scientific management. Theory X assumes that employees dislike work and will function effectively only in a highly controlled work environment.

Theory X is based on the following assumptions:

1. People dislike work and try to avoid it.
2. Because people dislike work, managers must coerce, control, and frequently threaten employees to achieve organizational goals.
3. People generally must be led because they have little ambition and will not seek responsibility; they are concerned mainly with security.

The logical outcome of such assumptions will be a highly controlled work environment—one in which managers make all the decisions and employees take all the orders.

On the other hand, **Theory Y** is a concept of employee motivation generally consistent with the ideas of the human relations movement. Theory Y assumes that employees accept responsibility and work toward organizational goals, and by so doing they also achieve personal rewards. Theory Y is based on the following assumptions:

1. People do not naturally dislike work; in fact, work is an important part of their lives.
2. People will work toward goals to which they are committed.
3. People become committed to goals when it is clear that accomplishing the goals will bring personal rewards.
4. People often seek out and willingly accept responsibility.
5. Employees have the potential to help accomplish organizational goals.
6. Organizations generally do not make full use of their human resources.

Obviously, this view is quite different from—and much more positive than—that of Theory X. McGregor argued that most managers behave in accordance with Theory X. But he maintained that Theory Y is more appropriate and effective as a guide for managerial action (see Table 10.1).

The human relations movement and Theories X and Y increased managers' awareness of the importance of social factors in the workplace. However, human motivation is a complex and dynamic process to which there is no simple key.

Theory X a concept of employee motivation generally consistent with Taylor's scientific management; assumes that employees dislike work and will function only in a highly controlled work environment

Theory Y a concept of employee motivation generally consistent with the ideas of the human relations movement; assumes that employees accept responsibility and work toward organizational goals if by so doing they also achieve personal rewards

TABLE 10.1: Theory X and Theory Y Contrasted

Area	Theory X	Theory Y
Attitude toward work	Dislike	Involvement
Control systems	External	Internal
Supervision	Direct	Indirect
Level of commitment	Low	High
Employee potential	Ignored	Identified
Use of human resources	Limited	Not limited

Neither money nor social factors alone can provide the answer. Rather, a number of factors must be considered in any attempt to increase motivation.

Theory Z

William Ouchi, a management professor at UCLA, studied business practices in American and Japanese firms. He concluded that different types of management systems dominate in these two countries.[4] In Japan, Ouchi found what he calls *type J* firms. They are characterized by lifetime employment for employees, collective (or group) decision making, collective responsibility for the outcomes of decisions, slow evaluation and promotion, implied control mechanisms, nonspecialized career paths, and a holistic concern for employees as people.

American industry is dominated by what Ouchi calls *type A* firms, which follow a different pattern. They emphasize short-term employment, individual decision making, individual responsibility for the outcomes of decisions, rapid evaluation and promotion, explicit control mechanisms, specialized career paths, and a segmented concern for employees only as employees.

A few very successful American firms represent a blend of the type J and type A patterns. These firms, called *type Z* organizations, emphasize long-term employment, collective decision making, individual responsibility for the outcomes of decisions, slow evaluation and promotion, informal control along with some formalized measures, moderately specialized career paths, and a holistic concern for employees.

Ouchi's **Theory Z** is the belief that some middle ground between his type A and type J practices is best for American business (see Figure 10.4). A major part of Theory Z is the emphasis on participative decision making. The focus is on "we" rather than on "us versus them." Theory Z employees and managers view the organization as a family. This participative spirit fosters cooperation and the dissemination of information and organizational values.

Reinforcement Theory

Reinforcement theory is based on the premise that behavior that is rewarded is likely to be repeated, whereas behavior that is punished is less likely to recur. A *reinforcement* is an action that follows directly from a particular behavior. It may be a pay raise following a particularly large sale to a new customer or a reprimand for coming to work late.

Reinforcements can take a variety of forms and can be used in a number of ways. A *positive reinforcement* is one that strengthens desired behavior by providing a reward. For example, many employees respond well to praise; recognition from their supervisors for a job well done increases (strengthens) their willingness

Theory Z the belief that some middle ground between Ouchi's type A and type J practices is best for American business

reinforcement theory a theory of motivation based on the premise that behavior that is rewarded is likely to be repeated, whereas behavior that is punished is less likely to recur

---

FIGURE 10.4: The Features of Theory Z The best aspects of Japanese and American management theories combine to form the nucleus of Theory Z.

TYPE J FIRMS (Japanese)
- Lifetime employment
- Collective decision making
- Collective responsibility
- Slow promotion
- Implied control mechanisms
- Nonspecialized career paths
- Holistic concern for employees

TYPE Z FIRMS (Best choice for American firms)
- Long-term employment
- Collective decision making
- Individual responsibility
- Slow promotion
- Informal control
- Moderately specialized career paths
- Holistic concern for employees

TYPE A FIRMS (American)
- Short-term employment
- Individual decision making
- Individual responsibility
- Rapid promotion
- Explicit control mechanisms
- Specialized career paths
- Segmented concern for employees

to perform well in the future. A *negative reinforcement* strengthens desired behavior by eliminating an undesirable task or situation. Suppose that a machine shop must be cleaned thoroughly every month—a dirty, miserable task. During one particular month when the workers do a less-than-satisfactory job at their normal work assignments, the boss requires the workers to clean the factory rather than bringing in the usual private maintenance service. The employees will be motivated to work harder the next month to avoid the unpleasant cleanup duty again.

Punishment is an undesired consequence of undesirable behavior. Common forms of punishment used in organizations include reprimands, reduced pay, disciplinary layoffs, and termination (firing). Punishment often does more harm than good. It tends to create an unpleasant environment, fosters hostility and resentment, and suppresses undesirable behavior only until the supervisor's back is turned.

Managers who rely on *extinction* hope to eliminate undesirable behavior by not responding to it. The idea is that the behavior eventually will become "extinct." Suppose, for example, that an employee has the habit of writing memo after memo to his or her manager about insignificant events. If the manager does not respond to any of these memos, the employee probably will stop writing them, and the behavior will have been squelched.

The effectiveness of reinforcement depends on which type is used and how it is timed. One approach may work best under certain conditions, but some situations lend themselves to the use of more than one approach. Generally, positive reinforcement is considered the most effective, and it is recommended when the manager has a choice.

Continual reinforcement can become tedious for both managers and employees, especially when the same behavior is being reinforced over and over in the same way. At the start, it may be necessary to reinforce a desired behavior every time it occurs. However, once a desired behavior has become more or less established, occasional reinforcement seems to be most effective.

Contemporary Views on Motivation

Maslow's hierarchy of needs and Herzberg's motivation-hygiene theory are popular and widely known theories of motivation. Each is also a significant step up from the relatively narrow views of scientific management and Theories X and Y. But they do have one weakness: Each attempts to specify *what* motivates people, but neither explains *why* or *how* motivation develops or is sustained over time. In recent years, managers have begun to explore three other models that take a more dynamic view of motivation. These are equity theory, expectancy theory, and goal-setting theory.

Equity Theory

The **equity theory** of motivation is based on the premise that people are motivated to obtain and preserve equitable treatment for themselves. As used here, *equity* is the distribution of rewards in direct proportion to the contribution of each employee to the organization. Everyone need not receive the *same* rewards, but the rewards should be in accordance with individual contributions.

According to this theory, we tend to implement the idea of equity in the following way: First, we develop our own input-to-outcome ratio. *Inputs* are the time, effort, skills, education, experience, and so on, that we contribute to the organization. *Outcomes* are the rewards we get from the organization, such as pay, benefits, recognition, and promotions. Next, we compare this ratio with what we perceive as the input-to-outcome ratio for some other person. It might be a coworker, a friend who works for another firm, or even an average of all the people in our organization. This person is called the *comparison other*. Note that our perception of this person's input-to-outcome ratio may be absolutely correct or completely wrong. However, we believe that it is correct.

equity theory a theory of motivation based on the premise that people are motivated to obtain and preserve equitable treatment for themselves

Concept Check

1. What are the major elements of Taylor's "scientific management"?

2. What were Elton Mayo's conclusions from the Hawthorne studies?

3. What are the different levels in Maslow's Hierarchy of Needs?

4. What are the major elements of Herzberg's Motivation-Hygiene theory?

5. What are the underlying assumptions of Theory X and Theory Y?

3 LEARNING OBJECTIVE

Describe three contemporary views of motivation: equity theory, expectancy theory, and goal-setting theory.

If the two ratios are roughly the same, we feel that the organization is treating us equitably. In this case, we are motivated to leave things as they are. However, if our ratio is the higher of the two, we feel under-rewarded and are motivated to make changes. We may (1) decrease our own inputs by not working so hard, (2) try to increase our total outcome by asking for a raise in pay, (3) try to get the comparison other to increase some inputs or receive decreased outcomes, (4) leave the work situation, or (5) do a new comparison with a different comparison other.

Equity theory is most relevant to pay as an outcome. Because pay is a very real measure of a person's worth to an organization, comparisons involving pay are a natural part of organizational life. Managers can try to avoid problems arising from inequity by making sure that rewards are distributed on the basis of performance and that everyone clearly understands the basis for his or her own pay.

Expectancy Theory

Expectancy theory, developed by Victor Vroom, is a very complex model of motivation based on a deceptively simple assumption. According to expectancy theory, motivation depends on how much we want something and on how likely we think we are to get it (see Figure 10.5). Consider, for example, the case of three sales representatives who are candidates for promotion to one sales manager's job. Bill has had a very good sales year and always gets good performance evaluations. However, he isn't sure that he wants the job because it involves a great deal of travel, long working hours, and much stress and pressure. Paul wants the job badly but doesn't think he has much chance of getting it. He has had a terrible sales year and gets only mediocre performance evaluations from his present boss. Susan wants the job as much as Paul, and she thinks that she has a pretty good shot at it. Her sales have improved significantly this past year, and her evaluations are the best in the company.

Expectancy theory would predict that Bill and Paul are not very motivated to seek the promotion. Bill doesn't really want it, and Paul doesn't think that he has much of a chance of getting it. Susan, however, is very motivated to seek the promotion because she wants it *and* thinks that she can get it.

Expectancy theory is complex because each action we take is likely to lead to several different outcomes; some we may want, and others we may not want. For example, a person who works hard and puts in many extra hours may get a pay raise, be promoted, and gain valuable new job skills. However, that person also may be forced to spend less time with his or her family and be forced to cut back on his or her social life.

For one person, the promotion may be paramount, the pay raise and new skills fairly important, and the loss of family and social life of negligible importance. For someone else, the family and social life may be most important, the pay raise of moderate importance, the new skills unimportant, and the promotion undesirable because of the additional hours it would require. The first person would be motivated to work hard and put in the extra hours, whereas the second person would not be at all motivated to do so. In other words, it is the entire bundle of

expectancy theory a model of motivation based on the assumption that motivation depends on how much we want something and on how likely we think we are to get it

FIGURE 10.5: Expectancy Theory Vroom's theory is based on the idea that motivation depends on how much people want something and on how likely they think they are to get it.

outcomes—and the individual's evaluation of the importance of each outcome—that determines motivation.

Expectancy theory is difficult to apply, but it does provide several useful guidelines for managers. It suggests that managers must recognize that (1) employees work for a variety of reasons, (2) these reasons, or expected outcomes, may change over time, and (3) it is necessary to clearly show employees how they can attain the outcomes they desire.

Goal-Setting Theory

Goal-setting theory suggests that employees are motivated to achieve goals that they and their managers establish together. The goal should be very specific, moderately difficult, and one the employee will be committed to achieve.[5] Rewards should be tied directly to goal achievement. Using goal-setting theory, a manager can design rewards that fit employee needs, clarify expectations, maintain equity, and provide reinforcement. A major benefit of this theory is that it provides a good understanding of the goal the employee is to achieve and the rewards that will accrue to the employee if the goal is accomplished.

Key Motivation Techniques

Today, it takes more than a generous salary to motivate employees. Increasingly, companies are trying to provide motivation by satisfying employees' less tangible needs. In this section, we discuss several specific techniques that help managers to boost employee motivation and job satisfaction.

Management by Objectives

Management by objectives (MBO) is a motivation technique in which managers and employees collaborate in setting goals. The primary purpose of MBO is to clarify the roles employees are expected to play in reaching the organization's goals. For example, Daymark Solutions has put MBO to use by establishing short-term goals for every employee. These quarterly objectives may be achieving a high level of customer satisfaction or receiving specific certifications. These smaller goals directly correlate with the larger company objectives, such as cost containment or revenue goals.[6]

By allowing individuals to participate in goal setting and performance evaluation, MBO increases their motivation. Most MBO programs consist of a series of five steps. The first step in setting up an MBO program is to secure the acceptance of top management. It is essential that top managers endorse and participate in the program if others in the firm are to accept it. The commitment of top management also provides a natural starting point for educating employees about the purposes and mechanics of MBO.

Next, preliminary goals must be established. Top management also plays a major role in this activity because the preliminary goals reflect the firm's mission and strategy. The intent of an MBO program is to have these goals filter down through the organization.

The third step, which actually consists of several smaller steps, is the heart of MBO:

1. The manager explains to each employee that he or she has accepted certain goals for the group (the manager as well as the employees) and asks the individual to think about how he or she can help to achieve these goals.
2. The manager later meets with each employee individually. Together they establish goals for the employee. Whenever possible, the goals should be measurable and should specify the time frame for completion (usually one year).
3. The manager and the employee decide what resources the employee will need to accomplish his or her goals.

As the fourth step, the manager and each employee meet periodically to review the employee's progress. They may agree to modify certain goals during these meetings if circumstances have changed. For example, a sales representative may have

Concept Check

1. What is equity theory?

2. How do managers use it in order to decide the pay structure of employees?

3. What is expectancy theory and how is it different from goal setting theory?

4 LEARNING OBJECTIVE

Explain several techniques for increasing employee motivation.

goal-setting theory a theory of motivation suggesting that employees are motivated to achieve goals that they and their managers establish together

management by objectives (MBO) a motivation technique in which managers and employees collaborate in setting goals

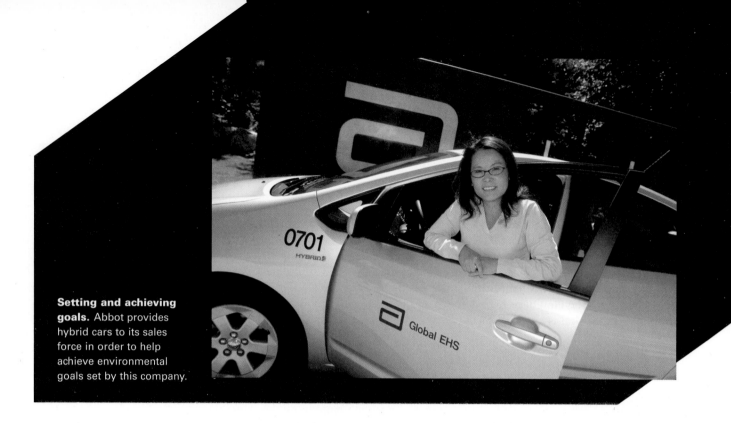

Setting and achieving goals. Abbot provides hybrid cars to its sales force in order to help achieve environmental goals set by this company.

accepted a goal of increasing sales by 20 percent. However, an aggressive competitor may have entered the marketplace, making this goal unattainable. In light of this circumstance, the goal may be revised downward to 10 or 15 percent.

The fifth step in the MBO process is evaluation. At the end of the designated time period, the manager and each employee meet again to determine which of the individual's goals were met, which were not met, and why. The employee's reward (in the form of a pay raise, praise, or promotion) is based primarily on the degree of goal attainment.

As with every other management method, MBO has advantages and disadvantages. MBO can motivate employees by involving them actively in the life of the firm. The collaboration on goal setting and performance appraisal improves communication and makes employees feel that they are an important part of the organization. Periodic review of progress also enhances control within an organization. A major problem with MBO is that it does not work unless the process begins at the top of an organization. In some cases, MBO results in excessive paperwork. Also, a manager may not like sitting down and working out goals with subordinates and may instead just assign them goals. Finally, MBO programs prove difficult to implement unless goals are quantifiable.

Job Enrichment

Job enrichment is a method of motivating employees by providing them with variety in their tasks while giving them some responsibility for, and control over, their jobs. At the same time, employees gain new skills and acquire a broader perspective about how their individual work contributes to the goals of the organization. Earlier in this chapter, we noted that Herzberg's motivation-hygiene theory is one rationale for the use of job enrichment; that is, the added responsibility and control that job enrichment confers on employees increases their satisfaction and motivation. At times, **job enlargement**, expanding a worker's assignments to include additional but similar tasks, can lead to job enrichment. Job enlargement might mean that a worker on an assembly line who used to connect three wires to components moving down the line, now connects five wires. Unfortunately, the added tasks often are just as routine as those the worker performed before the change. In such cases, enlargement may not be effective.

Whereas job enlargement does not really change the routine and monotonous nature of jobs, job enrichment does. Job enrichment requires that added tasks give an employee more responsibility for what he or she does. It provides workers with both more tasks to do and more control over how they perform them. In particular,

job enrichment a motivation technique that provides employees with more variety and responsibility in their jobs

job enlargement expanding a worker's assignments to include additional but similar tasks job enrichment removes many controls from jobs, gives workers more authority, and assigns work in complete, natural units. Moreover, employees frequently are given fresh and challenging job assignments. By blending more planning and decision making into jobs, job enrichment gives work more depth and complexity.

Job redesign is a type of job enrichment in which work is restructured in ways that cultivate the worker-job match. Job redesign can be achieved by combining tasks, forming work groups, or establishing closer customer relationships. Employees often are more motivated when jobs are combined because the increased variety of tasks presents more challenge and therefore more reward. Work groups motivate employees by showing them how their jobs fit within the organization as a whole and how they contribute to its success. Establishing client relationships allows employees to interact directly with customers. Not only does this type of redesign add a personal dimension to employment, but it also provides workers with immediate and relevant feedback about how they are doing their jobs.

Job enrichment works best when employees seek more challenging work. Of course, not all workers respond positively to job-enrichment programs. Employees must desire personal growth and have the skills and knowledge to perform enriched jobs. Lack of self-confidence, fear of failure, or distrust of management's intentions are likely to lead to ineffective performance on enriched jobs. In addition, some workers do not view their jobs as routine and boring, and others even prefer routine jobs because they find them satisfying. Companies that use job enrichment as an alternative to specialization also face extra expenses, such as the cost of retraining. Another motivation for job redesign is to reduce employees' stress at work. A job redesign that carefully matches worker to job can prevent stress-related injuries, which constitute about 60 to 80 percent of all work-related injuries.

Behavior Modification

Behavior modification is a systematic program of reinforcement to encourage desirable behavior. Behavior modification involves both rewards to encourage desirable actions and punishments to discourage undesirable actions. However, studies have shown that rewards, such as compliments and expressions of appreciation, are much more effective behavior modifiers than punishments, such as reprimands and scorn.

When applied to management, behavior modification strives to encourage desirable organizational behavior. Use of this technique begins with identification of a *target behavior*—the behavior that is to be changed. (It might be low production levels or a high rate of absenteeism, for example.) Existing levels of this behavior then are measured. Next, managers provide positive reinforcement in the form of a reward when employees exhibit the *desired behavior* (such as increased production or less absenteeism). The reward might be praise or a more tangible form of recognition, such as a gift, meal, or trip. Apple Company created the Corporate Gifting and Rewards Program in order to give companies the ability to reward their staff with iPods, iPod accessories, and iTunes gift cards.[7] Finally, the levels of the target behavior are measured again to determine whether the desired changes have been achieved. If they have, the reinforcement is maintained. However, if the target behavior has not changed significantly in the desired direction, the reward system must be changed to one that is likely to be more effective. John Kotter, a renowned Harvard Business School professor, states that this is difficult; the kind of emotional persuasion needed for these changes is not taught in business schools and is not often properly considered in many business settings.[8] The key is to devise effective rewards that not only will modify employees' behavior in desired ways but also will motivate them. To this end, experts suggest that management should reward quality, loyalty, and productivity.

Flextime

To most people, a work schedule means the standard nine-to-five, forty-hour work week. In reality, though, many people have work schedules that are quite different from this. S.C. Johnson and Sons' Flexible Work Schedule Program allows employees to create their own work schedule around their personal lives.[9] Police officers,

job redesign a type of job enrichment in which work is restructured to cultivate the worker-job match

behavior modification a systematic program of reinforcement to encourage desirable behavior

Job enrichment. Jobs can be enriched by expanding the number of tasks performed and allowing employees to make more decisions that are directly related to performing various tasks.

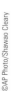

firefighters, restaurant personnel, airline employees, and medical personnel usually have work schedules that are far from standard. Some manufacturers also rotate personnel from shift to shift. Many professional people—such as managers, artists, and lawyers—need more than forty hours each week to get their work done.

The needs and lifestyles of today's workforce are changing. Dual-income families make up a much larger share of the workforce than ever before, and women are one of its fastest-growing sectors. Additionally, more employees are responsible for the care of elderly relatives. Recognizing that these changes increase the demand for family time, many employers are offering flexible work schedules that not only help employees to manage their time better but also increase employee motivation and job satisfaction.

Flextime is a system in which employees set their own work hours within certain limits determined by employers. Typically, the firm establishes two bands of time: the *core time*, when all employees must be at work, and the *flexible time*, when employees may choose whether to be at work. The only condition is that every employee must work a total of eight hours each day.

For example, the hours between 9 and 11 a.m. and 1 and 3 p.m. might be core time, and the hours between 6 and 9 a.m., between 11 a.m. and 1 p.m., and between 3 and 6 p.m. might be flexible time. This would give employees the option of coming in early and getting off early, coming in later and leaving later, or taking an extra long lunch break. But flextime also ensures that everyone is present at certain times, when conferences with supervisors and department meetings can be scheduled. Another type of flextime allows employees to work a forty-hour work week in four days instead of five. Workers who put in ten hours a day instead of eight get an extra day off each week. More than three-quarters of companies currently offer flextime.[10] At times, smaller firms use flextime to attract and retain employees, especially when they cannot match the salaries and benefit package provided by larger companies. For example, independent accounting firm Jefferson Wells uses flexible schedules as an incentive when recruiting high-quality candidates. By offering a customized work schedule and part-time positions with full-time benefits, the firm is able to remain competitive with larger companies.[11]

The sense of independence and autonomy employees gain from having a say in what hours they work can be a motivating factor. In addition, employees who have

flextime a system in which employees set their own work hours within employer-determined limits enough time to deal with nonwork issues often work more productively and with greater satisfaction when they are on the job. Two common problems associated with using flextime are (1) supervisors sometimes find their jobs complicated by having employees who come and go at different times, and (2) employees without flextime sometimes resent coworkers who have it.

Part-Time Work and Job Sharing

Part-time work is permanent employment in which individuals work less than a standard work week. The specific number of hours worked varies, but part-time jobs are structured so that all responsibilities can be completed in the number of hours an employee works. Part-time work is of special interest to parents who want more time with their children and people who simply desire more leisure time. One disadvantage of part-time work is that it often does not provide the benefits that come with a full-time position. This is not, however, the case at Starbucks, where approximately 80 percent of its employees work part time. Starbucks does not treat its part-time employees any differently from its full-time employees; all receive the same access to numerous benefits, which even includes a free pound of coffee every week.[12]

Job sharing (sometimes referred to as *work sharing*) is an arrangement whereby two people share one full-time position. One job sharer may work from 8 a.m. to noon, and the other may work from 1 to 5 p.m., or they may alternate work days. At Verizon Communications, Charlotte Schutzman and Sue Manix share the post of vice president of public affairs and communications. Each of them works two days a week along with alternating Wednesdays. By talking on the phone at least twice a week, they are able to handle a challenging administrative position and still be able to raise their children.[13] Job sharing combines the security of a full-time position with the flexibility of a part-time job. For firms, job sharing provides a unique opportunity to attract highly skilled employees who might not be available on a full-time basis. In addition, companies can save on expenses by reducing the cost of benefits and avoiding the disruptions of employee turnover. For employees, opting for the flexibility of job sharing may mean giving up some of the benefits received for full-time work. In addition, job sharing is difficult if tasks are not easily divisible or if two people do not work or communicate well with one another.

Telecommuting

A growing number of companies allow **telecommuting**, working at home all the time or for a portion of the work week. Personal computers, modems, fax machines, voice mail, cellular phones, and overnight couriers all facilitate the work-at-home trend. Working at home means that individuals can set their own hours and have more time with their families.

Companies that allow telecommuting experience several benefits, including increased productivity, lower real estate and travel costs, reduced employee absenteeism and turnover, increased work/life balance, improved morale, and access to additional labor pools. Telecommuting also helps improve the community by decreasing air pollutants, reducing traffic congestion, and lowering consumption of fossil fuels, which can give a company a green factor. Also, by having fewer employees commuting to work, the Reason Public Policy Institute estimates that approximately 350 lives are saved per year.[14] Of all the companies that give employees the option to telecommute or work from home, Cisco Systems is ranked number one with 70 percent of its employees classified as "regular" telecommuters.[15]

Spotlight
Getting a Life

Percentage of workers who plan to do these things to achieve a balance of home and work life.

Use all vacation time	Prioritize projects	Have weekly to-do list	Leave work at reasonable hour	Take lunch break consistently
49%	44%	42%	41%	36%

Source: Braun Research and Ketchum for FedEx Office, survey of 501 full-time U.S. workers conducted online, November 18–20, 2008.

part-time work permanent employment in which individuals work less than a standard work week

job sharing an arrangement whereby two people share one full-time position

telecommuting working at home all the time or for a portion of the work week

Part-time work. At Starbucks, part-time employees receive the same level of benefits as full-time employees.

Among the disadvantages to telecommuting are feelings of isolation, putting in longer hours, and being distracted by family or household responsibilities. In addition, some supervisors have difficulty monitoring productivity. Although most bosses say that they trust their staff to work from home, many think that home workers are work-shy and less productive than office-based staff. A survey conducted in the United Kingdom found that up to 38 percent of managers surveyed believe that home workers are less productive, and 22 percent think that working from home is an excuse for time off. In addition, some supervisors have difficulty monitoring productivity.[16]

Sun Microsystems, for example, is an industry leader at providing a virtual work environment. Approximately 80 percent of the company's 20,000-member workforce connects to the company remotely. Sun was awarded the Optimas Award for Global Outlook because of its new iWork Program that allows employees to connect to Sun all over the globe. The program has boosted employee satisfaction, reduced turnover, and saved the company $255 million on real estate over the past four years.[17]

Employee Empowerment

Many companies are increasing employee motivation and satisfaction through the use of empowerment. **Empowerment** means making employees more involved in their jobs and in the operations of the organization by increasing their participation in decision making. With empowerment, control no longer flows exclusively from the top levels of the organization downward. Empowered employees have a voice in what they do and how and when they do it. In some organizations, employees' input is restricted to individual choices, such as when to take breaks. In other companies, their responsibilities may encompass more far-reaching issues. For example, at Wegmans grocery stores, employees are empowered to ensure that the store achieves its primary objective: No customer leaves unhappy. Employees are allowed to make any concessions or decisions necessary to provide a good shopping experience. Anything is possible—from baking a family's Thanksgiving turkey in the store's oven to traveling to a customer's home to fix a botched order. Not only are Wegmans employees empowered to make on-the-spot customer-service decisions, but they also receive extensive training in the products they sell so as to guarantee that they can answer customers' questions about recipes, exotic items, and even food preparation.[18]

For empowerment to work effectively, management must be involved. Managers should set expectations, communicate standards, institute periodic evaluations, and

empowerment making employees more involved in their jobs by increasing their participation in decision making

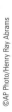

Do You Have What It Takes to Telecommute?

Is telecommuting right for you? Studies show that telecommuters are generally more satisfied and more productive than non-telecommuters. But before you arrange to work from home, ask yourself:

- *Do you have the motivation to work on your own for one or more days every week?* If you can gear up to tackle your tasks without constant supervision, telecommuting may be a good step for you. According to telecommuting expert Toby Johnson, "You have to wear multiple hats and have an entrepreneurial streak."
- *How will you stay in touch with your workplace?* "Communication is critical, and the onus is on you to ensure that out of sight doesn't mean out of mind," Johnson says. Be prepared to stay in contact via phone, fax, e-mail, or whatever methods your company requires or prefers. If you don't like taking the initiative or you don't like technology, you may not like telecommuting.
- *How will you know that you're doing a good job?* Some bosses look only at what telecommuters accomplish; others also expect telecommuters to work a certain number of hours every day. Either way, being a good telecommuter means getting things done on time.

Sources: Marci Alboher, "Your Own Map to Working from Home," *New York Times,* September 14, 2008, p. 12; Ann Meyer, "Telecommuting Is Working for Many," *Chicago Tribune,* September 8, 2008, www.chicagotribune.com; D. Schwartz and J. Chamberlin, "Employees Benefit from Flexible Hours, Telecommuting," *Monitor on Psychology,* January 1, 2008, p. 11.

guarantee follow-up. Effectively implemented, empowerment can lead to increased job satisfaction, improved job performance, higher self-esteem, and increased organizational commitment. Obstacles to empowerment include resistance on the part of management, distrust of management on the part of workers, insufficient training, and poor communication between management and employees.

Employee Ownership

Some organizations are discovering that a highly effective technique for motivating employees is **employee ownership**—that is, employees own the company they work for by virtue of being stockholders. Employee-owned businesses directly reward employees for success. When the company enjoys increased sales or lower costs, employees benefit directly. The National Center for Employee Ownership, an organization that studies employee-owned American businesses, reports that employee stock ownership plans (ESOPs) provide considerable employee incentive and increase employee involvement and commitment. In the United States today, about 8.5 million employees participate in 11,500 ESOPs and stock bonus plans.[19] As a means to motivate top executives and, frequently, middle-ranking managers who are working long days for what are generally considered poor salaries, some firms provide stock options as part of the employee compensation package. The option is simply the right to buy shares of the firm within a prescribed time at a set price. If the firm does well and its stock price rises past the set price (presumably because of all the work being done by the employee), the employee can exercise the option and immediately sell the stock and cash in on the company's success.

The difficulties of such companies as United Airlines have damaged the idea of employee ownership. United's ESOP has failed to solve problems between employees and management. In addition, Lowe's, the home-improvement retailer, recently stopped its long-running and mostly successful ESOP and transferred remaining money into 401(k) plans.

Teams and Teamwork

The concepts of teams and teamwork may be most commonly associated with sports, but they also are integral parts of business organizations. This organizational structure is popular because it encourages employees to participate more fully in business decisions. The growing number of companies organizing their

employee ownership a situation in which employees own the company they work for by virtue of being stockholders

Concept Check

1. What are the five steps of most MBO programs?

2. How can companies use job enrichment as a method for motivating employees?

3. What is behavior modification and how is it used in organizations?

4. What benefits does a company receive when using flextime, job sharing and telecommuting?

5. How do employee ownership and employee empowerment help in increasing employee motivation and satisfaction?

5 LEARNING OBJECTIVE

Understand the types, development, and uses of teams.

The Dark Side of Virtual Teamwork

Virtual teamwork has many benefits—but it can also have a dark side. The entire team's performance and morale can suffer if some members don't get their work done, don't meet deadlines, or don't communicate well with colleagues. There are ethical ways to counteract the dark side of virtual teamwork, however.

Implementing overall team guidelines is a fair and objective way to establish and enforce acceptable norms. For example, to prevent delays and communication gaps, the global energy company BP has companywide rules so virtual team members know how quickly they must reply to e-mails from their colleagues.

Another approach is to have team members collaborate in developing a charter that describes their group goals and the guidelines they commit to following. If possible, members should divide the work in such a way that they can progress at their own pace without holding back the entire team.

Finally, harness members' enthusiasm. Nokia, the international telecommunications firm, encourages employees to volunteer for virtual teams instead of being assigned. Why? When members ask to join a virtual team, they're more likely to be engaged and dedicated—important qualities for members of any type of team.

Sources: Amy Schurr, "Secrets to Virtual Team Success," *NetworkWorld*, October 7, 2008, www.networkworld.com; Lynda Gratton, "Working Together . . . When Apart," *Wall Street Journal*, June 16, 2007, p. R4; "Crash Course in . . . Managing a Virtual Team," *Management Today*, September 3, 2007, p. 20.

workforces into teams reflects an effort to increase employee productivity and creativity, because team members are working on specific goals and are given greater autonomy. This leads to greater job satisfaction as employees feel more involved in the management process.[20]

What Is a Team?

In a business organization, a **team** is a group of workers functioning together as a unit to complete a common goal or purpose. A team may be assigned any number of tasks or goals, from development of a new product to selling that product.[21] Jones Walker, a New Orleans–based law firm, assembled a team of business students, alumni, and faculty advisors from Harvard University to assist Mayor C. Ray Nagin's Bring New Orleans Back Commission.[22] While teamwork may seem like a simple concept learned on soccer or football fields, teams function as a microcosm of the larger organization, and it is important to understand the types, development, and general nature of teams.

Types of Teams

There are several types of teams within businesses that function in specific ways to achieve different purposes, including problem-solving teams, self-managed teams, cross-functional teams, and virtual teams.

Problem-Solving Teams

The most common type of team in business organizations is the **problem-solving team**. It is generally used temporarily in order to bring knowledgeable employees together to tackle a specific problem. Once the problem is solved, the team typically is disbanded.

In some extraordinary cases, an expert team may be needed to generate ground-breaking ideas. A **virtuoso team** consists of exceptionally highly skilled and talented individuals brought together to produce significant change. As with other kinds of problem-solving teams, virtuoso teams usually are assembled on a temporary basis. Instead of being task oriented, they focus on producing ideas and provoking change that could have an impact on the company and its industry. Because of the high skill level of their members, virtuoso teams can be difficult to manage. And unlike traditional teams, virtuoso teams place an emphasis on individuality over teamwork, which can cause further conflict. However, their conflicts usually are viewed as competitive and therefore productive in generating the most substantial ideas.[23]

Self-Managed Work Teams

Self-managed teams are groups of employees with the authority and skills to manage themselves. Experts suggest that workers on self-managed teams are more motivated and satisfied because they have more task variety and job control. On many work teams, members rotate through all the jobs for which the team is responsible. Some organizations cross-train the entire team so that everyone can perform everyone else's job. In a traditional business structure, management is responsible for hiring and firing employees, establishing budgets, purchasing supplies, conducting performance reviews, and taking corrective action. When self-managed teams are in place, they take over some or all of these management functions. Xerox, Procter & Gamble, Ferrari, as well as numerous other companies, have used self-managed teams successfully. The major advantages and disadvantages of self managed teams are mentioned in Figure 10.6.

team a group of workers functioning together as a unit to complete a common goal or purpose

problem-solving team a team of knowledgeable employees brought together to tackle a specific problem

virtuoso team a team of exceptionally highly skilled and talented individuals brought together to produce significant change

self-managed teams groups of employees with the authority and skills to manage themselves

FIGURE 10.6: Advantages and Disadvantages of Self-Managed Teams While self-managed teams provide benefits, managers must recognize their limitations.

ADVANTAGES	DISADVANTAGES
• Boosts employee morale	• Additional training costs
• Increases productivity	• Teams may be disorganized
• Aids innovation	• Conflicts may arise
• Reduces employee boredom	• Leadership role may be unclear

Cross-Functional Teams Traditionally, businesses have organized employees into departments based on a common function or specialty. However, increasingly, business organizations are faced with projects that require a diversity of skills not available within a single department. A **cross-functional team** consists of individuals with varying specialties, expertise, and skills that are brought together to achieve a common task. For example, a purchasing agent might create a cross-functional team with representatives from various departments to gain insight into useful purchases for the company. This structure avoids departmental separation and allows greater efficiency when there is a single goal. Although cross-functional teams aren't necessarily self-managed, most self-managed teams are cross-functional. They also can be cross-divisional, such as at Mercedes Benz, which assembles cross-functional teams to improve quality and cut costs in research and development. Instead of a single team per model, cross-functional teams will be developing standard parts to be used across different types of Mercedes' vehicles.[24] Cross-functional teams also can include a variety of people from outside the company, such as the cross-functional team of ergonomists, users, and university scientists that developed a new natural ergonomic keyboard for Microsoft.[25] Owing to their speed, flexibility, and increased employee satisfaction, it is likely that the use of cross-functional teams will increase.

Virtual Teams With the advent of sophisticated communications technology, it is no longer necessary for teams to be geographically close. A **virtual team** consists of members who are geographically dispersed but communicate electronically. In fact, team members may never meet in person but rely solely on e-mail, teleconferences, faxes, voice mail, and other technologic interactions. In the modern global environment, virtual teams connect employees on a common task across continents, oceans, time zones, and organizations. In some cases, the physical distances between participants and the lack of face-to-face interaction can be difficult when deadlines approach or communication is not clear.

Developing and Using Effective Teams

When a team is first developed, it takes time for the members to establish roles, relationships, delegation of duties, and other attributes of an effective team. As a team matures, it passes through five stages of development, as shown in Figure 10.7.

Forming In the first stage, *forming,* team members are introduced to one another and begin to develop a social dynamic. The members of the team are still unsure how to relate to one another, what behaviors are considered acceptable, and what the ground rules for the team are. Through group member interaction over time, team members become more comfortable, and a group dynamic begins to emerge.

Storming During the *storming* stage, the interaction may be volatile, and the team may lack unity. Because the team is still relatively new, this is the stage at which goals and objectives begin to develop. Team members will brainstorm to develop ideas and plans and establish a broad-ranging agenda. It is important at this stage

cross-functional team a team of individuals with varying specialties, expertise, and skills that are brought together to achieve a common task

virtual team a team consisting of members who are geographically dispersed but communicate electronically

FORMING
The team is new. Members get to know each other.

STORMING
The team may be volatile. Goals and objectives are developed.

NORMING
The team stabilizes. Roles and duties are accepted and recognized.

PERFORMING
The team is dynamic. Everyone makes a focused effort to accomplish goals.

ADJOURNING
The team is finished. The goals have been accomplished and the team is disbanded.

for team members to grow more comfortable around the others so that they can contribute openly. At this time, the leadership role likely will be formally undefined. A team member may emerge as the informal leader. The success or failure of the ideas in storming determines how long until the team reaches the next stage.

Norming After storming and the first large burst of activity, the team begins to stabilize during the *norming* stage. During this process, each person's role within the group starts to become apparent, and members begin to recognize the roles of others. A sense of unity will become stronger. If it hasn't already occurred, an identified leader will emerge. The group still may be somewhat volatile at this point and may regress back to the second stage if any conflict, especially over the leadership role, occurs.

Performing The fourth stage, *performing*, is when the team achieves its full potential. It is usually slow to develop and occurs when the team begins to focus strongly on the assigned task and away from team-development issues. The members of the team work in harmony under the established roles to accomplish the necessary goals.

Adjourning In the final stage, *adjourning*, the team is disbanded because the project has been completed. Team members may be reassigned to other teams or tasks. This stage does not always occur if the team is placed together for a task with no specific date of completion. For example, a marketing team for Best Buy may continue to develop promotional efforts for a store even after a specific promotional task has been accomplished. This stage is especially common in problem-solving teams that are dismantled after the assigned problem has been resolved.

Roles within a Team

Within any team, each member has a role to play in helping the team attain its objectives. Each of these roles adds important dimensions to team member interactions. The group member who pushes forward toward goals and places the objective first is playing the *task-specialist role* by concentrating fully on the assigned task. In a cross-functional team, this might be the person with the most expertise relating to the current task. The *socioemotional role* is played by the individual who supports and encourages the emotional needs of the other members. This person places the team members' personal needs over the task of the team. While this may sound unimportant, the socioemotional member's dedication to team cohesiveness will lead to greater unity and higher productivity. The leader of the team, and possibly others as well, will play a *dual role*. This dual role is a combination of both the socioemotional and task-specialist roles because this individual focuses on both the task and the team. The team leader might not always play a dual role, but the team is likely to be most successful when he or she does. Sometimes an individual assumes the *nonparticipant role*. This role behavior is characterized by a person who does not contribute to accomplishing the task and does not provide favorable input with respect to team members' socioemotional needs.

Team Cohesiveness

Developing a unit from a diverse group of personalities, specialties, backgrounds, and work styles can be challenging and complicated. In a cohesive team, the members get along and are able to accomplish their tasks effectively. There are factors that affect cohesiveness within a team. Teams generally are ideal when they contain five to twelve people. Fewer than five people is too few to accomplish tasks and generate a variety of ideas. More than twelve is too large because members do not develop relationships, may feel intimidated to speak, or may disconnect. It also may be beneficial to have team members introduce themselves and describe their past work experiences. This activity will foster familiarity and shared experiences. One of the most reliable ways to build cohesiveness within a team is through competition with other teams. When two teams are competing for a single prize or recognition, they are forced to put aside conflict and accomplish their goal. By adding an incentive to finishing the task, the team automatically becomes more goal oriented. Also, a favorable appraisal from an outsider may strengthen team cohesiveness. Since the team is being praised as a group, team members recognize their contribution as a unit. Teams are also more successful when goals have become agreed on. A team that is clear about its objective will focus more on accomplishing it. Frequent interaction also builds cohesiveness as relationships strengthen and familiarity increases.

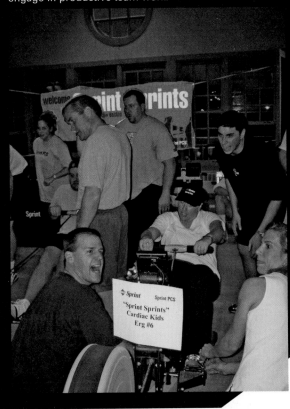

Team building. Employees at Sprint participate in team sports which helps them improve their overall ability to engage in productive team work.

Team Conflict and How to Resolve It

Conflict occurs when a disagreement arises between two or more team members. Conflict traditionally has been viewed as negative, but if handled properly, conflict can work to improve a team. For example, if two team members disagree about a certain decision, both may analyze the situation more closely to determine the best choice. As long as conflict is handled in a respectful and professional manner, it can improve the quality of work produced. If conflict turns hostile and affects the work environment, then steps must be taken to arrive at a suitable compromise. Compromises can be difficult in a business organization because neither party ends up getting everything he or she wants. The best solution is a middle-ground alternative in which each party is satisfied to some degree. It is best to avoid attempting to minimize or ignore conflicts within a group because this may cause the conflict to grow as members concentrate on the problem instead of the task. However the conflict is resolved, it is important to remember that conflict must be acknowledged if it is to be either resolved or serve a constructive purpose.

Benefits and Limitations of Teams

Teamwork within a company has been credited as a key to reducing turnover and costs and increasing production, quality, and customer service. There is also evidence that working in teams leads to higher levels of job satisfaction among employees and a harmonious work environment. Thus, an increasingly large number of companies are considering teams as a viable organizational structure. However, the process of reorganizing into teams can be stressful and time consuming with no guarantee that the team will develop effectively. If a team lacks cohesiveness and is unable to resolve conflict, the company may experience lower productivity.

©Susan Van Etten

Concept Check

1. What are the major types of teams?

2. Highlight some differences between cross functional teams and virtual teams?

3. Identify and describe the stages of team development.

4. How can team conflict be reduced?

5. What are some of the benefits and limitations of a team?

SUMMARY

1 Explain what motivation is.

Motivation is the individual internal process that energizes, directs, and sustains behavior. Motivation is affected by employee morale—that is, the employee's feelings about the job, superiors, and the firm itself. Motivation, morale, and job satisfaction are closely related.

2 Understand some major historical perspectives on motivation.

One of the first approaches to employee motivation was Frederick Taylor's scientific management, the application of scientific principles to the management of work and workers. Taylor believed that employees work only for money and that they must be closely supervised and managed. This thinking led to the piece-rate system, under which employees are paid a certain amount for each unit they produce. The Hawthorne Studies attempted to determine the effects of the work environment on productivity. Results of these studies indicated that human factors affect productivity more than do physical aspects of the workplace.

Maslow's hierarchy of needs suggests that people are motivated by five sets of needs. In ascending order of importance, these motivators are physiological, safety, social, esteem, and self-actualization needs. People are motivated by the lowest set of needs that remains unfulfilled. As needs at one level are satisfied, people try to satisfy needs at the next level.

Frederick Herzberg found that job satisfaction and dissatisfaction are influenced by two distinct sets of factors. Motivation factors, including recognition and responsibility, affect an employee's degree of satisfaction, but their absence does not necessarily cause dissatisfaction. Hygiene factors, including pay and working conditions, affect an employee's degree of dissatisfaction but do not affect satisfaction.

Theory X is a concept of motivation that assumes that employees dislike work and will function effectively only in a highly controlled work environment. Thus, to achieve an organization's goals, managers must coerce, control, and threaten employees. This theory generally is consistent with Taylor's scientific management. Theory Y is more in keeping with the results of the Hawthorne Studies and the human relations movement. It suggests that employees can be motivated to behave as responsible members of the organization. Theory Z emphasizes long-term employment, collective decision making, individual responsibility for the outcomes of decisions, informal control, and a holistic concern for employees. Reinforcement theory is based on the idea that people will repeat behavior that is rewarded and will avoid behavior that is punished.

3 Describe three contemporary views of motivation: equity theory, expectancy theory, and goal-setting theory.

Equity theory maintains that people are motivated to obtain and preserve equitable treatment for themselves. Expectancy theory suggests that our motivation depends on how much we want something and how likely we think we are to get it. Goal-setting theory suggests that employees are motivated to achieve a goal that they and their managers establish together.

4 Explain several techniques for increasing employee motivation.

Management by objectives (MBO) is a motivation technique in which managers and employees collaborate in setting goals. MBO motivates employees by getting them more involved in their jobs and in the organization as a whole. Job enrichment seeks to motivate employees by varying their tasks and giving them more responsibility for and control over their jobs. Job enlargement, expanding a worker's assignments to include additional tasks, is one aspect of job enrichment. Job redesign is a type of job enrichment in which work is restructured to improve the worker-job match.

Behavior modification uses reinforcement to encourage desirable behavior. Rewards for productivity, quality, and loyalty change employees' behavior in desired ways and also increase motivation.

Allowing employees to work more flexible hours is another way to build motivation and job satisfaction. Flextime is a system of work scheduling that allows workers to set their own hours as long as they fall within limits established by employers. Part-time work is permanent employment in which individuals work less than a standard work week. Job sharing is an arrangement whereby two people share one full-time position. Telecommuting allows employees to work at home all or part of the work week. All these types of work arrangements give employees more time outside the workplace to deal with family responsibilities or to enjoy free time.

Employee empowerment, self-managed work teams, and employee ownership are also techniques that boost employee motivation. Empowerment increases employees' involvement in their jobs by increasing their decision-making authority. Self-managed work teams are groups of employees with the authority and skills to manage themselves. When employees participate in ownership programs such as employee stock ownership plans (ESOPs), they have more incentive to make the company succeed and therefore work more effectively.

5 Understand the types, development, and uses of teams.

A large number of companies use teams to increase their employees' productivity. In a business organization, a team is a group of workers functioning together as a unit to complete a common goal or purpose.

There are several types of teams within businesses that function in specific ways to achieve different purposes. A problem-solving team is a team of knowledgeable employees brought together to tackle a specific problem. A virtuoso team is a team of highly skilled and talented individuals brought together to produce significant change. A virtual team is a team consisting of members who are geographically dispersed but communicate electronically. A cross-functional team is a team of individuals with varying specialties, expertise, and skills.

The five stages of team development are forming, storming, norming, performing, and adjourning. As a team develops, it should become more productive and unified. The four roles within teams are task specialist, socioemotional, dual, and nonparticipative. Each of these roles plays a specific part in the team's interaction. For a team to be successful, members must learn how to resolve and manage conflict so that the team can work cohesively to accomplish goals.

KEY TERMS

You should now be able to define and give an example relevant to each of the following terms:

motivation (261)
morale (262)
scientific management (262)
piece-rate system (262)
need (264)
Maslow's hierarchy of needs (264)
physiological needs (264)
safety needs (265)
social needs (265)
esteem needs (265)

self-actualization needs (265)
motivation-hygiene theory (266)
motivation factors (266)
hygiene factors (266)
Theory X (267)
Theory Y (267)
Theory Z (268)
reinforcement theory (268)
equity theory (269)
expectancy theory (270)

goal-setting theory (271)
management by objectives (MBO) (271)
job enrichment (272)
job enlargement (272)
job redesign (273)
behavior modification (273)
flextime (274)
part-time work (275)
job sharing (275)
telecommuting (275)

empowerment (276)
employee ownership (277)
team (278)
problem-solving team (278)
virtuoso team (278)
self-managed teams (278)
cross-functional team (279)
virtual team (279)

DISCUSSION QUESTIONS

1. How did the results of the Hawthorne Studies influence researchers' thinking about employee motivation?
2. What are the five sets of needs in Maslow's hierarchy? How are a person's needs related to motivation?
3. What are the two dimensions in Herzberg's theory? What kinds of elements affect each dimension?
4. According to equity theory, how does an employee determine whether he or she is being treated equitably?
5. According to expectancy theory, what two variables determine motivation?
6. Describe the steps involved in the MBO process.

7. What are the objectives of MBO? What do you think might be its disadvantages?
8. How does employee participation increase motivation?
9. Identify and describe the major types of teams.
10. What are the major benefits and limitations associated with the use of self-managed teams?
11. Explain the major stages of team development.
12. What combination of motivational techniques do you think would result in the best overall motivation and reward system?
13. In what ways are team cohesiveness and team conflict related?

Get Flash Cards, Quizzes, Games, Crosswords and more @ www.cengage.com/introbusiness/pride

Test Yourself

Matching Questions

1. _____ A force that causes people to behave in a particular way.
2. _____ Based on an assumption that people dislike work.
3. _____ Employees believe they will receive the rewards.
4. _____ When not provided, they become dissatisfiers.
5. _____ Needs that can be met by health care benefits.
6. _____ Promotions and rewards can fulfill these needs.

7. _____ Behavior that is rewarded is likely to be repeated.
8. _____ Employees become more involved in the decision-making process.
9. _____ Employees are given more variety and responsibility in their jobs.
10. _____ Groups that have more task variety and greater job control.

a. virtuoso teams
b. empowerment

Test Yourself

c. esteem needs

d. expectancy theory

e. hygiene factors

f. job enrichment

g. motivation

h. reinforcement theory

i. self-managed work teams

j. safety needs

k. Theory X

l. morale

True False Questions

11. **T F** Giving an employee recognition builds employee morale.

12. **T F** The Hawthorne Studies concluded that human factors were responsible for the results.

13. **T F** Maslow's higher-level needs are the easiest to satisfy.

14. **T F** MBO is an inflexible system that requires all goals to be met; if not, the employee is fired.

15. **T F** Theory Y is a set of assumptions that are consistent with the human relations movement.

16. **T F** Frederick W. Taylor made his most significant contribution to management practice by his involvement with the Hawthorne Studies.

17. **T F** According to the expectancy theory, motivation depends on how much we want something and how likely we think we are to get it.

18. **T F** Self-actualization needs are the most basic needs that Maslow discovered.

19. **T F** Herzberg's theory suggests that pay is a strong motivator.

20. **T F** A systematic program of reinforcement that encourages desirable behavior is called behavior modification.

Multiple-Choice Questions

21. _____ Herzberg cited _____ as a cause of dissatisfaction.

    a. working conditions

    b. promotions

    c. pay for special projects

    d. rewards

    e. challenging work

22. _____ According to Theory Y, which type of behavior would a supervisor expect from an employee?

    a. Delegate most of the work to others.

    b. Avoid working too hard.

    c. Spend time discussing job security.

    d. Ask to leave early several times a month.

    e. Seek opportunities to learn new skills.

23. _____ The idea that satisfaction and dissatisfaction are separate and distinct dimensions comes from which of the following theories?

    a. Frederick Herzberg's motivation-hygiene theory

    b. Maslow's hierarchy of needs

    c. Frederick Taylor's scientific management

    d. Reinforcement theory

    e. Hawthorne studies

24. _____ If Delta Airlines ticket agents discovered that they were being paid a lot less per ticket sold than Northwest Airlines ticket agents, we might expect the Delta ticket agents to

    a. increase their sales so that they will make as much as their Northwest peers.

    b. think their outcome-to-input ratios are lower than those of the Northwest ticket agents.

    c. have as a group very different personal needs than Northwest ticket agents.

    d. be very satisfied because they work for a great airline.

    e. feel that rewards are being distributed fairly and equitably.

25. _____ Randi Wood wants to become the best manager in the firm. She takes every available opportunity to learn new skills and improve her knowledge about management. Which need is Randi attempting to satisfy?

    a. Social

    b. Esteem

    c. Self-actualization

    d. Physiological

    e. Safety

26. _____ Developing an input-to-output ratio is the basis of the _____ theory.

    a. equity

    b. expectancy

    c. reward

    d. reinforcement

    e. quality circle

27. _____ Expectancy theory is difficult to apply, but it does provide several useful guidelines for managers. One such outcome that managers must realize is that

    a. everyone expects the same things.

    b. employees expect to be financially rewarded for hard work.

Test Yourself

c. employees work for a variety of reasons.

d. most employees tend to be unreasonable in their expectations.

e. managers need to use the authoritarian style to get tasks accomplished.

28. _____ Which of the following is a motivation technique that provides employees with more variety and responsibility in their jobs?

a. Job rotation

b. Job enrichment

c. Job redesign

d. Job evolution

e. Job analysis

29. _____ What stage of a team is usually slow to develop and occurs when the team begins to focus strongly on the assigned task and away from team-development issues?

a. Norming

b. Storming

c. Performing

d. Adjourning

e. Unifying

30. _____ The group member who pushes forward toward goals and places the objective first is playing the

a. task-specialist role.

b. socioemotional role.

c. nonparticipant role.

d. pusher role.

e. aggressor role.

Answers on p. TY-1

VIDEO CASE

American Flatbread Fires up Employees

George Schenk's passion is making work meaningful, sustainable, and personal. He learned about wood-fired cooking from his grandmother in Vermont and, years later, rekindled his love of it when he founded the American Flatbread Company. His company produces frozen wood-fired flatbread pizzas from all-natural, locally grown ingredients, handmade by 100 employees in Waitsfield and Middlebury, Vermont.

On Mondays, Tuesdays, Wednesdays, and Thursdays, two shifts of employees stoke the bakeries' wood-fired ovens to a temperature of 800°F and prepare the flatbreads. After the products are baked, frozen, and wrapped, they are shipped to grocery and specialty stores such as Whole Foods supermarkets. Both bakeries are transformed into casual pizza restaurants on Friday and Saturday nights, where diners sit in view of the gigantic ovens to enjoy salads and flatbreads. Schenk also has licensed American Flatbread's brand and wood-fired cooking methods to bakeries and restaurants in New England and in Los Alamos, California. One-third of American Flatbread's annual revenue comes from the licensing deals and restaurant receipts; the whole-sale frozen pizza operation contributes the remaining two-thirds.

Schenk's enthusiasm for wood-fired cooking is matched by his drive to build a business in which the work has long-term significance to both the employees and the community. Among American Flatbread's goals are to "create a pleasant, fulfilling, sustainable, and secure workplace" and "to trust one another and practice respectful relationships with everyone involved in this work."

Another goal mentioned in the mission statement is to be grateful, respectful, and forgiving—and to encourage the same in others. In line with this goal, Schenk has worked hard to avoid what he calls "founder's syndrome," the notion that the founder can do no wrong. Because Schenk is quick to admit he's not perfect, his managers and employees know they can speak up about their own mistakes and not lose the opportunity to try new things.

Jennifer Moffroid, the company's director of marketing, says Schenk has created an environment in which employees can do work in keeping with what they want for their lives. Making the work day fun is one of Schenk's priorities, as is making the workplace an inviting place to be. Moffroid also notes that Schenk not only delegates, but he also "empowers employees and celebrates their work." The company's seven senior managers are involved in decision making, and every suggestion is evaluated on its merit, not its source. "We're all in this together," Schenk says.

Since the beginning, American Flatbread has supported local food producers and given back to the community in a variety of ways. For example, the restaurants hold "benefit bakes" to raise money for causes such as public health clinics and habitat preservation. In turn, the community has come to the company's aid on more than one occasion. When flood waters inundated American Flatbread's bakery, people came from miles around to clean and rebuild the facility. Thanks to this outpouring of support, the bakery was able to reopen in only seven days. Without the help of the community, Schenk observes, the company might well have failed.

Today, the Vermont bakeries turn out 10,000 flatbreads every week; the California bakery produces another 4,000 for distribution in western states. The company now has its own Facebook page with news and images, and Schenk also keeps its values in the spotlight by writing a dedication for each week's menu. These dedications focus employees on what's important and provide "food for thought" for restaurant customers. Sharing values, being "a good neighbor," and building trusting, respectful relationships with stakeholders have enabled American Flatbread to keep employees happy and productive, minimize turnover, and strengthen financial performance.[26]

For more information about this company, go to **www.americanflatbread.com**.

Questions

1. Does George Schenk manage American Flatbread as a type A or a type Z firm? Support your answer.
2. Would you recommend that American Flatbread offer bakery and restaurant employees flextime arrangements? Why or why not?
3. How has George Schenk paved the way for empowerment at his company?

BUILDING SKILLS FOR CAREER SUCCESS

1. EXPLORING THE INTERNET

There are few employee incentives as motivating as owning "a piece of the action." Either through profit sharing or equity, many firms realize that the opportunity to share in the wealth generated by their effort is a primary force to drive employees toward better performance and a sense of ownership. The Foundation for Enterprise Development (www.fed.org/) is a nonprofit organization dedicated to helping entrepreneurs and executives use employee ownership and equity compensation as a fair and effective means of motivating the workforce and improving corporate performance. You can learn more about this approach at the foundation's website. Visit the text website for updates to this exercise.

Assignment

1. Describe the content and services provided by the Foundation for Enterprise Development through its website.
2. Do you agree with this orientation toward motivation of employees/owners, or does it seem contrived to you? Discuss.
3. How else might employees be motivated to improve their performance?

2. BUILDING TEAM SKILLS

By increasing employees' participation in decision making, empowerment makes workers feel more involved in their jobs and the operations of the organization. While empowerment may seem like a commonsense idea, it is a concept not found universally in the workplace. If you had empowerment in your job, how would you describe it?

Assignment

1. Use brainstorming to explore the concept of empowerment.
   a. Write each letter of the word *empowerment* in a vertical column on a sheet of paper or on the classroom chalkboard.
   b. Think of several words that begin with each letter.
   c. Write the words next to the appropriate letter.

2. Formulate a statement by choosing one word from each letter that best describes what empowerment means to you.
3. Analyze the statement.
   a. How relevant is the statement for you in terms of empowerment? Or empowerment in your workplace?
   b. What changes must occur in your workplace for you to have empowerment?
   c. How would you describe yourself as an empowered employee?
   d. What opportunities would empowerment give to you in your workplace?
4. Prepare a report of your findings.

3. RESEARCHING DIFFERENT CAREERS

Because a manager's job varies from department to department within firms, as well as among firms, it is virtually impossible to write a generic description of a manager's job. If you are contemplating becoming a manager, you may find it very helpful to spend time on the job with several managers learning first hand what they do.

Assignment

1. Make an appointment with managers in three firms, preferably firms of different sizes. When you make the appointments, request a tour of the facilities.
2. Ask the managers the following questions:
   a. What do you do in your job?
   b. What do you like most and least about your job? Why?
   c. What skills do you need in your job?
   d. How much education does your job require?
   e. What advice do you have for someone thinking about pursuing a career in management?
3. Summarize your findings in a two-page report. Include answers to these questions:
   a. Is management a realistic field of study for you? Why?
   b. What might be a better career choice? Why?

Inside the People Business at Finagle A Bagel

People are a vital ingredient in Finagle A Bagel's recipe for success. In fact, careful attention to human resources management has enabled Finagle A Bagel to continue expanding its market share without spending money on advertising. Low work force turnover means less money and time spent on recruiting and training—an important financial consideration for a fast-growing business. It also means that Finagle A Bagel has the human resources strength to combine super service with fresh food for a distinctive competitive advantage in a crowded marketplace.

The Right People in the Right Place

A sizable number of Finagle A Bagel's managers and employees (including Robertson) were hired years ago and became so excited about the product, the company, and the customers that they simply stayed. Many remain with Finagle A Bagel because they prefer the more personal atmosphere of a 320-employee business over the relatively faceless anonymity of a gigantic corporation. "It's really unusual to have one-on-one interaction on a daily basis with the president of the company or any senior executive member of the company," Robertson states. "Our cashiers, our café attendants, our bakers, and our managers know they can pick up the phone at any point and call anybody here and say, 'Here's my problem. How do I fix it?' or 'I need your help.' The size of our company allows us to do that, and the culture of the company encourages that."

Because bagels are an integral part of every menu item, employees who join Finagle A Bagel must "love" bagels, regardless of any other skills or experiences they bring to their jobs. When Robertson advertises to fill an open position in Finagle A Bagel's headquarters, for example, she always mentions this requirement.

Different Kinds of Managers for Different Locations

Alan Litchman, Finagle A Bagel's copresident, says that selecting a candidate to manage one of the Boston stores is easier than selecting one for a suburban store. Given the inner-city location of the company's support center, he or another executive can get to the Boston stores more quickly if a problem arises. Moreover, the city stores compete by providing speedy, accurate service to busy customers who have little time to waste waiting in line. Paulo Pereira, general manager of the Harvard Square store in Cambridge, has become an expert at squeezing inefficiencies from the city stores so that customers are in and out more quickly. By increasing the number of customers served each day and slashing the number of bagels left over at closing, Pereira boosts both sales revenues and profits.

When selecting a manager for a suburban store, Litchman looks for people with an "owner-operator mentality" who have the drive, initiative, and know-how to build business locally. His message to a potential general manager is: "If you want to be a franchisee but don't have the capital, or if you want to own your own business, we're going to put you in business. You

don't have to give us any money to do that. And if your store achieves more than a certain level of sales or profits, we'll start splitting the bottom line with you in a bonus program."

Hiring and Motivating Store Personnel

General managers are responsible for recruiting, interviewing, hiring, training, motivating, and evaluating store-level personnel. They assign job responsibilities according to the skills and strengths of each manager and employee, but they also expect everyone to work as a team during extremely busy periods. In addition to motivating general managers by offering bonuses based on meeting revenue and profit goals, Finagle A Bagel encourages crew members to take advantage of extra training and internal promotions.

"In a company our size," stresses co-president Laura Trust, "there is always opportunity. You just have to find the right fit for the individual." In fact, says her husband, "The best supervisors, coordinators, assistant managers, or managers in any unit—by far—are the ones who have started with us at a lower level and worked their way up."

Diverse Work Force, Family Business

Finagle A Bagel has an extremely diverse work force made up of people originally from Latin America, Europe, western Africa, and many other areas. Over the years, the company has served as a sponsor for new Americans who need government-issued work permits so that they can legally remain in the United States for work reasons. Despite diversity's many advantages—including creativity, flexibility, and the ability to relate to a broader customer base—it also can create communications challenges when English is not an employee's native language. To avoid confusion, Litchman and Trust insist that employees speak only in English when addressing customers.

As a small, family-run business, Finagle A Bagel sees its work force as a group of unique individuals, not interchangeable cogs in an impersonal corporate machine. Trust feels strongly that "there's a responsibility that you have to your employees and to your colleagues. These people work for you—they work hard to try and move your company forward—and their efforts need to be recognized."

Questions

1. What effect has diversity had on Finagle A Bagel?
2. If you were the general manager of a downtown Finagle A Bagel store, what job description and job specification would you prepare for a cashier? Based on these, what kinds of questions would you ask when interviewing candidates for this position?
3. Which of Herzberg's motivation factors are Trust and Litchman emphasizing for general managers?
4. Would it be feasible for Finagle A Bagel to apply the concept of flextime to store employees? To senior managers at the headquarters facility? Explain.

©Barbara Helgason

In this section of your business plan you will expand on the type and quantity of employees that will be required to operate the business. Your human resources requirements are determined by the type of business and by the size and scale of your operation. From the preceding section, you should have a good idea of how many people you will need. And Part 4 of your textbook, "Human Resources," especially Chapters 10 and 11, should help you in answering some of the questions in this part of the business plan.

THE HUMAN RESOURCES COMPONENT

To ensure successful performance by employees, you must inform workers of their specific job requirements. Employees must know what is expected on the job, and they are entitled to expect regular feedback on their work. It is vital to have a formal job description and job specification for every position in your business. Also, you should establish procedures for evaluating performance.

The labor force component should include the answers to at least the following questions:

4.1. How many employees will you require, and what are their qualifications—including skills, experience, and knowledge? How many jobs will be full time? Part time?

4.2. Will you have written job descriptions for each position?

4.3. Have you prepared a job-application form? Do you know what can legally be included in it?

4.4. What criteria will you use in selecting employees?

4.5. Have you made plans for the orientation process?

4.6. Who will do the training?

4.7. What can you afford to pay in wages and salaries? Is this in line with the going rate in your region and industry?

4.8. Who will evaluate your employees?

4.9. Will you delegate any authority to employees?

4.10. Have you developed a set of disciplinary rules?

4.11. Do you plan to interview employees when they resign?

REVIEW OF BUSINESS PLAN ACTIVITIES

Remember that your employees are the most valuable and important resource. Therefore, make sure that you expend a great deal of effort to acquire and make full use of this resource. Check and resolve any issues in this component of your business plan before beginning Part 5. Again, make sure that your answers to the questions in each part are consistent with the entire business plan. Finally, write a brief statement that summarizes all the information for this part of the business plan.

11 Building Customer Relationships through Effective Marketing

WHY THIS CHAPTER MATTERS. Marketers are concerned about building long-term customer relationships. To develop competitive product offerings, business people must identify acceptable target customer groups and understand their behaviors.

©Christian Wheatley/Shutterstock

LEARNING OBJECTIVES

1 Understand the meaning of *marketing* and the importance of management of customer relationships.

2 Explain how marketing adds value by creating several forms of utility.

3 Trace the development of the marketing concept and understand how it is implemented.

4 Understand what markets are and how they are classified.

5 Identify the four elements of the marketing mix and be aware of their importance in developing a marketing strategy.

6 Explain how the marketing environment affects strategic market planning.

7 Understand the major components of a marketing plan.

8 Describe how market measurement and sales forecasting are used.

9 Distinguish between a marketing information system and marketing research.

10 Identify the major steps in the consumer buying decision process and the sets of factors that may influence this process.

Get Flash Cards, Quizzes, Games, Crosswords and more @ www.cengage.com/introbusiness/pride

How Kimberly-Clark Builds Customer Loyalty

Kimberly-Clark has built a $19 billion empire marketing household and hygiene products such as tissues, paper towels, disposable diapers, and disposable hospital gowns—essentials that people need day in and day out, no matter what the economic climate. Founded as a Midwestern paper company during the 1860s, the company has grown into a multinational firm with 53,000 employees and a presence in 80 countries. Today, it markets such well-known brands as Kleenex, Viva, Huggies, and Scott to consumers and institutional customers.

Household and hygiene products are a marketing battleground, with Kimberly-Clark facing aggressive competition from Procter & Gamble, Georgia Pacific, and other major corporations. That's why the company's marketing plan calls for studying consumer behavior and influencing how people think about, talk about, and shop for its brands. For example, Kimberly-Clark's researchers have examined the ways in which consumers make brand decisions before and during shopping trips. Finding that consumers often make buying decisions at the point-of-sale, the company now supports product introductions with eye-catching store displays and free samples to encourage trial.

Although Kimberly-Clark is a heavy user of television, print, and direct mail advertising, it also reaches out to customers through online marketing. Its ScottCommonSense website has 600,000 brand fans who swap household cleaning and organizing tips, check out the latest Scott products, and download special offers. When the company introduced Huggies Pure & Natural disposable diapers, it set up a special website and invited consumers to register to receive free samples and product information. In the first four days, the site attracted more than 200,000 sample requests.

In the past, Kimberly-Clark has operated programs to reward consumers for their loyalty in buying its products. It recently added a new program that allows parents to earn points toward prizes for watching online videos about Huggies products, referring friends to the Huggies site, answering survey questions, and taking online quizzes about Huggies products. Parents "gain valuable information and offers," explains the senior brand manager, "and we can learn from their opinions."[1]

DID YOU KNOW?

Kimberly-Clark rings up $19 billion in annual worldwide sales by influencing how customers think about, talk about, and shop for its brands, which include Kleenex, Viva, Huggies, and Scott.

Numerous organizations, like Kimberly-Clark, use marketing efforts to provide customer satisfaction and value. Understanding customers' needs, such as "what's cool," is crucial to providing customer satisfaction. Although marketing encompasses a diverse set of decisions and activities performed by individuals and by both business and nonbusiness organizations, marketing always begins and ends with the customer. The American Marketing Association defines **marketing** as "The activity, set of institutions, and processes for creating, communicating, delivering, and exchanging offerings that have value for customers, clients, partners, and society at large."[2] The marketing process involves eight major functions and numerous related activities (see Table 11.1). All these functions are essential if the marketing process is to be effective.

In this chapter, we examine marketing activities that add value to products. We trace the evolution of the marketing concept and describe how organizations practice it. Next, our focus shifts to market classifications and marketing strategy. We analyze the four elements of a marketing mix and also discuss uncontrollable factors in the marketing environment. Then we examine the major components of a marketing plan. We consider tools for strategic market planning, including market measurement, sales forecasts, marketing information systems, and marketing research. Last, we look at the forces that influence consumer and organizational buying behavior.

marketing the activity, set of institutions, and processes for creating, communicating, delivering, and exchanging offerings that have value for customers, clients, partners, and society at large

TABLE 11.1: Major Marketing Functions

Exchange functions: All companies—manufacturers, wholesalers, and retailers—buy and sell to market their merchandise.

1. **Buying** includes obtaining raw materials to make products, knowing how much merchandise to keep on hand, and selecting suppliers.

2. **Selling** creates possession utility by transferring the title of a product from seller to customer.

Physical distribution functions: These functions involve the flow of goods from producers to customers. Transportation and storage provide time utility and place utility and require careful management of inventory.

3. **Transporting** involves selecting a mode of transport that provides an acceptable delivery schedule at an acceptable price.

4. **Storing** goods is often necessary to sell them at the best selling time.

Facilitating functions: These functions help the other functions take place.

5. **Financing** helps at all stages of marketing. To buy raw materials, manufacturers often borrow from banks or receive credit from suppliers. Wholesalers may be financed by manufacturers, and retailers may receive financing from the wholesaler or manufacturer. Finally, retailers often provide financing to customers.

6. **Standardizing** sets uniform specifications for products or services. Grading classifies products by size and quality, usually through a sorting process. Together, standardization and grading facilitate production, transportation, storage, and selling.

7. **Risk taking**—even though competent management and insurance can minimize risks—is a constant reality of marketing because of such losses as bad-debt expense, obsolescence of products, theft by employees, and product-liability lawsuits.

8. **Gathering market information** is necessary for making all marketing decisions.

---

relationship marketing establishing long-term, mutually satisfying buyer-seller relationships

customer relationship management (CRM) using information about customers to create marketing strategies that develop and sustain desirable customer relationships

Managing Customer Relationships

1 LEARNING OBJECTIVE

Understand the meaning of marketing and the importance of management of customer relationships.

Marketing relationships with customers are the lifeblood of all businesses. Maintaining positive relationships with customers is an important goal for marketers. The term **relationship marketing** refers to "marketing decisions and activities focused on achieving long-term, satisfying relationships with customers." Relationship marketing continually deepens the buyer's trust in the company, which, as the customer's loyalty grows, increases a company's understanding of the customer's needs and desires. Successful marketers respond to customer needs and strive to continually increase value to buyers over time. Eventually, this interaction becomes a solid relationship that allows for cooperation and mutual trust. For example, Chico's, a specialty women's retailer, offers a Passport Program that gives members such benefits as monthly coupons, free shipping, and 5 percent off all future purchases. Once a customer has spent over $500 on Chico's merchandise with a Preliminary Passport card, they are eligible to be a member of the Passport Program. Borders likewise offers Borders Rewards, a card-based system that provides incentives for frequent shoppers. Such initiatives give stores the opportunity to build stronger relationships with customers.[3]

To build long-term customer relationships, marketers increasingly are turning to marketing research and information technology. **Customer relationship management (CRM)** focuses on using information about customers to create

Concept Check

1. How can technology help to build long-term customer relationships?

2. What are the benefits of retaining customers?

Building long-term customer relationships. Airlines, like many other organizations, spend considerable resources to develop and maintain long-term customer relationships

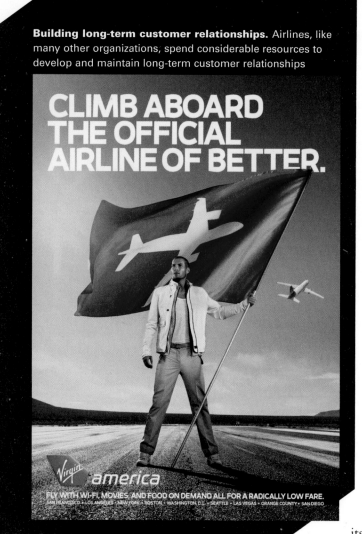

CLIMB ABOARD
THE OFFICIAL
AIRLINE OF BETTER.

virgin america

FLY WITH WI-FI, MOVIES, AND FOOD ON DEMAND ALL FOR A RADICALLY LOW FARE.
SAN FRANCISCO · LOS ANGELES · NEW YORK · BOSTON · WASHINGTON, D.C. · SEATTLE · LAS VEGAS · ORANGE COUNTY · SAN DIEGO

marketing strategies that develop and sustain desirable customer relationships. By increasing customer value over time, organizations try to retain and increase long-term profitability through customer loyalty.[4]

Managing customer relationships requires identifying patterns of buying behavior and using that information to focus on the most promising and profitable customers.[5] Companies must be sensitive to customers' requirements and desires and establish communication to build customers' trust and loyalty. In some instances, it may be more profitable for a company to focus on satisfying a valuable existing customer than to attempt to attract a new one who may never develop the same level of loyalty. This involves determining how much the customer will spend over his or her lifetime. The **customer lifetime value** is a combination of purchase frequency, average value of purchases, and brand-switching patterns over the entire span of a customer's relationship with a company.[6] However, there are also intangible benefits of retaining lifetime-value customers, such as their ability to provide feedback to a company and referring new customers of similar value. The amount of money a company is willing to spend to retain such customers is also a factor. In general, when marketers focus on customers chosen for their lifetime value, they earn higher profits in future periods than when they focus on customers selected for other reasons.[7] Because the loss of a potential lifetime customer can result in lower profits, managing customer relationships has become a major focus of marketers.

PR NewsFoto/Virgin Atlantic

Utility: The Value Added by Marketing

Explain how marketing adds value by creating several forms of utility.

customer lifetime value a combination of purchase frequency, average value of purchases, and brand-switching patterns over the entire span of a customer's relationship with a company

utility the ability of a good or service to satisfy a human need

form utility utility created by people converting raw materials, finances, and information into finished products

place utility utility created by making a product available at a location where customers wish to purchase it

As defined in Chapter 8, **utility** is the ability of a good or service to satisfy a human need. A lunch at a Pizza Hut, an overnight stay at a Holiday Inn, and a Mercedes S500L all satisfy human needs. Thus, each possesses utility. There are four kinds of utility.

Form utility is created by people converting raw materials, finances, and information into finished products. Marketing efforts may influence form utility indirectly because the data gathered as part of marketing research frequently are used to determine the size, shape, and features of a product.

The three kinds of utility that are created directly by marketing are place, time, and possession utility. **Place utility** is created by making a product available at a location where customers wish to purchase it. A pair of shoes is given place utility when it is shipped from a factory to a department store.

Time utility is created by making a product available when customers wish to purchase it. For example, Halloween costumes may be manufactured in April but not displayed until late September, when consumers start buying them. By storing the costumes until they are wanted, the manufacturer or retailer provides time utility.

Possession utility is created by transferring title (or ownership) of a product to a buyer. For a product as simple as a pair of shoes, ownership usually is transferred by means of a sales slip or receipt. For such products as automobiles and homes, the transfer of title is a more complex process. Along with the title to its products, the seller transfers the right to use that product to satisfy a need (see Figure 11.1).

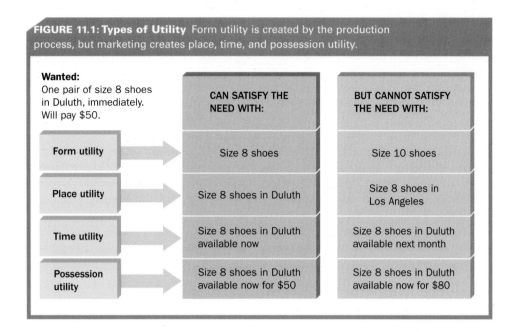

FIGURE 11.1: Types of Utility Form utility is created by the production process, but marketing creates place, time, and possession utility.

Wanted:
One pair of size 8 shoes in Duluth, immediately. Will pay $50.

	CAN SATISFY THE NEED WITH:	BUT CANNOT SATISFY THE NEED WITH:
Form utility	Size 8 shoes	Size 10 shoes
Place utility	Size 8 shoes in Duluth	Size 8 shoes in Los Angeles
Time utility	Size 8 shoes in Duluth available now	Size 8 shoes in Duluth available next month
Possession utility	Size 8 shoes in Duluth available now for $50	Size 8 shoes in Duluth available now for $80

Place, time, and possession utility have real value in terms of both money and convenience. This value is created and added to goods and services through a wide variety of marketing activities—from research indicating what customers want to product warranties ensuring that customers get what they pay for. Overall, these marketing activities account for about half of every dollar spent by consumers. When they are part of an integrated marketing program that delivers maximum utility to the customer, many would agree that they are worth the cost.

Place, time, and possession utility are only the most fundamental applications of marketing activities. In recent years, marketing activities have been influenced by a broad business philosophy known as the *marketing concept.*

The Marketing Concept

The **marketing concept** is a business philosophy that a firm should provide goods and services that satisfy customers' needs through a coordinated set of activities that allows the firm to achieve its objectives. Thus, initially, the firm must communicate with potential customers to assess their product needs. Then the firm must develop a good or service to satisfy those needs. Finally, the firm must continue to seek ways to provide customer satisfaction. This process is an application of the marketing concept, or marketing orientation. Ben & Jerry's, for example, constantly assesses customer demand for ice cream and sorbet. On its website, it maintains a "flavor graveyard" listing combinations that were tried and ultimately failed. It also notes its top ten flavors each month. Thus, the marketing concept emphasizes that marketing begins and ends with customers.

Evolution of the Marketing Concept

From the start of the Industrial Revolution until the early twentieth century, business effort was directed mainly toward the production of goods. Consumer demand for manufactured products was so great that manufacturers could almost bank on selling everything they produced. Business had a strong *production orientation,* in which emphasis was placed on increased output and production efficiency. Marketing was limited to taking orders and distributing finished goods.

In the 1920s, production caught up with and began to exceed demand. Now producers had to direct their efforts toward selling goods rather than just producing goods that consumers readily bought. This new *sales orientation* was characterized by increased advertising, enlarged sales forces, and occasion-

3 LEARNING OBJECTIVE

Trace the development of the marketing concept and understand how it is implemented.

time utility utility created by making a product available when customers wish to purchase it

possession utility utility created by transferring title (or ownership) of a product to a buyer

marketing concept a business philosophy that a firm should provide goods and services that satisfy customers' needs through a coordinated set of activities that allows the firm to achieve its objectives ally, high-pressure selling techniques. Manufacturers produced the goods they expected consumers to want, and marketing consisted primarily of promoting products through personal selling and advertising, taking orders, and delivering goods.

During the 1950s, however, businesspeople started to realize that even enormous advertising expenditures and the most thoroughly proven sales techniques were not enough. Something else was needed if products were to sell as well as expected. It was then that business managers recognized that they were not primarily producers or sellers but rather were in the business of satisfying customers' needs. Marketers realized that the best approach was to adopt a customer orientation—in other words, the organization had to first determine what customers need and then develop goods and services to fill those particular needs (see Table 11.2).

All functional areas—research and development (R&D), production, finance, human resources, and of course, marketing—are viewed as playing a role in providing customer satisfaction.

Implementing the Marketing Concept

The marketing concept has been adopted by many of the most successful business firms. Some firms, such as Ford Motor Company and Apple Computer, have gone through minor or major reorganizations in the process. Because the marketing concept is essentially a business philosophy, anyone can say, "I believe in it." To make it work, however, management must fully adopt and then implement it.

To implement the marketing concept, a firm first must obtain information about its present and potential customers. The firm must determine not only what customers' needs are but also how well those needs are being satisfied by products currently on the market—both its own products and those of competitors. It must ascertain how its products might be improved and what opinions customers have about the firm and its marketing efforts.

The firm then must use this information to pinpoint the specific needs and potential customers toward which it will direct its marketing activities and resources. (Obviously, no firm can expect to satisfy all needs. And not every individual or firm can be considered a potential customer for every product manufactured or sold by a firm.) Next, the firm must mobilize its marketing resources to (1) provide a product that will satisfy its customers, (2) price the product at a level that is acceptable to buyers and that will yield an acceptable profit, (3) promote the product so that potential customers will be aware of its existence and its ability to satisfy their needs, and (4) ensure that the product is distributed so that it is available to customers where and when needed.

Finally, the firm again must obtain marketing information—this time regarding the effectiveness of its efforts. Can the product be improved? Is it being promoted properly? Is it being distributed efficiently? Is the price too high or too low? The firm must be ready to modify any or all of its marketing activities based on information about its customers and competitors. Toyota, for example, has taken the lead in

TABLE 11.2: Evolution of Customer Orientation Business managers recognized that they were not primarily producers or sellers but rather were in the business of satisfying customers' needs.

Production Orientation	Sales Orientation	Customer Orientation
Take orders	Increase advertising	Determine customer needs
Distribute goods	Enlarge sales force	Develop products to fill these needs
	Intensify sales techniques	Achieve the organization's goals

What do customers want? Albertson's conducts customer surveys to help this company find out what customers want.

the American automotive industry through its promise of high-quality yet sensible cars. But Toyota isn't satisfied with producing practical cars and is launching a new campaign to make consumers passionate about its product. Toyota is revamping its relationship with customers by forgoing traditional advertising and bringing its cars straight to the consumer. The Toyota Camry, the no. 1 selling car in America, is being redesigned to integrate a flashier grill and a sportier body to add fun to its proven quality. When the hybrid version of the new Camry debuts, Toyota will team up with medical doctors to promote the vehicle as asthma friendly. Toyota will test out its new FJ Cruiser sport-utility vehicle (SUV) at off-road and trail events instead of using more traditional television advertising. As for its truck line, Toyota will focus on fishing and hunting events.[8]

Markets and Their Classification

A **market** is a group of individuals or organizations, or both, that need products in a given category and that have the ability, willingness, and authority to purchase such products. The people or organizations must want the product. They must be able to purchase the product by exchanging money, goods, or services for it. They must be willing to use their buying power. Finally, they must be socially and legally authorized to purchase the product.

Markets are broadly classified as consumer or business-to-business markets. These classifications are based on the characteristics of the individuals and organizations within each market. Because marketing efforts vary depending on the intended market, marketers should understand the general characteristics of these two groups.

Consumer markets consist of purchasers and/or household members who intend to consume or benefit from the purchased products and who do not buy products to make profits. *Business-to-business markets*, also called *industrial markets*, are grouped broadly into producer, reseller, governmental, and institutional categories. These markets purchase specific kinds of products for use in making other products for resale or for day-to-day operations. *Producer markets* consist of individuals and business organizations that buy certain products to use in the manufacture of other products. *Reseller markets* consist of intermediaries such as wholesalers and retailers

Concept Check

1. Identify the major components of the marketing concept.

2. How did the customer orientation evolve?

3. What steps are involved when implementing the marketing concept?

4 LEARNING OBJECTIVE

Understand what markets are and how they are classified.

market a group of individuals or organizations, or both, that need products in a given category and that have the ability, willingness, and authority to purchase such products that buy finished products and sell them for a profit. *Governmental markets* consist of federal, state, county, and local governments. They buy goods and services to maintain internal operations and to provide citizens with such products as highways, education, water, energy, and national defense. Governmental purchases total billions of dollars each year. *Institutional markets* include churches, not-for-profit private schools and hospitals, civic clubs, fraternities and sororities, charitable organizations, and foundations. Their goals are different from such typical business goals as profit, market share, or return on investment.

Developing Marketing Strategies

A **marketing strategy** is a plan that will enable an organization to make the best use of its resources and advantages to meet its objectives. A marketing strategy consists of (1) the selection and analysis of a target market and (2) the creation and maintenance of an appropriate **marketing mix**, a combination of product, price, distribution, and promotion developed to satisfy a particular target market.

Target Market Selection and Evaluation

marketing strategy a plan that will enable an organization to make the best use of its resources and advantages to meet its objectives

marketing mix a combination of product, price, distribution, and promotion developed to satisfy a particular target market

target market a group of individuals or organizations, or both, for which a firm develops and maintains a marketing mix suitable for the specific needs and preferences of that group

A **target market** is a group of individuals or organizations, or both, for which a firm develops and maintains a marketing mix suitable for the specific needs and preferences of that group. In selecting a target market, marketing managers examine potential markets for their possible effects on the firm's sales, costs, and profits. The managers attempt to determine whether the organization has the resources to produce a marketing mix that meets the needs of a particular target market and whether satisfying those needs is consistent with the firm's overall objectives. They also analyze the strengths and numbers of competitors already marketing to people in this target market. Marketing managers may define a target market as a vast number of people or a relatively small group. Rolls-Royce, for example, targets its automobiles toward a small, very exclusive market: wealthy people who want the ultimate in prestige in an automobile. Other companies target multiple markets with different products, prices, distribution systems, and promotion for each one. Nike uses this strategy, marketing different types of shoes to meet specific needs

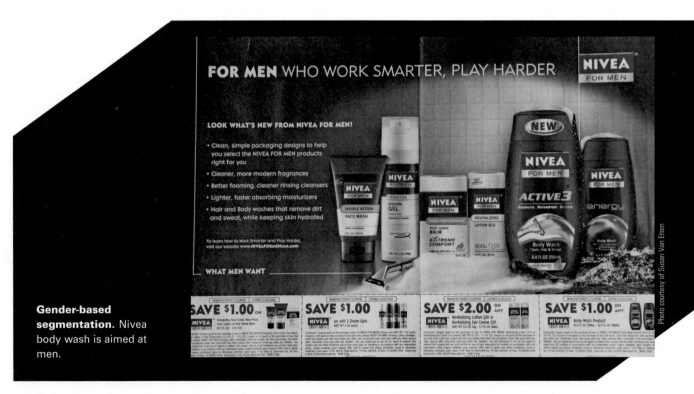

Gender-based segmentation. Nivea body wash is aimed at men.

of cross-trainers, rock climbers, basketball players, aerobics enthusiasts, and other athletic-shoe buyers. When selecting a target market, marketing managers generally take either the undifferentiated approach or the market segmentation approach.

Undifferentiated Approach A company that designs a single marketing mix and directs it at the entire market for a particular product is using an **undifferentiated approach** (see Figure 11.2). This approach assumes that individual customers in the target market for a specific kind of product have similar needs and that the organization therefore can satisfy most customers with a single marketing mix. This single marketing mix consists of one type of product with little or no variation, one price, one promotional program aimed at everyone, and one distribution system to reach all customers in the total market. Products that can be marketed successfully with the undifferentiated approach include staple food items, such as sugar and salt, and certain kinds of farm produce. An undifferentiated approach is useful in only a limited number of situations because for most product categories, buyers have different needs. When customers' needs vary, a company should use the market segmentation approach.

Market Segmentation Approach A firm that is marketing forty-foot yachts would not direct its marketing effort toward every person in the total boat market. Some might want a sailboat or a canoe. Others might want a speedboat or an outboard-powered fishing boat. Still others might be looking for something resembling a small ocean liner. Marketing efforts directed toward such boat buyers would be wasted.

Instead, the firm would direct its attention toward a particular portion, or *segment*, of the total market for boats. A **market segment** is a group of individuals or organizations within a market that shares one or more common characteristics. The process of dividing a market into segments is called **market segmentation**. As shown in Figure 11.2, there are two types of market-segmentation approaches: concentrated and differentiated. When an organization uses *concentrated* market segmentation, a single marketing mix is directed at a single market segment. If *differentiated* market segmentation is employed, multiple marketing mixes are focused on multiple market segments.

In our boat example, one common characteristic, or *basis*, for segmentation might be "end use of a boat." The firm would be interested primarily in that market segment whose uses for a boat could lead to the purchase of a forty-foot yacht. Another basis for segmentation might be income; still another might be geographic location. Each of these variables can affect the type of boat an individual might purchase. When choosing a basis for segmentation, it is important to select a characteristic that relates to differences in people's needs for a product. The yacht producer, for example, would not use religion to segment the boat market because people's needs for boats do not vary based on religion.

Marketers use a wide variety of segmentation bases. Those bases most commonly applied to consumer markets are shown in Table 11.3. Each may be used as a single basis for market segmentation or in combination with other bases. Best Buy has used multiple bases for market segmentation, catering to customers based on their specific issues. The company classified its most profitable customers into one of four typologies: Ray (price-conscious family guy), Buzz (young gadget fiend), Barry (affluent tech enthusiast), or Jill (busy suburban mom) and then began retooling each of its stores to target one or more of the typologies based on marketing research and demographics. Stores that tar-

undifferentiated approach directing a single marketing mix at the entire market for a particular product

market segment a group of individuals or organizations within a market that shares one or more common characteristics

market segmentation the process of dividing a market into segments and directing a marketing mix at a particular segment or segments rather than at the total market

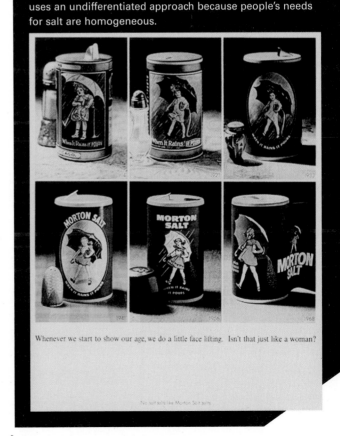

Undifferentiated approach. The producer of Morton Salt uses an undifferentiated approach because people's needs for salt are homogeneous.

Whenever we start to show our age, we do a little face lifting. Isn't that just like a woman?

FIGURE 11.2: General Approaches for Selecting Target Markets The undifferentiated approach assumes that individual customers have similar needs and that most customers can be satisfied with a single marketing mix. When customers' needs vary, the market segmentation approach—either concentrated or differentiated—should be used.

UNDIFFERENTIATED APPROACH

Organization → **Single marketing mix** (Product, Price, Distribution, Promotion) → **Target market**

```
A A A A A
A A A A A
A A A A A
A A A A A
A A A A A
A A A A A
A A A A A
```

CONCENTRATED MARKET SEGMENTATION APPROACH

Organization → **Single marketing mix** (Product, Price, Distribution, Promotion) → **Target market**

```
A A A A A
A A A A A A
A A A A A
B B B B B B
B B B B B
B B B B B
C C C C C
C C C C C
C C C C C
```

DIFFERENTIATED MARKET SEGMENTATION APPROACH

Organization → **Marketing mix I** (Product, Price, Distribution, Promotion) and **Marketing mix II** (Product, Price, Distribution, Promotion) → **Target markets**

```
A A A A A
A A A A A
A A A A A
B B B B B B
B B B B B
B B B B B
C C C C C
C C C C C
C C C C C
```

NOTE: The letters in each target market represent potential customers. Customers that have the same letters have similar characteristics and similar product needs.

Source: William M. Pride and O. C. Ferrell, *Marketing: Concepts and Strategies*, 15th ed. (Mason, Ohio: South-Western/Cengage Learning, 2010). Adapted with permission.

TABLE 11.3: Common Bases of Market Segmentation

Demographic	Psychographic	Geographic	Behavioristic
Age	Personality attributes	Region	Volume usage
Gender	Motives	Urban, suburban, rural	End use
Race	Lifestyles		Benefit expectations
Ethnicity		Market density	Brand loyalty
Income		Climate	Price sensitivity
Education		Terrain	
Occupation		City size	
Family size		County size	
Family life cycle		State size	
Religion			
Social class			

Source: William M. Pride and O. C. Ferrell, *Marketing: Concepts and Strategies*, 15th ed. (Mason, Ohio: South-Western/Cengage Learning, 2010). Adapted with permission.

get Jills, for example, include personal shopping assistants, whereas stores that target Buzzes offer lots of video games. Best Buy stores that use the customer-centric model have enjoyed sales growth that is three times that of the conventional stores.[9]

Creating a Marketing Mix

A business firm controls four important elements of marketing that it combines in a way that reaches the firm's target market. These are the *product* itself, the *price* of the product, the means chosen for its *distribution*, and the *promotion* of the product. When combined, these four elements form a marketing mix (see Figure 11.3). The maker of the Rogue developed a marketing mix that included an economical engine, stylish design, and performance handling; a price around $20,000; product placement and advertising during the hit show *Heroes;* and a five-car giveaway.[10]

A firm can vary its marketing mix by changing any one or more of these ingredients. Thus, a firm may use one marketing mix to reach one target market and a second, somewhat different marketing mix to reach another target market. For example, most automakers produce several different types and models of vehicles and aim them at different market segments based on age, income, and other factors.

The *product* ingredient of the marketing mix includes decisions about the product's design, brand name, packaging, warranties, and the like. When McDonald's decides on brand names, package designs, sizes of orders, flavors of sauces, and recipes, these choices are all part of the product ingredient.

The *pricing* ingredient is concerned with both base prices and discounts of various kinds. Pricing decisions are intended to achieve particular goals, such as to maximize profit or even to make room for new models. The rebates offered by automobile manufacturers are a pricing strategy developed to boost low auto sales. Product and pricing are discussed in detail in Chapter 12.

The *distribution* ingredient involves not only transportation and storage but also the selection of intermediaries. How many levels of intermediaries should be used in the distribution of a particular product? Should the product be distributed as widely as possible? Or should distribution be restricted to a few specialized outlets in each area? These and other questions related to distribution are considered in Chapter 13.

The *promotion* ingredient focuses on providing information to target markets. The major forms of promotion are advertising, personal selling, sales promotion, and public relations. These four forms are discussed in Chapter 13.

5 LEARNING OBJECTIVE

Identify the four elements of the marketing mix and be aware of their importance in developing a marketing strategy.

FIGURE 11.3: The Marketing Mix and the Marketing Environment The marketing mix consists of elements that the firm controls—product, price, distribution, and promotion. The firm generally has no control over forces in the marketing environment.

Source: William M. Pride and O. C. Ferrell, *Marketing: Concepts and Strategies*, 15th ed. (Mason Ohio: South-Western/Cengage Learning, 2010). Adapted with permission.

Creating a marketing mix. The maker of Slimfast created a complete marketing mix—product, price, distribution, and promotion. This ad is a part of the promotion ingredient of the marketing mix.

These ingredients of the marketing mix are controllable elements. A firm can vary each of them to suit its organizational goals, marketing goals, and target markets. As we extend our discussion of marketing strategy, we will see that the marketing environment includes a number of *uncontrollable* elements.

Marketing Strategy and the Marketing Environment

The marketing mix consists of elements that a firm controls and uses to reach its target market. In addition, the firm has control over such organizational resources as finances and information. These resources, too, may be used to accomplish marketing goals. However, the firm's marketing activities are also affected by a number of external—and generally uncontrollable—forces. As Figure 11.3 illustrates, the forces that make up the external *marketing environment* are

- *Economic forces*—the effects of economic conditions on customers' ability and willingness to buy
- *Sociocultural forces*—influences in a society and its culture that result in changes in attitudes, beliefs, norms, customs, and lifestyles
- *Political forces*—influences that arise through the actions of elected and appointed officials
- *Competitive forces*—the actions of competitors, who are in the process of implementing their own marketing plans
- *Legal and regulatory forces*—laws that protect consumers and competition and government regulations that affect marketing
- *Technological forces*—technological changes that, on the one hand, can create new marketing opportunities or, on the other, can cause products to become obsolete almost overnight

These forces influence decisions about marketing-mix ingredients. Changes in the environment can have a major impact on existing marketing strategies. In addition, changes in environmental forces may lead to abrupt shifts in customers' needs. For example, Hertz introduced a new service called "Green Collection" that allows customers to rent more fuel-efficient vehicles.[11]

Developing a Marketing Plan

A **marketing plan** is a written document that specifies an organization's resources, objectives, marketing strategy, and implementation and control efforts to be used in marketing a specific product or product group. The marketing plan describes the firm's current position or situation, establishes marketing objectives for the product, and specifies how the organization will attempt to achieve these objectives. Marketing plans vary with respect to the time period involved. Short-range plans are for one year or less, medium-range plans cover from over one year up to five years, and long-range plans cover periods of more than five years.

Although time-consuming, developing a clear, well-written marketing plan is important. The plan will be used for communication among the firm's employees. It covers the assignment of responsibilities, tasks, and schedules for implementation. It specifies how resources are to be allocated to achieve marketing objectives. It helps marketing managers monitor and evaluate the performance of the marketing strategy. Because the forces of the marketing environment are subject to change, marketing plans have to be updated frequently. Disney, for example, recently made changes to its marketing plans by combining all activities and licensing associated with the Power Rangers, Winnie the Pooh, and Disney Princess into one marketing plan with a $500 million budget. The primary goal is to send consistent messages about branding to customers. As the new marketing plan is implemented, Disney will have to respond quickly to customers' reactions and make adjustments to the plan. The major components of a marketing plan are shown in Table 11.4.

Concept Check

1. What are the major components of a marketing strategy?

2. Describe the major approaches used in target market selection.

3. Identify the four elements of marketing mix.

4. Describe the environmental forces that affect a firm's marketing activities.

7 LEARNING OBJECTIVE

Understand the major components of a marketing plan.

marketing plan a written document that specifies an organization's resources, objectives, strategy, and implementation and control efforts to be used in marketing a specific product or product group

Concept Check

1. What are the major components of a marketing plan?

2. Why is developing a well-written marketing plan important?

TABLE 11.4: Components of the Marketing Plan

Plan Component	Component Summary	Highlights
Executive summary	One- to two-page synopsis of the entire marketing plan	
Environmental analysis	Information about the company's current situation with respect to the marketing environment	1. Assessment of marketing environment factors 2. Assessment of target market(s) 3. Assessment of current marketing objectives and performance
SWOT analysis	Assessment of the organization's strengths, weaknesses, opportunities, and threats	1. Strengths 2. Weaknesses 3. Opportunities 4. Threats
Marketing objectives	Specification of the firm's marketing objectives	Qualitative measures of what is to be accomplished
Marketing strategies	Outline of how the firm will achieve its objectives	1. Target market(s) 2. Marketing mix
Marketing implementation	Outline of how the firm will implement its marketing strategies	1. Marketing organization 2. Activities and responsibilities 3. Implementation timetable
Evaluation and control	Explanation of how the firm will measure and evaluate the results of the implemented plan	1. Performance standards 2. Financial controls 3. Monitoring procedures (audits)

Source: William M. Pride and O. C. Ferrell, *Marketing: Concepts and Strategies*, 15th ed. (Mason, Ohio: South-Western/Cengage Learning, 2010). Reprinted with permission.

LEARNING OBJECTIVE 8 — Market Measurement and Sales Forecasting

Describe how market measurement and sales forecasting are used.

Measuring the sales potential of specific types of market segments helps an organization to make some important decisions. It can evaluate the feasibility of entering new segments. The organization also can decide how best to allocate its marketing resources and activities among market segments in which it is already active. All such estimates should identify the relevant time frame. As with marketing plans, these estimates may be short range, covering periods of less than one year; medium range, covering one to five years; or long range, covering more than five years. The estimates also should define the geographic boundaries of the forecast. For example, sales potential can be estimated for a city, county, state, or group of nations. Finally, analysts should indicate whether their estimates are for a specific product item, a product line, or an entire product category.

A **sales forecast** is an estimate of the amount of a product that an organization expects to sell during a certain period of time based on a specified level of marketing effort. Managers in different divisions of an organization rely on sales forecasts when they purchase raw materials, schedule production, secure financial resources, consider plant or equipment purchases, hire personnel, and plan inventory levels. Because the accuracy of a sales forecast is so important, organizations often use several forecasting methods, including executive judgments, surveys of buyers or sales personnel, time-series analyses, correlation analyses, and market tests. The specific methods used depend on the costs involved, type of product, characteristics of the market, time span of the forecast, purposes for which the forecast is used, stability of historical sales data, availability of the required information, and expertise and experience of forecasters.

sales forecast an estimate of the amount of a product that an organization expects to sell during a certain period of time based on a specified level of marketing effort

Concept Check

1. Why is sales forecasting important?

2. What methods do businesses use to forecast sales?

Marketing Information

The availability and use of accurate and timely information are critical to making effective marketing decisions. A wealth of marketing information is obtainable. There are two general ways to obtain it: through a marketing information system and through marketing research.

Marketing Information Systems

A **marketing information system** is a system for managing marketing information that is gathered continually from internal and external sources. Most of these systems are computer-based because of the amount of data the system must accept, store, sort, and retrieve. *Continual* collection of data is essential if the system is to incorporate the most up-to-date information.

In concept, the operation of a marketing information system is not complex. Data from a variety of sources are fed into the system. Data from *internal* sources include sales figures, product and marketing costs, inventory levels, and activities of the sales force. Data from *external* sources relate to the organization's suppliers, intermediaries, and customers; competitors' marketing activities; and economic conditions. All these data are stored and processed within the marketing information system. Its output is a flow of information in the form that is most useful for making marketing decisions. This information might include daily sales reports by territory and product, forecasts of sales or buying trends, and reports on changes in market share for the major brands in a specific industry. Both the information outputs and their form depend on the requirements of the personnel in the organization.

marketing information system a system for managing marketing information that is gathered continually from internal and external sources

marketing research the process of systematically gathering, recording, and analyzing data concerning a particular marketing problem

Marketing Research

Marketing research is the process of systematically gathering, recording, and analyzing data concerning a particular marketing problem. Thus, marketing research is used in specific situations to obtain information not otherwise available to decision makers. It is an intermittent, rather than a continual, source of marketing information. JC Penney, for example, conducted extensive research to learn more about a core segment of shoppers who weren't being adequately reached by department stores: middle-income mothers between the ages of 35 and 54. The research involved asking 900 women about their casual clothes preferences. Later, the firm conducted in-depth interviews with 30 women about their clothing needs, feelings about fashion, and shopping experiences. The research helped the company recognize that this "missing middle" segment of shoppers was frustrated with the choices and quality of the clothing available in their price range and stressed out by the experience of shopping for clothes for themselves. Armed with this information, Penney launched two new lines of moderately priced, quality casual women's clothing, including one by designer Nicole Miller.[12] A study by SPSS Inc. found that the most common reasons for conducting marketing research surveys included determining satisfaction (43 percent);

Does Highly-Targeted Marketing Invade Your Privacy?

Marketers are always looking for better ways to get the right offer to the right customer at the right time. But do today's highly-targeted marketing techniques invade your privacy?

Many marketers use cookies to track where consumers go and what they do on the Internet. This enables marketers to personalize their websites and tailor advertising messages for individual consumers. The Federal Trade Commission regulates some of this activity, seeking to ensure "that online advertisers best protect consumer privacy while collecting information about their online activities," according to an official.

However, privacy advocates worry about how much information is being collected, how it will be used, and for how long. With the rise of social networking sites such as Facebook and MySpace, marketers are able to use "a new form of behavioral targeting—a kind of conversational eavesdropping analysis," says the director of the Center for Digital Democracy. Marketers can fine-tune their targeting by analyzing gender, age, and other personal details that participants post. For example, one JC Penney online campaign presented dorm-room products to college students on Facebook.

Targeting is also getting more precise at the store level, now that millions of consumers have joined retailers' loyal shopper programs. Because the stores record what members buy, Nestlé and other marketers can tailor special offers to each customer's purchasing patterns—right at the checkout counter. Should marketers know so much about where you shop and what you buy?

Sources: Dianna Dilworth, "Self-regulation Is Still Key to Behavioral Targeting: FTC," *DM News*, February 18, 2009, www.dmnews.com; David Kesmodel, "Personalized Store Ads Take Off," *Wall Street Journal*, October 23, 2008, www.wsj.com; Becky Ebenkamp, "Behavioral Targeting: A Tricky Issue for Marketers," *Brandweek*, October 21, 2008, www.brandweek.com; Rachel Metz, "MySpace Taps Small Businesses in Ad Money Quest," *Associated Press*, October 13, 2008, ap.google.com.

product development (29 percent); branding (23 percent); segmentation (18 percent); awareness, trend tracking, and concept testing (18 percent); and business markets (11 percent).[13]

Table 11.5 outlines a six-step procedure for conducting marketing research. This procedure is particularly well suited to testing new products, determining various characteristics of consumer markets, and evaluating promotional activities. Food-processing companies, such as Kraft Foods and Kellogg's, use a variety of marketing research methods to avoid costly mistakes in introducing the wrong products or products in the wrong way or at the wrong time. They have been particularly interested in using marketing research to learn more about the African-American and Hispanic markets. Understanding of the food preferences, loyalties, and purchase motivators of these groups enables these companies to serve them better.

Using Technology to Gather and Analyze Marketing Information

Technology is making information for marketing decisions increasingly accessible. The ability of firms to track the purchase behaviors of customers electronically and to better determine what they want is changing the nature of marketing. The integration of telecommunications with computing technology provides marketers with access to accurate information not only about customers and competitors but also about industry forecasts and business trends. Among the communication tools that are radically changing the way marketers obtain and use information are databases, online information services, and the Internet.

A *database* is a collection of information arranged for easy access and retrieval. Using databases, marketers tap into internal sales reports, newspaper articles, company news releases, government economic reports, bibliographies, and more. Many marketers use commercial databases, such as LEXIS-NEXIS, to obtain useful information for marketing decisions. Many of these commercial databases are available in printed form (for a fee), online (for a fee), or on purchasable CD-ROMs. Other marketers develop their own databases in-house. Some firms sell their databases to other organizations. *Reader's Digest,* for example, markets a database that provides information on 100 million households. Dunn & Bradstreet markets a database that includes information on the addresses, phone numbers, and contacts of businesses located in specific areas.

Information provided by a single firm on household demographics, purchases, television viewing behavior, and responses to promotions such as coupons and free samples is called *single-source data.* For example, Behavior Scan, offered by Information Resources, Inc., screens about 60,000 households in twenty-six U.S. markets. This single-source information service monitors household televisions and records the programs and commercials viewed. When buyers from these households

TABLE 11.5: The Six Steps of Marketing Research

1. Define the problem	In this step, the problem is stated clearly and accurately to determine what issues are involved in the research, what questions to ask, and what types of solutions are needed. This is a crucial step that should not be rushed.
2. Make a preliminary investigation	The objective of preliminary investigation is to develop both a sharper definition of the problem and a set of tentative answers. The tentative answers are developed by examining internal information and published data and by talking with persons who have some experience with the problem. These answers will be tested by further research.
3. Plan the research	At this stage, researchers know what facts are needed to resolve the identified problem and what facts are available. They make plans on how to gather needed but missing data.
4. Gather factual information	Once the basic research plan has been completed, the needed information can be collected by mail, telephone, or personal interviews; by observation; or from commercial or government data sources. The choice depends on the plan and the available sources of information.
5. Interpret the information	Facts by themselves do not always provide a sound solution to a marketing problem. They must be interpreted and analyzed to determine the choices available to management.
6. Reach a conclusion	Sometimes the conclusion or recommendation becomes obvious when the facts are interpreted. However, in other cases, reaching a conclusion may not be so easy because of gaps in the information or intangible factors that are difficult to evaluate. If and when the evidence is less than complete, it is important to say so.

shop in stores equipped with scanning registers, they present Hotline cards (similar to credit cards) to cashiers. This enables each customer's identification to be coded electronically so that the firm can track each product purchased and store the information in a database.

Online information services offer subscribers access to e-mail, websites, files for downloading (such as with Acrobat Reader), news, databases, and research materials. By subscribing to mailing lists, marketers can receive electronic newsletters and participate in online discussions with other network users. This ability to communicate online with customers, suppliers, and employees improves the capability of a firm's marketing information system and helps the company track its customers' changing desires and buying habits.

The *Internet* has evolved as a powerful communication medium, linking customers and companies around the world via computer networks with e-mail, forums, Web pages, and more. Growth in Internet use has given rise to an entire industry that makes marketing information easily accessible to both companies and customers. Among the many Web pages useful for marketing research are the home pages of Nielsen marketing research and *Advertising Age*. While most Web pages are open to all Internet users, some companies, such as U.S. West and Turner Broadcasting System, also maintain internal Web pages, called *intranets*, that allow employees to access internal data and facilitate communication among departments.

Table 11.6 lists a number of websites that may serve as valuable resources for marketing research. The Bureau of the Census, for example, uses the Internet to disseminate information that may be useful to marketing researchers, particularly through the *Statistical Abstract of the United States* and data from the most recent Census. The "Census Lookup" option allows marketing researchers to create their own customized information. With this online tool, researchers can select tables by clicking boxes to select a state and then, within the state, the county, place, and urbanized area or metropolitan statistical area to be examined.

Courtesy, Western Wats

Concept Check

1. Data from a marketing information system is collected from which internal and external sources?

2. What are the major reasons for conducting marketing research?

3. Identify and describe the six steps of the marketing research process.

4. How does technology facilitate collecting and analyzing marketing information?

TABLE 11.6: Internet Sources of Marketing Information

Government Sources	Commercial Sources	Periodicals and Books
census.gov	acnielsen.com	adage.com
state.gov	usa.infores.com	salesandmarketing.com
fedworld.gov	gallup.com	Fortune.com
	arbitron.com	inc.com
	chamber-of-commerce.com	businessweek.com
	bloomberg.com	

Source: William M. Pride and O. C. Ferrell, *Marketing: Concepts and Strategies*, 15th ed. (Mason, Ohio: South-Western/Cengage Learning, 2010). Reprinted with permission.

buying behavior the decisions and actions of people involved in buying and using products

consumer buying behavior the purchasing of products for personal or household use, not for business purposes

business buying behavior the purchasing of products by producers, resellers, governmental units, and institutions

LEARNING OBJECTIVE 10

Identify the major steps in the consumer buying decision process and the sets of factors that may influence this process.

Types of Buying Behavior

Buying behavior may be defined as the decisions and actions of people involved in buying and using products.[14] **Consumer buying behavior** refers to the purchasing of products for personal or household use, not for business purposes. **Business buying behavior** is the purchasing of products by producers, resellers, governmental units, and institutions. Since a firm's success depends greatly on buyers' reactions to a particular marketing strategy, it is important to understand buying behavior. Marketing managers are better able to predict customer responses to marketing strategies and to develop a satisfying marketing mix if they are aware of the factors that affect buying behavior.

Consumer Buying Behavior

Consumers' buying behaviors differ when they buy different types of products. For frequently purchased low-cost items, a consumer employs routine response behavior involving very little search or decision-making effort. The buyer uses limited decision making for purchases made occasionally or when more information is needed about an unknown product in a well-known product category. When buying an unfamiliar, expensive item or one that is seldom purchased, the consumer engages in extensive decision making.

A person deciding on a purchase goes through some or all of the steps shown in Figure 11.4. First, the consumer acknowledges that a problem exists. A problem is usually the lack of a product or service that is desired or needed. Then the buyer looks for information, which may include brand names, product characteristics, warranties, and other features. Next, the buyer weighs the various alternatives he or she has discovered and then finally makes a choice and acquires the item. In the after-purchase stage, the consumer evaluates the suitability of the product. This judgment will affect future purchases. As Figure 11.4 shows, the buying process is influenced by situational factors (physical surroundings, social surroundings, time, purchase reason, and buyer's mood and condition), psychological factors (perception, motives, learning, attitudes, personality, and

Recognizing a problem. Some advertisements, such as this Winterfresh gum ad, are aimed at a particular stage of the consumer buying decision process. This ad is meant to stimulate the problem recognition stage of the consumer buying decision process.

©Graffiti BBDO/Romania

lifestyle), and social factors (family, roles, reference groups, online social networks, social class, culture, and subculture).

Consumer buying behavior is also affected by ability to buy or buying power, which is largely determined by income. As every taxpayer knows, not all income is available for spending. For this reason, marketers consider income in three different ways. **Personal income** is the income an individual receives from all sources *less* the Social Security taxes the individual must pay. **Disposable income** is personal income *less* all additional personal taxes. These taxes include income, estate, gift, and property taxes levied by local, state, and federal governments. About 3 percent of all disposable income is saved. **Discretionary income** is disposable income *less* savings and expenditures on food, clothing, and housing. Discretionary income is of particular interest to marketers because consumers have the most choice in spending it. Consumers use their discretionary income to purchase items ranging from automobiles and vacations to movies and pet food.

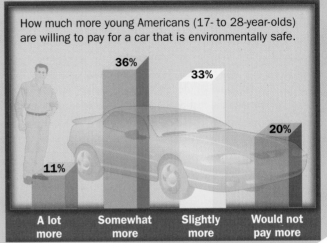

Spotlight
The Green Ride

How much more young Americans (17- to 28-year-olds) are willing to pay for a car that is environmentally safe.

- 11% — A lot more
- 36% — Somewhat more
- 33% — Slightly more
- 20% — Would not pay more

Source: Bayer Consulting for Deloitte LLP survey of 1,006 people ages 17 to 28.

Business Buying Behavior

Business buyers consider a product's quality, its price, and the service provided by suppliers. Business buyers usually are better informed than consumers about products and generally buy in larger quantities. In a business, a committee or group of people, rather than just one person, often decides on purchases. Committee members must consider the organization's objectives, purchasing policies, resources, and personnel. Business buying occurs through description, inspection, sampling, or negotiation. A number of organizations buy a variety of products online.

disposable income personal income *less* all additional personal taxes

discretionary income disposable income *less* savings and expenditures on food, clothing, and housing

personal income the income an individual receives from all sources *less* the Social Security taxes the individual must pay

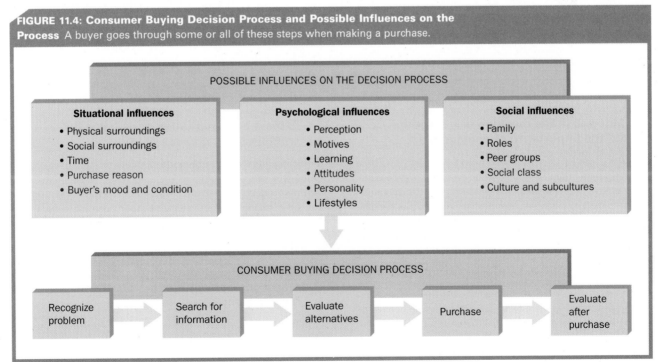

FIGURE 11.4: Consumer Buying Decision Process and Possible Influences on the Process A buyer goes through some or all of these steps when making a purchase.

POSSIBLE INFLUENCES ON THE DECISION PROCESS

Situational influences
- Physical surroundings
- Social surroundings
- Time
- Purchase reason
- Buyer's mood and condition

Psychological influences
- Perception
- Motives
- Learning
- Attitudes
- Personality
- Lifestyles

Social influences
- Family
- Roles
- Peer groups
- Social class
- Culture and subcultures

CONSUMER BUYING DECISION PROCESS

Recognize problem → Search for information → Evaluate alternatives → Purchase → Evaluate after purchase

Source: William M. Pride and O. C. Ferrell, *Marketing: Concepts and Strategies*, 15th ed. (Mason, Ohio: South-Western/Cengage Learning, 2010). Adapted with permission.

Global Economic Challenges

Can Coca-Cola Win Big in China?

Coca-Cola is spending big to win big in China, where consumers have ever-higher purchasing power because of rising household income. From 1979 to 2009, the company spent $1.6 billion to market soft drinks, fruit juices, and other beverages in China. Now the company will invest an additional $2 billion dollars to dramatically increase its market share in the fast-growing Chinese economy.

Although Coca-Cola leads the market in carbonated drinks, it knows Chinese consumers have a special taste for fruit juices. Until Coca-Cola entered this segment, large national brands such as Beijing-based Huiyuan and major regional brands such as Taiwan-based Uni-President dominated. Everything changed in 2004, when Coca-Cola introduced Minute Maid Pulpy, an orange juice beverage. It was a huge success: last year alone, Chinese consumers bought more than one billion bottles of Pulpy.

At one point, Coca-Cola tried to buy Huiyuan as a way of accelerating its growth in China. While the Chinese government considered whether to allow the acquisition, Coca-Cola opened a new innovation facility in Shanghai to develop beverages specifically for China. Just months after the government rejected the acquisition, citing antitrust concerns, Coca-Cola's innovation facility was ready to launch its first new product, a white grape and aloe vera beverage. The high-profile introductory campaign featured the Hong Kong pop star Eason Chan and signaled a new competitive era in the battle for market share among fruit-juice producers. Will Coca-Cola be the big winner?

Sources: "Coke Steps Up China Juice Marketing," Associated Press, May 19, 2009, http://www.bangkokpost.com/business/marketing/143736/coke-steps-up-china-juice-marketing; Tu Lei, "Minute Maid Trying to Unseat Uni-President," *China Daily*, February 23, 2009, p. 9; Daniel Inman, "Coke Spends on Technology and Infrastructure in China," *BusinessWeek*, March 9, 2009, www.businessweek.com. http://www.google.com/hostednews/afp/article/ALeqM5gzzY6ETW9ahaHmLi4kzdQtwlYnIw

Concept Check

1. Why is it important to understand buying behavior?

2. How does a customer's decision making time vary with the type of product?

3. What are the five stages of the consumer buying decision process?

4. What are the possible influences on this process?

5. What is the difference between disposable income and discretionary income?

SUMMARY

1 Understand the meaning of marketing and the importance of management of customer relationships.

Marketing is an organizational function and a set of processes for creating, communicating, and delivering value to customers and for managing customer relationships in ways that benefit the organization and its stake-holders. Maintaining positive relationships with customers is crucial. Relationship marketing is establishing long-term, mutually satisfying buyer-seller relationships. Customer relationship management uses information about customers to create marketing strategies that develop and sustain desirable customer relationships. Managing customer relationships requires identifying patterns of buying behavior and focusing on the most profitable customers. Customer lifetime value is a combination of purchase frequency, average value of purchases, and brand-switching patterns over the entire span of a customer's relationship with the company.

2 Explain how marketing adds value by creating several forms of utility.

Marketing adds value in the form of utility or the power of a product or service to satisfy a need. It creates place utility by making products available where customers want them, time utility by making products available when customers want them, and possession utility by transferring the ownership of products to buyers.

3 Trace the development of the marketing concept and understand how it is implemented.

From the Industrial Revolution until the early twentieth century, businesspeople focused on the production of goods; from the 1920s to the 1950s, the emphasis moved to the selling of goods. During the 1950s, however, businesspeople recognized that their enterprises involved not only producing and selling products but also satisfying customers' needs. They began to implement the marketing concept, a business philosophy that involves the entire organization in the dual processes of meeting the customers' needs and achieving the organization's goals.

Implementation of the marketing concept begins and ends with customers—first to determine what customers' needs are and later to evaluate how well the firm is meeting those needs.

4 Understand what markets are and how they are classified.

A market consists of people with needs, the ability to buy, and the desire and authority to purchase. Markets are classified as consumer and industrial (producer, reseller, governmental, and institutional) markets.

5 Identify the four elements of the marketing mix and be aware of their importance in developing a marketing strategy.

A marketing strategy is a plan for the best use of an organization's resources to meet its objectives. Developing a marketing strategy involves selecting and analyzing a target market and creating and maintaining a marketing mix that will satisfy that target market. A target market is chosen through either the undifferentiated approach or the market-segmentation approach. A market segment is a group of individuals or organizations within a market that have similar characteristics and needs. Businesses that use an undifferentiated approach design a single marketing mix and direct it at the entire market for a particular product. The market-segmentation approach directs a marketing mix at a segment of a market.

The four elements of a firm's marketing mix are product, price, distribution, and promotion. The product ingredient includes decisions about the product's design, brand name, packaging, and warranties. The pricing ingredient is concerned with both base prices and various types of discounts. Distribution involves not only transportation and storage but also the selection of intermediaries. Promotion focuses on providing information to target markets. The elements of the marketing mix can be varied to suit broad organizational goals, marketing objectives, and target markets.

6 Explain how the marketing environment affects strategic market planning.

To achieve a firm's marketing objectives, marketing-mix strategies must begin with an assessment of the marketing environment, which, in turn, will influence decisions about marketing-mix ingredients. Marketing activities are affected by a number of external forces that make up the marketing environment. These forces include economic forces, sociocultural forces, political forces, competitive forces, legal and regulatory forces, and technological forces. Economic forces affect customers' ability and willingness to buy. Sociocultural forces are societal and cultural factors, such as attitudes, beliefs, and lifestyles, that affect customers' buying choices. Political forces and legal and regulatory forces influence marketing planning through laws that protect consumers and regulate competition. Competitive forces are the actions of competitors who

are implementing their own marketing plans. Technological forces can create new marketing opportunities or quickly cause a product to become obsolete.

7 Understand the major components of a marketing plan.

A marketing plan is a written document that specifies an organization's resources, objectives, strategy, and implementation and control efforts to be used in marketing a specific product or product group. The marketing plan describes a firm's current position, establishes marketing objectives, and specifies the methods the organization will use to achieve these objectives. Marketing plans can be short range, covering one year or less; medium range, covering two to five years; or long range, covering periods of more than five years.

8 Describe how market measurement and sales forecasting are used.

Market measurement and sales forecasting are used to estimate sales potential and predict product sales in specific market segments.

9 Distinguish between a marketing information system and marketing research.

Strategies are monitored and evaluated through marketing research and the marketing information system that stores and processes internal and external data in a form that aids marketing decision making. A marketing information system is a system for managing marketing information that is gathered continually from internal and external sources. Marketing research is the process of systematically gathering, recording, and analyzing data concerning a particular marketing problem. It is an intermittent rather than a continual source of marketing information. Technology is making information for marketing decisions more accessible. Electronic communication tools can be very useful for accumulating accurate information with minimal customer interaction. Information technologies that are changing the way marketers obtain and use information are databases, online information services, and the Internet.

10 Identify the major steps in the consumer buying decision process and the sets of factors that may influence this process.

Buying behavior consists of the decisions and actions of people involved in buying and using products. Consumer buying behavior refers to the purchase of products for personal or household use. Organizational buying behavior is the purchase of products by producers, resellers, governments, and institutions. Understanding buying behavior helps marketers to predict how buyers will respond to marketing strategies. The consumer buying decision process consists of five steps, including recognizing the problem, searching for information, evaluating alternatives, purchasing, and evaluating after purchase. Factors affecting the consumer buying decision process fall into three categories: situational influences, psychological influences, and social influences.

KEY TERMS

You should now be able to define and give an example relevant to each of the following terms:

marketing (290)
relationship marketing (291)
customer relationship
    management (CRM) (291)
customer lifetime value (292)
utility (292)
form utility (292)
place utility (292)
time utility (293)

possession utility (293)
marketing concept (293)
market (295)
marketing strategy (296)
marketing mix (296)
target market (296)
undifferentiated approach
    (297)
market segment (297)

market segmentation (297)
marketing plan (301)
sales forecast (302)
marketing information
    system (302)
marketing research (303)
buying behavior (306)
consumer buying behavior
    (306)

business buying behavior
    (306)
personal income (307)
disposable income (307)
discretionary income (307)

DISCUSSION QUESTIONS

1. What is relationship marketing?
2. How is a marketing-oriented firm different from a production-oriented firm or a sales-oriented firm?
3. What are the major requirements for a group of individuals and organizations to be a market? How does a consumer market differ from a business-to-business market?
4. What are the major components of a marketing strategy?
5. What is the purpose of market segmentation? What is the relationship between market segmentation and the selection of target markets?
6. Describe the forces in the marketing environment that affect an organization's marketing decisions.

7. What is a marketing plan, and what are its major components?
8. What new information technologies are changing the ways that marketers keep track of business trends and customers?
9. Why do marketers need to understand buying behavior?
10. Are there any problems for a company that focuses mainly on the most profitable customers?
11. How might adoption of the marketing concept benefit a firm? How might it benefit the firm's customers?
12. Is marketing information as important to small firms as it is to larger firms? Explain.
13. How does the marketing environment affect a firm's marketing strategy?

**Get Flash Cards, Quizzes,
Games, Crosswords and more
@ www.cengage.com/introbusiness/
pride**

Test Yourself

Matching Questions

1. _____ The process of planning and executing the conception, pricing, promotion, and distribution of ideas, goods, and services.

2. _____ A business philosophy that involves the satisfying of customer's needs while achieving a firm's goals.

3. _____ Value is added through converting raw materials into finished goods.

4. _____ It is the individuals in a market who share common characteristics.

5. _____ Income that is left after savings, food, clothing, and housing are paid.

6. _____ It is a combination of marketing elements designed to reach a target market.

7. _____ It is a plan of actions intended to accomplish a marketing goal.

8. _____ The decision-making process that is used when purchasing personal-use items.

9. _____ Marketing activities that focus on a particular group such as teenagers.

10. _____ The marketing objectives for a product are established.

    a. consumer buying behavior
    b. discretionary income
    c. form utility

Test Yourself

    d. possession utility
    e. market segment
    f. marketing
    g. marketing concept
    h. customer lifetime value
    i. marketing mix
    j. marketing plan
    k. marketing strategy
    l. target market

True False Questions

11. **T F** Marketing is a process that fulfills consumers' needs.

12. **T F** The first step in implementing the marketing concept is to provide a product that satisfies customers.

13. **T F** The marketing mix is composed of product, price, distribution, and promotion.

14. **T F** Markets are classified as consumer markets or business-to-business markets.

15. **T F** Financing and risk taking are physical distribution functions of marketing.

16. **T F** The four common bases of market segmentation are demographic, strategic, geographic, and discretionary.

17. **T F** The Internet *Advertising Age,* and the *Statistical Abstract of the United States* are important resources for marketing research.

18. **T F** When the Ford Motor Company focuses its advertising for the Explorer on the population between the ages of twenty and thirty-four, it is targeting a market.

19. **T F** Understanding factors that affect buying behavior helps marketing managers to predict consumer responses to marketing strategies and helps to develop a market mix.

20. **T F** Pricing is an uncontrollable element of the marketing environment.

Multiple-Choice Questions

21. _____ When fresh vegetables are shipped to Oklahoma from Mexico, which utility is added?
    a. Form
    b. Place
    c. Price
    d. Possession
    e. Time

22. _____ Sales orientation predominated primarily during the
    a. late 1800s.
    b. 1920s.
    c. 1940s.
    d. late 1950s.
    e. 1970s.

23. _____ Which facilitating function of marketing is riddled with thefts, obsolescence, and lawsuits?
    a. Risk taking
    b. Standardizing
    c. Financing
    d. Information gathering
    e. Selling

24. _____ Women in the market can be classified as
    a. market segmentation.
    b. a marketing mix.
    c. a market segment.
    d. an independent market.
    e. a producer market.

25. _____ What element in the market mix provides information to consumers?
    a. Product
    b. Price
    c. Promotion
    d. Distribution
    e. Quality

26. _____ Which ingredient in the marketing mix focuses on transportation, storage, and intermediaries?
    a. Product
    b. Price
    c. Distribution
    d. Promotion
    e. Buying

27. _____ Which environmental force influences change in consumers' attitudes, customs, and lifestyles?
    a. Legal, political, and regulatory
    b. Competitive
    c. Technological
    d. Economic
    e. Sociocultural

28. _____ Consumers buy products because
    a. they have uses for the products.
    b. they like the convenience that products provide.
    c. they take pride in ownership of products.

Test Yourself

d. they believe that products will enhance their wealth.

e. all of the above.

29. _____ To implement the marketing concept, the firm must mobilize its marketing resources to

a. price the product at a level that is acceptable to buyers and the seller.

b. provide a product that will satisfy the firm's objectives.

c. minimize promotion.

d. reduce the number of distribution sites.

e. all of the above.

30. _____ What type of income is Ramona's $2,450 monthly *net* take-home amount?

a. Ordinary

b. Personal

c. Disposable

d. Gross

e. Discretionary

Answers on p. TY-1

VIDEO CASE

Harley-Davidson: More Than Just a Motorcycle

Harley-Davidson's customers can spot each other instantly by the iconic black, white, and orange logo on their motorcycles, clothing, and saddlebags. More than a century after the first Harley-Davidson motorcycle hit the road, the company's annual worldwide sales have risen as high as $5 billion. Harley-Davidson dominates the U.S. motorcycle market, and sales are also strong in Japan and Europe. Its annual output covers 31 models in five product lines (Sportster, Dyna, Softail, VRSC, and Touring).

Although Harley-Davidson teetered on the brink of bankruptcy in the 1980s, it roared back by limiting production to focus on a consistently high level of quality. Many of its newer products marry the brand's image of freedom and individuality to motorcycles with styling, performance, and features that appeal to younger buyers and women buyers. To attract first-time buyers as well as experienced riders trading up to better bikes, Harley-Davidson prices its motorcycles starting at $6,695 and offers financing and insurance, as well. To help build showroom traffic when recession recently slashed sales by about 10% domestically and 12% worldwide, the company developed a special "Ride Free" promotion offering new-bike trade-in value to buyers of the inexpensive Sportster model. Restructuring, reduced production, and some layoffs make up the company's other recession-fighting strategies.

Buyers can also order limited-edition motorcycles custom built with distinctive paint designs and accessories. Customers see their bikes as a way of expressing their individuality. However, Harley-Davidson selects only a small number of orders annually for custom-built bikes. Not surprisingly, these custom products are usually in high demand.

To encourage the next generation of biking enthusiasts to learn to drive a motorcycle and then buy the Harley-Davidson bike of their dreams, many of the company's dealers offer the Rider's Edge driving course. Since 2000, when the course was first offered, nearly 140,000 people have graduated and earned a motorcycle license. The Rider's Edge also helps experienced riders to hone their driving skills and learn special techniques for riding in groups.

Group riding is such an important part of the overall product experience that the company founded the Harley Owners Group (HOG) to foster a sense of community among its customers. Today, the 1 million HOG members enjoy benefits such as access to dozens of exclusive group rides, a special customer service hotline, and a members-only website. They also receive two magazines: *Hog Tales,* with articles about members and member events, and *Enthusiast,* with articles about Harley-Davidson's goods and services. In addition, customers can use the Harley-Davidson website to plan travel, book hotels, rent bikes, or ship their bikes for their next riding adventure.

Knowing that customers are passionate about motorcycles and about Harley-Davidson in particular, the company arranges tours at four of its factories in Wisconsin, Pennsylvania, and Missouri. It recently opened the Harley-Davidson Museum in Milwaukee, Wisconsin, home of its headquarters, with 130,000 square feet of exhibits. Many of the exhibits feature products from Harley-Davidson's past, including a sample of the bikes, boats, golf carts, and snowmobiles the company once manufactured. Museum-goers can get a taste of the Harley experience by climbing onto one of the company's current bikes for a virtual ride through beautiful country scenery projected on a big screen.

The museum also looks ahead by highlighting Harley-Davidson's latest technology, its newest engines, and the inner workings of its new-product development process. One exhibit shows how a new motorcycle starts life as a sketch, is transformed into a clay model, becomes a testable prototype, and ultimately enters full production. "In creating this museum, we wanted to make sure that it told an evolving story," says the museum director. "We have a rich heritage, but we also have an exciting future."[15]

For more information about this company, go to www.harley-davidson.com.

Questions

1. Why would Harley-Davidson put as much emphasis on consistency of quality as it does on level of quality?
2. How does Harley-Davidson use customer services to differentiate its motorcycle products?
3. What role do you think the Harley-Davidson Museum might play in influencing how consumers perceive the company and its products?

BUILDING SKILLS FOR CAREER SUCCESS

1. EXPLORING THE INTERNET

Consumer products companies with a variety of famous brand names known around the world are making their presence known on the Internet through websites and online banner advertising. The giants in consumer products include U.S.-based Procter & Gamble (www.pg.com/), Swiss-based Nestlé (www.nestle.com/), and British-based Unilever (www.unilever.com/).

According to a spokesperson for the Unilever Interactive Brand Center in New York, the firm is committed to making the Internet part of its marketing strategy. The center carries out research and development (R&D) and serves as a model for others now in operation in the Netherlands and Singapore. Information is shared with interactive marketers assigned to specific business units. Eventually, centers will be established globally, reflecting the fact that most of Unilever's $52 billion in sales takes place in about 100 countries around the world.

Unilever's view that online consumer product sales are the way of the future was indicated by online alliances established with Microsoft Network, America Online, and NetGrocer.com. Creating an online dialogue with consumers on a global scale is no simple task. Cultural differences often are subtle and difficult to explain but nonetheless are perceived by the viewers interacting with a site. Unilever's website, which is its connection to customers all over the world, has a global feel to it. The question is whether or not it is satisfactory to each target audience. Visit the text website for updates to this exercise.

Assignment

1. Examine the Unilever, Procter & Gamble, and Nestlé sites and describe the features that you think would be most interesting to consumers.
2. Describe those features you do not like and explain why.
3. Do you think that the sites can contribute to better consumer buyer behavior? Explain your thinking.

2. BUILDING TEAM SKILLS

Review the text definitions of *market* and *target market*. Markets can be classified as consumer or industrial. Buyer behavior consists of the decisions and actions of those involved in buying and using products or services. By examining aspects of a company's products, you usually can determine the company's target market and the characteristics important to members of that target market.

Assignment

1. Working in teams of three to five, identify a company and its major products.
2. List and discuss characteristics that customers may find important. These factors may include price, quality, brand name, variety of services, salespeople, customer service, special offers, promotional campaign, packaging, convenience of use, convenience of purchase, location, guarantees, store/office decor, and payment terms.
3. Write a description of the company's primary customer (target market).

3. RESEARCHING DIFFERENT CAREERS

Before interviewing for a job, you should learn all you can about the company. With this information, you will be prepared to ask meaningful questions about the firm during the interview, and the interviewer no doubt will be impressed with your knowledge of the business and your interest in it. To find out about a company, you can conduct some market research.

Assignment

1. Choose at least two local companies for which you might like to work.
2. Contact your local Chamber of Commerce. (The Chamber of Commerce collects information about local businesses, and most of its services are free.) Ask for information about the companies.
3. Call the Better Business Bureau in your community and ask if there are any complaints against the companies.
4. Prepare a report summarizing your findings.

12
Creating and Pricing Products That Satisfy Customers

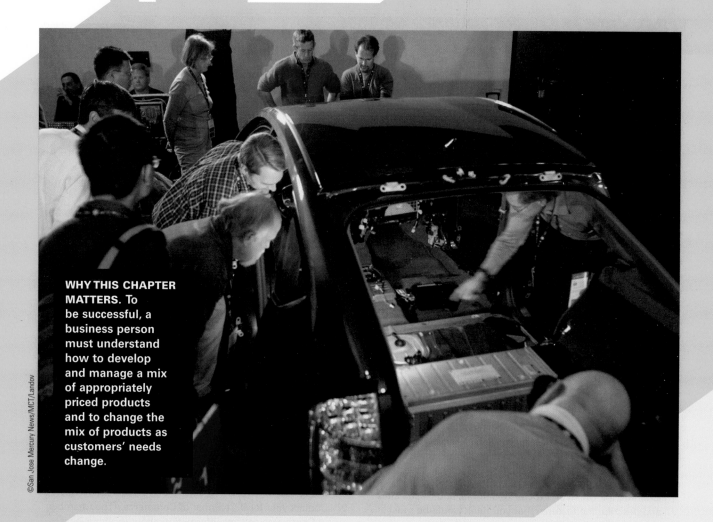

WHY THIS CHAPTER MATTERS. To be successful, a business person must understand how to develop and manage a mix of appropriately priced products and to change the mix of products as customers' needs change.

©San Jose Mercury News/MCT/Landov

LEARNING OBJECTIVES

1 Explain what a product is and how products are classified.

2 Discuss the product life cycle and how it leads to new product development.

3 Define *product line* and *product mix* and distinguish between the two.

4 Identify the methods available for changing a product mix.

5 Explain the uses and importance of branding, packaging, and labeling.

6 Describe the economic basis of pricing and the means by which sellers can control prices and buyers' perceptions of prices.

7 Identify the major pricing objectives used by businesses.

8 Examine the three major pricing methods that firms employ.

9 Explain the different strategies available to companies for setting prices.

10 Describe three major types of pricing associated with business products.

How Goya Cooks up Growth

Since Don Prudencio Unanue and his wife Carolina founded Goya Foods in 1936, the company has made quality the top ingredient in its recipe for decades of profitable growth. Initially, Goya imported a small number of condiments and canned goods from Spain. Over the years, it expanded its product mix to include authentic foods and ingredients from the Caribbean region, Mexico, and both Central and South America.

Today Goya is one of the largest family-owned businesses in the United States. It rings up $1 billion in annual sales and offers 1,600 different Latino food products made in its facilities in several U.S. states, Puerto Rico, the Dominican Republic, and Spain. The company introduces as many as 400 new items every year, drawing on its knowledge of Hispanic tastes and customs. For example, its 38 varieties of bean products include something for every palate and lifestyle, from refried beans to organic beans to low-sodium beans. Families on a budget can buy Goya's packaged dry beans to cook favorite dishes from scratch, while convenience-seekers can choose Goya's heat-and-eat canned or frozen meals.

Goya has increased its prices in recent years because of higher costs for ingredients such as wheat, rice, beans, and corn, as well as for transportation. To control costs, the company manufactures its own cans and bottles. Also, it has streamlined its distribution and delivery routes to save time and money.

Bringing its brand to a wider audience, Goya has opened the Goya Food Latin Café in Minute Maid Park in Houston. During the baseball season, fans can enjoy such specialties as Cuban sandwiches with plantain chips while they cheer on the Houston Astros. Why would Goya team up with the Astros? "Since we sell such a varied line of products, it's a way to introduce just some of them to the consumers in the area," the CEO explains. "The more we get our name out there, the more we become synonymous with the Latino community, the better we do."[1]

DID YOU KNOW?

Goya Foods, one of the largest family-owned businesses in America, markets more than 1,600 products and rings up more than $1 billion in annual sales.

A **product** is everything one receives in an exchange, including all tangible and intangible attributes and expected benefits. An Apple iPod purchase, for example, includes not only the iPod itself but also earphones, instructions, and a warranty. A car includes a warranty, an owner's manual, and perhaps free emergency road service for a year. Some of the intangibles that may go with an automobile include the status associated with ownership and the memories generated from past rides. Developing and managing products effectively are crucial to an organization's ability to maintain successful marketing mixes.

A product may be a good, a service, or an idea. A *good* is a real, physical thing that we can touch, such as a Classic Sport football. A *service* is the result of applying human or mechanical effort to a person or thing. Basically, a *service* is a change we pay others to make for us. A real estate agent's services result in a change in the ownership of real property. A barber's services result in a change in your appearance. An *idea* may take the form of philosophies, lessons, concepts, or advice. Often ideas are included with a good or service. Thus, we might buy a book (a good) that provides ideas on how to lose weight. Or we might join Weight Watchers for ideas on how to lose weight and for help (services) in doing so.

We look first in this chapter at products. We examine product classifications and describe the four stages, or life cycle, through which every product moves. Next, we illustrate how firms manage products effectively by modifying or deleting existing products and by developing new products. We also discuss branding, packaging, and labeling of products. Then our focus shifts to pricing. We explain competitive factors that influence sellers' pricing decisions and also explore buyers'

product everything one receives in an exchange, including all tangible and intangible attributes and expected benefits; it may be a good, service, or idea

consumer product a product purchased to satisfy personal and family needs

perceptions of prices. After considering organizational objectives that can be accomplished through pricing, we outline several methods for setting prices. Finally, we describe pricing strategies by which sellers can reach target markets successfully.

LEARNING OBJECTIVE **1**

Explain what a product is and how products are classified.

business product a product bought for resale, for making other products, or for use in a firm's operations

convenience product a relatively inexpensive, frequently purchased item for which buyers want to exert only minimal effort

shopping product an item for which buyers are willing to expend considerable effort on planning and making the purchase

specialty product an item that possesses one or more unique characteristics for which a significant group of buyers is willing to expend considerable purchasing effort

Classification of Products

Different classes of products are directed at particular target markets. A product's classification largely determines what kinds of distribution, promotion, and pricing are appropriate in marketing the product.

Products can be grouped into two general categories: consumer and business (also called *business-to-business* or *industrial products*). A product purchased to satisfy personal and family needs is a **consumer product**. A product bought for resale, for making other products, or for use in a firm's operations is a **business product**. The buyer's use of the product determines the classification of an item. Note that a single item can be both a consumer and a business product. A broom is a consumer product if you use it in your home. However, the same broom is a business product if you use it in the maintenance of your business. After a product is classified as a consumer or business product, it can be categorized further as a particular type of consumer or business product.

Consumer Product Classifications

The traditional and most widely accepted system of classifying consumer products consists of three categories: convenience, shopping, and specialty products. These groupings are based primarily on characteristics of buyers' purchasing behavior.

A **convenience product** is a relatively inexpensive, frequently purchased item for which buyers want to exert only minimal effort. Examples include bread, gasoline, newspapers, soft drinks, and chewing gum. The buyer spends little time in planning the purchase of a convenience item or in comparing available brands or sellers.

A **shopping product** is an item for which buyers are willing to expend considerable effort on planning and making the purchase. Buyers allocate ample time for comparing stores and brands with respect to prices, product features, qualities, services, and perhaps warranties. Appliances, upholstered furniture, men's suits, bicycles, and cellular phones are examples of shopping products. These products are expected to last for a fairly long time and thus are purchased less frequently than convenience items.

A **specialty product** possesses one or more unique characteristics for which a group of buyers is willing to expend considerable purchasing effort. Buyers actually plan the purchase of a specialty product; they know exactly what they want and will not accept a substitute. In searching for specialty products, purchasers do not compare alternatives. Examples include unique sports cars, a specific type of antique dining table, a rare imported beer, or perhaps special handcrafted stereo speakers.

One problem with this approach to classification is that buyers may behave differently when purchasing a specific type of product. Thus, a single product can fit into more than one category. To minimize this problem, marketers think in terms of how buyers are most likely to behave when purchasing a specific item.

Business Product Classifications

Based on their characteristics and intended uses, business products can be classified into the following categories: raw materials, major equipment, accessory equipment,

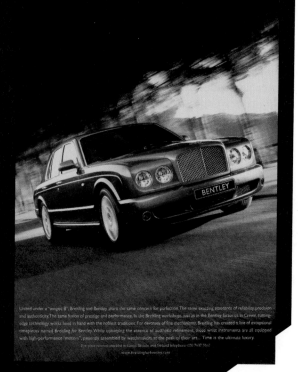

Specialty products. Most cars are classified as shopping products. However, a few automobiles, such as the Bentley, are extremely expensive, have distinctive styling and amenities, and are distributed exclusively through just a few dealers. These distinctive vehicles are specialty products.

The greatest luxury in life is time. Savour every second.

component parts, process materials, supplies, and services.

A **raw material** is a basic material that actually becomes part of a physical product. It usually comes from mines, forests, oceans, or recycled solid wastes. Raw materials usually are bought and sold according to grades and specifications.

Major equipment includes large tools and machines used for production purposes. Examples of major equipment are lathes, cranes, and stamping machines. Some major equipment is custom-made for a particular organization, but other items are standardized products that perform one or several tasks for many types of organizations.

Accessory equipment is standardized equipment used in a firm's production or office activities. Examples include hand tools, fax machines, fractional-horsepower motors, and calculators. Compared with major equipment, accessory items are usually much less expensive and are purchased routinely with less negotiation.

A **component part** becomes part of a physical product and is either a finished item ready for assembly or a product that needs little processing before assembly. Although it becomes part of a larger product, a component part often can be identified easily. Clocks, tires, computer chips, and switches are examples of component parts.

A **process material** is used directly in the production of another product. Unlike a component part, however, a process material is not readily identifiable in the finished product. Like component parts, process materials are purchased according to industry standards or to the specifications of the individual purchaser. Examples include industrial glue and food preservatives.

A **supply** facilitates production and operations but does not become part of a finished product. Paper, pencils, oils, and cleaning agents are examples.

A **business service** is an intangible product that an organization uses in its operations. Examples include financial, legal, online, janitorial, and marketing research services. Purchasers must decide whether to provide their own services internally or to hire them from outside the organization.

©J. Heigason/Shutterstock

raw material a basic material that actually becomes part of a physical product; usually comes from mines, forests, oceans, or recycled solid wastes

major equipment large tools and machines used for production purposes

accessory equipment standardized equipment used in a firm's production or office activities

component part an item that becomes part of a physical product and is either a finished item ready for assembly or a product that needs little processing before assembly

process material a material that is used directly in the production of another product but is not readily identifiable in the finished product

supply an item that facilitates production and operations but does not become part of a finished product

business service an intangible product that an organization uses in its operations

Concept Check

1. Identify the general categories of products.

2. Describe the classifications of consumer products.

3. Based on their characteristics, business products can be classified into what categories?

The Product Life Cycle

In a way, products are like people. They are born, they live, and they die. Every product progresses through a **product life cycle**, a series of stages in which a product's sales revenue and profit increase, reach a peak, and then decline. A firm must be able to launch, modify, and delete products from its offering of products in response to changes in product life cycles. Otherwise, the firm's profits will disappear, and the firm will fail. Depending on the product, life-cycle stages will vary in length. In this section, we discuss the stages of the life cycle and how marketers can use this information.

2 LEARNING OBJECTIVE

Discuss the product life cycle and how it leads to new product development.

product life cycle a series of stages in which a product's sales revenue and profit increase, reach a peak, and then decline

Stages of the Product Life Cycle

Generally, the product life cycle is assumed to be composed of four stages—introduction, growth, maturity, and decline—as shown in Figure 12.1. Some products progress through these stages rapidly, in a few weeks or months. Others may take years to go through each stage. The Rubik's Cube had a relatively short life cycle. Parker Brothers' Monopoly game, which was introduced over seventy years ago, is still going strong.

Introduction In the *introduction stage,* customer awareness and acceptance of the product are low. Sales rise gradually as a result of promotion and distribution activities, but initially, high development and marketing costs result in low profit or even in a loss. There are relatively few competitors. The price is sometimes high, and purchasers are primarily people who want to be "the first" to own the new product. The marketing challenge at this stage is to make potential customers aware of the product's existence and its features, benefits, and uses.

A new product is seldom an immediate success. Marketers must watch early buying patterns carefully and be prepared to modify the new product promptly if necessary. The product should be priced to attract the particular market segment that has the greatest desire and ability to buy the product. Plans for distribution and promotion should suit the targeted market segment. As with the product itself, the initial price, distribution channels, and promotional efforts may need to be adjusted quickly to maintain sales growth during the introduction stage.

Growth In the *growth stage,* sales increase rapidly as the product becomes well known. Other firms probably have begun to market competing products. The competition and lower unit costs (owing to mass production) result in a lower price, which reduces the profit per unit. Note that industry profits reach a peak and begin to decline during this stage. To meet the needs of the growing market, the originating firm offers modified versions of its product and expands its distribution. The 3M Company, the maker of Post-it Notes, has developed a variety of sizes, colors, and designs.

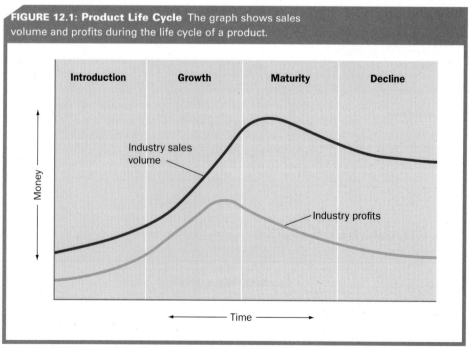

FIGURE 12.1: Product Life Cycle The graph shows sales volume and profits during the life cycle of a product.

Source: William M. Pride and O. C. Ferrell, *Marketing: Concepts and Strategies,* 15th ed. (Mason, Ohio: South-Western/Cengage Learning, 2010). Adapted with permission.

Management's goal in the growth stage is to stabilize and strengthen the product's position by encouraging brand loyalty. To beat the competition, the company may further improve the product or expand the product line to appeal to additional market segments. Apple, for example, has introduced several variations of its wildly popular iPod MP3 player. The iPod Shuffle is the smallest and most affordable version, while the iPod Nano offers song, photo, and video support in a thin, lightweight version. The iPod Classic provides 120 GB of hard drive space, the most of any of the versions. The iPod Touch has a vibrant touch screen display and an additional Wi-Fi connection with a built-in map location-based service. Apple has expanded its iTunes Music Store to include downloadable versions of popular TV shows in high definition that can be purchased per episode or as an entire season, along with exclusive music video downloads. Apple greatly expanded its product mix with the release of the iPhone, a combination iPod Touch and cell phone. Continuous product innovation and service expansion have helped to expand Apple's market penetration in the competitive MP3 player industry.[2] Management also may compete by lowering prices if increased production efficiency has resulted in savings for the company. As the product becomes more widely accepted, marketers may be able to broaden the network of distributors. Marketers also can emphasize customer service and prompt credit for defective products. During this period, promotional efforts attempt to build brand loyalty among customers.

Maturity Sales are still increasing at the beginning of the *maturity stage,* but the rate of increase has slowed. Later in this stage, the sales curve peaks and begins to decline. Industry profits decline throughout this stage. Product lines are simplified, markets are segmented more carefully, and price competition increases. The increased competition forces weaker competitors to leave the industry. Refinements and extensions of the original product continue to appear on the market.

During a product's maturity stage, its market share may be strengthened by redesigned packaging or style changes. Also, consumers may be encouraged to use the product more often or in new ways. Pricing strategies are flexible during this stage. Markdowns and price incentives are not uncommon, although price increases may work to offset production and distribution costs. Marketers may offer incentives and assistance of various kinds to dealers to encourage them to support mature products, especially in the face of competition from private-label brands. New promotional efforts and aggressive personal selling may be necessary during this period of intense competition.

Decline During the *decline stage,* sales volume decreases sharply. Profits continue to fall. The number of competing firms declines, and the only survivors in the marketplace are firms that specialize in marketing the product. Production and marketing costs become the most important determinant of profit.

When a product adds to the success of the overall product line, the company may retain it; otherwise, management must determine when to eliminate the product. A product usually declines because of technological advances or environmental factors or because consumers have switched to competing brands. Therefore, few changes are made in the product itself during this stage. Instead, management may raise the price to cover costs, reprice to maintain market share, or lower the price to reduce inventory. Similarly, management will narrow distribution of the declining product to the most profitable existing markets. During this period, the company probably will not spend heavily on promotion, although it may use some advertising and sales incentives to slow the product's decline. The company may choose to eliminate less profitable versions of the product from the product line or may decide to drop the product entirely. For example, although Procter & Gamble's Sure deodorant had been around for nearly three decades, sharply declining sales led the company to delete the product.[3]

Using the Product Life Cycle

Marketers should be aware of the life-cycle stage of each product for which they are responsible. And they should try to estimate how long the product is expected to remain in that stage. Both must be taken into account in making decisions about the marketing strategy for a product. If a product is expected to remain in the maturity stage for a long time, a replacement product might be introduced later in the maturity stage. If the maturity stage is expected to be short, however, a new product should be introduced much earlier. In some cases, a firm may be willing to take the chance of speeding up the decline of existing products. In other situations, a company will attempt to extend a product's life cycle. For example, General Mills has extended the life of Bisquick baking mix (launched in the mid-1930s) by improving the product's formulation significantly and creating and promoting a variety of uses.

Concept Check

1. Explain the four stages of the product life cycle.

2. How does knowledge of product life cycle relate to introduction of new products?

LEARNING OBJECTIVE 3

Define *product line* and *product mix* and distinguish between the two.

Product Line and Product Mix

A **product line** is a group of similar products that differ only in relatively minor characteristics. Generally, the products within a product line are related to each other in the way they are produced, marketed, or used. Procter & Gamble, for example, manufactures and markets several shampoos, including Prell, Head & Shoulders, and Ivory.

Many organizations tend to introduce new products within existing product lines. This permits them to apply the experience and knowledge they have acquired to the production and marketing of new products. Other firms develop entirely new product lines.

An organization's **product mix** consists of all the products the firm offers for sale. For example, Procter & Gamble, which acquired Gillette, has more than 90 brands that fall into one of twenty-four product lines ranging from deodorants to paper products.[4] Two "dimensions" are often applied to a firm's product mix. The *width* of the mix is the number of product lines it contains. The *depth* of the mix is the average number of individual products within each line. These are general measures; we speak of a *broad* or a *narrow* mix rather than a mix of exactly three or five product lines. Some organizations provide broad product mixes to be competitive.

Concept Check

1. Differentiate product line and product mix.

2. Describe two dimensions of the product mix.

LEARNING OBJECTIVE 4

Identify the methods available for changing a product mix.

Managing the Product Mix

To provide products that satisfy people in a firm's target market or markets and that also achieve the organization's objectives, a marketer must develop, adjust, and maintain an effective product mix. Seldom can the same product mix be effective for long. Because customers' product preferences and attitudes change, their desire for a product may diminish or grow. In some cases, a firm needs to alter its product mix to adapt to competition. A marketer may have to eliminate a product from the mix because one or more competitors dominate that product's specific market segment. Similarly, an organization may have to introduce a new product or modify an existing one to compete more effectively. A marketer may expand the firm's product mix to take advantage of excess marketing and production capacity. For example, both Coca-Cola and Pepsi have expanded their lines by adding to their existing brands and acquiring new brands as well. In response to the increasing popularity of energy drinks, Coca-Cola has acquired brands including AMP. In an effort to seem more health-conscious, both companies came out with new sugar-free or zero calorie soda products, along with more juice brands. Coca-Cola contains brands such as Minute Maid, Simply Orange, and FUZE, while Pepsi contains Tropicana, Ocean Spray, Dole, and SoBe. For tea and coffee brands, Coca-Cola has Nestea and Georgia coffee, while Pepsi has Lipton and a recent partnership with Starbucks. Both companies are also involved in the fast-growing sports drink category, with Coca-Cola's POWERADE and Pepsi's Gatorade among the top competitors. Coca-Cola even has a brand in the alcohol category: BACARDI Mixers.[5] For whatever reason a

product line a group of similar products that differ only in relatively minor characteristics

product mix all the products a firm offers for sale

product mix is altered, the product mix must be managed to bring about improvements in the mix. There are three major ways to improve a product mix: change an existing product, delete a product, or develop a new product.

Managing Existing Products

A product mix can be changed by deriving additional products from existing ones. This can be accomplished through product modifications and by line extensions.

Product Modifications

Product modification refers to changing one or more of a product's characteristics. For this approach to be effective, several conditions must be met. First, the product must be modifiable. Second, existing customers must be able to perceive that a modification has been made, assuming that the modified item is still directed at the same target market. Third, the modification should make the product more consistent with customers' desires so that it provides greater satisfaction. For example, Energizer increased its product's durability by using better materials—a larger cathode and anode interface—that make batteries last longer.

Existing products can be altered in three primary ways: in quality, function, and aesthetics. *Quality modifications* are changes that relate to a product's dependability and durability and usually are achieved by alterations in the materials or production process. *Functional modifications* affect a product's versatility, effectiveness, convenience, or safety; they usually require redesign of the product. Typical product categories that have undergone extensive functional modifications include home appliances, office and farm equipment, and consumer electronics. *Aesthetic modifications* are directed at changing the sensory appeal of a product by altering its taste, texture, sound, smell, or visual characteristics. Because a buyer's purchasing decision is affected by how a product looks, smells, tastes, feels, or sounds, an aesthetic modification may have a definite impact on purchases. Through aesthetic modifications, a firm can differentiate its product from competing brands and perhaps gain a sizable market share if customers find the modified product more appealing.

Line Extensions

A **line extension** is the development of a product closely related to one or more products in the existing product line but designed specifically to meet somewhat different customer needs. For example, Nabisco extended its cookie line to include Reduced Fat Oreos and Double Stuf Oreos.

Many of the so-called new products introduced each year are in fact line extensions. Line extensions are more common than new products because they are a less expensive, lower-risk alternative for increasing sales. A line extension may focus on a different market segment or be an attempt to increase sales within the same market segment by more precisely satisfying the needs of people in that segment. Line extensions are also used to take market share from competitors.

Deleting Products

To maintain an effective product mix, an organization often has to eliminate some products. This is called **product deletion**. A weak product costs a firm time,

Product mix. These products represent a part of Procter and Gamble's product mix.

product modification the process of changing one or more of a product's characteristics

line extension development of a new product that is closely related to one or more products in the existing product line but designed specifically to meet somewhat different customer needs

product deletion the elimination of one or more products from a product line

©Susan Van Etten

The Entrepreneurial Spirit

Big Innovations from Small Business Partners

Big businesses are on the lookout for innovative product ideas from small businesses. Even corporate giants such as Kraft, General Mills, and Procter & Gamble, which have strong track records in product development, are actively inviting the input and innovation of outside entrepreneurs.

Consider the story of Kraft's Bagel-Fuls, a bagel-like roll filled with Philadelphia Cream Cheese (also a Kraft product). Gary Schwartzberg invented an early version of this product but when he had difficulty getting national supermarket distribution, he sent samples to Kraft. Kraft's executives were so impressed that they negotiated an alliance with Schwartzberg's company. Working together, the partners spent two years developing, researching, refining, and test-marketing several flavors of Bagel-Fuls. Today the product is available under the Kraft brand in supermarkets across the United States and in Canada.

Kraft has also set up an "innovate with Kraft" website to solicit ideas for new products and new packaging. "We realize there's a very large body of innovators outside of Kraft," says the vice-president for open innovation and investment. "The world has gotten much smaller, and innovation is happening at small businesses."

Since 2005, General Mills has had a special innovation group working with entrepreneurs to partner on new food products backed by the big company's marketing might. Its small-business partnerships have already resulted in more than a dozen new products, with another 30 on the way. Will its next big hit start out as a recipe cooked up in some entrepreneur's kitchen?

Sources: James Townsend, "Episode 8: Interview with Jeff Bellairs, director of General Mills' Worldwide Innovation Network," *National Products Expo West 2009 Show Daily,* March 30, 2009, http://naturalfoodsmerchandiser.com/tabId/123/itemId/3719/Episode-8-Interview-with-Jeff-Bellairs-director.aspx; Simona Covel, "Running the Show: My Brain, Your Brawn," *Wall Street Journal,* October 13, 2008, p. R12; Anjali Cordeiro, "P&G Looks Outside for Ideas," *Wall Street Journal,* April 23, 2008, www.wsj.com.

money, and resources that could be used to modify other products or develop new ones. Also, when a weak product generates an unfavorable image among customers, the negative image may rub off on other products sold by the firm.

Most organizations find it difficult to delete a product. Some firms drop weak products only after they have become severe financial burdens. A better approach is some form of systematic review of the product's impact on the overall effectiveness of a firm's product mix. Such a review should analyze a product's contribution to a company's sales for a given period. It should include estimates of future sales, costs, and profits associated with the product and a consideration of whether changes in the marketing strategy could improve the product's performance.

A product-deletion program definitely can improve a firm's performance. M&M Mars, for example, discontinued all but one variety of its M-Azing candy bar with embedded M&M candies after two years of disappointing performance. However, the company intends to rebrand the remaining M-Azing Crunchy Singles bar.[6]

Developing New Products

Developing and introducing new products is frequently time consuming, expensive, and risky. Thousands of new products are introduced annually. Depending on how we define it, the failure rate for new products ranges between 60 and 75 percent. Although developing new products is risky, failing to introduce new products can be just as hazardous. New products generally are grouped into three categories on the basis of their degree of similarity to existing products. *Imitations* are products designed to be similar to—and to compete with—existing products of other firms. Examples are the various brands of whitening toothpastes that were developed to compete with Rembrandt. *Adaptations* are variations of existing products that are intended for an established market. Product refinements and extensions are the adaptations considered most often, although imitative products also may include some refinement and extension. *Innovations* are entirely new products. They may give rise to a new industry or revolutionize an existing one. The introduction of CDs, for example, has brought major changes to the recording industry. Innovative products take considerable time, effort, and money to develop. They are therefore less common than adaptations and imitations. As shown in Figure 12.2, the process of developing a new product consists of seven phases.

Idea Generation Idea generation involves looking for product ideas that will help a firm to achieve its objectives. Although some organizations get their ideas almost by chance, firms trying to maximize product-mix effectiveness usually develop systematic approaches for generating new product ideas. Ideas may come from managers, researchers, engineers, competitors, advertising agencies, management consultants, private research organizations, customers, salespersons, or top executives. Procter & Gamble gets 35 percent of its ideas from inventors and outside consultants. Consultants are often used as sources for stimulating new-product ideas. For example, Fahrenheit 212 serves as an "idea factory" that provides ready-to-go product ideas, including market potential analysis.[7]

Screening During screening, ideas that do not match organizational resources and objectives are rejected. In this phase, a firm's managers consider whether the organization has personnel with the expertise to develop and market the proposed product. Management may reject a good idea because the company lacks the necessary skills and abilities. The largest number of product ideas are rejected during the screening phase.

Concept Testing Concept testing is a phase in which a product idea is presented to a small sample of potential buyers through a written or oral description (and perhaps a few drawings) to determine their attitudes and initial buying intentions regarding the product. For a single product idea, an organization can test one or several concepts of the same product. Concept testing is a low-cost means for an organization to determine consumers' initial reactions to a product idea before investing considerable resources in product research and development (R&D). Product development personnel can use the results of concept testing to improve product attributes and product benefits that are most important to potential customers. The types of questions asked vary considerably depending on the type of product idea being tested. The following are typical questions:

- Which benefits of the proposed product are especially attractive to you?
- Which features are of little or no interest to you?
- What are the primary advantages of the proposed product over the one you currently use?
- If this product were available at an appropriate price, how often would you buy it?
- How could this proposed product be improved?

Business Analysis Business analysis provides tentative ideas about a potential product's financial performance, including its probable profitability. During this stage, the firm considers how the new product, if it were introduced, would affect the firm's sales, costs, and profits. Marketing personnel usually work up preliminary sales and cost projections at this point, with the help of R&D and production managers.

Product Development In the product development phase, the company must find out first if it is technically feasible to produce the product and then if the product can be made at costs low enough to justify a reasonable price. If a product idea makes it to this point, it is transformed into a working model, or *prototype*. Honda Motor, for example, developed a prototype minivan that targets Japan's growing population of pet owners with pet-friendly features such as paneled floors and seats that convert to a holding pen. Displayed at the Tokyo Auto Show, the prototype helped Honda assess interest in the concept.[8]

Test Marketing Test marketing is the limited introduction of a product in several towns or cities chosen to be representative of the intended target market. Its aim is to determine buyers' probable reactions. The product is left in the test markets long enough to give buyers a chance to repurchase the product if they are so inclined. Marketers can experiment with advertising, pricing, and packaging in different test areas and can measure the extent of brand awareness, brand switching, and repeat purchases that result from alterations in the marketing mix.

FIGURE 12.2: Phases of New Product Development
Generally, marketers follow these seven steps to develop a new product.

1 Idea generation

2 Screening

3 Concept testing

4 Business analysis

5 Product development

6 Test marketing

7 Commercialization

Source: William M. Pride and O. C. Ferrell, *Marketing: Concepts and Strategies*, 15th ed. (Mason, Ohio: South-Western/Cengage Learning, 2010). Adapted with permission.

Line extensions. The maker of Breathe Right products has developed several line extensions that include vapor strips, throat spray, throat rinse, and child-size nasal strips.

PR NewsFoto/Glaxo Smith Kline Consumer Heathcare

Commercialization During commercialization, plans for full-scale manufacturing and marketing must be refined and completed, and budgets for the project must be prepared. In the early part of the commercialization phase, marketing management analyzes the results of test marketing to find out what changes in the marketing mix are needed before the product is introduced. The results of test marketing may tell the marketers, for example, to change one or more of the product's physical attributes, to modify the distribution plans to include more retail outlets, to alter promotional efforts, or to change the product's price. Products usually are not introduced nationwide overnight. Most new products are marketed in stages, beginning in selected geographic areas and expanding into adjacent areas over a period of time.

Why Do Products Fail? Despite this rigorous process for developing product ideas, most new products end up as failures. In fact, many well-known companies have produced market failures (see Table 12.1).

Why does a new product fail? Mainly because the product and its marketing program are not planned and tested as completely as they should be. For example, to save on development costs, a firm may market-test its product but not its entire marketing mix. Or a firm may market a new product before all the "bugs" have been worked out. Or, when problems show up in the testing stage, a firm may try to recover its product development costs by pushing ahead with full-scale marketing anyway. Finally, some firms try to market new products with inadequate financing.

brand a name, term, symbol, design, or any combination of these that identifies a seller's products as distinct from those of other sellers

brand name the part of a brand that can be spoken

Concept Check

1. What are the ways to improve a product mix? Describe two approaches to use existing products to strengthen a product mix.

2. Why is it important to delete certain products? The largest number of product ideas are rejected during which stage?

3. What is the aim of test marketing?

4. Describe seven phases of new product development.

TABLE 12.1: Examples of Product Failures

Company	Product
Gillette	For Oily Hair shampoo
3M	Floptical storage disk
IncrEdibles Breakaway Foods	Push n' Eat
General Mills	Betty Crocker MicroRave Singles
Adams (Pfizer)	Body Smarts nutritional bars
Anheuser-Busch	Companies Bud Dry and Michelob Dry beer
Coca-Cola	Surge Citrus drink
Heinz	Ketchup Salsa
Noxema	Noxema Skin Fitness

Sources: www.newproductworks.com, accessed January 23, 2006; Robert M. McMath, "Copycat Cupcakes Don't Cut It," *American Demographics*, January 1997, p. 60; Eric Berggren and Thomas Nacher, "Why Good Ideas Go Bust," *Management Review*, February 2000, pp. 32–36.

Branding, Packaging, and Labeling

Three important features of a product (particularly a consumer product) are its brand, package, and label. These features may be used to associate a product with a successful product line or to distinguish it from existing products. They may be designed to attract customers at the point of sale or to provide information to potential purchasers. Because the brand, package, and label are very real parts of the product, they deserve careful attention during product planning.

What Is a Brand?

A **brand** is a name, term, symbol, design, or any combination of these that identifies a seller's products and distinguishes it from other sellers' products. A **brand name** is the part of a brand that can be spoken. It may include letters, words, numbers, or pronounceable symbols, such as the ampersand in *Procter & Gamble*. A **brand mark**, on the other hand, is the part of a brand that is a symbol or distinctive design, such as the Nike "swoosh." A **trademark** is a brand name or brand mark that is registered with the U.S. Patent and Trademark Office and thus is legally protected from use by anyone except its owner. A **trade name** is the complete and legal name of an organization, such as Pizza Hut or Cengage Learning (the publisher of this text).

Types of Brands

Brands often are classified according to who owns them: manufacturers or stores. A **manufacturer (or producer) brand**, as the name implies, is a brand that is owned by a manufacturer. Many foods (Frosted Flakes), major appliances (Whirlpool), gasolines (Exxon), automobiles (Honda), and clothing (Levis) are sold as manufacturers' brands. Some consumers prefer manufacturer brands because they usually are nationally known, offer consistent quality, and are widely available.

A **store (or private) brand** is a brand that is owned by an individual wholesaler or retailer. Among the better-known store brands are Kenmore and Craftsman, both owned by Sears, Roebuck. Owners of store brands claim that they can offer lower prices, earn greater profits, and improve customer loyalty with their own brands. Some companies that manufacture private brands also produce their own manufacturer brands. They often find such operations profitable because they can use excess capacity and at the same time avoid most marketing costs. Many private-branded grocery products are produced by companies that specialize in making private-label products. About 20 percent of products sold in supermarkets are private-branded items.[9]

Consumer confidence is the most important element in the success of a branded product, whether the brand is owned by a producer or by a retailer. Because branding identifies each product completely, customers can easily repurchase products that provide satisfaction, performance, and quality. And they can just as easily avoid or ignore products that do not. In supermarkets, the products most likely to keep their shelf space are the brands with large market shares and strong customer loyalty.

A **generic product (sometimes called a generic brand)** is a product with no brand at all. Its plain package carries only the name of the product—applesauce, peanut butter, potato chips, or whatever. Generic products, available in supermarkets since 1977, sometimes are made by the major producers that manufacture name brands. Even though generic brands may have accounted for as much as 10 percent of all grocery sales several years ago, they currently represent less than one-half of 1 percent.

Benefits of Branding

Both buyers and sellers benefit from branding. Because brands are easily recognizable, they reduce the amount of time buyers must spend shopping; buyers can quickly identify the brands they prefer. Choosing particular brands, such as Tommy Hilfiger, Polo, Nautica, and Nike, can be a way of expressing oneself.

brand mark the part of a brand that is a symbol or distinctive design

trademark a brand name or brand mark that is registered with the U.S. Patent and Trademark Office and thus is legally protected from use by anyone except its owner

trade name the complete and legal name of an organization

manufacturer (or producer) brand a brand that is owned by a manufacturer

store (or private) brand a brand that is owned by an individual wholesaler or retailer

generic product (or brand) a product with no brand at all

Private brand. A number of supermarkets, like Kroger, develop numerous private branded products.

PRNewsFoto/Kroger

When buyers are unable to evaluate a product's characteristics, brands can help them to judge the quality of the product. For example, most buyers are not able to judge the quality of stereo components but may be guided by a well-respected brand name. Brands can symbolize a certain quality level to a customer, allowing that perception of quality to represent the actual quality of the item. Brands thus help to reduce a buyer's perceived risk of purchase. Finally, customers may receive a psychological reward that comes from owning a brand that symbolizes status. The Lexus brand is an example.

Because buyers are already familiar with a firm's existing brands, branding helps a firm to introduce a new product that carries the same brand name. Branding aids sellers in their promotional efforts because promotion of each branded product indirectly promotes other products of the same brand. H.J. Heinz, for example, markets many products with the Heinz brand name, such as ketchup, vinegar, vegetarian beans, gravies, barbecue sauce, and steak sauce. Promotion of one Heinz product indirectly promotes the others.

One chief benefit of branding is the creation of **brand loyalty**, the extent to which a customer is favorable toward buying a specific brand. The stronger the brand loyalty, the greater is the likelihood that buyers will consistently choose the brand. There are three levels of brand loyalty: recognition, preference, and insistence. *Brand recognition* is the level of loyalty at which customers are aware that the brand exists and will purchase it if their preferred brands are unavailable or if they are unfamiliar with available brands. This is the weakest form of brand loyalty. *Brand preference* is the level of brand loyalty at which a customer prefers one brand over competing brands. However, if the preferred brand is unavailable, the customer is willing to substitute another brand. *Brand insistence* is the strongest level of brand loyalty. Brand-insistent customers strongly prefer a specific brand and will not buy substitutes. Brand insistence is the least common type of brand loyalty. Partly owing to marketers' increased dependence on discounted prices, coupons, and other short-term promotions, and partly because of the enormous array of new products with similar characteristics, brand loyalty in general seems to be declining.

Brand equity is the marketing and financial value associated with a brand's strength in a market. Although difficult to measure, brand equity represents the value of a brand to an organization. Some of the world's most valuable brands include Coca-Cola, IBM, Microsoft, General Electric, and Nokia.[10] The four major factors that contribute to brand equity are brand awareness, brand associations, perceived brand quality, and brand loyalty. Brand awareness leads to brand familiarity, and buyers are more likely to select a familiar brand than an unfamiliar one. The associations linked to a brand can connect a personality type or lifestyle with a particular brand. For example, customers associate Michelin tires with protecting family members; a De Beers diamond with a loving, long-lasting relationship ("A Diamond Is Forever"); and Dr Pepper with a unique taste. When consumers are unable to judge for themselves the quality of a product, they may rely on their perception of the quality of the product's brand. Finally, brand loyalty is a valued element of brand equity because it reduces both a brand's vulnerability to competitors and the need to spend tremendous resources to attract new customers; it also provides brand visibility and encourages retailers to carry the brand. New companies, for example, have much work to do in establishing new brands to compete with well-known brands.

Marketing on the Internet sometimes is best done in collaboration with a better-known Web brand. For instance, Weight Watchers, Tire Rack, wine.com, Office Depot, Toys "R" Us, and Shutterfly all rely on partnerships with Internet retail giant Amazon to increase their sales. Amazon provides special sections on its website to promote its partners and their products. As with its own products, Amazon gives users the ability to post online reviews of its partners' products or to add them to an Amazon "wish list" that can be saved or e-mailed to friends. Amazon even labels its partners as "Amazon Trusted" when customers browse their sites, giving even these well-known real-world companies credibility in the online marketplace.[11]

brand loyalty extent to which a customer is favorable toward buying a specific brand

brand equity marketing and financial value associated with a brand's strength in a market

Choosing and Protecting a Brand

A number of issues should be considered when selecting a brand name. The name should be easy for customers to say, spell, and recall. Short, one-syllable names such as *Tide* often satisfy this requirement. Letters and numbers are used to create such brands as Volvo's S60 sedan or RIM's BlackBerry 8100. Words, numbers, and letters are combined to yield brand names such as Motorola's RAZR V3 phone or BMW's Z4 Roadster. The brand name should suggest, in a positive way, the product's uses, special characteristics, and major benefits and should be distinctive enough to set it apart from competing brands. Choosing the right brand name has become a challenge because many obvious product names already have been used.

It is important that a firm select a brand that can be protected through registration, reserving it for exclusive use by that firm. Some brands, because of their designs, are infringed on more easily than others. Although registration protects trademarks domestically for ten years and can be renewed indefinitely, a firm should develop a system for ensuring that its trademarks will be renewed as needed. To protect its exclusive right to the brand, the company must ensure that the selected brand will not be considered an infringement on any existing brand already registered with the U.S. Patent and Trademark Office. This task may be complicated by the fact that infringement is determined by the courts, which base their decisions on whether a brand causes consumers to be confused, mistaken, or deceived about the source of the product. McDonald's is one company that aggressively protects its trademarks against infringement; it has brought charges against a number of companies with *Mc* names because it fears that the use of the prefix will give consumers the impression that these companies are associated with or owned by McDonald's.

A firm must guard against a brand name's becoming a generic term that refers to a general product category. Generic terms cannot be legally protected as exclusive brand names. For example, names such as *yo-yo, aspirin, escalator,* and *thermos*—all exclusively brand names at one time—eventually were declared generic terms that refer to product categories. As such, they could no longer be protected. To ensure that a brand name does not become a generic term, the firm should spell the name with a capital letter and use it as an adjective to modify the name of the general product class, as in Jell-O Brand Gelatin. An organization can deal directly with this problem by advertising that its brand is a trademark and should not be used generically. Firms also can use the registered trademark symbol ® to indicate that the brand is trademarked.

Branding Strategies

The basic branding decision for any firm is whether to brand its products. A producer may market its products under its own brands, private brands, or both. A retail store may carry only producer brands, its own brands, or both. Once either type of firm decides to brand, it chooses one of two branding strategies: individual branding or family branding.

Individual branding is the strategy in which a firm uses a different brand for each of its products. For example, Procter & Gamble uses individual branding for its line of bar soaps, which includes Ivory, Camay, Zest, Safeguard, Coast, and Oil of Olay. Individual branding offers two major advantages. A problem with one product will not affect the good name of the firm's other products, and the different brands can be directed toward different market segments. For example, Marriott's Fairfield Inns are directed toward budget-minded travelers and Marriott Hotels toward upscale customers.

Family branding is the strategy in which a firm uses the same brand for all or most of its products. Sony, Dell, IBM, and Xerox use family branding for their entire product mixes. A major advantage of family branding is that the promotion of any one item that carries the family brand tends to help all other products with the same brand name. In addition, a new product has a head start when its brand name is already known and accepted by customers.

individual branding the strategy in which a firm uses a different brand for each of its products

family branding the strategy in which a firm uses the same brand for all or most of its products

Brand Extensions

A **brand extension** occurs when an organization uses one of its existing brands to brand a new product in a different product category. For example, Procter & Gamble employed a brand extension when it named a new product Ivory Body Wash. A brand extension should not be confused with a line extension. A *line extension* refers to using an existing brand on a new product in the same product category, such as a new flavor or new sizes. For example, when the makers of Tylenol introduced Extra Strength Tylenol PM, the new product was a line extension because it was in the same product category. One thing marketers must be careful of, however, is extending a brand too many times or extending too far outside the original product category, which may weaken the brand.

Packaging

Packaging consists of all the activities involved in developing and providing a container with graphics for a product. The package is a vital part of the product. It can make the product more versatile, safer, or easier to use. Through its shape, appearance, and printed message, a package can influence purchasing decisions.

Packaging Functions Effective packaging means more than simply putting products in containers and covering them with wrappers. The basic function of packaging materials is to protect the product and maintain its functional form. Fluids such as milk, orange juice, and hair spray need packages that preserve and protect them; the packaging should prevent damage that could affect the product's usefulness and increase costs. Since product tampering has become a problem for marketers of many types of goods, several packaging techniques have been developed to counter this danger. Some packages are also designed to foil shoplifting.

Another function of packaging is to offer consumer convenience. For example, small, aseptic packages—individual-serving boxes or plastic bags that contain liquids and do not require refrigeration—appeal strongly to children and to young adults with active lifestyles. The size or shape of a package may relate to the product's storage, convenience of use, or replacement rate. Small, single-serving cans of vegetables, for instance, may prevent waste and make storage easier. A third function of packaging is to promote a product by communicating its features, uses, benefits, and image. Sometimes a firm develops a reusable package to make its product more desirable. For example, the Cool Whip package doubles as a food-storage container.

Package Design Considerations Many factors must be weighed when developing packages. Obviously, one major consideration is cost. Although a number of packaging materials, processes, and designs are available, some are rather expensive. While U.S. buyers have shown a willingness to pay more for improved packaging, there are limits.

Marketers also must decide whether to package the product in single or multiple units. Multiple-unit packaging can increase demand by increasing the amount of the product available at the point of consumption (in the home, for example). However, multiple-unit packaging does not work for infrequently used products because buyers do not like to tie up their dollars in an excess supply or to store those products for a long time. However, multiple-unit packaging can make storage and handling easier (as in the case of six-packs used for soft drinks); it also can facilitate special price offers, such as two-for-one sales. In addition, multiple-unit packaging may increase consumer acceptance of a product by encouraging the buyer to try it

Package design. PBM Products' Parent's Choice Baby Food employs reusable plastic tubs that are designed to be sturdy, spill less, and keep its contents fresh longer.

PR NewsFoto/PBM Products, LLC

several times. On the other hand, customers may hesitate to try the product at all if they do not have the option to buy just one.

Marketers should consider how much consistency is desirable among an organization's package designs. To promote an overall company image, a firm may decide that all packages must be similar or include one major element of the design. This approach, called *family packaging*, is sometimes used only for lines of products, as with Campbell's soups, Weight Watchers entrees, and Planters nuts. The best policy is sometimes no consistency, especially if a firm's products are unrelated or aimed at vastly different target markets.

Packages also play an important promotional role. Through verbal and nonverbal symbols, the package can inform potential buyers about the product's content, uses, features, advantages, and hazards. Firms can create desirable images and associations by choosing particular colors, designs, shapes, and textures. Many cosmetics manufacturers, for example, design their packages to create impressions of richness, luxury, and exclusiveness. The package performs another promotional function when it is designed to be safer or more convenient to use if such features help to stimulate demand.

Packaging also must meet the needs of intermediaries. Wholesalers and retailers consider whether a package facilitates transportation, handling, and storage. Resellers may refuse to carry certain products if their packages are cumbersome.

Finally, firms must consider the issue of environmental responsibility when developing packages. Companies must balance consumers' desires for convenience against the need to preserve the environment. About one-half of all garbage consists of discarded plastic packaging, such as plastic soft drink bottles and carryout bags. Plastic packaging material is not biodegradable, and paper necessitates destruction of valuable forest lands. Consequently, many companies are exploring packaging alternatives and recycling more materials.

Labeling

Labeling is the presentation of information on a product or its package. The *label* is the part that contains the information. This information may include the brand name and mark, the registered trademark symbol ®, the package size and contents, product claims, directions for use and safety precautions, a list of ingredients, the name and address of the manufacturer, and the Universal Product Code (UPC) symbol, which is used for automated checkout and inventory control.

A number of federal regulations specify information that *must* be included in the labeling for certain products. For example,

- Garments must be labeled with the name of the manufacturer, country of manufacture, fabric content, and cleaning instructions.
- Food labels must contain the most common term for ingredients.
- Any food product for which a nutritional claim is made must have nutrition labeling that follows a standard format.
- Food product labels must state the number of servings per container, the serving size, the number of calories per serving, the number of calories derived from fat, and the amounts of specific nutrients.
- Nonedible items such as shampoos and detergents must carry safety precautions as well as instructions for their use.

Such regulations are aimed at protecting customers from both misleading product claims and the improper (and thus unsafe) use of products.

Labels also may carry the details of written or express warranties. An **express warranty** is a written explanation of the responsibilities of the producer in the event that a product is found to be defective or otherwise unsatisfactory. As a result of consumer discontent (along with some federal legislation), firms have begun to simplify the wording of warranties and to extend their duration. The L.L. Bean warranty states, "Our products are guaranteed to give 100 percent satisfaction in every way. Return anything purchased from us at any time if it proves otherwise. We will replace it, refund your purchase price or credit your credit card, as you wish."

labeling the presentation of information on a product or its package

express warranty a written explanation of the responsibilities of the producer in the event that a product is found to be defective or otherwise unsatisfactory

Concept Check

1. Describe the major types of brands.

2. How do brands help customers in product selection? How do brands help companies introduce new products? Explain the three levels of brand loyalty.

3. Define brand equity and describe the four major factors that contribute toward brand equity. What issues must be considered while choosing a brand name?

4. What are the major functions of packaging?

Pricing Products

Describe the economic basis
of pricing and the means
by which sellers can control
prices and buyers' perceptions
of prices.

A product is a set of attributes and benefits that has been carefully designed to satisfy its market while earning a profit for its seller. No matter how well a product is designed, however, it cannot help an organization to achieve its goals if it is priced incorrectly. Few people will purchase a product with too high a price, and a product with too low a price will earn little or no profit. Somewhere between too high and too low there is a "proper," effective price for each product. Let's take a closer look at how businesses go about determining a product's right price.

The Meaning and Use of Price

The **price** of a product is the amount of money a seller is willing to accept in exchange for the product at a given time and under given circumstances. At times, the price results from negotiations between buyer and seller. In many business situations, however, the price is fixed by the seller. Suppose that a seller sets a price of $10 for a particular product. In essence, the seller is saying, "Anyone who wants this product can have it here and now in exchange for $10."

Each interested buyer then makes a personal judgment regarding the utility of the product, often in terms of some dollar value. A particular person who feels that he or she will get at least $10 worth of want satisfaction (or value) from the product is likely to buy it. If that person can get more want satisfaction by spending $10 in some other way, however, he or she will not buy the product.

Price thus serves the function of *allocator*. First, it allocates goods and services among those who are willing and able to buy them. (As we noted in Chapter 1, the answer to the economic question "For whom to produce?" depends primarily on prices.) Second, price allocates financial resources (sales revenue) among producers according to how well they satisfy customers' needs. And third, price helps customers to allocate their own financial resources among various want-satisfying products.

Supply and Demand Affect Prices

In Chapter 1, we defined the **supply** of a product as the quantity of the product that producers are willing to sell at each of various prices. We can draw a graph of the supply relationship for a particular product, say, jeans (see the left graph in Figure 12.3). Note that the quantity supplied by producers *increases* as the price increases along this *supply curve*.

As defined in Chapter 1, the **demand** for a product is the quantity that buyers are willing to purchase at each of various prices. We also can draw a graph of the

price the amount of money a seller is willing to accept in exchange for a product at a given time and under given circumstances

supply the quantity of a product that producers are willing to sell at each of various prices

demand the quantity of a product that buyers are willing to purchase at each of various prices

FIGURE 12.3: Supply and Demand Curves Supply curve (left): The upward slope means that producers will supply more jeans at higher prices. Demand curve (center): The downward slope (to the right) means that buyers will purchase fewer jeans at higher prices. Supply and demand curves together (right): Point E indicates equilibrium in quantity and price for both sellers and buyers.

Price competition. Consumer electronics stores compete on the basis of price.

demand relationship (see the center graph in Figure 12.3). Note that the quantity demanded by purchasers *increases* as the price decreases along the *demand curve*. The buyers and sellers of a product interact in the marketplace. We can show this interaction by superimposing the supply curve onto the demand curve for our product, as shown in the right graph in Figure 12.3. The two curves intersect at point *E*, which represents a quantity of 15 million pairs of jeans and a price of $30 per pair. Point *E* is on the *supply curve*; thus, producers are willing to supply 15 million pairs at $30 each. Point *E* is also on the demand curve; thus, buyers are willing to purchase 15 million pairs at $30 each. Point *E* represents *equilibrium*. If 15 million pairs are produced and priced at $30, they all will be sold. And everyone who is willing to pay $30 will be able to buy a pair of jeans.

Price and Nonprice Competition

Before the price of a product can be set, an organization must decide on the basis on which it will compete—on the basis of price alone or some combination of factors. The choice influences pricing decisions as well as other marketing-mix variables.

Price competition occurs when a seller emphasizes the low price of a product and sets a price that equals or beats competitors' prices. To use this approach most effectively, a seller must have the flexibility to change prices often and must do so rapidly and aggressively whenever competitors change their prices. Price competition allows a marketer to set prices based on demand for the product or in response to changes in the firm's finances. Competitors can do likewise, however, which is a major drawback of price competition. They, too, can quickly match or outdo an organization's price cuts. In addition, if circumstances force a seller to raise prices, competing firms may be able to maintain their lower prices. Consider that when Wal-Mart and Amazon.com reduced the price of a Toshiba high definition DVD player to $200, consumer interest rose. But when Wal-Mart slashed the price by another $100 for 48 hours, consumers snatched up 90,000 to 100,000 of the players. Best Buy also boosted sales when it dropped the price of a Sony Blue-ray DVD player to $399.[12]

The Internet makes price comparison relatively easy for users. This ease of price comparison helps to drive competition. Examples of websites where customers can compare prices include mysimon.com, pricescan.com, bizrate.com, pricegrabber.com, pricecomparison.com, shopping.yahoo.com, nextag.com, and froogle.google.com.

price competition an emphasis on setting a price equal to or lower than competitors' prices to gain sales or market share

Grocery Shopping

How important price is when deciding where to shop for groceries:

52% — Very
45% — Somewhat
3% — Not too

Source: 2009 National Grocers Association—SupermarketGuru Consumer Panel Survey, November 2008–January 2009.

Nonprice competition is competition based on factors other than price. It is used most effectively when a seller can make its product stand out from the competition by distinctive product quality, customer service, promotion, packaging, or other features. Buyers must be able to perceive these distinguishing characteristics and consider them desirable. Once customers have chosen a brand for nonprice reasons, they may not be attracted as easily to competing firms and brands. In this way, a seller can build customer loyalty to its brand. A method of nonprice competition is **product differentiation** which is the process of developing and promoting differences between one's product and all similar products. Mars, for example, markets not only Snickers and M&Ms, but also has an upscale candy line called Ethel's Chocolates. Using the tagline, "no mystery middles," Ethel's chocolates bases its competition on taste, appearance, and packaging, so it doesn't need to compete on price.[13]

Buyers' Perceptions of Price

In setting prices, managers should consider the price sensitivity of people in the target market. How important is price to them? Is it always "very important"? Members of one market segment may be more influenced by price than members of another. For a particular product, the price may be a bigger factor to some buyers than to others. For example, buyers may be more sensitive to price when purchasing gasoline than when purchasing running shoes.

Buyers will accept different ranges of prices for different products; that is, they will tolerate a narrow range for certain items and a wider range for others. Consider the wide range of prices that consumers pay for soft drinks—from 15 cents per ounce at the movies down to 1.5 cents per ounce on sale at the grocery store. Management should be aware of these limits of acceptability and the products to which they apply. The firm also should take note of buyers' perceptions of a given product in relation to competing products. A premium price may be appropriate if a product is considered superior to others in its category or if the product has inspired strong brand loyalty. On the other hand, if buyers have even a hint of a negative view of a product, a lower price may be necessary.

Sometimes buyers relate price to quality. They may consider a higher price to be an indicator of higher quality. Managers involved in pricing decisions should determine whether this outlook is widespread in the target market. If it is, a higher price may improve the image of a product and, in turn, make the product more desirable.

Concept Check

1. What factors must be considered when pricing products?

2. How does a change in price affect the demand and supply of a product?

3. Differentiate price competition and nonprice competition.

4. Why is it important to consider the buyer's sensitivity to price when pricing products?

LEARNING OBJECTIVE 7

Identify the major pricing objectives used by businesses.

Pricing Objectives

Before setting prices for a firm's products, management must decide what it expects to accomplish through pricing. That is, management must set pricing objectives that are in line with both organizational and marketing objectives. Of course, one objective of pricing is to make a profit, but this may not be a firm's primary objective. One or more of the following factors may be just as important.

Survival

A firm may have to price its products to survive—either as an organization or as a player in a particular market. This usually means that the firm will cut its price to attract customers, even if it then must operate at a loss. Obviously, such a goal hardly can be pursued on a long-term basis, for consistent losses would cause the business to fail.

nonprice competition competition based on factors other than price

product differentiation the process of developing and promoting differences between one's product and all similar products

Profit Maximization

Many firms may state that their goal is to maximize profit, but this goal is impossible to define (and thus impossible to achieve). What, exactly, is the *maximum* profit? How does a firm know when it has been reached? Firms that wish to set profit goals should express them as either specific dollar amounts or percentage increases over previous profits.

Target Return on Investment

The *return on investment* (ROI) is the amount earned as a result of that investment. Some firms set an annual percentage ROI as their pricing goal. ConAgra, the company that produces Healthy Choice meals and a multitude of other products, has a target after-tax ROI of 20 percent.

Market-Share Goals

A firm's *market share* is its proportion of total industry sales. Some firms attempt, through pricing, to maintain or increase their market shares. To gain market share, both U.S. cola giants try to gain market share through aggressive pricing and other marketing efforts.

Status-Quo Pricing

In pricing their products, some firms are guided by a desire to avoid "making waves," or to maintain the status quo. This is especially true in industries that depend on price stability. If such a firm can maintain its profit or market share simply by meeting the competition—charging about the same price as competitors for similar products—then it will do so.

Concept Check

1. Explain the various types of pricing objectives.

2. Which ones usually will result in a firm having lower prices?

Pricing Methods

8 LEARNING OBJECTIVE

Examine the three major pricing methods that firms employ.

Once a firm has developed its pricing objectives, it must select a pricing method to reach that goal. Two factors are important to every firm engaged in setting prices. The first is recognition that the market, and not the firm's costs, ultimately determines the price at which a product will sell. The second is awareness that costs and expected sales can be used only to establish some sort of *price floor,* the minimum price at which the firm can sell its product without incurring a loss. In this section, we look at three kinds of pricing methods: cost-based, demand-based, and competition-based pricing.

Cost-Based Pricing

Using the simplest method of pricing, *cost-based pricing,* the seller first determines the total cost of producing (or purchasing) one unit of the product. The seller then adds an amount to cover additional costs (such as insurance or interest) and profit. The amount that is added is called the **markup**. The total of the cost plus the markup is the selling price of the product.

A firm's management can calculate markup as a percentage of its total costs. Suppose, for example, that the total cost of manufacturing and marketing 1,000 DVD players is $100,000, or $100 per unit. If the manufacturer wants a markup that is 20 percent above its costs, the selling price will be $100 plus 20 percent of $100, or $120 per unit.

Markup pricing is easy to apply, and it is used by many businesses (mostly retailers and wholesalers). However, it has two major flaws. The first is the difficulty of determining an effective markup percentage. If this percentage is too high, the product may be overpriced for its market; then too few units may be sold to return the total cost of producing and marketing the product. In contrast, if the markup percentage is too low, the seller is "giving away" profit it could have earned simply by assigning a higher price. In other words, the markup percentage needs to be set to account for the workings of the market, and that is very difficult to do.

The second problem with markup pricing is that it separates pricing from other business functions. The product is priced *after* production quantities are determined, *after* costs are incurred, and almost without regard for the market or the marketing

markup the amount a seller adds to the cost of a product to determine its basic selling price mix. To be most effective, the various business functions should be integrated. *Each should have an impact on all marketing decisions.*

Cost-based pricing also can be facilitated through the use of breakeven analysis. For any product, the **breakeven quantity** is the number of units that must be sold for the total revenue (from all units sold) to equal the total cost (of all units sold). **Total revenue** is the total amount received from the sales of a product. We can estimate projected total revenue as the selling price multiplied by the number of units sold.

The costs involved in operating a business can be broadly classified as either fixed or variable costs. A **fixed cost** is a cost incurred no matter how many units of a product are produced or sold. Rent, for example, is a fixed cost; it remains the same whether 1 or 1,000 units are produced. A **variable cost** is a cost that depends on the number of units produced. The cost of fabricating parts for a stereo receiver is a variable cost. The more units produced, the higher is the cost of parts. The **total cost** of producing a certain number of units is the sum of the fixed costs and the variable costs attributed to those units.

If we assume a particular selling price, we can find the breakeven quantity either graphically or by using a formula. Figure 12.4 graphs the total revenue earned and the total cost incurred by the sale of various quantities of a hypothetical product. With fixed costs of $40,000, variable costs of $60 per unit, and a selling price of $120, the breakeven quantity is 667 units. To find the breakeven quantity, first deduct the variable cost from the selling price to determine how much money the sale of one unit contributes to offsetting fixed costs. Then divide that contribution into the total fixed costs to arrive at the breakeven quantity. (The breakeven quantity in Figure 12.4 is the quantity represented by the intersection of the total revenue and total cost axes.) If the firm sells more than 667 units at $120 each, it will earn a profit. If it sells fewer units, it will suffer a loss.

Demand-Based Pricing

Rather than basing the price of a product on its cost, companies sometimes use a pricing method based on the level of demand for the product: *demand-based pricing*. This method results in a high price when product demand is strong and a low price when demand is weak. Some long-distance telephone companies use demand-based pricing. Buyers of new cars that are in high demand, such as Ford Mustang GT and Toyota Prius, pay sticker prices plus a premium. To use this method, a marketer estimates the amount of a product that customers will demand at different prices and then chooses

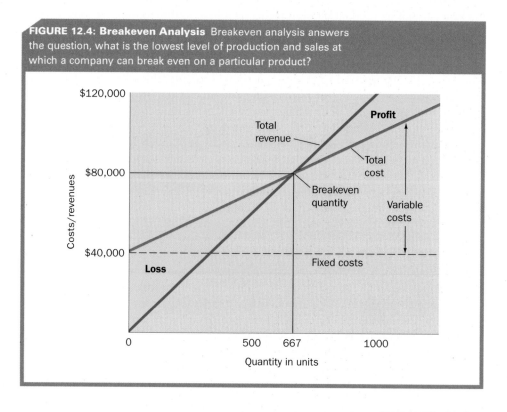

FIGURE 12.4: Breakeven Analysis Breakeven analysis answers the question, what is the lowest level of production and sales at which a company can break even on a particular product?

breakeven quantity the number of units that must be sold for the total revenue (from all units sold) to equal the total cost (of all units sold)

total revenue the total amount received from sales of a product

fixed cost a cost incurred no matter how many units of a product are produced or sold

variable cost a cost that depends on the number of units produced

total cost the sum of the fixed costs and the variable costs attributed to a product the price that generates the highest total revenue. Obviously, the effectiveness of this method depends on the firm's ability to estimate demand accurately.

A firm may favor a demand-based pricing method called *price differentiation* if it wants to use more than one price in the marketing of a specific product. Price differentiation can be based on such considerations as time of the purchase, type of customer, or type of distribution channel. For example, Florida hotel accommodations are more expensive in winter than in summer; a home owner pays more for air-conditioner filters than does an apartment complex owner purchasing the same size filters in greater quantity; and Christmas tree ornaments usually are cheaper on December 26 than on December 16. For price differentiation to work correctly, the company first must be able to segment a market on the basis of different strengths of demand and then must be able to keep the segments separate enough so that segment members who buy at lower prices cannot sell to buyers in segments that are charged a higher price. This isolation could be accomplished, for example, by selling to geographically separated segments.

Compared with cost-based pricing, demand-based pricing places a firm in a better position to attain higher profit levels, assuming that buyers value the product at levels sufficiently above the product's cost. To use demand-based pricing, however, management must be able to estimate demand at different price levels, which may be difficult to do accurately.

Competition-Based Pricing

In using *competition-based pricing*, an organization considers costs and revenue secondary to competitors' prices. The importance of this method increases if competing products are quite similar and the organization is serving markets in which price is the crucial variable of the marketing strategy. A firm that uses competition-based pricing may choose to be below competitors' prices, slightly above competitors' prices, or at the same level. The price that your bookstore paid to the publishing company of this text was determined using competition-based pricing. Competition-based pricing can help to attain a pricing objective to increase sales or market share. Competition-based pricing may be combined with other cost approaches to arrive at profitable levels.

Pricing Strategies

A *pricing strategy* is a course of action designed to achieve pricing objectives. Generally, pricing strategies help marketers to solve the practical problems of setting prices. The extent to which a business uses any of the following strategies depends on its pricing and marketing objectives, the markets for its products, the degree of product differentiation, the life-cycle stage of the product, and other factors. Figure 12.5 contains a

FIGURE 12.5: Types of Pricing Strategies Companies have a variety of pricing strategies available to them.

PRICING STRATEGIES

New-Product Pricing	Differential Pricing	Psychological Pricing	Product-Line Pricing	Promotional Pricing
• Price skimming • Penetration pricing	• Negotiated pricing • Secondary-market pricing • Periodic discounting • Random discounting	• Odd-number pricing • Multiple-unit pricing • Reference pricing • Bundle pricing • Everyday low prices • Customary pricing	• Captive pricing • Premium pricing • Price lining	• Price leaders • Special-event pricing • Comparison discounting

Inside the Rent-to-Own Business

Do rent-to-own companies take advantage of poor consumers by pricing products too high? A $7 billion industry, rent-to-own businesses offer appliances, furniture, musical instruments, and electronics priced to rent by the week or the month. Their customers generally don't have the cash or the credit to buy big-ticket items outright. Although renting is affordable in the short term, it's costly in the long run.

Consider a flat-screen television renting for $86.25 per month at a rent-to-own store. The store informs prospective renters that after 12 monthly payments, they will own the television, at a total cost of $1,035. Yet that same television sells in a nearby electronics store for only $500.

An executive at Rent-A-Center, which operates more than 3,000 rent-to-own stores nationwide, says renting allows consumers to try a product for a short period. If they don't like it or they can't keep up the payments, they can stop renting. "It gives them the flexibility to end it if they want, with no further obligation," he explains.

Through rent-to-own, consumers with bad credit records can take home merchandise that they couldn't otherwise buy. Aaron's, an Atlanta-based rent-to-own retailer, asks customers for the names of three references—and finds that mothers are a good source of information about their children's ability to pay.

Still, customers who rent by the week or month wind up paying roughly twice as much to own a product as consumers who buy it elsewhere, with cash or credit. Is the price too high?

Sources: Suzanne Kapner, "Rent-to-own Makes a Comeback," *Fortune*, May 27, 2009, http://money.cnn.com; Jim Dwyer, "For Just a Few Dollars, A Big TV and Years of Debt," *New York Times*, February 2, 2008, p. B1; Jessica Heffner, "Rent-to-Own Plans Can Cost Cash-Poor Customers in the Long Run," *Middletown (Ohio) Journal*, September 7, 2008, www.middletown.com; Marc Heller, "Schumer Targeting Rent-to-Own Stores," *Watertown Daily Times*, June 5, 2008.

price skimming the strategy of charging the highest possible price for a product during the introduction stage of its life cycle

penetration pricing the strategy of setting a low price for a new product

negotiated pricing establishing a final price through bargaining

list of the major types of pricing strategies. We discuss these strategies in the remainder of this section.

New Product Pricing

The two primary types of new product pricing strategies are price skimming and penetration pricing. An organization can use either one or even both over a period of time.

Price Skimming Some consumers are willing to pay a high price for an innovative product either because of its novelty or because of the prestige or status that ownership confers. **Price skimming** is the strategy of charging the highest possible price for a product during the introduction stage of its life cycle. The seller essentially "skims the cream" off the market, which helps to recover the high costs of R&D more quickly. Also, a skimming policy may hold down demand for the product, which is helpful if the firm's production capacity is limited during the introduction stage. The greatest disadvantage is that a skimming price may make the product appear lucrative to potential competitors, who then may attempt to enter that market.

Penetration Pricing At the opposite extreme, **penetration pricing** is the strategy of setting a low price for a new product. The main purpose of setting a low price is to build market share for the product quickly. The seller hopes that the building of a large market share quickly will discourage competitors from entering the market. If the low price stimulates sales, the firm also may be able to order longer production runs, which result in lower production costs per unit. A disadvantage of penetration pricing is that it places a firm in a less flexible position. It is more difficult to raise prices significantly than it is to lower them.

Differential Pricing

An important issue in pricing decisions is whether to use a single price or different prices for the same product. A single price is easily understood by both employees and customers, and since many salespeople and customers do not like having to negotiate a price, it reduces the chance of a marketer developing an adversarial relationship with a customer.

Differential pricing means charging different prices to different buyers for the same quality and quantity of product. For differential pricing to be effective, the market must consist of multiple segments with different price sensitivities. When this method is employed, caution should be used to avoid confusing or antagonizing customers. Differential pricing can occur in several ways, including negotiated pricing, secondary-market pricing, periodic discounting, and random discounting.

Negotiated Pricing **Negotiated pricing** occurs when the final price is established through bargaining between the seller and the customer. Negotiated pricing occurs in a number of industries and at all levels of distribution. Even when there is a predetermined stated price or a price list, manufacturers, wholesalers, and retailers still may negotiate to establish the final sales price. Consumers commonly negotiate prices for houses, cars, and used equipment.

Secondary-Market Pricing **Secondary-market pricing** means setting one price for the primary target market and a different price for another market. Often the price charged in the secondary market is lower. However, when the costs of serving a secondary market are higher than normal, secondary-market customers may have to pay a higher price. Examples of secondary markets include a geographically isolated domestic market, a market in a foreign country, and a segment willing to purchase a product during off-peak times (such as "early bird" diners at restaurants and off-peak users of cellular phones).

Periodic Discounting **Periodic discounting** is the temporary reduction of prices on a patterned or systematic basis. For example, many retailers have annual holiday sales, and some women's apparel stores have two seasonal sales each year—a winter sale in the last two weeks of January and a summer sale in the first two weeks of July. From the marketer's point of view, a major problem with periodic discounting is that customers can predict when the reductions will occur and may delay their purchases until they can take advantage of the lower prices.

Random Discounting To alleviate the problem of customers' knowing when discounting will occur, some organizations employ **random discounting**. That is, they reduce their prices temporarily on a nonsystematic basis. When price reductions of a product occur randomly, current users of that brand are not likely to be able to predict when the reductions will occur and so will not delay their purchases in anticipation of buying the product at a lower price. Marketers also use random discounting to attract new customers.

Psychological Pricing

Psychological pricing strategies encourage purchases based on emotional responses rather than on economically rational responses. These strategies are used primarily for consumer products rather than business products.

Odd-Number Pricing Many retailers believe that consumers respond more positively to odd-number prices such as $4.99 than to whole-dollar prices such as $5. **Odd-number pricing** is the strategy of setting prices using odd numbers that are slightly below whole-dollar amounts. Nine and five are the most popular ending figures for odd-number prices.

Sellers who use this strategy believe that odd-number prices increase sales. The strategy is not limited to low-priced items. Auto manufacturers may set the price of a car at $11,999 rather than $12,000. Odd-number pricing has been the subject of various psychological studies, but the results have been inconclusive.

Multiple-Unit Pricing Many retailers (and especially supermarkets) practice **multiple-unit pricing**, setting a single price for two or more units, such as two cans for 99 cents rather than 50 cents per can. Especially for frequently purchased products, this strategy can increase sales. Customers who see the single price and who expect eventually to use more than one unit of the product regularly purchase multiple units to save money.

Reference Pricing **Reference pricing** means pricing a product at a moderate level and positioning it next to a more expensive model or brand in the hope that the customer will use the higher price as a reference price (i.e., a comparison price). Because of the comparison, the customer is expected to view the moderate price favorably. When you go to Sears to buy a DVD recorder, a moderately priced DVD recorder may appear especially attractive because it offers most of the important attributes of the more expensive alternatives on display and at a lower price.

secondary-market pricing setting one price for the primary target market and a different price for another market

periodic discounting temporary reduction of prices on a patterned or systematic basis

random discounting temporary reduction of prices on an unsystematic basis

odd-number pricing the strategy of setting prices using odd numbers that are slightly below whole-dollar amounts

multiple-unit pricing the strategy of setting a single price for two or more units

reference pricing pricing a product at a moderate level and positioning it next to a more expensive model or brand

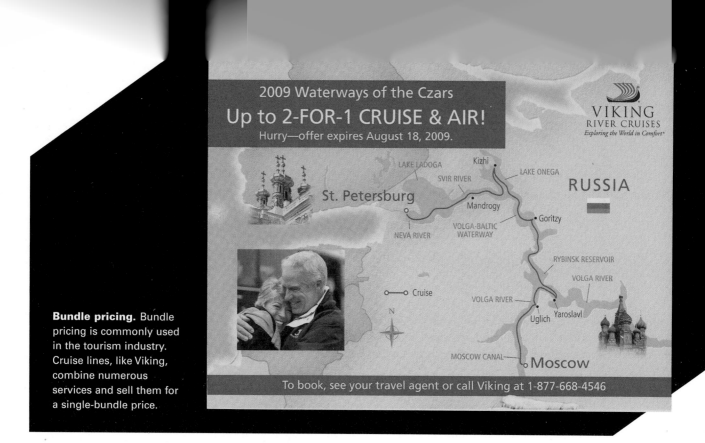

2009 Waterways of the Czars
Up to 2-FOR-1 CRUISE & AIR!
Hurry—offer expires August 18, 2009.

VIKING
RIVER CRUISES
Exploring the World in Comfort

RUSSIA

To book, see your travel agent or call Viking at 1-877-668-4546

Bundle pricing. Bundle pricing is commonly used in the tourism industry. Cruise lines, like Viking, combine numerous services and sell them for a single-bundle price.

Bundle Pricing

Bundle pricing is the packaging together of two or more products, usually of a complementary nature, to be sold for a single price. To be attractive to customers, the single price usually is considerably less than the sum of the prices of the individual products. Being able to buy the bundled combination of products in a single transaction may be of value to the customer as well. Bundle pricing is used commonly for banking and travel services, computers, and automobiles with option packages. Bundle pricing can help to increase customer satisfaction. Bundling slow-moving products with ones with a higher turnover, an organization can stimulate sales and increase its revenues. Selling products as a package rather than individually also may result in cost savings. As regulations in the telecommunications industry continue to evolve, many experts agree that telecom services will be provided together using bundled pricing in the near future. The new term *all-distance* has emerged, but the bundling of services goes beyond just combined pricing for local and long-distance services. Verizon, for example, is offering the Verizon Triple Play plan that gives customers unlimited local, long-distance, wireless, DSL, and DirectTV for a bundled price of about $80 per month.[14]

Everyday Low Prices (EDLPs)

To reduce or eliminate the use of frequent short-term price reductions, some organizations use an approach referred to as **everyday low prices (EDLPs)**. When EDLPs are used, a marketer sets a low price for its products on a consistent basis rather than setting higher prices and frequently discounting them. EDLPs, though not deeply discounted, are set far enough below competitors' prices to make customers feel confident that they are receiving a fair price. EDLPs are employed by retailers such as Wal-Mart and by manufacturers such as Procter & Gamble. A company that uses EDLPs benefits from reduced promotional costs, reduced losses from frequent markdowns, and more stability in its sales. A major problem with this approach is that customers have mixed responses to it. In some instances, customers simply do not believe that EDLPs are what they say they are but are instead a marketing gimmick.

Customary Pricing

In **customary pricing**, certain goods are priced primarily on the basis of tradition. Examples of customary, or traditional, prices would be those set for candy bars and chewing gum.

bundle pricing packaging together two or more complementary products and selling them for a single price

everyday low prices (EDLPs) setting a low price for products on a consistent basis

customary pricing pricing on the basis of tradition

Product-Line Pricing

Rather than considering products on an item-by-item basis when determining pricing strategies, some marketers employ product-line pricing. *Product-line pricing* means establishing and adjusting the prices of multiple products within a product line. Product-line pricing can provide marketers with flexibility in price setting. For example, marketers can set prices so that one product is quite profitable, whereas another increases market share by virtue of having a lower price than competing products.

When marketers employ product-line pricing, they have several strategies from which to choose. These include captive pricing, premium pricing, and price lining.

Captive Pricing
When **captive pricing** is used, the basic product in a product line is priced low, but the price on the items required to operate or enhance it are set at a higher level. For example, a manufacturer of cameras and film may price a camera at a low level to attract customers but price the film at a relatively high level because customers must continue to purchase film in order to use their cameras.

Premium Pricing
Premium pricing occurs when the highest-quality product or the most-versatile version of similar products in a product line is given the highest price. Other products in the line are priced to appeal to price-sensitive shoppers or to those who seek product-specific features. Marketers that use premium pricing often realize a significant portion of their profits from premium-priced products. Examples of product categories in which premium pricing is common are small kitchen appliances, beer, ice cream, and television cable service.

Price Lining
Price lining is the strategy of selling goods only at certain predetermined prices that reflect definite price breaks. For example, a shop may sell men's ties only at $22 and $37. This strategy is used widely in clothing and accessory stores. It eliminates minor price differences from the buying decision—both for customers and for managers who buy merchandise to sell in these stores.

Promotional Pricing

Price, as an ingredient in the marketing mix, often is coordinated with promotion. The two variables sometimes are so interrelated that the pricing policy is promotion oriented. Examples of promotional pricing include price leaders, special-event pricing, and comparison discounting.

Price Leaders
Sometimes a firm prices a few products below the usual markup, near cost, or below cost, which results in prices known as **price leaders**. This type of pricing is used most often in supermarkets and restaurants to attract customers by giving them especially low prices on a few items. Management hopes that sales of regularly priced products will more than offset the reduced revenues from the price leaders.

Special-Event Pricing
To increase sales volume, many organizations coordinate price with advertising or sales promotions for seasonal or special situations. **Special-event pricing** involves advertised sales or price cutting linked to a holiday, season, or event. If the pricing objective is survival, then special sales events may be designed to generate the necessary operating capital.

Comparison Discounting
Comparison discounting sets the price of a product at a specific level and simultaneously compares it with a higher price. The higher price may be the product's previous price, the price of a competing brand, the product's price at another retail outlet, or a manufacturer's suggested retail price. Customers may find comparative discounting informative, and it can have a significant impact on them. However, because this pricing strategy on occasion has led to deceptive pricing practices, the Federal Trade Commission has established guidelines for comparison discounting. If the higher price against which the comparison is made is the price formerly charged for the product, sellers must have made the previous

---

captive pricing pricing the basic product in a product line low, but pricing related items at a higher level

premium pricing pricing the highest-quality or most-versatile products higher than other models in the product line

price lining the strategy of selling goods only at certain predetermined prices that reflect definite price breaks

price leaders products priced below the usual markup, near cost, or below cost

special-event pricing advertised sales or price cutting linked to a holiday, season, or event

comparison discounting setting a price at a specific level and comparing it with a higher price

Concept Check

1. Identify the five categories of pricing strategies.

2. Describe two specific pricing strategies in each category.

price available to customers for a reasonable period of time. If sellers present the higher price as the one charged by other retailers in the same trade area, they must be able to demonstrate that this claim is true. When they present the higher price as the manufacturer's suggested retail price, then the higher price must be similar to the price at which a reasonable proportion of the product was sold. Some manufacturers' suggested retail prices are so high that very few products actually are sold at those prices. In such cases, it would be deceptive to use comparison discounting.

LEARNING OBJECTIVE 10

Describe three major types of pricing associated with business products.

Pricing Business Products

Many of the pricing issues discussed thus far in this chapter deal with pricing in general. Setting prices for business products can be different from setting prices for consumer products owing to several factors such as size of purchases, transportation considerations, and geographic issues. We examine three types of pricing associated with business products, including geographic pricing, transfer pricing, and discounting.

Geographic Pricing

Geographic pricing strategies deal with delivery costs. The pricing strategy that requires the buyer to pay the delivery costs is called *FOB origin pricing*. It stands for "free on board at the point of origin," which means that the price does not include freight charges, and thus the buyer must pay the transportation costs from the seller's warehouse to the buyer's place of business. *FOB destination* indicates that the price does include freight charges, and thus the seller pays these charges.

Transfer Pricing

When one unit in an organization sells a product to another unit, **transfer pricing** occurs. The price is determined by calculating the cost of the product. A transfer price can vary depending on the types of costs included in the calculations. The choice of the costs to include when calculating the transfer price depends on the company's management strategy and the nature of the units' interaction. An organization also must ensure that transfer pricing is fair to all units involved in the purchases.

Discounting

A **discount** is a deduction from the price of an item. Producers and sellers offer a wide variety of discounts to their customers, including the following:

transfer pricing prices charged in sales between an organization's units

discount a deduction from the price of an item

- *Trade discounts* are discounts from the list prices that are offered to marketing intermediaries, or middlemen. A furniture retailer, for example, may receive a 40 percent discount from the manufacturer. The retailer then would pay $60 for a lamp carrying a list price of $100. Intermediaries, discussed in Chapter 14, perform various marketing activities in return for trade discounts.
- *Quantity discounts* are discounts given to customers who buy in large quantities. The seller's per-unit selling cost is lower for larger purchases. The quantity discount is a way of passing part of these savings on to the buyer.
- *Cash discounts* are discounts offered for prompt payment. A seller may offer a discount of "2/10, net 30," meaning that the buyer may take a 2 percent discount if the bill is paid within ten days and that the bill must be paid in full within thirty days.
- A *seasonal discount* is a price reduction to buyers who purchase out of season. This discount lets the seller maintain steadier production during the year. For example, automobile rental agencies offer seasonal discounts in winter and early spring to encourage firms to use automobiles during the slow months of the automobile rental business.
- An *allowance* is a reduction in price to achieve a desired goal. Trade-in allowances, for example, are price reductions granted for turning in used equipment when purchasing new equipment. This type of discount is popular in the aircraft industry. Another example is a promotional allowance, which is a price reduction granted to dealers for participating in advertising and sales-support programs intended to increase sales of a particular item.

Concept Check

1. Describe the three types of pricing associated with business products.

2. Differentiate between FOB origin and FOB destination pricing.

3. Explain the five types of discounts for business products.

SUMMARY

1 Explain what a product is and how products are classified.

A product is everything one receives in an exchange, including all attributes and expected benefits. The product may be a manufactured item, a service, an idea, or some combination of these.

Products are classified according to their ultimate use. Classification affects a product's distribution, promotion, and pricing. Consumer products, which include convenience, shopping, and specialty products, are purchased to satisfy personal and family needs. Business products are purchased for resale, for making other products, or for use in a firm's operations. Business products can be classified as raw materials, major equipment, accessory equipment, component parts, process materials, supplies, and services.

2 Discuss the product life cycle and how it leads to new product development.

Every product moves through a series of four stages—introduction, growth, maturity, and decline—which together form the product life cycle. As the product progresses through these stages, its sales and profitability increase, peak, and then decline. Marketers keep track of the life-cycle stage of products in order to estimate when a new product should be introduced to replace a declining one.

3 Define product line and product mix and distinguish between the two.

A product line is a group of similar products marketed by a firm. The products in a product line are related to each other in the way they are produced, marketed, and used. The firm's product mix includes all the products it offers for sale. The width of a mix is the number of product lines it contains. The depth of the mix is the average number of individual products within each line.

4 Identify the methods available for changing a product mix.

Customer satisfaction and organizational objectives require marketers to develop, adjust, and maintain an effective product mix. Marketers may improve a product mix by changing existing products, deleting products, and developing new products.

New products are developed through a series of seven steps. The first step, idea generation, involves the accumulation of a pool of possible product ideas. Screening, the second step, removes from consideration those product ideas that do not mesh with organizational goals or resources. Concept testing, the third step, is a phase in which a small sample of potential buyers is exposed to a proposed product through a written or oral description in order to determine their initial reaction and buying intentions. The fourth step, business analysis, generates information about the potential sales, costs, and profits. During the development step, the product idea is transformed into mock-ups and actual prototypes to determine if the product is technically feasible to build and can be produced at reasonable costs. Test marketing is an actual launch of the product in several selected cities. Finally, during commercialization, plans for full-scale production and market-

ing are refined and implemented. Most product failures result from inadequate product planning and development.

5 Explain the uses and importance of branding, packaging, and labeling.

A brand is a name, term, symbol, design, or any combination of these that identifies a seller's products as distinct from those of other sellers. Brands can be classified as manufacturer brands, store brands, or generic brands. A firm can choose between two branding strategies—individual branding or family branding. Branding strategies are used to associate (or *not* associate) particular products with existing products, producers, or intermediaries. Packaging protects goods, offers consumer convenience, and enhances marketing efforts by communicating product features, uses, benefits, and image. Labeling provides customers with product information, some of which is required by law.

6 Describe the economic basis of pricing and the means by which sellers can control prices and buyers' perceptions of prices.

Under the ideal conditions of pure competition, an individual seller has no control over the price of its products. Prices are determined by the workings of supply and demand. In our real economy, however, sellers do exert some control, primarily through product differentiation. Product differentiation is the process of developing and promoting differences between one's product and all similar products. Firms also attempt to gain some control over pricing through advertising. A few large sellers have considerable control over prices because each controls a large proportion of the total supply of the product. Firms must consider the relative importance of price to buyers in the target market before setting prices. Buyers' perceptions of prices are affected by the importance of the product to them, the range of prices they consider acceptable, their perceptions of competing products, and their association of quality with price.

7 Identify the major pricing objectives used by businesses.

Objectives of pricing include survival, profit maximization, target return on investment, achieving market goals, and maintaining the status quo. Firms sometimes have to price products to survive, which usually requires cutting prices to attract customers. Return on investment (ROI) is the amount earned as a result of the investment in developing and marketing the product. The firm sets an annual percentage ROI as the pricing goal. Some firms use pricing to maintain or increase their market share. And in industries in which price stability is important, firms often price their products by charging about the same as competitors.

8 Examine the three major pricing methods that firms employ.

The three major pricing methods are cost-based pricing, demand-based pricing, and competition-based pricing. When cost-based pricing is employed, a proportion of the cost is added to the total cost to determine the selling price. When demand-based pricing is used, the price will be higher when demand is higher, and the price will be lower when demand is lower. A firm that uses competition-based pricing may choose to price below competitors' prices, at the same level as competitors' prices, or slightly above competitors' prices.

9 Explain the different strategies available to companies for setting prices.

Pricing strategies fall into five categories: new product pricing, differential pricing, psychological pricing, product-line pricing, and promotional pricing. Price skimming and penetration pricing are two strategies used for pricing new products. Differential pricing can be accomplished through negotiated pricing, secondary-market pricing, periodic discounting, and random discounting. The types of psychological pricing strategies are odd-number pricing, multiple-unit pricing, reference pricing,

bundle pricing, everyday low prices, and customary pricing. Product-line pricing can be achieved through captive pricing, premium pricing, and price lining. The major types of promotional pricing are price-leader pricing, special-event pricing, and comparison discounting.

10 Describe three major types of pricing associated with business products.

Setting prices for business products can be different from setting prices for consumer products as a result of several factors, such as size of purchases, transportation considerations, and geographic issues. The three types of pricing associated with the pricing of business products are geographic pricing, transfer pricing, and discounting.

KEY TERMS

You should now be able to define and give an example relevant to each of the following terms:

product (315)
consumer product (316)
business product (316)
convenience product (316)
shopping product (316)
specialty product (316)
raw material (317)
major equipment (317)
accessory equipment (317)
component part (317)
process material (317)
supply (317)
business service (317)
product life cycle (317)
product line (320)
product mix (320)
product modification (321)
line extension (321)

product deletion (321)
brand (324)
brand name (324)
brand mark (325)
trademark (325)
trade name (325)
manufacturer (or producer) brand (325)
store (or private) brand (325)
generic product (or brand) (325)
brand loyalty (326)
brand equity (326)
individual branding (327)
family branding (327)
brand extension (328)
packaging (328)
labeling (329)

express warranty (329)
price (330)
supply (330)
demand (330)
price competition (331)
nonprice competition (332)
product differentiation (332)
markup (333)
breakeven quantity (334)
total revenue (334)
fixed cost (334)
variable cost (334)
total cost (334)
price skimming (336)
penetration pricing (336)
negotiated pricing (336)
secondary-market pricing (337)

periodic discounting (337)
random discounting (337)
odd-number pricing (337)
multiple-unit pricing (337)
reference pricing (337)
bundle pricing (338)
everyday low prices (EDLPs) (338)
customary pricing (338)
captive pricing (339)
premium pricing (339)
price lining (339)
price leaders (339)
special-event pricing (339)
comparison discounting (339)
transfer pricing (340)
discount (340)

DISCUSSION QUESTIONS

1. What does the purchaser of a product obtain besides the good, service, or idea itself?
2. What major factor determines whether a product is a consumer or a business product?
3. What are the four stages of the product life cycle? How can a firm determine which stage a particular product is in?
4. Under what conditions does product modification work best?
5. Why do products have to be deleted from a product mix?
6. Why must firms introduce new products?
7. What is the difference between manufacturer brands and store brands? Between family branding and individual branding?
8. What is the difference between a line extension and a brand extension?
9. For what purposes is labeling used?
10. Compare and contrast the characteristics of price and nonprice competition.

11. How might buyers' perceptions of price influence pricing decisions?
12. What are the five major categories of pricing strategies? Give at least two examples of specific strategies that fall into each category.
13. Identify and describe the main types of discounts that are used in the pricing of business products.
14. Some firms do not delete products until they become financially threatening. What problems may result from relying on this practice?
15. Under what conditions would a firm be most likely to use nonprice competition?
16. Under what conditions would a business most likely decide to employ one of the differential pricing strategies?
17. For what types of products are psychological pricing strategies most likely to be used?

Get Flash Cards, Quizzes,
Games, Crosswords and more
@ www.cengage.com/introbusiness/
pride

Test Yourself

Matching Questions

1. _____ Quantities of products that producers are willing to sell.

2. _____ Quantities of products that buyers are willing to purchase.

3. _____ Presentation of information on a package.

4. _____ The amount earned for investing.

5. _____ Changes that make a product more dependable.

6. _____ Different prices are set for each market.

7. _____ It represents the value of an organization's brand.

8. _____ Customers consistently choose specific brands.

9. _____ It is the legal name of an organization.

10. _____ Bargaining occurs between seller and buyer.

    a. labeling
    b. supply
    c. demand
    d. product differentiation
    e. return on investment (ROI)
    f. secondary-market pricing
    g. quality product modification
    h. trade name
    i. brand loyalty
    j. brand equity
    k. consumer product
    l. negotiated pricing

True False Questions

11. **T F** Tobacco products, alcoholic beverages, and Del Monte brand fruits are considered a product line.

12. **T F** Screening is the first step in the evolution of a new product.

13. **T F** Once established, a product mix remains effective.

14. **T F** Commercialization is the final stage in the development of a new product.

15. **T F** Product differentiation makes products more competitive with similar products.

16. **T F** "Peanut Butter" written on a plain white wrapper is an example of a generic product.

17. **T F** Packaging has little influence on buying decisions.

18. **T F** Total revenue is the selling price times the number of units sold.

19. **T F** Labels may carry details of written or express warranties.

20. **T F** The breakeven quantity includes the desired profit level.

Multiple-Choice Questions

21. _____ Heinz, IBM, and Xerox use a strategy that helps promote all their products. This strategy is called
    a. family branding.
    b. generic brands.
    c. store brands.
    d. individual branding.
    e. none of the above.

22. _____ Sales rise gradually as a result of promotion and distribution activities, but initially, high development and marketing costs result in low profit or even in a loss. This best describes which stage of the product life cycle.
    a. Maturity
    b. Introduction
    c. Decline
    d. Growth
    e. Steady

23. _____ The manager of a local restaurant wants to add new desserts to the menu. Customers were asked to complete a survey about what they like. The restaurant is in which stage of the new product development process?
    a. Test marketing
    b. Product development
    c. Idea generation
    d. Screening
    e. Business analysis

24. _____ Product modification makes changes to existing products in three primary ways. They are
    a. screening, testing, and changing.
    b. growth, maturity, and decline.

Test Yourself

c. quality, function, and aesthetics.

d. quantity, description, and appearance.

e. product, price, and service.

25. _____ Western Day was a special day at the office. Janice wanted to dress in the latest western fashion, but she had limited funds. She visited several shops before finding the right outfit. For Janice, what type of product is the clothing?

   a. Specialty product
   b. Major equipment
   c. Industrial product
   d. Shopping product
   e. Convenience product

26. _____ The larger number of product ideas are rejected during this phase.

   a. Concept testing
   b. Screening
   c. Test marketing
   d. Idea generation
   e. Business analysis

27. _____ A customer who consistently buys Sony television whenever he or she needs to replace his or her TV set demonstrates

   a. the importance of trademarks.
   b. the importance of trade names.
   c. the importance of brand awareness.
   d. brand loyalty.
   e. brand equity.

28. _____ Plastic water bottles, while convenient for customers, are a clear example that manufacturers are not considering _____ when designing packaging.

   a. the needs of intermediaries
   b. the needs of retailers
   c. environmental consciousness
   d. family needs
   e. cost-effectiveness

29. _____ When there is a shortage of citrus fruit, the economic forces of supply and demand would suggest that

   a. price will stay constant.
   b. price will decrease.
   c. price will stay constant.
   d. price, all things remaining equal, will increase.
   e. it will take a long time before the shortage is felt in the market.

30. _____ Like many other food establishments, Denny's offers senior citizen's discount. This is an example of

   a. periodic discounting.
   b. random discounting.
   c. differential pricing.
   d. negotiated pricing.
   e. senior market pricing.

Answers on p. TY-1

VIDEO CASE

The Smart Car: Tiny with a Price Tag to Match

Tiny car, tiny price tag, tiny gasoline bill. The Smart Car, made by Daimler's Mercedes Car Group in Hambach, France, first appeared on U.S. roads in 2008, just as prices at the gas pump were hitting record highs week after week. The timing could not have been better. Tired of emptying their wallets every time they filled their gas tanks, many U.S. drivers were thinking about downsizing from a big sport-utility vehicle or pickup truck to a smaller vehicle. But were they ready for a 106-inch-long car that seats only two people? Daimler was ready to find out.

The Smart Car had a good track record in other parts of the world. From 1998 to 2008, Daimler sold more than 900,000 Smart Cars in Europe, the Middle East, Asia, Australia, Mexico, and Canada. The car was cute, nimble, and unconventional—a good size for getting through crowded, narrow city streets and fitting into any tight parking spot. Not only was the purchase price highly affordable, but the excellent fuel efficiency made the car especially popular in countries where gas prices were generally high.

To bring the Smart Car to the United States, Daimler redesigned the body and engineering to meet U.S. safety standards. It added six inches to the car's length and included four air bags, an antilock braking system, a collapsing steering column, and other safety features. It also installed a fuel-saving 71-horsepower engine so that the Smart Car would go about 40 highway miles on a gallon of gasoline.

Daimler set the list price of the Smart Fortwo Pure model—the basic version of the two-seater—at $11,590. The list price of the Smart Fortwo Passion Coupe, equipped with more features, was $13,590. The list price of the Smart Fortwo Passion Cabriolet, a convertible with leather seats and additional features, was $16,590. Buyers had the option of ordering extras, such as a metallic-paint finish or an alarm system, for an additional fee. Keeping the list price as tiny as the car allowed Daimler to build market share quickly.

Rather than selling Smart Cars through its regular dealer network, Daimler contracted with the Penske Automotive Group to handle distribution and sales. In another unusual move, Daimler set up a website to let buyers reserve the model of their choice and choose from six interior colors and six exterior colors on the car body's removable panels. Three of the exterior colors were offered as part of the purchase price, while the three metallic exterior colors were offered at an extra cost. The $99 reservation fee was applied to the buyer's purchase price once the ordered model became available. By the time Smart Cars arrived in U.S. showrooms, 30,000 people had paid for reservations.

To build customer interest prior to the introduction, Daimler sent a number of Smart Cars on a 50-city U.S. tour. Nearly 50,000 members of the media and prospective car buyers took test drives. Although many reporters couldn't resist poking fun at the tiny car (*USA Today* called it a "breadbox on wheels"), they all noted its high fuel efficiency and low purchase price.

Soon, demand became so strong that even buyers who had reserved their cars well in advance had to wait months for delivery. A few U.S. customers who didn't want to wait paid as much as $39,000 for European Smart Cars adapted to meet U.S. safety and emissions standards. Down the road, as more auto manufacturers gear up to bring gas-sipping cars to U.S. markets, will the Smart Car maintain its popularity?[15]

For more information about this company, go to www.daimler.com.

Questions

1. Why is bundle pricing appropriate for the various models of Smart Cars?
2. How is demand likely to affect dealers' willingness to negotiate prices with Smart Car buyers?
3. Imagine that Daimler is considering whether to sell unpainted Smart Cars and reduce the list price by $1,500. The Smart Car exterior consists of ten removable panels that can be easily painted. Buyers could paint their own panels, leave the panels unpainted, or pay the dealer an additional fee to personalize their cars by having the panels custom finished in almost any color or design. What are the advantages and disadvantages of this pricing idea?

BUILDING SKILLS FOR CAREER SUCCESS

1. EXPLORING THE INTERNET

The Internet has quickly taken comparison shopping to a new level. Several websites such as bizrate.com, pricescan.com, and mysimon.com have emerged boasting that they can find the consumer the best deal on any product. From computers to watches, these sites offer unbiased price and product information to compare virtually any product. Users may read reviews about products as well as provide their own input from personal experience. Some of these sites also offer special promotions and incentives in exchange for user information. Visit the text website for updates to this exercise.

Assignment

1. Search all three of the websites listed above for the same product.
2. Did you notice any significant differences between the sites and the information they provide?
3. What percentage of searches do you think lead to purchases as opposed to browsing? Explain your answer.
4. Which site are you most likely to use on a regular basis? Why?
5. In what ways do these websites contribute to price competition?

2. BUILDING TEAM SKILLS

In his book, *The Post-Industrial Society,* Peter Drucker wrote:
Society, community, and family are all conserving institutions. They try to maintain stability and to prevent, or at least slow down, change. But the organization of the post-capitalist society of organizations is a destabilizer. Because its function is to put knowledge to work—on tools, processes, and products; on work; on knowledge itself—it must be organized for constant change. It must be organized for innovation.

New product development is important in this process of systematically abandoning the past and building a future. Current customers can be sources of ideas for new products and services and ways of improving existing ones.

Assignment

1. Working in teams of five to seven, brainstorm ideas for new products or services for your college.
2. Construct questions to ask currently enrolled students (your customers). Sample questions might include:
   a. Why did you choose this college?
   b. How can this college be improved?
   c. What products or services do you wish were available?
3. Conduct the survey and review the results.
4. Prepare a list of improvements and/or new products or services for your college.

3. RESEARCHING DIFFERENT CAREERS

Standard & Poor's Industry Surveys, designed for investors, provides insight into various industries and the companies that compete within those industries. The "Basic Analysis" section gives overviews of industry trends and issues. The other sections define some basic industry terms, report the latest revenues and earnings of more than 1,000 companies, and occasionally list major reference books and trade associations.

Assignment

1. Identify an industry in which you might like to work.
2. Find the industry in *Standard & Poor's.* (*Note: Standard & Poor's* uses broad categories of industry. For example, an apparel or home-furnishings store would be included under "Retail" or "Textiles.")
3. Identify the following:
   a. Trends and issues in the industry
   b. Opportunities and/or problems that might arise in the industry in the next five years
   c. Major competitors within the industry (These companies are your potential employers.)
4. Prepare a report of your findings.

Distributing and Promoting Products

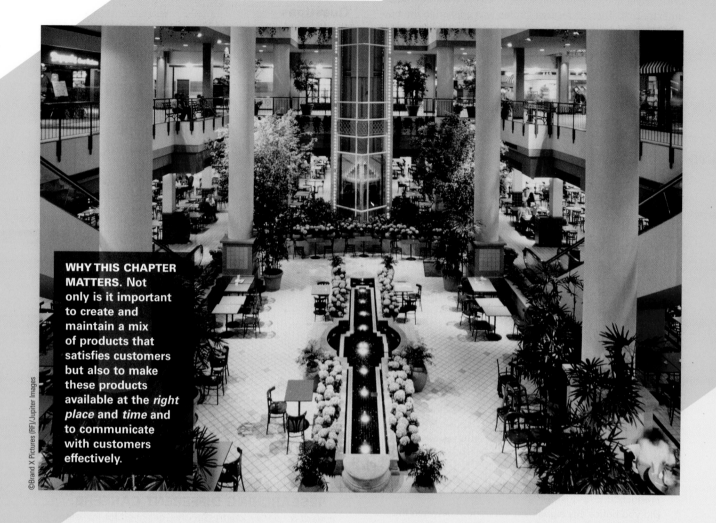

WHY THIS CHAPTER MATTERS. Not only is it important to create and maintain a mix of products that satisfies customers but also to make these products available at the *right place* and *time* and to communicate with customers effectively.

©Brand X Pictures (RF)/Jupiter Images

LEARNING OBJECTIVES

1 Identify the various distribution channels and explain the concept of market coverage.

2 Understand how supply chain management facilitates partnering among channel members.

3 Discuss the need for wholesalers, describe the services they provide, and identify the major types of wholesalers.

4 Distinguish among the major types of retailers and shopping centers.

5 Explain the five most important physical distribution activities.

6 Explain how integrated marketing communications works to have the maximum impact on the customer.

7 Understand the basic elements of the promotion mix.

8 Explain the three types of advertising and describe the major steps of developing an advertising campaign.

9 Recognize the kinds of salespersons, the steps in the personal selling process, and the major sales management tasks.

10 Describe sales promotion objectives and methods.

11 Understand the types and uses of public relations.

Get Flash Cards, Quizzes, Games, Crosswords and more @ www.cengage.com/introbusiness/pride

Best Buy's Burst of Retailing Speed

At a time when many stores are saving money by cutting back on store openings, inventory, and customer service, Best Buy is gaining market share by opening new stores, expanding its assortment, and providing expert service before, during, and after a sale. Best Buy is already the world's largest electronics retailer, ringing up $45 billion annual revenue. Its global empire consists of 4,000 stores with a total of 54 million square feet of retail space.

Best Buy picked up some market share when its main U.S. rival, Circuit City, went bankrupt, closed 567 stores, and sold its brand and website. The company has also been gaining ground by opening dozens of new stores every year, both in the United States and abroad. Two things really set it apart from the competition—its ever-evolving assortment of high-tech merchandise and its approach to customer service.

Although Best Buy began retailing cell phones and service only a few years ago, this has become one of its fastest-growing product categories. The company is also prospering from moving beyond its traditional music, television, and appliance merchandise to offer tech products such as computers, printers, and networking equipment for home and office. To increase profit margins, Best Buy retails some tech items under store brands such as Dynex and Rocketfish. "Technology is becoming ever more important in people's lives," observes Best Buy's chief marketing officer. "The technology is a central part of who you are and how you get things done."

Best Buy has put on its biggest burst of speed in the area of customer service, which is increasingly important for customers buying sophisticated technology products. "Our value proposition is our people: How they help you before, during, and after the sale," explains its chief marketing officer. Expert service from in-store personnel and members of its Geek Squad may be Best Buy's best weapon against the aggressive competitive moves of Costco, Wal-Mart, and Amazon.com, retailers that see electronics as a major opportunity to win new customers and build sales revenue. Can Best Buy maintain its lead in the race for higher market share?[1]

DID YOU KNOW?

Best Buy rings up $45 billion in annual revenue from the sale of electronics in 4,000 stores worldwide with a total of 54 million square feet of retail space.

Some companies, like Best Buy, use a particular approach to distribution and marketing channels that gives them a sustainable competitive advantage. More than two million firms in the United States help to move products from producers to consumers. Store chains such as Dollar General Stores, Starbucks, Sears, and Wal-Mart operate retail outlets where consumers make purchases. Some retailers, such as Avon Products and Amway, send their salespeople to the homes of customers. Other retailers, such as Lands' End and L. L. Bean, sell online, through catalogs, or both. Still others, such as Amazon, sell online to customers.

In this chapter, we initially examine various distribution channels that products follow as they move from producer to ultimate user. Then we discuss wholesalers and retailers and examine the major types of shopping centers. Next, we explore the physical distribution function and the major modes of transportation that are used to move goods. Then we discuss integrated marketing communication and the major elements that can be a part of a promotion mix: advertising, personal selling, sales promotion, and public relations.

distribution channel (or marketing channel) a sequence of marketing organizations that directs a product from the producer to the ultimate user

middleman (or marketing intermediary) a marketing organization that links a producer and user within a marketing channel

Distribution Channels and Market Coverage

1 LEARNING OBJECTIVE

Identify the various distribution channels and explain the concept of market coverage.

A **distribution channel, or marketing channel**, is a sequence of marketing organizations that directs a product from the producer to the ultimate user. Every marketing channel begins with the producer and ends with either the consumer or the business user.

A marketing organization that links a producer and user within a marketing channel is called a **middleman, or marketing intermediary**. For the most part, middlemen are concerned with the transfer of *ownership* of products. A **merchant middleman** (or, more simply, a *merchant*) is a middleman that actually takes title to products by buying them. A **functional middleman** on the other hand, helps in the transfer of ownership of products but does not take title to the products.

Commonly Used Distribution Channels

Different channels of distribution generally are used to move consumer and business products. The four most commonly used channels for consumer products and the two most commonly used business product channels are illustrated in Figure 13.1.

Producer to Consumer This channel, often called the *direct channel*, includes no marketing intermediaries. Practically all services and a few consumer goods are distributed through a direct channel. Examples of marketers that sell goods directly to consumers include Dell Computer, Mary Kay Cosmetics, and Avon Products.

Producers sell directly to consumers for several reasons. They can better control the quality and price of their products. They do not have to pay (through discounts) for the services of intermediaries. Also, they can maintain closer ties with customers.

Producer to Retailer to Consumer A **retailer** is a middleman that buys from producers or other middlemen and sells to consumers. Producers sell directly to retailers when retailers (such as Wal-Mart) can buy in large quantities. This channel is used most often for products that are bulky, such as furniture and automobiles, for which additional handling would increase selling costs. It is also the usual channel for perishable products, such as fruits and vegetables, and for high-fashion products that must reach the consumer in the shortest possible time.

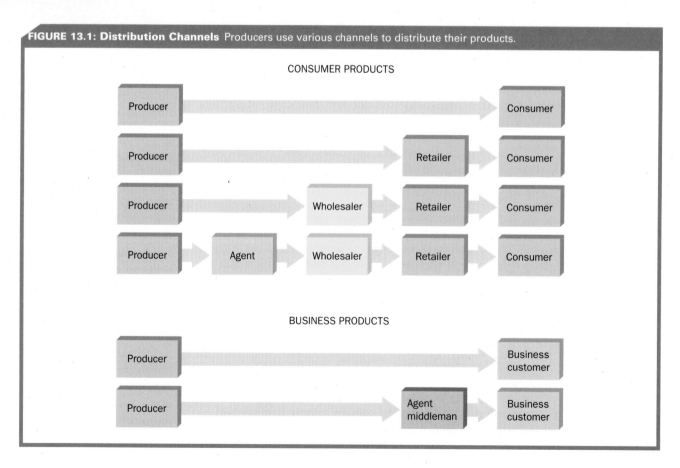

FIGURE 13.1: Distribution Channels Producers use various channels to distribute their products.

Producer to Wholesaler to Retailer to Consumer This channel is known as the *traditional channel* because many consumer goods (especially convenience goods) pass through wholesalers to retailers. A **wholesaler** is a middleman that sells products to other firms. These firms may be retailers, industrial users, or other wholesalers. A producer uses wholesalers when its products are carried by so many retailers that the producer cannot deal with all of them. For example, the maker of Wrigley's gum uses this type of channel.

Producer to Agent to Wholesaler to Retailer to Consumer Producers may use agents to reach wholesalers. Agents are functional middlemen that do not take title to products and that are compensated by commissions paid by producers. Often these products are inexpensive, frequently purchased items. For example, to reach a large number of potential customers, a small manufacturer of gas-powered lawn edgers might choose to use agents to market its product to wholesalers, which, in turn, sell the lawn edgers to a large number of retailers. This channel is also used for highly seasonal products (such as Christmas tree ornaments) and by producers that do not have their own sales forces.

Producer to Business User In this direct channel, the manufacturer's own sales force sells directly to business users. Heavy machinery, airplanes, and major equipment usually are distributed in this way. The very short channel allows the producer to provide customers with expert and timely services, such as delivery, machinery installation, and repairs.

Producer to Agent Middleman to Business User Manufacturers use this channel to distribute such items as operating supplies, accessory equipment, small tools, and standardized parts. The agent is an independent intermediary between the producer and the user. Generally, agents represent sellers.

Using Multiple Channels Often a manufacturer uses different distribution channels to reach different market segments. For example, candy bars are sold through channels containing wholesalers and retailers as well as channels in which the producer sells them directly through large retailers. Multiple channels are also used to increase sales or to capture a larger share of the market with the goal of selling as much merchandise as possible.

Level of Market Coverage

How does a producer decide which distribution channels (and which particular intermediaries) to use? As with every other marketing decision, this one should be based on all relevant factors. These include the firm's production capabilities

The Entrepreneurial Spirit

Are You Ready to Own a Store?

You need more than the right location, the right merchandise, creative ideas, and hard work to succeed as an independent retailer. Before you open a store, ask yourself:

- *Do you have competitive spirit?* Every small store has competition. Karl Benson, who owns two kitchen and gourmet stores in Minnesota, faced a challenge when a national chain opened an outlet nearby. Benson fought back by expanding his line of imported foods and rewarding customer loyalty with special events and discounts.
- *Do you like people?* Personalized service can be a big advantage for a small store. Greg Larson, the owner of Larson's Toys and Games in Arlington, Ohio, enjoys helping customers select age-appropriate toys and offers free gift-wrapping. Dean Holborn, who owns two small stores in Great Britain, is on a first-name basis with customers and will order what they suggest.
- *Do you understand business?* Startups, in particular, must have the business savvy to select and pay for sufficient merchandise to stock their stores before holidays and other peak shopping periods. In addition, store owners must be ready to balance customer needs with business realities. When Holborn bought his first store, he didn't continue the previous owner's informal practice of letting customers sign for purchases and pay later, because he was concerned about being able to collect. Despite this change, most customers remained loyal because they liked Holborn's personal service.

Sources: Emily Chasan, "Retail Bankruptcies Seen Picking Up," *Reuters*, June 11, 2009, www.reuters.com; Dick Youngblood, "Small Business: Cooks of Crocus Hill Finds New Recipes for Success," *Star Tribune (Minneapolis)*, July 23, 2008, p. 1D; Stefan Chomka, "Store Visit: Holborn's," *Grocer*, April 19, 2008, pp. 34+; Anne Field, "Small Shops See Smallness As Their Big Selling Point," *New York Times*, December 15, 2007, p. C1.

retailer a middleman that buys from producers or other middlemen and sells to consumers

wholesaler a middleman that sells products to other firms

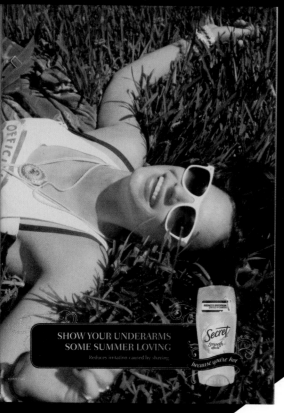

Intensive distribution. Deodorants, like Secret, are widely available and distributed through intensive distribution.

SHOW YOUR UNDERARMS
SOME SUMMER LOVING
Reduces irritation caused by shaving

Secret
Smooth effects
because you're hot

and marketing resources, the target market and buying patterns of potential customers, and the product itself. After evaluating these factors, the producer can choose a particular *intensity of market coverage.* Then the producer selects channels and intermediaries to implement that coverage.

Intensive distribution is the use of all available outlets for a product. The producer that wants to give its product the widest possible exposure in the marketplace chooses intensive distribution. The manufacturer saturates the market by selling to any intermediary of good financial standing that is willing to stock and sell the product. For the consumer, intensive distribution means being able to shop at a convenient store and spend minimum time buying the product. Many convenience goods, including candy, gum, and soft drinks, are distributed intensively. Companies such as Procter & Gamble that produce consumer packaged items rely on intensive distribution for many of their products because consumers want ready availability.

Selective distribution is the use of only a portion of the available outlets for a product in each geographic area. Manufacturers of goods such as furniture, major home appliances, and clothing typically prefer selective distribution. For example, Apple distributes its iPhone through Best Buy, AT&T, and Apple retail stores in the United States.

Exclusive distribution is the use of only a single retail outlet for a product in a large geographic area. Exclusive distribution usually is limited to very prestigious products. It is appropriate, for instance, for specialty goods such as upscale pianos, fine china, and expensive jewelry. The producer usually places many requirements (such as inventory levels, sales training, service quality, and warranty procedures) on exclusive dealers. For example, Patek Philippe watches, which may sell for $10,000 or more, are available in only a few select locations.

LEARNING OBJECTIVE 2 — Partnering through Supply-Chain Management

Understand how supply-chain management facilitates partnering among channel members.

Supply-chain management is a long-term partnership among channel members working together to create a distribution system that reduces inefficiencies, costs, and redundancies while creating a competitive advantage and satisfying customers. Supply-chain management requires cooperation throughout the entire marketing channel, including manufacturing, research, sales, advertising, and shipping. Supply chains focus not only on producers, wholesalers, retailers, and customers but also on component-parts suppliers, shipping companies, communication companies, and other organizations that participate in product distribution. Suppliers are having a greater impact on determining what items retail stores carry. This phenomenon, called *category management,* is becoming common for mass merchandisers, supermarkets, and convenience stores. Through category management, the retailer asks a supplier in a particular category how to stock the shelves. Many retailers and suppliers claim this process delivers maximum efficiency.

Traditionally, buyers and sellers have been adversarial when negotiating purchases. Supply-chain management, however, encourages cooperation in reducing the costs of inventory, transportation, administration, and handling; in speeding order-cycle times; and in increasing profits for all channel members. When buyers, sellers, marketing intermediaries, and facilitating agencies work together, custom-

intensive distribution the use of all available outlets for a product

selective distribution the use of only a portion of the available outlets for a product in each geographic area

exclusive distribution the use of only a single retail outlet for a product in a large geographic area

350

Part 5: Marketing

ers' needs regarding delivery, scheduling, packaging, and other requirements are better met. Home Depot, North America's largest home-improvement retailer, is working to help its suppliers improve productivity and thereby supply Home Depot with better-quality products at lower costs. The company has even suggested a cooperative partnership with its competitors so that regional trucking companies making deliveries to all these organizations can provide faster, more efficient delivery.

Technology has enhanced the implementation of supply-chain management significantly. Through computerized integrated information sharing, channel members reduce costs and improve customer service. At Wal-Mart, for example, supply-chain management has almost eliminated the occurrence of out-of-stock items. Using barcode and electronic data interchange (EDI) technology, stores, warehouses, and suppliers communicate quickly and easily to keep Wal-Mart's shelves stocked with items customers want. Furthermore, there are currently about four hundred electronic trading communities made up of businesses selling to other businesses, including auctions, exchanges, e-procurement hubs, and multisupplier online catalogs. As many major industries transform their processes over the next five to ten years, the end result will be increased productivity by reducing inventory, shortening cycle time, and removing wasted human effort.

supply-chain management long-term partnership among channel members working together to create a distribution system that reduces inefficiencies, costs, and redundancies while creating a competitive advantage and satisfying customers

Concept Check

1. How does supply-chain management encourage cooperation between buyers and sellers?

2. How has technology enhanced the implementation of supply-chain management?

Marketing Intermediaries: Wholesalers

3 LEARNING OBJECTIVE

Discuss the need for wholesalers, describe the services they provide, and identify the major types of wholesalers.

Wholesalers may be the most misunderstood of marketing intermediaries. Producers sometimes try to eliminate them from distribution channels by dealing directly with retailers or consumers. Yet wholesalers provide a variety of essential marketing services. Although wholesalers can be eliminated, their functions cannot be eliminated; these functions *must* be performed by other channel members or by the consumer or ultimate user. Eliminating a wholesaler may or may not cut distribution costs.

Wholesalers Provide Services to Retailers and Manufacturers

Wholesalers help retailers

- Buying in large quantities and then selling to retailers in smaller quantities and by delivering goods to retailers.
- Stocking in one place the variety of goods that retailers otherwise would have to buy from many producers.
- Providing assistance in other vital areas, including promotion, market information, and financial aid.

Wholesalers help manufacturers by

- Performing functions similar to those provided to retailers.
- Providing a sales force, reducing inventory costs, assuming credit risks, and furnishing market information.

Types of Wholesalers

Wholesalers generally fall into two categories: merchant wholesalers; agents and brokers. Of these, merchant wholesalers constitute the largest portion. They account for about four-fifths of all wholesale establishments and employees.

Wholesalers. Grainger, a facilities maintenance products provider, is an example of a wholesaler.

PR NewsFoto/W.W. Grainger, Inc.

Merchant Wholesalers A **merchant wholesaler** is a middleman that purchases goods in large quantities and then sells them to other wholesalers or retailers and to institutional, farm, government, professional, or industrial users.

Characteristics of a Merchant Wholesaler

- Merchant wholesalers usually operate one or more warehouses at which they receive, take title to, and store goods. These wholesalers are sometimes called *distributors* or *jobbers*.
- Most merchant wholesalers are businesses composed of salespeople, order takers, receiving and shipping clerks, inventory managers, and office personnel.
- The successful merchant wholesaler must analyze available products and market needs. It must be able to adapt the type, variety, and quality of its products to changing market conditions.
- Merchant wholesalers may be classified as full-service or limited-service wholesalers depending on the number of services they provide. A **full-service wholesaler** performs the entire range of wholesaler functions described earlier in this section. These functions include delivering goods, supplying warehousing, arranging for credit, supporting promotional activities, and providing general customer assistance.

A full-service wholesaler can be of three different types:

- A **general-merchandise wholesaler** deals in a wide variety of products, such as drugs, hardware, nonperishable foods, cosmetics, detergents, and tobacco.
- A **limited-line wholesaler** stocks only a few product lines but carries numerous product items within each line.
- A **specialty-line wholesaler** carries a select group of products within a single line. Food delicacies such as shellfish represent the kind of product handled by this type of wholesaler.

Agents and Brokers Agents and brokers are functional middlemen. Functional middlemen do not take title to products. They perform a small number of marketing activities and are paid a commission that is a percentage of the sales price.

An **agent** is a middleman that expedites exchanges, represents a buyer or a seller, and often is hired permanently on a commission basis. When agents represent producers, they are known as *sales agents* or *manufacturer's agents*. As long as the products represented do not compete, a sales agent may represent one or several manufacturers on a commission basis. The agent solicits orders for the manufacturers within a specific territory. As a rule, the manufacturers ship the merchandise and bill the customers directly. The manufacturers also set the prices and other conditions of the sales.

What do the manufacturers gain by using a sales agent? The sales agent provides immediate entry into a territory, regular calls on customers, selling experience, and a known, predetermined selling expense (a commission that is a percentage of sales revenue).

A **broker** is a middleman that specializes in a particular commodity, represents either a buyer or a seller, and is likely to be hired on a temporary basis. However, food brokers, which sell grocery products to resellers, generally have long-term relationships with their clients. Brokers may perform only the selling function or both buying and selling using established contacts or special knowledge of their fields.

Marketing Intermediaries: Retailers

Retailers are the final link between producers and consumers. Retailers may buy from either wholesalers or producers. They sell not only goods but also such services as auto repairs, haircuts, and dry cleaning. Some retailers sell both. Sears, Roebuck sells consumer goods, financial services, and repair services for home appliances bought at Sears.

---

merchant wholesaler a middleman that purchases goods in large quantities and then sells them to other wholesalers or retailers and to institutional, farm, government, professional, or industrial users

full-service wholesaler a middleman that performs the entire range of wholesaler functions

general-merchandise wholesaler a middleman that deals in a wide variety of products

limited-line wholesaler a middleman that stocks only a few product lines but carries numerous product items within each line

specialty-line wholesaler a middleman that carries a select group of products within a single line

agent a middleman that expedites exchanges, represents a buyer or a seller, and often is hired permanently on a commission basis

broker a middleman that specializes in a particular commodity, represents either a buyer or a seller, and is likely to be hired on a temporary basis

Concept Check

1. What services do wholesalers provide to producers and to retailers?

2. Identify and describe the various types of wholesalers.

LEARNING OBJECTIVE 4

Distinguish among the major types of retailers and shopping centers.

Of approximately 3 million retailers in the United States, about 90 percent have annual sales of less than $1 million. On the other hand, some large retail organizations realize well over $1 million in sales revenue per day. Table 13.1 lists the ten largest retail organizations and their approximate sales revenues and yearly profits.

Types of Retail Stores

One way to classify retailers is by the number of stores owned and operated by the firm.

1. An **independent retailer** is a firm that operates only one retail outlet. Approximately three-fourths of retailers are independent. One-store operators, like all small businesses, generally provide personal service and a convenient location.
2. A **chain retailer** is a company that operates more than one retail outlet. By adding outlets, chain retailers attempt to reach new geographic markets. As sales increase, chains usually buy merchandise in larger quantities and thus take advantage of quantity discounts. They also wield more power in their dealings with suppliers. About one-fourth of retail organizations operate chains.

Another way to classify retail stores is by store size and the kind and number of products carried. Let's take a closer look at store types based on these dimensions.

Department Stores These large retail establishments consist of several sections, or departments, that sell a wide assortment of products. According to the U.S. Bureau of the Census, a **department store** is a retail store that (1) employs twenty-five or more persons and (2) sells at least home furnishings, appliances, family apparel, and household linens and dry goods, each in a different part of the store. Marshall Field's in Chicago (and several other cities), Harrods in London, and Au Printemps in Paris are examples of large department stores. Sears, Roebuck and JCPenney are also department stores. Traditionally, department stores have been service oriented. Along with the goods they sell, these retailers provide credit, delivery, personal assistance, liberal return policies, and pleasant shopping atmospheres.

Discount Stores A **discount store** is a self-service general-merchandise outlet that sells products at lower-than-usual prices. These stores can offer lower prices

TABLE 13.1: The Ten Largest Retail Firms in the United States

Rank	Company	2007 Revenues (000)	2007 Earnings (000)	No. of Stores
1	Wal-Mart	$378,799,000	$12,731,000	7,262
2	Home Depot	$77,349,000	$4,395,000	2,234
3	CVS Caremark	$76,329,500	$2,622,800	6,301
4	Kroger	$70,235,000	$1,180,500	3,662
5	Costco	$64,400,155	$1,082,772	520
6	Target	$63,367,000	$2,849,000	1,591
7	Walgreen	$53,762,000	$2,041,300	5,997
8	Sears Holdings	$50,703,000	$826,000	3,800
9	Lowe's	$48,283,000	$2,809,000	1,525
10	SUPERVALU	$44,048,000	$593,000	2,474

Sources: 2008 Top 100 Retailers, **www.stores.org**; accessed April 13, 2009.

independent retailer a firm that operates only one retail outlet

chain retailer a company that operates more than one retail outlet

department store a retail store that (1) employs twenty-five or more persons and (2) sells at least home furnishings, appliances, family apparel, and household linens and dry goods, each in a different part of the store

discount store a self-service general-merchandise outlet that sells products at lower-than-usual prices

Department store.
Macy's is an example of a
department store.

by operating on smaller markups and by offering minimal customer services. To keep prices low, discount stores operate on the basic principle of high turnover of such items as appliances, toys, clothing, automotive products, and sports equipment. Popular discount stores include KMart, Wal-Mart, Dollar General, and Target.

Warehouse Showrooms A **warehouse showroom** is a retail facility with five basic characteristics: (1) a large, low-cost building, (2) warehouse materials-handling technology, (3) vertical merchandise displays, (4) a large, on-premises inventory, and (5) minimal service. Some of the best-known showrooms are operated by big furniture retailers. These operations employ few personnel and offer few services. Most customers carry away purchases in the manufacturer's carton, although some warehouse showrooms will deliver for a fee.

Convenience Stores A **convenience store** is a small food store that sells a limited variety of products but remains open well beyond normal business hours. Almost 70 percent of convenience store customers live within a mile of the store. White Hen Pantry, 7-Eleven, Circle K, and Open Pantry stores, for example, are found in some areas, as are independent convenience stores. Convenience stores are the fastest growing category of retailer, with an 8.6 percent growth in sales over the past year compared with a 9 percent decline in overall retail sales.[2]

Supermarkets A **supermarket** is a large self-service store that sells primarily food and household products. It stocks canned, fresh, frozen, and processed foods; paper products; and cleaning supplies. Supermarkets also may sell such items as housewares, toiletries, toys and games, drugs, stationery, books and magazines, plants and flowers, and a few clothing items. Supermarkets are large-scale operations that emphasize low prices and one-stop shopping for household needs.

Superstores A **superstore** is a large retail store that carries not only food and nonfood products ordinarily found in supermarkets but also additional product lines—housewares, hardware, small appliances, clothing, personal-care products,

warehouse showroom a retail facility in a large, low-cost building with a large on-premises inventory and minimal service

convenience store a small food store that sells a limited variety of products but remains open well beyond normal business hours

supermarket a large self-service store that sells primarily food and household products

superstore a large retail store that carries not only food and nonfood products ordinarily found in supermarkets but also additional product lines

Global Economic Challenges

Wrapping the World in Wal-Marts?

Wal-Mart is by far the world's largest retailer, with $400 billion in annual sales and 7,900 stores in 15 nations. Yet the company didn't expand beyond the United States until 1991, when it opened a store in downtown Mexico City. Despite that late start, more than 25 percent of Wal-Mart's sales revenue today comes from retail operations in Central and South America, Japan, and China.

Not all of Wal-Mart's international expansion efforts have been successful. The company had high hopes when it entered the fast-growing South Korean market. However, eight years later, with no profits in sight, Wal-Mart sold all its South Korean stores to a local competitor. It also pushed hard for market share when it began opening stores in Germany. But local discounters proved to be tough competitors, and Wal-Mart sold its 85 German stores to a rival when it left the market in 2006 with a $1 billion loss.

These days, Wal-Mart studies local conditions very carefully before entering new markets. It has opened an office in Russia to learn more about that country's retailing situation. It also bought a controlling interest in a Chilean grocery chain to edge into that market. In India, where local laws limit foreign competition, Wal-Mart opened a wholesale outlet and will monitor reaction as it expands. "The easiest thing is to roll out stores, but the most difficult is to sustain and feed them," comments the head of Wal-Mart India.

Sources: Mark Choueke, "Marketing at Heart of All Retail Success," *Marketing Week*, June 11, 2009, http://www.marketingweek.co.uk/marketing-at-heart-of-all-retail-success/3001315.article; Andria Cheng, "Wal-Mart Taps Color, Brands to Retail Shoppers," *Wall Street Journal*, June 5, 2009, www.wsj.com; Nandini Lakshman, "Why Wal-Mart's First India Store Isn't a Wal-Mart," *Time*, May 15, 2009, www.time.com.

garden products, and automotive merchandise. Superstores also provide a number of services to entice customers. Typically, these include automotive repair, snack bars and restaurants, film developing, and banking.

Warehouse Clubs The **warehouse club** is a large-scale members-only establishment that combines features of cash-and-carry wholesaling with discount retailing. For a nominal annual fee (about $25), small retailers may purchase products at wholesale prices for business use or for resale. Warehouse clubs also sell to ultimate consumers. Individual purchasers usually can choose to pay yearly dues for membership cards that allow them to avoid the 5 percent additional charge.

Because their product lines are shallow and sales volumes are high, warehouse clubs can offer a broad range of merchandise, including perishable and nonperishable foods, beverages, books, appliances, housewares, automotive parts, hardware, furniture, and sundries.

Traditional Specialty Stores A **traditional specialty store** carries a narrow product mix with deep product lines. Traditional specialty stores are sometimes called *limited-line retailers*. If they carry depth in one particular product category, they may be called *single-line retailers*. Specialty stores usually sell such products as clothing, jewelry, sporting goods, fabrics, computers, flowers, baked goods, books, and pet supplies. Specialty stores usually offer deeper product mixes than department stores. They attract customers by emphasizing service, atmosphere, and location. Consumers who are dissatisfied with the impersonal atmosphere of large retailers often find the attention offered by small specialty stores appealing. Specialty stores include the Gap, Radio Shack, Bath and Body Works, and Foot Locker.

warehouse club a large-scale members-only establishment that combines features of cash-and-carry wholesaling with discount retailing

traditional specialty store a store that carries a narrow product mix with deep product lines

off-price retailer a store that buys manufacturers' seconds, overruns, returns, and off-season merchandise for resale to consumers at deep discounts

Off-Price Retailers An **off-price retailer** is a store that buys manufacturers' seconds, overruns, returns, and off-season merchandise

©Anne Kitzman/Shutterstock

at below-wholesale prices and sells them to consumers at deep discounts. Off-price retailers sell limited lines of national-brand and designer merchandise, usually clothing, shoes, or housewares. Off-price retailers include T.J. Maxx, Burlington Coat Factory, and Marshalls. Off-price stores charge up to 50 percent less than department stores do for comparable merchandise but offer few customer services. They often include community dressing rooms and central checkout counters, and some off-price retailers have a no-returns, no-exchanges policy.

Category Killers A **category killer** is a very large specialty store that concentrates on a single product line and competes by offering low prices and an enormous number of products. These stores are called *category killers* because they take business away from smaller, high-cost retail stores. Category killers include Home Depot (building materials), Office Depot (office supplies and equipment), and Best Buy (electronics), all of which are leaders in their niche. Some experts are predicting a decrease in the number of large-scale category killers in the not so distant future owing to other stores focusing on even smaller niches.[3]

Types of Nonstore Selling

Nonstore retailing is selling that does not take place in conventional store facilities; consumers purchase products without visiting a store. This form of retailing accounts for an increasing percentage of total retail sales. Nonstore retailers use direct selling, direct marketing, and vending machines.

Direct Selling **Direct selling** is the marketing of products to customers through face-to-face sales presentations at home or in the workplace. Traditionally called *door-to-door selling*, direct selling in the United States began with peddlers more than a century ago and has grown to about $30 billion in U.S. sales annually.[4] Instead of the door-to-door approach, many companies today—such as Mary Kay, Kirby, Amway, and Avon—use other approaches. They identify customers by mail, telephone, the Internet, or at shopping malls and then set up appointments. Direct selling sometimes involves the "party plan," which can occur in the customer's home or workplace. Direct selling through the party plan requires effective salespeople who can identify potential hosts and provide encouragement and incentives for them to organize a gathering of friends and associates. Companies that commonly use the party plan are Tupperware, Stanley Home Products, Pampered Chef, and Sarah Coventry.

Direct Marketing **Direct marketing** is the use of the telephone, Internet, and nonpersonal media to communicate product and organizational information to customers, who then can purchase products via mail, telephone, or the Internet. Direct marketing is one type of nonstore retailing. Direct marketing can occur through catalog marketing, direct-response marketing, telemarketing, television home shopping, and online retailing.

In **catalog marketing**, an organization provides a catalog from which customers make selections and place orders by mail, telephone, or the Internet. Catalog marketing began in 1872 when Montgomery Ward issued its first catalog to rural families. Today, there are more than 7,000 catalog marketing companies in the United States, as well as a number of retail stores, such as JCPenney, that engage in catalog marketing. Some organizations, including Spiegel and JCPenney, offer a broad array of products spread over multiple product lines. Catalog companies such as Lands' End, Pottery Barn, and J. Crew offer considerable depth in one major line of products. Still other catalog companies specialize in only a few products within a single line. The advantages of catalog marketing include efficiency and convenience for customers. The retailer benefits by being able to locate in remote, low-cost areas, save on expensive store fixtures, and reduce both personal selling and store operating expenses. Disadvantages, on the other hand, are that catalog marketing is inflexible, provides limited service, and is most effective for only a selected set of products.

category killer a very large specialty store that concentrates on a single product line and competes on the basis of low prices and product availability

nonstore retailing a type of retailing whereby consumers purchase products without visiting a store

direct selling the marketing of products to customers through face-to-face sales presentations at home or in the workplace

direct marketing the use of the telephone, Internet, and nonpersonal media to introduce products to customers, who then can purchase them via mail, telephone, or the Internet

catalog marketing a type of marketing in which an organization provides a catalog from which customers make selections and place orders by mail, telephone, or the Internet

Direct-response marketing occurs when a retailer advertises a product and makes it available through mail, telephone, or online orders. Examples of direct-response marketing would include a television commercial offering a recording artist's musical collection or a newspaper or magazine advertisement for a series of children's books. Direct-response marketing is also conducted by sending letters, samples, brochures, or booklets to prospects on a mailing list and asking that they order the advertised products by mail, by telephone, or online.

Telemarketing is the performance of marketing-related activities by telephone. Some organizations use a prescreened list of prospective clients. Telemarketing has many advantages such as generating sales leads, improving customer service, speeding up payments on past-due accounts, raising funds for nonprofit organizations, and gathering market data.

Currently, the laws and regulations regarding telemarketing, while in a state of flux, are becoming more restrictive. On October 1, 2003, the U.S. Congress implemented a national do-not-call registry for consumers who do not want to receive telemarketing calls. So far, the do-not-call registry has listed over 172 million phone numbers. Regulations associated with the national do-not-call registry are enforced by the Federal Trade Commission (FTC). Companies are subject to fines of up to $12,000 for each call made to consumers listed on the national do-not-call registry. In February 2008, The Do-Not-Call Fee Extension Act of 2007 came into effect, settling the annual fees telemarketers must pay to access the registry at $54 for each area code of data accessed or $14,850 for access to every area code in the registry, whichever is less.[5] For example, DirecTV recently was ordered to pay $5.3 million in fines by the FTC for violating the do-not-call list.[6] Certain exceptions apply to no-call lists. A company still can use telemarketing to communicate with existing customers. In addition, charitable, political, and telephone survey organizations are not restricted by the national registry.

Television home shopping presents products to television viewers, encouraging them to order through toll-free numbers and pay with credit cards. Home Shopping Network (HSN) originated and popularized this format. The most popular products sold through television home shopping are jewelry (40 percent of total sales), clothing, housewares, and electronics. Home shopping channels have grown so rapidly in recent years that more than 60 percent of U.S. households have access to home shopping programs.

HSN and QVC are two of the largest home shopping networks. Approximately 60 percent of home shopping sales revenues come from repeat purchasers.

Online retailing makes products available to buyers through computer connections. Most bricks-and-mortar retailers have websites to sell products, provide information about their company, or distribute coupons. Netflix has changed the video rental industry by offering its completely online movie rental service. Customers pay a monthly fee for unlimited rentals and browse the Netflix site to compose a list of videos they want to rent. Selections are mailed to their home, and customers are free to keep the rental as long as they want without the late fees typically charged by traditional stores.[7] Although online retailing represents a major retailing venue, security remains an issue. In a recent survey conducted

direct-response marketing a type of marketing in which a retailer advertises a product and makes it available through mail, telephone, or online orders

telemarketing the performance of marketing-related activities by telephone

television home shopping a form of selling in which products are presented to television viewers, who can buy them by calling a toll-free number and paying with a credit card

online retailing retailing that makes products available to buyers through computer connections

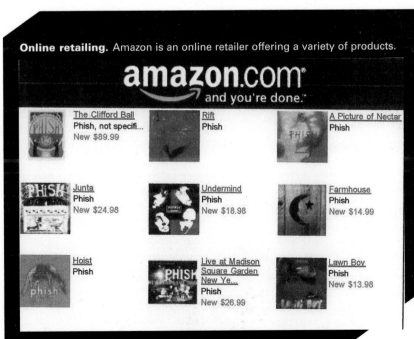

Online retailing. Amazon is an online retailer offering a variety of products.

by the Business Software Alliance, some Internet users still expressed concerns about shopping online. The major problems are identity theft and credit-card theft.

Automatic vending is the use of machines to dispense products. It accounts for less than 2 percent of all retail sales. Video game machines provide an entertainment service, and many banks offer automatic teller machines (ATMs), which dispense cash and perform other services.

Automatic vending is one of the most impersonal forms of retailing. Small, standardized, routinely purchased products (e.g., chewing gum, candy, newspapers, cigarettes, soft drinks, and coffee) can be sold in machines because consumers usually buy them at the nearest available location. Machines in areas of heavy traffic provide efficient and continuous service to consumers. Such high-volume areas may have more diverse product availability—for example, hot and cold sandwiches, DVD rentals, or even iPods (yes, $200 iPods are available in machines with coin slots). San Francisco–based Zoom Systems has expanded its vending machine offerings from snacks to digital cameras. Its number one seller, though, is the iPod vending machine that offers Apple's popular MP3 players as well as accessories such as headphones, speakers, and battery chargers.[8]

Types of Shopping Centers

The *planned shopping center* is a self-contained retail facility constructed by independent owners and consisting of various stores. Shopping centers are designed and promoted to serve diverse groups of customers with widely differing needs. The management of a shopping center strives for a coordinated mix of stores, a comfortable atmosphere, adequate parking, pleasant landscaping, and special events to attract customers. The convenience of shopping for most family and household needs in a single location is an important part of shopping-center appeal.

A planned shopping center is one of four types: lifestyle, neighborhood, community, or regional. Although shopping centers vary, each offers a complementary mix of stores for the purpose of generating consumer traffic.

Lifestyle Shopping Centers
A **lifestyle shopping center** is a shopping center that has an open-air configuration and is occupied by upscale national chain specialty stores.

The lifestyle center is more convenient than a traditional enclosed mall but offers the same quality of upscale retail and department stores, movie theaters, and dining. A strong emphasis is placed on the architecture of the center and creating a pleasant and "hip" shopping environment. Most lifestyle centers are found in affluent neighborhoods.[9]

Neighborhood Shopping Centers
A **neighborhood shopping center** typically consists of several small convenience and specialty stores. Businesses in neighborhood shopping centers might include small grocery stores, drugstores, gas stations, and fast-food restaurants. These retailers serve consumers who live less than ten minutes away, usually within a two- to three-mile radius of the stores. Because most purchases in the neighborhood shopping center are based on convenience or personal contact, these retailers generally make only limited efforts to coordinate promotional activities among stores in the shopping center.

Community Shopping Centers
A **community shopping center** includes one or two department stores and some specialty stores, along with convenience stores. It attracts consumers from a wider geographic area who will drive longer distances to find products and specialty items unavailable in neighborhood shopping centers. Community shopping centers, which are carefully planned and coordinated, generate traffic with special events such as art exhibits, automobile shows, and sidewalk sales. The management of a community shopping center maintains a balance of tenants so that the center can offer wide product mixes and deep product lines.

automatic vending the use of machines to dispense products

lifestyle shopping center an open-air-environment shopping center with upscale chain specialty stores

neighborhood shopping center a planned shopping center consisting of several small convenience and specialty stores

community shopping center a planned shopping center that includes one or two department stores and some specialty stores, along with convenience stores

Lifestyle shopping centers. The Village of Rochester Hills shopping center is one example of a lifestyle shopping center.

Regional Shopping Centers A **regional shopping center** usually has large department stores, numerous specialty stores, restaurants, movie theaters, and sometimes even hotels. It carries most of the merchandise offered by a downtown shopping district. Downtown merchants, in fact, often have renovated their stores and enlarged their parking facilities to meet the competition of successful regional shopping centers. Urban expressways and improved public transportation also have helped many downtown shopping areas to remain vigorous.

Regional shopping centers carefully coordinate management and marketing activities to reach the 150,000 or more customers in their target market. These large centers usually advertise, hold special events, and provide transportation to certain groups of customers. They also maintain a suitable mix of stores. National chain stores can gain leases in regional shopping centers more easily than small independent stores because they are better able to meet the centers' financial requirements.

Physical Distribution

Physical distribution is all those activities concerned with the efficient movement of products from the producer to the ultimate user. Physical distribution therefore is the movement of the products themselves—both goods and services—through their channels of distribution. It is a combination of several interrelated business functions. The most important of these are inventory management, order processing, warehousing, materials handling, and transportation. These functions and their costs are highly interrelated. For example, using expensive air freight may reduce warehousing and inventory costs. Because of such interrelationships, marketers view physical distribution as an integrated effort that supports other important marketing activities, such as getting the right product to the right place at the right time and at minimal total cost.

Inventory Management

In Chapter 8 we discussed inventory management from the standpoint of operations. We defined **inventory management** as the process of managing inventories in such a way as to minimize inventory costs, including both holding costs and potential stock-out costs. Both the definition and the objective of inventory control apply here as well.

Holding costs are the costs of storing products until they are purchased or shipped to customers. *Stock-out costs* are the costs of sales lost when items are not

---

Concept Check

1. Describe the major types of retail stores. Give an example of each.

2. How does nonstore retailing occur?

3. What are the four most common types of shopping centers, and what type of store does each typically contain?

5 LEARNING OBJECTIVE

Explain the five most important physical distribution activities.

regional shopping center a planned shopping center containing large department stores, numerous specialty stores, restaurants, movie theaters, and sometimes even hotels

physical distribution all those activities concerned with the efficient movement of products from the producer to the ultimate user

inventory management the process of managing inventories in such a way as to minimize inventory costs, including both holding costs and potential stock-out costs in inventory. Of course, holding costs can be reduced by minimizing inventories, but then stock-out costs could be financially threatening to the organization. And stock-out costs can be minimized by carrying very large inventories, but then holding costs would be enormous.

Inventory management therefore is a sort of balancing act between stock-out costs and holding costs. The latter include the cost of money invested in inventory, the cost of storage space, insurance costs, and inventory taxes. Often even a relatively small reduction in inventory investment can provide a relatively large increase in working capital. And sometimes this reduction can best be accomplished through a willingness to incur a reasonable level of stock-out costs. Companies frequently rely on technology and software to help manage inventory on a regular basis.

Order Processing

Order processing consists of activities involved in receiving and filling customers' purchase orders. It may include not only the means by which customers order products but also procedures for billing and for granting credit.

Fast, efficient order processing is an important marketing service—one that can provide a dramatic competitive edge. The people who purchase goods for intermediaries are especially concerned with their suppliers' promptness and reliability in order processing. To them, promptness and reliability mean minimal inventory costs as well as the ability to order goods when they are needed rather than weeks in advance. The Internet is providing new opportunities for improving services associated with order processing.

Warehousing

Warehousing is the set of activities involved in receiving and storing goods and preparing them for reshipment. Goods are stored to create time utility; that is, they are held until they are needed for use or sale. Warehousing includes the following activities:

- *Receiving goods.* The warehouse accepts delivered goods and assumes responsibility for them.
- *Identifying goods.* Records are made of the quantity of each item received. Items may be marked, coded, or tagged for identification.
- *Sorting goods.* Delivered goods may have to be sorted before being stored.
- *Dispatching goods to storage.* Items must be moved to specific storage areas, where they can be found later.
- *Holding goods.* The goods are kept in storage under proper protection until needed.
- *Recalling, picking, and assembling goods.* Items that are to leave the warehouse must be selected from storage and assembled efficiently.
- *Dispatching shipments.* Each shipment is packaged suitably and directed to the proper transport vehicle. Shipping and accounting documents are prepared.

A firm may use its own private warehouses or rent space in public warehouses. A *private warehouse,* owned and operated by a particular firm, can be designed to serve the firm's specific needs. However, the organization must take on the task of financing the facility, determining the best location for it, and ensuring that it is used fully. Generally, only companies that deal in large quantities of goods can justify private warehouses. With a total of almost 96 million square feet in warehouse space, United Parcel Service (UPS) owns the largest amount of private warehouse space in the world. Wal-Mart is second with 80 million, and Sears is third with 40 million.[10]

Public warehouses offer their services to all individuals and firms. Most are huge, one-story structures on the outskirts of cities, where rail and truck transportation is easily available. They provide storage facilities, areas for sorting and assembling shipments, and office and display spaces for wholesalers and retailers.

order processing activities involved in receiving and filling customers' purchase orders

warehousing the set of activities involved in receiving and storing goods and preparing them for reshipment

Public warehouses also will hold—and issue receipts for—goods used as collateral for borrowed funds.

Materials Handling

Materials handling is the actual physical handling of goods—in warehouses as well as during transportation. Proper materials-handling procedures and techniques can increase the usable capacity of a warehouse or that of any means of transportation. Proper handling can reduce breakage and spoilage as well.

Modern materials handling attempts to reduce the number of times a product is handled. One method is called *unit loading*. Several smaller cartons, barrels, or boxes are combined into a single standard-size load that can be handled efficiently by forklift, conveyer, or truck.

Transportation

As a part of physical distribution, **transportation** is simply the shipment of products to customers. The greater the distance between seller and purchaser, the more important is the choice of the means of transportation and the particular carrier.

A firm that offers transportation services is called a **carrier**. A *common carrier* is a transportation firm whose services are available to all shippers. Railroads, airlines, and most long-distance trucking firms are common carriers. A *contract carrier* is available for hire by one or several shippers. Contract carriers do not serve the general public. Moreover, the number of firms they can handle at any one time is limited by law. A *private carrier* is owned and operated by the shipper.

In addition, a shipper can hire agents called *freight forwarders* to handle its transportation. Freight forwarders pick up shipments from the shipper, ensure that the goods are loaded on selected carriers, and assume responsibility for safe delivery of the shipments to their destinations. Freight forwarders often can group a number of small shipments into one large load (which is carried at a lower rate). This, of course, saves money for shippers.

The six major criteria used for selecting transportation modes are compared in Table 13.2. These six criteria are cost, speed, dependability, load flexibility, accessibility, and frequency.

materials handling the actual physical handling of goods, in warehouses as well as during transportation

transportation the shipment of products to customers

carrier a firm that offers transportation services

TABLE 13.2: Characteristics of Transportation Modes

Selection Criteria	Railroads	Trucks	Pipelines	Waterways	Airplanes
Cost	Moderate	High	Low	Very low	Very high
Speed	Average	Fast	Slow	Very slow	Very fast
Dependability	Average	High	High	Average	High
Load flexibility	High	Average	Very low	Very high	Low
Accessibility	High	Very high	Very limited	Limited	Average
Frequency	Low	High	Very high	Very low	Average
Percent of use	36.8%	29.0%	19.9%	13.9%	0.3%
Products carried	Coal, grain, lumber, heavy equipment, paper and pulp products, chemicals	Clothing, computers, books, groceries and produce, livestock	Oil, processed coal, natural gas, wood chips	Chemicals, bauxite, grain, motor vehicles, agricultural implements	Flowers, food (highly perishable), technical instruments, emergency parts and equipment, overnight mail

Sources: U.S. Bureau of Transportation Statistics, National Transportation Statistics 2005, **www.bts.gov**; accessed July 12, 2006.

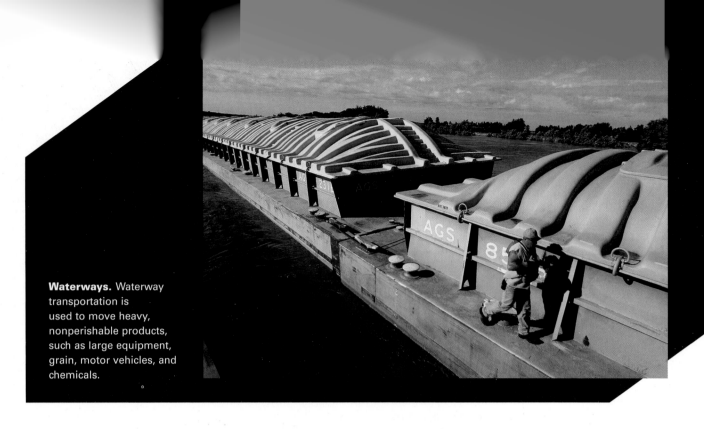

Waterways. Waterway transportation is used to move heavy, nonperishable products, such as large equipment, grain, motor vehicles, and chemicals.

Obviously, the *cost* of a transportation mode is important to marketers. At times, marketers choose higher-cost modes of transportation because of the benefits they provide. *Speed* is measured by the total time that a carrier possesses the products, including time required for pickup and delivery, handling, and movement between point of origin and destination. Usually there is a direct relationship between cost and speed; that is, faster modes of transportation are more expensive. A transportation mode's *dependability* is determined by the consistency of service provided by that mode. *Load flexibility* is the degree to which a transportation mode can provide appropriate equipment and conditions for moving specific kinds of products and can be adapted for moving other kinds of products. For example, certain types of products may need controlled temperatures or humidity levels. *Accessibility* refers to a transportation mode's ability to move goods over a specific route or network. *Frequency* refers to how often a marketer can ship products by a specific transportation mode. Whereas pipelines provide continuous shipments, railroads and waterways follow specific schedules for moving products from one location to another. In Table 13.2, each transportation mode is rated on a relative basis for these six selection criteria and the percentage of use (ton-miles) for each mode.

Railroads In terms of total freight carried, railroads are America's most important mode of transportation. They are also the least expensive for many products. Almost all railroads are common carriers, although a few coal-mining companies operate their own lines. Many commodities carried by railroads could not be transported easily by any other means.

Trucks The trucking industry consists of common, contract, and private carriers. Trucks can move goods to suburban and rural areas not served by railroads. They can handle freight quickly and economically, and they carry a wide range of shipments. Many shippers favor this mode of transportation because it offers door-to-door service, less stringent packaging requirements than ships and airplanes, and flexible delivery schedules. Railroad and truck carriers have teamed up to provide a form of transportation called *piggyback*. Truck trailers are carried from city to city on specially equipped railroad flatcars. Within each city, the trailers are then pulled in the usual way by truck tractors.

Airplanes Air transport is the fastest but most expensive means of transportation. All certified airlines are common carriers. Supplemental or charter lines are contract carriers. Because of the high cost, lack of airport facilities in many areas, and reliance on weather conditions, airlines carry less than 1 percent of all intercity freight. Only high-value, perishable items or goods that are needed immediately usually are shipped by air.

Waterways Cargo ships and barges offer the least expensive but slowest form of transportation. They are used mainly for bulky, nonperishable goods such as iron ore, bulk wheat, motor vehicles, and agricultural implements. Of course, shipment by water is limited to cities located on navigable waterways.

Pipelines Pipelines are a highly specialized mode of transportation. They are used primarily to carry petroleum and natural gas. Pipelines have become more important as the nation's need for petroleum products has increased. Such products as semiliquid coal and wood chips also can be shipped through pipelines continuously, reliably, and with minimal handling.

Concept Check

1. How is inventory management a balancing act between stock-out costs and holding costs?

2. Explain the seven major warehousing activities.

3. What is the goal of materials handling?

4. Describe the major characteristics of the primary transportation modes.

What Is Integrated Marketing Communications?

6 LEARNING OBJECTIVE

Explain how integrated marketing communications works to have the maximum impact on the customer.

Integrated marketing communications is the coordination of promotion efforts to ensure maximal informational and persuasive impact on customers. A major goal of integrated marketing communications is to send a consistent message to customers.

Integrated marketing communications provides an organization with a way to coordinate and manage its promotional efforts to ensure that customers do receive consistent messages. This approach fosters not only long-term customer relationships but also the efficient use of promotional resources. The concept of integrated marketing communications has been increasingly accepted for several reasons. Mass-media advertising, a very popular promotional method in the past, is used less today because of its high costs and less predictable audience sizes. Marketers now can take advantage of more precisely targeted promotional tools, such as cable TV, direct mail, DVDs, the Internet, special-interest magazines, and podcasts. Database marketing is also allowing marketers to be more precise in targeting individual customers. Until recently, suppliers of marketing communications were specialists. Advertising agencies provided advertising campaigns, sales promotion companies provided sales promotion activities and materials, and public-relations organizations engaged in public-relations efforts. Today, a number of promotion-related companies provide one-stop shopping to the client seeking advertising, sales promotion, and public relations, thus reducing coordination problems for the sponsoring company.

integrated marketing communications coordination of promotion efforts to ensure maximal informational and persuasive impact on customers

promotion communication about an organization and its products that is intended to inform, persuade, or remind target-market members

Because the overall costs of marketing communications are significant, management demands systematic evaluations of communications efforts to ensure that promotional resources are being used efficiently. Although the fundamental role of promotion is not changing, the specific communication vehicles employed and the precision with which they are used are changing.

Concept Check

1. What is the major goal of integrated marketing communications?

2. Why is integrated marketing communications being increasingly accepted?

The Promotion Mix: An Overview

7 LEARNING OBJECTIVE

Understand the basic elements of the promotion mix.

Promotion is communication about an organization and its products that is intended to inform, persuade, or remind target-market members. The promotion with which we are most familiar—advertising—is intended to inform, persuade, or remind us to buy particular products. But there is more to promotion than advertising, and it is used for other purposes as well. Charities use promotion to inform us of their need

Source: Wiliam M. Pride and O. C. Ferrell, *Marketing: Concepts and Strategies* (Mason, OH: South-Western/Cengage Learning), 2010.

for donations, to persuade us to give, and to remind us to do so in case we have forgotten. Even the Internal Revenue Service uses promotion (in the form of publicity) to remind us of its April 15 deadline for filing tax returns.

A **promotion mix** (sometimes called a *marketing-communications mix*) is the particular combination of promotion methods a firm uses to reach a target market. The makeup of a mix depends on many factors, including the firm's promotional resources and objectives, the nature of the target market, the product characteristics, and the feasibility of various promotional methods. The four major elements that can be a part of an organization's mix are advertising, personal selling, sales promotion, and public relations (see Figure 13.2).

Advertising is a paid nonpersonal message communicated to a select audience through a mass medium. Advertising is flexible enough that it can reach a very large target group or a small, carefully chosen one. **Personal selling** is personal communication aimed at informing customers and persuading them to buy a firm's products. It is more expensive to reach a consumer through personal selling than through advertising, but this method provides immediate feedback and often is more persuasive than advertising. **Sales promotion** is the use of activities or materials as direct inducements to customers or salespersons. It adds extra value to the product or increases the customer's incentive to buy the product. **Public relations** is a broad set of communication activities used to create and maintain favorable relationships between an organization and various public groups, both internal and external. Public-relations activities are numerous and varied and can be a very effective form of promotion.

While it is possible that one ingredient may be used, it is likely that two, three, or four of these ingredients will be used in a promotion mix depending on the type of product and target market involved.

LEARNING OBJECTIVE 8

Explain the three types of advertising and describe the major steps of developing an advertising campaign.

Advertising

In the U.S., organizations spent $285 billion on advertising last year.[11] In this section, we discuss the types of advertising and how to develop an advertising campaign.

Types of Advertising by Purpose

Depending on its purpose and message, advertising may be classified into one of three groups: primary demand, selective demand, or institutional.

Primary-Demand Advertising **Primary-demand advertising** is advertising aimed at increasing the demand for all brands of a product within a specific industry. Trade and industry associations, such as the California Milk Processor Board ("got milk?"), are the major users of primary-demand advertising. Their advertisements promote broad product categories, such as beef, milk, pork, potatoes, and prunes, without mentioning specific brands.

Selective-Demand Advertising **Selective-demand (or brand) advertising** is advertising that is used to sell a particular brand of product. It is by far the most common type of advertising, and it accounts for the lion's share of advertising expenditures. Producers use brand-oriented advertising to convince us to buy everything from Bubble Yum to Buicks.

Selective-demand advertising that aims at persuading consumers to make purchases within a short time is called *immediate-response advertising*. Most local advertising is of this type.

promotion mix the particular combination of promotion methods a firm uses to reach a target market

advertising a paid nonpersonal message communicated to a select audience through a mass medium

personal selling personal communication aimed at informing customers and persuading them to buy a firm's products

sales promotion the use of activities or materials as direct inducements to customers or salespersons

Often local advertisers promote products with immediate appeal. Selective advertising aimed at keeping a firm's name or product before the public is called *reminder advertising*.

Comparative advertising compares the sponsored brand with one or more identified competing brands. Of course, the comparison shows the sponsored brand to be as good as or better than the other identified competing brands.

Institutional Advertising Institutional advertising is advertising designed to enhance a firm's image or reputation. Many public utilities and larger firms use part of their advertising dollars to build goodwill rather than to stimulate sales directly. A positive public image helps an organization to attract customers, employees, and investors.

Major Steps in Developing an Advertising Campaign

An advertising campaign is developed in several stages. These stages may vary in number and the order in which they are implemented depending on the company's resources, products, and audiences. The development of a campaign in any organization, however, will include the following steps in some form:

1. Identify and Analyze the Target Audience
The target audience is the group of people toward which a firm's advertisements are directed. To pinpoint the organization's target audience and develop an effective campaign, marketers must analyze such information as the geographic distribution of potential customers; their age, sex, race, income, and education; and their attitudes toward both the advertiser's product and competing products. How marketers use this information will be influenced by the features of the product to be advertised and the nature of the competition. Precise identification of the target audience is crucial to the proper development of subsequent stages and, ultimately, to the success of the campaign itself.

2. Define the Advertising Objectives
The goals of an advertising campaign should be stated precisely and in measurable terms. The objectives should include the current position of the firm, indicate how far and in what direction from that original reference point the company wishes to move, and specify a definite period of time for the achievement of the goals. Advertising objectives that focus on sales will stress increasing sales by a certain percentage or dollar amount or expanding the firm's market share. Communication objectives will emphasize increasing product or brand awareness, improving consumer attitudes, or conveying product information.

3. Create the Advertising Platform
An advertising platform includes the important selling points or features that an advertiser wishes to incorporate into the advertising campaign. These features should be important to customers in their selection and use of a product, and if possible, they should be features that competing products lack. Although research into what consumers view as important issues is expensive, it is the most productive way to determine which issues to include in an advertising platform.

Spotlight

Small-Business Internet Advertising

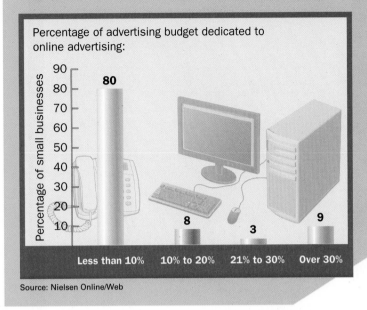

Percentage of advertising budget dedicated to online advertising:

Percentage of small businesses

| Less than 10% | 10% to 20% | 21% to 30% | Over 30% |

80 — Less than 10%
8 — 10% to 20%
3 — 21% to 30%
9 — Over 30%

Source: Nielsen Online/Web

public relations communication activities used to create and maintain favorable relationships between an organization and various public groups, both internal and external

primary-demand advertising advertising whose purpose is to increase the demand for *all* brands of a product within a specific industry

selective-demand (or brand) advertising advertising that is used to sell a particular brand of product

institutional advertising advertising designed to enhance a firm's image or reputation

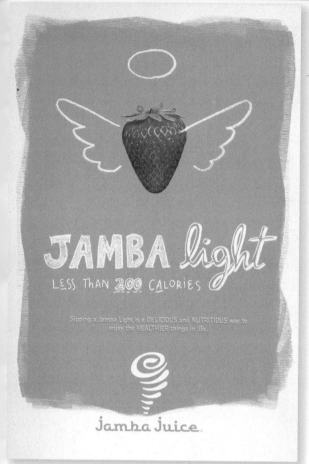

Selective demand advertising. This advertisement promotes a specific brand indicating that the maker of Jamba Juice is attempting to stimulate selective demand.

4. Determine the Advertising Appropriation The advertising appropriation is the total amount of money designated for advertising in a given period. This stage is critical to the success of the campaign because advertising efforts based on an inadequate budget will understimulate customer demand, and a budget too large will waste a company's resources. Advertising appropriations may be based on last year's (or next year's forecasted) sales, on what competitors spend on advertising, or on executive judgment. The top ten U.S. companies that spend the most on advertising are shown in Table 13.3.

5. Develop the Media Plan A media plan specifies exactly which media will be used in the campaign and when advertisements will appear. Although cost-effectiveness is not easy to measure, the primary concern of the media planner is to reach the largest number of persons in the target audience for each dollar spent. In addition to cost, media planners must consider the location and demographics of people in the advertising target, the content of the message, and the characteristics of the audiences reached by various media. The media planner begins with general media decisions, selects subclasses within each medium, and finally chooses particular media vehicles for the campaign. The advantages and disadvantages (and the proportion of ad spending) of the major media classes are shown in Table 13.4.

6. Create the Advertising Message The content and form of a message are influenced by the product's features, the characteristics of people in the target

TABLE 13.3: Advertising Expenditures and Sales Volume for the Top Ten National Advertisers

Rank	Company	Advertising Expenditures (in millions)	Sales (in millions)	Advertising Expenditures as Percentage of Sales
1	Procter & Gamble	$5,230	$ 31,946	16.4
2	AT&T	3,207	118,928	2.7
3	Verizon Communications	3,016	89,504	3.4
4	General Motors	3,010	100,545	3.0
5	Time Warner	2,962	38,256	7.7
6	Ford Motor Co.	2,525	80,874	3.1
7	GlaxoSmithKline	2,457	18,563	13.2
8	Johnson & Johnson	2,409	32,444	7.4
9	Walt Disney Co.	2,293	27,286	8.4
10	Unilever	2,246	18,372	12.2

Source: Reprinted with permission from the June 23, 2008 issue of Advertising Age. Copyright, Craine Communications Inc. 2008.

TABLE 13.4: Percent Use and Advantages and Disadvantages of Major Media Classes

	Percent of Total*	Advantages	Disadvantages
Television	24.4%	Reaches large audiences; high frequency available; dual impact of audio and video; highly visible; high prestige; geographic and demographic selectivity; difficult to ignore	Very expensive; highly perishable message; size of audience not guaranteed; amount of prime time limited; lack of selectivity in target market
Direct mail	21.7%	Little wasted circulation; highly selective; circulation controlled by advertiser; few distractions; personal; stimulates actions; use of novelty; relatively easy to measure performance; hidden from competitors	Very expensive; lacks editorial content to attract readers; often thrown away unread as junk mail; criticized as invasion of privacy; consumers must choose to read the ad
Newspapers	13.7%	Reaches large audience; purchased to be read; geographic flexibility; short lead time; frequent publication; favorable for cooperative advertising; merchandising services	Not selective for socioeconomic groups or target market; short life; limited reproduction capabilities; large advertising volume limits exposure to any one advertisement
Radio	6.6%	Reaches 95 percent of consumers; highly mobile and flexible; very low relative costs; ad can be changed quickly; high level of geographic and demographic selectivity; encourages use of imagination	Lacks visual imagery; short life of message; listeners' attention limited because of other activities; market fragmentation; difficult buying procedures; limited media and audience research
Yellow Pages	5.0%	Wide availability; action and product category oriented; low relative costs; ad frequency and longevity; nonintrusive	Market fragmentation; extremely localized; slow updating; lack of creativity; long lead times; requires large space to be noticed
Magazines	4.9%	Demographic selectivity; good reproduction; long life; prestige; geographic selectivity when regional issues are available; read in leisurely manner	High costs; 30- to 90-day average lead time; high level of competition; limited reach; communicates less frequently
Internet	4.1%	Immediate response; potential to reach a precisely targeted audience; ability to track customers and build databases; highly interactive medium	Costs of precise targeting are high; inappropriate ad placement; effects difficult to measure; concerns about security and privacy
Outdoor	2.6%	Allows for frequent repetition; low cost; message can be placed close to point of sale; geographic selectivity; operable 24 hours a day; high creativity and effectiveness	Message must be short and simple; no demographic selectivity; seldom attracts readers' full attention; criticized as traffic hazard and blight on countryside; much wasted coverage; limited capabilities

*Spending on miscellaneous advertising accounts for 17% of total expenditures.
Sources: William F. Arens, Michael Weigold, and Christian Arens, Contemporary Advertising (Burr Ridge, IL: Irwin/McGraw-Hill, 2008); George E. Belch and Michael Belch, Advertising and Promotion (Burr Ridge, IL: Irwin/McGraw-Hill, 2009), Robert Coen, "Insider's Report," July 2008, p. 4.

audience, the objectives of the campaign, and the choice of media. An advertiser must consider these factors to choose words and illustrations that will be meaningful and appealing to persons in the advertising target. The copy, or words, of an advertisement will vary depending on the media choice but should attempt to move the audience through attention, interest, desire, and action. Artwork and visuals should complement copy by attracting the audience's attention and communicating an idea quickly. Creating a cohesive advertising message is especially difficult for a company such as eBay that offers such a broad mix of products. eBay developed a "whatever it is" campaign that features a variety of consumers of every age using a variety of products (a car, a television, a dress, and a laptop) all shaped like the letters "it". The tagline, "Whatever it is, you can get it on eBay," emphasizes the massive range of products available from the site and showcases the service that the company provides effectively.

7. Execute the Campaign Execution of an advertising campaign requires extensive planning, scheduling, and coordinating because many tasks must be completed on time. The efforts of many people and firms are involved. Production companies, research organizations, media firms, printers, photo-engravers, and commercial artists are just a few of the people and firms that may contribute to a campaign. Advertising managers constantly must assess the quality of the work and take corrective action when necessary. In some instances, advertisers make changes during the campaign to meet objectives more effectively.

8. Evaluate Advertising Effectiveness A campaign's success should be measured in terms of its original objectives before, during, and/or after the campaign. An advertiser should at least be able to estimate whether sales or market share went up because of the campaign or whether any change occurred in customer attitudes or brand awareness. Data from past and current sales and responses to coupon offers and customer surveys administered by research organizations are some of the ways in which advertising effectiveness can be evaluated.

Advertising Agencies

Advertisers can plan and produce their own advertising with help from media personnel, or they can hire advertising agencies. An **advertising agency** is an independent firm that plans, produces, and places advertising for its clients. Many large ad agencies offer help with sales promotion and public relations as well. The media usually pay a commission of 15 percent to advertising agencies. Thus the cost to the agency's client can be quite moderate. The client may be asked to pay for selected services that the agency performs. Other methods for compensating agencies are also used.

Firms that do a lot of advertising may use both an in-house advertising department and an independent agency. This approach gives the firm the advantage of being able to call on the agency's expertise in particular areas of advertising. An agency also can bring a fresh viewpoint to a firm's products and advertising plans.

Social and Legal Considerations in Advertising

Critics of U.S. advertising have two main complaints—that it is wasteful and that it can be deceptive. Although advertising (like any other activity) can be performed inefficiently, it is far from wasteful. Let's look at the evidence:

- Advertising is the most effective and least expensive means of communicating product information to a large number of individuals and organizations.
- Advertising encourages competition and is, in fact, a means of competition. It thus leads to the development of new and improved products, wider product choices, and lower prices.
- Advertising revenues support our mass-communications media—newspapers, magazines, radio, and television. This means that advertising pays for much of our news coverage and entertainment programming.
- Advertising provides job opportunities in fields ranging from sales to film production.

A number of government and private agencies scrutinize advertising for false or misleading claims or offers. At the national level, the Federal Trade Commission (FTC), the Food and Drug Administration (FDA), and the Federal Communications Commission (FCC) oversee advertising practices. The FDA conducted a survey of

advertising agency an independent firm that plans, produces, and places advertising for its clients doctors about the impact of direct-to-consumer advertising for prescription drugs and found that 92 percent could recall a patient initiating conversation about a drug he or she had seen advertised. Direct-to-consumer prescription ads, a controversial type of advertising, make patients more aware of potential treatments according to 72 percent of the physicians surveyed, and they also caused 47 percent of these doctors to feel pressured into prescribing a particular drug.[12] Advertising also may be monitored by state and local agencies, better business bureaus, and industry associations.

Concept Check

1. Describe the major types of advertising by purpose.

2. Explain the eight major steps in developing an advertising campaign.

Personal Selling

9 LEARNING OBJECTIVE

Recognize the kinds of salespersons, the steps in the personal-selling process, and the major sales management tasks.

Personal selling is the most adaptable of all promotional methods because the person who is presenting the message can modify it to suit the individual buyer. However, personal selling is also the most expensive method of promotion. Most successful salespeople are able to communicate with others on a one-to-one basis and are strongly motivated. They strive to have a thorough knowledge of the products they offer for sale. And they are willing and able to deal with the details involved in handling and processing orders. Sales managers tend to emphasize these qualities when recruiting and hiring. Many selling situations demand the face-to-face contact and adaptability of personal selling. This is especially true of industrial sales, in which a single purchase may amount to millions of dollars. Obviously, sales of that size must be based on carefully planned sales presentations, personal contact with customers, and thorough negotiations.

Kinds of Salespersons

Because most businesses employ different salespersons to perform different functions, marketing managers must select the kinds of sales personnel that will be most effective in selling the firm's products. Salespersons may be identified as order getters, order takers, and support personnel. A single individual can, and often does, perform all three functions.

Order Getters An **order getter** is responsible for what is sometimes called **creative selling**—selling a firm's products to new customers and increasing sales to current customers. An order getter must perceive buyers' needs, supply customers with information about the firm's product, and persuade them to buy the product. Some order getters focus on current customers, whereas others focus on new customers.

Order Takers An **order taker** handles repeat sales in ways that maintain positive relationships with customers. An order taker sees that customers have products when and where they are needed and in the proper amounts. *Inside order takers* receive incoming mail and telephone orders in some businesses; salespersons in retail stores are also inside order takers. *Outside* (or *field*) *order takers* travel to customers. Often the buyer and the field salesperson develop a mutually beneficial relationship of placing, receiving, and delivering orders. Both inside and outside order takers are active salespersons and often produce most of their companies' sales.

Support Personnel **Sales support personnel** aid in selling but are more involved in locating prospects (likely first-time customers), educating customers, building goodwill for the firm, and providing follow-up service. The most common categories of support personnel are missionary, trade, and technical salespersons.

A **missionary salesperson**, who usually works for a manufacturer, visits retailers to persuade them to buy the manufacturer's products. If the retailers agree, they buy the products from wholesalers, who are the manufacturer's actual customers.

order getter a salesperson who is responsible for selling a firm's products to new customers and increasing sales to present customers

creative selling selling products to new customers and increasing sales to present customers

order taker a salesperson who handles repeat sales in ways that maintain positive relationships with customers

sales support personnel employees who aid in selling but are more involved in locating prospects, educating customers, building goodwill for the firm, and providing follow-up service

missionary salesperson a salesperson—generally employed by a manufacturer—who visits retailers to persuade them to buy the manufacturer's products

©Andresr/Shutterstock

A **trade salesperson**, who generally works for a food producer or processor, assists customers in promoting products, especially in retail stores. A trade salesperson may obtain additional shelf space for the products, restock shelves, set up displays, and distribute samples. Because trade salespersons usually are order takers as well, they are not strictly support personnel.

A **technical salesperson** assists a company's current customers in technical matters. He or she may explain how to use a product, how it is made, how to install it, or how a system is designed. A technical salesperson should be formally educated in science or engineering.

Marketers usually need sales personnel from several of these categories. Factors that affect hiring and other personnel decisions include the number of customers and their characteristics; the product's attributes, complexity, and price; the distribution channels used by the company; and the company's approach to advertising.

The Personal-Selling Process

No two selling situations are exactly alike, and no two salespeople perform their jobs in exactly the same way. Most salespeople, however, follow the six-step procedure illustrated in Figure 13.3.

Prospecting The first step in personal selling is to research potential buyers and choose the most likely customers, or prospects. Sources of prospects include business associates and customers, public records, telephone and trade-association directories, and company files. The salesperson concentrates on those prospects who have the financial resources, willingness, and authority to buy the product.

Approaching the Prospect First impressions are often lasting impressions. Thus the salesperson's first contact with the prospect is crucial to successful selling. The best approach is one based on knowledge of the product, of the prospect's needs, and of how the product can meet those needs. Salespeople who understand each customer's particular situation are likely to make a good first impression—and to make a sale.

Making the Presentation The next step is actual delivery of the sales presentation. In many cases this includes demonstrating the product. The salesperson points out the product's features, its benefits, and how it is superior to competitors' merchandise. If the product has been used successfully by other firms, the salesperson may mention this as part of the presentation.

During a demonstration, the salesperson may suggest that the prospect try out the product personally. The demonstration and product trial should underscore specific points made during the presentation.

Answering Objections The prospect is likely to raise objections or ask questions at any time. This gives the salesperson a chance to eliminate objections that might prevent a sale, to point out additional features, or to mention special services the company offers.

Closing the Sale To close the sale, the salesperson asks the prospect to buy the product. This is considered the critical point in the selling process. Many experienced salespeople make use of a *trial closing*, in which they ask questions based on the assumption that the customer is going to buy the product. The questions "When would you want delivery?" and "Do you want the standard model or the one with the special options package?" are typical of trial closings. They allow the reluctant prospect to make a purchase without having to say, "I'll take it."

Following Up The salesperson must follow up after the sale to ensure that the product is delivered on time, in the right quantity, and in proper operating condition. During follow-up, the salesperson also makes it clear that he or she is

FIGURE 13.3: The Six Steps of the Personal-Selling Process Personal selling is not only the most adaptable of all promotional methods but also the most expensive.

1. Prospecting
2. Approaching the prospect
3. Making the presentation
4. Answering objections
5. Closing the sale
6. Following up

Source: William M. Pride and O. C. Ferrell, *Marketing: Concepts and Strategies* (Mason, OH: South-Western/Cengage Learning) 2010. Adapted with permission.

available in case problems develop. Follow-up leaves a good impression and eases the way toward future sales. Hence it is essential to the selling process. The salesperson's job does not end with a sale. It continues as long as the seller and the customer maintain a working relationship.

Major Sales Management Tasks

A firm's success often hinges on the competent management of its sales force. Although some companies operate efficiently without a sales force, most firms rely on a strong sales force—and the sales revenue it brings in—for their success.

Responsibilities of Sales Managers

- Sales managers must set sales objectives in concrete, quantifiable terms and specify a certain period of time and a certain geographic area.
- Sales managers must adjust the size of the sales force to meet changes in the firm's marketing plan and the marketing environment.
- Sales managers must attract and hire effective salespersons. Guitar Center, the largest musical instrument chain in the United States, has only one requirement for members of its sales force—that they be able to play a musical instrument. The company believes that a rocking sales force will care more deeply about the product and sell it more effectively to customers.[13]
- Sales managers must develop a training program and decide where, when, how, and for whom to conduct the training.
- Sales managers must formulate a fair and adequate compensation plan to keep qualified employees.
- Sales managers must motivate salespersons to boost their productivity.
- Sales managers must define sales territories and determine scheduling and routing of the sales force.
- Finally, sales managers must evaluate the operation as a whole through sales reports, communications with customers, and invoices.

Concept Check

1. What are the advantages and disadvantages of using personal selling?

2. Identify the three types of salespersons.

3. Describe the six steps of the personal-selling process.

Sales Promotion

10 LEARNING OBJECTIVE

Describe sales promotion objectives and methods.

Sales promotion consists of activities or materials that are direct inducements to customers or salespersons. Are you a member of an airline frequent-flyer program? Did you recently receive a free sample in the mail or at a supermarket? Have you recently received a rebate from a manufacturer? Do you use coupons? All these are examples of sales promotion efforts. Sales promotion techniques often are used to enhance and supplement other promotional methods. They can have a significant impact on sales.

The dramatic increase in spending for sales promotion shows that marketers have recognized the potential of this promotional method. Many firms now include numerous sales promotion efforts as part of their overall promotion mix.

Sales Promotion Objectives

Sales promotion activities may be used singly or in combination, both offensively and defensively, to achieve one goal or a set of goals. Marketers use sales promotion activities and materials for a number of purposes, including

1. To attract new customers
2. To encourage trial of a new product
3. To invigorate the sales of a mature brand
4. To boost sales to current customers
5. To reinforce advertising
6. To increase traffic in retail stores
7. To steady irregular sales patterns
8. To build up reseller inventories
9. To neutralize competitive promotional efforts
10. To improve shelf space and displays[14]

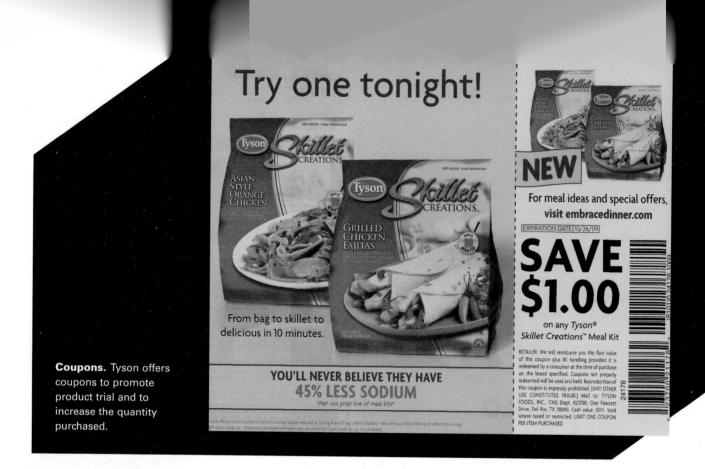

Coupons. Tyson offers coupons to promote product trial and to increase the quantity purchased.

Any sales promotion objectives should be consistent with the organization's general goals and with its marketing and promotional objectives.

Sales Promotion Methods

Most sales promotion methods can be classified as promotional techniques for either consumer sales or trade sales.

A **consumer sales promotion method** attracts consumers to particular retail stores and motivates them to purchase certain new or established products.

A **trade sales promotion method** encourages wholesalers and retailers to stock and actively promote a manufacturer's product. Incentives such as money, merchandise, marketing assistance, and gifts are commonly awarded to resellers who buy products or respond positively in other ways. Of the combined dollars spent on sales promotion and advertising last year, about one-half was spent on trade promotions, one-fourth on consumer promotions, and one-fourth on advertising.

Selection of Sales Promotion Methods

Several factors affect the choice of sales promotion methods to be used. Of greatest importance are

1. The objectives of the promotional effort
2. Product characteristics—size, weight, cost, durability, uses, features, and hazards
3. Target-market profiles—age, gender, income, location, density, usage rate, and buying patterns
4. Distribution channels and availability of appropriate resellers
5. The competitive and regulatory forces in the environment

consumer sales promotion method a sales promotion method designed to attract consumers to particular retail stores and to motivate them to purchase certain new or established products

trade sales promotion method a sales promotion method designed to encourage wholesalers and retailers to stock and actively promote a manufacturer's product

rebate a return of part of the purchase price of a product

Rebates A **rebate** is a return of part of the purchase price of a product. Usually the refund is offered by the producer to consumers who send in a coupon along with a specific proof of purchase. Rebating is a relatively low-cost promotional method.

One problem with rebates is that many people perceive the redemption process as too complicated. Only about half of individuals who purchase rebated products actually apply for the rebates.

Coupons A **coupon** reduces the retail price of a particular item by a stated amount at the time of purchase. Coupons may be worth anywhere from a few cents to a few dollars. They are made available to customers through newspapers, magazines, direct mail, online, and shelf dispensers in stores. Some coupons are precisely targeted at customers. All Online Coupons is an Internet site that provides visitors with links to all online coupons currently being offered. Customers can find coupons by category or store name. Other companies, such as Old Navy and The Gap, offer coupons on their websites that can be used online or in stores. Billions of coupons are distributed annually. Of these, just under 2 percent are redeemed by consumers. Still, 73 percent of consumers say that coupons save them a lot of money.[15]

Samples A **sample** is a free product given to customers to encourage trial and purchase. Marketers use free samples to stimulate trial of a product, increase sales volume in the early stages of a product's life cycle, and obtain desirable distribution. Samples may be offered via online coupons, direct mail, or in stores. Many customers prefer to receive their samples by mail. It is the most expensive sales promotion technique, and while it is used often to promote new products, it can be used to promote established brands, too, such as cosmetics companies that use samples to attract customers. In designing a free sample, organizations must consider such factors as seasonal demand for the product, market characteristics, and prior advertising.

Premiums A **premium** is a gift that a producer offers a customer in return for buying its product. They are used to attract competitors' customers, introduce different sizes of established products, add variety to other promotional efforts, and stimulate consumer loyalty. Creativity is essential when using premiums; to stand out and achieve a significant number of redemptions, the premium must match both the target audience and the brand's image. Premiums also must be easily recognizable and desirable. Premiums are placed on or inside packages and also can be distributed through retailers or through the mail.

Frequent-User Incentives A **frequent-user incentive** is a program developed to reward customers who engage in repeat (frequent) purchases. Such programs are used commonly by service businesses such as airlines, hotels, and auto rental agencies. Frequent-user incentives foster customer loyalty to a specific company or group of cooperating companies because the customer is given an additional reason to continue patronizing the business. For example, most major airlines offer frequent-flier programs that reward customers who have flown a specified number of miles with free tickets for additional travel. Research shows that 93 percent of people with household incomes above $100,000 participate in

coupon reduces the retail price of a particular item by a stated amount at the time of purchase

sample a free product given to customers to encourage trial and purchase

premium a gift that a producer offers a customer in return for buying its product

frequent-user incentive a program developed to reward customers who engage in repeat (frequent) purchases

Trade show. Trade show participants look at Hitachi's 1.5 inch thick LCD television display at the Consumer Electronics trade show held annually in Las Vegas.

©AP Photo/Jae C. Hong

frequent-user programs, whereas only 58 percent of people with incomes below $50,000 participate.[16]

Point-of-Purchase Displays

A **point-of-purchase display** is promotional material placed within a retail store. The display is usually located near the product being promoted. It actually may hold merchandise (as do L'eggs hosiery displays) or inform customers about what the product offers and encourage them to buy it. Most point-of-purchase displays are prepared and set up by manufacturers and wholesalers.

Trade Shows

A **trade show** is an industry-wide exhibit at which many sellers display their products. Some trade shows are organized exclusively for dealers—to permit manufacturers and wholesalers to show their latest lines to retailers. Others are promotions designed to stimulate consumer awareness and interest. Among the latter are boat shows, home shows, and flower shows put on each year in large cities.

Buying Allowances

A **buying allowance** is a temporary price reduction to resellers for purchasing specified quantities of a product. A laundry detergent manufacturer might give retailers $1 for each case of detergent purchased. A buying allowance may serve as an incentive to resellers to handle new products and may stimulate purchase of items in large quantities. While the buying allowance is simple, straightforward, and easily administered, competitors can respond quickly by offering a better buying allowance.

Cooperative Advertising

Cooperative advertising is an arrangement whereby a manufacturer agrees to pay a certain amount of a retailer's media cost for advertising the manufacturer's products. To be reimbursed, a retailer must show proof that the advertisements actually did appear. A large percentage of all cooperative advertising dollars are spent on newspaper advertisements. Not all retailers take advantage of available cooperative advertising offers because they cannot afford to advertise or do not choose to do so.

Concept Check

1. Why do marketers use sales promotion?

2. What are the two classifications of sales promotion methods?

3. What factors affect the choice of sales promotion used?

LEARNING OBJECTIVE 11

Understand the types and uses of public relations.

Public Relations

As noted earlier, public relations is a broad set of communication activities used to create and maintain favorable relationships between an organization and various public groups, both internal and external. These groups can include customers, employees, stockholders, suppliers, educators, the media, government officials, and society in general.

Types of Public-Relations Tools

Organizations use a variety of public-relations tools to convey messages and to create images. Public-relations professionals prepare written materials such as brochures, newsletters, company magazines, annual reports, and news releases. They also create corporate-identity materials such as logos, business cards, signs, and stationery. Speeches are another public-relations tool. Speeches can affect an organization's image and therefore must convey the desired message clearly.

Another public-relations tool is event sponsorship, in which a company pays for all or part of a special event such as a concert, sports competition, festival, or play. Sponsoring special events is an effective way for organizations to increase brand recognition and receive media coverage with comparatively little investment. Pharmaceutical company Bristol-Myers Squibb sponsored the Tour of Hope, a nine-day bike trek from San Diego, California, to Washington, D.C., to raise money for cancer research. Bristol-Myers spokesman, seven-time Tour de France winner and cancer survivor Lance Armstrong, led twenty-four other bikers on the tour.[17]

Some public-relations tools traditionally have been associated specifically with publicity, which is a part of public relations. **Publicity** is communication in news-story form about an organization, its products, or both. Publicity is transmitted through a mass medium, such as newspapers or radio, at no charge. Organizations use publicity to provide information about products; to announce new product launches, expansions, or research; and to strengthen the company's image. Public-relations personnel sometimes organize events, such as grand openings with prizes and celebrities, to create news stories about a company.

The most widely used type of publicity is the **news release**. It is generally one typed page of about 300 words provided by an organization to the media as a form of publicity. The release includes the firm's name, address, phone number, and contact person. There are also several other kinds of publicity-based public-relations tools. A **feature article**, which may run as long as 3,000 words, is usually written for inclusion in a particular publication. For example, a software firm might send an article about its new product to a computer magazine. A **captioned photograph**, a picture accompanied by a brief explanation, is an effective way to illustrate a new or improved product. A **press conference** allows invited media personnel to hear important news announcements and to receive supplementary textual materials and photographs. Finally, letters to the editor, special newspaper or magazine editorials, films, and tapes may be prepared and distributed to appropriate media for possible use.

Uses of Public Relations

Public relations can be used to promote people, places, activities, ideas, and even countries. Public relations focuses on enhancing the reputation of the total organization by making people aware of a company's products, brands, or activities and by creating specific company images such as that of innovativeness or dependability. Ice-cream maker Ben and Jerry's uses news stories and other public-relations efforts to reinforce its reputation as a socially responsible company. By getting the media to report on a firm's accomplishments, public relations helps a company to maintain positive public visibility. Effective management of public-relations efforts also can reduce the unfavorable effects of negative events.

Event sponsorship. Target dog, Bullseye, at the start of the 36th Annual Iditarod Trail Sled Dog Race, one of Alaska's most favored sports events. Target is currently opening stores in Alaska. (Sarah Palin or Tina Fey?)

©AP Photo/Rob Stapleton

Concept Check

1. What are the common tools of public relations?

2. What is publicity, and why do organizations use it?

3. What are the four common types of publicity?

SUMMARY

1 Identify the various distribution channels and explain the concept of market coverage.

A marketing channel is a sequence of marketing organizations that directs a product from producer to ultimate user. The marketing channel for a particular product is concerned with the transfer of ownership of that product. Merchant middlemen (merchants) actually take title to products, whereas functional middlemen simply aid in the transfer of title.

The channels used for consumer products include the direct channel from producer to consumer; the channel from producer to retailer to consumer; the channel from producer to wholesaler to retailer to consumer; and the channel from producer to agent to wholesaler to retailer to consumer. There are two major channels of industrial products: (1) producer to user and (2) producer to agent middleman to user.

Channels and intermediaries are chosen to implement a given level of market coverage. Intensive distribution is the use of all available outlets for a product, providing the widest market coverage. Selective distribution uses only a portion of the available outlets in an area. Exclusive distribution uses only a single retail outlet for a product in a large geographic area.

2 Understand how supply chain management facilitates partnering among channel members.

Supply-chain management is a long-term partnership among channel members working together to create a distribution system that reduces inefficiencies, costs, and redundancies while creating a competitive advantage and satisfying customers. Cooperation is required among all channel members, including manufacturing, research, sales, advertising, and shipping. When all channel partners work together, delivery, scheduling, packaging, and other customer requirements are better met. Technology, such as bar coding and electronic data interchange (EDI), makes supply-chain management easier to implement.

3 Discuss the need for wholesalers, describe the services they provide, and identify the major types of wholesalers.

Wholesalers are intermediaries that purchase from producers or other intermediaries and sell to industrial users, retailers, or other wholesalers. Wholesalers perform many functions in a distribution channel. If they are eliminated, other channel members—such as the producer or retailers—must perform these functions. Wholesalers provide retailers with help in promoting products, collecting information and financing. They provide manufacturers with sales help, reduce their inventory costs, furnish market information, and extend credit to retailers.

Merchant wholesalers buy and then sell products. Commission merchants and brokers are essentially agents and do not take title to the goods they distribute. Sales branches and offices are owned by the manufacturers and resemble merchant wholesalers and agents, respectively.

4 Distinguish among the major types of retailer s and shopping centers.

Retailers are intermediaries that buy from producers or wholesalers and sell to consumers. In-store retailers include department stores, discount stores, catalog and warehouse showrooms, convenience stores, supermarkets, superstores, warehouse clubs, traditional specialty stores, off-price retailers, and category killers. Non store retailers do not sell in conventional store facilities. Instead they use direct selling, direct marketing, and automatic vending. Types of direct marketing include catalog marketing, direct response marketing, telemarketing, television home shopping, and online retailing.

There are four major types of shopping centers: lifestyle, neighborhood, community, and regional. A center fits one of these categories based on its mix of stores and the size of the geographic area it serves.

5 Explain the five most important physical distribution activities.

Physical distribution consists of activities designed to move products from producers to ultimate users. Its five major

functions are inventory management, order processing, warehousing, materials handling, and transportation. These interrelated functions are integrated into the marketing effort.

6 Explain how integrated marketing communications works to have the maximum impact on the customer.

Integrated marketing communications is the coordination of promotion efforts to achieve maximum informational and persuasive impact on customers.

7 Understand the basic elements of the promotion mix.

Promotion is communication about an organization and its products that is intended to inform, persuade, or remind target market members. The major ingredients of a promotion mix are advertising, personal selling, sales promotion, and public relations. The role of promotion is to facilitate exchanges directly or indirectly and to help an organization maintain favorable relationship with groups in the marketing environment.

8 Explain the three types of advertising and describe the major steps of developing an advertising campaign.

Advertising is a paid nonpersonal message communicated to a specific audience through a mass medium. Primary-demand advertising promotes the products of an entire industry rather than just a single brand. Selective demand advertising promotes a particular brand of product. Institutional advertising is image-building advertising for a firm.

An advertising campaign is developed in several stages. A firm's first task is to identify and analyze its advertising target. The goals of the campaign also must be clearly defined. Then the firm must develop the advertising platform, or statement of important selling points, and determine the size of advertising budget. The next steps are to develop a media plan, to create the advertising message, and to execute the campaign. Finally, promotion managers must evaluate the effectiveness of the advertising efforts before, during, and/or after the campaign.

9 Recognize the kinds of salespersons, the steps in the personal selling process, and the major sales management tasks.

Personal selling is personal communication aimed at informing customers and persuading them to buy a firm's products. It is the most adaptable promotional method because the salesperson can modify the message to fit each buyer. Three major kinds of salespeople are order getters, order takers, and support personnel. The six steps in the personal-selling process are prospecting, approaching the prospect, making the presentation, answering objections, closing the sale, and following up. Sales managers are involved directly in setting sales force objectives; recruiting; selecting, and training salespersons; compensating and motivating sales personnel; creating sales territories; and evaluating sales performance.

10 Describe sales promotion objectives and methods.

Sales promotion is the use of activities and materials as direct inducements to customers and salespersons. The primary objective of sales promotion methods is to enhance and supplement other promotional methods. Methods of sales promotion include rebates, coupons, samples, premiums, frequent-user incentives, point-of-purchase displays, trade shows, buying allowances, and cooperative advertising.

11 Understand the types and uses of public relations.

Public relations is a broad set of communication activities used to create and maintain favorable relationships between an organization and various public groups, both internal and external. Organizations use a variety of public relations tools to convey messages and create images. Brochures, newsletters, company magazines and annual reports are written public-relations tools. Speeches, event sponsorship, and publicity are other public-relations tools. Publicity is communication in news-story form about an organization, its products, or both. Types of publicity include news releases, feature articles, captioned photographs, and press conferences. Public relations can also be used to promote people, places, activities, ideas, and even countries. It can be used to enhance the reputation of an organization and also to reduce the unfavorable effects of negative events.

KEY TERMS

You should now be able to define and give an example relevant to each of the following terms:

distribution channel (or marketing channel) (347)
middleman (or marketing intermediary) (347)
merchant middleman (348)
functional middleman (348)
retailer (349)
wholesaler (349)
intensive distribution (350)
selective distribution (350)
exclusive distribution (350)
supply-chain management (351)
merchant wholesaler (352)
full-service wholesaler (352)
general-merchandise wholesaler (352)
limited-line wholesaler (352)
specialty-line wholesaler (352)
agent (352)
broker (352)
independent retailer (353)
chain retailer (353)
department store (353)

discount store (353)
warehouse showroom (354)
convenience store (354)
supermarket (354)
superstore (354)
warehouse club (355)
traditional specialty store (355)
off-price retailer (355)
category killer (356)
nonstore retailing (356)
direct selling (356)
direct marketing (356)
catalog marketing (356)
direct-response marketing (357)
telemarketing (357)
television home shopping (357)
online retailing (357)
automatic vending (358)
lifestyle shopping center (358)
neighborhood shopping center (358)

community shopping center (358)
regional shopping center (359)
physical distribution (359)
inventory management (359)
order processing (360)
warehousing (360)
materials handling (361)
transportation (361)
carrier (361)
integrated marketing communications (363)
promotion (363)
promotion mix (364)
advertising (364)
personal selling (364)
sales promotion (364)
public relations (365)
primary-demand advertising (365)
selective-demand (or brand) advertising (365)
institutional advertising (365)
advertising agency (368)
order getter (369)

creative selling (369)
order taker (369)
sales support personnel (369)
missionary salesperson (369)
trade salesperson (370)
technical salesperson (370)
consumer sales promotion method (372)
trade sales promotion method (372)
rebate (372)
coupon (373)
sample (373)
premium (373)
frequent-user incentive (373)
point-of-purchase display (374)
trade show (374)
buying allowance (374)
cooperative advertising (374)
publicity (374)
news release (374)
feature article (374)
captioned photograph (374)
press conference (374)

DISCUSSION QUESTIONS

1. What are the most common marketing channels for consumer products? For industrial products?
2. What are the three levels of market coverage? What types of products is each used for?
3. List the services performed by wholesalers. For whom is each service performed?
4. Identify three kinds of full-service wholesalers. What factors are used to classify wholesalers into one of these categories?
5. What can nonstore retailers offer their customers that in-store retailers cannot?
6. What is physical distribution? Which major functions does it include?

7. Many producers sell to consumers both directly and through middlemen. How can such a producer justify competing with its own middlemen?
8. In what situations might a producer use agents or commission merchants rather than its own sales offices or branches.
9. If a middleman is eliminated from a marketing channel, under what conditions will costs decrease? Under what conditions will costs increase? Will the middleman's functions be eliminated? Explain.
10. What is integrated marketing communications, and why is it becoming increasingly accepted?
11. Identify and describe the major ingredients of a promotion mix.

12. Identify and give examples of the three major types of salespersons.
13. What are the major tasks involved in managing a sales force?
14. What are the major differences between consumer and trade sales promotion methods? Give examples of each.

15. What is the difference between publicity and public relations? What is the purpose of each?
16. Why do firms use event sponsorship?

Get Flash Cards, Quizzes, Games, Crosswords and more @ www.cengage.com/introbusiness/pride

Test Yourself

Matching Questions

1. _____ This type of market coverage provides the widest possible exposure in the marketplace.

2. _____ A middleman often hired on a commission basis.

3. _____ This middleman carries a few lines with many products within each line.

4. _____ The process involves receiving and filling customers, purchase orders.

5. _____ Manufacturer's seconds or off-season merchandise are examples of products sold.

6. _____ The process includes any nonpersonal, paid form of communication.

7. _____ The purpose is to increase demand for all brands of a product.

8. _____ A program-length commercial message placed on television.

9. _____ It is the most selective medium for advertising products.

10. _____ News stories about products, employees, or a company that appear in the newspaper are examples.

    a. agent
    b. intensive distribution
    c. limited-line wholesaler
    d. category killer
    e. off-price retailer
    f. order processing
    g. advertising
    h. direct-mail advertising
    i. infomercial
    j. primary-demand advertising
    k. publicity
    l. order taker

True False Questions

11. **T F** A direct channel of distribution includes both wholesalers and retailers.

12. **T F** Exclusive distribution makes use of all available outlets for a product.

13. **T F** Piggyback service is unique to air freight.

14. **T F** A retailer buys and sells merchandise.

15. **T F** Inventory holding costs consist of money invested in inventory, cost of storage space, insurance costs, and inventory taxes.

16. **T F** Institutional advertising promotes specific brands of products.

17. **T F** A major disadvantage of magazines is their lack of timeliness.

18. **T F** Radio advertising offers a high degree of selectivity.

19. **T F** News releases are the least used type of publicity.

20. **T F** Advertising can be broadly classified into three groups: selective-demand, institutional, and primary-demand.

Multiple-Choice Questions

21. _____ Which activity combines inventory management, order processing, warehousing, material handling, and transportation?
    a. Marketing
    b. Merchandising
    c. Warehousing
    d. Physical distribution
    e. Transporting

22. _____ Haley is shopping for a new outfit to wear to an awards banquet where

Test Yourself

she will be honored. She has found a beautiful outfit at The Gap and a new pair of shoes at the Foot Locker. What type of stores are these?

a. Warehouse club
b. Convenience
c. Specialty
d. Department
e. Off-price

23. _____ Category management is

a. a producer deciding which category to concentrate on for the next season.
b. a retailer asking the supplier in a particular category how to stock the shelves.
c. when suppliers tell the manufacturer which category to produce more of.
d. when Home Depot decides which category sells the best and decides to concentrate on that category of goods.
e. the combined efforts of producers and wholesalers to manage the wholesaler's inventory.

24. _____ A women's apparel manufacturer most likely will use

a. intensive distribution
b. selective distribution
c. exclusive distribution
d. high-style distribution
e. popular-style distribution

25. _____ Which one of the following is an example of a category killer?

a. KMart
b. 7-Eleven
c. Home Depot
d. Burlington Coat Factory
e. Macy's

26. _____ Closing the sale is considered the critical point in the selling process. Many salespeople use a trial closing. Based on an assumption that the customer is going to buy, which of the following statements is an appropriate trial closing?

a. "Will you be placing an order, Mrs. Johnston?"
b. "Do you like the standard or the deluxe model best?"
c. "Here's my card. Give me a call if you would like to place an order."
d. "Shall I give you a week to consider the offer?"
e. "I'll put you down for the deluxe model. Is that your natural hair color?"

27. _____ Deloitte & Touche, a public accounting firm, helps to underwrite the musical production "Mama Mia" currently playing at the Theater Center. Why would the accounting firm do this? What is Deloitte & Touche creating?

a. Point-of-purchase activity
b. Sales promotion
c. Public-relations activity
d. Community-service activity
e. Cooperative advertising

28. _____ Choose the correct order of the following three of the eight steps in developing an advertising campaign.

a. Create the advertising platform; identify and analyze the target audience; define the advertising objectives.
b. Identify and analyze the target audience; create the advertising platform; define the advertising objectives.
c. Identify and analyze the target audience; define the advertising objectives; create the advertising platform.
d. Define the advertising objectives, identify and analyze the target audience, create the advertising platform.
e. Define the advertising objectives, create the advertising platform; identify and analyze the target audience.

29. _____ Salespeople may be identified as

a. experts, order makers, and support personnel.
b. order preparers, order trackers, and order receivers.
c. order getters, order trackers, and support personnel.
d. order getters, order makers, and order receivers.
e. order getters, order dictators, and support personnel.

30. _____ The first step in the personal selling process is

a. product display.
b. prospecting.
c. approaching the prospect.
d. organizing the sales pitch.
e. making the presentation.

Answers on p. TY-1

VIDEO CASE

Netflix Uses Distribution to Compete

Netflix was originally an online version of a traditional video rental store, a website where customers chose the films they wanted to rent and paid $4 for each, along with a $2 shipping fee and late fees if applicable. This model wasn't very price-competitive, or even very efficient compared to brick-and-mortar video rental retailers. So, to gain a competitive advantage, the company slowly transformed itself, focusing on technological advances and improving product offerings. Today Netflix is membership-based, has over 10 million subscribers, and relies on a unique business model.

Members subscribe to various packages based on the number of movies they want to rent per month, from two all the way to an unlimited number, which allows them to keep up to eight films at a time. Online, they list the movies they want to see in order of preference, and Netflix delivers them. Customers can keep any movie as long as they like, with no late fees, but they are not sent a new one until they have returned an old one to their local Netflix distribution center, using the company's special prepaid mailers.

As its service became more popular, Netflix expanded its film and television show collection to include Blu-Ray disks. To stay ahead of the competition, it added a Play Instantly feature, which allows subscribers to download movies from the Netflix website and watch them on their computers. This service gives customers instant access to a wide selection of films and saves Netflix shipping fees.

Recently, Netflix started offering a direct-to-television streaming box rental option. To gain access to more than 12,000 movies and television shows from the Netflix library, customers must purchase a box that hooks up to a television set and sign up for a plan. The box costs around $100 and streams video directly to television via high-speed Internet. Customers must sign up for a plan, but rather than wait for DVDs to come in the mail, they can watch movies instantly on their televisions. Apple and Vudu offer similar products, but their boxes cost two to three times Netflix's price. Netflix also recently formed a partnership with Microsoft to stream movies through Xbox systems to the television.

Most recently, Netflix partnered with TiVo to provide movies directly through the Internet. Netflix subscribers who also subscribe to TiVo (and have a Series 3 or HD DVR connected to broadband) can use this service.

Netflix has a number of competitive advantages over companies such as Movielink, Blockbuster, and Wal-Mart. First and foremost, it offers more selections—as many as 100,000 titles—including more independent and foreign films, documentaries, and television shows, than anyone else. Wal-Mart attempted to compete with Netflix starting in 2002 but admitted that Netflix had won and bowed out of the race less than three years later.

Blockbuster, a company that lost market share as some customers moved away from traditional brick-and-mortar video stores, continues to be Netflix's strongest competitor. The company, which remains the largest in-store movie rental chain in the world, entered the online rental competition about five years ago and originally tried to compete with Netflix on price. The two eventually settled on similar prices, but their competitive battle also landed in court when Netflix sued Blockbuster for infringing on two of its patents. The suit was settled a year later, but competition between the rivals remains fierce.[18]

For more information about this company, go to www.netflix.com.

Questions

1. What type of retailer is Netflix?
2. To compete more efficiently with Blockbuster, should Netflix open brick-and-mortar retail stores? Why or why not?
3. Should Netflix consider other forms of nonstore retailing along with its current distribution activities? Why or why not?

BUILDING SKILLS FOR CAREER SUCCESS

1. EXPLORING THE INTERNET

One reason the Internet has generated so much excitement and interest among both buyers and distributors of products is that it is a highly effective method of direct marketing. Already a multibillion dollar industry, e-commerce is growing as more businesses recognize the power of the Internet to reach customers twenty-four hours a day anywhere in the world. In addition to using the Internet to provide product information to potential customers, businesses can use it to process orders and accept payment from customers. Quick delivery from warehouses or stores by couriers such as UPS and FedEx adds to the convenience of Internet shopping.

Businesses whose products traditionally have sold well through catalogs are clear leaders in the electronic marketplace. Books, CDs, clothing, and other frequently purchased, relatively low-cost items sell well through both the Internet and catalogs. As a result, many successful catalog companies are including the Internet as a means of communicating about products. Many of their customers are finding that they prefer the more dynamic online versions of the catalogs.

Assignment

1. Explore the websites listed below, or just enter "shopping" on one of the web search engines—then stand back! Also visit the text website for updates to this exercise.
   www.llbean.com
   www.jcpenney.com
   www.sears.com
   www.landsend.com

www.barnesandnoble.com
www.amazon.com

2. Which website does the best job of marketing merchandise? Explain your answer.
3. Find a product that you would be willing to buy over the Internet, and explain why you would buy it. Name the website and describe the product.
4. Find a product that you would be unwilling to buy over the Internet, and again, explain your reasoning. Name the website and describe the product.

2. BUILDING TEAM SKILLS

Surveys are a commonly used tool in marketing research. The information they provide can reduce business risk and facilitate decision making. Retail outlets often survey their customers' wants and needs by distributing comment cards or questionnaires. The customer survey (below) is an example of a survey that a local photography shop might distribute to its customers.

Assignment

1. Working in teams of three to five, choose a local retailer.
2. Classify the retailer according to the major types of retailers.
3. Design a survey to help the retailer improve customer service. (You may find it beneficial to work with the retailer and actually administer the survey to the retailer's customers. Prepare a report of the survey results for the retailer.)
4. Present your findings to the class.

3. RESEARCHING DIFFERENT CAREERS

Most public libraries maintain relatively up-to-date collections of occupational or career materials. Begin your library search by looking at the computer listings under "vocations" or "careers" and then under specific fields. Check the library's periodicals section, where you will find trade and professional magazines and journals about specific occupations and industries. (*Business Periodicals Index,* published by H. W. Wilson, is an index to articles in major business publications. Arranged alphabetically, it is easy to use.) Familiarize yourself with the concerns and activities of potential employers by skimming their annual reports and other information they distribute to the public. You can also find occupational information on videocassettes, in kits, and through computerized information systems.

Assignment

1. Choose a specific occupation.
2. Conduct a library search of the occupation.
3. Prepare an annotated bibliography for the occupation.

Customer Survey

To help us serve you better, please take a few minutes while your photographs are being developed to answer the following questions. Your opinions are important to us.

1. Do you live/work in the area? (Circle one or both if they apply.)

2. Why did you choose us? (Circle all that apply.)

   Close to home
   Close to work
   Convenience
   Good service
   Quality
   Full-service photography shop
   Other

3. How did you learn about us? (Circle one.)

   Newspaper
   Flyer/coupon
   Passing by
   Recommended by someone
   Other

4. How frequently do you have film developed? (Please estimate.)

   _____ Times per month
   _____ Times per year

5. Which aspects of our photography shop do you think need improvement?

6. Our operating hours are from 8:00 A.M. to 7:00 P.M. weekdays and Saturdays from 9:30 A.M. to 6:00 P.M. We are closed on Sundays and legal holidays. If changes in our operating hours would serve you better, please specify how you would like them changed.

7. Age (Circle one.)

   Under 25
   26–39
   40–59
   Over 60

Comments:

Round, flat, seeded, plain, crowned with cheese, or cut into croutons, bagels form the basis of every menu item at Finagle A Bagel. "So many other shops will just grab onto whatever is hot, whatever is trendy, in a 'me too' strategy," observes Heather Robertson, the director of marketing, human resources, and research and development. In contrast, she says, "We do bagels—that's what we do best. And any menu item in our stores really needs to reaffirm that as our core concept." That's the first of Finagle A Bagel's marketing rules.

In addition to its retailing activities, the company wholesales its bagels in bulk to hospitals, schools, and other organizations. It also wholesales a line of Finagle A Bagel–branded bagels for resale in Shaw's Market stores. Whether selling wholesale or retail, the company is always hunting for new product ideas involving bagels.

Product Development: Mix, Bake, Bite, and Try Again

To identify a new product idea, Robertson and her colleagues conduct informal research by talking with both customers and employees. They also browse food magazines and cookbooks for ideas about out-of-the-ordinary flavors, taste combinations, and preparation methods. When developing a new bagel variety, for example, Robertson says that she looks for ideas that are uncommon and innovative yet appealing: "If someone else has a sun-dried tomato bagel, that's all the more reason for me not to do it. People look at Finagle A Bagel as kind of the trendsetter."

Once the marketing staff comes up with a promising idea, the next step is to write up a formula or recipe, walk downstairs to the dough factory, and mix up a test batch. Through trial and error, they refine the idea until they like the way the bagel or sandwich looks and tastes. Occasionally, Finagle A Bagel has to put an idea on hold until it can find just the right ingredients.

For example, when Robertson was working on a new bagel with jalapeno peppers and cheddar cheese, she had difficulty finding a cheese that would melt during baking but not dissolve and disappear into the batter. Ultimately, she found a supplier willing to cook up cheese formulas especially for Finagle A Bagel. The supplier would send a batch of cheese overnight for Robertson to incorporate into the next day's test batch of bagels. After baking, Robertson would send some of the bagels overnight to the supplier so that the two of them could discuss the flavor, consistency, and other details.

The cheeses and bagels flew back and forth for eight months until Finagle A Bagel hit on a recipe that worked well. "When we finally got it done," Robertson says, "we shipped test batches to our stores, three stores at a time. And we just gave the product away. We'd make several batches during the week, and guess who would come back wanting to

buy dozens of these bagels?" That's when she knew the new product was going to be a hit. Not every new flavor becomes popular, however. Dark chocolate bagels with white chocolate chips sold poorly, as did pineapple-mango-coconut bagels. Today, plain bagels remain the best-selling flavor, followed by sesame.

Samples and Coupons Spark Word-Of-Mouth Communication

The story of the jalapeno-and-cheese bagel illustrates another of Finagle A Bagel's marketing rules: Spend nothing on advertising. Many quick-serve food companies use television and radio commercials, newspaper advertisements, and other mass-media messages to build brand awareness, promote products, and attract customers. However, Robertson and her colleagues believe that the best way to build the Finagle A Bagel brand and whet customers' appetites for a new menu item is to give them a free taste.

Consider what happened when Finagle A Bagel used samples and coupons to build lunchtime sales by promoting bagel sandwiches in one of the suburban stores. Instead of placing an ad in the local newspaper, Robertson and her staff went to the store and prepared 100 bagel sandwiches. They cut each in half and wrapped the halves individually. Then they set up 200 Finagle A Bagel bags, put a half-sandwich into each, and added a coupon for a free bagel sandwich without any risk. They piled all the bags into a big basket, attached a sign reading, "Free Bagel Sandwiches," and headed to a large intersection just a block from the store.

"Every time the light turned red, we would run out into the middle of the street and throw a bag through someone's car window," Robertson recalls. "We got a lot of strange looks. A few people would roll up their car windows . . . but a lot of people just thought it was hysterically funny. They would be motioning, waving us over, saying, 'What have you got?' And then they'd go back to their office and tell their coworkers, 'Hey, you know what happened to me today? Some crazy lady threw a bagel through my car window, and it was great. You should check it out.'" The entire effort cost $100—and convinced a large number of customers to look around the store, try a sandwich risk-free, and talk up the experience to colleagues, friends, and family.

The popular Finagle A Bagel headquarters tour has become an effective public-relations tool. Community groups, students, and bagel lovers of all ages can visit the "World Headquarters" building and walk through exhibits representing the company's successes and mistakes. In the factory area, visitors watch through a huge window as hundreds of pounds of dough are mixed, cut, and shaped into bagels. The window is set low so even the youngest visitors can get a great view of the process.

©Barbara Helgason

Buy a Branded Bagel—Again and Again

Although some restaurant companies want each unit to look distinctly different, Finagle A Bagel uses consistency to reinforce the brand image—another of its marketing rules. "We believe the stores should have a very similar look and feel so that you can walk into any Finagle A Bagel and know what to expect," says copresident Alan Litchman. For example, every Finagle A Bagel store sports an eye-catching burgundy-and-yellow sign featuring an oversized bagel with a few bites taken out. This bagel icon is repeated on posters highlighting menu items as well as on other store decorations.

Still, the suburban stores are not exactly like the downtown stores. Many of the suburban stores have children's furniture and cushiony chairs so that families can sit and relax. Free weekly concerts by the "Music Man"—a local musician—make these stores decidedly family friendly. The city stores have no children's furniture because they cater to busy working people who want to be in and out in a hurry. The Harvard Square store is unique: It has a liquor license and attracts a large student crowd, which means it is busier on weekends than on weekdays.

One of the most effective sales promotion techniques the company uses is the Frequent Finagler loyalty card, which rewards customers for making repeat purchases. For every dollar customers spend on bagels or other menu items, they receive Frequent Finagler points that can be redeemed for free coffee, free sandwiches, and so on. Customers are pleased because they receive extra value for the money they spend—and Finagle A Bagel is pleased because its average sale to loyal customers is higher.

Pricing a Bagel

Pricing is an important consideration in the competitive world of quick-serve food. This is where another of Finagle A Bagel's marketing rules comes in. Regardless of cost, the company will not compromise quality. Therefore, the first step in pricing a new product is to find the best possible ingredients and then examine the costs and calculate an approximate retail price. After thinking about what a customer might expect to pay for such a menu item, shopping the competition, and talking with some customers, the company settles on a price that represents "a great product for a fair value," says Robertson.

Although Finagle A Bagel's rental costs vary, the copresidents price menu items the same in higher-rent stores as in lower-rent stores. "We have considered adjusting prices based upon the location of the store, but we haven't done it because it can backfire in a very significant way," copresident Laura Trust explains. "People expect to be treated fairly, regardless of where they live."

Questions

1. Does Finagle A Bagel apply all seven phases of the new product development process when working on a new menu item such as the jalapeno-and-cheese bagel? Explain.

2. Do you agree with Laura Trust's assessment that adjusting prices based on store location can backfire? What arguments can you offer for and against Finagle A Bagel raising prices in higher-rent stores?

3. Finagle A Bagel is both a wholesaler and a retailer. Which of these two marketing intermediary roles do you think the company should develop more aggressively in the next few years? Why?

4. Should Finagle A Bagel continue to spend nothing on media advertising and rely instead primarily on sales promotion techniques such as samples and coupons?

This part is one of the most important components of your business plan. In this part, you will present the facts that you have gathered on the size and nature of your market(s). State market size in dollars and units. How many units and what is the dollar value of the products you expect to sell in a given time period? Indicate your primary and secondary sources of data and the methods you used to estimate total market size and your market share. Part 5 of your textbook covers all marketing-related topics. These chapters should help you to answer the questions in this part of the business plan.

THE MARKETING PLAN COMPONENT

The marketing plan component is and should be unique to your business. Many assumptions or projections used in the analysis may turn out differently; therefore, this component should be flexible enough to be adjusted as needed. The marketing plan should include answers to at least the following questions:

5.1. What are your target markets, and what common identifiable need(s) can you satisfy?

5.2. What are the competitive, legal, political, economic, technological, and sociocultural factors affecting your marketing efforts?

5.3. What are the current needs of each target market? Describe the target market in terms of demographic, geographic, psychographic, and product-usage characteristics. What changes in the target market are anticipated?

5.4. What advantages and disadvantages do you have in meeting the target market's needs?

5.5. How will your product distribution, promotion, and price satisfy customer needs?

5.6. How effectively will your products meet these needs?

5.7. What are the relevant aspects of consumer behavior and product use?

5.8. What are your company's projected sales volume, market share, and profitability?

5.9. What are your marketing objectives? Include the following in your marketing objectives:

- Product introduction, improvement, or innovation
- Sales or market share
- Profitability
- Pricing
- Distribution
- Advertising (Prepare advertising samples for the appendix.)

  Make sure that your marketing objectives are clearly written, measurable, and consistent with your overall marketing strategy.

5.10. How will the results of your marketing plan be measured and evaluated?

REVIEW OF BUSINESS PLAN ACTIVITIES

Remember that even though it will be time consuming, developing a clear, well-written marketing plan is important. Therefore, make sure that you have checked the plan for any weaknesses or problems before proceeding to Part 6. Also, make certain that all your answers to the questions in this and other parts are consistent throughout the business plan. Finally, write a brief statement that summarizes all the information for this part of the business plan.

The information contained in this section will also assist you in completing the online *Interactive Business Plan*.

Understanding Information and e-Business

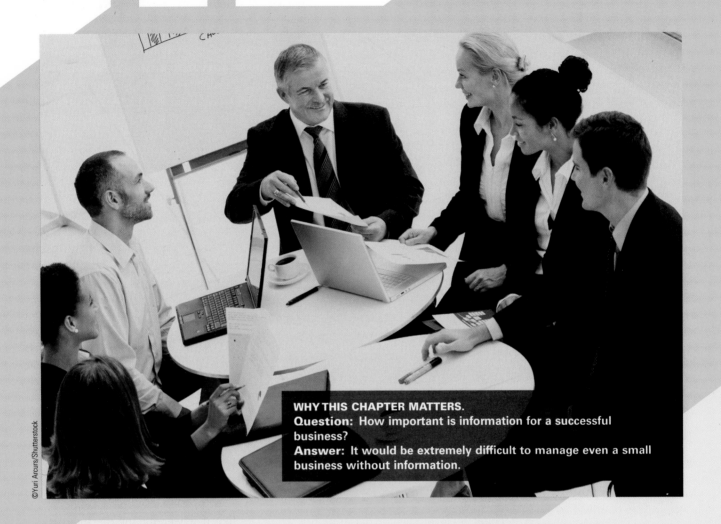

WHY THIS CHAPTER MATTERS.
Question: How important is information for a successful business?
Answer: It would be extremely difficult to manage even a small business without information.

©Yuri Arcurs/Shutterstock

LEARNING OBJECTIVES

1 Examine how information can reduce risk when making a decision.

2 Discuss management's information requirements.

3 Outline the five functions of an information system.

4 Describe how the Internet helps in decision making, communications, sales, and recruiting and training.

5 Analyze how computers and technology change the way information is acquired, organized, and used.

6 Explain the meaning of e-business.

7 Describe the fundamental models of e-business.

8 Explore the factors that will affect the future of e-business.

Facebook Faces Privacy Issues

Four Harvard University students founded Facebook in February, 2004 as an online place for classmates to connect with each other. One month later, they opened the site to students at other colleges—and by the end of the first year, they had 1 million users. Today Facebook has 200 million users worldwide uploading 850 million photos and 10 million videos every month. That's a lot of connecting—and a lot of data contained in one site's pages. Facebook's revenue, which comes mainly from advertising sales, has been growing as the site's usage increases.

Despite Facebook's meteoric growth and popularity, it's been criticized for violating users' privacy in some instances. A few years ago, as part of a new advertising program, it instituted a system that automatically displayed certain online purchases to users' "friends." After receiving thousands of complaints, the CEO apologized, changed the system, and added privacy controls to prevent such information from being released without users' permission.

Facebook faced even more controversy when it later announced that its terms of service gave it the right to continue copying and distributing users' photos, videos, and messages after accounts are closed. Privacy advocates joined users in protesting the rules, and once again, Facebook backed down. Although the company said it was clarifying existing policy, it quickly reverted to the old terms of service, created an online discussion forum, and established a Facebook Bill of Rights and Responsibilities Group to solicit user input. In an unprecedented move, it also invited users to vote on revised rules. Based on this feedback, Facebook agreed not to copy or distribute content after any user closes an account.

Now Facebook's rules state that it will provide advance notice of any changes to its terms of service, give users an opportunity to comment on proposed changes, and put some proposals to a user vote. Still, privacy remains a concern when millions of people share personal information through a single site. Facebook estimates that only 20 percent of its users currently use the site's privacy settings to control who has access to their content. What new privacy issues will Facebook face as U.S. and European officials consider new online data protection regulations?[1]

DID YOU KNOW?

Founded in 2004, Facebook now has more than 200 million users worldwide who upload 850 million photos and 10 million videos every month.

Think for a moment what your life would be like if it weren't for the Internet? Everyday tasks such as using the Web to obtain the weather forecast or movie reviews or tracking the value of your investments would be much more difficult. And today, more and more people are even using the Internet to meet people by sharing messages, photos, and videos. The phenomenal success of Facebook, the company profiled in the Inside Business case for this chapter, illustrates yet one more way that people are getting the information they need to "stay connected." And information is just as important for business decision makers. The fact is that information helps people become better managers and employees.

To improve the decision-making process, the information used by both individuals and business firms must be relevant or useful to meet a specific need. Using relevant information results in better decisions.

Relevant information → Better intelligence and knowledge → Better decisions

For businesses, better intelligence and knowledge that lead to better decisions are especially important because they can provide a *competitive edge* over competitors and improve a firm's *profits*. We begin this chapter by describing why employees need information.

The first three major sections in this chapter answer the following questions:

- How can information reduce risk when making a decision?
- What is a management information system?
- How do employees use an information system?

Next, we discuss how computers, the Internet, and software—all topics covered in this chapter—are used to obtain the information needed to make decisions on a daily basis. In the last three parts of this chapter, we take a close look at how firms conduct business on the Internet and what growth opportunities may be available to both new and existing firms.

How Can Information Reduce Risk When Making a Decision?

1 LEARNING OBJECTIVE

Examine how information can reduce risk when making a decision.

As we noted in Chapter 1, information is one of the four major resources (along with material, human, and financial resources) managers must have to operate a business. While a successful business uses all four resources efficiently, it is information that helps managers reduce risk when making a decision.

Information and Risk

Theoretically, with accurate and complete information, there is no risk whatsoever. On the other hand, a decision made without any information is a gamble. These two extreme situations are rare in business. For the most part, business decision makers see themselves located someplace between either extreme. As illustrated in Figure 14.1, when the amount of available information is high, there is less risk; when the amount of available information is low, there is more risk.

Suppose that a marketing manager for Procter & Gamble (P&G) responsible for the promotion of a well-known shampoo such as Pantene Pro-V has called a meeting of her department team to consider the selection of a new magazine advertisement. The company's advertising agency has submitted two new advertisements in sealed envelopes. Neither the manager nor any of her team has seen them before. Only one selection will be made for the new advertising campaign. Which advertisement should be chosen?

Without any further information, the team might as well make the decision by flipping a coin. If, however, team members were allowed to open the envelopes and examine the advertisements, they would have more information. If, in addition to allowing them to examine the advertisements, the marketing manager circulated a report containing the reactions of a group of target consumers to each of the two advertisements, the team would have even more information with which to work. Thus, information, when understood properly, produces knowledge and empowers managers and employees to make better decisions.

FIGURE 14.1: The Relationship Between Information and Risk When the amount of available information is high, managers tend to make better decisions. On the other hand, when the amount of information is low, there is a high risk of making a poor decision.

More risk ← *Less* **Information** *More* → Less risk

Information Rules

Marketing research continues to show that discounts influence almost all car buyers. Simply put, if dealers lower their prices, they will sell more cars. This relationship between buyer behavior and price can be thought of as an information rule that usually will guide the marketing manager correctly. An information rule emerges when research confirms the same results each time that it studies the same or a similar set of circumstances.

Because of the volume of information they receive each day and their need to make decisions on a daily basis, businesspeople try to accumulate information rules to shorten the time they spend analyzing choices. Information rules are the "great simplifiers" for all decision makers. Business research is continuously looking for new rules that can be put to good use and looking to discredit old ones that are no longer valid. This ongoing process is necessary because business conditions rarely stay the same for very long.

The Difference between Data and Information

Many people use the terms *data* and *information* interchangeably, but the two differ in important ways. **Data** are numerical or verbal descriptions that usually result from some sort of measurement. (The word *data* is plural; the singular form is datum.) Your current wage level, the amount of last year's after-tax profit for Intel, and the current retail prices of Honda automobiles are all data. Most people think of data as being numerical only, but they can be nonnumerical as well. A description of an individual as a "tall, athletic person with short, dark hair" certainly would qualify as data.

Information is data presented in a form that is useful for a specific purpose. Suppose that a human resources manager wants to compare the wages paid to male and female employees over a period of five years. The manager might begin with a stack of computer printouts listing every person employed by the firm, along with each employee's current and past wages. The manager would be hard pressed to make any sense of all the names and numbers. Such printouts consist of data rather than information.

Now suppose that the manager uses a computer to graph the average wages paid to men and to women in each of the five years. The result is information because the manager can use it for the purpose at hand—to compare wages paid to men with those paid to women over the five-year period. When summarized in the graph, the wage *data* from the printouts become *information*. For a manager, information presented in a practical, useful form such as a graph simplifies the decision-making process.

The average company maintains a great deal of data that can be transformed into information. Typical data include records pertaining to personnel, inventory, sales, manufacturing costs, and expenses. Often each type of data is stored in individual departments within an organization. However, the data can be used more effectively when they are organized into a database. A **database** is a single collection of data stored in one place that can be used by people throughout an organization to make decisions. Today, most companies have several different types of databases. While databases are important, the way the data and information are used is even more

---

data numerical or verbal descriptions that usually result from some sort of measurement

information data presented in a form that is useful for a specific purpose

database a single collection of data stored in one place that can be used by people throughout an organization to make decisions

Concept Check

1. In your own words, describe how information reduces risk when you make a personal or work-related decision.

2. What are information rules? How do they simplify the process of making decisions?

3. What is the difference between data and information? Give one example of accounting data and one example of accounting information.

important—and more valuable to the firm. As a result, management information experts now use the term **knowledge management (KM)** to describe a firm's procedures for generating, using, and sharing the data and information contained in the firm's databases. Typically, data, information, databases, and knowledge management all become important parts of a firm's management information system.

What Is a Management Information System?

2 LEARNING OBJECTIVE

Discuss management's information requirements.

A **management information system (MIS)** is a system that provides managers and employees with the information they need to perform their jobs as effectively as possible (see Figure 14.2).

The purpose of an MIS (sometimes referred to as an information technology system or simply IT system) is to distribute timely and useful information from both internal and external sources to the managers and employees who need it. Today, most medium-sized to large business firms have an information technology (IT) officer. An **information technology (IT) officer** is a manager at the executive level who is responsible for ensuring that a firm has the equipment necessary to provide the information the firm's employees and managers need to make effective decisions.

Today's typical MIS is built around a computerized system of record-keeping and communications software so that it can provide information based on a wide variety of data. After all, the goal is to provide needed information to all managers and employees.

Managers' Information Requirements

Managers have to plan for the future, implement their plans in the present, and evaluate results against what has been accomplished in the past. Of course, the specific types of information they need depend on their area of management and on their level within the firm.

Today, many firms are organized into five areas of management: *finance, operations, marketing, human resources,* and *administration.* Managers in each of these areas need specific information in order to make decisions.

knowledge management (KM) a firm's procedures for generating, using, and sharing the data and information contained in the firm's databases

management information system (MIS) a system that provides managers and employees with the information they need to perform their jobs as effectively as possible

information technology (IT) officer a manager at the executive level who is responsible for ensuring that a firm has the equipment necessary to provide the information the firm's employees and managers need to make effective decisions

FIGURE 14.2: Management Information System (MIS) After an MIS is installed, a user can get information directly from the MIS without having to go through other people in the organization.

MANAGEMENT INFORMATION SYSTEM

Integrated database capable of receiving, organizing, summarizing, and calculating data and information from functional areas, and providing information to managers from functional areas networked into the system

| Finance | Operations | Marketing | Human resources | Administration |

Source: Ricky W. Griffin, MANAGEMENT, 9/e (Boston: Houghton Mifflin Company, 2008). Reprinted by permission.

Building employee diversification at Home Depot. Barbara Serret, a human resources manager at Home Depot, knows the value of bilingual employees for Home Depot—the world's largest home improvement chain. Like many retailers, Home Depot is recruiting Hispanic employees who can provide information to Hispanic customers.

- *Financial managers* obviously are most concerned with their firm's finances. They study its debts and receivables, cash flow, future capitalization needs, financial statements, and other accounting information. Of equal importance to financial managers is information about the present state of the economy, interest rates, and predictions of business conditions in the future.

- *Operations managers* are concerned with present and future sales levels, current inventory levels of work in process and finished goods, and the availability and cost of the raw materials required to produce products and services. They also must keep abreast of any innovative production technology that might be useful to the firm.

- *Marketing managers* need to have detailed information about their firm's products and the products offered by competitors. Such information includes pricing strategies, new promotional campaigns, and products that competitors are test marketing. Information concerning the firm's customers, current and projected market share, and new and pending product legislation is also important to marketing managers.

- *Human resources managers* must be aware of anything that pertains to the firm's employees. Key examples include current wage levels and benefits packages both within the firm and in firms that compete for valuable employees, current legislation and court decisions that affect employment practices, union activities, and the firm's plans for growth, expansion, or mergers.

- *Administrative managers* are responsible for the overall management of the organization. Thus, they are concerned with the coordination of information—just as they are concerned with the coordination of material, human, and financial resources.

First, administrators must ensure that all employees have access to the information they need to do their jobs. Then administrative managers must ensure that the information is used in a consistent manner throughout the firm. Administrative managers must also make sure that all managers and employees are able to use the information technology that is available. Certainly, this requires that all employees receive the skills training required to use the firm's MIS. Finally, administrative managers must commit to the costs of updating the firm's MIS and providing additional training when necessary.

Size and Complexity of the System

An MIS must be tailored to the needs of the organization it serves. In some firms, a tendency to save on initial costs may result in a system that is too small or overly simple. Such a system generally ends up serving only one or two management levels or a single department. Managers in other departments "give up" on the system as soon as they find that it cannot process their data. Often, they look elsewhere for information, process their own data, or simply do without.

Almost as bad is an MIS that is too large or too complex for the organization. Unused capacity and complexity do nothing but increase the cost of owning and operating the system. In addition, a system that is difficult to use probably will not be used at all. Obviously, much is expected of an effective MIS system. Let's examine the functions an MIS system must perform to provide the information managers need.

©AP Photo/Luis M. Alvarez

Going Green

The Future of the Paperless Office

Is the paperless office finally at hand? Since the dawn of the information age, people have talked about doing away with printed documents to save trees and spare landfills. However, as businesses computerized their operations, they actually printed and filed, faxed, or mailed more and more documents. In 1975, before the personal computer was invented, U.S. offices used an average of 62 pounds of paper per worker per year. By 1999, with a PC on nearly every business desk, annual paper usage per office worker had soared to 143 pounds.

Today that trend has turned around: Office workers now use about 127 pounds of paper per year. In fact, U.S. firms still print 1.5 trillion pages every year. However, paper use is definitely decreasing as companies learn to digitally manage documents, photographs, maps, and other business information that once existed only on paper.

Businesses of all sizes are going as paperless as possible by scanning documents for electronic storage and retrieval and using web-based applications to invoice customers and pay employees and suppliers. Increasingly, they're exchanging information through e-mail, text messaging, instant messaging, file sharing, and other electronic methods. And to save paper and cut waste, many offices print on both sides of the page and squeeze more onto a single sheet.

Sources: Steve Kaelble, "What Paperless Office?" *Indiana Business,* February 2009, p. 30; Stephen H. Wildstrom, "The Paperless Office—Really," *BusinessWeek,* October 29, 2008, www.businessweek.com; "On Its Way, At Last: The Paperless Office," *The Economist,* October 11, 2008, p. 79; Arik Hesseldahl, "The New Push to Get Rid of Paper," *BusinessWeek Online,* May 28, 2008, www.businessweek.com.

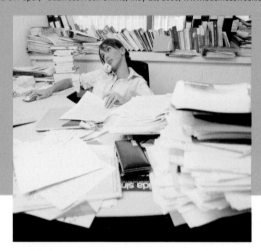

How Do Employees Use an Information System?

3 LEARNING OBJECTIVE

Outline the five functions of an information system.

To provide information, an MIS must perform five specific functions. It must collect data, store the data, update the data, process the data into information, and present information to users (See Figure 14.3).

Collecting Data

A firm's employees, with the help of an MIS system, must gather the data needed to establish the firm's *data bank*. The data bank should include all past and current data that may be useful in managing the firm. Clearly, the data entered into the system must be *relevant* to the needs of the firm's managers. And perhaps most important, the data must be *accurate*. Irrelevant data are simply useless; inaccurate data can be disastrous. There are two data sources: *internal* and *external*.

Internal Sources of Data Typically, most of the data gathered for an MIS come from internal sources. The most common internal sources of information are managers and employees, company records and reports, and minutes of meetings.

Past and present accounting data also can provide information about the firm's transactions with customers, creditors, and suppliers. Sales reports are a source of data on sales, pricing strategies, and the effectiveness of promotional campaigns. Human resources records are useful as a source of data on wage and benefits levels, hiring patterns, employee turnover, and other personnel variables.

Present and past production forecasts also should be included in the firm's data bank, along with data indicating how well these forecasts predicted actual events. And specific plans and management decisions—regarding capital expansion and new product development, for example—should be incorporated into the MIS system.

External Sources of Data External sources of data include customers, suppliers, bankers, trade and financial publications, industry conferences, online computer

©Commercial Eye/Iconica/Getty Images

1 Collects data

2 Stores data

3 Updates data

4 Processes data into information

5 Presents information to users

services, government sources, and firms that specialize in gathering data for organizations. For example, a marketing research company may acquire forecasts pertaining to product demand, consumer tastes, and other marketing variables. Suppliers are also an excellent source of information about the future availability and costs of raw materials and component parts. Bankers often can provide valuable economic insights and projections. And the information furnished by trade publications and industry conferences usually is concerned as much with future projections as with present conditions. Legal issues and court decisions that may affect a firm are discussed occasionally in local newspapers and, more often, in specialized publications such as the *Wall Street Journal, Fortune, and BusinessWeek*. Government publications such as the *Monthly Labor Review* and the *Federal Reserve Bulletin* also are quite useful as sources of external data, as are a number of online computer services.

Whether the source of the data is internal or external, always remember the following three cautions:

1. The cost of obtaining data from some external sources, such as marketing research firms, can be quite high.
2. Outdated or incomplete data usually yield inaccurate information.
3. Although computers generally do not make mistakes, the people who use them can make or cause errors. When data (or information) and your judgment disagree, always check the data.

Storing Data

An MIS must be capable of storing data until they are needed. Typically, the method chosen to store data depends on the size and needs of the organization. Small businesses may enter data and then store them directly on the hard drive inside an employee's computer. Generally, medium-sized to large businesses store data in a larger computer system and provide access to employees through a computer network. Today, networks take on many configurations and are designed by specialists who work with a firm's IT personnel to decide on what's best for the company.

Updating Data

Today, an MIS must be able to update stored data regularly to ensure that the information presented to managers and employees is accurate, complete, and up to date. The frequency with which data are updated depends on how fast they change and how often they are used. When it is vital to have current data, updating may occur as soon as the new data are available. For example, Giant Food, a grocery store chain operating in the eastern part of the United States, has cash registers that automatically transmit data on each item sold to a central computer. The computer adjusts the store's inventory records accordingly. In some systems, the computer even may be programmed to reorder items whose inventories fall below some specified level. Data and information also may be updated according to a predetermined time schedule.

Processing Data

Some data are used in the form in which they are stored, whereas other data require processing to extract, highlight, or summarize the information they contain. **Data processing** is the transformation of data into a form that is useful for a specific purpose.

For verbal data, this processing consists mainly of extracting the pertinent material from storage and combining it into a report. Most business data, however, are in the form of numbers—large groups of numbers, such as daily sales totals or production costs for a specific product. Such groups of numbers are difficult to handle and to comprehend, but their contents can be summarized through the use of statistics. A **statistic** is a measure that summarizes a particular characteristic of an entire group of numbers. Figure 14.4 is an example of statistics in use. This figure contains only eleven items of data, but most business situations involve hundreds or even thousands of items. Fortunately, computers can be programmed to process such large volumes of numbers quickly.

data processing the transformation of data into a form that is useful for a specific purpose

statistic a measure that summarizes a particular characteristic of an entire group of numbers

Presenting Information

An MIS must be capable of presenting information in a usable form. That is, the method of presentation—reports, tables, graphs, or charts, for example—must be appropriate for the information itself and for the uses to which it will be put.

Verbal information may be presented in list or paragraph form. Employees often are asked to prepare formal business reports. A typical business report includes (1) an introduction, (2) the body of the report, (3) the conclusions, and (4) the recommendations.

The *introduction*, which sets the stage for the remainder of the report, describes the problem to be studied in the report, identifies the research techniques that were used, and previews the material that will be presented in the report. The *body of the report* should objectively describe the facts that were discovered in the process of completing the report. The body also should provide a foundation for the conclusions and the recommendations. The *conclusions* are statements of fact that describe the findings contained in the report. They should be specific, practical, and based on the evidence contained in the report. The *recommendations* section presents suggestions on how the problem might be solved. Like the conclusions, the recommendations should be specific, practical, and based on the evidence.

A *visual display* can also be used to present information and may be a diagram that represents several items of information in a manner that makes comparison easier. Figure 14.5 illustrates examples of visual displays generated by a computer. Typical visual displays include:

- Graphs
- Bar charts
- Pie charts

Spotlight

To Collect Information, Consumers Often Use the Internet

(Data for March 2009)

Computer time per person per month: 39 Hours
Sessions per person per month: 38
Web pages viewed each session: 43

Source: The Nielsen/NetRatings website, www.netratings.com, accessed April 30, 2009.

FIGURE 14.4: Statistics Managers often examine statistics that describe trends in employee compensation.

Sky Cloud Manufacturing

Employee Salaries for November 2009

Employee	Monthly Salary
Thomas P. Ouimet	$ 3,500
Marina Ruiz	3,500
Ronald F. Washington	3,000
Sarah H. Abrams	3,000
Kathleen L. Norton	3,000
Martin C. Hess	2,800
Jane Chang	2,500
Margaret S. Fernandez	2,400
John F. O'Malley	2,000
Robert Miller	2,000
William G. Dorfmann	1,800
Total	$29,500

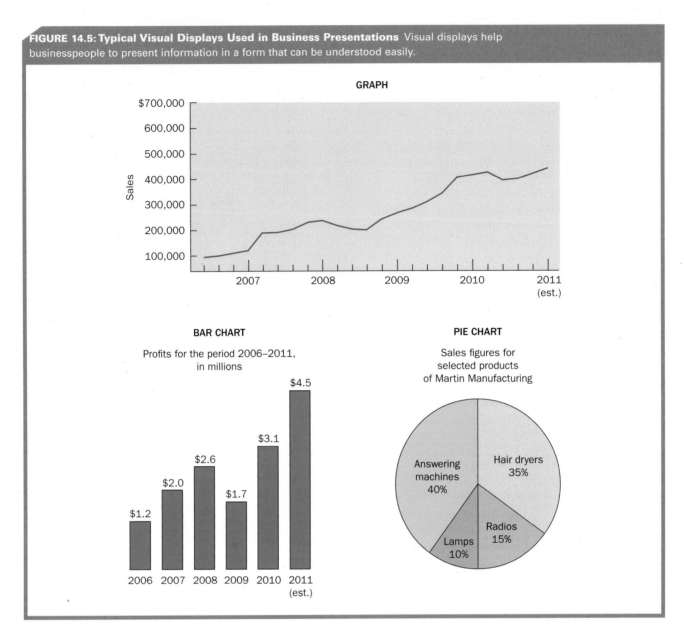

A *tabular* display is used to present verbal or numerical information in columns and rows. It is most useful in presenting information about two or more related variables. A table, for example, can be used to illustrate the number of salespeople in each region of the country, sales for different types of products, and total sales for all products (see Table 14.1). And information that is to be manipulated—for example, to calculate loan payments—is usually displayed in tabular form.

TABLE 14.1: Typical Three-Column Table Used in Business Presentations Tables are most useful for displaying information about two or more variables.

All-Star Technology Projected Sales			
Section of the Country	Number of Salespeople	Consumer Products	Industrial Products
Eastern territory	15	$1,500,000	$3,500,000
Midwestern territory	20	$2,000,000	$5,000,000
Western territory	10	$1,000,000	$4,000,000
TOTAL	45	$4,500,000	$12,500,000

Slumber interrupted

Men and women were asked:
What disturbs you most when sleeping?

Men	
Partner	44%
Pets	42%
Don't know	14%

Women	
Partner	55%
Pets	36%
Don't know	9%

Source: Sealy Snooze Report

Tabular displays generally have less impact than visual displays. However, displaying the information that could be contained in a multicolumn table such as Table 14.1 would require several bar or pie charts.

Improving Productivity with the Help of Computers and Technology

4 LEARNING OBJECTIVE

Describe how the Internet helps in decision making, communications, sales, and recruiting and training.

In this section, we examine several solutions to challenges created when a firm or its employees use computers and the Internet. In each case, a solution is always evaluated in terms of its costs and compared with the benefits a firm receives, generally referred to as a *cost/benefit analysis*. Typical areas of concern for a business include decision making, communications, sales, recruiting and training employees, and business software applications.

Making Smart Decisions

How do managers and employees sort out relevant and useful information from the spam, junk mail, and useless data? Three different applications actually can help to improve and speed the decision-making process for people at different levels within an organization. First, a **decision-support system (DSS)** is a type of computer program that provides relevant data and information to help a firm's employees make decisions. It also can be used to determine the effect of

decision-support system (DSS) a type of computer program that provides relevant data and information to help a firm's employees make decisions

PR NewsFoto/Sealy, Inc.

changing different variables and answer "what if " type questions. For example, a manager at California-based KB Homes may use a DSS to determine prices for new homes built in an upscale, luxury subdivision. By entering the number of homes that will be built along with different costs associated with land, labor, materials, building permits, promotional costs, and all other costs, a DSS can help to determine a base price for each new home. It is also possible to increase or decrease the building costs and determine new home prices for each set of assumptions with a DSS.

Although similar to a DSS, an **executive information system (EIS)** is a computer-based system that facilitates and supports the decision-making needs of top managers and senior executives by providing easy access to both internal and external information. With an EIS, executives can obtain information by touching a computer screen, using a mouse, or using voice recognition and simply talking to the computer. Needed data and information can be displayed in graphs, charts, and spreadsheets.

An **expert system** is a type of computer program that uses artificial intelligence to imitate a human's ability to think. An expert system uses a set of rules that analyze information supplied by the user about a particular activity or problem. Based on the information supplied, the expert system then provides recommendations or suggests specific actions in order to help make decisions. Expert systems, for example, have been used to schedule manufacturing tasks, diagnose illnesses, determine credit limits for credit-card customers, and develop electronic games.

Improving productivity is just a hand-held device away. In a competitive business environment, a company's sales representatives must stay in contact with their customers. In this photo, a sales representative is text messaging information about current inventory levels and product availability to one of his customers.

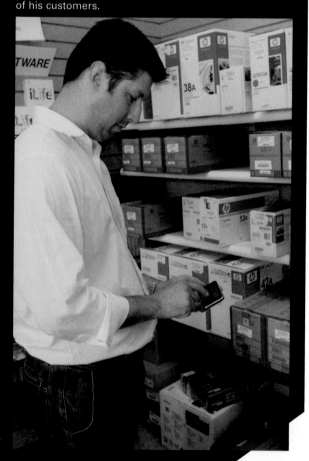

©Vicki Beaver

Helping Employees Communicate

One of the first business applications of computer technology was e-mail. Once software was chosen and employees trained, communications could be carried out globally within and outside a firm at any time, twenty-four hours a day, seven days a week. Today, e-mail is also being used as a direct link between businesses and customers. For example, many brokerage and financial firms like Charles Schwab and Fidelity Investments use e-mail to stay in contact with customers and promote different investment products.

Groupware is one of the latest types of software that facilitates the management of large projects among geographically dispersed employees, as well as such group activities as problem solving and brainstorming. Suppose that the home office of a software development firm in a major city has been hired to prepare customized software for a client in another city. The project team leader uses groupware to establish guidelines for the project, check availability of employees around the world, give individuals specific work assignments, and set up a schedule for work completion, testing, and final installation on the client's computer. The team leader is able to monitor work progress and may intervene if asked or if problems develop. When needed, people from various locations, possessing an array of knowledge and skills, can be called to the "workspace" created on the computer system for their contribution. When the work is finally completed, it can be forwarded to the client's computer and installed.

Besides being useful in project management, groupware provides an opportunity to establish a collaborative learning system to help solve a specific problem.

A **collaborative learning system** is a work environment that allows problem-solving participation by all team members. By posting a question or problem on the groupware site, the team leader invites members, who may be located anywhere in the world, to submit messages that can help to move the group toward a solution.

Assisting the Firm's Sales Force

Internet-based software application programs sometimes referred to as *customer relationship management* (CRM) programs focus on the special informational needs of sales personnel. For example, sales force automation programs support sales representatives with organized databases of information such as names of clients, status of pending orders, and sales leads and opportunities, as well as any related advice or recommendations from other company personnel. Consider what happens when a sales representative for the pharmaceutical division of a company such as Johnson & Johnson is planning to visit doctors, health care providers, and hospitals in the Chicago area. A sales force automation software program can provide information about what the results were of the last contacts, who else in the pharmaceutical division has interacted with the client, and previous purchases the client has made. As sales representatives complete their visits, information about what was learned should be entered into the sales force automation system as soon as possible so that everyone can use the latest information.

Recruiting and Training Employees

A common icon on most corporate websites is a link to "Careers" or "Employment Opportunities." Firms looking for people with specialized skills can post their employee needs on their websites and reach potential candidates from around the globe. This is an extremely important method of recruiting employees for positions where labor shortages are common and individuals with the *right* skills are in high demand.

Furthermore, software programs can help large firms such as General Electric and Exxon Mobil to establish a database of potential employees. This is an especially important function for a firm that receives thousands of unsolicited employment resumes from people all over the world. The cost of organizing and processing this information is high, but software can reduce this expense when compared with a paper-based system.

Large and midsize companies also spend a great deal of money on educational and training programs for employees. By distributing information about the firm, products and services, new procedures, and general information to employees through the Internet for reading and study at convenient times and places, firms can reduce training costs dramatically. Furthermore, revision and distribution of changes to this type of information are much easier if the information is provided on the company's website.

Business Applications Software

Early software typically performed a single function. Today, however, *integrated software* combines many functions in a single package. Integrated packages allow for the easy *linking* of text, numerical data, graphs, photos, and even audiovisual clips. A business report prepared using the Microsoft Office package, for instance, can include all these components.

Integration offers at least two other benefits. Once data have been entered into an application in an integrated package, the data can be used in another integrated package without having to re-enter the data again. Also, once a user learns one application, it is much easier to learn another application in an integrated package. From a career standpoint, you should realize that firms will assume that you possess, or will possess after training, a high degree of working comfort with several of the software applications described in Table 14.2.

collaborative learning system a work environment that allows problem-solving participation by all team members

TABLE 14.2: Current Business Application Software Used to Improve Productivity

Word processing	Users can prepare and edit written documents and store them in the computer or on a memory device.
Desktop publishing	Users can combine text and graphics in reports, newsletters, and pamphlets in professional reports.
Accounting	Users can record routine financial transactions and prepare financial reports at the end of the accounting period.
Database management	Users can electronically store large amounts of data and transform the data into information.
Graphics	Users can display and print pictures, drawings, charts, and diagrams.
Spreadsheets	Users can organize numerical data into a grid of rows and columns.

Concept Check

1. Describe the three types of computer applications that help employees, managers, and executives make smart decisions.

2. How can computers and software help the firm's employees communicate, increase sales, and recruit and train employees?

LEARNING OBJECTIVE 5

Analyze how computers and technology change the way information is acquired, organized, and used.

Using Computers and the Internet to Obtain Information

We live in a rapidly changing **information society**—that is, a society in which large groups of employees generate or depend on information to perform their jobs. The need for more and better information will only continue to grow. Today, businesses are using the Internet to find and distribute information to global users. The Internet is also used for communicating between the firm's employees and its customers. Finally, businesses use the Internet to gather information about competitors' products, prices, and other business strategies. Clearly, the Internet is here to stay.

The Internet, the Intranet, and Networks

The **Internet** is a worldwide network of computers linked through telecommunications. Enabling users around the world to communicate with each other electronically, the Internet provides access to a huge array of information sources. The Internet's most commonly used network for finding information is the World Wide Web. The **World Wide Web** (or more simply, **the Web**) is the Internet's multimedia environment of audio, visual, and text data. To get on the Internet, you need a computer, a modem, and an **Internet service provider (ISP)**, such as AT&T, America Online, Verizon, Comcast, or other companies that provide a connection to the Web. Internet service providers (ISPs) provide customers with a connection to the Internet through various phone plugs and cables. Today, connections to the Internet include simple telephone lines or faster digital subscriber lines (DSLs) and cabled broadband that carry larger amounts of data at quicker transfer speeds. **Broadband technology** is a general term referring to higher speed Internet connections that deliver data, voice, and video material. And with new wireless technology, it is possible to access the Internet by using your laptop computer, cellular phone, and other wireless communications devices. (Wireless technology is especially attractive for many people because not only does it enable them to access the Internet, but it also enables computers and other electronic components to communicate with each other without the multitude of cables and wires common in many offices and homes.)

In addition to business sites, the World Wide Web has a wide array of government and institutional sites that provide information to a firm's employees and the general public. There are also online sites available for most of the popular business periodicals.

An **intranet** is a smaller version of the Internet for use within a firm. Using a series of customized Web pages, employees can quickly find information about

information society a society in which large groups of employees generate or depend on information to perform their jobs

Internet a worldwide network of computers linked through telecommunications

World Wide Web (the Web) the Internet's multimedia environment of audio, visual, and text data

Internet service providers (ISPs) provide customers with a connection to the Internet through various phone plugs and cables

broadband technology a general term referring to higher-speed Internet connections that deliver data, voice, and video material

intranet a smaller version of the Internet for use within a firm's computer network

Managing Your Career

Your Digital Rep

What do you want future employers to find when they search for you online? Think about that as you post messages, photos, or videos on a blog, on Facebook or MySpace, or on any publicly-available web page. Employers often use search engines to check on candidates before making a job offer. A good online impression can give your career a boost; a revealing YouTube video or a post describing questionable activities might stall your career even before it begins.

To protect your digital reputation:

- *Search yourself.* See what others see when they do a web search for your name. Do the results confirm or contradict what's on your résumé? Are there any posts or images you should remove?

- *Preserve your privacy.* Be sure your MySpace or Facebook profile is private and avoid disclosing personal details, especially on public sites.

- *Check photos.* Think, before you post any photos, about whether these are appropriate for potential employers (and anyone else) to see. Also check whether you've been tagged in inappropriate photos posted on other people's sites or pages.

- *Pause before you post.* Information has a long life online—and nearly anything can be forwarded to a huge audience with just a click or two. So think ahead: Will what you post today be an embarrassment tomorrow?

Sources: Scott Sarvay, "Use Caution When Posting to the Web," *Indiana's NewsCenter,* May 8, 2009, http://www.indianasnewscenter.com/news/local/44609387.html; Lisa Bolivar, "Can Facebook Ruin You?" *Miami Herald,* November 9, 2008, www.miamiherald.com; Liz Wolgemuth, "Using Facebook to Fire Up Your Career," *U.S. News & World Report,* August 6, 2008, n.p.; Andy Simmons, "How to Click and Clean," *Reader's Digest,* April 2008, pp. 155–159.

their firm as well as connect to external sources. For instance, an employee might use the intranet to access the firm's policy documents on customer warranties or even take a company-designed course on new products and how to introduce them to customers. Generally, intranet sites are protected, and users must supply both a user name and a password to gain access to a company's intranet site.

Both the Internet and intranets are examples of a computer network. A **computer network** is a group of two or more computers linked together that allows users to share data and information. Today, two basic types of networks affect the way employees and the general public obtain data and information. A **wide-area network (WAN)** is a network that connects computers over a large geographic area, such as a city, a state, or even the world. The world's most popular WAN is the Internet.[2] In addition to the Internet, other WANs include private corporate networks (sometimes referred to as virtual private networks, or VPNs) and research networks. A **local-area network (LAN)** is a network that connects computers that are in close proximity to each other, such as an office building or a college campus. LANs allow users to share files, printers, games, or other applications.[3] Typically, LANs also will allow users to connect to the Internet.

Accessing the Internet

In order to access the Internet or an intranet, computers and software must be standardized. Establishing standards is vital to ensuring that a Hewlett-Packard computer in McPherson, Kansas, can "talk" with a Dell computer in San Francisco, California. It is just as important for software to be standardized if businesses and individuals are going to use computers to communicate and conduct business activities through the Internet.

The search for available information often begins with a specific website address or a search engine. Every website on the Internet is identified by its *Uniform Resource Locator* (URL), which acts as its address. To connect to a site, you enter its URL in your Web browser. A Web browser such as Windows Internet Explorer or Firefox is software that helps users to navigate around the Internet and connect to different websites. The URLs of most corporate sites are similar to the organizations' real names. For instance, you can reach IBM by entering **http://www.ibm.com**.

computer network a group of two or more computers linked together that allows users to share data and information

wide-area network (WAN) a network that connects computers over a large geographic area, such as a city, a state, or even the world

local-area network (LAN) a network that connects computers that are in close proximity to each other, such as an office building or a college campus

The first part of the entry, *http*, sets the software protocols for proper transfer of information between your computer and the one at the site to which you are connecting. *Http* stands for *HyperText Transfer Protocol* and frequently is omitted from a URL because your computer adds it automatically when you enter the rest of the address. *HyperText* refers to words or phrases highlighted or underlined on a Web page; when you select these, they link you to other websites.

To find a particular website, you can take advantage of several free search programs available on the Web, such as Google, Yahoo!, and AltaVista. To locate a search engine, enter its URL in your browser. Some URLs for popular search engines are **www.altavista.com, www.google.com,** and **www.yahoo.com.**

The home page for many search engines provides a short list of primary topic divisions, such as *careers, news, shopping, yellow pages,* and *weather,* as well as a search window where you can enter the particular topic you are looking for.

Creating Web Pages

Today, employees and the general public connect to the Internet, enter a Web address, or use a Web search engine to access information. That information is presented on a website created and maintained by business firms; agencies of federal, state, or local governments; or educational or similar organizations. Because a website should provide accurate information, great care is required when creating a website. Generally, once a *template* or structure for the Web page has been created, content such as text or images can be inserted or changed readily, allowing the site to remain current.

What the website says about a company is important and should be developed carefully to portray the "right" image. Therefore, it is understandable that a firm without the internal human resources to design and launch its website will turn to the talents of creative experts available through Web consulting firms. Regardless of whether the website is developed by the firm's employees or outside consultants, the suggestions listed in Table 14.3 should be considered when creating materials for a firm's website.

Once a website is established, most companies prefer to manage their sites on their own computers. An alternative approach is to pay a hosting service that often will provide guaranteed user accessibility, e-business shopping software, site-updating services, and other specialized services.

TABLE 14.3: Tips for Website Development Whether you build your site from scratch, use a Web design software program, or hire outside professionals, make sure that your website conveys not only the "right" image but also useful information about your company or organization.

1. Develop a theme.	A website is like a book and needs a theme to tie ideas together and tell an interesting story.
2. Determine how much information to include on your site.	Get a handle on the type and amount of information that will be contained on your site. Although it is tempting to include "everything," you must be selective.
3. Plan the layout of your site.	Think about how you want your site to look. Websites that combine color, art, and links to narrative material are the most useful.
4. Add graphics.	Obtain graphics that illustrate the types of data and information contained on your site. Choose colors and photos carefully to make sure that they add rather than detract from the site.
5. Outline the material for each page.	Generally, the opening, or home, page contains basic information with links to additional pages that provide more detailed information.
6. Develop plans to update the site.	It is important to develop a plan to update your site on a regular basis. Too often, sites are "forgotten" and contain dated or inaccurate material.
7. Make sure that your site is easy to use.	Stand back and take a look at your site. Is your site confusing, or does it provide a road map to get from point A to point B? If you have trouble getting information, others will too.

Concept Check

1. Explain the differences between the Internet and an intranet. What types of information does each of these networks provide?

2. What is the difference between a wide-area network (WAN) and a local-area network (LAN)?

3. What factors should be considered when a firm is developing a Web page?

Defining e-Business

6 LEARNING OBJECTIVE

Explain the meaning of e-business.

In Chapter 1, we defined *business* as the organized effort of individuals to produce and sell, for a profit, the goods and services that satisfy society's needs. In a simple sense, then, **e-business, or electronic business,** can be defined as the organized effort of individuals to produce and sell, for a profit, the goods and services that satisfy society's needs *through the facilities available on the Internet.* As you will see in the remainder of this chapter, e-business is transforming key business activities.

Organizing e-Business Resources

As noted in Chapter 1, to be organized, a business must combine *human, material, informational,* and *financial resources.* This is true of e-business, too, but in this case, the resources may be more specialized than in a typical business (see Figure 14.6). For example, people who can design, create, and maintain websites are only a fraction of the specialized human resources required by e-businesses. Material resources must include specialized computers, sophisticated equipment and software, and high-speed Internet connections. Computer programs that track the number of customers to view a firm's website are generally among the specialized informational resources required. Financial resources, the money required to start and maintain the firm and allow it to grow, usually reflect greater participation by individual entrepreneurs and investors willing to invest in a high-tech firm instead of conventional financial sources such as banks.

In an effort to reduce the cost of specialized resources that are used in e-business, many firms have turned to outsourcing. **Outsourcing** is the process of finding

e-business (electronic business) the organized effort of individuals to produce and sell, for a profit, the goods and services that satisfy society's needs *through the facilities available on the Internet*

outsourcing the process of finding outside vendors and suppliers that provide professional help, parts, or materials at a lower cost

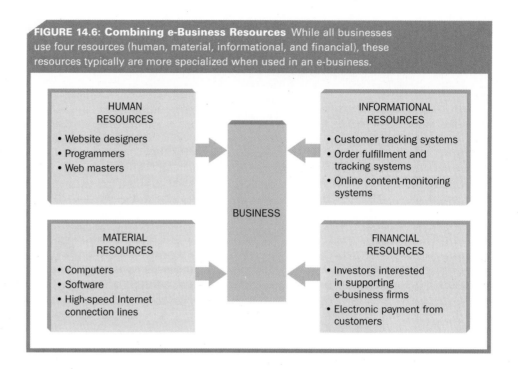

FIGURE 14.6: Combining e-Business Resources While all businesses use four resources (human, material, informational, and financial), these resources typically are more specialized when used in an e-business.

HUMAN RESOURCES
- Website designers
- Programmers
- Web masters

INFORMATIONAL RESOURCES
- Customer tracking systems
- Order fulfillment and tracking systems
- Online content-monitoring systems

BUSINESS

MATERIAL RESOURCES
- Computers
- Software
- High-speed Internet connection lines

FINANCIAL RESOURCES
- Investors interested in supporting e-business firms
- Electronic payment from customers

outside vendors and suppliers that provide professional help, parts, or materials at a lower cost. For example, a firm that needs specialized software to complete a project may turn to an outside firm located in another part of the United States, India, or some Eastern European country.

Satisfying Needs Online

Think for a moment, why do people use the Internet? For most people, the Internet can be used to purchase products or services and as a source of information and interaction with other people. Today, more people use the Internet to

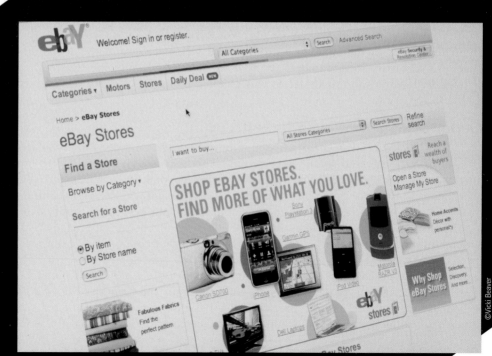

Got something to sell, then use eBay. For many consumers, the search for that hard-to-find item starts with accessing the eBay Website. Started one weekend in 1995 when Pierre Omidyar wrote the software code for an auction Website, eBay is now the world's largest online marketplace that enables trade on a local, national, and international basis.

©Vicki Beaver

satisfy these needs than ever before, and the number of people who use the Internet will continue to grow in the years to come. Because of the explosive growth of the Internet, let's start with two basic assumptions.

- The Internet has created some new customer needs that did not exist before creation of the Internet.
- e-businesses can satisfy those needs, as well as more traditional ones.

Restoration Hardware (**www.restorationhardware.com**), for instance, gives customers anywhere in the world access to the same virtual store of hardware and decorative items. And at eBay's global auction site (**www.ebay.com**), customers can, for a small fee, buy and sell almost anything. In each of these examples, customers can use the Internet to purchase a product or service.

In addition to purchasing products, the Internet can be used by both individuals and business firms to obtain information. For example,

- Internet users can access newspapers and magazines and radio and television programming at a time and place convenient to them.
- The Internet provides the opportunity for two-way interaction between the online program and the viewer. CNN.com (**www.cnn.com**) and other news-content sites encourage dialogue among viewers in chat rooms and exchanges with the writers of articles posted to the site.
- Customers can respond to Internet programming by requesting more information about a product or posing specific questions, which may lead to purchasing a product or service.
- Finally, the Internet allows customers to choose the content they are offered. For example, individuals can custom design the home page for a search engine like Yahoo! with topics and articles that are of interest to them. Knowing what is of interest to a customer allows an Internet firm to direct appropriate, smart advertising to a specific customer. For example, someone wanting to read articles about the New York Yankees might be a potential customer for products and services related to baseball. For the advertiser, knowing that its advertisements are being directed to the most likely customers represents a better way to spend advertising dollars.

Creating e-Business Profit

Business firms can increase profits either by increasing sales revenue or by reducing expenses through a variety of e-business activities.

Increasing Sales Revenue Each source of sales revenue flowing into a firm is referred to as a **revenue stream**. One way to increase revenues is to sell merchandise on the Internet. Online merchants can reach a global customer base twenty-four hours a day, seven days a week because the opportunity to shop on the Internet is virtually unrestricted. And yet shifting revenues earned from customers inside a real store to revenues earned from *those same customers online* does not create any real new revenue for a firm. The goal is to find *new customers* and generate *new sales* so that *total revenues are increased*.

Intelligent informational systems also can help to generate sales revenue for Internet firms such as Amazon (**www.amazon.com**). Such systems store information about each customer's purchases, along with a variety of other information about the buyer's preferences. Using this information, the system can assist the customer the next time he or she visits the website. For example, if the customer has bought a Taylor Hicks or Carrie Underwood CD in the past, the system might suggest CDs by similar artists who have appeared on the popular televised talent-search program *American Idol*.

While some customers in certain situations may not make a purchase online, the existence of the firm's website and the services and information it provides may lead to increased sales in the firm's physical stores. For example, Toyota (**www.toyota.com**)

revenue stream a source of revenue flowing into a firm

can provide basic comparative information for shoppers so that they are better prepared for their visit to an automobile showroom.

In addition to selling products or services online, e-business revenue streams are created by advertising placed on Web pages and by subscription fees charged for access to online services and content. For example, Hoover's Online (**www.hoovers.com**), a comprehensive source for company and industry information, makes some of its online content free for anyone who visits the site, but more detailed data are available only by paid subscription. In addition, it receives revenue from companies that are called sponsors, who advertise their products and services on Hoover's website.

Many Internet firms that distribute news, magazine and newspaper articles, and similar content generate revenue from commissions earned from sellers of products linked to the site. Online shopping malls, for example, now provide groups of related vendors of electronic equipment and computer hardware and software with a new method of selling their products and services. In many cases, the vendors share online sales revenues with the site owners.

Reducing Expenses Reducing expenses is the second major way in which e-business can help to increase profitability. Providing online access to information customers want can reduce the cost of dealing with customers. Sprint Nextel (**www.sprint.com**), for instance, is just one company that maintains an extensive website where potential customers can learn more about its wireless communication products and services and current customers can access personal account information, send e-mail questions to customer service, and purchase additional products or services. With such extensive online services, Sprint Nextel does not have to maintain as many physical store locations as it would without these online services. We examine more examples of how e-business contributes to profitability throughout this chapter, especially as we focus on some of the business models for activity on the Internet.

Concept Check

1. What are the four major factors contained in the definition of e-business?

2. How do e-businesses generate revenue streams and earn a profit?

LEARNING OBJECTIVE 7

Describe the fundamental models of e-business.

Fundamental Models of e-Business

One way to get a better sense of how businesses are adapting to the opportunities available on the Internet is to identify e-business models. A **business model** represents a group of common characteristics and methods of doing business to generate sales revenues and reduce expenses. Each of the models discussed below represents a primary e-business model. Regardless of the type of business model, planning often depends on if the e-business is a new firm or an existing firm adding an online presence—see Figure 14.7.

Business-to-Business (B2B) Model

Many e-businesses can be distinguished from others simply by their customer focus. For instance, some firms use the Internet mainly to conduct business with other businesses. These firms generally are referred to as having a **business-to-business (or B2B) model**.

When examining B2B business firms, two clear types emerge. In the first type, the focus is simply on facilitating sales transactions between businesses. For example, Dell manufactures computers to specifications that customers enter on the Dell website. A large portion of Dell's online orders are from corporate clients who are well informed about the products they need and are looking for fairly priced, high-quality computer products that will be delivered quickly. By dealing directly with Dell, customers eliminate costs associated with wholesalers and retailers, thereby helping to reduce the price they pay for equipment.

A second, more complex type of B2B model involves a company and its suppliers. Today, suppliers use the Internet to bid on products and services they wish to sell to a customer and learn about the customer's rules and procedures that must be

business model represents a group of common characteristics and methods of doing business to generate sales revenues and reduce expenses

business-to-business (or B2B) model a model used by firms that conduct business with other businesses

FIGURE 14.7: Planning for a New Internet Business or Building an Online Presence for an Existing Business The approach taken to creating an e-business plan will depend on whether you are establishing a new Internet business or adding an online component to an existing business.

- Will the new e-business provide a product or service that meets customer needs?
- Who are the new firm's potential customers?
- How do promotion, pricing, and distribution affect the new e-business?
- Will the potential market generate enough sales and profits to justify the risk of starting an e-business?

- Is going online a logical way to increase sales and profits for the existing business?
- Are potential online customers different from the firm's traditional customers?
- Will the new e-business activities complement the firm's traditional activities?
- Does the firm have the time, talent, and financial resources to develop an online presence?

Starting a new Internet business

Building an online presence for an existing business

SUCCESSFUL E-BUSINESS PLANNING

followed. For example, Ford has developed B2B models to link thousands of suppliers that sell the automobile maker parts worth billions of dollars each year. While the B2B sites are expensive to start and maintain, there are significant savings for Ford. Given the potential savings, it is no wonder that many other manufacturers and their suppliers are beginning to use the same kind of B2B systems that are used by the automaker.

Business-to-Consumer (B2C) Model

In contrast to the B2B model, firms such as **Barnesandnoble.com** and **Landsend.com** clearly are focused on individual consumers and so are referred to as having a **business-to-consumer (or B2C) model**. In a B2C situation, understanding how consumers behave online is critical to a firm's success. Typically, a business firm that uses a B2C model must answer the following questions:

- Will consumers use websites merely to simplify and speed up comparison shopping?
- Will consumers purchase services and products online or end up buying at a traditional retail store?
- What sorts of products and services are best suited for online consumer shopping?
- Which products and services are simply not good choices at this stage of online development?

In addition to providing round-the-clock global access to all kinds of products and services, B2C firms often attempt to build long-term relationships with their customers. Often, firms will make a special effort to make sure that the customer

business-to-consumer (or B2C) model a model used by firms that focus on conducting business with individual consumers

The magic of Microsoft. Microsoft uses a business-to-business (B2B) approach to reach potential business customers. One of its newest software applications is called "virtual product placement" and allows advertisers to place a photo of a product or advertising image into an existing video or movie—such as the Coca-Cola image shown in this photo.

©AP Photo/Ted S. Warren

is satisfied and that problems, if any, are solved quickly. While a "little special attention" may increase the cost of doing business for a B2C firm, the customer's repeated purchases will repay the investment many times over.

Today, B2B and B2C models are the most popular business models for e-business. And yet, there are other business models that perform specialized e-business activities to generate revenues. Most of the business models described in Table 14.4 are modified versions of the B2B and B2C models.

Concept Check

1. What are the two fundamental e-business models?

2. Assume that you are the owner of a small company that produces outdoor living furniture. Describe how you could use the B2C business model to sell your products to consumers.

TABLE 14.4: Other Business Models That Perform Specialized e-Business Activities Although modified versions of B2B or B2C, these business models perform specialized e-business activities to generate revenues.

Advertising e-business model	Advertisements that are displayed on a firm's website in return for a fee. Examples include pop-up and banner advertisements on search engines and other popular Internet sites.
Brokerage e-business model	Online marketplaces where buyers and sellers are brought together to facilitate exchange of goods and services. Examples include eBay (www.ebay.com), which provides a site for buying and selling virtually anything.
Consumer-to-consumer model	Peer-to-peer software that allows individuals to share information over the Internet. Examples include LimeWire (www.limewire.com), which allows users to exchange video and music files.
Subscription and pay-per-view e-business models	Content that is available only to users who pay a fee to gain access to a website. Examples include investment information provided by Standard & Poor's (www2.standardandpoors.com) and business research provided by Forrester Research, Inc. (www.forrester.com).

The Future of e-Business: Growth, Opportunities, and Challenges

8 LEARNING OBJECTIVE

Explore the factors that will affect the future of e-business.

Since the beginning of commercial activity on the Internet, developments in e-business have been rapid and formidable with spectacular successes such as Google, eBay, and Yahoo!. However, the slowdown in e-business activity that began in 2000 caused a shakeout of excessive optimism in this new-business environment. Today, most firms involved in e-business use a more intelligent approach to development. The long-term view held by the vast majority of analysts is that the Internet will continue to expand along with related technologies. For example, according to Forrester Research, Inc., the popularity and growth of consumer broadband access to the Internet have pushed marketers to allocate more money to advertising online in order to reach customers who are moving to the Web and away from traditional media such as television and radio. As a result, Forrester predicts that by 2010, more than $26 billion, or about 8 percent of all advertising spending, will be online.[4]

Internet Growth Potential

To date, only a small percentage of the global population uses the Internet. Current estimates suggest that about 1.8 billion of the nearly 7 billion people in the world use the Web. Clearly, there is much more growth opportunity. Americans comprise 12 percent of all Internet users. Of the approximately 300 million people making up the American population, 223 million use the Internet. With approximately 75 percent of the American population already being Internet users, potential growth in the United States is limited.[5] On the other hand, the number of Internet users in the world's developing countries is expected to increase dramatically. Because of worldwide growth and an increase in wireless computing devices, Computer Industry Almanac projects that worldwide users will exceed 2.1 billion by 2012.[6]

Firms that adapt existing business models to an online environment will continue to dominate development. For example, books, CDs, clothing, hotel accommodations, car rentals, and travel reservations are products and services well suited to online buying

PR NewsFoto/Language Technologies

A new way to enhance your reading enjoyment. Back in 1864 when Lewis Carroll wrote Alice in Wonderland, he had no idea that his now famous book would be read on Apple iPhones and iPods. While converting printed text to electronic files is just one application of technology, there will be many more applications of technology in the future that will change the way we live, work, and play.

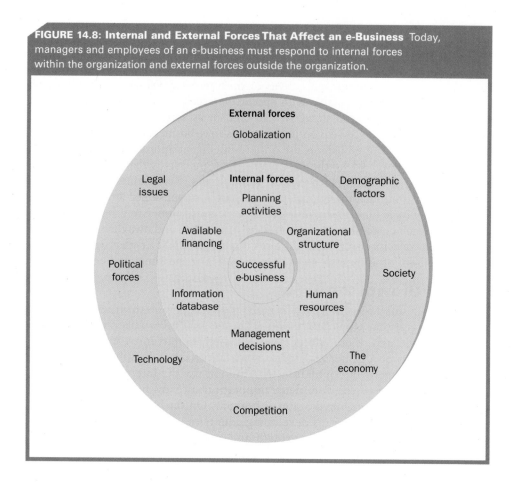

FIGURE 14.8: Internal and External Forces That Affect an e-Business Today, managers and employees of an e-business must respond to internal forces within the organization and external forces outside the organization.

and selling. These products or services will continue to be sold in the traditional way, as well as in a more cost-effective and efficient fashion over the Internet.

Environmental Forces Affecting e-Business

Although the environmental forces at work are complex, it is useful to think of them as either *internal* or *external* forces that affect an e-business. Internal environmental forces are those that are closely associated with the actions and decisions taking place within a firm. As shown in Figure 14.8, typical internal forces include a firm's planning activities, organization structure, human resources, management decisions, information database, and available financing. A shortage of skilled employees needed for a specialized project, for instance, can undermine a firm's ability to sell its services to clients. Unlike the external environmental forces affecting the firm, internal forces such as this one are more likely to be under the direct control of management. In this case, management can either hire the needed staff or choose to pass over a prospective project.

In contrast, external environmental forces are factors affecting e-business planning that originate from outside the organization. These forces are unlikely to be controllable by an e-business firm. Instead, managers and employees of an e-business firm generally will react to these forces, attempting to shield the organization from any undue negative effects and finding ways to take advantage of opportunities in the ever-changing e-business environment. The primary external environmental forces affecting e-business planning include globalization, demographic, societal, economic, competitive, technological, and political and legal forces.

In this chapter, we have explored a business firm's need for information and how a computer, the Internet, and technology can help people to obtain the information they need. We also examined how e-business is changing the way that firms do business. In Chapter 15, we examine the accounting process, which is a major source of information for business.

SUMMARY

1 Examine how information can reduce risk when making a decision.

The more information a manager has, the less risk there is that a decision will be incorrect. Information produces knowledge and empowers managers and employees to make better decisions. Without accurate and timely information, individual performance will be undermined, and consequently, so will the performance of the entire organization. Because of the volume of information they receive each day and their need to make decisions on a daily basis, businesspeople use information rules to shorten the time spent analyzing choices. Information rules emerge when business research confirms the same results each time it studies the same or a similar set of circumstances. Although many people use the terms *data* and *information* interchangeably, there is a difference. Data are numerical or verbal descriptions that usually result from some sort of measurement. Information is data presented in a form that is useful for a specific purpose. A database is a single collection of data stored in one place that can be used by people throughout an organization to make decisions. While databases are important, the way the data and information are used is even more important. As a result, management information experts now use the term knowledge management (KM) to incorporate a firm's procedures for generating, using, and sharing the data and information contained in the firm's databases.

2 Discuss management's information requirements.

A management information system (MIS) is a means of providing managers with the information they need to perform their jobs as effectively as possible. The purpose of an MIS, (sometimes referred to as an information technology system or simply IT system) is to distribute timely and useful information from both internal and external sources to the decision makers who need it. The specific types of information managers need depend on their area of management and level within the firm. The size and complexity of an MIS must be tailored to the information needs of the organization it serves.

3 Outline the five functions of an information system.

The five functions performed by an MIS system are collecting data, storing data, updating data, processing data into information, and presenting information. Data may be collected from such internal sources as company records, reports, and minutes of meetings, as well as from the firm's managers. External sources include customers, suppliers, bankers, trade and financial publications, industry conferences, online computer services, and information-gathering organizations. An MIS must be able to store data until they are needed and to update them regularly to ensure that the information presented to managers is accurate, complete, and timely. Data processing is the MIS function that transforms stored data into a form useful for a specific purpose. Large groups of numerical data usually are processed into summary numbers called

statistics. Finally, the processed data (which now can be called information) must be presented for use. Verbal information generally is presented in the form of a report. Numerical information most often is displayed in graphs, charts, or tables.

4 Describe how the Internet helps in decision making, communications, sales, and recruiting and training.

Today, many employees use computers and the Internet to improve productivity and performance and communicate with other employees while at the office or away from the office. Three different applications—decision-support systems, executive information systems, and expert systems—can help managers and employees to speed and improve the decision-making process. Another application in the workplace is electronic mail, or simply e-mail, which provides for communication within and outside the firm at any time, twenty-four hours a day, seven days a week. An extension of e-mail is groupware, which is software that facilitates the management of large projects among geographically dispersed employees as well as such group activities as problem solving and brainstorming. The Internet and a sales force automation software program can provide a database of information that can be used to assist a sales representative. The Internet also can be used to improve employee training and recruitment while lowering costs. A number of software applications—word processing, desktop publishing, accounting, database management, graphics, and spreadsheets—can all help employees improve productivity.

5 Analyze how computers and technology change the way information is acquired, organized, and used.

We live in an information society—one in which large groups of employees generate or depend on information to perform their jobs. To find needed information, many businesses and individuals use the Internet. The Internet is a worldwide network of computers linked through telecommunications. Firms also can use an intranet to distribute information within the firm. Both the Internet and intranets are examples of a computer network. A computer network is a group of two or more computers linked together to allow users to share data and information. Two basic types—local-area networks (LANs) and wide-area networks (WANs)—affect the way employees and the general public obtain data and information. Today, employees and the general public connect to the Internet, enter a Web address, or use a Web search engine to access information. That information is presented on a website created and maintained by business firms; agencies of federal, state, and local governments; or educational or similar organizations. Because a website should provide accurate information, great care is required when creating a website.

6 Explain the meaning of e-business.

e-Business, or electronic business, can be defined as the organized effort of individuals to produce and sell, for a profit, the goods and services that satisfy society's needs *through the facilities available on the Internet.* The human, material, information, and financial resources that any business requires are highly specialized for e-business. In an effort to reduce the cost of e-business resources, many firms have turned to outsourcing.

Using e-business activities, it is possible to satisfy new customer needs created by the Internet as well as traditional ones in unique ways. Meeting customer needs is especially important when an e-business is trying to earn profits by increasing sales and reducing expenses. Each source of revenue flowing into the firm is referred to as a revenue stream.

7 Describe the fundamental models of e-business.

e-Business models focus attention on the identity of a firm's customers. Firms that use the Internet mainly to conduct business with other businesses generally are referred to as having a business-to-business, or B2B, model. When examining B2B business firms, two clear types emerge. In the first type of B2B, the focus is simply on facilitating sales transactions between businesses. A second, more complex type of the B2B model involves a company and its suppliers. In contrast to the focus of the B2B model, firms such as Amazon or eBay clearly are focused on individual buyers and so are referred to as having a business-to-consumer, or B2C, model. In a B2C situation,

understanding how consumers behave online is critical to the firm's success. And successful B2C firms often make a special effort to build long-term relationships with their customers. While B2B and B2C models are the most popular e-business models, there are other models that perform specialized e-business activities to generate revenues (see Table 14.4).

8 Explore the factors that will affect the future of e-business.

Since the advent of commercial activity on the Internet, developments in e-business have been rapid and formidable. Clearly, the slowdown in e-business activity that began in 2000 caused a shakeout of excessive optimism in this new business environment. Today, most firms involved in e-business use a more intelligent approach to development. The long-term view held by the vast majority of analysts is that the Internet will continue to expand along with related technologies. While approximately 75 percent of Americans now have access to the Internet, it is expected that worldwide users will exceed 2.1 billion by 2012. Although the environmental forces at work are complex, it is useful to think of them as either internal or external forces that affect an e-business. Internal environmental forces are those that are closely associated with the actions and decisions taking place within a firm. In contrast, external environmental forces are those factors affecting an e-business originating outside an organization.

KEY TERMS

You should now be able to define and give an example relevant to each of the following terms:

data (388)
information (388)
database (388)
knowledge management (KM) (389)
management information system (MIS) (389)
information technology (IT) officer (389)
data processing (392)

statistic (392)
decision-support system (DSS) (395)
executive information system (EIS) (396)
expert system (396)
groupware (396)
collaborative learning system (397)
information society (398)

Internet (398)
World Wide Web (the Web) (398)
Internet service providers (ISPs) (398)
broadband technology (398)
intranet (398)
computer network (399)
wide-area network (WAN) (399)

local-area network (LAN) (399)
e-business (electronic business) (401)
outsourcing (401)
revenue stream (403)
business model (404)
business-to-business (B2B) model (404)
business-to-consumer (B2C) model (405)

DISCUSSION QUESTIONS

1. Do managers really need all the kinds of information discussed in this chapter? If not, which kinds can they do without?
2. How can confidential data and information (such as the wages of individual employees) be kept confidential and yet still be available to managers who need them?
3. Why are computers so well suited to management information systems (MISs)? What are some things computers *cannot* do in dealing with data and information?

4. How could the Internet help you to find information about employment opportunities at Coca-Cola, Johnson & Johnson, or Microsoft? Describe the process you would use to access this information.
5. Can advertising provide enough revenue for an e-business to succeed in the long run?
6. Is outsourcing good for an e-business firm? The firm's employees? Explain your answer.
7. What distinguishes a B2B from a B2C e-business model?

Test Yourself

Matching Questions

1. _____ Data that have been processed.

2. _____ It incorporates a firm's procedures for generating, using, and sharing the data and information contained in the firm's database.

3. _____ It is a work environment that allows groups to solve problems.

4. _____ It transforms data into useful information.

5. _____ This tool organizes numerical data into grids of rows and columns.

6. _____ All business activities that are conducted on the Internet.

7. _____ Its focus is to facilitate sales transactions between businesses.

8. _____ Amazon.com makes a special effort to build long-term relationships with its customers.

9. _____ It provides customers with a connection to the Internet.

10. _____ Two or more computers that are linked together.

   a. data processing
   b. business-to-business model
   c. knowledge management
   d. spreadsheet program
   e. convergence of technologies
   f. e-business
   g. broadband technology
   h. information
   i. internet service provider
   j. business-to-consumer model
   k. collaborative learning system
   l. computer network

True False Questions

11. **T F** The more information a manager has, the less risk there is that a decision will be incorrect.

12. **T F** Information rules help businesspeople make everyday decisions.

13. **T F** Most data gathered for an MIS come from external sources.

14. **T F** An expert system uses artificial intelligence to imitate a human's ability to think.

15. **T F** A society in which large groups of employees generate or depend on information to perform their jobs is referred to as a data society.

16. **T F** A LAN is a network that connects computers over a large geographic area.

17. **T F** Companies such as Sprint reduce their expenses by offering product information online.

18. **T F** Sources of revenue flowing into the firm are referred to as channels.

19. **T F** Firms that tend to focus on conducting e-business with other businesses are referred to as having a B2B focus.

20. **T F** When Ford Motor Company uses the Internet to purchase materials from its suppliers, it is using a B2C business model.

Multiple-Choice Questions

21. _____ You are a purchasing manager in a large firm and are responsible for deciding on and ordering the appropriate software program that allows the user to prepare and edit letters and store them on a computer memory stick. What type of program will you order?

   a. Spreadsheet
   b. Word processing
   c. Graphics
   d. Communications
   e. Database

22. _____ Management information systems

   a. collect data, hire personnel, and compensate workers.
   b. store data, present data to users, and make final decisions.
   c. collect, store, update, process, and present data.
   d. supervise personnel, reprimand workers, and conduct follow-ups.
   e. collect relevant information.

Test Yourself

23. _____ As an MIS manager, you are charged with establishing a management information system that is capable of presenting information in a useable form. Which item below do you feel is not appropriate for presenting information in business report format?

    a. The introduction describes the problem and techniques used to gather data.
    b. The body of the report describes the facts.
    c. The conclusions describe the findings.
    d. The recommendations present suggestions for solving the problem.
    e. The database of research methods used by the author of the report.

24. _____ As an information manager, you must ensure that

    a. information is protected from employees.
    b. information is used in a consistent manner.
    c. the smart group receives the data first.
    d. the promotional campaigns are aired on time.
    e. new product planning is on schedule.

25. _____ A single collection of data stored in one place and used by employees throughout an organization is called a(n)

    a. data collection.
    b. information center.
    c. database.
    d. data center.
    e. management data center.

26. _____ A manager at the executive level responsible for ensuring that a firm has the equipment necessary to provide the information the firm's employees and managers need to make effective decisions is often called a(n)

    a. information expert.
    b. technology expert.

    c. MIS officer.
    d. information technology officer.
    e. database manager.

27. _____ A customer tracking system is an example of e-business _____ resources.

    a. human
    b. informational
    c. material
    d. financial
    e. supplemental

28. _____ Which of the types of resources needed for an e-business is Storybook.com most likely to receive from a venture capitalist?

    a. Financial
    b. Human
    c. Software
    d. Material
    e. Informational

29. _____ When Microsoft allows workers in a foreign country to provide technical assistance to its customers, it is engaging in

    a. external recruiting
    b. employment sourcing.
    c. insourcing.
    d. outsourcing.
    e. revenue stream buildup.

30. _____ An Internet distributor of office supplies has a system of bidding and awarding contracts online for its purchases and acquisitions from suppliers. This is most likely a _____ model.

    a. B2B
    b. C2C
    c. B2C
    d. C2B
    e. Cross functional

Answers on p. TY-1

VIDEO CASE

Manifest Digital Helps Clients Upgrade the Customer Experience

Manifest Digital, based in Chicago, is an award-winning young marketing and design firm of about 50 people that provides interactive marketing services to traditional brick-and-mortar firms and to e-businesses. Companies looking to improve their online presence, to better integrate their website with their other marketing communications, and to offer their customers the rewards of belonging to an exciting online community are likely to ask Manifest for its expert help. Manifest's revenues are in the $7 million range; it works with firms of all sizes and counts among its clients Sony, Texas Instruments, Playboy Enterprises, Kraft Foods, and the Field Museum.

Though it started out executing individual online ads and campaigns, Manifest has moved on to creating integrated marketing strategies for its business customers, including building and remodeling entire websites and crafting inter-active product-related games. Along the way it has grown tremendously, but it's retained its focus on user-centered principles that put the ultimate consumer at the center of all its design decisions. The purpose of a company website, Manifest's designers believe, is to acquire, retain, and stimu-late the firm's customers.

Manifest first sits down with its client companies to address the question, "What do your users need and want to get from their online experience?" Manifest's software design-ers, who have widely different skills and backgrounds, know the answer isn't always going to mean creating the flashiest graphics or the hottest animation. Most website visitors want above all to find the information they came for, though it's not a bad idea to also offer them a new and rewarding experience they might not have expected.

What's inside the user's head isn't always so obvious. Wilson Sporting Goods, Inc., for example, had organized its website the same way its executives think of the company's offerings—by product. But Manifest's staff pointed out that most of the site's visitors, often 10–15-year-old boys, used the baseball section of the site, for instance, mainly to find out about their favorite play-ers. So its designers undertook a redesign that gave users new player-centric portals to Wilson's site, letting them first find the player bios and videos they most wanted, and then making it easy for them to explore beyond that for product details, dealers, company news and sponsorships, and other information. The new design thus meets Wilson's goals as well—to educate users about the products and to strengthen the brand so customers will choose Wilson products when they get to the store. The rede-sign was so successful that Wilson asked Manifest to repeat the process for its football, tennis, and basketball website pages too.

Other Manifest clients have other needs. NEC Visual Systems, for instance, makes professional-grade plasma displays and projectors. NEC asked Manifest to help it intro-duce a new plasma display to its customers, and the result was a wildly successful online "advergame"—an interactive game with a marketing purpose. The prize for winning the game was a huge plasma display, and the IT professionals at whom the game was targeted dove in to compete, creat-ing an online community to compare notes and share game strategies. Some enthusiasts even tried to hack the game, which NEC saw as the seal of approval on the game's success. Manifest's engineers kept tinkering with the game to slow the hackers and raise the suspense, and even the ongoing "battle" between them and the players became part of the fun.

Manifest relies on customer focus groups and feedback from site users to help improve its software and website designs. It also looks at successful firms like Amazon.com, eBay, and MySpace for benchmarks on creating self-sustaining user communities with the carefully balanced degrees of struc-ture and freedom these firms have designed into their web-sites. One of Manifest's most recent successful online com-munity builds was a prize-winning digital scrapbook, in which Chicago residents were invited to post photos and videos on personalized pages to explain why they think Chicago should become the host of the 2016 Olympics.[7]

For more information about this company, go to **www.manifestdigital.com**.

Questions

1. What type of business model is Manifest using?
2. How does Manifest Digital help its client companies acquire, retain, and stimulate their customers while providing a unique interactive experience?
3. What external factors do you think will change the types of services Manifest Digital may offer its clients in the future, and how?

BUILDING SKILLS FOR CAREER SUCCESS

1. EXPLORING THE INTERNET

Computer technology is a fast-paced, highly competitive industry in which product life cycles sometimes are mea-sured in months or even weeks. To keep up with changes and trends in hardware and software, MIS managers routinely must scan computer publications and websites that discuss new products.

A major topic of interest among MIS managers is group-ware, software that facilitates the management of large proj-ects among geographically dispersed employees, as well as group activities such as problem solving and brainstorming.

Assignment

1. Use a search engine and enter the keyword "groupware" to locate companies that provide this type of software. Try the demonstration edition of the groupware if it is available.
2. Based on your research of this business application, why do you think groupware is growing in popularity?
3. Describe the structure of one of the groupware programs you examined as well as your impressions of its value to users.

2. BUILDING TEAM SKILLS

To provide marketing managers with information about con-sumer reactions to a particular product or service, business researchers often conduct focus groups. The participants in these groups are representative of the target market for the product or service under study. The leader poses questions and lets members of the group express their feelings and ideas about the product or service. The ideas are recorded, transcribed, and analyzed.

Assignment

1. Working in a small team, select a product or service to research—for example, your college's food service or bookstore or a new item you would like to see stocked in your local grocery store.
2. Create a list of questions that can be used to generate discussion about the product or service with focus-group members.
3. Form a focus group of five to seven people representative of the market for the product or service your team has selected.

4. During the group sessions, record the input. Later, transcribe it into printed form, analyze it, and process it into information. On the basis of this information, make recommendations for improving the product or service.

5. In a report, describe your team's experiences in forming the focus groups and the value of focus groups in collecting data. Use the report as the basis for a three- to five-minute class presentation.

3. RESEARCHING DIFFERENT CAREERS

Firms today expect employees to be proficient in using computers and computer software. Typical business applications include e-mail, word processing, spreadsheets, and graphics. By improving your skills in these areas, you can increase your chances not only of being employed but also of being promoted once you are employed.

Assignment

1. Assess your computer skills by placing a check in the appropriate column in the following table:

Software	Skill Level			
	None	Low	Average	High
e-mail				
Word processing				
Desktop publishing				
Accounting				
Database management				
Graphics				
Spreadsheets				
Groupware				

2. Describe your self-assessment in a written report. Specify the software programs in which you need to become more proficient, and outline a plan for doing this.

15 Using Accounting Information

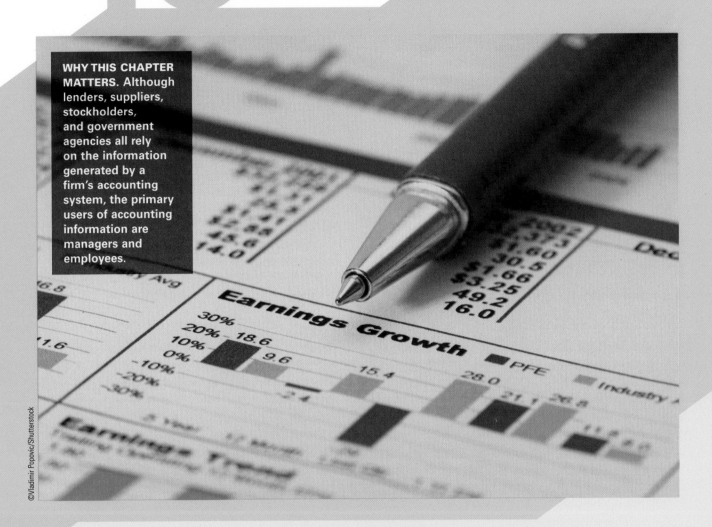

WHY THIS CHAPTER MATTERS. Although lenders, suppliers, stockholders, and government agencies all rely on the information generated by a firm's accounting system, the primary users of accounting information are managers and employees.

©Vladimir Popovic/Shutterstock

LEARNING OBJECTIVES

1 Explain why accurate accounting information and audited financial statements are important.

2 Identify the people who use accounting information and possible careers in the accounting industry.

3 Discuss the accounting process.

4 Read and interpret a balance sheet.

5 Read and interpret an income statement.

6 Describe business activities that affect a firm's cash flow.

7 Summarize how managers evaluate the financial health of a business.

PricewaterhouseCoopers Peeks behind the Numbers

Johnson & Johnson, Bank of America, and thousands of other corporations—large and small—count on PricewaterhouseCoopers to peek behind their accounting numbers. The firm's 150,000 employees provide corporate clients in 150 nations with a wide range of accounting, financial reporting, auditing, tax, and consulting services. They also guide corporations in complying with the many local, state, national, regional, and international laws and regulations that apply to their business operations.

Formed from the merger of several well-established accounting firms founded more than 100 years ago, PricewaterhouseCoopers now rings up $28 billion in annual revenue worldwide. Although its professionals serve corporations in many industries, they have developed special expertise in 22 industries, ranging from aerospace and automotive to technology and transportation. PricewaterhouseCoopers experts know how to go behind the numbers and examine not only what clients are doing but how they could be doing it more efficiently and more effectively. They also offer consulting assistance to help corporate clients address key challenges such as operating in the 24/7 global economy, using technology to boost productivity, and doing business in a sustainable way.

To keep all employees up-to-date on the latest accounting regulations, auditing tools, business trends, and technology, the PricewaterhouseCoopers Learning & Education group offers classroom training, self-paced online courses, Webcasts, and best-practices reports. The firm has also established a Fraud Academy to help accounting and financial personnel share ideas about uncovering, analyzing, and preventing corporate corruption and fraud.

Over the years, PricewaterhouseCoopers has worked with government agencies and nonprofit organizations such as the U.S. Department of Homeland Security and the World Bank to manage and secure accounting data, evaluate internal processes and procedures, and plan for the future. The firm is part of an industry group seeking to promote new, interactive approaches to presenting complex accounting and financial data. And, looking ahead to its own future, PricewaterhouseCoopers uses the web, Facebook, Twitter, and other 21st-century technology to reach out to companies, employees, and the workforce of tomorrow.[1]

DID YOU KNOW?

PricewaterhouseCoopers rings up $28 billion in annual revenue by providing clients in 150 nations with accounting, financial reporting, auditing, tax, and consulting services.

What is an average day in the life of an accountant like? Many people have the idea that accountants spend their day working with endless columns of numbers in a small office locked away from other people. In fact, accountants do spend a lot of time at their desks, but their job entails far more than just adding or subtracting numbers. Accountants are expected to share their ideas and the information they possess with people who need the information. Accounting is serious business, but it can also be an exciting and rewarding career—one that offers higher than average starting salaries. Today, many accounting firms, like PricewaterhouseCoopers, are eager to hire both women and men to help them in their task of providing accounting information to individuals and businesses. For business firms, accounting information is especially important. Without accounting information, managers can't make decisions, investors can't evaluate potential investments, and lenders and suppliers can't extend credit to a business firm. Simply put, without accounting information a business firm cannot operate in a very competitive world.

We begin this chapter by looking at why accounting information is important, the recent problems in the accounting industry, and attempts to improve financial reporting. Then we look at how managers, employees, individuals, and groups outside a firm use accounting information. We also identify different types of accountants and career opportunities in the accounting industry. Next, we focus on the accounting process and the basics of an accounting system. We also examine the three most important financial statements: the balance sheet, the income statement, and the statement of cash flows. Finally, we show how ratios are used to measure specific aspects of a firm's financial health.

Why Accounting Information Is Important

1 LEARNING OBJECTIVE

Explain why accurate accounting information and audited financial statements are important.

Accounting is the process of systematically collecting, analyzing, and reporting financial information. Today, it is impossible to manage a business without accurate and up-to-date information supplied by the firm's accountants. Just for a moment, think about the following three questions:

1. How much profit did a business earn last year?
2. How much tax does a business owe the Internal Revenue Service?
3. How much cash does a business have on hand?

In each case, the firm's accountants and its accounting system provide the answers to these questions and many others. And while accounting information can be used to answer questions about what has happened in the past, it also can be used to help make decisions about the future. For these reasons, accounting is one of the most important areas within a business organization.

Because the information provided by a firm's accountants and its accounting system is so important, managers and other groups interested in a business firm's financial records must be able to "trust the numbers." Unfortunately, a large number of accounting scandals have caused people to doubt not only the numbers but also the accounting industry.

accounting the process of systematically collecting, analyzing, and reporting financial information

Recent Accounting Problems for Corporations and Their Auditors

Which of the following firms has been convicted or accused of accounting fraud?

a. Enron
b. WorldCom
c. Fannie Mae
d. Freddie Mac
e. All of the above

Unfortunately, the answer to the question is e—all of the above. While you may not recognize all of the companies included in the above question, each company is (or was) a major U.S. business that has been plagued by accounting problems. These problems led to Enron's bankruptcy, prison time for Bernard Ebbers, the CEO of WorldCom, and a massive federal bailout for mortgage giants Fannie Mae and Freddie Mac. The accounting problems at these companies—and similar problems at even more companies—have forced many investors, lenders and suppliers, and government regulators to question the motives behind fraudulent and unethical accounting practices.

Today, much of the pressure on corporate executives to "cook" the books is driven by the desire to look good to Wall Street analysts and investors. Every three months companies report their revenues, expenses, profits, and projections for the future. If

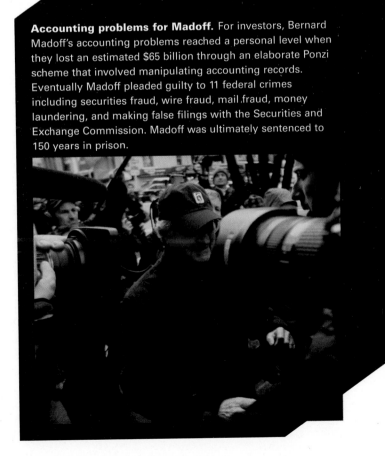

Accounting problems for Madoff. For investors, Bernard Madoff's accounting problems reached a personal level when they lost an estimated $65 billion through an elaborate Ponzi scheme that involved manipulating accounting records. Eventually Madoff pleaded guilty to 11 federal crimes including securities fraud, wire fraud, mail fraud, money laundering, and making false filings with the Securities and Exchange Commission. Madoff was ultimately sentenced to 150 years in prison.

©Chip East/Reuters/Landov

a company meets or exceeds "the street's" expectations, everything is usually fine. However, if a company reports financial numbers that are lower than expected, the company's stock value can drop dramatically. An earnings report that is lower by even a few pennies per share than what is expected can cause a company's stock value to drop immediately by as much as 30 to 40 percent or more. Greed—especially when salary and bonuses are tied to a company's stock value—is another factor that can lead some corporate executives to use questionable accounting methods to inflate a firm's financial performance.

In a perfect world, the accountants who inspect the corporate books would catch mistakes and disclose questionable accounting practices. Unfortunately, we do not live in a perfect world. Consider the part that auditors for the accounting firm Arthur Andersen played in the Enron meltdown. When the Securities and Exchange Commission (SEC) launched its inquiry into Enron's financial affairs, Andersen employees shredded the documents related to the audit. As a result, both the SEC and the Department of Justice began to investigate Andersen's role in the failure of Enron. Eventually, Andersen was convicted of obstruction of justice and was forced to cease auditing public companies. Simply put, Andersen—the once-proud accounting firm—was found guilty.[2] Note: On May 31, 2005, the U.S. Supreme Court overturned the Andersen conviction.[3] In theory, Andersen could resume its accounting and audit operations. However, Arthur Andersen had not returned as a viable business even on a limited scale. It seems that no company wanted the Andersen name on its audit work because of the accounting firm's tarnished reputation. The consequences for Enron were just as devastating. Less than a month after admitting accounting errors that inflated earnings by almost $600 million since 1994, Enron filed for bankruptcy.[4]

Unfortunately, the ones hurt when companies (and their accountants) report inaccurate or misleading accounting information often are not always the high-paid corporate executives. In many cases, it's the employees who lose their jobs and often the money they invested in the company's retirement program and investors, lenders, and suppliers who relied on fraudulent accounting information in order to make a decision to invest in or lend money to the company.

In an indirect way, the recent accounting scandals underscore how important accurate accounting information is for a corporation. To see how the auditing process can improve accounting information, read the next section.

Why Audited Financial Statements Are Important

Assume that you are a bank officer responsible for evaluating loan applications. How do you make a decision to approve or reject a loan request? In this situation, most bank officers rely on the information contained in the firm's balance sheet, income statement, and statement of cash flows, along with other information provided by the prospective borrower. In fact, most lenders insist that these financial statements be audited by a certified public accountant (CPA). An **audit** is an examination of a company's financial statements and the accounting practices that produced them. The purpose of an audit is to make sure that a firm's financial statements have been prepared in accordance with generally accepted accounting principles. **Generally accepted accounting principles (GAAPs)** have been developed to provide an accepted set of guidelines and practices for U.S. companies reporting financial information and the accounting profession. At the time of publication, the Financial Accounting Standards Board, which establishes and improves accounting standards for U.S. companies, is working toward establishing a new set of standards that combines GAAPs with the International Financial Reporting Standards (IFRS) to create one set of accounting standards that can be used by both U.S. firms and multinational firms. Created by the International Accounting Standards Board, IFRS are now used in more than 100 different countries around the world. For multinational firms, the benefits of global accounting standards are huge because preparing financial statements and accounting records that meet global standards saves both time and money. According to many accounting experts, it's not a question if IFRS guidelines will be adopted in the U.S., but when.[5]

audit an examination of a company's financial statements and the accounting practices that produced them

generally accepted accounting principles (GAAPs) an accepted set of guidelines and practices for companies reporting financial information and for the accounting profession

If an accountant determines that a firm's financial statements present financial information fairly and conform to accepted accounting standards, then he or she will issue the following statement:

In our opinion, the financial statements ... present fairly, in all material respects ... in conformity with generally accepted accounting principles.

While an audit and the resulting report do not *guarantee* that a company has not "cooked" the books, it does imply that, on the whole, the company has followed accepted accounting standards. Bankers, creditors, investors, and government agencies are willing to rely on an auditor's opinion because of the historically ethical reputation and independence of auditors and accounting firms. With the recent scandals involving corporations and their accountants that falsified or misled the general public, it is easy to indict an entire profession because of the actions of a few. And yet there are many more accountants who adhere to the rules and are honest, hard-working professionals. Finally, it should be noted that without the audit function, there would be very little oversight or supervision. The validity of a firm's financial statements and its accounting records would drop quickly, and firms would find it difficult to obtain debt financing, acquire goods and services from suppliers, find investor financing, or prepare documents requested by government agencies.

Reform: The Sarbanes-Oxley Act of 2002

According to John Bogle, founder of Vanguard Mutual Funds, "Investing is an act of faith. Without that faith—that reported numbers reflect reality, that companies are being run honestly, that Wall Street is playing it straight, and that investors aren't being hoodwinked—our capital markets simply can't function."[6] In reality, what Mr. Bogle says is true. To help ensure that corporate financial information is accurate and in response to the many accounting scandals, Congress enacted the Sarbanes-Oxley Act. Key components include the following:[7]

- The SEC is required to establish a full-time five-member federal oversight board that will police the accounting industry.
- Chief executive and financial officers are required to certify periodic financial reports and are subject to criminal penalties for violations of securities reporting requirements.
- Accounting firms are prohibited from providing many types of nonaudit and consulting services to the companies they audit.
- Auditors must maintain financial documents and audit work papers for five years.
- Auditors, accountants, and employees can be imprisoned for up to twenty years for destroying financial documents and willful violations of the securities laws.
- A public corporation must change its lead auditing firm every five years.
- There is added protection for whistle-blowers who report violations of the Sarbanes-Oxley Act.

While most people welcome the Sarbanes-Oxley Act, complex rules make compliance more expensive and time consuming for corporate management and more difficult for accounting firms. And yet, most people agree that the cost of compliance is justified. As you read the next section, you will see just how important accurate accounting information is.

Who Uses Accounting Information

Managers and employees, lenders, suppliers, stockholders, and government agencies all rely on the information contained in three financial statements, each no more than one page in length. These three reports—the balance sheet, the income statement, and the statement of cash flows—are concise summaries of a firm's activities during a specific time period. Together they represent the results of perhaps

2 LEARNING OBJECTIVE

Identify people who use accounting information and possible careers in the accounting industry.

Does this man have enough money to buy Girl Scout cookies? You bet! Although there are many reasons why Warren Buffett, chairman of the board of Berkshire Hathaway, has become one of the richest people in the world, his ability to understand accounting information has enabled him to identify investments that are extremely profitable.

tens of thousands of transactions that have occurred during the accounting period. Moreover, the form of the financial statements is pretty much the same for all businesses, from a neighborhood video store to giant conglomerates such as Home Depot, Boeing, and United Parcel Service. This information has a variety of uses both within the firm and outside it. However, first and foremost, accounting information is management information.

The People Who Use Accounting Information

The primary users of accounting information are *managers*. The firm's accounting system provides information that can be compiled for the entire firm—for each product; for each sales territory, store, or salesperson; for each division or department; and generally in any way that will help those who manage the organization. At a company such as Kraft Foods, for example, financial information is gathered for all its hundreds of food products: Maxwell House Coffee, A1 Steak Sauce, Chips Ahoy Cookies, Jell-O Desserts, Kool Aid, and so on. The president of the company would be interested in total sales for all these products. The vice president for marketing would be interested in national sales for Maxwell House Coffee and Jell-O Desserts. The northeastern sales manager might want to look at sales figures for Kool Aid in New England. For a large, complex organization like Kraft, the accounting system must enable managers to get the information they need.

Much of this accounting information is *proprietary*; it is not divulged to anyone outside the firm. This type of information is used by a firm's managers and employees to plan and set goals, organize, lead, motivate, and control—all the management functions that were described in Chapter 6.

In addition to proprietary information used inside the firm, certain financial information must be supplied to individuals and organizations outside the firm (see Table 15.1).

- *Lenders* require information contained in the firm's financial statements before they will commit themselves to either short- or long-term loans. *Suppliers* who provide the raw materials, component parts, or finished goods a firm needs also generally ask for financial information before they will extend credit to a firm.

©AP Photo/Nik Harnik

TABLE 15.1: Users of Accounting Information The primary users of accounting information are a company's managers, but individuals and organizations outside the company also require information on its finances.

Management	Lenders and Suppliers	Stockholders and Potential Investors	Government Agencies
Plan and set goals, organize, lead, motivate, and control	Evaluate credit risks before committing to short- or long-term financing	Evaluate the financial health of the firm before purchasing stocks or bonds	Confirm tax liabilities Confirm payroll deductions Approve new issues of stocks and bonds

- *Stockholders and potential investors* are concerned not only about a company's current financial health but also about the financial risk associated with an investment in its stock.
- *Government agencies* require a variety of information about the firm's tax liabilities, payroll deductions for employees, and new issues of stocks and bonds.

An important function of accountants is to ensure that such information is accurate and thorough enough to satisfy these outside groups.

Different Types of Accounting

While many people think that all accountants do the same tasks, there are special areas of expertise within the accounting industry. In fact, accounting usually is broken down into two broad categories: managerial and financial.

Managerial accounting provides managers and employees with the information needed to make decisions about a firm's financing, investing, and operating activities. By using managerial accounting information, both managers and employees can evaluate how well they have done in the past and what they can expect in the future. **Financial accounting**, on the other hand, generates financial statements and reports for interested people outside of an organization. Typically, stockholders, financial analysts, bankers, lenders, suppliers, government agencies, and other interested groups use the information provided by financial accounting to determine how well a business firm has achieved its goals. In addition to managerial and financial accounting, additional special areas of accounting include the following:

- *Cost accounting*—determining the cost of producing specific products or services.
- *Tax accounting*—planning tax strategy and preparing tax returns for firms or individuals.
- *Government accounting*—providing basic accounting services to ensure that tax revenues are collected and used to meet the goals of state, local, and federal agencies.
- *Not-for-profit accounting*—helping not-for-profit organizations to account for all donations and expenditures.

Careers in Accounting

Wanted: An individual with at least two years of college accounting courses. Must be honest, dependable, and willing to complete all routine accounting activities for a manufacturing business. Salary dependent on experience.

Want a job? Positions such as the one described in this newspaper advertisement increasingly are becoming available to those with the required training. According to the *Occupational Outlook Handbook,* published by the Department of Labor, job opportunities for accountants and auditors in the accounting area are expected to experience strong growth between now and the year 2016.[8]

Many people have the idea that accountants spend their day working with endless columns of numbers in a small office locked away from other people. In fact, accountants do spend a lot of time at their desks, but their job entails far more than just adding or subtracting numbers. Accountants are expected to share their ideas and the information they possess with people who need the information. Accounting can be an exciting and rewarding career—one that offers higher-than-average starting salaries. To be successful in the accounting industry, employees must

- Be responsible, honest, and ethical.
- Have a strong background in financial management.
- Know how to use a computer and software to process data into accounting information.
- Be able to communicate with people who need accounting information.

Today, accountants generally are classified as either private accountants or public accountants. A *private accountant* is employed by a specific organization.

managerial accounting provides managers and employees with the information needed to make decisions about a firm's financing, investing, and operating activities

financial accounting generates financial statements and reports for interested people outside an organization

A medium-sized or large firm may employ one or more private accountants to design its accounting information system, manage its accounting department, and provide managers with advice and assistance.

Individuals, self-employed business owners, and smaller firms that do not require their own full-time accountants can hire the services of public accountants. A *public accountant* works on a fee basis for clients and may be self-employed or be the employee of an accounting firm. Accounting firms range in size from one-person operations to huge international firms with hundreds of accounting partners and thousands of employees. Today, the largest accounting firms, sometimes referred to as the "Big Four," are PricewaterhouseCoopers, Ernst & Young, KPMG, and Deloitte Touche Tohmatsu.

Typically, public accounting firms include on their staffs at least one **certified public accountant (CPA)**, an individual who has met state requirements for accounting education and experience and has passed a rigorous accounting examination prepared by the AICPA. The AICPA uniform CPA examination covers four areas: (1) regulation, taxation, business law, and professional responsibilities, (2) auditing, (3) business environment and concepts, and (4) financial accounting and reporting. More information about general requirements and the CPA profession can be obtained by contacting the AICPA at **www.aicpa.org**.[9] State requirements usually include a college degree or a specified number of hours of college coursework and generally from one to three years of on-the-job experience. Details regarding specific state requirements for practice as a CPA can be obtained by contacting the state's board of accountancy.

Once an individual becomes a CPA, he or she must participate in continuing-education programs to maintain state certification. These specialized programs are designed to provide the current training needed in today's changing business environment.

Certification as a CPA brings both status and responsibility. In addition to auditing a corporation's financial statements, typical services performed by CPAs include planning and preparing tax returns, determining the true cost of producing and marketing a firm's goods or services, and compiling the financial information needed to make major management decisions. Fees for the services provided by CPAs generally range from $50 to $300 an hour.

In addition to certified public accountants, there are also certified management accountants. A **certified management accountant (CMA)** is an accountant who has met the requirements for education and experience, passed a rigorous exam, and is certified by the Institute of Management Accountants. The CMA exam is designed to develop and measure not only accounting skills but also decision-making and critical-thinking skills. For more information about the CMA exam, visit the Institute of Management Accountants website at **www.imanet.org**. While both CPAs and CMAs can work for the public, a CMA is more likely to work within a large organization. Also, both types of accountants are excellent career choices.

LEARNING OBJECTIVE 3

Discuss the accounting process.

The Accounting Process

In Chapter 14, *information* was defined as data presented in a form that is useful for a specific purpose. In this section, we examine accounting as the system for transforming raw financial *data* into useful financial *information*. Then, in the next sections we describe the three most important financial statements provided by the accounting process.

The Accounting Equation

The accounting equation is a simple statement that forms the basis for the accounting process. This important equation shows the relationship between a firm's assets, liabilities, and owners' equity.

- **Assets** are the resources a business owns—cash, inventory, equipment, and real estate.
- **Liabilities** are the firm's debts—what it owes to others.
- **Owners' equity** is the difference between total assets and total liabilities—what would be left for the owners if the firm's assets were sold and the money used to pay off its liabilities.

The relationship between assets, liabilities, and owners' equity is shown by the following **accounting equation**:

$$\text{Assets} = \text{liabilities} + \text{owners' equity}$$

Whether a business is a small corner grocery store or a giant corporation such as General Mills, its assets must equal the sum of its liabilities and owners' equity. To use this equation, a firm's accountants must record raw data—that is, the firm's day-to-day financial transactions—using the double-entry system of bookkeeping. The **double-entry bookkeeping system** is a system in which each financial transaction is recorded as two separate accounting entries to maintain the balance shown in the accounting equation. With the double-entry system, an accountant can use the steps in the accounting cycle to generate accounting information and financial statements.

The Accounting Cycle

In the typical accounting system, raw data are transformed into financial statements in specific steps. The first three—analyzing, recording, and posting—are performed on a regular basis throughout the accounting period. The last two—preparation of the trial balance and preparation of the financial statements and closing the books— are performed at the end of the accounting period.

Analyzing Source Documents Basic accounting data are contained in *source documents,* the receipts, invoices, sales slips, and other documents that show the dollar amounts of day-to-day business transactions. The accounting cycle begins with the analysis of each of these documents. The purpose of the analysis is to determine which of the firm's accounts are affected by the documents and how they are affected.

Recording Transactions Every financial transaction then is recorded in a journal—a process called *journalizing.* Transactions must be recorded in the firm's general journal or in specialized journals. The *general journal* is a book of original entry in which typical transactions are recorded in order of their occurrence. An accounting system also may include *specialized journals* for specific types of transactions that occur frequently. Thus, a retail store might have journals for cash receipts, cash disbursements, purchases, and sales in addition to its general journal.

Posting Transactions After the information is recorded in the general journal and specialized journals, it is transferred to the general ledger. The *general ledger* is a book of accounts containing a separate sheet or section for each account. Today, most businesses use a computer and software to record accounting entries in the general journal or specialized journals and then to post journal entries to the general ledger.

Preparing the Trial Balance A **trial balance** is a summary of the balances of all general ledger accounts at the end of the accounting period. To prepare a trial balance, the accountant determines and lists the balances for all ledger accounts. If the trial balance totals are correct and the accounting equation is still in balance, the accountant can prepare the financial statements. If not, a mistake has occurred somewhere, and the accountant must find it and correct it before proceeding.

Preparing Financial Statements and Closing the Books The firm's financial statements are prepared from the information contained in the trial balance. This information is presented in a standardized format to make the statements as accessible as possible to the various people who may be interested in the firm's financial affairs—managers, employees, lenders, suppliers, stockholders, potential investors, and government agencies. A firm's financial statements are prepared at least once a year and included in the firm's annual report. An **annual report** is a report distributed to stockholders and other interested parties that describes a firm's operating activities and its financial condition. Most firms also have financial statements prepared semiannually, quarterly, or monthly.

Once these statements have been prepared and checked, the firm's books are "closed" for the accounting period, and a *postclosing* trial balance is prepared. Although, like

accounting equation the basis for the accounting process: *assets = liabilities + owners' equity*

double-entry bookkeeping system a system in which each financial transaction is recorded as two separate accounting entries to maintain the balance shown in the accounting equation

trial balance a summary of the balances of all general ledger accounts at the end of the accounting period

annual report a report distributed to stockholders and other interested parties that describes a firm's operating activities and its financial condition

Concept Check

1. State the accounting equation, and list two specific examples of each term in the equation.

2. How is double-entry bookkeeping related to the accounting equation?

3. Briefly, describe the specific steps of the accounting cycle in order.

the trial balance just described, the postclosing trial balance generally is prepared after *all* accounting work is completed for one accounting period. If the postclosing trial balance totals agree, the accounting equation is still in balance at the end of the cycle. Only then can a new accounting cycle begin for the next accounting period.

With this brief information about the steps of the accounting cycle in mind, let's now examine the three most important financial statements generated by the accounting process: the balance sheet, the income statement, and the statement of cash flows.

The Balance Sheet

Question: *Where could you find the total amount of assets, liabilities, and owners' equity for Hershey Foods Corporation?*

Answer: The firm's balance sheet.

A **balance sheet** (sometimes referred to as a **statement of financial position**) is a summary of the dollar amounts of a firm's assets, liabilities, and owners' equity accounts at the end of a specific accounting period. The balance sheet must demonstrate that assets are equal to liabilities plus owners' equity. Most people think of a balance sheet as a statement that reports the financial condition of a business firm such as Hershey, but balance sheets apply to individuals, too. For example, Marty Campbell graduated from college three years ago and obtained a position as a sales representative for an office supply firm. After going to work, he established a checking and savings account and purchased an automobile, stereo, television, and a few pieces of furniture. Marty paid cash for some purchases, but he had to borrow money to pay for the larger ones. Figure 15.1 shows Marty's current personal balance sheet.

Marty Campbell's assets total $26,500, and his liabilities amount to $10,000. While the difference between total assets and total liabilities is referred to as *owners' equity* or *stockholders' equity* for a business, it is normally called *net worth* for an

FIGURE 15.1: Personal Balance Sheet Often individuals determine their net worth, or owner's equity, by subtracting the value of their debts from the value of their assets.

Marty Campbell
Personal Balance Sheet
December 31, 20XX

ASSETS		
Cash	$ 2,500	
Savings account	5,000	
Automobile	15,000	
Stereo	1,000	
Television	500	
Furniture	2,500	
TOTAL ASSETS		$26,500
LIABILITIES		
Automobile loan	$ 9,500	
Credit card balance	500	
TOTAL LIABILITIES		$10,000
NET WORTH (Owner's Equity)		16,500
TOTAL LIABILITIES AND NET WORTH		$26,500

balance sheet (or statement of financial position) a summary of the dollar amounts of a firm's assets, liabilities, and owners' equity accounts at the end of a specific accounting period individual. As reported on Marty's personal balance sheet, net worth is $16,500. The total assets ($26,500) and the total liabilities *plus* net worth ($26,500) are equal.

Figure 15.2 shows the balance sheet for Northeast Art Supply, a small corporation that sells picture frames, paints, canvases, and other artists' supplies to retailers in New England. Note that assets are reported at the top of the statement, followed by liabilities and stockholders' equity. Let's work through the different accounts in Figure 15.2 from top to bottom.

FIGURE 15.2: Business Balance Sheet A balance sheet (sometimes referred to as a statement of financial position) summarizes a firm's accounts at the end of an accounting period, showing the various dollar amounts that enter into the accounting equation. Note that assets ($340,000) equal liabilities plus owners' equity ($340,000).

NORTHEAST ART SUPPLY, INC.

Balance Sheet
December 31, 20XX

ASSETS

Current assets		
Cash		$ 59,000
Marketable securities		10,000
Accounts receivable	$ 40,000	
Less allowance for doubtful accounts	2,000	38,000
Notes receivable		32,000
Merchandise inventory		41,000
Prepaid expenses		2,000
Total current assets		$182,000
Fixed assets		
Delivery equipment	$110,000	
Less accumulated depreciation	20,000	$ 90,000
Furniture and store equipment	$62,000	
Less accumulated depreciation	15,000	47,000
Total fixed assets		137,000
Intangible assets		
Patents		$ 6,000
Goodwill		15,000
Total intangible assets		21,000
TOTAL ASSETS		$340,000

LIABILITIES AND STOCKHOLDERS' EQUITY

Current liabilities		
Accounts payable	$ 35,000	
Notes payable	25,675	
Salaries payable	4,000	
Taxes payable	5,325	
Total current liabilities		$ 70,000
Long-term liabilities		
Mortgage payable on store equipment	$ 40,000	
Total long-term liabilities		$ 40,000
TOTAL LIABILITIES		$110,000
Stockholders' equity		
Common stock	$150,000	
Retained earnings	80,000	
TOTAL OWNERS' EQUITY		230,000
TOTAL LIABILITIES AND OWNERS' EQUITY		$340,000

Assets

On a balance sheet, assets are listed in order from the *most liquid* to the *least liquid*. The **liquidity** of an asset is the ease with which it can be converted into cash.

Current Assets **Current assets** are assets that can be converted quickly into cash or that will be used in one year or less. Because cash is the most liquid asset, it is listed first. Next are *marketable securities*—stocks, bonds, and other investments—that can be converted into cash in a matter of days.

Next are the firm's receivables. Its *accounts receivable,* which result from allowing customers to make credit purchases, generally are paid within thirty to sixty days. However, the firm expects that some of these debts will not be collected. Thus, it has reduced its accounts receivables by a 5 percent *allowance for doubtful accounts.* The firm's *notes receivable* are receivables for which customers have signed promissory notes. They generally are repaid over a longer period of time than the firm's accounts receivable.

Northeast's *merchandise inventory* represents the value of goods on hand for sale to customers. Since Northeast Art Supply is a wholesale operation, the inventory listed in Figure 15.2 represents finished goods ready for sale to retailers. For a manufacturing firm, merchandise inventory also may represent raw materials that will become part of a finished product or work that has been partially completed but requires further processing.

Northeast's last current asset is *prepaid expenses,* which are assets that have been paid for in advance but have not yet been used. An example is insurance premiums. They are usually paid at the beginning of the policy year. The unused portion (say, for the last four months of the time period covered by the policy) is a prepaid expense. For Northeast Art, all current assets total $182,000.

Fixed Assets **Fixed assets** are assets that will be held or used for a period longer than one year. They generally include land, buildings, and equipment used in the continuing operation of the business. Although Northeast owns no land or buildings, it does own *delivery equipment* that originally cost $110,000. It also owns *furniture and store equipment* that originally cost $62,000.

Note that the values of both fixed assets are decreased by their *accumulated depreciation.* **Depreciation** is the process of apportioning the cost of a fixed asset over the period during which it will be used, that is, its useful life. The depreciation amount allotted to each year is an expense for that year, and the value of the asset must be reduced by the amount of depreciation expense. Although the actual methods used to calculate the dollar amounts for depreciation expense reported on a firm's financial statements are beyond the scope of this text, you should know that there are a number of different methods that can be used. In the case of Northeast's delivery equipment, $20,000 of its value has been depreciated (or used up) since it was purchased. Its value at this time is thus $110,000 less $20,000, or $90,000. In a similar fashion, the original value of furniture and store equipment ($62,000) has been reduced by depreciation totaling $15,000. Furniture and store equipment now has a reported value of $47,000. For Northeast Art, all fixed assets total $137,000.

Intangible Assets **Intangible assets** are assets that do not exist physically but that have a value based on the rights or privileges they confer on a firm. They include patents, copyrights, trademarks, franchises, and goodwill. By their nature, intangible assets are long-term assets—they are of value to the firm for a number of years.

liquidity the ease with which an asset can be converted into cash

current assets assets that can be converted quickly into cash or that will be used in one year or less

fixed assets assets that will be held or used for a period longer than one year

depreciation the process of apportioning the cost of a fixed asset over the period during which it will be used

intangible assets assets that do not exist physically but that have a value based on the rights or privileges they confer on a firm

current liabilities debts that will be repaid in one year or less

long-term liabilities debts that need not be repaid for at least one year

Northeast Art Supply lists two intangible assets. The first is a *patent* for a special oil paint that the company purchased from the inventor. The firm's accountants estimate that the patent has a current market value of $6,000. The second intangible asset, *goodwill,* is the value of a firm's reputation, location, earning capacity, and other intangibles that make the business a profitable concern. Goodwill normally is not listed on a balance sheet unless the firm has been purchased from previous owners. In such a case, the new owners actually have paid an additional amount over and above the fair market value of the firm's assets for goodwill. Goodwill exists because most businesses are worth more as going concerns than as a collection of assets. Northeast Art's accountants included a $15,000 amount for goodwill. The firm's intangible assets total $21,000. Now it is possible to total all three types of assets for Northeast Art. As calculated in Figure 15.2, total assets are $340,000.

Liabilities and Owners' Equity

The liabilities and the owners' equity accounts complete the balance sheet. The firm's liabilities are separated into two categories—current and long term.

Current Liabilities A firm's **current liabilities** are debts that will be repaid in one year or less. Northeast Art Supply purchased merchandise from its suppliers on credit. Thus, its balance sheet includes an entry for accounts payable. *Accounts payable* are short-term obligations that arise as a result of a firm making credit purchases.

Notes payable are obligations that have been secured with promissory notes. They are usually short-term obligations, but they may extend beyond one year. Only those that must be paid within the year are listed under current liabilities.

Northeast also lists *salaries payable* and *taxes payable* as current liabilities. These are both expenses that have been incurred during the current accounting period but will be paid in the next accounting period. For Northeast Art, current liabilities total $70,000.

Long-Term Liabilities **Long-term liabilities** are debts that need not be repaid for at least one year. Northeast lists only one long-term liability—a $40,000 *mortgage payable* for store equipment. Bonds and other long-term loans would be included here as well, if they existed. As you can see in Figure 15.2, Northeast's current and long-term liabilities total $110,000.

©AndreyArmyagov/Shutterstock

Concept Check

1. How are current assets distinguished from fixed assets?

2. Why are fixed assets depreciated on a firm's balance sheet?

3. How do you determine the dollar amount of owner's equity for a sole proprietorship or a partnership or a corporation?

Owners' or Stockholders' Equity For a sole proprietorship or partnership, the owners' equity is shown as the difference between assets and liabilities. In a partnership, each partner's share of the ownership is reported separately in each owner's name. For a corporation, the owners' equity usually is referred to as *stockholders' equity*. The dollar amount reported on the balance sheet is the total value of stock plus retained earnings that have accumulated to date. **Retained earnings** are the portion of a business's profits *not* distributed to stockholders.

The original investment by the owners of Northeast Art Supply was $150,000. In addition, $80,000 of Northeast's earnings have been reinvested in the business since it was founded. Thus, owners' equity totals $230,000.

As the two grand totals in Figure 15.2 show, Northeast's assets and the sum of its liabilities and owners' equity are equal—at $340,000. The accounting equation (assets = liabilities + owners' equity) is still in balance.

LEARNING OBJECTIVE 5

Read and interpret an income statement.

The Income Statement

Question: *Where can you find the profit or loss amount for Gap Inc.?*

Answer: The firm's income statement.

An **income statement** is a summary of a firm's revenues and expenses during a specified accounting period—one month, three months, six months, or a year. The income statement is sometimes called the *earnings statement* or *the statement of income and expenses*. Let's begin our discussion by constructing a personal income statement for Marty Campbell. Having worked as a sales representative for an office supply firm for the past three years, Marty now earns $33,600 a year, or $2,800 a month. After deductions, his take-home pay is $1,900 a month. As illustrated in Figure 15.3, Marty's typical monthly expenses include payments for an automobile

FIGURE 15.3: Personal Income Statement By subtracting expenses from income, anyone can construct a personal income statement and determine if they have a surplus or deficit at the end of each month.

Marty Campbell
Personal Income Statement
For the month ended December 31, 20XX

INCOME (Take-home pay)		$1,900
LESS MONTHLY EXPENSES		
Automobile loan	$ 250	
Credit card payment	100	
Apartment rent	500	
Utilities	200	
Food	250	
Clothing	100	
Recreation & entertainment	250	
TOTAL MONTHLY EXPENSES		1,650
CASH SURPLUS (or profit)		$ 250

retained earnings the portion of a business's profits not distributed to stockholders

income statement a summary of a firm's revenues and expenses during a specified accounting period loan, credit card purchases, apartment rent, utilities, food, clothing, and recreation and entertainment.

While the difference between income and expenses is referred to as *profit* or *loss* for a business, it is normally referred to as a *cash surplus* or *cash deficit* for an individual. Fortunately for Marty, he has a surplus of $250 at the end of each month. He can use this surplus for savings, investing, or paying off debts.

Figure 15.4 shows the income statement for Northeast Art Supply. Generally, revenues *less* cost of goods sold *less* operating expenses equals net income.

Revenues

Revenues are the dollar amounts earned by a firm from selling goods, providing services, or performing business activities. Like most businesses, Northeast

revenues the dollar amounts earned by a firm from selling goods, providing services, or performing business activities

FIGURE 15.4: Business Income Statement An income statement summarizes a firm's revenues and expenses during a specified accounting period. For Northeast Art, net income after taxes is $30,175.

NORTHEAST ART SUPPLY, INC.

Income Statement
For the Year Ended
December 31, 20XX

Revenues			
Gross sales			$465,000
Less sales returns and allowances		$ 9,500	
Less sales discounts		4,500	14,000
Net sales			$451,000
Cost of goods sold			
Beginning inventory, January 1, 20XX			$ 40,000
Purchases		$346,000	
Less purchase discounts		11,000	
Net purchases			335,000
Cost of goods available for sale			$375,000
Less ending inventory December 31, 20XX			41,000
Cost of goods sold			334,000
Gross profit			$117,000
Operating expenses			
Selling expenses			
Sales salaries		$ 22,000	
Advertising		4,000	
Sales promotion		2,500	
Depreciation—store equipment		3,000	
Depreciation—delivery equipment		4,000	
Miscellaneous selling expenses		1,500	
Total selling expenses			$ 37,000
General expenses			
Office salaries		$ 28,500	
Rent		8,500	
Depreciation—office furniture		1,500	
Utilities expense		2,500	
Insurance expense		1,000	
Miscellaneous expense		500	
Total general expense			42,500
Total operating expenses			79,500
Net income from operations			$ 37,500
Less interest expense			2,000
NET INCOME BEFORE TAXES			$ 35,500
Less federal income taxes			5,325
NET INCOME AFTER TAXES			$ 30,175

Spotlight

Income for Accountants and Auditors

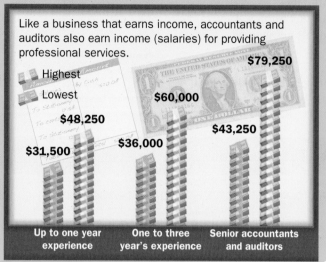

Like a business that earns income, accountants and auditors also earn income (salaries) for providing professional services.

Highest

Lowest

$79,250

$60,000

$48,250

$43,250

$31,500 $36,000

| Up to one year experience | One to three year's experience | Senior accountants and auditors |

Source: The Bureau of Labor Statistics website at www.bls.gov, May 18, 2009.

gross sales the total dollar amount of all goods and services sold during the accounting period

net sales the actual dollar amounts received by a firm for the goods and services it has sold after adjustment for returns, allowances, and discounts

Art obtains its revenues solely from the sale of its products or services. The revenues section of its income statement begins with gross sales. **Gross sales** are the total dollar amount of all goods and services sold during the accounting period. From this amount are deducted the dollar amounts of

- *Sales returns*—merchandise returned to the firm by its customers
- *Sales allowances*—price reductions offered to customers who accept slightly damaged or soiled merchandise
- *Sales discounts*—price reductions offered to customers who pay their bills promptly

The remainder is the firm's net sales. **Net sales** are the actual dollar amounts received by the firm for the goods and services it has sold after adjustment for returns, allowances, and discounts. For Northeast Art, net sales are $451,000.

Cost of Goods Sold

The standard method of determining the **cost of goods sold** by a retailing or wholesaling firm can be summarized as follows:

Cost of goods sold = beginning inventory + net purchases − ending inventory

A manufacturer must include raw materials inventories, work in progress, finished goods inventory, and direct manufacturing costs in this computation.

According to Figure 15.4, Northeast began its accounting period on January 1 with a merchandise inventory that cost $40,000. During the next twelve months, the firm purchased merchandise valued at $346,000. After taking advantage of *purchase discounts*, however, it paid only $335,000 for this merchandise. Thus,

One necessary business expense! Without jet airplanes, FedEx could not provide overnight delivery services to its customers. Started in 1971 by entrepreneur Fred Smith in Memphis, Tennessee, Federal Express now employs 280,000 people and provides worldwide delivery services that generate annual revenues of $35 billion.

©AP Photo/Chris Kasson

during the year, Northeast had total *goods available for sale* valued at $40,000 plus $335,000, or $375,000.

Twelve months later, at the end of the accounting period on December 31, Northeast had sold all but $41,000 worth of the available goods. The cost of goods sold by Northeast was therefore $375,000 less ending inventory of $41,000, or $334,000. It is now possible to calculate gross profit. A firm's **gross profit** is its net sales *less* the cost of goods sold. For Northeast, gross profit was $117,000.

Operating Expenses

A firm's **operating expenses** are all business costs other than the cost of goods sold. Total operating expenses generally are divided into two categories: selling expenses or general expenses.

Selling expenses are costs related to the firm's marketing activities. For Northeast Art, selling expenses total $37,000. *General expenses* are costs incurred in managing a business. For Northeast Art, general expenses total $42,500. Now it is possible to total both selling and general expenses. As Figure 15.4 shows, total operating expenses for the accounting period are $79,500.

Net Income

When revenues exceed expenses, the difference is called **net income**. When expenses exceed revenues, the difference is called **net loss**. As Figure 15.4 shows, Northeast Art's *net income from operations* is computed as gross profit ($117,000) less total operating expenses ($79,500). For Northeast Art, net income from operations is $37,500. From this amount, *interest expense* of $2,000 is deducted to obtain a *net income before taxes* of $35,500. The interest expense is deducted in this section of the income statement because it is not an operating expense. Rather, it is an expense that results from financing the business.

Northeast's *federal income taxes* are $5,325. Although these taxes may or may not be payable immediately, they are definitely an expense that must be deducted from income. This leaves Northeast Art with a *net income after taxes* of $30,175. This amount may be used to pay a dividend to stockholders, it may be retained or reinvested in the firm, it may be used to reduce the firm's debts, or all three.

The Statement of Cash Flows

Cash is the lifeblood of any business. In 1987, the SEC and the Financial Accounting Standards Board required all publicly traded companies to include a statement of cash flows, along with their balance sheet and income statement, in their annual report. The **statement of cash flows** illustrates how the operating, investing, and financing activities of a company affect cash during an accounting period. A statement of cash flows for Northeast Art Supply is illustrated in Figure 15.5. It provides information concerning the company's cash receipts and cash payments and is organized around three different activities: operations, investing, and financing.

- *Cash flows from operating activities.* This is the first section of a statement of cash flows. It addresses the firm's primary revenue source—providing goods and services. The amounts paid to suppliers, employees, interest, taxes, and other expenses are deducted from the amount received from customers. Finally, the interest and dividends received by the firm are added to determine the total. After all adjustments are made, the total represents a true picture of cash flows from operating activities.
- *Cash flows from investing activities.* The second section of the statement is concerned with cash flow from investments. This includes the purchase and sale of land, equipment, and other assets and investments.

cost of goods sold the dollar amount equal to beginning inventory *plus* net purchases *less* ending inventory

Concept Check

1. What is the difference between a balance sheet and an income statement?

2. Explain how a retailing firm would determine the cost of goods sold during an accounting period.

3. How does a firm determine its net income after taxes?

6 LEARNING OBJECTIVE

Describe business activities that affect a firm's cash flow.

gross profit a firm's net sales *less* the cost of goods sold

operating expenses all business costs other than the cost of goods sold

net income occurs when revenues exceed expenses

net loss occurs when expenses exceed revenues

statement of cash flows a statement that illustrates how the operating, investing, and financing activities of a company affect cash during an accounting period

NORTHEAST ART SUPPLY, INC.

Statement of Cash Flows
For the Year Ended
December 31, 20XX

Cash flows from operating activities

Cash received from customers	$ 451,000	
Cash paid to suppliers and employees	(385,500)	
Interest paid	(2,000)	
Income taxes paid	(5,325)	
Net cash provided by operating activities		$ 58,175

Cash flows from investing activities

Purchase of equipment	$ (2,000)	
Purchase of investments	(10,000)	
Sale of investments	10,000	
Net cash provided by investing activities		(2,000)

Cash flows from financing activities

Payment of short-term debt	$ (9,000)	
Payment of long-term debt	(17,000)	
Payment of dividends	(15,000)	
Net cash provided by financing activities		(41,000)
NET INCREASE (DECREASE) IN CASH		$ 15,175
Cash at beginning of year		43,825
CASH AT END OF YEAR		$ 59,000

Concept Check

1. What is the purpose of a statement of cash flows?

2. In a statement of cash flows, what is included in the operating activities section? In the investing activities section? In the financing activities section?

- *Cash flows from financing activities.* The third and final section deals with the cash flow from all financing activities. It reports changes in debt obligation and owners' equity accounts. This includes loans and repayments, the sale and repurchase of the company's own stock, and cash dividends.

The totals of all three activities are added to the beginning cash balance to determine the ending cash balance. For Northeast Art Supply, the ending cash balance is $59,000. Note that this is the same amount reported for the cash account on the firm's balance sheet. Together, the cash flow statement, balance sheet, and income statement illustrate the results of past business decisions and reflect the firm's ability to pay debts and dividends and to finance new growth.

LEARNING OBJECTIVE 7

Summarize how managers evaluate the financial health of a business.

Evaluating Financial Statements

All three financial statements—the balance sheet, the income statement, and the statement of cash flows—can provide answers to a variety of questions about a firm's ability to do business and stay in business, its profitability, its value as an investment, and its ability to repay its debts. Even more information can be obtained

Going Green

Annual Reports Go Green

It's not easy being green when investors are accustomed to printed annual reports. Although public corporations must post certain investor materials online, many are making their annual reports more eco-friendly by:

- *Offering electronic options.* Interactive online annual reports help investors find the exact information they want. Kellogg, known for its breakfast cereals, invites the public to click through its interactive online report. It also allows investors to download and read an electronic version of the printed annual report or click to order a printed copy. Wal-Mart's printed annual report is as slim as possible, and the company encourages investors to view more details online. The online annual report of Endurance Specialty Holdings, an insurance firm, includes video of its top executives explaining the year's results.

- *Using earth-friendly paper, inks, and energy.* Itron, which makes water and energy metering systems, prints its annual report with vegetable-based inks on recycled paper and produces it using wind-generated power. The paper choice alone saves 23 trees and 10,000 gallons of waste water.

Can annual reports be even greener? Although hospitals are not required to issue annual reports, Akron General Medical Center traditionally mailed a 30-page report to thousands of community members. Now it mails a postcard showing where to find the report on the web and offering a DVD version for people who lack Internet access.

Sources: Matt Krantz, "Companies Cut Back on Fancy Annual Reports," *USA Today,* May 6, 2009, www.usatoday.com; Cheryl Powell, "Akron General Saves by Putting Annual Report Online Only," *Akron Beacon Journal,* April 4, 2008, n.p.; www.itron.com; www.walmart.com; www.kellogg.com.

by comparing present financial statements with those prepared for past accounting periods.

Using Annual Reports to Compare Data for Different Accounting Periods

Typically, an annual report contains a great deal of information about the company, its operations, current financial statements, and its past and current financial health. The following five suggestions can help you get to the "bottom line" of a corporation's annual report.

1. Look at the firm's income statement to determine whether the company is profitable or not.
2. Read the letters from the chairman of the board and chief executive officer (CEO) that describe the corporation's operations, prospects for the future, new products or services, financial strengths, *and* any potential problems.
3. Compare the corporation's current income statement, balance sheet, and statement of cash flows with previous financial statements. Look at trends for sales, expenses, profits or losses, assets, liabilities, and owners' equity.
4. Examine the footnotes closely, and look for red flags that may be in the fine print. Often, the footnotes contain (and sometimes hide) important information about the company and its finances.
5. Learn how to calculate financial ratios. Some of the most important financial ratios are discussed in the last part of this section.

Most corporations include in their annual reports comparisons of the important elements of their financial statements for recent years. Figure 15.6 shows such comparisons—of revenue, research and development (R&D), operating income, and sales and marketing expenses—for Microsoft Corporation, a world leader in the computer software industry. By examining these data, an operating manager can tell whether R&D expenditures are increasing or decreasing over the past three years. The vice president of marketing can determine if the total amount of sales and marketing expenses is changing. Stockholders and potential investors, on the other hand, may be more concerned with increases or decreases in Microsoft's revenues and operating income over the same time period.

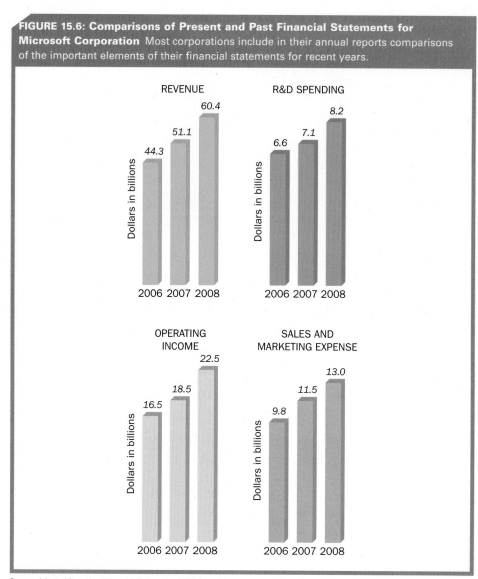

FIGURE 15.6: Comparisons of Present and Past Financial Statements for Microsoft Corporation Most corporations include in their annual reports comparisons of the important elements of their financial statements for recent years.

REVENUE

Dollars in billions

44.3 51.1 60.4

2006 2007 2008

R&D SPENDING

Dollars in billions

6.6 7.1 8.2

2006 2007 2008

OPERATING INCOME

Dollars in billions

16.5 18.5 22.5

2006 2007 2008

SALES AND MARKETING EXPENSE

Dollars in billions

9.8 11.5 13.0

2006 2007 2008

Source: Adapted from the Microsoft Corporation 2008 Annual Report, www.microsoft.com, May 16, 2009.

Comparing Data with Other Firms' Data

Many firms also compare their financial results with those of competing firms and with industry averages. Comparisons are possible as long as accountants follow generally accepted accounting principles.

Except for minor differences in format and terms, the balance sheet and income statement of Procter & Gamble, for example, will be similar to those of other large corporations, such as Alberto-Culver, Clorox, Colgate-Palmolive, and Unilever, in the consumer goods industry. Comparisons among firms give managers a general idea of a firm's relative effectiveness and its standing within the industry. Competitors' financial statements can be obtained from their annual reports—if they are public corporations. Industry averages are published by reporting services such as D&B (formerly Dun & Bradstreet) and Standard & Poor's, as well as by some industry trade associations.

Still another type of analysis of a firm's financial health involves computation of financial ratios. A **financial ratio** is a number that shows the relationship between two elements of a firm's financial statements. Among the most useful ratios are profitability ratios, short-term financial ratios, activity ratios, and the debt-to-owners'-equity ratio. Like the individual elements in financial statements, these ratios can be compared with the firm's past ratios, with those of competitors, and with industry averages. The information required to form these ratios is found

financial ratio a number that shows the relationship between two elements of a firm's financial statements

Part 6: Managing Information, Accounting, and Financing

in a firm's balance sheet and income statement (in our examples for Northeast Art Supply, Figures 15.2 and 15.4).

Profitability Ratios

A firm's net income after taxes indicates whether the firm is profitable. It does not, however, indicate how effectively the firm's resources are being used. For this latter purpose, three ratios can be computed.

Return on Sales **Return on sales**, sometimes called *profit margin*, is a financial ratio calculated by dividing net income after taxes by net sales. For Northeast Art Supply,

$$\text{Return on sales} = \frac{\text{net income after taxes}}{\text{net sales}} = \frac{\$30,175}{\$451,000}$$
$$= 0.067, \text{ or } 6.7 \text{ percent}$$

The return on sales indicates how effectively the firm is transforming sales into profits. A higher return on sales is better than a low one. Today, the average return on sales for all business firms is between 4 and 5 percent. With a return on sales of 6.7 percent, Northeast Art Supply is above average. A low return on sales can be increased by reducing expenses, increasing sales, or both.

Return on Owners' Equity **Return on owners' equity** is a financial ratio calculated by dividing net income after taxes by owners' equity. For Northeast Art Supply,

$$\text{Return on owners' equity} = \frac{\text{net income after taxes}}{\text{owners' equity}} = \frac{\$30,175}{\$230,000}$$
$$= 0.13, \text{ or } 13 \text{ percent}$$

Return on owners' equity indicates how much income is generated by each dollar of equity. Northeast is providing income of 13 cents per dollar invested in the business. The average for all businesses is between 12 and 15 cents. A higher return on owners' equity is better than a low one, and the only practical ways to increase return on owners' equity is to reduce expenses, increase sales, or both.

Earnings per Share From the point of view of stockholders, **earnings per share** is one of the best indicators of a corporation's success. It is calculated by dividing net income after taxes by the number of shares of common stock outstanding. If we assume that Northeast Art Supply has issued 25,000 shares of stock, then its earnings per share are

$$\text{Earnings per share} = \frac{\text{net income after taxes}}{\text{common stock shares outstanding}} = \frac{\$30,175}{25,000}$$
$$= \$1.21 \text{ per share}$$

There is no meaningful average for this ratio mainly because the number of outstanding shares of a firm's stock is subject to change as a result of stock splits and stock dividends. Also, some corporations choose to issue more stock than others. As a general rule, however, an increase in earnings per share is a healthy sign for any corporation.

Short-Term Financial Ratios

Two short-term financial ratios permit managers (and lenders) to evaluate the ability of a firm to pay its current liabilities. Before we discuss these ratios, we should examine one other easily determined measure: working capital.

Working Capital **Working capital** is the difference between current assets and current liabilities. For Northeast Art,

Current assets	$182,000
Less current liabilities	70,000
Equals working capital	$112,000

return on sales (or profit margin) a financial ratio calculated by dividing net income after taxes by net sales

return on owners' equity a financial ratio calculated by dividing net income after taxes by owners' equity

earnings per share a financial ratio calculated by dividing net income after taxes by the number of shares of common stock outstanding

working capital the difference between current assets and current liabilities

Bouncing checks is not a good idea! As part of the accounting process, a firm must evaluate the information on its financial statements to establish its ability to pay everyday expenses. To make sure it has enough available cash to "pay the bills," accountants track the amount of working capital a firm has and often calculate a current ratio and an acid-test ratio.

Working capital indicates how much would remain if a firm paid off all current liabilities with cash and other current assets. The "proper" amount of working capital depends on the type of firm, its past experience, and its particular industry. A firm with too little working capital may have to borrow money to finance its operations.

Current Ratio A firm's **current ratio** is computed by dividing current assets by current liabilities. For Northeast Art Supply,

$$\text{Current ratio} = \frac{\text{current assets}}{\text{current liabilities}} = \frac{\$182,000}{\$70,000} = 2.6$$

This means that Northeast Art Supply has $2.60 of current assets for every $1 of current liabilities. The average current ratio for all industries is 2.0, but it varies greatly from industry to industry. A high current ratio indicates that a firm can pay its current liabilities. A low current ratio can be improved by repaying current liabilities, by reducing dividend payments to stockholders to increase the firm's cash balance, or by obtaining additional cash from investors.

Acid-Test Ratio This ratio, sometimes called the *quick ratio,* is a measure of the firm's ability to pay current liabilities *quickly*—with its cash, marketable securities, and receivables. The **acid-test ratio** is calculated by adding cash, marketable securities, and receivables and dividing the total by current liabilities. The value of inventory and other current assets is "removed" from current assets because these assets are not converted into cash as easily as cash, marketable securities, and receivables. For Northeast Art Supply,

$$\text{Acid-test ratio} = \frac{\text{cash} + \text{marketable securities} + \text{receivables}}{\text{current liabilities}} = \frac{\$139,000}{\$70,000}$$
$$= 1.99$$

For all businesses, the desired acid-test ratio is 1.0. Northeast Art Supply is above average with a ratio of 1.99, and the firm should be well able to pay its current liabilities. To increase a low acid-test ratio, a firm would have to repay current liabilities, reduce dividend payments to stockholders to increase the firm's cash balance, or obtain additional cash from investors.

Activity Ratios

Two activity ratios permit managers to measure how many times each year a company collects its accounts receivables or sells its inventory.

Accounts Receivable Turnover A firm's **accounts receivable turnover** is the number of times the firm collects its accounts receivable in one year. If the data are available, this ratio should be calculated using a firm's net credit sales. Since data for Northeast Art Supply's credit sales are unavailable, this ratio can be calculated by dividing net sales by accounts receivable. For Northeast Art,

$$\text{Accounts receivable turnover} = \frac{\text{net sales}}{\text{accounts receivable}} = \frac{\$451,000}{\$38,000}$$
$$= 11.9 \text{ times per year}$$

current ratio a financial ratio computed by dividing current assets by current liabilities

acid-test ratio a financial ratio calculated by adding cash, marketable securities, and receivables and dividing the total by current liabilities

Northeast Art Supply collects its accounts receivables 11.9 times each year, or about every thirty days. If a firm's credit terms require customers to pay in twenty-five days, a collection period of thirty days is considered acceptable. There is no meaningful average for this measure mainly because credit terms differ among companies. A high accounts receivable turnover is better than a low one. As a general rule, a low accounts receivable turnover ratio can be improved by pressing for payment of past-due accounts and by tightening requirements for prospective credit customers.

Inventory Turnover A firm's **inventory turnover** is the number of times the firm sells its merchandise inventory in one year. It is approximated by dividing the cost of goods sold in one year by the average value of the inventory.

The average value of the inventory can be found by adding the beginning inventory value and the ending inventory value (given on the income statement) and dividing the sum by 2. For Northeast Art Supply, average inventory is $40,500. Thus

$$\text{Inventory turnover} = \frac{\text{cost of goods sold}}{\text{average inventory}} = \frac{\$334,000}{\$40,500}$$

$$= 8.2 \text{ times per year}$$

Northeast Art Supply sells its merchandise inventory 8.2 times each year, or about once every forty-five days. The average inventory turnover for all firms is about 9 times per year, but turnover rates vary widely from industry to industry. For example, supermarkets may have inventory turnover rates of 20 or higher, whereas inventory turnover rates for furniture stores are generally well below the national average. The quickest way to improve inventory turnover is to order merchandise in smaller quantities at more frequent intervals.

Debt-to-Owners'-Equity Ratio

Our final category of financial ratios indicates the degree to which a firm's operations are financed through borrowing. Although other ratios can be calculated, the debt-to-owners'-equity ratio is used often to determine whether a firm has too much debt. The **debt-to-owners'-equity ratio** is calculated by dividing total liabilities by owners' equity. For Northeast Art Supply,

$$\text{Debt-to-owners'-equity ratio} = \frac{\text{total liabilities}}{\text{owner's equity}} = \frac{\$110,000}{\$230,000}$$

$$= 0.48, \text{ or } 48 \text{ percent}$$

A debt-to-owners'-equity ratio of 48 percent means that creditors have provided about 48 cents of financing for every dollar provided by the owners. The higher this ratio, the riskier the situation is for lenders. A high debt-to-owners'-equity ratio may make borrowing additional money from lenders difficult. It can be reduced by paying off debts or by increasing the owners' investment in the firm.

Northeast's Financial Ratios: A Summary

Table 15.2 compares the financial ratios of Northeast Art Supply with the average financial ratios for all businesses. It also lists the formulas we used to calculate Northeast's ratios. Northeast seems to be in good financial shape. Its return on sales, current ratio, and acid-test ratio are all above average. Its other ratios are about average, although its inventory turnover and debt-to-equity ratio could be improved.

This chapter ends our discussion of accounting information. In Chapter 16, we see why firms need financing, how they obtain it, and how they ensure that funds are used efficiently in keeping with their organizational objectives.

accounts receivable turnover a financial ratio calculated by dividing net sales by accounts receivable

inventory turnover a financial ratio calculated by dividing the cost of goods sold in one year by the average value of the inventory

debt-to-owners'-equity ratio a financial ratio calculated by dividing total liabilities by owners' equity

Concept Check

1. What type of information is contained in an annual report? How does the information help to identify financial trends?

2. Explain the calculation procedure for and significance of each of the following:
   a. One of the profitability ratios.
   b. A short-term financial ratio.
   c. An activity ratio.
   d. Debt-to-owners'-equity ratio.

TABLE 15.2: Financial Ratios of Northeast Art Supply Compared with Average Ratios for all Businesses

Ratio	Formula	Northeast Ratio	Average Business Ratio	Direction for Improvement
Profitability Ratios				
Return on sales	$\dfrac{\text{net income after taxes}}{\text{net sales}}$	6.7%	4%–5%	Higher
Return on owners' equity	$\dfrac{\text{net income after taxes}}{\text{owners' equity}}$	13%	12%–15%	Higher
Earnings per share	$\dfrac{\text{net income after taxes}}{\text{common stock shares outstanding}}$	$1.21 per share	—	Higher
Short-Term Financial Ratios				
Working capital	current assets – current liabilities	$112,000	—	Higher
Current ratio	$\dfrac{\text{current assets}}{\text{current liabilities}}$	2.6	2.0	Higher
Acid-test ratio	$\dfrac{\text{cash + marketable securites + receivables}}{\text{current liabilities}}$	1.99	1.0	Higher
Activity Ratios				
Accounts receivable turnover	$\dfrac{\text{net sales}}{\text{accounts receivable}}$	11.9	—	Higher
Inventory turnover	$\dfrac{\text{cost of goods sold}}{\text{average inventory}}$	8.2	9	Higher
Debt-to-owners'-equity ratio	$\dfrac{\text{total liabilities}}{\text{owners' equity}}$	48%	—	Lower

SUMMARY

1 Explain why accurate accounting information and audited financial statements are important.

Accounting is the process of systematically collecting, analyzing, and reporting financial information. It can be used to answer questions about what has happened in the past; it also can be used to help make decisions about the future. In fact, it's the firm's accountants and its accounting system that often translate goals, objectives, and plans into dollars and cents to help determine if a decision or plan of action makes "financial sense." Unfortunately, a large number of accounting scandals have caused people to doubt not only the financial information reported by a corporation but also the accounting industry. In a perfect world, accountants and auditors would catch mistakes and disclose questionable accounting practices in a firm's audit. The purpose of an audit is to make sure that a firm's financial statements have been prepared in accordance with accepted accounting principles. To help ensure that corporate financial information is accurate and in response to the many accounting scandals that surfaced in the last part of the 1990s and the first part of the twenty-first century, the Sarbanes-Oxley Act was signed into law. This law contains a

number of provisions designed to restore public confidence in the accounting industry.

2 Identify the people who use accounting information and possible careers in the accounting industry.

To be successful in the accounting industry, employees must be responsible, honest, and ethical; have a strong background in financial management; know how to use a computer and software to process data into accounting information; and be able to communicate with people who need accounting information. Primarily, management uses accounting information, but it is also demanded by lenders, suppliers, stockholders, potential investors, and government agencies. While many people think that all accountants do the same tasks, there are special areas of expertise within the accounting industry. Typical areas of expertise include managerial, financial, cost, tax, government, and not-for-profit accounting. A private accountant is employed by a specific organization to operate its accounting system. A public accountant performs these functions for various individuals or firms on a fee basis. Most accounting firms include on their staffs at least one certified public accountant (CPA). In addition to CPAs, there are also certified management accountants (CMAs). Both types of accountants are excellent career choices.

3 Discuss the accounting process.

The accounting process is based on the accounting equation: Assets = liabilities + owners' equity. Double-entry bookkeeping ensures that the balance shown by the accounting equation is maintained. The accounting process involves five steps: (1) source documents are analyzed, (2) each transaction is recorded in a journal, (3) each journal entry is posted in the appropriate general ledger accounts, (4) at the end of each accounting period, a trial balance is prepared to make sure that the accounting equation is in balance, and (5) financial statements are prepared from the trial balance. A firm's financial statements are included in its annual report. An annual report is a report distributed to stockholders and other interested parties that describes a firm's operating activities and its financial condition. Once statements are prepared, the books are closed. A new accounting cycle then is begun for the next accounting period.

4 Read and interpret a balance sheet.

A balance sheet (sometimes referred to as a statement of financial position) is a summary of a firm's assets, liabilities, and owners' equity accounts at the end of an accounting period. This statement must demonstrate that the accounting equation is in balance. On the balance sheet, assets are categorized as current, fixed, or intangible. Similarly, liabilities can be divided into current liabilities and long-term ones. For a sole proprietorship or partnership, owners' equity is shown as the difference between assets and liabilities. For corporations, the owners' equity section reports the values of stock and retained earnings.

5 Read and interpret an income statement.

An income statement is a summary of a firm's financial operations during the specified accounting period. On the income statement, the company's gross profit is computed by subtracting the cost of goods sold from net sales. Operating expenses and interest expense then are deducted to compute net income before taxes. Finally, income taxes are deducted to obtain the firm's net income after taxes.

6 Describe business activities that affect a firm's cash flow.

Since 1987, the Securities and Exchange Commission (SEC) and the Financial Accounting Standards Board (FASB) have required all publicly traded companies to include a statement of cash flows in their annual reports. This statement illustrates how the operating, investing, and financing activities of a company affect cash during an accounting period. Together, the cash flow statement, balance sheet, and income statement illustrate the results of past decisions and the business's ability to pay debts and dividends and to finance new growth.

7 Summarize how managers evaluate the financial health of a business.

The firm's financial statements and its accounting information become more meaningful when compared with corresponding information for previous years, for competitors, and for the industry in which the firm operates. Such comparisons permit managers and other interested people to pick out trends in growth, borrowing, income, and other business variables and to determine whether the firm is on the way to accomplishing its long-term goals. A number of financial ratios can be computed from the information in a firm's financial statements. These ratios provide a picture of the firm's profitability, its short-term financial position, its activity in the area of accounts receivable and inventory, and its debt financing. Like the information on the firm's financial statements, these ratios can and should be compared with those of past accounting periods, those of competitors, and those representing the average of the industry as a whole.

KEY TERMS

You should now be able to define and give an example relevant to each of the following terms:

accounting (417)
audit (418)
generally accepted
    accounting principles
    (GAAPs) (418)
managerial accounting (421)
financial accounting (421)
certified public accountant
    (CPA) (422)
certified management
    accountant (CMA) (422)
assets (422)
liabilities (422)
owners' equity (422)

accounting equation (423)
double-entry bookkeeping
    system (423)
trial balance (423)
annual report (423)
balance sheet (or statement
    of financial position)
    (424)
liquidity (426)
current assets (426)
fixed assets (426)
depreciation (426)
intangible assets (426)
current liabilities (426)

long-term liabilities (426)
retained earnings (428)
income statement (428)
revenues (429)
gross sales (430)
net sales (430)
cost of goods sold (431)
gross profit (431)
operating expenses (431)
net income (431)
net loss (431)
statement of cash flows
    (431)
financial ratio (434)

return on sales (or profit
    margin) (435)
return on owners' equity
    (435)
earnings per share (435)
working capital (435)
current ratio (436)
acid-test ratio (436)
accounts receivable
    turnover (437)
inventory turnover (437)
debt-to-owners'-equity
    ratio (437)

1. Why do you think there have been so many accounting scandals involving public companies in recent years?
2. Bankers usually insist that prospective borrowers submit audited financial statements along with a loan application. Why should financial statements be audited by a CPA?
3. What can be said about a firm whose owners' equity is a negative amount? How could such a situation come about?
4. Do the balance sheet, income statement, and statement of cash flows contain all the information you might want as a potential lender or stockholder? What other information would you like to examine?
5. Why is it so important to compare a firm's current financial statements with those of previous years, those of competitors, and the average of all firms in the industry in which the firm operates?
6. Which do you think are the two or three most important financial ratios? Why?

Get Flash Cards, Quizzes, Games, Crosswords and more @ www.cengage.com/introbusiness/pride

Test Yourself

Matching Questions

1. _____ It is the process of collecting, analyzing, and reporting data.
2. _____ All the firm's debts are included.
3. _____ It is the difference between a firm's assets and its liabilities.
4. _____ A person who is employed by PricewaterhouseCoopers.
5. _____ Inventories are an example.
6. _____ The ease with which assets can be converted into cash.
7. _____ This statement reveals the financial position of the firm.
8. _____ It illustrates how operating, investing, and financing activities affect cash.
9. _____ A promissory note secures this obligation.
10. _____ The result of dividing current assets by current liabilities.

   a. accounting
   b. assets
   c. balance sheet
   d. cost of goods sold
   e. current ratio
   f. double-entry bookkeeping
   g. liabilities
   h. liquidity
   i. notes payable
   j. owners' equity
   k. public accountant
   l. statement of cash flows

True False Questions

11. **T F** A private accountant is an accountant whose services may be hired on a fee basis by individuals or business firms.
12. **T F** The accounting equation is assets + liabilities = owners' equity.
13. **T F** A cash receipts journal is a specialized journal.
14. **T F** Return on owners' equity indicates a measure of the amount earned per share.
15. **T F** An acid-test ratio is a measure of the firm's ability to pay current liabilities.
16. **T F** There is added protection for whistle-blowers who report violations of the Sarbanes-Oxley Act.
17. **T F** The debt-to-to-owners' equity ratio is used to indicate the degree to which a firm's operations are financed through borrowing.
18. **T F** Recording transactions in the general ledger is the first step in the accounting cycle.
19. **T F** Marketable securities can be converted into cash in a matter of days.
20. **T F** Stockholders' equity represents the total value of a corporation's stock plus retained earnings that have accumulated to date.

Test Yourself

21. _____ Which statement is not true about a balance sheet?

    a. It provides proof that assets = liabilities + owners' equity.
    b. It lists the current, fixed, and intangible assets.
    c. It summarizes the firm's revenues and expenses during one accounting period.
    d. It gives the liabilities of the firm.
    e. It shows the owners' equity in the business.

22. _____ The board of directors decided to pay 50 percent of the $460,000 earnings in dividends to the stockholders. The firm has retained earnings of $680,000 on the books. After the dividends are paid, which of the following statements is true about the firm's retained earnings account?

    a. The new value of the firm's retained earnings is $910,000.
    b. The new value of the firm's retained earnings is $450,000.
    c. The firm failed to reach its profit goal.
    d. Each shareholder will received more than he or she received last year.
    e. The firm's retained earnings are too high.

23. _____ A firm had gross profits from sales in the amount of $180,000, operating expenses of $90,000, and federal incomes taxes of $20,000. What was the firm's net income after taxes?

    a. $10,000
    b. $20,000
    c. $70,000
    d. $90,000
    e. $200,000

24. _____ The Sarbanes-Oxley Act

    a. requires the SEC to police the accounting industry.
    b. requires CEO to certify periodic financial statements.
    c. subjects CEOs to criminal penalties for violations of security reporting.
    d. prohibits many types of consulting services by accounting firms.
    e. All of the above are true.

25. _____ A high debt-to-owners'-equity ratio

    a. reduces the risk for lenders.
    b. will increase as debts are paid off.
    c. will increase the owner's investment.
    d. makes borrowing money from lenders difficult.
    e. makes investors want to invest more money in the firm.

26. _____ An income statement is sometimes called the

    a. statement of financial position.
    b. owners' equity statement.
    c. earnings statement.
    d. statement of cash inflow.
    e. statement of revenues.

27. _____ When a company reports financial numbers that are lower than expected, generally

    a. the company's stock value will increase.
    b. the company's stock value will decrease.
    c. the company will restate its earnings amount.
    d. the stockholders' will immediately ask for an audit.
    e. the corporate officers will resign and new officers will be appointed.

28. _____ An audit is

    a. performed by the firm's private bookkeepers.
    b. not necessary if the firm used accepted bookkeeping procedures.
    c. required by many lenders who are trying to validate a firm's accounting statements.
    d. a waste of the firm's resources.
    e. a guarantee that a firm hasn't "cooked" the books.

29. _____ People who purchased stock in Morgan Oil Exploration are most interested in its _____ reports.

    a. financial accounting
    b. schedule of accounting
    c. cost accounting
    d. managerial accounting
    e. tax accounting

30. _____ The process of transferring information from a general journal to a general ledger is referred to as

    a. journalizing.
    b. posting.
    c. constructing a trial balance.
    d. debiting.
    e. crediting.

Answers on p. TY-1

VIDEO CASE

The Ethics of "Making the Numbers"

Will sales and profits meet the expectations of investors and Wall Street analysts? Managers at public corporations must answer this vitally important question quarter after quarter, year after year. In an ideal world—one in which the economy never contracts, expenses never go up, and customers never buy competing products—the corporation's share price would soar, and investors would cheer as every financial report showed ever-higher sales revenues, profit margins, and earnings.

In the real world, however, many uncontrollable and unpredictable factors can affect a corporation's performance. Customers may buy fewer units or postpone purchases, competitors may introduce superior products, energy costs and other expenses may rise, interest rates may climb, and buying power may plummet. Faced with the prospect of releasing financial results that fall short of Wall Street's expectations, managers may feel intense pressure to "make the numbers" using a variety of accounting techniques.

For example, some executives at WorldCom made earnings look better by booking billions of dollars in ordinary expenses as capital investments. The company was forced into bankruptcy a few weeks after the accounting scam was exposed. As another example, top managers at the drug retailer Rite Aid posted transactions improperly to inflate corporate earnings. Ultimately, Rite Aid had to lower its earnings figures by $1.6 billion, and investors fled, driving the share price down.

Under the Sarbanes-Oxley Act, the CEO and CFO now must certify the corporation's financial reports. This has led hundreds of companies to restate their earnings in recent years, a sign that stricter controls on accounting practices are having the intended effect. "I don't mean to sugarcoat the figure on restatements," says Steve Odland, CEO of Office Depot, "but I think it is positive—it shows a healthy system." Yet not all earnings restatements are due to accounting irregularities. "The general impression of the public is that accounting rules are black and white," Odland adds. "They are often anything but that, and in many instances the changes in earnings came after new interpretations by the chief accountant of the SEC."

Because accounting rules are open to interpretation, managers sometimes find themselves facing ethical dilemmas when a corporation feels pressure to live up to Wall Street's expectations. Consider the hypothetical situation at Commodore Appliances, a fictional company that sells to Home Depot, Lowe's, and other major retail chains. Margaret, the vice president of sales, has told Rob, a district manager, that the company's sales are down 10 percent in the current quarter. She points out that sales in Rob's district are down 20 percent and states that higher-level managers want him to improve this month's figures using "book and hold," which means recording future sales transactions in the current period.

Rob hesitates, saying that the company is gaining market share and that he needs more time to get sales momentum going. He thinks "book and hold" is not good business practice, even if it is legal. Margaret hints that Rob will lose his job if his sales figures don't look better and stresses that he will need the book-and-hold approach for one month only. Rob realizes that if he doesn't go along, he won't be working at Commodore for very much longer.

Meeting with Kevin, one of Commodore's auditors, Rob learns that book and hold meets generally accepted accounting principles. Kevin emphasizes that customers must be willing to take title to the goods before they're delivered or billed. Any book-and-hold sales must be real, backed by documentation such as e-mails to and from buyers, and the transactions must be completed in the near future.

Rob is at a crossroads: His sales figures must be higher if Commodore is to achieve its performance targets, yet he doesn't know exactly when (or if) he actually would complete any book-and-hold sales he might report this month. He doesn't want to mislead anyone, but he also doesn't want to lose his job or put other people's jobs in jeopardy by refusing to do what he is being asked to do. Rob is confident that he can improve his district's sales over the long term. On the other hand, Commodore's executives can't wait—they are pressuring Rob to make the sales figures look better right now. What should he do?[10]

For more information about the Sarbanes-Oxley Act, go to **www.aicpa.org**. (This is the website for the American Institute of Certified Public Accountants and is a good source of information about the act.)

Questions

1. What are the ethical and legal implications of using accounting practices such as the book-and-hold technique to inflate corporate earnings?
2. Why would Commodore's auditor insist that Rob document any sales booked under the book-and-hold technique?
3. If you were in Rob's situation, would you agree to use the book-and-hold technique this month? Justify your decision.
4. Imagine that Commodore has taken out a multimillion-dollar loan that must be repaid next year. How might the lender react if it learned that Commodore was using the book-and-hold method to make revenues look higher than they really are?

BUILDING SKILLS FOR CAREER SUCCESS

1. EXPLORING THE INTERNET

At the time of this text's publication, the U.S. economy was experiencing a financial crisis. Obtaining business loans, home and automobile loans, and consumer credit was more difficult because of tightening of credit policies by major lenders. At the heart of the problem were two large home mortgage lenders—Fannie Mae and Freddie Mac—that provide funds to home mortgage lenders by either purchasing mortgage assets or issuing home mortgage loan guarantees that facilitate the flow of funds into the home mortgage market in the United States. Both firms have also been accused of doctoring earnings and questionable accounting practices.

Assignment

1. Using an Internet search engine such as Google or Yahoo!, locate two or three sites providing information about the recent accounting scandals at these two firms.
2. After examining these sites and reading journal articles, report information about the accounting scandals for each firm. What type of questionable accounting practices occurred in these firms?
3. Based on your assessment of the information you have read, what were the consequences of the questionable accounting practices that occurred?
4. In a two-page report, summarize the questionable accounting practices and what the consequences were for each firm and the executives involved in the scandal.

2. BUILDING TEAM SKILLS

This has been a bad year for Miami-based Park Avenue Furniture. The firm increased sales revenues to $1,400,000, but total expenses ballooned to $1,750,000. Although management realized that some of the firm's expenses were out of control, including cost of goods sold ($700,000), salaries ($450,000), and advertising costs ($140,000), it could not contain expenses. As a result, the furniture retailer lost $350,000. To make matters worse, the retailer applied for a $350,000 loan at Fidelity National Bank and was turned down. The bank officer, Mike Nettles, said that the firm already had too much debt. At that time, liabilities totaled $420,000; owners' equity was $600,000.

Assignment

1. In groups of three or four, analyze the financial condition of Park Avenue Furniture.
2. Discuss why you think the bank officer turned down Park Avenue's loan request.
3. Prepare a detailed plan of action to improve the financial health of Park Avenue Furniture over the next twelve months.

3. RESEARCHING DIFFERENT CAREERS

As pointed out in this chapter, job opportunities for accountants and auditors in the accounting area are expected to experience strong growth between now and the year 2016. Employment opportunities range from entry-level positions for clerical workers and technicians to professional positions that require a college degree in accounting, management consulting, or computer technology. Typical job titles in the accounting field include bookkeeper, corporate accountant, public accountant, auditor, managerial accountant, and controller.

Assignment

1. Answer the following questions based on information obtained from interviews with people employed in accounting, from research in the library or by using the Internet, or from information gained from your college's career center.
   a. What types of activities would a person employed in one of the accounting positions listed above perform on a daily basis?
   b. Would you choose this career? Why or why not?
2. Summarize your findings in a report.

16

Mastering Financial Management

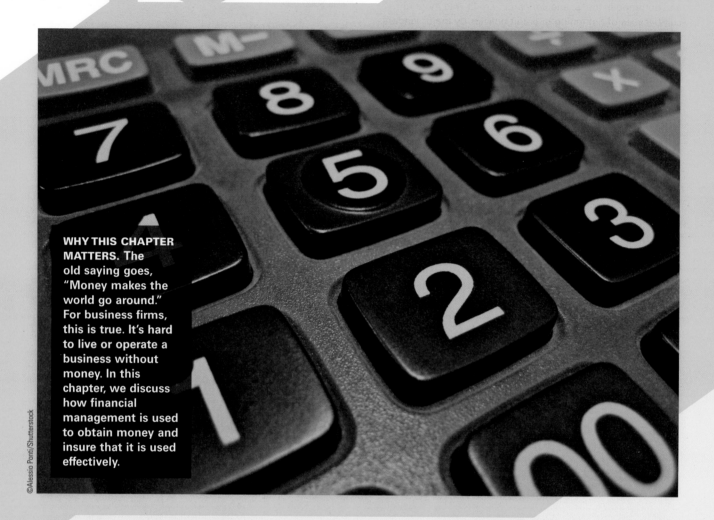

©Alessio Ponti/Shutterstock

WHY THIS CHAPTER MATTERS. The old saying goes, "Money makes the world go around." For business firms, this is true. It's hard to live or operate a business without money. In this chapter, we discuss how financial management is used to obtain money and insure that it is used effectively.

LEARNING OBJECTIVES

1 Explain the need for financial management in business.

2 Summarize the process of planning for financial management.

3 Identify the services provided by banks and financial institutions for their business customers.

4 Describe the advantages and disadvantages of different methods of short-term debt financing.

5 Evaluate the advantages and disadvantages of equity financing.

6 Evaluate the advantages and disadvantages of long-term debt financing.

SCORE, "Counselors to America's Small Business"

When Laura Dessauer started Creativity Queen, her art therapy business, she had never written a business plan. When Joel Erb started INM United, his marketing agency, he knew a lot about web design but not as much about finances. Both learned to master financial management by meeting with volunteer counselors at their local SCORE offices.

Founded in 1964 as the Service Corps of Retired Executives, SCORE has helped more than 8 million small businesses in America prepare for a profitable future. The organization, which calls itself "Counselors to America's Small Business," has 11,200 knowledgeable volunteers in more than 370 offices nationwide, ready to offer free advice in person or online. Whether an entrepreneur has an idea for opening a new business, needs guidance in finding financing, or wants to brainstorm ways of improving profitability, SCORE can help.

Experienced volunteer counselors, some retired and some still active in big corporations or small businesses, have the skills and savvy to point entrepreneurs toward the information and resources appropriate for virtually any situation. They can answer one-time questions, discuss an entrepreneur's specific concerns, and even offer long-term mentoring.

Laura Dessauer of Creativity Queen has met with her SCORE counselors more than two dozen times. Early on, she needed advice about financing and launching her business; later, she sought assistance with generating additional revenue through new products and services. "With a clear vision and action plan, I was able to create a profit in the first year," she notes. In recognition of Dessauer's success, SCORE recently named Creativity Queen as its Small Business of the Year.

Small business owners can get started with SCORE by contacting a nearby office, visiting its website (www.score.org), reading one of its blogs, listening to one of its podcasts, or subscribing to its e-newsletter. SCORE is also affiliated with the U.S. Small Business Administration, which offers many programs for entrepreneurs and guarantees some small-business loans made by participating banks. With all that SCORE has to offer, it's a valuable free resource for any entrepreneur seeking to master financial management.[1]

DID YOU KNOW?

Since its founding in 1964 as the Service Corps of Retired Executives, SCORE has helped more than 8 million small businesses in America prepare for a profitable future.

In Chapter 1, we defined a *business* as the organized effort of individuals to produce and sell, for a profit, the goods and services that satisfy society's needs. Now after reflecting on this definition, imagine that you are a would-be entrepreneur. You have a good idea for a successful business and with hard work, a little luck, *and* some financing you could turn your dream into a reality. That's the situation that many would-be entrepreneurs around the world face when attempting to start a business. For some, like Laura Dessauer and Joel Erb—the two entrepreneurs profiled in the Inside Business case for this chapter—the financial advice provided by SCORE volunteers made the difference between success and failure. And while many entrepreneurs start a business without help from SCORE, the fact is that once a business is open, all businesses need financial management to stay in business and earn a profit.

Regardless of whether the business is a new start-up or an existing business with a track record, they all need money. This continuing need for money became apparent during the recent economic crisis. In reality, the crisis was a wake-up call for many corporate executives, managers, and business owners because one factor became obvious. The ability to borrow money (debt capital) or obtain money from the owners of a business (equity capital) is necessary for the efficient operation of a business firm *and* our economic system.

In this chapter we focus on how firms find the financing required to meet two needs of all business organizations: the need for money to start a business and keep it going, and the need to manage that money effectively. We also look at how firms develop financial plans and evaluate financial performance. Then we examine typical banking services and compare various methods of obtaining short-term financing. We also examine sources of long-term financing.

What Is Financial Management?

Financial management consists of all the activities concerned with obtaining money and using it effectively. Within a business organization, the financial manager not only must determine the best way (or ways) to raise money, but he or she also must ensure that projected uses are in keeping with the organization's goals.

The Need for Financing

Money is needed both to start a business and to keep it going. The original investment of the owners, along with money they may have borrowed, should be enough to open the doors. After that, it would seem that sales revenues could be used to pay the firm's expenses and to provide a profit as well.

This is exactly what happens in a successful firm—over the long run. However, income and expenses may vary from month to month or from year to year. Temporary financing may be needed when expenses are high or sales are low. Then, too, situations such as the opportunity to purchase a new facility or expand an existing plant may require more money than is currently available within a firm. In either case, the firm must look for outside sources of financing.

Short-Term Financing Short-term financing is money that will be used for one year or less. As illustrated in Table 16.1, there are many short-term financing needs, but two deserve special attention. First, certain business practices may affect a firm's cash flow and create a need for short-term financing. **Cash flow** is the movement of money into and out of an organization. The ideal is to have sufficient money coming into the firm in any period to cover the firm's expenses during that period. The ideal, however, is not always achieved. For example, California-based Callaway Golf offers credit to retailers and wholesalers that carry the firm's golf clubs and balls. Credit purchases made by Callaway's retailers generally are not paid until thirty to sixty days (or more) after the transaction. Callaway therefore may need short-term financing to pay its bills until its customers have paid theirs.

A second major need for short-term financing is inventory. For most manufacturers, wholesalers, and retailers, inventory requires considerable investment. Moreover, most goods are manufactured four to nine months before they are actually sold to the ultimate customer. This type of manufacturing is often referred to as *speculative production*. **Speculative production** refers to the time lag between

financial management all the activities concerned with obtaining money and using it effectively

short-term financing money that will be used for one year or less

cash flow the movement of money into and out of an organization

speculative production the time lag between the actual production of goods and when the goods are sold

TABLE 16.1: Comparison of Short- and Long-Term Financing Whether a business seeks short- or long-term financing depends on what the money will be used for.

Corporate Cash Needs	
Short-Term Financing Needs	**Long-Term Financing Needs**
Cash-flow problems	Business start-up costs
Current inventory needs	Mergers and acquisitions
Monthly expenses	New product development
Speculative production	Long-term marketing activities
Short-term promotional needs	Replacement of equipment
Unexpected emergencies	Expansion of facilities

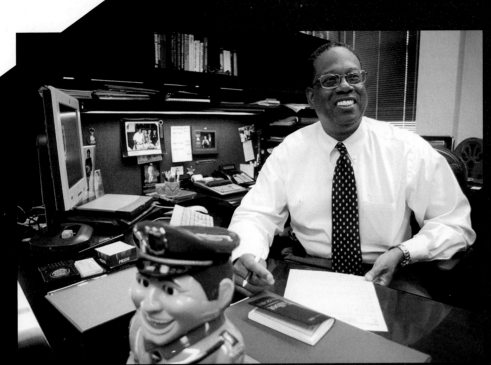

This banker wants to help. Bob Harvey, president and CEO of Seattle Metropolitan Credit Union, likes to help people and business owners achieve their financial goals. Still, like most bankers, Harvey is concerned with two questions: What will the loan money be used for, and can the applicant repay the loan as scheduled? The answers to these questions often determine if a loan will be approved.

PR NewsFoto/Seattle Metropolitan Credit Union

the actual production of goods and when the goods are sold. Consider what happens when a firm such as Black & Decker begins to manufacture electric tools and small appliances for sale during the Christmas season. Manufacturing begins in February, March, and April, and Black & Decker negotiates short-term financing to buy materials and supplies, to pay wages and rent, and to cover inventory costs until its products eventually are sold to wholesalers and retailers later in the year. Take a look at Figure 16.1. Although Black & Decker manufactures and sells finished products all during the year, expenses peak during the first part of the year. During this same period, sales revenues are low. Once the firm's finished products are shipped

FIGURE 16.1: Cash Flow for a Manufacturing Business Manufacturers such as Black & Decker often use short-term financing to pay expenses during the production process. Once goods are shipped to retailers and wholesalers and payment is received, sales revenues are used to repay short-term financing.

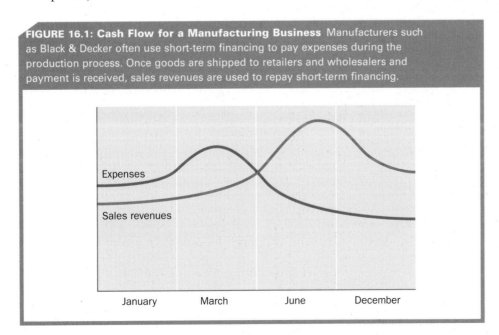

Chapter 16: Mastering Financial Management

to retailers and wholesalers and payment is received (usually within thirty to sixty days), sales revenues are used to repay short-term financing.

Retailers that range in size from Wal-Mart to the neighborhood drugstore also need short-term financing to build up their inventories before peak selling periods. For example, Dallas-based Bruce Miller Nurseries must increase the number of shrubs, trees, and flowering plants that it makes available for sale during the spring and summer growing seasons. To obtain this merchandise inventory from growers or wholesalers, it uses short-term financing and repays the loans when the merchandise is sold.

Long-Term Financing **Long-term financing** is money that will be used for longer than one year. Long-term financing obviously is needed to start a new business. As Table 16.1 shows, it is also needed for business mergers and acquisitions, new product development, long-term marketing activities, replacement of equipment that has become obsolete, and expansion of facilities.

The amounts of long-term financing needed by large firms can seem almost unreal. For example, Pfizer invested $8 billion in research and development (R&D) to create new or improved prescription drugs in 2008—the last year that complete dollar amounts were available at the time of this publication.[2]

The Need for Financial Management

To some extent, financial management can be viewed as a two-sided problem. On one side, the uses of funds often dictate the type or types of financing needed by a business. On the other side, the activities a business can undertake are determined by the types of financing available. Financial managers must ensure that funds are available when needed, that they are obtained at the lowest possible cost, and that they are used as efficiently as possible. Financial managers also must consider the risk-return ratio when making decisions. The **risk-return ratio** is based on the principle that a high-risk decision should generate higher financial returns for a business. On the other hand, more conservative decisions (with less risk) often generate lesser returns. While financial managers want higher returns, they often must strive for a balance between risk and return. For example, American Electric Power may consider investing millions of dollars to fund research into new solar technology that could enable the company to use the sun to generate electrical power. And yet, financial managers (along with other managers throughout the organization) must determine the potential return before committing to such a costly research project.

Finally, financial managers must ensure that funds are available for the repayment of debts in accordance with lenders' financing terms. Prompt repayment is essential to protect the firm's credit rating and its ability to obtain financing in the future.

Many firms have failed because their managers did not pay enough attention to finances. In fact, poor financial management was one of the major reasons why over 43,500 businesses filed for bankruptcy in 2008—the most recent year for which complete statistics are available.[3] In addition, many fairly successful firms could be highly successful if they managed their finances more carefully. However, many people often take finances for granted. Their first focus may be on production or marketing. As long as there is sufficient financing today, they don't worry about how well it is used or whether it will be there tomorrow. Proper financial management can ensure that:

- Financing priorities are established in line with organizational goals and objectives.
- Spending is planned and controlled.
- Sufficient financing is available when it is needed, both now and in the future.
- A firm's credit customers pay their bills on time, and the number of past-due or delinquent accounts is reduced.
- Bills are paid promptly to protect the firm's credit rating and its ability to borrow money.
- The funds required for paying the firm's taxes are available when needed to meet tax deadlines.
- Excess cash is invested in certificates of deposit (CDs), government securities, or conservative, marketable securities.

long-term financing money that will be used for longer than one year

risk-return ratio a ratio based on the principle that a high-risk decision should generate higher financial returns for a business and more conservative decisions often generate lesser returns

Inventory management: A complex problem. For retailers like Best Buy, managing inventory can be a problem, especially before Christmas and other peak selling periods. Although retailers don't want to get stuck with unsold inventory, they must have the right mix and amount of inventory to meet consumer demand. Despite the problems associated with inventory, it's a good feeling to see customers at the cash register purchasing the products they need.

These functions define effective management as applied to a particular resource—money. And like all effective management, financial management begins with people who must set goals and plan for the future.

Careers in Finance

When you hear the word *finance,* you may think of highly paid executives who determine what a corporation can afford to do and what it can't. At the executive level, most large business firms have a chief financial officer for financial management. A **chief financial officer (CFO)** is a high-level corporate executive who manages a firm's finances and reports directly to the company's chief executive officer or president. Some firms prefer to use the titles vice president of financial management, treasurer, or controller instead of the CFO title for executive-level positions in the finance area.

While some executives in finance do make $300,000 a year or more, many entry-level and lower-level positions that pay quite a bit less are available. Banks, insurance companies, and investment firms obviously have a need for workers who can manage and analyze financial data. So do businesses involved in manufacturing, services, and marketing. Colleges and universities, not-for-profit organizations, and government entities at all levels also need finance workers.

People in finance must have certain traits and skills. In addition to honesty, managers and employees in the finance area must:

1. Have a strong background in accounting or mathematics.
2. Know how to use a computer to analyze data.
3. Be an expert at both written and oral communication.

Typical job titles in finance include bank officer, consumer credit officer, financial analyst, financial planner, loan officer, insurance analyst, and investment account executive. Depending on qualifications, work experience, and education, starting salaries

chief financial officer (CFO) a high-level corporate executive who manages a firm's finances and reports directly to the company's chief executive officer or president

Concept Check

1. How does short-term financing differ from long-term financing? Give two business uses for each type of financing.

2. What is speculative production? How is it related to a firm's cash flow problems?

3. In your own words, define the risk-return ratio.

4. To be successful, what traits and skills does an employee in the finance area need?

©AP Photo/Wide World

generally begin at $30,000 to $40,000 a year, but it is not uncommon for college graduates to earn higher salaries. In addition to salary, many employees have attractive benefits and other perks that make a career in financial management attractive.

Planning—The Basis of Sound Financial Management

In Chapter 6, we defined a *plan* as an outline of the actions by which an organization intends to accomplish its goals. A **financial plan**, then, is a plan for obtaining and using the money needed to implement an organization's goals.

Developing the Financial Plan

Financial planning (like all planning) begins with establishing a set of valid goals and objectives. Financial managers next must determine how much money is needed to accomplish each goal and objective. Finally, financial managers must identify available sources of financing and decide which to use. The three steps involved in financial planning are illustrated in Figure 16.2.

Establishing Organizational Goals and Objectives As pointed out in Chapter 6, a *goal* is an end result that an organization expects to achieve over a one- to ten-year period. *Objectives* are specific statements detailing what the organization intends to accomplish within a shorter period of time. If goals and objectives are not specific and measurable, they cannot be translated into dollar costs, and financial planning cannot proceed. Goals and objectives also must be realistic. Otherwise, they may be impossible to finance or achieve. For large corporations, goals and objectives can be expensive. For example, when Pepsi wanted to revamp its image in the marketplace, it planned to spend at least $1.2 billion over three years. The goal was to redesign many of Pepsi's packaging graphics for its carbonated soft drink products as well as a redesign of the Pepsi corporate logo.[4]

financial plan a plan for obtaining and using the money needed to implement an organization's goals

Budgeting for Financial Needs Once planners know what the firm's goals and objectives are for a specific period—say, the next calendar year—they can

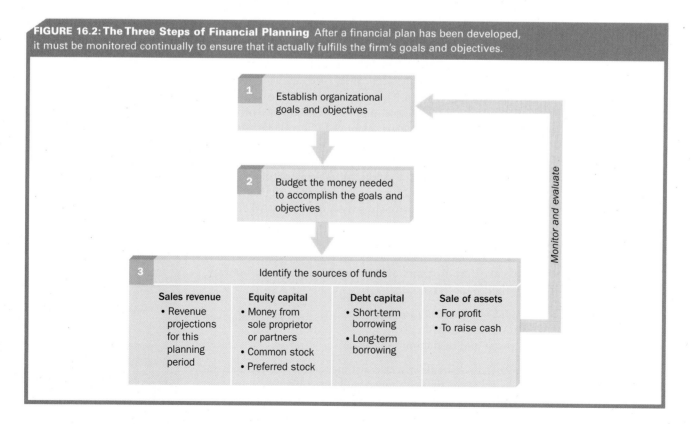

FIGURE 16.2: The Three Steps of Financial Planning After a financial plan has been developed, it must be monitored continually to ensure that it actually fulfills the firm's goals and objectives.

1. Establish organizational goals and objectives

2. Budget the money needed to accomplish the goals and objectives

3. Identify the sources of funds

Sales revenue	Equity capital	Debt capital	Sale of assets
• Revenue projections for this planning period	• Money from sole proprietor or partners • Common stock • Preferred stock	• Short-term borrowing • Long-term borrowing	• For profit • To raise cash

Monitor and evaluate

budget the costs the firm will incur and the sales revenues it will receive. Specifically, a **budget** is a financial statement that projects income and/or expenditures over a specified future period.

Usually, the budgeting process begins with the construction of budgets for sales and various types of expenses. (A typical sales budget—for Stars and Stripes Clothing, a California-based retailer—is shown in Figure 16.3.) Financial managers can easily combine each department's budget for sales and expenses into a company-wide cash budget. A **cash budget** estimates cash receipts and cash expenditures over a specified period. Notice in the cash budget for Stars and Stripes Clothing, shown in Figure 16.4, that cash sales and collections are listed at the top for each calendar quarter. Payments for purchases and routine expenses are listed in the middle section. Using this information, it is possible to calculate the anticipated cash gain or loss at the end of each quarter.

To develop a plan for long-term financing needs, managers often construct a capital budget. A **capital budget** estimates a firm's expenditures for major assets, including new product development, expansion of facilities, replacement of obsolete equipment, and mergers and acquisitions. For example, software giant Oracle constructed a capital budget to determine the best way to finance the $5.6 billion acquisition of Sun Microsystems.[5]

Identifying Sources of Funds The four primary sources of funds, listed in Figure 16.2, are sales revenue, equity capital, debt capital, and proceeds from the sale of assets. Future sales revenue generally provides the greatest part of a firm's financing. Figure 16.4 shows that for Stars and Stripes Clothing, sales for the year are expected to cover all expenses and to provide a cash gain of $106,000, or about 16 percent of sales. However, Stars and Stripes has a problem in the first quarter, when sales are expected to fall short of expenses by $7,000. In fact, one of the primary reasons for financial planning is to provide management with adequate lead time to solve this type of cash-flow problem.

A second type of funding is **equity capital**. For a sole proprietorship or partnership, equity capital is provided by the owner or owners of the business. For a corporation, equity capital is money obtained from the sale of shares of ownership in the business. Equity capital is used almost exclusively for long-term financing. Thus, it might be used to start a business and to fund expansions or mergers. It would not be considered for short-term financing needs, such as Stars and Stripes Clothing's first-quarter $7,000 shortfall.

A third type of funding is **debt capital**, which is borrowed money. Debt capital may be borrowed for either short- or long-term use—and a short-term loan seems made to order for Stars and Stripes Clothing's shortfall problem. The firm probably would borrow the needed $7,000 (or perhaps a bit more) at some point during the first quarter and repay it from second-quarter sales revenue.

budget a financial statement that projects income and/or expenditures over a specified future period

cash budget a financial statement that estimates cash receipts and cash expenditures over a specified period

capital budget a financial statement that estimates a firm's expenditures for major assets and its long-term financing needs

equity capital money received from the owners or from the sale of shares of ownership in a business

debt capital borrowed money obtained through loans of various types

FIGURE 16.3: Sales Budget for Stars and Stripes Clothing Usually, the budgeting process begins with the construction of departmental budgets for sales.

STARS AND STRIPES CLOTHING
Sales Budget For January 1, 2010 to December 31, 2010

Department	First Quarter	Second Quarter	Third Quarter	Fourth Quarter	Totals
Infants'	$ 50,000	$ 55,000	$ 60,000	$ 70,000	$235,000
Children's	45,000	45,000	40,000	40,000	170,000
Women's	35,000	40,000	35,000	50,000	160,000
Men's	20,000	20,000	15,000	25,000	80,000
Totals	$150,000	$160,000	$150,000	$185,000	$645,000

FIGURE 16.4: Cash Budget for Stars and Stripes Clothing A company-wide cash budget projects sales, collections, purchases, and expenses over a specified period to anticipate cash surpluses and deficits.

STARS AND STRIPES CLOTHING
Cash Budget

For January 1, 2010 to December 31, 2010

	First Quarter	Second Quarter	Third Quarter	Fourth Quarter	Totals
Cash sales and collections	$150,000	$160,000	$150,000	$185,000	$645,000
Less payments					
Purchases	$110,000	$ 80,000	$ 90,000	$ 60,000	$340,000
Wages/salaries	25,000	20,000	25,000	30,000	100,000
Rent	10,000	10,000	12,000	12,000	44,000
Other expenses	4,000	4,000	5,000	6,000	19,000
Taxes	8,000	8,000	10,000	10,000	36,000
Total payments	$157,000	$122,000	$142,000	$118,000	$539,000
Cash gain or (loss)	$ (7,000)	$ 38,000	$ 8,000	$ 67,000	$106,000

Proceeds from the sale of assets are the fourth type of funding. Selling assets is a drastic step. However, it may be a reasonable last resort when neither equity capital nor debt capital can be found. Assets also may be sold when they are no longer needed or do not "fit" with the company's core business. To concentrate on its core business and to raise financing, food giant ConAgra sold its commodity trade operations to an affiliate of New York-based Ospraie Management for about $2.1 billion. At the time of the

Financial Bailout: A move to stabilize the economy! Senators Corker, Dodd, Martinez, Schumer, and Bennett (left to right) all got involved in the government's recent bailout plan commonly referred to as the Economic Stabilization Act. While politicians, business leaders, and the general public still debate the merits of a federal rescue plan, one factor became very apparent. Something had to be done to correct what some experts described as the nation's worst economic problems since the Great Depression.

©Roger L. Wollenberg/UPI/Landov

sale, ConAgra's management said it would use the proceeds from the sale to repurchase stock, reduce debt, and to remake itself as a force in consumer packaged goods.[6]

Monitoring and Evaluating Financial Performance

It is important to ensure that financial plans are being implemented properly and to catch potential problems before they become major ones. For example, many Internet-based businesses have reduced various expenses in order to become profitable. Even so, many of these high-tech companies have failed in the past few years. Pets.com is an example of a dotcom start-up that lost control of its finances. Backed by Amazon, the firm spent millions on television and other media advertising to generate awareness and sales. The funny advertisements presented by the famous talking-dog sock puppet could not create the critical mass of buyers quickly enough to offset the advertising and other operational costs. As a result, the firm lost $5 for every dollar of pet supplies revenue received. This quickly created a cash crisis and eventually led to failure. (*Note:* The firm's URL—**www.pets.com**—was purchased by competitor PetSmart.)

To prevent problems such as those just described, financial managers should establish a means of monitoring financial performance. Interim budgets (weekly, monthly, or quarterly) may be prepared for comparison purposes. These comparisons point up areas that require additional or revised planning—or at least areas calling for a more careful investigation. Budget comparisons also can be used to improve the firm's future budgets.

Concept Check

1. What is the function of a cash budget? A capital budget?

2. What is the difference between equity capital and debt capital?

3. Describe the four sources of funds for a business.

4. How does a financial manager monitor and evaluate a firm's financing?

Financial Services Provided by Banks and Other Financial Institutions

3 LEARNING OBJECTIVE

Identify the services provided by banks and financial institutions for their business customers.

For a business owner, it helps to know your banker. Banking services can be divided into three broad categories: traditional services, electronic banking services, and international services.

Traditional Banking Services for Business Clients

Traditional services provided by banks and other financial institutions include savings and checking accounts, loans, processing credit- and debit-card transactions, and providing professional advice.

Savings and Checking Accounts Savings accounts provide a safe place to store money and a very conservative means of investing. The usual *passbook savings account* earns between 0.50 and 1 percent in banks and savings and loan associations (S&Ls) and slightly more in credit unions. A business with excess cash that is willing to leave money on deposit with a bank for a set period of time can earn a higher rate of interest. To do so, the business firm buys a certificate of deposit. A **certificate of deposit (CD)** is a document stating that the bank will pay the depositor a guaranteed interest rate on money left on deposit for a specified period of time.

Business firms (and individuals) also deposit money in checking accounts so that they can write checks to pay for purchases. A **check** is a written order for a bank or other financial institution to pay a stated dollar amount to the business or person indicated on the face of the check. For businesses, monthly charges are based on the average daily balance in the checking account and/or the number of checks written.

Business Loans Banks, savings and loan associations, credit unions, and other financial institutions provide short- and long-term loans to businesses. *Short-term business loans* must be repaid within one year or less. Typical uses for the money obtained through short-term loans include solving cash-flow problems, purchasing inventory, and meeting unexpected emergencies. To help ensure that short-term money will be available when needed, many firms establish a line of credit. A **line of credit** is a loan that is approved before the money is actually needed. Because all the necessary paperwork is already completed and the loan is preapproved, the business can obtain the money later without delay, as soon as it is required. Even with

certificate of deposit (CD) A document stating that the bank will pay the depositor a guaranteed interest rate on money left on deposit for a specified period of time

check a written order for a bank or other financial institution to pay a stated dollar amount to the business or person indicated on the face of the check

line of credit a loan that is approved before the money is actually needed

Without proper financial management, a firm cannot exist. Linens' n Things is just one of many firms that closed its doors during the recent financial crisis. Unfortunately, there are many far-reaching side effects when a company goes out of business. Customers can no longer buy the firm's products or services, the firm's employees lose their jobs, suppliers can't sell products or services to the firm, and investors lose the money they invested in the firm.

a line of credit, a firm may not be able to borrow money if the bank does not have sufficient funds available. For this reason, some firms prefer a **revolving credit agreement**, which is a guaranteed line of credit. Under this type of agreement, the bank guarantees that the money will be available when the borrower needs it. In return for the guarantee, the bank charges a commitment fee ranging from 0.25 to 1.0 percent of the *unused* portion of the revolving credit agreement. The usual interest is charged for the portion that *is* borrowed.

Long-term business loans are repaid over a period of years. The average length of a long-term business loan is generally three to seven years but sometimes as long as fifteen to twenty years. Long-term loans are used most often to finance the expansion of buildings and retail facilities, mergers and acquisitions, replacement of equipment, or product development. Most lenders require some type of collateral for long-term loans. **Collateral** is real estate or property (e.g., stocks, bonds, equipment, or any other asset of value) pledged as security for a loan.

Repayment terms and interest rates for both short- and long-term loans are arranged between the lender and the borrower. For businesses, repayment terms may include monthly, quarterly, semiannual, or annual payments.

Why Has the Use of Credit Transactions Increased?

By 2010, 181 million Americans will use credit cards to pay for everything from tickets on American Airlines to Zebco fishing gear.[7] Why have credit cards become so popular? For a merchant, the answer is obvious. By depositing charge slips in a bank or other financial institution, the merchant can convert credit-card sales into cash. In return for processing the merchant's credit-card transactions, the financial institution charges a fee that generally ranges between 1.5 and 4 percent. Typically, small, independent businesses pay more than larger stores or chain stores. Let's assume that you use a Visa credit card to purchase a microwave oven for $300 from Gold Star Appliances, a small retailer in Richardson, Texas. At the end of the day, the retailer deposits your charge slip, along with other charge slips, checks, and currency collected during the day, at its bank. If the bank charges Gold Star Appliances 4

revolving credit agreement a guaranteed line of credit

collateral real estate or property pledged as security for a loan percent to process each credit-card transaction, the bank deducts a processing fee of $12 ($300 × 0.04 = $12) for your credit-card transaction and immediately deposits the remainder ($288) in Gold Star Appliances' account. The number of credit-card transactions, the total dollar amount of credit sales, and how well the merchant can negotiate the fees the financial institution charges determine actual fees.

Do not confuse debit cards with credit cards. Although they may look alike, there are important differences. A **debit card** electronically subtracts the amount of a customer's purchase from her or his bank account at the moment the purchase is made. (By contrast, when you use your credit card, the credit-card company extends short-term financing, and you do not make payment until you receive your next statement.) Debit cards are used most commonly to obtain cash at automatic teller machines (ATMs) and to purchase products and services from retailers.

Electronic Banking Services

An **electronic funds transfer (EFT) system** is a means of performing financial transactions through a computer terminal or telephone hookup. The following three EFT applications are changing how banks help firms do business:

1. *Automated clearinghouses (ACHs)*. Designed to reduce the number of paper checks, automated clearinghouses process checks, recurring bill payments, Social Security benefits, and employee salaries. For example, large companies use ACHs to transfer wages and salaries directly into their employees' bank accounts, thus eliminating the need to make out individual paychecks.
2. *Point-of-sale (POS) terminals*. A POS terminal is a computerized cash register located in a retail store and connected to a bank's computer. At the cash register, you pull your bank credit or debit card through a magnetic card reader. A central processing center notifies a computer at your bank that you want to make a purchase. The bank's computer immediately adds the amount to your account for a credit-card transaction. In a similar process, the bank's computer deducts the amount of the purchase from your bank account if you use a debit card. Finally, the amount of your purchase is added to the store's account. The store then is notified that the transaction is complete, and the cash register prints out your receipt.
3. *Electronic check conversion (ECC)*. Electronic check conversion is a process used to convert information from a paper check into an electronic payment for merchandise, services, or bills. When you give your completed check to a store cashier, the check is processed through an electronic system that captures your banking information and the dollar amount of the check. Once the check is processed, you are asked to sign a receipt, and you get a voided (canceled) check back for your records. Finally, the funds to pay for your transaction are transferred into the business firm's account. ECC also can be used for checks you mail to pay for a purchase or to pay on an account.

Bankers and business owners generally are pleased with EFT systems. EFTs are fast, and they eliminate the costly processing of checks. However, many customers are reluctant to use online banking or EFT systems. Some simply do not like "the technology," whereas others fear that the computer will garble their accounts. Early on, in 1978, Congress responded to such fears by passing the Electronic Funds Transfer Act, which protects the customer in case the bank makes an error or the customer's credit or debit card is stolen.

International Banking Services

For international businesses, banking services are extremely important. Depending on the needs of an international firm, a bank can help by providing a letter of credit or a banker's acceptance.

A **letter of credit** is a legal document issued by a bank or other financial institution guaranteeing to pay a seller a stated amount for a specified period of time—usually thirty to sixty days. (With a letter of credit, certain conditions, such as delivery of the merchandise, may be specified before payment is made.)

debit card a card that electronically subtracts the amount of a customer's purchase from her or his bank account at the moment the purchase is made

electronic funds transfer (EFT) system a means of performing financial transactions through a computer terminal or telephone hookup

letter of credit a legal document issued by a bank or other financial institution guaranteeing to pay a seller a stated amount for a specified period of time

Global Economic Challenges

Microfinance Goes Global

Pioneered by Grameen Bank in Bangladesh, microfinance—lending small amounts of money to small businesses—has become a credit lifeline for entrepreneurs all over the world. Since 1982, Grameen Bank has loaned a total of $6 billion to 8 million small businesses worldwide. Most of its borrowers are poor women who are building businesses to support their families. They apply for loans that average $220 to buy materials or equipment or to bring their wares to a distant but lucrative marketplace.

Although borrowers must explain what they will do with the money, their loans are short-term and unsecured, backed only by their promise to repay. Conventional banks shy away from such borrowers, yet nearly 98 percent of Grameen Bank's borrowers repay their loans in full. In fact, the bank has steadily expanded its microfinance activities throughout the world, including several U.S. cities.

Microfinance is now a $25 billion industry, with a growing online presence through microfinance organizations such as Kiva.org. Founded in 2005, Kiva has raised $75 million from individuals and made short-term microloans to 180,000 small businesses in 44 nations. Anyone who wants to lend money can visit the Kiva site, read about would-be borrowers and their businesses, select one or more loans to fund, and send money (at least $25) to Kiva via PayPal or credit card. Lenders receive no interest, but they do have the satisfaction of participating in what Kiva calls "loans that change lives."

Sources: Mac Margolis, "Microfinance: The Next Bubble?" *Newsweek*, June 29, 2009, www.newsweek.com; Michael Liedtke, "Kiva to Feed Cash-Starved US Small Businesses," *Associated Press*, June 10, 2009, www.google.com/hostednews/ap; Alison Benjamin, "Money Well Lent," *Guardian (UK)*, June 3, 2009, www.guardian.co.uk.

Concept Check

1. Describe the traditional banking services provided by financial institutions.

2. What are the major advantages of electronic banking services?

3. How can a bank or other financial institution help American businesses to compete in the global marketplace?

A **banker's acceptance** is a written order for a bank to pay a third party a stated amount of money on a specific date. (With a banker's acceptance, no conditions are specified. It is simply an order to pay without any strings attached.)

Both a letter of credit and a banker's acceptance are popular methods of paying for import and export transactions. Imagine that you are a business owner in the United States who wants to purchase some leather products from a small business in Florence, Italy. You offer to pay for the merchandise with your company's check drawn on an American bank, but the Italian business owner is worried about payment. To solve the problem, your bank can issue either a letter of credit or a banker's acceptance to guarantee that payment will be made. In addition to a letter of credit and a banker's acceptance, banks also can use EFT technology to speed international banking transactions.

One other international banking service should be noted. Banks and other financial institutions provide for currency exchange. If you place an order for Japanese merchandise valued at $50,000, how do you pay for the order? Do you use U.S. dollars or Japanese yen? To solve this problem, you can use the bank's currency-exchange service. To make payment, you can use either currency, and if necessary, the bank will exchange one currency for the other to complete your transaction.

LEARNING OBJECTIVE 4

Describe the advantages and disadvantages of different methods of short-term debt financing.

Sources of Short-Term Debt Financing

During the recent financial crisis, many business firms found that it was much more difficult to borrow money for short periods of time. Typically, short-term debt financing is money that will be repaid in one year or less. To help free up the credit markets, the government passed a $700 billion financial rescue plan in October 2008. While not all the money was used to meet short-term financing needs, the availability of more money did provide funds for businesses that needed short-term financing.

The decision to borrow money does not necessarily mean that a firm is in financial trouble. On the contrary, astute financial management often means regular, responsible borrowing of many different kinds to meet different needs. In this section, we examine the sources of *short-term debt financing* available to businesses. In the next two sections, we look at long-term financing options: equity capital and debt capital.

banker's acceptance a written order for a bank to pay a third party a stated amount of money on a specific date

Sources of Unsecured Short-Term Financing

Short-term debt financing is usually easier to obtain than long-term debt financing for three reasons:

1. For the lender, the shorter repayment period means less risk of nonpayment.
2. The dollar amounts of short-term loans usually are smaller than those of long-term loans.
3. A close working relationship normally exists between the short-term borrower and the lender.

Most lenders do not require collateral for short-term financing. When they do, it is usually because they are concerned about the size of a particular loan, the borrowing firm's poor credit rating, or the general prospects of repayment. **Unsecured financing** is financing that is not backed by collateral. A company seeking unsecured short-term financing has several options.

Trade Credit Manufacturers and wholesalers often provide financial aid to retailers by allowing them thirty to sixty days (or more) in which to pay for merchandise. This delayed payment, known as **trade credit**, is a type of short-term financing extended by a seller who does not require immediate payment after delivery of merchandise. It is the most popular form of short-term financing, because most manufacturers and wholesalers don't charge interest for trade credit. In fact, from 70 to 90 percent of all transactions between businesses involve some trade credit.

Let's assume that a Barnes & Noble bookstore receives a shipment of books from a publisher. Along with the merchandise, the publisher sends an invoice that states the terms of payment. Barnes & Noble now has two options for payment. First, the book retailer may pay the invoice promptly and take advantage of any cash discount the publisher offers. Cash-discount terms are specified on the invoice. For instance, "2/10, net 30" means that the customer—Barnes & Noble—may take a 2 percent discount if it pays the invoice within ten days of the invoice date. Cash discounts can generate substantial savings and lower the cost of purchasing merchandise for a retailer such as Barnes & Noble. Let's assume that the dollar amount of the invoice is $140,000. In this case, the cash discount is $2,800 ($140,000 × 0.02 = $2,800).

A second option is to wait until the end of the credit period before making payment. If payment is made between eleven and thirty days after the date of the invoice, the customer must pay the entire amount. As long as payment is made before the end of the credit period, the customer maintains the ability to purchase additional merchandise using the trade-credit arrangement.

Promissory Notes Issued to Suppliers A **promissory note** is a written pledge by a borrower to pay a certain sum of money to a creditor at a specified future date. Suppliers uneasy about extending trade credit may be less reluctant to offer credit to customers who sign promissory notes. Unlike trade credit, however, promissory notes usually require the borrower to pay interest. Although repayment periods may extend to one year, most short-term promissory notes are repaid in 60 to 180 days.

A promissory note offers two important advantages to the firm extending the credit. First, a promissory note is a legally binding and enforceable document that

Trade credit helped build this helicopter. Many companies like California-based Robinson Helicopter use trade credit to purchase the materials they need to manufacture products. When trade credit is used, manufacturers obtain short-term financing and don't have to pay suppliers and vendors for thirty to sixty days or more. As an added bonus, typically there is no finance or interest charge when trade credit is used to purchase materials.

unsecured financing financing that is not backed by collateral

trade credit a type of short-term financing extended by a seller who does not require immediate payment after delivery of merchandise

promissory note a written pledge by a borrower to pay a certain sum of money to a creditor at a specified future date has been signed by the individual or business borrowing the money. Second, most promissory notes are negotiable instruments, and the supplier (or company extending credit) may be able to discount, or sell, the note to its own bank. If the note is discounted, the dollar amount the supplier would receive is slightly less than the maturity value because the bank charges a fee for the service. The supplier would recoup most of its money immediately, and the bank would collect the maturity value when the note matured.

Unsecured Bank Loans Banks and other financial institutions offer unsecured short-term loans to businesses at interest rates that vary with each borrower's credit rating. The **prime interest rate**, sometimes called the *reference rate*, is the lowest rate charged by a bank for a short-term loan. This lowest rate generally is reserved for large corporations with excellent credit ratings. Organizations with good to high credit ratings may pay the prime rate plus 2 percent. Firms with questionable credit ratings may have to pay the prime rate plus 4 percent. (The fact that a banker charges a higher interest rate for a higher-risk loan is a practical application of the risk-return ratio discussed earlier in this chapter.) Of course, if the banker believes that loan repayment may be a problem, the borrower's loan application may well be rejected.

Banks generally offer unsecured short-term loans through promissory notes, a line of credit, or a revolving credit agreement. A bank promissory note is similar to the promissory note issued to suppliers described in the preceding section. For both types of promissory notes, interest rates and repayment terms may be negotiated between the borrower and a bank or supplier. A bank that offers a promissory note or line of credit may require that a *compensating balance* be kept on deposit at the bank. This balance may be as much as 20 percent of the borrowed funds. Assume that Bank of America requires a 20 percent compensating balance on a short-term promissory note. If you borrow $50,000, at least $10,000 ($50,000 × 0.20 = $10,000) of the loan amount must be kept on deposit at the bank. In this situation, the effective interest rate you must pay on the original $50,000 loan increases because you have the use of only $40,000. The bank also may require that every commercial borrower *clean up* (pay off completely) its short-term promissory note or line of credit at least once each year and not use it again for a period of thirty to sixty days.

Commercial Paper **Commercial paper** is a short-term promissory note issued by a large corporation. Commercial paper is secured only by the reputation of the issuing firm; no collateral is involved. It is usually issued in large denominations, ranging from $5,000 to $100,000. Corporations issuing commercial paper pay interest rates slightly below the interest rates charged by banks for short-term loans. Thus, issuing commercial paper is cheaper than getting short-term financing from a bank. The interest rate a corporation pays when it issues commercial paper is tied to its credit rating and its ability to repay the commercial paper. It is most often used to purchase inventory, pay salaries and other necessary expenses, and solve cash-flow problems.

Large firms with excellent credit reputations like Microsoft, Procter & Gamble, and Caterpillar can raise large sums of money quickly by issuing commercial paper. However, during the recent financial crisis, even companies that had always been able to sell commercial paper had difficulty finding buyers. For example, both GE and AT&T—two premier names in corporate America—couldn't get the short-term financing they were looking for.[8] To help provide additional short-term financing, the Federal Reserve Bank stepped in and began to purchase the commercial paper from firms in need of financing to pay for day-to-day business operations.[9]

Sources of Secured Short-Term Financing

If a business cannot obtain enough capital through unsecured financing, it must put up collateral to obtain additional short-term financing. Almost any asset can serve as collateral. However, *inventories* and *accounts receivable* are the assets most com-

prime interest rate the lowest rate charged by a bank for a short-term loan

commercial paper a short-term promissory note issued by a large corporation monly pledged for short-term financing. Even when it is willing to pledge collateral to back up a loan, a firm that is financially weak may have difficulty obtaining short-term financing.

Loans Secured by Inventory Normally, manufacturers, wholesalers, and retailers have large amounts of money invested in finished goods. In addition, manufacturers carry raw materials and work-in-process inventories. All three types of inventory may be pledged as collateral for short-term loans. However, lenders prefer the much more salable finished merchandise to raw materials or work-in-process inventories.

A lender may insist that inventory used as collateral be stored in a public warehouse. In such a case, the receipt issued by the warehouse is retained by the lender. Without this receipt, the public warehouse will not release the merchandise. The lender releases the warehouse receipt—and the merchandise—to the borrower when the borrowed money is repaid. In addition to paying the interest on the loan, the borrower must pay for storage in the public warehouse. As a result, this type of loan is more expensive than an unsecured short-term loan.

Loans Secured by Receivables As defined in Chapter 15, *accounts receivable* are amounts owed to a firm by its customers. They are created when trade credit is given to customers and usually are due within thirty to sixty days. A firm can pledge its accounts receivable as collateral to obtain short-term financing. A lender may advance 70 to 80 percent of the dollar amount of the receivables. First, however, it conducts a thorough investigation to determine the *quality* of the receivables. (The quality of the receivables is the credit standing of the firm's customers, coupled with the customers' ability to repay their credit obligations.) If a favorable determination is made, the loan is approved. When the borrowing firm collects from a customer whose account has been pledged as collateral, it must turn the money over to the lender as partial repayment of the loan. An alternative approach is to notify the borrower's credit customers to make their payments directly to the lender.

Factoring Accounts Receivable

Accounts receivable may be used in one other way to help raise short-term financing: They can be sold to a factoring company (or factor). A **factor** is a firm that specializes in buying other firms' accounts receivable. The factor buys the accounts receivable for less than their face value, but it collects the full dollar amount when each account is due. The factor's profit thus is the difference between the face value of the accounts receivable and the amount the factor has paid for them. Generally, the amount of profit the factor receives is based on the risk the factor assumes. Risk, in this case, is the probability that the accounts receivable will not be repaid when they mature.

Even though the firm selling its accounts receivable gets less than face value, it does receive needed cash immediately. Moreover, it has shifted both the task of collecting and the risk of nonpayment to the factor, which now owns the accounts receivable. In many cases, the firm selling its accounts receivable must obtain approval from the factor *before* selling merchandise to a credit customer. Thus, the firm receives instant feedback on whether the factor will purchase the credit customer's account. Generally, customers whose accounts receivable have been factored are given instructions to make their payments directly to the factor.

Cost Comparisons

Table 16.2 compares the various types of short-term financing. As you can see, trade credit is the least expensive. Factoring of accounts receivable is typically the highest-cost method shown.

For many purposes, short-term financing suits a firm's needs perfectly. At other times, however, long-term financing may be more appropriate. In this case, a business may try to raise equity capital or long-term debt capital.

factor a firm that specializes in buying other firms' accounts receivable

Concept Check

1. How important is trade credit as a source of short-term financing?

2. Why would a supplier require a customer to sign a promissory note?

3. What is the prime rate? Who gets the prime rate?

4. Explain how factoring works. Of what benefit is factoring to a firm that sells its receivables?

TABLE 16.2: Comparison of Short-Term Financing Methods

Type of Financing	Cost	Repayment Period	Businesses That May Use It	Comments
Trade credit	Low, if any	30–60 days	All businesses with good credit	Usually no finance charge
Promissory note issued to suppliers	Moderate	1 year or less	All businesses	Usually unsecured but requires legal document
Unsecured bank loan	Moderate	1 year or less	All businesses	Promissory note, a line of credit, or revolving credit agreement generally required
Commercial paper	Moderate	1 year or less	Large corporations with high credit ratings	Available only to large firms
Secured loan	High	1 year or less	Firms with questionable credit ratings	Inventory or accounts receivable often used as collateral
Factoring	High	None	Firms that have large numbers of credit customers	Accounts receivable sold to a factor

Sources of Equity Financing

Evaluate the advantages and disadvantages of equity financing.

Sources of long-term financing vary with the size and type of business. As mentioned earlier, a sole proprietorship or partnership acquires equity capital (sometimes referred to as *owner's equity*) when the owner or owners invest money in the business. For corporations, equity-financing options include the sale of stock and the use of profits not distributed to owners. All three types of businesses also can obtain venture capital and use long-term debt capital (borrowed money) to meet their financial needs. Different types of debt capital are discussed in the next section. Regardless of the type of long-term financing chosen, most financial managers have found that financing is more expensive and harder to obtain since the recent financial crisis. Both investors and lenders are more cautious than they were before the crisis.

initial public offering (IPO) when a corporation sells common stock to the general public for the first time

investment banking firm an organization that assists corporations in raising funds, usually by helping to sell new issues of stocks, bonds, or other financial securities

Selling Stock

Some equity capital is used to start every business—sole proprietorship, partnership, or corporation. In the case of corporations, stockholders who buy shares in the company provide equity capital.

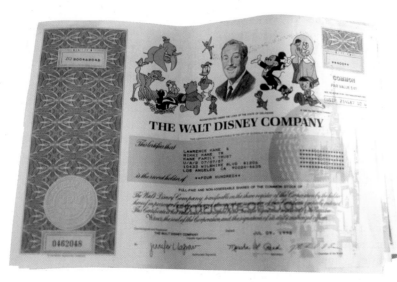

Initial Public Offerings An **initial public offering (IPO)** occurs when a corporation sells common stock to the general public for the first time. In 2009, Rosetta Stone, a company known for providing software that helps people learn foreign languages, used an IPO to raise $112.5 million that could be used to fund business expansion and other business activities.[10] Established companies that plan to raise capital by selling subsidiaries to the public also can use IPOs. For example, Bristol Myers Squibb sold shares in its Mead Johnson Nutrition subsidiary. The Mead Johnson IPO raised approximately $700 million. Bristol Meyers

Squibb used the money it received from the IPO to repay intercompany obligations and expansion of its current business activities.[11]

A corporation selling stock often will use an **investment banking firm**—an organization that assists corporations in raising funds, usually by helping to sell new issues of stocks, bonds, or other financial securities. The investment banking firm generally charges a fee of 2 to 20 percent of the proceeds received by the corporation issuing the securities. The size of the commission depends on the financial health of the corporation issuing the new securities and the size of the new security issue.

Even though the cost of selling stock (often referred to as *flotation costs*) is high, the *ongoing* costs associated with this type of equity financing are low for two reasons. First, the corporation does not have to repay money obtained from the sale of stock because the corporation is under no legal obligation to do so. If you purchase corporate stock and later decide to sell your stock, you may sell it to another investor—not the corporation.

A second advantage of selling stock is that a corporation is under no legal obligation to pay dividends to stockholders. In Chapter 4, a *dividend* was defined as a distribution of earnings to the stockholders of a corporation. For any reason (if a company has a bad year, for example), the board of directors can vote to omit dividend payments. Earnings then are retained for use in funding business operations. Of course, corporate management may hear from unhappy stockholders if expected dividends are omitted too frequently.

There are two types of stock: common and preferred. Each type has advantages and drawbacks as a means of long-term financing.

Common Stock As discussed in Chapter 4, a share of *common stock* represents the most basic form of corporate ownership. In return for the financing provided by selling common stock, management must make certain concessions to stockholders that may restrict or change corporate policies. By law, every corporation must hold an annual meeting, at which the holders of common stock may vote for the board of directors and approve or disapprove major corporate actions. Among such actions are:

1. Amendments to the corporate charter or corporate by-laws
2. Sale of certain assets
3. Mergers and acquisitions
4. New issues of preferred stock or bonds
5. Changes in the amount of common stock issued

Few investors will buy common stock unless they believe that their investment will increase in value.

Is it Ethical?

AIG Pays out after the Bailout

The ailing insurer American International Group—known as AIG—received access to more than $100 billion in bailout loans from the U.S. government to keep it afloat during the recent economic crisis. However, even as AIG sold off units and slashed costs to stabilize its finances, a controversial decision to pay executive bonuses sparked widespread outrage.

Although multimillion-dollar bonuses are not uncommon in the financial services industry, critics objected to AIG paying bonuses to the senior managers who headed the division that was largely responsible for its losses. The insurer argued that it was contractually obligated to pay and could not legally withhold the bonuses. It also noted that these managers had the specialized knowledge and skill needed to help fix AIG's problems. Therefore, keeping them as employees would be in the best interests of the firm and the American taxpayers who funded the bailout.

Under extraordinary pressure, AIG's CEO asked managers to return at least half their bonuses. Many did, giving back more than $30 million in bonus payments. The CEO also stated that "the recent vilification and harassment of AIG employees is grossly unfair and unwarranted" because they had successfully reduced the firm's risk. Still, when Congress voted to let AIG borrow another $30 billion, it deducted $165 million—the total amount of the controversial bonuses—and set strict rules limiting executive compensation and corporate expenses. Weeks later, the U.S. Treasury appointed a Washington lawyer to set compensation for top executives at AIG and six other firms receiving bailout loans.

Sources: Stephen Labaton, "Treasury to Set Executives' Pay at 7 Ailing Firms," *New York Times*, June 11, 2009, p. A1; Liam Pleven, "AIG Rescue Didn't End Bonus Pay," *Wall Street Journal*, May 14, 2009, p. C3; Randall Sith, Jonathan Weisman, and Liam Pleven, "Some at AIG Buck Efforts to Give Back Bonus Pay," *Wall Street Journal*, March 29, 2009, p. C1; Lavonne Kuykendall and Bhattiprolu Murti, "Moving the Market: AIG Gets Aid, Minus Bonus Pay," *Wall Street Journal*, April 21, 2009, p. C3.

Spotlight

IPOs Can Raise Billions!

The four all time largest IPOs are listed below.

$17.9 billion — Visa
$10.6 billion — AT&T Wireless
$8.7 billion — Kraft Foods
$5.5 billion — UPS

Source: The Renaissance Capital IPO Home website, www.ipohome.com, accessed May 24, 2009.

Basically, there are three ways to profit from stock investments:

• From dividend payments.
• From an increase in the value of the stock.
• Because of stock splits.

More information on the reasons why investors purchase stocks and how to evaluate stock investments is provided in Appendix A on Personal Finances and Investments.

Preferred Stock As noted in Chapter 4, the owners of *preferred stock* must receive their dividends before holders of common stock receive theirs. Moreover, the preferred stock dividend amount is specified on the stock certificate. Even so, as with common stock, the board of directors must approve dividends on preferred stock. Also, the owners of preferred stock have first claim, after bond owners and general creditors, on corporate assets if the firm is dissolved or enters bankruptcy. For investors, these features make preferred stock a more conservative investment with an added degree of safety and a more predictable source of income when compared with common stock. In return for preferential treatment, preferred stockholders generally give up the right to vote at a corporation's annual meeting.

To make preferred stock more attractive to investors, some corporations include a conversion feature. **Convertible preferred stock** is preferred stock that an owner may exchange for a specified number of shares of common stock. The Textron Corporation—a manufacturer of component parts for the automotive and aerospace industries—has issued convertible preferred stock. Each share of Textron preferred stock is convertible to 8.8 shares of the firm's common stock.[12] This conversion feature provides the investor with the safety of preferred stock and the hope of greater speculative gain through conversion to common stock.

Retained Earnings

Most large corporations distribute only a portion of their after-tax earnings to stockholders. The portion of a corporation's profits *not* distributed to stockholders is called **retained earnings**. Because they are undistributed profits, retained earnings are considered a form of equity financing.

The amount of retained earnings in any year is determined by corporate management and approved by the board of directors. Most small and growing corporations pay no cash dividend—or a very small dividend—to their stockholders. All or most earnings are reinvested in the business for research and development, expansion, or the funding of major projects. Reinvestment tends to increase the value of the firm's stock while it provides essentially cost-free financing for the business. More mature corporations may distribute 40 to 60 percent of their after-tax profits as dividends. Utility companies and other corporations with very stable earnings often pay out as much as 80 to 90 percent of what they earn. For a large corporation, retained earnings can amount to a hefty bit of financing. For example, in 2008, the total amount of retained earnings for IBM was just over $70 billion.[13]

Venture Capital and Private Placements

To establish a new business or expand an existing one, an entrepreneur may try to obtain venture capital. In Chapter 5, we defined *venture capital* as money invested

convertible preferred stock preferred stock that an owner may exchange for a specified number of shares of common stock

retained earnings the portion of a corporation's profits not distributed to stockholders in small (and sometimes struggling) firms that have the potential to become very successful. Most venture capital firms do not invest in the typical small business—a neighborhood convenience store or a local dry cleaner—but in firms that have the potential to become extremely profitable. Generally, a venture capital firm consists of a pool of investors, a traditional partnership established by a wealthy family, or a joint venture formed by corporations with money to invest. In return for financing, these investors generally receive an equity position in the business and share in its profits. Venture capital firms vary in size and scope of interest. Some offer financing for start-up businesses, whereas others finance only established businesses.

Another method of raising capital is through a private placement. A **private placement** occurs when stock and other corporate securities are sold directly to insurance companies, pension funds, or large institutional investors. When compared with selling stocks and other corporate securities to the public, there are often fewer government regulations and the cost is generally less when the securities are sold through a private placement. Typically, terms between the buyer and seller are negotiated when a private placement is used to raise capital.

Sources of Long-Term Debt Financing

6 LEARNING OBJECTIVE

Evaluate the advantages and disadvantages of long-term debt financing.

As we pointed out earlier in this chapter, businesses borrow money on a short-term basis for many valid reasons other than desperation. There are equally valid reasons for long-term borrowing. In addition to using borrowed money to meet the long-term needs listed in Table 16.1, successful businesses often use the financial leverage it creates to improve their financial performance. **Financial leverage** is the use of borrowed funds to increase the return on owners' equity. The principle of financial leverage works as long as a firm's earnings are larger than the interest charged for the borrowed money.

To understand how financial leverage can increase a firm's return on owners' equity, study the information for Texas-based Cypress Springs Plastics presented in Table 16.3. Pete Johnston, the owner of the firm, is trying to decide how best to finance a $100,000 purchase of new high-tech manufacturing equipment. He could borrow the money and pay 9 percent annual interest. As a second option, Johnston could invest an additional $100,000 in the firm. Assuming that the firm

Concept Check

1. What are the advantages of financing through the sale of stock?

2. From a corporation's point of view, how does preferred stock differ from common stock?

3. Where do a corporation's retained earnings come from? What are the advantages of this type of financing?

4. What is venture capital?

TABLE 16.3: Analysis of the Effect of Additional Capital from Debt or Equity for Cypress Springs Plastics, Inc.

Additional Debt		Additional Equity	
Owners' equity	$ 500,000	Owners' equity	$ 500,000
Additional equity	+0	Additional equity	+100,000
Total equity	$ 500,000	Total equity	$ 600,000
Loan (@ 9 percent)	+100,000	No loan	+0
Total capital	$ 600,000	Total capital	$ 600,000
Year-End Earnings			
Gross profit	$ 95,000	Gross profit	$ 95,000
Less loan interest	−9,000	No interest	−0
Operating profit	$ 86,000	Operating profit	$ 95,000
Return on owners' equity	17.2%	Return on owners' equity	15.8%
($86,000 ÷ $500,000 = 17.2%)		($95,000 ÷ $600,00 0 = 15.8%)	

private placement occurs when stock and other corporate securities are sold directly to insurance companies, pension funds, or large institutional investors

financial leverage the use of borrowed funds to increase the return on owners' equity earns $95,000 a year and that annual interest for this loan totals $9,000 ($100,000 × 0.09 = $9,000), the return on owners' equity for Cypress Springs Plastics would be higher if the firm borrowed the additional financing. Return on owners' equity—a topic covered in Chapter 15—is determined by dividing a firm's net income by the dollar amount of owners' equity. For Cypress Springs Plastics, return on owners' equity equals 17.2 percent ($86,000 ÷ $500,000 = 0.172, or 17.2 percent) if Johnston borrows the additional $100,000. The firm's return on owners' equity would decrease to 15.8 percent ($95,000 ÷ $600,000 = 0.158, or 15.8 percent) if Johnston invests an additional $100,000 in the business.

The most obvious danger when using financial leverage is that the firm's earnings may be less than expected. If this situation occurs, the fixed interest charge actually works to reduce or eliminate the return on owners' equity. Of course, borrowed money eventually must be repaid. Finally, because lenders always have the option to turn down a loan request, many managers are reluctant to rely on borrowed money.

For a small business, long-term debt financing generally is limited to loans. Large corporations have the additional option of issuing corporate bonds.

Long-Term Loans

Many businesses finance their long-range activities such as those listed in Table 16.1 with loans from commercial banks, and other financial institutions. Manufacturers and suppliers of heavy machinery also may provide long-term debt financing by granting extended credit to their customers.

Term-Loan Agreements When the loan repayment period is longer than one year, the borrower must sign a term-loan agreement. A **term-loan agreement** is a promissory note that requires a borrower to repay a loan in monthly, quarterly, semiannual, or annual installments. Although repayment may be as long as fifteen to twenty years, long-term business loans normally are repaid in three to seven years.

Assume that Pete Johnston, the owner of Cypress Springs Plastics, decides to borrow $100,000 and take advantage of the principle of financial leverage illustrated in Table 16.3. Although the firm's return on owners' equity does increase, interest must be paid each year, and eventually, the loan must be repaid. To pay off a $100,000 loan over a three-year period with annual payments, Cypress Springs Plastics must pay $33,333 on the loan balance plus $9,000 annual interest, or a total of $42,333 the first year. While the amount of interest decreases each year because of the previous year's payment on the loan balance, annual payments of this amount are still a large commitment for a small firm such as Cypress Springs Plastics.

The interest rate and repayment terms for term loans often are based on such factors as the reasons for borrowing, the borrowing firm's credit rating, and the value of collateral. Although long-term loans occasionally may be unsecured, the lender usually requires some type of collateral. Acceptable collateral includes real estate, machinery, and equipment. Lenders also may require that borrowers maintain a minimum amount of working capital.

The Basics of Getting a Loan According to many financial experts, preparation is the key when applying for a long-term business loan. In reality, preparation begins before you ever apply for the loan. To begin the process, you should get to know potential lenders before requesting debt financing. While there may be many potential lenders that can provide the money you need, the logical place to borrow money is where your business does its banking. This fact underscores the importance of maintaining adequate balances in the firm's bank accounts. Before applying for a loan, you also may want to check your firm's credit rating with a national credit bureau such as D&B (formerly known as Dun & Bradstreet).

Typically, business owners will be asked to fill out a loan application. In addition to the loan application, the lender also will want to see your current business plan. Be sure to explain what your business is, how much funding you require to

term-loan agreement a promissory note that requires a borrower to repay a loan in monthly, quarterly, semiannual, or annual installments accomplish your goals and objectives, and how the loan will be repaid. Next, have your certified public accountant (CPA) prepare financial statements. Most lenders insist that you submit current financial statements that have been prepared by an independent CPA. Then compile a list of references that includes your suppliers, other lenders, or the professionals with whom you are associated. Once you submit your application, business plan, and supporting financial documents, a bank officer or a loan committee will examine the loan application. You also may be asked to discuss the loan request with a loan officer. Hopefully, your loan request will be approved. If not, try to determine why your loan request was rejected. Think back over the loan process and determine what you could do to improve your chances of getting a loan the next time you apply.

Corporate Bonds

In addition to loans, large corporations may choose to issue bonds in denominations of $1,000 to $50,000. Although the usual face value for corporate bonds is $1,000, the total face value of all the bonds in an issue usually amounts to millions of dollars. In fact, one of the reasons why corporations sell bonds is that they can borrow a lot of money from a lot of different bondholders and raise larger amounts of money than could be borrowed from one lender. A **corporate bond** is a corporation's written pledge that it will repay a specified amount of money with interest. The **maturity date**, for a corporate bond, is the date on which the corporation is to repay the borrowed money.

Until a bond's maturity, a corporation pays interest to the bond owner at the stated rate. Owners of the Alcoa corporate bond that matures in 2013 receive 6 percent per year for each bond. Because interest for corporate bonds is usually paid semi-annually, bond owners receive a payment every six months for each bond they own.

Types of Bonds Today, most corporate bonds are registered bonds. A **registered bond** is a bond registered in the owner's name by the issuing company. Until the maturity date, the registered owner receives periodic interest payments. On the maturity date, the owner receives cash equaling the face value. Corporate bonds generally are classified as debentures, mortgage bonds, or convertible bonds. Most corporate bonds are debenture bonds.

- *Debenture bonds* are backed only by the reputation of the issuing corporation.
- *Mortgage bonds* are secured by various assets of the issuing firm.
- *Convertible bonds* can be exchanged, at the owner's option, for a specified number of shares of the corporation's common stock.

Repayment Provisions for Corporate Bonds Maturity dates for bonds generally range from ten to thirty years after the date of issue. If the interest is not paid or the firm becomes insolvent, bond owners' claims on the assets of the corporation take precedence over the claims of both common and preferred stockholders. Some bonds are callable before the maturity date; that is, a corporation can buy back, or redeem them. For these bonds, the corporation may pay the bond owner a call premium. The amount of the call premium, if any, is specified, along with other provisions, in the bond indenture. The **bond indenture** is a legal document that details all the conditions relating to a bond issue.

Before deciding if bonds are the best way to obtain corporate financing, managers must determine if the company can afford to pay the interest on the corporate bonds. It should be obvious that the larger the bond issue, the higher the dollar amount of interest will be. For example, assume that American Express issues bonds with a face value of $100 million. If the interest rate is 4.875 percent, the interest on this bond issue is $4,875,000 ($100 million $\times$ 0.04875 = $4,875,000) each year until the bonds are repaid. In addition, corporate bonds must be redeemed for their face value at maturity. If the corporation defaults on (does not pay) either interest payments or repayment of the bond at maturity, owners of bonds can force the firm into bankruptcy.

corporate bond a corporation's written pledge that it will repay a specified amount of money with interest

maturity date the date on which a corporation is to repay borrowed money

registered bond a bond registered in the owner's name by the issuing company

bond indenture a legal document that details all the conditions relating to a bond issue

A corporation may use one of three methods to ensure that it has sufficient funds available to redeem a bond issue. First, it can issue the bonds as **serial bonds**, which are bonds of a single issue that mature on different dates. For example, a company may use a twenty-five-year $50 million bond issue to finance its expansion. None of the bonds mature during the first fifteen years. Thereafter, 10 percent of the bonds mature each year until all the bonds are retired at the end of the twenty-fifth year. Second, the corporation can establish a sinking fund. A **sinking fund** is a sum of money to which deposits are made each year for the purpose of redeeming a bond issue. When Union Pacific Corporation sold a $275 million bond issue, the company agreed to contribute to a sinking fund until the bond's maturity in the year 2025.[14] Third, a corporation can pay off an old bond issue by selling new bonds. Although this may appear to perpetuate the corporation's long-term debt, a number of utility companies and railroads use this repayment method.

A corporation that issues bonds also must appoint a **trustee**, an individual or an independent firm that acts as the bond owners' representative. A trustee's duties are handled most often by a commercial bank or other large financial institution. The corporation must report to the trustee periodically regarding its ability to make interest payments and eventually redeem the bonds. In turn, the trustee transmits this information to the bond owners, along with its own evaluation of the corporation's ability to pay.

Cost Comparisons

Table 16.4 compares some of the methods that can be used to obtain long-term equity *and* debt financing. Although the initial flotation cost of issuing stock is high, selling common stock generally is the first choice for most financial managers. Once the stock is sold and upfront costs are paid, the *ongoing* costs of using stock to finance a business are low. The type of long-term financing that generally has the highest *ongoing* costs is a long-term loan (debt).

To a great extent, firms are financed through the investments of individuals—money that people have deposited in banks or have used to purchase stocks, mutual funds, and bonds. In Appendix A, we look at personal finance and how people invest their money in business.

TABLE 16.4: Comparison of Long-Term Financing Methods

Type of Financing	Repayment	Repayment Period	Cost/Dividends Interest	Businesses That May Use It
Equity				
Common stock	No	None	High initial cost; low ongoing costs because dividends not required	All corporations that sell stock to investors
Preferred stock	No	None	Dividends not required but must be paid before common stockholders receive any dividends	Large corporations that have an established investor base of common stockholders
Debt				
Long-term loan	Yes	Usually 3–7 years	Interest rates between 6 and 12 percent depending on economic conditions and the financial stability of the company requesting the loan	All firms that can meet the lender's repayment and collateral requirements
Corporate bond	Yes	Usually 10–30 years	Interest rates between 5 and 10 percent depending on economic conditions and the financial stability of the company issuing the bonds	Large corporations that are financially healthy

SUMMARY

1 Explain the need for financial management in business.

Financial management consists of all activities concerned with obtaining money and using it effectively. Short-term financing is money that will be used for one year or less. There are many short-term needs, but cash flow and inventory are two for which financing is often required. Long-term financing is money that will be used for more than one year. Such financing may be required for a business start-up, for a merger or an acquisition, for new product development, for long-term marketing activities, for replacement of equipment, or for expansion of facilities. Financial management can be viewed as a two-sided problem. On one side, the uses of funds often dictate the type or types of financing needed by a business. On the other side, the activities a business can undertake are determined by the types of financing available. Financial managers also must consider the risk-return ratio when making decisions. The risk-return ratio is based on the principle that a high-risk decision should generate higher financial returns for a business. On the other hand, more conservative decisions generate lesser returns. Financial managers must ensure that funds are available when needed, that they are obtained at the lowest possible cost, and that they are available for the repayment of debts.

2 Summarize the process of planning for financial management.

A financial plan begins with an organization's goals and objectives. Next, these goals and objectives are "translated" into departmental budgets that detail expected income and expenses. From these budgets, which may be combined into an overall cash budget, the financial manager determines what funding will be needed and where it may be obtained. Whereas departmental and cash budgets emphasize short-term financing needs, a capital budget can be used to estimate a firm's expenditures for major assets and its long-term financing needs. The four principal sources of financing are sales revenues, equity capital, debt capital, and proceeds from the sale of assets. Once the needed funds have been obtained, the financial manager is responsible for ensuring that they are used properly. This is accomplished through a system of monitoring and evaluating the firm's financial activities.

3 Identify the services provided by banks and financial institutions for their business customers.

Banks and other financial institutions offer today's customers a tempting array of services. Among the most important and attractive banking services are savings accounts, checking accounts, short- and long-term loans, and credit-card and debit-card processing. The use of technology will increase as financial institutions continue to offer online banking. Increased use of electronic funds transfer systems (automated clearinghouses, point-of-sale terminals, and electronic check conversion) also will change the way people bank. For firms in the global marketplace, a bank can provide letters of credit and banker's acceptances that will reduce the risk of nonpayment for sellers. Banks and financial institutions also can provide currency exchange to reduce payment problems for import or export transactions.

4 Describe the advantages and disadvantages of different methods of short-term debt financing.

Most short-term financing is unsecured; that is, no collateral is required. Sources of unsecured short-term financing include trade credit, promissory notes issued to suppliers, unsecured bank loans, and commercial paper. Sources of secured short-term financing include loans secured by inventory and accounts receivable. A firm also may sell its receivables to factors. Trade credit is the least expensive source of short-term financing. The cost of financing through other sources generally depends on the source and on the credit rating of the firm that requires the financing. Factoring generally is the most expensive approach.

5 Evaluate the advantages and disadvantages of equity financing.

A corporation can raise equity capital by selling either common or preferred stock. Common stock is voting stock; holders of common stock elect the corporation's directors and must approve changes to the corporate charter. Investors can profit from common stock investments from dividend payments, from an increase in the value of the stock, and because of stock splits. Holders of preferred stock must be paid dividends before holders of common stock are paid any dividends. Another source of equity funding is retained earnings, which is the portion of a business's profits not distributed to stockholders. Venture capital—money invested in small (and sometimes struggling) firms that have the potential to become very successful—is yet another source of equity funding. Generally, the venture capital is provided by investors, partnerships established by wealthy families, or a joint venture formed by corporations with money to invest. In return, they receive an equity position in the firm and share in the profits of the business. Finally, a private placement can be used to sell stocks and other corporate securities.

6 Evaluate the advantages and disadvantages of long-term debt financing.

For a small business, debt financing generally is limited to loans. Large corporations have the additional option of issuing corporate bonds. Regardless of whether the business is small or large, it can take advantage of financial leverage. Financial leverage is the use of borrowed funds to increase the return on owners' equity. The rate of interest for long-term loans usually depends on the financial status of the borrower, the reason for borrowing, and the kind of collateral pledged to back up the loan. Long-term business loans normally are repaid in three to seven years but can be as long as fifteen to twenty years. Money realized from the sale of corporate bonds must be repaid when the bonds mature. In addition, the corporation must pay interest on that money from the time the bonds are sold until maturity. Maturity dates for bonds generally range from ten to thirty years after the date of issue. Three types of bonds—debentures, mortgage bonds, and convertible bonds—are sold to raise debt capital. When comparing the cost of equity and debt long-term financing, the ongoing costs of using stock (equity) to finance a business are low. The most expensive is a long-term loan (debt).

KEY TERMS

You should now be able to define and give an example relevant to each of the following terms:

financial management (446)
short-term financing (446)
cash flow (446)
speculative production (446)
long-term financing (448)
risk-return ratio (448)
chief financial officer (CFO) (449)
financial plan (450)
budget (451)
cash budget (451)
capital budget (451)
equity capital (451)
debt capital (451)

certificate of deposit (453)
check (453)
line of credit (453)
revolving credit agreement (454)
collateral (454)
debit card (455)
electronic funds transfer (EFT) system (455)
letter of credit (455)
banker's acceptance (456)
unsecured financing (457)
trade credit (457)
promissory note (457)

prime interest rate (458)
commercial paper (458)
factor (459)
initial public offering (IPO) (460)
investment banking firm (460)
convertible preferred stock (462)
retained earnings (462)
private placement (463)
financial leverage (463)
term-loan agreement (464)
corporate bond (465)

maturity date (465)
registered bond (465)
bond indenture (465)
serial bonds (466)
sinking fund (466)
trustee (466)

DISCUSSION QUESTIONS

1. During the recent financial crisis, many financial managers and corporate officers have been criticized for (a) poor decisions, (b) lack of ethical behavior, (c) large salaries, (d) lucrative severance packages worth millions of dollars, and (e) extravagant lifestyles. Is this criticism justified? Justify your opinion.

2. What does a financial manager do? How can he or she monitor a firm's financial success?

3. If you were the financial manager of Stars and Stripes Clothing, what would you do with the excess cash that the firm expects in the second and fourth quarters? (See Figure 16.4.)

4. Develop a *personal* cash budget for the next six months. Explain what you would do if there are budget shortfalls or excess cash amounts at the end of any month during the six-month period.

5. Why would a lender offer unsecured loans when it could demand collateral?

6. How can a small-business owner or corporate manager use financial leverage to improve the firm's profits and return on owners' equity?

7. In what circumstances might a large corporation sell stock rather than bonds to obtain long-term financing? In what circumstances would it sell bonds rather than stock?

Get Flash Cards, Quizzes, Games, Crosswords and more @ www.cengage.com/introbusiness/pride

Test Yourself

Matching Questions

1. _____ It is the movement of money into and out of a business organization.

2. _____ Determining a firm's financial needs is one of its important functions.

3. _____ A loan that is approved before the money is actually needed

4. _____ Funding that comes from the sale of stock.

5. _____ Payments are usually made in 30 to 60 days from the invoice date.

6. _____ Must receive dividends before common stockholders.

7. _____ It is pledged as security for a loan.

8. _____ A method of financing that is a legally binding and enforceable and often issued to suppliers.

9. _____ The deposits are used for redeeming a bond issue.

10. _____ This investment is backed by the reputation of the issuing corporation.

Test Yourself

a. cash flow
b. collateral
c. debenture bond
d. equity capital
e. financial management
f. letter of credit
g. line of credit
h. preferred stock
i. private placement
j. promissory note
k. sinking fund
l. trade credit

True False Questions

11. **T F** Long-term financing is generally used to open new businesses.

12. **T F** A budget is a historical record of the previous year's financial activities.

13. **T F** When you use a debit card to make a purchase, a financial institution is extending credit to you and expects to be paid in the future.

14. **T F** With a banker's acceptance, certain conditions, such as delivery of the merchandise, may be specified before payment is made.

15. **T F** Most lenders do not require collateral for short-term financing.

16. **T F** A revolving credit agreement is a guaranteed line of credit.

17. **T F** Factoring of accounts receivable typically is the highest cost method of short-term financing.

18. **T F** Normally, the usual repayment period for a long-term loan is 3 to 7 years.

19. **T F** The face value for most corporate bonds is $5,000.

20. **T F** A capital budget estimates a firm's expenditures for labor costs.

Multiple-Choice Questions

21. _____ A written order for a bank or other financial institution to pay a stated dollar amount to a specified business or person is called a
    a. check
    b. deposit slip
    c. notes receivable
    d. receipt
    e. debit memorandum

22. _____ Judy Martinez, owner of Judy's Fashions, received a $12,000 tax refund. She deposited the money in Chase Bank. The terms of the agreement are that she must leave the money on deposit for three years and the bank will pay her 3 percent interest. Her account is a
    a. line of credit.
    b. certificate of deposit.
    c. checking account.
    d. commercial paper agreement.
    e. savings account.

23. _____ An invoice in the amount of $200 carries cash terms of "2/10, net 30." If the buyer takes advantage of the discount terms, how much will the buyer pay?
    a. $100
    b. $120
    c. $140
    d. $160
    e. $196

24. _____ When a firm sells its accounts receivable to raise short-term cash, it is engaging in a strategy called
    a. factoring.
    b. financial planning.
    c. equity financing.
    d. debt financing.
    e. drafting.

25. _____ Retained earnings, as a form of equity financing, are
    a. gross earnings.
    b. profits before taxes.
    c. profits after taxes.
    d. undistributed profits.
    e. total owners' equity.

26. _____ Since prices are extremely low, the Pipeline Supply Company wants to purchase a special line of pipes from a company going out of business. Pipeline, however, will need to borrow money to make this deal. Which assets will Pipeline most commonly pledge as collateral for this short-term loan?
    a. delivery equipment
    b. notes payable
    c. manufacturing equipment
    d. owners' equity
    e. inventory

27. _____ The most basic form of corporate ownership that has voting rights is
    a. preferred stock.
    b. common stock.
    c. retained stock.
    d. deferred value stock.
    e. treasury stock.

Test Yourself

28. _____ A short-term promissory note issued by large corporations is known as

    a. debenture agreement.
    b. equity agreement.
    c. commercial paper.
    d. draft agreement.
    e. loan commitment.

29. _____ Each of the following causes a cash flow problem except

    a. embezzlement of company funds.
    b. an unexpected slow selling season.
    c. a large number of credit sales.
    d. slow-paying customers.
    e. customers who pay early.

30. _____ The primary sources of funds available to a business include all of the following except

    a. debt capital.
    b. equity capital.
    c. sales revenue.
    d. government grants.
    e. sale of assets.

Answers on p. TY-2

VIDEO CASE

Pizzeria Uno

Profit margins in the restaurant business average three to five cents of every dollar of revenue. When you're managing pennies, accounting for them is critical to growing a successful business. Pizzeria Uno has learned to manage its financials effectively and grow dramatically.

The Pizzeria Uno Restaurant Corporation started in 1943 and was taken public in 1987. Currently the chain operates in 31 states and four foreign countries with more than 200 restaurants, both franchised and company-owned. Its average restaurant generates $2 million in revenues annually.

Financial management for Uno starts at the store level, where the firm employs sophisticated accounting mechanisms to manage the cost structure of the business. The management team in each restaurant is primarily responsible for collecting data through point-of-sale computers that send information to a corporate database every night. These computers collect data about sales (what people are buying), supplies needed to replenish inventories (what items have been sold that day), and employees' hours and wage rates.

Uno has developed a cost control model that determines what its food and drink costs should be, based on experience and the current menu mix. For example, based on the model, Uno expects each restaurant to sell twenty ounces of Jack Daniels liquor in a particular day. However, if the cost control system shows one restaurant incurring a cost for twenty-five ounces but selling only twenty, the company is paying for five ounces that cannot be accounted for. If Uno is planning to run the business at 25 percent of the cost of sales, and the data indicate one of the restaurants is actually running at 27 percent of the cost of sales, then corporate management will want to know why there is a discrepancy. Either the drink has been given away or the bartenders have been overportioning the beverages

The restaurant business is a cash business, and Uno is able to use working capital to its advantage. Because the company is dealing with rapidly consumed products, it has the luxury of using its vendors'/suppliers' money to fund its operations.

If the restaurants buy a food product on a thirty-day net pay basis and sell the item within a day, Uno can have the use of that money for more than three weeks before it has to pay the supplier. Compare that to a manufacturing company. When an auto company builds an automobile, it has to buy the steel to make the car long before it sells the car. Manufacturing companies have to spend working capital to build up their inventory before they can sell that inventory for cash.

Effectively managing its balance sheet is a key component in ensuring that Uno continues to improve shareholder value. Debt is an important tool that it uses to build equity. If Uno can borrow money at 7 percent and put it to use in its restaurants that return 30 percent, it has earned 23 percent on someone else's money—an impressive return on debt.

Building restaurants is capital-intensive. The average Uno restaurant costs $1.6–$1.7 million in upfront capital to build, excluding the land. The company has typically bought the land, which can be a risk since ownership does not result in a high return on assets. However, it does allow the company to control its own destiny and future, and to lock in a large component of its expansion costs. The company uses long-term debt and, in some cases, mortgage debt to finance its land purchases. By using debt, Uno increases its return on equity as long as its earnings are higher than the interest charged for the borrowed money. And history shows that, more often than not, land values increase over time. The bottom line is that Uno has been able to manage its balance sheet and avoid tipping its debt-equity ratio.

Pizzeria Uno's goal is to operate in the top echelon of restaurant companies. The company believes that despite a recession that has hammered the restaurant industry, it can continue to manage its business to improve profitability, return on sales, and return on capital and to drive net income and earnings per share. Uno's stated goal is to grow its business 20–25 percent annually, measured in earnings per share.

For more information on this company, go to www.pizzeria-uno.com.

Questions

1. What are the primary sources of funds that Pizzeria Uno uses to run its business, and how does it use these funds?
2. How does Uno monitor and evaluate the financial performance of its restaurants?
3. Pizzeria Uno typically buys the land on which it builds new restaurants because it allows the company "to control its own destiny and future." What are some possible disadvantages to this practice?

BUILDING SKILLS FOR CAREER SUCCESS

1. EXPLORING THE INTERNET

Finding capital for new business start-ups is never an easy task. Besides a good business plan, those seeking investor funds must be convincing and clear about how their business activities will provide sufficient revenue to pay back investors who help to get them going in the first place. To find out what others have done, it is useful to read histories of successful start-ups as well as failures in journals that specialize in this area. Visit the text website for updates to this exercise.

Assignment

1. Examine articles that profile at least three successes or failures in the following publications and highlight the main points that led to either result.
   Business 2.0 (**www.business2.com**)
   Red Herring (**www.redherring.com**)
   Fast Company (**www.fastcompany.com**)
2. What are the shared similarities?
3. What advice would you give to a start-up venture after reading these stories?

2. BUILDING TEAM SKILLS

Suppose that for the past three years you have been repairing lawn mowers in your garage. Your business has grown steadily, and recently, you hired two part-time workers. Your garage is no longer adequate for your business; it is also in violation of the city code, and you have been fined twice for noncompliance. You have decided that it is time to find another location for your shop and that it also would be a good time to expand your business. If the business continues to grow in the new location, you plan to hire a full-time employee to repair small appliances. You are concerned, however, about how you will get the money to move your shop and get it established in a new location.

Assignment

1. With all class members participating, use brainstorming to identify the following:

   a. The funds you will need to accomplish your business goals
   b. The sources of short-term financing available to you
   c. Problems that might prevent you from getting a short-term loan
   d. How you will repay the money if you get a loan
2. Have a classmate write the ideas on the board.
3. Discuss how you can overcome any problems that might hamper your current chances of getting a loan and how your business can improve its chances of securing short-term loans in the future.
4. Summarize what you learned from participating in this exercise.

3. RESEARCHING DIFFERENT CAREERS

Financial managers are responsible for determining the best way to raise funds, for ensuring that the funds are used to accomplish their firm's goals and objectives, and for developing and implementing their firm's financial plan. Their decisions have a direct impact on the firm's level of success. When managers do not pay enough attention to finances, a firm is likely to fail.

Assignment

1. Investigate the job of financial manager by searching the library or Internet and/or by interviewing a financial manager.
2. Find answers to the following questions:
   a. What skills do financial managers need?
   b. How much education is required?
   c. What is the starting salary? Top salary?
   d. What will the job of financial manager be like in the future?
   e. What opportunities are available?
   f. What types of firms are most likely to hire financial managers? What is the employment potential?
3. Prepare a report on your findings.

Like the hole in a bagel, any hole in Finagle A Bagel's accounting and financial management systems means less dough for the company. Copresidents Alan Litchman and Laura Trust could not profitably build the business without quick access to details such as how much money the stores take in, how much money is spent on ingredients, how much money is needed for rent, and so on.

Tracking Sales, Cash, and Profits

Regina Jerome is Finagle A Bagel's director of information systems. She and her assistant are responsible for running the computerized accounting system as well as for the point-of-sale system that stores use to ring up all customer orders. "Every transaction in every store is recorded and can be retrieved by minute, by day, by store, by cashier, and by terminal," notes Jerome. The copresidents use all this financial data to reconcile daily store sales with daily bank deposits.

As a result, copresident Litchman knows by 7:30 each morning how much money was deposited on the previous day and the total amount the company has to cover payroll, food purchases, and other expenses. He also knows if a store's reported sales match its bank deposit. If not, a senior manager immediately looks into the discrepancy, which usually turns out to be some kind of error. Once in a while, however, the discrepancy is a sign of store-level theft that requires further investigation and—when warranted—legal action.

Although Finagle A Bagel makes about 8 cents in profit from every sales dollar, Litchman is aiming to make a profit of 10 cents per dollar. He needs timely reports showing retailing and wholesaling revenues, the cost of goods sold, and operating expenses to calculate the company's pretax profit and measure progress toward this profit goal. Food and labor cost constitute more than two-thirds of Finagle A Bagel's costs—so the faster managers can see these numbers, the faster they can act if expenses are higher than expected.

Bagels, Banking, and Borrowing

Like many other entrepreneurs, when Laura Trust and Alan Litchman decided to buy a business, they raised some money from friends and family. Unlike many entrepreneurs, however, they were so adamant about retaining full control of Finagle A Bagel that they never considered venture capital financing or going public. Instead, Litchman says, "We made the decision to get banks to finance this company, which is a difficult thing."

Banks prefer to make loans secured by assets such as inventory or accounts receivable. However, Finagle A Bagel has no inventory aside from each day's raw ingredients and fresh-baked bagels, which cannot be repossessed and resold if the company is unable to repay a loan. Nor does it have

significant accounts receivable because most of its revenues come from cash transactions in the seventeen stores. The company has commercial ovens and other equipment, but, says copresident Litchman, banks do not consider such assets sufficient collateral for a secured loan. And not every bank is willing to offer an unsecured line of credit to a small, fast-growing company like Finagle A Bagel.

Fortunately, the copresidents bought Finagle A Bagel after the previous owner (who stayed on for a time after the purchase) had built the business into a highly successful chain. To a bank, a company with a proven record of success and a detailed, practical business plan for continued growth looks less risky as a borrower than a newly established company without customers, assets, or cash flow. Thus Finagle A Bagel was able to negotiate an unsecured line of credit of nearly $4 million. As long as Trust and Litchman could show that the company was healthy and achieving certain financial ratios, they were allowed to draw on the credit line to open new stores or for other business purposes.

Initially, the copresidents only paid the interest on borrowed money so that they would have more money available for growth. Within a few years, however, they began repaying the principal as well as the interest. This meant less money to fuel growth, but it also lightened the company's debt load.

Juggling Three Banks and Two Checking Accounts

Even though Finagle A Bagel operates numerous stores plus a wholesale division, it deals with three banks and needs only two corporate checking accounts. Here's how the system works: For safety reasons, management does not want general managers or their assistants traveling too far to deposit each day's receipts. So the company deals with three New England banks that have local branches located near the stores. For each store, Finagle A Bagel opens an account in the closest branch of one of these three banks. After the day's deposits are made, money is transferred using an electronic funds transfer system to the company's main checking account.

Every morning, Litchman looks at the current balance in the main checking account and examines the report showing the previous day's sales and deposits. That tells him how much money he has to cover the bills to be paid that day. Given the slim profit margin in the food-service business—only pennies per sales dollar—Finagle A Bagel uses most of its cash to pay for food and labor.

Clearly, cash flow is critical for a small, fast-growing business. Especially on slower sales days, Litchman observes, "You may be one check away from being cash-negative." If its main checking account balance is too low to cover checks that are presented for payment that day, the company may have to draw on its line of credit. Once this happens, the company must pay interest on any money it borrows, even for just a day.

Finagle A Bagel uses its second checking account only for payroll. This is a zero-balance account containing no money because its sole function is to clear payroll checks. Having two checking accounts allows the company to separate its payroll payments from its payments for supplies, rent, and other business expenses, a convenience for tax and accounting purposes. It also helps the copresidents maintain tight financial control: No check can be issued without either Litchman's or Trust's signature.

The Future of Finagle A Bagel

The future of Finagle A Bagel could take a very different turn. "The opportunity to be bought by, just for an example, a McDonald's or a Wendy's or one of the larger operators becomes more plausible as you start to prove to people that you can survive as a multiunit chain with twenty or more stores," says Trust. Because big companies are always on the lookout for innovative food-service concepts, Finagle A Bagel's owners might receive an acquisition offer that's too good to pass up.

A few years ago the company was named Greater Boston's Small Business of the Year, and *Boston* magazine put it on the "Best of Boston" list for two consecutive years. The company also has been named to the list of Top 100 Women-Led Businesses in Massachusetts. As important and gratifying as such honors may be for a small business, money always must be—literally—the bottom line for Finagle A Bagel. "You have to make money," Trust emphasizes. "If you don't make money, you're not in business."

Questions

1. Finagle A Bagel tracks cash, sales revenue, and expenses on a daily basis. How does this type of accounting system encourage effective decision making and discourage store-level theft?
2. As a small business, which of the financial ratios might Finagle A Bagel want to track especially closely? Why?
3. If the copresidents of Finagle A Bagel had approached venture capitalists for funding, they probably would have been able to open more new stores in less time. Instead, they opted to use bank financing that has to be repaid. Do you agree with their decision? Why?
4. Given their growth plans, why would the copresidents repay principal and interest on borrowed money rather than pay interest only? Which repayment plan would Finagle A Bagel's bank prefer?

Now that you have a marketing plan, the next big and important step is to prepare a financial plan. One of the biggest mistakes an entrepreneur makes when faced with a need for financing is not being prepared. Completing this section will show you that if you are prepared and you are creditworthy, the task may be easier than you think. Remember, most lenders and investors insist that you submit current financial statements that have been prepared by an independent certified public accountant (CPA). Chapter 15, "Using Accounting Information," should help you to answer the questions in this part of the business plan.

In this last section, you should provide some information about your exit strategy, and discuss any potential trends, problems, or risks that you may encounter. Now is also the time to go back and prepare the executive summary, which should be placed at the beginning of the business plan.

THE FINANCIAL PLAN COMPONENT

Your financial plan should answer at least the following questions about the investment needed, sales and cash-flow forecasts, breakeven analysis, and sources of funding.

6.1. What is the actual amount of money you need to open your business (start-up budget) and the amount needed to keep it open (operating budget)? Prepare a realistic budget.

6.2. How much money do you have, and how much money will you need to start your business and stay in business?

6.3. Prepare a projected income statement by month for the first year of operation and by quarter for the second and third years.

6.4. Prepare projected balance sheets for each of the first three years of operation.

6.5. Prepare a breakeven analysis. How many units of your products or service will have to be sold to cover your costs?

6.6. Reinforce your final projections by comparing them with industry averages for your chosen industry.

THE EXIT STRATEGY COMPONENT

Your exit strategy component should at least include answers to the following questions:

6.7. How do you intend to get yourself (and your money) out of the business?

6.8. Will your children take over the business, or do you intend to sell it later?

6.9. Do you intend to grow the business to the point of an IPO?

6.10. How will investors get their money back?

THE CRITICAL RISKS AND ASSUMPTIONS COMPONENT

Your critical risks and assumptions component should answer at least the following questions:

6.11. What will you do if your market does not develop as quickly as you predicted? What if your market develops too quickly?

6.12. What will you do if your competitors underprice or make your product obsolete?

6.13. What will you do if there is an unfavorable industrywide trend?

6.14. What will happen if trained workers are not available as predicted?

6.15. What will you do if there is an erratic supply of products or raw materials?

THE APPENDIX COMPONENT

Supplemental information and documents often are included in an appendix. Here are a few examples of some documents that can be included:

- Résumés of owners and principal managers
- Advertising samples and brochures
- An organization chart
- Floor plans

REVIEW OF BUSINESS PLAN ACTIVITIES

As you have discovered, writing a business plan involves a long series of interrelated steps. As with any project involving a number of complex steps and calculations, your business plan should be reviewed carefully and revised before you present it to potential investors.

Remember, there is one more component you need to prepare after your business plan is completed: The executive summary should be written last, but because of its importance, it appears after the introduction.

THE EXECUTIVE SUMMARY COMPONENT

In the executive summary, give a one- to two-page overview of your entire business plan. This is the most important part of the business plan and is of special interest to busy bankers, investors, and other interested parties. Remember, this section is a summary; more detailed information is provided in the remainder of your business plan.

Make sure that the executive summary captures the reader's attention instantly in the first sentence by using a key selling point or benefit of the business.

Your executive summary should include answers to at least the following:

6.16. *Company information.* What product or service do you provide? What is your competitive advantage? When will the company be formed? What are your company objectives? What is the background of you and your management team?

6.17. *Market opportunity.* What is the expected size and growth rate of your market, your expected market share, and any relevant market trends?

Once again, review your answers to all the questions in the preceding parts to make sure that they are all consistent throughout the entire business plan.

Although many would-be entrepreneurs are excited about the prospects of opening their own business, remember that it takes a lot of hard work, time, and in most cases a substantial amount of money. While the business plan provides an enormous amount of information about your business, it is only the first step. Once it is completed, it is now your responsibility to implement the plan. Good luck in your business venture.

The information contained in "Building a Business Plan" will also assist you in completing the online *Interactive Business Plan.*

As the saying goes, "I've been rich and I've been poor, but believe me, rich is better." And yet, just dreaming of being rich doesn't make it happen. In order to be successful, you must be willing to invest the time and effort required to become a good money manager and a good investor. And don't underestimate how important you are when it comes to managing your money. No one is going to make you manage your money. No one is going to make you save the money you need to fund an investment program. These are your decisions—important decisions that literally can change your life.

Many people ask the question: Why begin an investment program now? At the time of publication, this is a very important question given the recent economic crisis. While it's true that many investors have lost a great deal of money as a result of the crisis, the experts all agree that the best investment program is one that stresses long-term growth over a twenty- to forty-year period. Although the dollar value of your investments may decrease over a short time period, historically the value of securities has always increased over a long time period. To illustrate this point, it may help to think of the financial markets as a roller coaster ride with ups (periods of increasing values) and downs (periods of declining values). The recent crisis is a very real example of how worldwide economic problems can cause the value of stocks, bonds, mutual funds, real estate, and other investments to decline. Faced with large dollar losses, many investors make a decision to sell their investments at the bottom of the roller coaster ride. Those investors who decide to hold their investments will eventually see their investments recover and increase in value over time. In fact, many experts recommend buying quality stocks, mutual funds, and real estate during an economic downturn.

A second compelling reason to start an investment program is that the sooner you start an investment program, the more time your investments have to work for you. So why do people wait to begin investing? In most cases, there are two reasons. First, they don't have the money needed to fund an investment program. And yet, once you begin managing your personal finances and get your spending under control, you will be able to save the money needed to fund an investment program. The second reason people don't begin investing is because they don't know anything about investing. Again, the material in this appendix provides the basics to get you started. It is time! Take the first step, and begin managing your personal finances.

Preparing for an Investment Program

While it would be nice if you could accumulate wealth magically, it's not magic. For most people, the first step is to make sure that their "financial house" is in order. In this section, we examine several steps for effective money management that will help you to prepare for an investment program.

Managing Your Personal Finances

Many personal finance experts recommend that you begin the process of managing your money by determining your current financial condition. The first step often is to construct a personal balance sheet and a personal income statement. A *personal balance sheet* lists your assets and liabilities on a specific date. By subtracting the

©Lidija Tomic

total amount of liabilities from the total amount of assets, you can determine your net worth. A *personal income statement* lists your income and your expenses for a specific period of time—usually a month. By subtracting expenses from income, you can determine if you have a surplus or a deficit at the end of the time period. (*Note:* Both personal balance sheets and personal income statements were examined in more detail in Chapter 15.) Based on the information contained in these statements, you can determine your current financial condition and where you spend your money. You also can take the next step: Construct a personal budget.

A **personal budget** is a specific plan for spending your income. You begin by estimating your income for a specific period—for example, next month. For most people, their major source of income is their salary. The second step is to list your expenditures for the same time period. Typical expenditures include savings and investments, housing, food, transportation, entertainment, and so on. For most people, this is the area where you can make choices and increase or decrease the amount spent on different items listed in your budget. Above all, it is important to balance your budget so that your income is equal to the money you spend, save, or invest each month. Unfortunately, many individuals spend more than they make. They purchase items on credit and then must make monthly payments and pay finance charges ranging from 10 to 21 percent. By reducing or eliminating credit purchases, eventually the amount of cash remaining after the bills are paid will increase and can be used to start a savings program or finance investments.

Investment Goals

Personal investment is the use of your personal funds to earn a financial return. Thus, in the most general sense, the goal of investing is to earn money with money. However, such a goal is completely useless for the individual because it is so vague and so easily attained.

In reality, an investment goal must be specific and measurable. It must be tailored to you so that it takes into account your particular financial needs. It also must be oriented toward the future because investing is usually a long-term undertaking. A long-term investment program has a number of advantages. By investing small amounts of money each year over a twenty- to forty-year period, you can accumulate money for emergencies and retirement. Also, if you choose quality investments, the value of your investments will grow over a long period of time. Despite the recent economic crisis, financial experts believe that long-term investors will not only see the value of their investment portfolio recover, but also increase over the next few years. Finally, an investment goal must be realistic in terms of current economic conditions and available investment opportunities.

Some financial planners suggest that investment goals should be stated in terms of money: "By January 1, 2020, I will have total assets of $80,000." Others believe that people are more motivated to work toward goals that are stated in terms of the particular things they desire: "By May 1, 2021, I will have accumulated enough money so that I can take a year off from work to travel around the world." Like the goals themselves, the way they are stated depends on you.

A Personal Investment Program

Once you have formulated specific goals and have some money to invest, investment planning is similar to planning for a business. It begins with the evaluation of different investment opportunities—including the potential return and risk involved in each. At the very least, this process requires some careful study and maybe some expert advice. Investors should beware of people who call themselves "financial planners" but who are in reality nothing more than salespersons for various financial investments, tax shelters, or insurance plans.

A true **financial planner** has had at least two years of training in investments, insurance, taxation, retirement planning, and estate planning and has passed a rigorous examination. As evidence of training and successful completion of the qualifying examination, the Certified Financial Planner Board of Standards (**www.cfp.net**)

personal budget a specific plan for spending your income

personal investment the use of your personal funds to earn a financial return

financial planner an individual who has had at least two years of training in investments, insurance, taxation, retirement planning, and estate planning and has passed a rigorous examination in Washington, D.C., allows individuals to use the designation Certified Financial Planner (CFP). Similarly, the American College (**www.theamericancollege.edu**) in Bryn Mawr, Pennsylvania, allows individuals who have completed the necessary requirements to use the designation Chartered Financial Consultant (ChFC). Most CFPs and ChFCs do not sell a particular investment product or receive commissions for their investment recommendations. Instead, they charge consulting fees that range from $100 to $250 an hour.

Many financial planners suggest that you accumulate an "emergency fund"—a certain amount of money that can be obtained quickly in case of immediate need—before beginning an investment program. The amount of money that should be salted away in a savings account varies from person to person. However, most financial planners agree that an amount equal to at least three months' living expenses is reasonable.

After the emergency account is established, you may invest additional funds according to your investment program. Some additional funds already may be available, or money for further investing may be saved out of earnings. For suggestions to help you obtain the money needed to fund your investment program, see Table A.1.

Once your program has been put into operation, you must monitor it and, if necessary, modify it. Your circumstances and economic conditions are both subject to change. Therefore, all investment programs should be reevaluated regularly.

Important Factors in Personal Investment

How can you (or a financial planner) tell which investments are "right" for your investment program and which are not? One way to start is to match potential investments with your investment goals in terms of safety, risk, income, growth, and liquidity.

Safety and Risk Safety and risk are two sides of the same coin. *Safety* in an investment means minimal risk of loss; *risk* in an investment means a measure of uncertainty about the outcome. If you want a steady increase in value over an extended period of time, choose safe investments, such as certificates of deposit (CDs), highly rated corporate and municipal bonds, and the stocks of highly regarded corporations. Selected mutual funds and real estate also may be very safe investments.

If you want higher dollar returns on investments, you generally must give up some safety. In general, *the potential return should be directly related to the assumed risk.* That is, the greater the risk assumed by the investor, the greater the potential

---

TABLE A.1: Suggestions to Help You Accumulate the Money Needed to Fund an Investment Program

1. *Pay yourself first.* Many financial experts recommend that you (1) pay your monthly bills, (2) save a reasonable amount of money, and (3) use whatever money is left over for personal expenses.

2. *Take advantage of employer-sponsored retirement programs.* Many employers will match part or all of the contributions you make to a retirement account.

3. *Participate in an elective savings program.* Elect to have money withheld from your paycheck each payday and automatically deposited in a savings account.

4. *Make a special savings effort one or two months each year.* By cutting back to the basics, you can obtain money for investment purposes.

5. *Take advantage of gifts, inheritances, and windfalls.* During your lifetime, you likely will receive gifts, inheritances, salary increases, year-end bonuses, or federal income tax refunds. Instead of spending these windfalls, invest these funds.

Source: Jack R. Kapoor, Les R. Dlabay, and Robert J. Hughes, *Personal Finance*, 9th ed. Copyright © 2009 by The McGraw Hill Companies Inc. Reprinted with permission of The McGraw Hill Companies Inc., p. 415.

monetary reward should be. As you will see shortly, there are a number of risky—and potentially profitable—investments.

Investment Income CDs, corporate and government bonds, and certain stocks pay interest or dividends each year. Some mutual funds and real estate also may offer steady income potential. Such investments generally are used by conservative investors or retired individuals who need a predictable source of income.

Investors in CDs and bonds know exactly how much income they will receive each year. The dividends paid to stockholders can and do vary, even for the largest and most stable corporations. As with dividends from stock, the income from mutual funds and real estate also may vary from one year to the next.

Investment Growth To investors, *growth* means that their investments will increase in value. For example, growing corporations such as eBay, Adobe Systems, and CNX Gas Corporation usually pay a small cash dividend or no dividend at all. Instead, profits are reinvested in the business (as retained earnings) to finance additional expansion. In this case, the value of their stock increases as the corporation expands.

Other investments that may offer growth potential include selected mutual funds and real estate. For example, many mutual funds are referred to as growth funds or aggressive growth funds because of the growth potential of the individual securities included in the fund.

Investment Liquidity Liquidity is the ease with which an investment can be converted into cash. Investments range from cash or cash equivalents (such as investments in government securities or money-market accounts) to the other extreme of frozen investments, which you cannot convert easily into cash.

Although you may be able to sell stock, mutual-fund, and corporate-bond investments quickly, you may not regain the amount of money you originally invested because of market conditions, economic conditions, or many other reasons. It also may be difficult to find buyers for real estate. And finding a buyer for investments in certain types of collectibles also may be difficult.

Surviving a Financial Crisis

Although monitoring your investment program and reevaluating your investment choices are always important, the recent economic crisis underscores the importance of managing your personal finances *and* your investment program. Because of the nation's economic problems, many people were caught off guard and had to scramble to find the money to pay their monthly bills. Many of these same individuals had to borrow money or use their credit cards to survive from one payday to the next. And some individuals were forced to sell some or all of their investments at depressed prices just to buy food for the family and pay for everyday necessities.

To survive a financial crisis, many experts recommend that you take action before the crisis to make sure your financial affairs are in order. Seven steps you can take include:

1. *Establish a larger than usual emergency fund.* While under normal circumstances, an emergency fund of three months' living expenses is considered adequate, you may want to increase your fund in anticipation of a crisis.
2. *Know what you owe.* It helps to make a list of all your debts, expenses, and the amount of the required monthly payments. Then identify the debts and expenses that *must* be paid. Typically these include the mortgage or rent, medicine, utilities, food, and transportation costs.
3. *Reduce spending.* Cut back to the basics and reduce the amount of money spent on entertainment, dining at restaurants, and vacations. Although not pleasant, the money saved from reduced spending can be used to increase your emergency fund or pay for everyday necessities.

liquidity the ease with which an investment can be converted into cash

4. *Pay off credit cards.* Get in the habit of paying your credit-card bill in full each month. If you have credit-card balances, begin by paying off the balance on the credit card with the highest interest rate.

5. *Apply for a line of credit at your bank, credit union, or financial institution.* As defined in Chapter 16, a line of credit is a pre-approved loan and will provide access to cash if needed for future emergencies.

6. *Notify credit-card companies and lenders if you are unable to make payments.* Although not all lenders are willing to help, many will work with you and lower your interest rate, reduce your monthly payment, or extend the time for repayment.

7. *Monitor the value of your investment accounts.* Tracking the value of your stock, mutual-fund, and retirement accounts, for example, will help you decide which investments to sell if you need cash for emergencies. Continued evaluation of your investments can also help you reallocate your investments to reduce investment risk.

Above all, don't panic. While financial problems are stressful, it helps to stay calm and consider all the options. Keep in mind that bankruptcy should be a last resort. The reason is simple: A bankruptcy will remain on your credit report for up to 10 years.

How Securities Are Bought and Sold

To purchase a Geoffrey Beene sweater, you simply walk into a store that sells these sweaters, choose one, and pay for it. To purchase stocks, bonds, mutual funds, and many other investments, you often work with an account executive employed by a brokerage firm.

The Role of an Account Executive

An **account executive**—sometimes called a *stockbroker* or *registered representative*—is an individual who buys and sells securities for clients. Choosing an account executive can be difficult for at least two reasons. First, you must exercise a shrewd combination of trust and mistrust when you approach an account executive. Remember that you are interested in the broker's recommendations to increase your wealth, but the account executive is interested in your investment trading as a means to swell commissions. Unfortunately, some account executives are guilty of *churning*—a practice that generates commissions by excessive buying and selling of securities.

Second, you must decide whether you need a *full-service* broker or a *discount* broker. A full-service broker usually charges higher commissions but gives you personal investment advice and provides detailed research information. When compared to a full-service broker, a discount broker simply executes buy and sell orders, usually over the phone or online. Most discount brokers offer no or very little investment advice; you must make your own investment decisions.

Before deciding if you should use a full-service or a discount brokerage firm, you should consider how much help you need when making an investment decision. Many full-service brokerage firms argue that you need a professional to help you make important investment decisions. While this may be true for some investors, most account executives employed by full-service brokerage firms are too busy to spend unlimited time with you on a one-on-one basis, especially if you are investing a small amount. On the other side, many discount brokerage firms argue that you alone are responsible for making your investment decisions. And they argue that discount brokerage firms have both the personnel and research materials to help you to become a better investor.

The Mechanics of a Transaction

Once investors have decided on a particular security, most simply telephone their account executive and place a market or limit order. A **market order** is a request that a security be purchased or sold at the current market price. Figure A.1 illustrates one method of executing a market

account executive an individual, sometimes called a stockbroker or registered representative, who buys and sells securities for clients

market order a request that a security be purchased or sold at the current market price

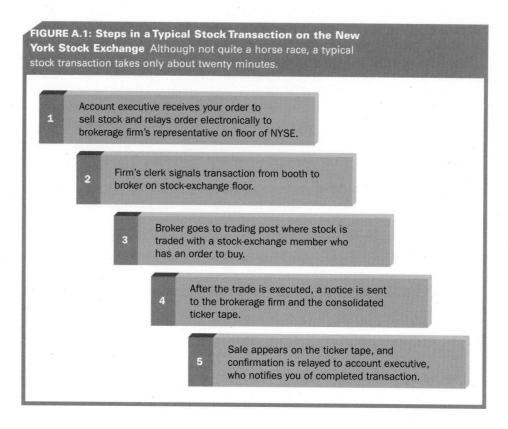

FIGURE A.1: Steps in a Typical Stock Transaction on the New York Stock Exchange Although not quite a horse race, a typical stock transaction takes only about twenty minutes.

1. Account executive receives your order to sell stock and relays order electronically to brokerage firm's representative on floor of NYSE.

2. Firm's clerk signals transaction from booth to broker on stock-exchange floor.

3. Broker goes to trading post where stock is traded with a stock-exchange member who has an order to buy.

4. After the trade is executed, a notice is sent to the brokerage firm and the consolidated ticker tape.

5. Sale appears on the ticker tape, and confirmation is relayed to account executive, who notifies you of completed transaction.

order to sell a stock listed on the NYSE at its current market value. It is also possible for a brokerage firm to match a buy order for a security for one of its customers with a sell order for the same security from another of its customers. Regardless of how the security is bought or sold, payment for stocks and many other financial securities generally is required within three business days of the transaction.

A **limit order** is a request that a security be bought or sold at a price equal to or better than (lower for buying, higher for selling) some specified price. Suppose that you place a limit order to *sell* Coca-Cola common stock at $48 per share. Your broker's representative sells the stock only if the price is $48 per share or *more*. If you place a limit order to *buy* Coca Cola at $48, the representative buys it only if the price is $48 per share or *less*. Usually, a limit order is good for one day, one week, one month, or good until canceled (GTC).

Online Security Transactions A computer and access to the Internet can help you to evaluate potential investments, manage your investments, monitor their value more closely, *and* place buy and sell orders online. As a rule of thumb, the more active an investor is, the more it makes sense to invest online. As you will see in the next section, one very good reason for trading securities online is the lower cost.

Commissions Most full-service brokerage firms have a minimum commission ranging from $25 to $55 for buying and selling stock. Additional commission charges are based on the number of shares and the value of stock bought and sold.

Table A.2 shows typical commission fees charged by online brokerage firms. Generally, online transactions are less expensive when compared with the costs of trading securities through a full-service brokerage firm. As a rule of thumb, full-service brokerage firms charge as much as 1.5 to 2 percent of the transaction amount. Commissions for trading bonds, commodities, and options usually are lower than those for trading stocks. With the exception of most mutual funds, the investor generally pays a commission when buying *and* selling securities.

It should be apparent that vast sums of money are involved in securities trading. In an effort to protect investors from unfair treatment, both federal and state governments have acted to regulate securities trading.

limit order a request that a security be bought or sold at a price that is equal to or better than some specified price

TABLE A.2: Typical Commission Costs Charged by Online Brokerage Firms for a Transaction in which 1,000 Shares Are Bought or Sold

	Internet	Interactive Voice-Response Telephone System	Broker-Assisted
TD Ameritrade	$ 9.99	$34.99	$ 44.99
E*Trade	$12.99	$12.99	$ 57.99
Fidelity	$19.95	$ 67.50	$181.00
Schwab	$12.95	$ 17.95	$ 37.95

Source: TD Ameritrade website, **www.tdameritrade.com**, accessed May 26, 2009.

Regulation of Securities Trading

Today, a regulatory pyramid consisting of four different levels exists to make sure that investors are protected. The U.S. Congress is at the top of the pyramid. Early on, Congress passed the Securities Act of 1933 (sometimes referred to as the Truth in Securities Act). This act provides for full disclosure. **Full disclosure** means that investors should have access to all important facts about stocks, bonds, and other securities so that they can make informed decisions. This act also requires that corporations issuing new securities file a registration statement and publish a prospectus. A **prospectus** is a detailed, written description of a new security, the issuing corporation, and the corporation's top management. Since 1933, Congress has passed additional legislation that includes creating the Securities Investor Protection Corporation (SIPC) to protect investors. More recently, Congress passed the Sarbanes-Oxley Act to improve corporate accountability and financial reporting (see Chapter 15).

On the next level of the regulatory pyramid is the Securities and Exchange Commission (SEC). In 1934, Congress passed the Securities Exchange Act of 1934, which created the SEC. The SEC is the agency that enforces federal securities regulations. The SEC also supervises all national exchanges, investment companies, the over-the-counter market, brokerage firms, and just about every other organization involved in trading securities.

On the next level of the regulatory pyramid is individual states. Today, most states require that new security issues be registered with a state agency and that brokers and securities dealers operating within the state be licensed. Most state regulations also provide for the prosecution of individuals accused of the fraudulent sale of stocks, bonds, and other securities.

The foundation and most important level of the regulatory pyramid is self-regulation by securities exchanges and brokerage firms. According to the New York Stock Exchange (NYSE), self-regulation—the way the securities industry monitors itself to create a fair and orderly trading environment—begins here.[1] To provide guidelines of ethical behavior, the NYSE has published rules, policies, and standards of conduct. These standards are applied to every member in the NYSE's investment community. The NYSE also conducts a thorough examination of each member firm that does business with the public at least once a year.[2] In addition, there are more than 300 brokerage firms that buy and sell securities for their customers. These firms are responsible for ensuring that their employees are highly trained and meet rigorous ethical standards.

full disclosure requirement that investors should have access to all important facts about stocks, bonds, and other securities so that they can make informed decisions

prospectus a detailed, written description of a new security, the issuing corporation, and the corporation's top management

Traditional Investment Alternatives

In this section, we look at different investment alternatives. A number of the investments listed in Table A.3 have been discussed. Others have only been mentioned and will be examined in more detail. We begin this section with an overview of how portfolio management can reduce investment risk. Then we describe how specific investments can help you to reach your investment goals.

TABLE A.3: Investment Alternatives Traditional investments involve less risk than high-risk investments.

Traditional	High Risk
Bank accounts	Selling short stock transactions
Corporate and government bonds	Margin stock transactions
Common stock	Stock options
Preferred stock	Commodities
Mutual funds	Precious metals
Real estate	Gemstones
	Coins/antiques/collectibles

Portfolio Management

"How can I choose the right investment?" Good question! Unfortunately, there are no easy answers because your investment goals, age, tolerance for risk, and financial resources are different from those of the next person. To help you to decide what investment is right for you, consider the following: Since 1926, as measured by the Standard and Poor's 500 stock index, stocks have returned almost 10 percent a year. During the same period, long-term government bonds have returned about 6 percent.[3] And projections by well-respected finance professor Roger Ibbotson indicate that these same investments will perform at about the same pace between now and the year 2025.[4] Therefore, why not just invest all your money in stocks or mutual funds that invest in stocks? After all, they offer the largest potential return? In reality, stocks may have a place in every investment portfolio, but there is more to investing than just picking a bunch of stocks or stock mutual funds.

Asset Allocation, the Time Factor, and Your Age

Asset allocation is the process of spreading your money among several different types of investments to lessen risk. While the term *asset allocation* is a fancy way of saying it, simply put, it really means that you need to diversify and avoid the pitfall of putting all of your eggs in one basket—a common mistake made by investors. Asset allocation often is expressed in percentages. For example, what percentage of my assets do I want to put in stocks and mutual funds? What percentage do I want to put in more conservative investments such as CDs and government bonds? In reality, the answers to these questions are determined by:

- Your investment objectives.
- Your ability to tolerate risk.
- How much you can save and invest each year.
- The dollar value of your current investments.
- The economic outlook for the economy.
- And several other factors.

The amount of time you have before you need your investment money is crucial. If you can leave your investments alone and let them work for five to ten years or more, then you can invest in stocks, mutual funds, and real estate. On the other hand, if you need your investment money in two years, you probably should invest in short-term government bonds, highly rated corporate bonds, or CDs. By taking a more conservative approach for short-term investments, you reduce the possibility of having to sell your investments at a loss because of depressed market value or a staggering economy.

You also should consider your age when developing an investment program. Younger investors tend to invest a large percentage of their nest egg in growth-oriented investments. On the other hand, older investors tend to choose more

asset allocation the process of spreading your money among several different types of investments to lessen risk conservative investments. How much of your portfolio should be in growth-oriented investments? Well-known personal financial expert Suze Orman suggests that you subtract your age from 110, and the difference is the percentage of your assets that should be invested in growth investments. For example, if you are 30 years old, subtract 30 from 110, which gives you 80. Therefore, 80 percent of your assets should be invested in growth-oriented investments, whereas the remaining 20 percent should be kept in safer conservative investments.[5] Now it's time to take a closer look at specific investment alternatives.

Bank Accounts

Bank accounts that pay interest—and therefore are investments—include passbook savings accounts, CDs, and interest-bearing accounts. The interest paid on bank accounts can be withdrawn to serve as income, or it can be left on deposit and increase the value of the bank account and provide for growth. At the time of this publication, one-year CDs were paying between 2 and 3 percent. While CDs and other bank accounts are risk-free for all practical purposes, many investors often choose other investments because of the potential for larger returns.

Corporate and Government Bonds

In Chapter 16, we discussed the issuing of bonds by corporations to obtain financing. The U.S. government and state and local governments also issue bonds for the same reason. Investors generally choose bonds because they provide a predictable source of income.

Corporate Bonds Because they are a form of long-term debt financing that must be repaid, bonds generally are considered a more conservative investment. One of the principal advantages of corporate bonds is that they are primarily long-term, income-producing investments. Between the time of purchase and the maturity date, the bondholder will receive interest payments—usually semiannually, or every six months. For example, assume that you purchase a $1,000 bond that matures in 2018 issued by the rail-based transportation giant CSX Corporation and that the interest rate for this bond is 6.25 percent. In this situation, you receive interest of $62.50 ($1,000 × 0.0625 = $62.50) a year from the corporation. CSX pays the interest every six months in $31.25 installments.

Most beginning investors think that a $1,000 bond is always worth $1,000. In reality, the price of a bond may fluctuate until its maturity date. Changes in the overall interest rates in the economy are the primary cause of most bond price fluctuations. For example, when overall interest rates in the economy are rising, the market value of existing bonds with a fixed interest rate typically declines. They then may be purchased for less than their face value. By holding such bonds until maturity or until overall interest rates decline (causing the bond's market value to increase), bond owners can sell their bonds for more than they paid for them. In this case, the difference between the purchase price and the selling price is profit and is in addition to annual interest income. However, remember that the price of a corporate bond can decrease and that interest payments and eventual repayment may be a problem for a corporation that encounters financial difficulty. To compare potential risk and return on corporate bond issues, many investors rely on the bond ratings provided by Moody's Investors Service, Inc. and Standard & Poor's Corporation.

Government Bonds The federal government sells bonds and securities to finance both the national debt and the government's ongoing activities. Generally, investors choose from five different types of U.S. government bonds:

1. *Treasury bills.* Treasury bills, sometimes called *T-bills*, are sold in minimum units of $100, with additional increments of $100 above the minimum. Although the maturities may be as long as one year, the Treasury Department currently only sells T-bills with four-, thirteen-, twenty-six-, and fifty-two-week maturities.

T-bills are sold at a discount, and the actual purchase price is less than the face value. When the T-bill matures, you receive the face value.

2. *Treasury notes.* Treasury notes are issued in $100 units with a maturity of more than one year but not more than ten years. Typical maturities are two, three, five, seven, and ten years. Treasury notes pay interest every six months until maturity.

3. *Treasury inflation-protected securities (TIPS).* TIPS are sold in $100 units and are sold with five, ten, or twenty-year maturities. The principal of TIPS increases with inflation and decreases with deflation, as measured by the consumer price index. When TIPS mature, you are paid the adjusted principal or original principal, which ever is greater. TIPS also pay interest twice a year, at a fixed rate.

4. *Treasury bonds.* Treasury bonds are issued in minimum units of $100 and have a thirty-year maturity. Like Treasury notes, Treasury bonds pay interest every six months until maturity.

5. *Savings bonds.* Series EE paper bonds, often called *U.S. savings bonds*, are purchased for one-half their maturity value. Thus, a $100 bond costs $50 when purchased. Series EE bonds purchased electronically are sold at their face value. With either paper or electronic-issue bonds, interest is added to the bond and paid when you cash in the bond.[6] (*Note:* If the interest derived from savings bonds is used to pay qualified college expenses, it may be exempt from federal taxation.)

The main reason investors choose U.S. government bonds is that they consider them risk-free. The other side of the coin is that these bonds pay lower interest than most other investments. Interest paid on U.S. government securities is taxable for federal income tax purposes, but is exempt from state and local taxation.

Like the federal government, state and local governments sell bonds to obtain financing. A **municipal bond**, sometimes called a *muni*, is a debt security issued by a state or local government. One of the most important features of municipal bonds is that the interest on them may be exempt from federal taxes. Whether or not the interest on municipal bonds is tax exempt often depends on how the funds obtained from their sale are used. *Caution: It is your responsibility, as an investor, to determine whether or not the interest paid by municipal bonds is taxable. It is also your responsibility to evaluate municipal bonds.* Although most municipal bonds are relatively safe, defaults have occurred in recent years.

Common Stock

As mentioned in Chapter 16, corporations issue common stock to finance their business start-up costs and help pay for expansion and their ongoing business activities. Before investing in stock, keep in mind that corporations don't have to repay the money a stockholder pays for stock. Usually, a stockholder may sell her or his stock to another individual.

How do you make money by buying common stock? Basically, there are three ways: through dividend payments, through an increase in the value of the stock, or through stock splits.

Dividend Payments One of the reasons why many stockholders invest in common stock is *dividend income.* Generally, dividends are paid on a quarterly basis. Although corporations are under no legal obligation to pay dividends, most corporate board members like to keep stockholders happy (and prosperous). A corporation may pay stock dividends in place of—or in addition to—cash dividends. A **stock dividend** is a dividend in the form of additional stock. It is paid to shareholders just as cash dividends are paid—in proportion to the number of shares owned.

Increase in Dollar Value Another way to make money on stock investments is through capital gains. A **capital gain** is the difference between a security's purchase price and its selling price. To earn a capital gain, you must sell when the

municipal bond sometimes called a muni, a debt security issued by a state or local government

stock dividend a dividend in the form of additional stock

capital gain the difference between a security's purchase price and its selling price market value of the stock is higher than the original purchase price. The **market value** is the price of one share of a stock at a particular time. Let's assume that on May 26, 2004, you purchased 100 shares of General Mills at a cost of $46 a share and that you paid $55 in commission charges, for a total investment of $4,655. Let's also assume that you held your 100 shares until May 26, 2009, and then sold the General Mills stock for $53. Your total return on investment is shown in Table A.4. You realized a profit of $1,242 because you received dividends totaling $6.67 a share during the five-year period and because the stock's market value increased by $7 a share. Of course, if the stock's market value had decreased, or if the firm's board of directors had voted to reduce or omit dividends, your return would have been less than the total dollar return illustrated in Table A.4.

Stock Splits Directors of many corporations feel that there is an optimal price range within which their firm's stock is most attractive to investors. When the market value increases beyond that range, they may declare a *stock split* to bring the price down. A **stock split** is the division of each outstanding share of a corporation's stock into a greater number of shares.

The most common stock splits result in one, two, or three new shares for each original share. For example, in 2009, the board of directors of Village Super Market, approved a two-for-one stock split. After this split, a stockholder who originally owned 100 shares owned 200 shares. The value of an original share was proportionally reduced. In the case of Village Super Market, the value per share was reduced to half the stock's value before the two-for-one stock split. There is no evidence to support that a corporation's long-term performance is improved by a stock split; however, some investors do profit from stock splits on a short-term basis. *BE WARNED: There are no guarantees that the stock will increase in value after a split.* However, the stock may be more attractive to the investing public because of the potential for a rapid increase in dollar value. This attraction is based on the belief that most corporations split their stock only when their financial future is improving and on the upswing.

Preferred Stock

As we noted in Chapter 16, a firm's preferred stockholders must receive their dividends before common stockholders are paid any dividend. Moreover, the preferred-stock dividend amount is specified on the stock certificate. And the owners

TABLE A.4: Sample Common-Stock Transaction for General Mills *Assumptions*: 100 shares of common stock purchased on May 26, 2004, for $46 a share; 100 shares sold on May 26, 2009, for $53 a share; dividends for 5 years total $6.67 a share.

Cost When Purchased		Return When Sold	
100 shares @ $46	$4,600	100 shares @ $53	$5,300
Plus commission	+55	Minus commission	−70
Total investment	$4,655	Total return	$5,230

Transaction Summary	
Total return	$ 5,230
Minus total investment	−4,655
Profit from stock sale	$ 575
Plus total dividends (5 years)	+667
Total return for this transaction	$ 1,242

Source: Price data and dividend amounts were taken from the Yahoo Finance website, http://finance.yahoo.com, accessed May 26, 2009.

market value the price of one share of a stock at a particular time

stock split the division of each outstanding share of a corporation's stock into a greater number of shares of preferred stock have first claim, after bond owners and general creditors, on corporate assets if the firm is dissolved or enters bankruptcy. These features make preferred stock a more conservative investment with an added degree of safety and a more predictable source of income when compared with common stock.

Mutual Funds

For many investors, mutual funds are the investment of choice. And there are plenty of funds from which to choose. In 1970, there were only about 400 mutual funds. In 2009, there were just over 10,000 mutual funds.[7]

According to the Mutual Fund Education Alliance (**www.mfea.com**), a **mutual fund** is a company that pools the money of many investors—its shareholders—to invest in a variety of different securities.[8] The major advantages of a mutual fund are its professional management and its diversification, or investment in a wide variety of securities. Diversification spells safety because an occasional loss incurred with one security usually is offset by gains from other investments.

Mutual-Fund Basics There are basically three types of mutual funds: (1) closed-end funds, (2) exchange-traded funds, and (3) open-end funds. A *closed-end fund* sells shares in the fund to investors only when the fund is originally organized. Once all the shares are sold, an investor must purchase shares from some other investor who is willing to sell them. The mutual fund itself is under no obligation to buy back shares from investors. An *exchange-traded fund* (ETF) is a fund that invests in the stocks contained in a specific stock index, such as the Standard & Poor's 500 Stock Index, the Dow Jones Industrial Average, or the Nasdaq Composite Index. With both a closed-end fund and an ETF, an investor can purchase as little as one share of a fund because both types are traded on a stock exchange or in the OTC market. The investment company sponsoring an *open-end fund* issues and sells new shares to any investor who requests them. It also buys back shares from investors who wish to sell all or part of their holdings.

The share value for any mutual fund is determined by calculating its net asset value. **Net asset value (NAV)** per share is equal to the current market value of the mutual fund's portfolio minus the mutual fund's liabilities divided by the number of outstanding shares. For most mutual funds, NAV is calculated at least once a day and is reported in newspapers and financial publications and on the Internet.

Mutual-Fund Sales Charges and Fees With regard to costs, there are two types of mutual funds: load and no-load funds. An individual who invests in a *load fund* pays a sales charge every time he or she purchases shares. This charge may be as high as 8.5 percent. While many exceptions exist, the average load charge for mutual funds is between 3 and 5 percent. Instead of charging investors a fee when they purchase shares in a mutual fund, some mutual funds charge a *contingent deferred sales fee*. Generally, this fee ranges from 1 to 5 percent of the amount withdrawn during the first five to seven years. Typically, the amount of the contingent deferred sales fee declines each year that you own the fund until there is no withdrawal fee. The purchaser of shares in a *no-load fund* pays no sales charges at all. Since no-load funds offer the same type of investment opportunities as load funds, you should investigate them further before deciding which type of fund is best for you.

Mutual funds also collect a yearly management fee of about 0.25 to 2 percent of the total dollar amount of assets in the fund. While fees vary considerably, the average management fee is between 0.50 and 1 percent of the fund's assets. Finally, some mutual funds charge a 12b-1 fee (sometimes referred to as a *distribution fee*) to defray the costs of advertising and marketing the mutual fund. Annual 12b-1 fees are calculated on the value of a fund's assets and cannot exceed 1 percent of the fund's assets. Unlike the one-time sales fees that some mutual funds charge to purchase *or* sell mutual-fund shares, the management fee and the 12b-1 fee are ongoing fees charged each year.

Managed Funds versus Indexed Funds Most mutual funds are managed funds. In other words, there is a professional fund manager (or team of

mutual fund a company that pools the money of many investors—its shareholders—to invest in a variety of different securities

net asset value (NAV) is equal to the current market value of a mutual fund's portfolio minus the mutual fund's liabilities divided by the number of outstanding shares managers) who chooses the securities that are contained in the fund. The fund manager also decides when to buy and sell securities in the fund. Ultimately, the fund manager is responsible for the fund's success.

Instead of investing in a managed fund, some investors choose to invest in an index fund. Why? The answer to this question is simple: Over many years, index funds have outperformed managed funds. The exact statistics vary depending on the year and the specific fund, but a common statistic is that the Standard & Poor's 500 stock index outperforms 80 percent of all managed mutual funds.[9] Simply put: It is hard to beat an index such as the Standard & Poor's 500. If the individual securities included in an index increase in value, the index goes up. Because an index mutual fund is a mirror image of a specific index, the dollar value of a share in an index fund also increases when the index increases. Unfortunately, the reverse is true. A second reason why investors choose index funds is the lower fees charged by these passively managed funds.

Types of Mutual-Fund Investments Based on the type of securities they invest in, mutual funds generally fall into three broad categories: stocks, bonds, and other. The majority of mutual funds are *stock funds* that invest in stocks issued by small, medium-size, and large corporations that provide investors with income, growth, or a combination of income and growth. *Bond funds* invest in corporate, government, or municipal bonds that provide investors with interest income. The third category includes funds that stress asset allocation and money-market investments or strive for a balance between stocks and bonds. In most cases, the name of the category gives a pretty good clue to the type of investments included in the fund.

To help investors obtain their investment objectives, most investment companies now allow shareholders to switch from one fund to another fund within the same family of funds. A **family of funds** exists when one investment company manages a group of mutual funds. For example, shareholders, at their option, can change from the AIM Global Equity Fund to the AIM Basic Value Fund. Generally, investors may give instructions to switch from one fund to another fund within the same family either in writing, over the telephone, or via the Internet. Charges for exchanges, if any, are small for each transaction. For funds that do charge, the fee may be as low as $5 per transaction.

Real Estate

Real estate ownership represents one of the best hedges against inflation, but it—like all investments—has its risks. A piece of property in a poor location, for example, actually can decrease in value. Table A.5 lists some of the many factors you should consider before investing in real estate.

family of funds a group of mutual funds managed by one investment company

TABLE A.5: Real Estate Checklist Although real estate offers one of the best hedges against inflation, not all property increases in value. Many factors should be considered before investing in real estate.

Evaluation of Property	Inspection of the Surrounding Neighborhood	Other Factors
Is the property priced competitively with similar property?	What are the present zoning requirements?	Why are the present owners selling the property?
What type of financing, if any, is available?	Is the neighborhood's population increasing or decreasing?	How long will you have to hold the property before selling it to someone else?
How much are the taxes?	What is the average income of people in the area?	How much profit can you reasonably expect to obtain?
	What is the state of repair of surrounding property? Do most of the buildings and homes need repair?	Is there a chance that the property value will decrease?

There are, of course, disadvantages to any investment, and real estate is no exception. If you want to sell your property, you must find an interested buyer with the ability to obtain enough money to complete the transaction. Finding such a buyer can be difficult if loan money is scarce, the real estate market is in a decline, or you overpaid for a piece of property. For example, many real estate investors were forced to hold some properties longer than they wanted because buyers could not obtain financing during the recent economic crisis. If you are forced to hold your investment longer than you originally planned, taxes, interest, and installment payments can be a heavy burden. As a rule, real estate increases in value and eventually sells at a profit, but there are no guarantees. The degree of your success depends on how well you evaluate different alternatives.

High-Risk Investment Alternatives

A **high-risk investment** is an investment made in the uncertain hope of earning a relatively large profit in a short time. Most high-risk investments become so because of the methods used by investors to earn a quick profit. Although a discussion of the actual methods used by speculative investors to earn profits with high-risk investments is beyond the scope of this text, they should not be used by anyone who does not fully understand the risks involved. Typical high-risk investments include the following:

- Stock investments that use margin or borrowed money
- Stock investments that use the selling short technique
- Stock options
- Commodities
- Precious metals
- Gemstones
- Coins
- Antiques and collectibles

Without exception, investments of this kind normally are referred to as high-risk investments for one reason or another. For example, the gold market has many unscrupulous dealers who sell worthless gold-plated lead coins to unsuspecting, uninformed investors. It pays to be careful. *Although investments in this category can lead to large dollar gains, they should not be used by anyone who does not fully understand all the potential risks involved.*

Sources of Financial Information

A wealth of information is available to investors. Sources include the Internet, newspapers, investors' services, brokerage firm reports, business periodicals, corporate reports, and securities averages.

The Internet

By using the Internet, investors can access a wealth of information on most investment and personal finance topics. For example, you can obtain interest rates for CDs; current price information for stocks, bonds, and mutual funds; and experts' recommendations to buy, hold, or sell an investment. You can even trade securities online.

Because the Internet makes so much information available, you need to use it selectively. One of the Web search engines such as Yahoo! (**www.yahoo.com**), MSN (**www.msn.com**), or Google (**www.google.com**) can help you locate the information you really need. These search engines allow you to do a word search for the personal finance or investment alternative you want to explore. Why not take a look? To access one of the preceding search engines, enter the website address and then type in a key term such as *personal finance* and see the results.

Corporations, investment companies that sponsor mutual funds, and federal, state, and local governments also have home pages where you can obtain valuable

high-risk investment an investment made in the uncertain hope of earning a relatively large profit in a short time investment information. You may want to explore these websites for two reasons. First, they are easily accessible. All you have to do is type in the Web address or use one of the above mentioned search engines to locate the site. Second, the information on these sites may be more up to date than printed material obtained from published sources.

In addition, you can access professional advisory services—a topic discussed later in the next section—for information on stocks, bonds, mutual funds, and other investment alternatives. While some of the information provided by these services is free, there is a charge for the more detailed information you may need to evaluate an investment.

Other Sources of Financial Information

In addition to the Internet, other sources, which include investors' services, newspapers, brokerage firm reports, business periodicals, corporate reports, and security averages offer detailed information about different investment alternatives.

- *Investors' services.* For a fee, various investors' services provide detailed information about different investment alternatives. For example, many investors use Value Line, Morningstar, and Standard and Poor's to research stock and mutual fund investments.
- *Newspapers.* Most local newspapers carry several pages of business news, including reports of securities transactions. The *Wall Street Journal* (published on weekdays) and *Barron's* (published once a week) are devoted almost entirely to financial and economic news.
- *Brokerage firm reports.* Brokerage firms employ financial analysts to prepare detailed reports on individual corporations and their securities. Such reports are based on the corporation's sales, profits or losses, management, and planning plus other information on the company, its industry, demand for its products, its efforts to develop new products, and the current economic environment.
- *Business periodicals.* Business magazines such as *Business Week, Fortune,* and *Forbes* provide not only general economic news but also detailed financial information about individual corporations. News magazines such as *U.S. News and World Report, Time,* and *Newsweek* feature financial news regularly. *Money, Kiplinger's Personal Finance Magazine, Smart Money,* and similar magazines provide information and advice designed to improve your financial planning and investment skills.
- *Corporate reports.* Publicly held corporations must publish annual reports which include a description of the company's performance, information about the firm's products or services, and detailed financial statements that readers can use to evaluate the firm. In addition, a corporation issuing a new security must—by law—prepare a prospectus and ensure that copies are distributed to potential investors.
- *Security Averages.* Investors often gauge the stock market and other investments through the security averages reported in newspapers and on television news programs. Over a period of time, these averages indicate price trends, but they do not predict the performance of individual investments. Typical examples of security averages include the Dow Jones Industrial Average, the Standard & Poor's 500 Stock Index, and the New York Stock Exchange Index. In addition to stock averages, there are averages for bonds, mutual funds, real estate, commodities, precious metals, fine art, most collectibles, and many other potential investments.

A Final Note

Before you can start investing, you must decide on a career and obtain a job that will provide the money needed to finance an investment program. To help you find the right job (and the money needed to fund an investment program), read Appendix B where we provide information that can help you to explore different career options.

SUMMARY

Many personal finance experts recommend that you begin the process of managing your money by determining your current financial condition. The first step often is to construct a personal balance sheet and a personal income statement. You also can construct a personal budget. For most people, the next step is to formulate measurable and realistic investment goals. A personal investment program then is designed to implement those goals. Many financial planners also suggest that the investor should establish an emergency fund equivalent to at least three months' living expenses. Then additional funds may be invested according to the investment program. Finally, all investments should be monitored carefully, and if necessary, the investment program should be modified.

Depending on their particular investment goals, investors seek varying degrees of safety, risk, income, growth, and liquidity from their investments. Safety is, in essence, freedom from the risk of loss. Generally, the greater the risk, the greater should be the potential return on an investment. Income is the periodic return from an investment. Growth is an increase in the value of the investment. Liquidity is the ease with which an investment can be converted to cash.

If you invest in securities, chances are that you will use the services of an account executive who works for a brokerage firm. It is also possible to use a discount broker or trade securities online with a computer. Today, a regulatory pyramid consisting of four different levels exists to make sure that investors are protected. The U.S. Congress, the Securities and Exchange Commission (SEC), individual states, and securities exchanges and brokerage firms all are involved in regulating the securities industry.

Asset allocation is the process of spreading your money among several different types of investments to lessen risk. Two other factors—the time your investments have to work for you and your age—also should be considered before deciding where to invest your money. Different investment alternatives include bank accounts, corporate bonds, government bonds, common stock, preferred stock, mutual funds, and real estate. You can also choose a high-risk investment. A high-risk investment is an investment made in the uncertain hope of earning a relatively large profit in a short time. Typical high-risk investments include selling short stock transactions, margin stock transactions, stock options, commodities, precious metals, gemstones, coins, and antiques and collectibles.

Today, there is a wealth of information on stocks, bonds, and other securities and the firms that issue them. There is also a wealth of investment information on other types of investments, including mutual funds, real estate, and high-risk investments. The Internet can be used to obtain current price information and detailed financial information about different investment alternatives. Often, the most detailed research information about securities—and the most expensive—is obtained from investors' services. In addition, newspapers, brokerage firm reports, business periodicals, and corporate reports also can be used to evaluate different investment alternatives. Finally, there are a number of security indexes or averages that indicate price trends but reveal nothing about the performance of individual securities.

Careers in Business

Words such as *excited, challenged, scared,* and *frustrated* have been used to describe someone involved in a job search. The reality, however, is that everyone who is employed must have looked for a job at one time or another, and survived. Although first-time employees often think that they will work for the same company for their entire career, most people change jobs and even careers during their lifetime. In fact, according to the Bureau of Labor Statistics, today's job applicants will change jobs over ten times. Therefore, the employment information that follows will be of lasting value. Let's begin our discussion with a look at the factors affecting an individual's career choices.

The Importance of Career Choices

Most people think that career planning begins with an up-to-date résumé and a job interview. In reality, it begins long before you prepare your résumé. It starts with you and what you want to become. In some ways, you have been preparing for a career ever since you started first grade. Everything you have experienced during your lifetime you can now use as a resource to help define your career goals. Let's start with a basic assumption: It is likely that you will spend more time at work than at any other single place during your lifetime. It therefore makes sense to spend those hours doing something you enjoy. Unfortunately, some people just work at a *job* because they need money to survive. Other people choose a *career* because there is a commitment not only to a profession but also to their own interests and talents. Whether you are looking for a job or a career, you should examine your own priorities. Before reading the next section, you may want to evaluate your priorities by completing the exercise in Figure B.1.

Personal Factors Influencing Career Choices

Before you choose your career or job, you need to have a pretty good idea of what motivates you and what skills you can offer an employer. The following five questions may help you to refine further what you consider important in life.

1. *What types of activities do you enjoy?* Although most people know what they enjoy in a general way, a number of interest inventories exist that can help you to determine specific interests and activities that can help you land a job that will lead to a satisfying career. In some cases, it may help just to list the interests or activities you enjoy, along with those you dislike. Watch for patterns that may influence your career choices.

2. *What do you do best?* All jobs in all careers require employees to be able to "do something." It is extremely important to assess what you do best. Be honest with yourself about your ability to succeed in a specific job. It may help to make a list of your strongest job-related skills. Also try looking at your skills from an employer's perspective. What can you do that an employer would be willing to pay for?

3. *What kind of education will you need?* The amount of education you need is determined by the type of career you choose. In some careers, it is impossible to get an entry-level position without at least a college degree. In other careers, technical or hands-on skills are more important than formal education.

©Lidija Tomic

FIGURE B.1: Which Priorities Are Important to You? Look over the list of job and personal variables. In the left-hand column, number them in order of current priority to you. Then renumber them in the right-hand column based on the priorities you anticipate having five or ten years down the road.

Priorities Now	Job and Personal Variables	Priorities in 5–10 years
_____	Salary	_____
_____	Family (children/spouse/parents)	_____
_____	Personal time	_____
_____	Job location	_____
_____	Work-related travel	_____
_____	Potential for advancement	_____
_____	Commuting time	_____
_____	Friendly coworkers/boss	_____
_____	Job responsibilities	_____
_____	Personal hobbies	_____
_____	Prestige	_____
_____	Benefits	_____
_____	Vacation time	_____
_____	Retirement plan	_____
_____	Security/stability	_____
_____	Personal growth/fulfillment	_____
_____	Exposure to new skills	_____

Source: Susan D. Greene and Melanie C. L. Martel, *The Ultimate Job Hunter's Guidebook*, 4th ed. Copyright © 2008 by Houghton Mifflin Company, p. 21. Reprinted with permission.

4. *Where do you want to live?* When you enter the job market, you may want to move to a different part of the country. According to the *Occupational Outlook Handbook*, the western and southern sections of the United States will experience the greatest population increase between now and the year 2012. The population in the Midwest will stay about the same, whereas the Northeast will decrease slightly in population. These population changes will affect job prospects in each of those areas. Before entering the job market, most people think that they are free to move any place they want. In reality, job applicants may be forced to move to a town, city, or metropolitan area that has jobs available.

5. *Are you willing to work long hours?* In some occupations you usually work long hours and receive relatively high pay, perhaps due, in part, to the time you spend working. According to data from the U.S. Bureau of Labor Statistics, time-consuming occupations often have average weekly earnings that are higher than those of other occupations.

Trends in Employment

The new millennium has brought change in employment opportunities to the U.S. labor market. Employment in 2016 is expected to reach 166.2 million, an increase of 15.6 million, or 10 percent, above the 2006 level. For the latest information, visit the Office of Occupational Statistics and Employment Projections website at **www.bls.gov/emp/**.

As you look ahead to your own career, you should consider the effects that the trends described below will have on employment and employment opportunities.

- Jobs in service industries will account for a larger proportion of total employment.
- Training, and retraining, will become increasingly important as firms require their employees to use the latest technology. Good jobs will require strong educational qualifications.

- Automation of factories and offices will create new types of jobs. Many of these will be computer related.
- The number of women, Hispanics, Asians, two-income families, and older workers in the workforce will increase.
- There will be a greater emphasis on job sharing, flexible hours, and other innovative work practices to accommodate employees. In some cases, employees will be able to complete assignments at home on remote computer terminals.

College graduates with majors in business and management, computer science, education, engineering, and health professions will be in high demand according to human resources experts. There will be fewer manufacturing jobs, and those that remain will require high-tech skills.

Occupational Search Activities

When most people begin to search for a job, they immediately think of the classified ads in the local newspaper. Those ads are an important source of information about jobs in your particular area, but they are only one source. Many other sources can lead to employment and a satisfying career. As illustrated in Figure B.2, a wealth of information about career planning is available. Therefore, you must be selective in both the type and amount of information you use to guide your job search.

The library, a traditional job-hunting tool, has been joined in recent years by the Internet. Both the library and the Internet are sources of everything from classified newspaper ads and government job listings to detailed information on individual companies and industries. You can use either of them to research an area of employment that interests you or a particular company. In addition, the Internet allows you to check electronic bulletin boards for current job information, exchange ideas with other job seekers through online discussion groups or e-mail, and get career advice from professional counselors. You also can create your own Web page to inform prospective employers of your qualifications. And you may even have a job interview online. Many prominent companies are now using their websites to post job openings, accept applications, and interview candidates. In fact, the Internet has been called the future of recruiting.

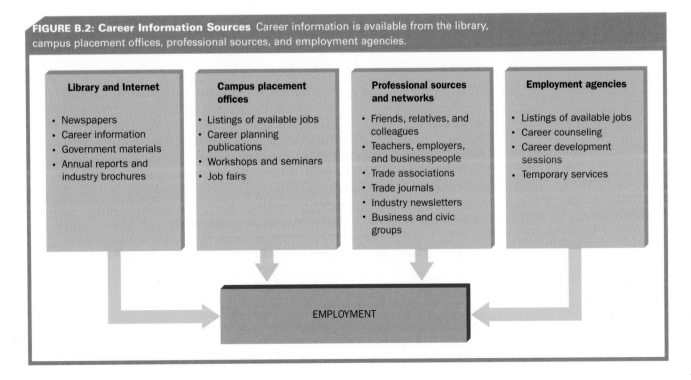

FIGURE B.2: Career Information Sources Career information is available from the library, campus placement offices, professional sources, and employment agencies.

Library and Internet	Campus placement offices	Professional sources and networks	Employment agencies
• Newspapers • Career information • Government materials • Annual reports and industry brochures	• Listings of available jobs • Career planning publications • Workshops and seminars • Job fairs	• Friends, relatives, and colleagues • Teachers, employers, and businesspeople • Trade associations • Trade journals • Industry newsletters • Business and civic groups	• Listings of available jobs • Career counseling • Career development sessions • Temporary services

EMPLOYMENT

As you start a job search, you may find websites helpful. In addition to the library and the Internet, the following sources can be of great help when you are trying to find the "perfect job":

1. *Campus placement offices.* Colleges and universities have placement offices staffed by trained personnel specialists. In most cases, these offices serve as clearinghouses for career information. The staff also may be able to guide you in creating your résumé and preparing for a job interview.

2. *Professional sources and networks.* A network is a group of people, friends, relatives, and professionals, who are in a position to exchange information (including information about job openings) in your field of business. And according to many job applicants, networking is one of the best sources of career information and job leads. Start with as many people as you can think of to establish your initial network. (The Internet can be very useful in this regard.) Contact these individuals, and ask specific questions about job opportunities that they may be aware of. Also ask each of these individuals to introduce or refer you to someone else who may be able to help you to continue your job search. For networking to work, you must continue this process. Remember that you must follow all leads. Even if you have referrals and introductions, you must still "get" the job. Finally, remember to thank the people who have helped you.

3. *Private employment agencies.* Private employment agencies charge a fee for helping people find jobs. Typical fees can be as high as 15 to 20 percent of an employee's first-year salary. The fee may be paid by the employer or the employee. As with college placement offices, private employment agencies provide career counseling, help to create résumés, and provide preparation for job interviews. Before you use a private employment agency, be sure you understand the terms of any contract or agreement you sign. Above all, make sure that you know who is responsible for paying the agency's fee.

4. *State employment agencies.* Another source of information about job openings in your immediate area is the local office of your state employment agency. Some job applicants are reluctant to use state agencies because the majority of jobs available through these agencies are for semiskilled or unskilled workers. From a practical standpoint, it can't hurt to consult state employment agencies. They will have information about some professional and managerial positions available in your area, and you will not be charged a fee if you obtain a job through a state employment agency.

Many people want a job immediately and are discouraged at the thought of an occupational search taking months. The fact is, though, that people seeking entry-level jobs should expect their job search to take three to six months. Job applicants who want higher-paying positions can expect to be looking for work for as long as a year, eighteen months, or more. Of course, the state of the economy and whether employers are hiring or not can shorten or extend a job search for anyone.

Regardless of how long it takes, most people will tell you that a job search always takes too long. During a job search, you should use the same work habits that effective employees use on the job. When searching for a job, resist the temptation to "take the day off." Instead, make a master list of activities that you want to accomplish each day. If necessary, force yourself to make contacts, do job research, or schedule interviews that might lead to job opportunities. (Actually, many job applicants look at the job hunt as their job and work from eight to five, five days a week until they find the job they want.) Above all, realize that an occupational search requires patience and perseverance. And according to many individuals who have been through the process of trying to find a job, perseverance may be the most important trait that successful job hunters need.

Planning and Preparation

It is generally agreed that competition for the better jobs will get tougher and tougher. The key to landing the job you want is planning and preparation, and planning begins with goals. In particular, it is important to determine your *personal goals,* to decide on the role your career will play in reaching those goals, and then to develop your career goals. Once you know where you are going, you can devise a reasonable plan for getting there.

The time to begin planning is as early as possible. You must, of course, satisfy the educational requirements for the occupational area you wish to enter. Early planning will give you the opportunity to do so. But those people with whom you will be competing for the better jobs also will be fully prepared. Can you do more?

The answer is yes. Corporate recruiters say that the following factors give job candidates a definite advantage:

- *Work experience.* You can get valuable work experience in cooperative work/school programs, during summer vacations, or in part-time jobs during the school year. Experience in your chosen occupational area carries the most weight, but even unrelated work experience is important.
- *The ability to communicate well.* Verbal and written communication skills are increasingly important in all aspects of business. Yours will be tested in your letters to recruiters, in your résumé, and in interviews. You will use these same communication skills throughout your career.
- *Clear and realistic job and career goals.* Recruiters feel most comfortable with candidates who know where they are headed and why they are applying for a specific job.

Again, early planning can make all the difference in defining your goals, in sharpening your communication skills (through elective courses, if necessary), and in obtaining solid work experience. See Table B.1 to learn about online career planning resources.

TABLE B.1: Online Career Planning Every day, more and more people are using the Internet for their career planning activities. Obtaining information about employers, picking up helpful résumé writing and interviewing tips, making contacts, and upgrading employment skills are just a few of the Web-based career tasks growing in popularity. (Visit the text website for updates and additions to these URLs.)

American Marketing Association	www.marketingpower.com
America's Job Bank	www.ajb.dni.us
CareerBuilder.com	www.careerbuilder.com
CareerJournal	www.careerjournal.com
CollegeGrad.com	http://collegegrad.com
D&B's Million Dollar Database	http://mddi.dnb.com
FedWorld	www.fedworld.gov/
Hoover's Online	http://premium.hoovers.com
HotJobs	http://hotjobs.yahoo.com
job-interview.net	http://job-interview.net
JobStar	http://jobstar.org
JobWeb	www.jobweb.com
Monster	www.monster.com
The Riley Guide	http://rileyguide.com
Vault	http://vault.com
WetFeet	http://wetfeet.com

Letter and Résumé

Preparation is also important when it is time to apply for a position. Your college placement office and various publications available in your library (including such directories as *Standard & Poor's Register of Corporations* and the *Thomas Register*) can help you find firms to apply to for jobs. As already mentioned, help-wanted ads, the Internet, networking, and employment agencies also may provide leads.

Your first contact with a prospective employer probably will be through the mail, in a letter in which you express your interest in working for that firm. This letter should be clear and straightforward, and it should follow proper business-letter form (see Figure B.3). It (and any other letters you write to potential employers) will be considered part of your employment credentials.

This first letter should be addressed to the personnel or human resources manager, by name, if possible. You may include in this letter, very briefly, some information regarding your qualifications and your reason for writing to that particular firm. If your source of information (newspaper advertisement, employment agency, current employee of the firm, and so on) indicates that this employer is looking for specific job skills, you also may want to state and describe in the cover letter the skills you possess. You should request an interview and, if the firm requires it, an employment application.

You should include a copy of your résumé with your first letter (most applicants do). In any case, you should already have prepared the résumé, which is a summary of all your attention-getting employment achievements and capabilities. Your goal in preparing both the cover letter and the résumé is to give the potential employer the impression that you are someone who deserves an interview.

A résumé should highlight and summarize your abilities and work achievements. The résumé should fit on a single sheet of white high-quality bond letter paper. It should be carefully thought out; rework it as many times as necessary to get it right and put your best foot forward. Make your résumé concise, but be sure to note everything important. You need not include explanations or details; you will have an opportunity to discuss your qualifications during the interviews. It should be written to grab a potential employer's interest. The employer reading your résumé should want to meet you to find out more. Your résumé needs to show that despite your current job title, you are qualified for the higher-level position you seek.

Remember that you are writing a résumé that will sell you to a potential employer. If necessary, ask former supervisors and colleagues to tell you what happened to projects or work that you produced. Then use action verbs to describe your major contributions. Words such as *managed, created, developed,* and *coordinated* sound high powered. Passive words or phrases such as *was responsible* for and *performed* are not attention-getting. Highlight your work achievements by using percentages, numbers, or dollar amounts. Such concrete details demonstrate just how important your contributions were. In some cases, personal traits or the ability to "do something," may be more important than technical skills. Employers may be looking for someone who has the ability to

1. Prepare letters, memos, and other written communications
2. Answer the telephone and talk with customers
3. Analyze and solve problems related to a specific job
4. Work independently and make decisions
5. Be flexible and get the job done
6. Get along with others and be a team player

These traits may be extremely important to some employers. And a job applicant who does not have a lot of occupational experience can use these traits to beef up a slim résumé.

Figures B.4, B.5, and B.6 show a chronological résumé, a functional résumé, and a new database résumé, respectively. The chronological résumé presents your

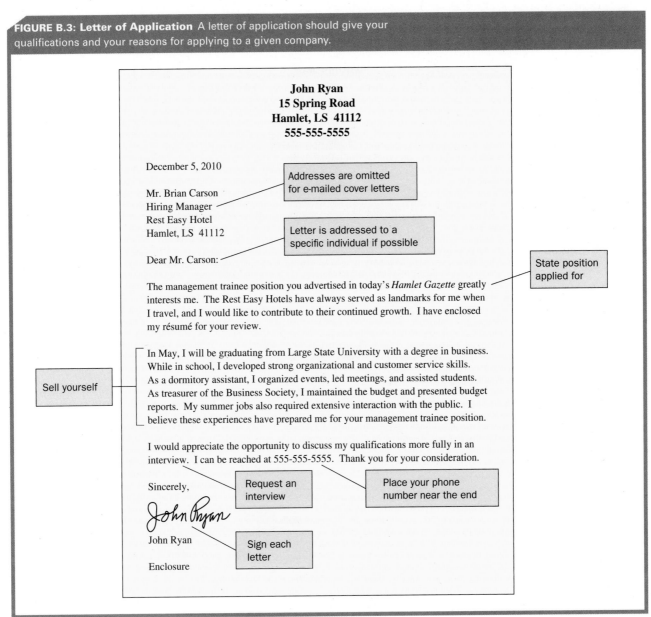

Source: U.S. Bureau of Labor Statistics website, **www.bls.gov/opub/ooq/1999/summer/art01.pdf,** accessed July 12, 2009.

education, work experience, and other information in a reverse-time sequence (the most recent item first). The functional résumé emphasizes your abilities and skills in categories such as communication, supervision, project planning, human relations, and research. The database résumé, also called a *plain text* or *e-mail résumé,* includes the same basic information, except that the database résumé is written without columns, bullets, or bold or italic styles. Regardless of the form used, a résumé should include the following: your name, address, and telephone number; your work experience and major accomplishments on the job; your educational background; and any awards you have won. Avoid all extraneous information (such as weight, age, marital status, and the names and addresses of references) that could be supplied during an interview. Reserve your employment and/or career objectives for mention in the one-page cover letters you send to potential employers with copies of your résumé.

Job Application Forms

Once you have mailed your cover letter and résumé, the next step generally depends on the employer. Most interested prospective employers will ask that

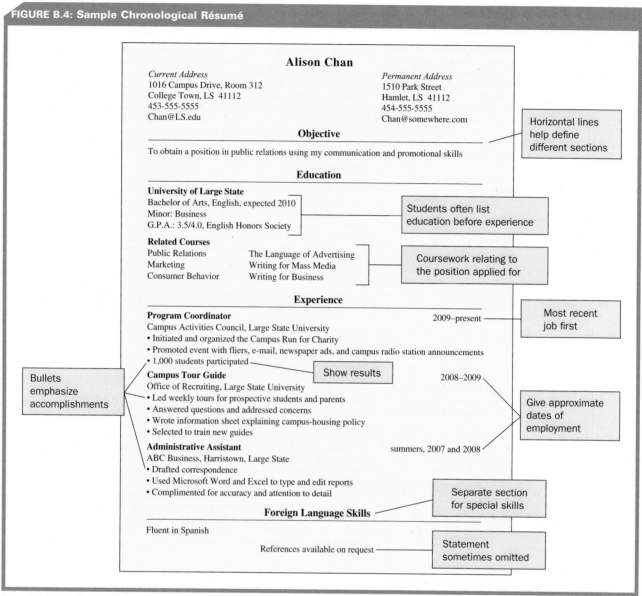

Source: U.S. Bureau of Labor Statistics website, **www.bls.gov/opub/ooq/1999/summer/art01.pdf,** accessed July 12, 2009.

you complete an employment application form, come in for a job interview, or both. Regardless of what happens next, you should view both the application form and the interview as opportunities to tell the prospective employer about any special skills and talents that make you the type of employee the company is looking for.

The typical job application form asks for the following information:

- Personal data
- Educational background
- Military record
- Employment history
- Criminal record
- Character references

Do the best job you can when answering questions in each of these areas. The way you complete an application form demonstrates your ability to follow directions and to communicate effectively. The suggestions listed in Table B.2 can help you to avoid some of the most common mistakes applicants make.

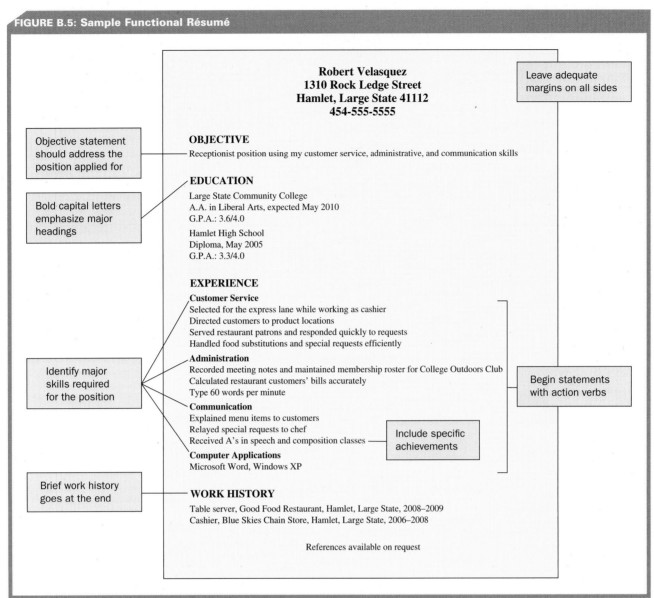

Robert Velasquez
1310 Rock Ledge Street
Hamlet, Large State 41112
454-555-5555

Leave adequate margins on all sides

Objective statement should address the position applied for

OBJECTIVE
Receptionist position using my customer service, administrative, and communication skills

Bold capital letters emphasize major headings

EDUCATION
Large State Community College
A.A. in Liberal Arts, expected May 2010
G.P.A.: 3.6/4.0

Hamlet High School
Diploma, May 2005
G.P.A.: 3.3/4.0

EXPERIENCE
Customer Service
Selected for the express lane while working as cashier
Directed customers to product locations
Served restaurant patrons and responded quickly to requests
Handled food substitutions and special requests efficiently

Identify major skills required for the position

Administration
Recorded meeting notes and maintained membership roster for College Outdoors Club
Calculated restaurant customers' bills accurately
Type 60 words per minute

Begin statements with action verbs

Communication
Explained menu items to customers
Relayed special requests to chef
Received A's in speech and composition classes

Include specific achievements

Computer Applications
Microsoft Word, Windows XP

Brief work history goes at the end

WORK HISTORY
Table server, Good Food Restaurant, Hamlet, Large State, 2008–2009
Cashier, Blue Skies Chain Store, Hamlet, Large State, 2006–2008

References available on request

Source: U.S. Bureau of Labor Statistics website, **www.bls.gov/opub/ooq/1999/summer/art01.pdf,** accessed July 12, 2009

The Job Interview

Your résumé and cover letter are, in essence, an introduction. The deciding factor in the hiring process is the interview (or several interviews) with representatives of the firm. It is through the interview that the firm gets to know you and your qualifications. At the same time, the interview provides a chance for you to learn about the firm.

Here, again, preparation is the key to success. Research the firm before your first interview. Learn all you can about its products, its subsidiaries, the markets it operates in, its history, the locations of its facilities, and so on. If possible, obtain and read the firm's most recent annual report. Be prepared to ask questions about the firm and the opportunities it offers. Interviewers welcome such questions. They expect you to be interested enough to spend some time thinking about your potential relationship with their firm.

Prepare also to respond to questions the interviewer may ask. Table B.3 is a list of typical interviewer questions that job applicants often find difficult to answer. However, do not expect interviewers to stick to the list given in the table or to the items appearing in your résumé. They will be interested in anything that helps them to decide what kind of person and worker you are.

FIGURE B.6: Sample Plain-Text Résumé

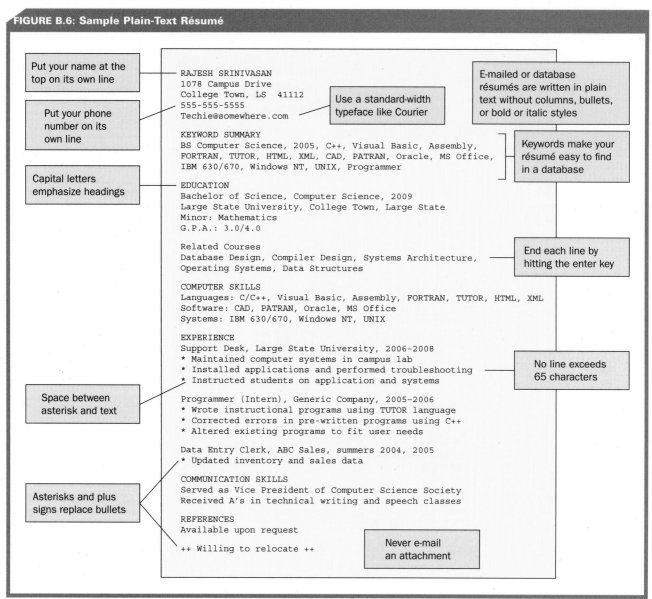

Put your name at the top on its own line

Put your phone number on its own line

Capital letters emphasize headings

Space between asterisk and text

Asterisks and plus signs replace bullets

Use a standard-width typeface like Courier

E-mailed or database résumés are written in plain text without columns, bullets, or bold or italic styles

Keywords make your résumé easy to find in a database

End each line by hitting the enter key

No line exceeds 65 characters

Never e-mail an attachment

```
RAJESH SRINIVASAN
1078 Campus Drive
College Town, LS  41112
555-555-5555
Techie@somewhere.com

KEYWORD SUMMARY
BS Computer Science, 2005, C++, Visual Basic, Assembly,
FORTRAN, TUTOR, HTML, XML, CAD, PATRAN, Oracle, MS Office,
IBM 630/670, Windows NT, UNIX, Programmer

EDUCATION
Bachelor of Science, Computer Science, 2009
Large State University, College Town, Large State
Minor: Mathematics
G.P.A.: 3.0/4.0

Related Courses
Database Design, Compiler Design, Systems Architecture,
Operating Systems, Data Structures

COMPUTER SKILLS
Languages: C/C++, Visual Basic, Assembly, FORTRAN, TUTOR, HTML, XML
Software: CAD, PATRAN, Oracle, MS Office
Systems: IBM 630/670, Windows NT, UNIX

EXPERIENCE
Support Desk, Large State University, 2006-2008
* Maintained computer systems in campus lab
* Installed applications and performed troubleshooting
* Instructed students on application and systems

Programmer (Intern), Generic Company, 2005-2006
* Wrote instructional programs using TUTOR language
* Corrected errors in pre-written programs using C++
* Altered existing programs to fit user needs

Data Entry Clerk, ABC Sales, summers 2004, 2005
* Updated inventory and sales data

COMMUNICATION SKILLS
Served as Vice President of Computer Science Society
Received A's in technical writing and speech classes

REFERENCES
Available upon request

++ Willing to relocate ++
```

Source: U.S. Bureau of Labor Statistics website, **www.bls.gov/opub/ooq/1999/summer/art01.pdf,** accessed July 12, 2009

Make sure that you are on time for your interview and are dressed and groomed in a businesslike manner. Interviewers take note of punctuality and appearance, just as they do of other personal qualities. Have a copy of your résumé with you, even if you have already sent one to the firm. You also may want to bring a copy of your course transcript and letters of recommendation. If you plan to furnish interviewers with the names and addresses of references rather than with letters of recommendation, make sure that you have your references' permission to do so.

Consider the interview itself as a two-way conversation rather than as a question-and-answer session. Volunteer any information that is relevant to the interviewer's questions. If an important point is skipped in the discussion, do not hesitate to bring it up. Be yourself, but emphasize your strengths. Good eye contact and posture are important, too. They should come naturally if you take an active part in the interview.

At the conclusion of the interview, thank the recruiter for taking the time to see you. Then, a day or two later, follow up by sending a short letter of thanks In this letter, you can ask a question or two that may have occurred to you after the interview or add pertinent information that may have been overlooked.

TABLE B.2: Tips for Completing Employment Application Forms

1. Do a "dry run" to practice answering the questions on a typical employment application.

2. If it is not possible to take the application home, complete the application in ink. Print clearly. Use one lettering style. Be neat.

3. Follow the directions on the employment application.

4. Read all questions before you begin answering them.

5. Judge the amount of space that you have to answer each question.

6. Fill in every blank even if you must write not applicable (N/A) or none.

7. Use only recognizable abbreviations.

8. Know your work history.

9. Answer all questions honestly.

10. Choose references carefully.

11. Be careful when writing salary requirements. Avoid committing yourself to a specific number, and know the going rate in your field.

12. Read over the completed application, and look for grammatical or spelling errors.

Sources: Susan D. Greene and Melanie C. L. Martel, *The Ultimate Job Hunter's Guidebook*, 5th ed. Copyright © 2008 by Houghton Mifflin Company, pp. 177–179. Adapted with permission.

TABLE B.3: Interview Questions Job Applicants Often Find Difficult to Answer

1. Tell me about yourself.

2. What do you know about our organization?

3. What can you do for us? Why should we hire you?

4. What qualifications do you have that make you feel that you will be successful in your field?

5. What have you learned from the jobs that you have held?

6. If you could write your own ticket, what would be your ideal job?

7. What are your special skills, and how did you acquire them?

8. Have you had any special accomplishments in your lifetime that you are particularly proud of?

9. Why did you leave your most recent job?

10. How do you spend your spare time? What are your hobbies?

11. What are your strengths and weaknesses?

12. Discuss five major accomplishments.

13. What kind of boss would you like? Why?

14. If you could spend a day with someone you have known or known of, who would it be?

15. What personality characteristics rub you the wrong way?

16. How do you show your anger? What type of things make you angry?

17. With what type of person do you spend the majority of your time?

18. What activities have you ever quit?

19. Define cooperation.

Sources: Adapted from Susan D. Greene and Melanie C. L. Martel, *The Ultimate Job Hunter's Guidebook*, 5th ed. Copyright © 2008 by Houghton Mifflin Company, pp. 196–197. Used with permission.

In most cases, the first interview is used to *screen* applicants, or to choose those who are best qualified. These applicants are then given a second interview and perhaps a third, usually with one or more department heads. If the job requires relocation to a different area, applicants may be invited there for these later interviews. After the interviewing process is complete, applicants are told when to expect a hiring decision.

Accepting an Offer

"We'd like to offer you the job" may be the best news a job applicant can hear. To accept the job, you should send the firm a letter in which you express your appreciation, accept the offer, and restate the conditions of employment as you understand them. These conditions should include the starting salary, employee benefits, and a general description of the job (responsibilities, training, the immediate supervisor's name, and such). If you have any concerns regarding the job, make sure that they are cleared up before you send your letter of acceptance: The job offer and your acceptance constitute a contract between you and the firm.

Less exciting is the news that begins, "We thank you for your interest in our firm, *but. ...*" The fact is that there are many more applicants for jobs than there are jobs. (This is so because most people apply for several positions at the same time.) As a result, most people are turned down for some jobs during their careers. Do not be discouraged if you don't get the first position you apply for. Instead, think back over the application process, analyze it, and try to determine what you might improve. In other words, learn from your experience, and keep trying. Success will come if you persevere.

A Final Note about Careers

A job is for today, but a career can last a lifetime. Although most applicants are excited when they get their first job, the employment process does not stop with your first job, it continues throughout your career. Additional training and education, promotions and advancement, and even changing jobs or careers are all part of a continuing process.

Although different people measure success in different ways, success in a career means more than just knowing how to do a job. You must combine technical skills and managerial skills with the ability to get along with people. A number of traits that successful people usually possess are presented in Table B.4. Generally, people

TABLE B.4: Traits That Successful People Usually Possess

1. An ability to work well with others in a variety of settings

2. A desire to do tasks better than they have to be done

3. An interest in reading a wide variety and large quantity of material

4. A willingness to cope with conflict and adapt to change

5. An ability to anticipate problems

6. A knowledge of technology and computer software such as word-processing, spreadsheet, and database programs

7. An ability to solve problems creatively

8. A knowledge of research techniques and library resources

9. Well-developed written and oral communication skills

10. An understanding of both their own motivations and the motivations of others.

Sources: From *Personal Finance*, 9th ed., by Jack R. Kapoor, Les R. Dlabay, and Robert J. Hughes. Copyright © 2009 by The McGraw-Hill Companies Inc. Reprinted by permission.

who are promoted know how to make decisions, communicate well, and handle stress. These same people also can manage another valuable asset, their time.

In any career there will be times when you need to reevaluate your decisions and opportunities. It may be necessary to determine what you can do to get your career back on track. It may even be necessary to change jobs or careers to obtain a better or more rewarding position. Although there are no guarantees, workers who can adapt to change and who are willing to pursue further education and training are more likely to be successful. The world is changing, and it is your responsibility to make the right decisions. Your teachers, friends, and relatives are willing to help you to make decisions, but it is your life and you must take charge. Good luck!

SUMMARY

Many people work at a job because they need money to survive. A career, on the other hand, is a commitment not only to a profession but also to an individual's own interests and talents. Before choosing a career, you must evaluate what you like to do, what you are good at, how much education you have, and where you want to live. Also, are you willing to work long hours?

Individuals should also consider future trends in employment before deciding on a career. It is expected that college graduates with degrees in business and management, computer science, education, engineering, and health professions will be in high demand between now and the year 2016. It is also expected that there will be an increased emphasis on training, retraining, and automation and that job seekers must incorporate each of these trends into their career plans. Finally, the experts predict that the number of women, two-income families, and older workers in the work force will increase between now and the year 2016. Furthermore, there will be a greater emphasis on job sharing, flexible hours, and other innovative work practices.

When job applicants begin their career search, they usually obtain information from a number of sources—the library, campus placement offices, a network of friends and professionals, and employment agencies. Employment agencies may be divided into two categories: private and state. Both types help individuals obtain jobs, but private employment agencies do charge a fee for their services. Although most people want a job immediately, an occupational job search takes time. During the occupational job search, you should use the same effective work habits that employees use on the job. Above all you should realize that an occupational search requires patience and perseverance.

The time to begin career planning is as early as possible. According to the corporate recruiters, work experience, the ability to communicate well, and realistic job and career goals are essential. Preparation again becomes important when it is time to apply for a position. You should develop both your resume and cover letter very carefully. Your goal in preparing both is to give the potential employer the impression that you are someone who deserves an interview.

Once you have mailed your cover letter and resume, the next step generally depends on the employer. If interested, most prospective employers will ask you to complete an employment application. Although employment applications vary in form and length, the typical application asks for the following information: personal data; military record; criminal record; educational background; employment history; and character references. You should always view the application as an opportunity to tell the prospective employer about your special skills and talents. Above all, completing an application allows you to demonstrate your ability to follow directions and to communicate effectively.

Your cover letter, resume, and application are, in essence, an introduction. The deciding factor in the hiring process is the interview with representatives of the firm. Once again, preparation is the key. Learn as much as you can about the firm and the opportunities it offers. Also prepare to answer questions that the interviewer may ask. In most cases, the first interview is used to screen applicants, or choose those that are the best qualified. These applicants are then given a second, and perhaps a third interview—usually with one or more department heads. If a job is offered, you should send the firm a letter expressing your appreciation, accepting the offer, restating the conditions of employment as you understand them.

To be competitive in today's world, you must realize that career planning doesn't stop when you get your first job. Additional training and education, promotions and advancements, and even changing jobs or careers are all part of a continuing process. In any career, there will be times when you need to reevaluate your decisions and opportunities. The world is changing, and workers who can adapt to change and who are willing to pursue further education and training are most likely to be successful.

NOTES

Chapter 1

1. Jeffrey M. O'Brien, "IBM's Grand Plan to Save the Planet," *Fortune,* May 4, 2009, p. 84; William M. Bulkeley, "IBM to Cut U.S. Jobs, Expand in India," *Wall Street Journal,* March 26, 2009, p. B1; John Hechinger, William M. Bulkeley, and Ben Worthen, "IBM Signals Strategy Shift with Talks to Buy Sun," *Wall Street Journal,* March 19, 2009, p. B9; www.ibm.com.
2. The Horatio Alger website at www.horatioalger.com, March 17, 2009.
3. Ibid.
4. The Wikipedia website at www.wikipedia.com, March 17, 2009.
5. Idy Fernandez, "Julie Stav," *Hispanic,* June-July 2005, p. 24.
6. The Wal-Mart, Inc., website at www.walmart.com, March 18, 2009.
7. The Bureau of Economic Analysis website at www.bea.gov, March 20, 2009.
8. The Bureau of Labor Statistics website at www.bls.gov, March 20, 2009.
9. Bill Weir, "Made in China: Your Job, Your Future, Your Fortune," ABC News website at www.abcnews.com, September 20, 2005.
10. The Bureau of Economic Analysis website at www.bea.gov, March 20, 2009.
11. The Bureau of Economic Analysis website at www.bea.gov, March 21, 2009.
12. The Treasury Direct website at www.treasurydirect.gov, March 21, 2009.
13. The Investopedia website at www.investopedia.com, March 28, 2009.
14. The Bureau of Labor Statistics website at www.bls.gov, March 21, 2009.
15. Bill Weir, "Made in China: Your Job, Your Future, Your Fortune," ABC News website at www.abcnews.com, September 20, 2005.
16. The Environmental Protection Agency website at www.epa.com, March 22, 2009.
17. Company website, http://www.peetscoffee.com, accessed May 11, 2009; "Peet's Coffee and Tea 1Q Jumps 46 Percent," Associated Press, April 28, 2009, http://www.forbes.com/feeds/ap/2009/04/28/ap6351274.html

Chapter 2

1. Michael Burnham, "FedEx to Boost Biofuel Use to Cut Costs, Emissions," *New York Times,* April 29, 2009, www.nytimes.com; Harriet Baskas, "Solar-Powered Airports? It Could Happen," *USA Today,* April 28, 2009, www.usatoday.com; "World's Most Admired Companies," *Fortune,* March 16, 2009, http://money.cnn.com/magazines/fortune/mostadmired/2009/index.html.
2. MSNBC website at www.msnbc.msn.com, accessed April 27, 2009.
3. The United States Department of Justice, www.usdoj.gov, accessed April 2, 2009.
4. *Frontlines* (Washington: U.S. Agency for International Development), September 2005, p. 16.
5. Deere & Company Corporate Governance—Code of Ethics, http://www.deere.com/en_US/ir/corporategovernance/pf_ethics.html, accessed April 20,2009.
6. "Corporate Convicts: Where are they Now?" CNNMoney.com, accessed April 20, 2009.
7. General Mills: 2009 Corporate Social Responsibility Report http://www.generalmills.com/corporate/commitment/corp.aspx, accessed April 25, 2009.
8. Dell Community and Employee Engagement,, http://content.dell.com/us/en/corp/d/corp-comm/employee-engagement. aspx, accessed April 26, 2009.
9. GE Citizenship, http://www.ge.com/citizenship/performance_areas/communities_philanthropy_people.jsp, accessed April 27, 2009.
10. The Charles Schwab Coporation, http://www.aboutschwab.com/community/corporate-giving/index.html, accessed April 28, 2009.
11. The Verizon Foundation, http://fooundation.verizon.com/abou8t/press/newstory_verizon_csahv09.shtml, April 28, 2009.
12. ExxonMobil-Higher Education, http:www.exxonmobile.com/Corporate/community_ed_higher.aspx, accessed April 29, 2009.
13. AT&T News Release, http://www.att.com/gen/press-room?pid=4800&cdvn=news&newsarticleid=26457, accessed April 27, 2009.
14. Based on information from "New Belgium Brewery: Four Principles of Sustainable Business," Triplepundit.com, June 7, 2008, http://www.triplepundit.com/pages/new-belgium-bre.php; "New Belgium Brewing Wins Ethics Award," *Denver Business Journal,* January 2, 2003, Denver .bizjournals.com/Denver/stories/2002/12/30/daily21.html; Richard Brandes, "Beer Growth Brands," *Beverage Dynamics,* September–October 2002, pp. 37ff; www.newbelgium.com.

Chapter 3

1. Julie Jargon, "New Ads Will Stir Up Coffee Wars," *Wall Street Journal,* May 4, 2009, www.wsj.com; Emma Hall, "McD's Opened Dialogue to Turn Itself Around," *Advertising Age,* February 23, 2009, p. 12; Gregg Cebrzynski, "McDonald's Overhauls Global Packaging to Send a Strong, Food-Driven Message about Quality," *Nation's Restaurant News,* November 10, 2008, p. 22.
2. The White House, Office of the Press Secretary, Press Release, August 6, 2002.
3. U.S. Bureau of Economic Analysis, U.S. Bureau of Commerce, http://bea.gov/international/bp_web/saction.cfm, accessed April `6, 2009.
4. This section draws heavily from *The World Economic Outlook Update,* International Monetary Fund, accessed January 28, 2009.
5. Micheal Chriszt and Elena Whisler, "China's Economic Emergence," *Econ South,* First Reserve Bank of Atlanta, Second Quarter 2005, pp. 4–7.
6. Office of the United States Trade Representative, *NAFTA Facts,* March 2008, p. 1, www.ustr.gov, accessed May 2, 2009.
7. Office of the United States Trade Representative, *USTR News,* February 27, 2008, www.ustr.gov, accessed May 2, 2009.
8. Office of the United States Trade Representative, *Fact Sheet,* http://www.ustr.gov/Trade_Agreements/Regional/Enterprice_for_ASEAN_Initiative/, accessed September 26, 2008.
9. William M. Pride and O. C. Ferrell, *Marketing,* Library Edition, (Boston: Houghton Mifflin, 2008) p. 194.
10. Based on video entitled *Fossil—Keeping Watch on a Global Business* © Cengage Learning.

Chapter 4

1. Sam Schechner and Elizabeth Holmes, "Disney Climbs Aboard Video Site Hulu," *Wall Street Journal,* May 1, 2009, www.wsj.com; Staci D. Kramer, "Hulu's Kilar: Great To Have Disney But 'We're Still An Extremely Young Company,'" *PaidContent.org,* May 5, 2009, www.washingtonpost.com; "Hulu Who?" *The Economist,* February 7, 2009, p. 59; www.hulu.com.
2. The Ivy Planning Group website at www.ivygroupllc.com, accessed April 3, 2009.
3. The National Association of Publicly Traded Partnerships website at www.naptp.org, accessed April 3, 2009.
4. The Procter & Gamble website at www.pg.com, accessed April 3, 2009.

©Grant Dougal

5. The AllBusiness website at www.allbusiness.com, accessed April 13, 2009.
6. The Hispanic PR Wire website at www.hispanicprwire.com, accessed April 13, 2009.
7. The Internal Revenue Service website at www.irs.gov, accessed April 13, 2009.
8. The Ocean Spray Cranberries, Inc. website at www.oceanspray.com, accessed April 14, 2009.
9. The BusinessWeek website at www.businessweek.com, accessed August 7, 2007.
10. The Sony Ericsson website at www.sonyericsson.com, accessed April 14, 2009.
11. "Visa IPO Prices at Record 417.9B," The CNNMoney.com website at www.money.cnn.com, March 19,2008.
12. The Wal-Mart Stores, Inc. website at www.walmart.com, accessed March 18, 2009.
13. The Yahoo! Finance website at http://finance.yahoo.com, accessed April 16, 2009.
14. The IBM website at www.ibm.com, accessed September 18, 2008.
15. Based on information from Keith Reed, "Bowing Out at Jordan's," *Boston Globe*, December 22, 2006, p. C1; David Gianatasio, "Rooms to Grow," *Adweek*, January 14, 2003, p. 3; Jon Chesto, "Buffet Helps Jordan's Flip Switch," *Boston Herald*, August 22, 2002, p. 37; "At the Movies with Buffet," *Financial Express*, October 28, 2002; Barry Tatelman, "You Can't Take That Away from Us," *Operations Management* (n.d.), http://www.entrepreneurship.org/Resources/Detail/Default.aspx?id=10676; www.jordansfurniture.com.

Chapter 5

1. "Mobile Apps To Hit $25 Billion By 2014," *InformationWeek*, April 29, 2009, www.informationweek.com; Eliot Van Buskirk, "Billionth iPhone App Downloader Scores Freebies; Developer Wins Too," *Wired*, April 24, 2009, www.wired.com; Jenna Wortham, "The iPhone Gold Rush," *New York Times*, April 5, 2009, pp. ST-1, ST-8; John Cook, "Get Out Your Picks and Shovels, the iPhone App Gold Rush Is On," *Techflash*, May 1, 2009, www.techflash.com.
2. U.S. Small Business Administration, http://www.sba.gov/services/contractingopportunities/OWNERS/BASICS/GC_SMALL_BUSINESS.html, accessed May 5, 2009.
3. Office of Advocacy estimates based on data from the U.S. Department of Commerce, Bureau of the Census, and U.S. Department of Labor, Employment and Training Administration, http://web.sba.gov/faqs/faqindex.cfm?areaID=24, accessed May 5, 2009.
4. Ibid.
5. Small Business Administration, Office of Advocacy, *Quarterly Indicators*, Second Quarter 2008, www.sba.gov/advo, accessed October 3, 2008.
6. Thomas A. Garrett, "Entrepreneurs Thrive in America," *Bridges*, Federal Reserve Bank of St. Louis, Spring 2005, p. 2.
7. U.S. Small Business Administration, SBA Office of Advocacy, *Small Business Research Summary*, Number 341, February 2009, accessed May 12, 2009; U.S. Small Business Administration, SBA Press Office, *News Release*, September 10, 2008; and 2008 *The Small Business Economy*, a Report to the President, U.S. Business Administration, Washington, D.C., December 2008, pp. 61–63, and 99.
8. U.S. Small Business Administration News Release, www.sba.gov/teens/brian_hendricks.html. accessed May 7, 2009.
9. U.S. Small Business Administration, Office of Advocacy, *Frequently Asked Questions*, September 2008, http://web.sba.gov/faqs/faqIndexAll.cfm?areaID=24, accessed May 9, 2009.
10. U.S. Small Business Administration, www.sba.gov/advo/, accessed May 6, 2009.
11. U.S. Small Business Administration, SBA Office of Advocacy, *Small Business Research Summary*, Number 341, February 2009, accessed May 12, 2009; and SBA *Quarterly Indicators*, First Quarter 2009, released May 8, 2009, p. 1.
12. Timothy S. Hatten, *"Small Business Management: Entrepreneurship and Beyond,"* 4th ed., Copyright © 2009 by Houghton Mifflin Company, p. 238. Reprinted with permission.
13. U.S. Small Business Administration, http://www.sba.gov/aboutsba/sbaprograms/sbdc/aboutus/index.html, accessed May 14, 2009.
14. SCORE *FY2007 Annual Report*, p. 2, www.score.org/pdf/SCORE_FY08_Annual_Report.pdf, accessed May 13, 2009.
15. U.S. Small Business Administration, *2007 The Year in Review*, p. 7, www.sba.gov, accessed October 5, 2008.
16. Ibid.
17. SBA Press Release, *Fact Sheet*, September 11, 2008, p. 2.
18. U.S. Small Business Administration, *Small Business Investment Companies*, http://www.sba.gov/aboutsba/sbaprograms/inv/index/html, accessed August 17, 2009.
19. Cindy Elmore, "Putting the Power into the Hands of Small Business Owners," *Marketwise*, Federal Reserve Bank of Richmond, Issue II, 2005, p. 13.
20. U.S. Small Business Administration, www.sba.gov/managing/marketing/intlsales.html, accessed October 4, 2008.
21. The U.S. Commercial Service, http://www.buyusa.gov/home/worldwide_us.html, accessed May 13, 2009.
22. Based on information from Krystal Grow, "Newbury Comics Coming Back," The Norwood Record, May 8, 2008, http://norwoodrecord.com; Donna Goodison, "Norwood Superstore Sets Newbury Comics Record," Boston Herald, August 20, 2008, p. 21; Ed Christman, "Newbury Comics Cuts Staff," *Billboard*, September 10, 2005, p. 8; Wendy Wilson, "Newbury Comics," *Video Business*, December 20, 2004, p. 18; Ed Christman, "'We Have All Had to Grow Up a Little,'" *Billboard*, September 27, 2003, pp. N3ff; www.newburycomics.com.

Chapter 6

1. Adam Bryant, "The Keeper of that Tapping Pen," *New York Times*, March 22, 2009, p. BU-2; Joanne Wojcik, "Volunteer Work Benefits Employers, Employees as Well as the Community," *Business Insurance*, June 23, 2008, p. 14; Thomas Hoffman, "Career Nurturing at Xerox," *Computerworld*, June 23, 2008, p. 36; www.xerox.com.
2. www.google.com/corporate/, accessed April 15, 2009.
3. Lucas Conley, "Climbing Back up the Mountain," *Fast Company*, April 2005, p. 84.
4. www.cosmeticdesign.com, accessed April 13, 2009.
5. Procter & Gamble, www.pg.com.
6. www.bizjournals.com, accessed April 13, 2009.
7. www.fastcompany.com; www.ge.com.
8. http://ajax.sys_con/node/530686, accessed April 16, 2009.
9. Henry Mintzberg, "The Manager's Job: Folklore and Fact," *Harvard Business Review*, July-August 1975, pp. 49–61.
10. Chana R. Shoenberger, "The Greenhouse Effect," www.forbes.com/global/2003/0203/030.html, accessed April 16, 2009.
11. Ricky W. Griffin, *Management*, 9th ed. (Boston: Houghton Mifflin, 2008), p. 234.
12. Based on video entitled Student Advantage Helps College Students Stay Organized © Cengage Learning. For more information, please see http://www.studentadvantage.com/content/?id=1205.

Chapter 7

1. Ashlee Vance, "Does H.P. Need a Dose of Anarchy?" *New York Times*, April 26, 2009, pp. BU1–BU8; "HP Labs Thriving with More Focused Approach," *San Francisco Chronicle*, March 16, 2009, www.sfgate.com; Brandon Bailey, "HP Labs director calls reorganization success," *San Jose Mercury News*, March 30, 2009, http://seattletimes.nwsource.com/html/businesstechnology/2008945990_bthplabs30.html?syndication=rss; www.hpl.hp.com.
2. "Mercedes-Benz USA Selects Workstream," *Business Editors; Automotive Writers*, March 2005.
3. Robert Kreitner, *Foundations of Management: Basics and Best Practices* (Boston: Houghton Mifflin, 2008), pp. 175–176.
4. Kreitner, *Foundations of Management*, p. 183.
5. www.hoovers.com, accessed April 16, 2009.
6. Rob Goffee and Gareth Jones, "The Character of a Corporation: How Your Company's Culture Can Make or Break Your Business," *Jones Harper Business*, p. 182.
7. Kreitner, *Foundations of Management*, p. 47.
8. Based on information from Paul Rolfes, "Green Mountain Coffee Roasters: Grounds for Growth," SmallCapInvestor.com, July 23, 2008, http://www.smallcapinvestor.com/stockresearch/spotlight/2008-07-23-green_mountain_coffee_roasters_grounds_for_growth; Tony Baer, "Brewing a New Kind of Connection," *Manufacturing Business Technology*, January 2005, pp. 40–42; Mark Pendergrast, "Green Mountain Coffee Roasters: Doing Well by Doing Good," *Tea & Coffee Trade Journal*, April 20, 2004, pp. 100+; Ellyn Spragins, "The Three-Peat," *Fortune Small Business*, July–August 2003, n.p.; www.greenmountaincoffee.com.

Chapter 8

1. Warren Staley, "Cargill Follows Vision Set by Lincoln," *Star Tribune (Minneapolis),* May 11, 2009, www.startribune.com; "Cargill Corn Milling Honored with Malcolm Baldrige Quality Award," *Food Processing,* November 25, 2008, www.foodprocessing.com; Jill Jusko, "Performance by Design," *Industry Week,* January 2008, p. 40; "Baldrige Award Recipient Profile," *National Institute of Standards and Technology,* November 25, 2008, www.nist.gov.
2. The Bureau of Labor Statistics website at www.bls.gov, accessed April 21, 2009.
3. Robert Kreitner, *Management* 11th ed. (Boston: Houghton Mifflin, 2009), p.474.
4. The 3M Corporate website at www.3M.com, accessed April 23, 2009.
5. The Campbell Soup Company website at www.campbellsoup.com, accessed April 23, 2009.
6. The Berry Plastics Corporation website at www.berryplastics. Com, accessed April 27, 2009.
7. The ATT Suppliers website at www.attsuppliers.com/diversity.asp, accessed April 27, 2009.
8. The National Institute for Standards and Technology (NIST) website at www.nist.gov, accessed April 27, 2009.
9. The iSixSigma website at www.isixsigma.com, accessed April 27, 2009.
10. The Bureau of Labor Statistics website at www.bls.gov, accessed April 27, 2009.
11. Ibid.
12. Ibid.
13. The Illumina Corporation website at www.illumina.com, accessed April 28, 2009.
14. The Dell Computer website at www.dell.com, accessed April 28, 2009.
15. Based on video entitled *Washburn Guitar* © Cengage Learning; and the Washburn Guitar Web site at www.washburn.com, accessed May 19, 2009.

Chapter 9

1. "Google: #4, 100 Best Companies to Work For," *Fortune,* February 2, 2009, www.fortune.com; "Despite Layoffs, Google Looks to Fill About 360 Openings," *Boston Globe,* March 29, 2009, p. G5; Jessica E. Vascellaro, "Google Plans 100 Layoffs of Recruiters," *Wall Street Journal,* January 15, 2009, p. B2; Jessica E. Vascellaro and Scott Morrison, "Google Gears Down for Tougher Times," *Wall Street Journal,* December 3, 2008, p. A1; www.google.com.
2. David Kiley, "Ford: Smaller-Than-Expected Loss Boosts the Stock," *BusinessWeek,* April 24, 2009.
3. U.S. Department of Labor, Bureau of Labor Statistics, www.bls.gov, accessed April 16, 2009.
4. "Diversity Training," *Virginia Business,* VirginiaBusiness.com, May 2007, www.virginiabusiness.com/edit/magazine/yr2007/may07/diver3.shtml.
5. http://hr.blr.com/about/about.aspx, accessed May 1, 2009.
6. Procter & Gamble, www.pg.com, accessed April 16, 2009.
7. Nanette Byrnes, "Start Search," *Business Week,* October 10, 2005, pp. 74–76.
8. U.S. Department of Labor, Bureau of Labor Statistics, News Release, September 10, 2008, www.bls.gov.
9. "100 Top Companies to Work For," *Fortune,* January 22, 2009, http://money.cnn.com/magazines/fortune/bestcompanies/2009/full_list/.
10. Cynthia D. Fisher, Lyle F. Schoenfeldt, and James B. Shaw, *Human Resource Management* (Boston: Houghton Mifflin, 2006), p. 464.
11. Ibid., pp. 465.
12. Naomi R. Kooker, "Aquarium Chief Doesn't See Economy Tanking," *Boston Business Journal,* January 4, 2008, boston.bizjournals.com; Geoff Edgers, "With Eye on Growth, Aquarium Names New Chief," *Boston Globe,* June 15, 2005, www.bostonglobe.com; Stephanie Vosk, "It's February, But on Summer Jobs, Hope Springs Eternal," *Boston Globe,* February 20, 2005, p. 3; Jeffrey Krasner, "New England Aquarium Plunges into Financial Turmoil," *Boston Globe,* December 13, 2002, www.boston.com/global; www.neaq.org.

Chapter 10

1. "100 Best Companies to Work For: #20 SAS," *Fortune,* February 2, 2009, www.fortune.com; Rich Whiting, "SAS Vows No Layoffs in 2009," *ChannelWeb,* March 24, 2009, www.crn.com/software; "SAS, NetSuite, Salesforce.com Announce Cloud Computing Efforts," *InformationWeek,* March 19, 2009, www.informationweek.com; www.sas.com.
2. Sheree R. Curry, "Retention Getters," *Incentive,* April 2005, pp. 14+, www.sap.com/usa/about/careers/benefits/index.epx, accessed April 17, 2009.
3. Douglas McGregor, *The Human Side of Enterprise* (New York: McGraw-Hill, 1960).
4. William Ouchi, *Theory Z* (Reading, MA: Addison-Wesley, 1981).
5. Ricky W. Griffin, *Fundamentals of Management,* 3d ed. (Boston: Houghton Mifflin, 2006), p. 300.
6. Rochelle Garner, "Company Growth and Rankings," *Computer Reseller,* January 31, 2005.
7. Filip Truta, "Apple Offers Corporate Gifting and Rewards Program," May 21, 2008, http://news.softpedia.com/news/Apple-Offers-Corporate-Gifting-and-Rewards-Program-86164.shtml.
8. Alan Deutschman, "Making Change," *Fast Company,* May 2005, p. 52.
9. SC Johnson, www.scjohnson.com/careers/car_aie.asp, accessed May 1, 2009.
10. "Companies Find Benefits in Flex-Time," http://marketplace.publicradio.org/display/web/2008/05/21/flex_time/, accessed May 1, 2009.
11. Nanette Byrnes, "Star Search," *BusinessWeek,* October 10, 2005, p. 78.
12. Starbucks, http://www.starbucks.com/aboutus/jobcenter.asp, accessed May 1, 2009.
13. Carolyn Hirschman, "Share and Share Alike," *HR Magazine,* September 2005.
14. www.judywolf.com/articles_pr/articles_news/convincing_your_boss.html, accessed May 1, 2009.
15. http://money.cnn.com/magazines/fortune/bestcompanies/2008/benefits/telecommuting.html, February 4, 2008.
16. Art Mohamed, "Bosses Split Over Productivity of Teleworkers," *Computer Weekly,* March 29, 2005, p. 55.
17. Samuel Greengard, "Sun's Shining Example," *Workforce Management,* March 2005, pp. 48+.
18. Matthew Boyle and Ellen Florian Kratz, "The Wegmans Way," *Fortune,* January 24, 2005, p. 62.
19. "A Short History of ESOP," www.nceo.org, January 2006.
20. Ricky W. Griffin, *Fundamentals of Management* (Boston: Houghton Mifflin, 2008), pp. 385–404.
21. Barry L. Reece and Rhonda Brandt, *Effective Human Relations: Personal and Organizational Applications* (Boston: Houghton Mifflin, 2005), pp. 280–285.
22. "Jones Walker Law Firm Taps Harvard for New Orleans Rebuild Advice," *New Orleans CityBusiness,* News Section, January 3, 2006, n.p.
23. Bill Fischer and Andy Boynton, "Virtuoso Teams," *Harvard Business Review,* July–August 2005, pp. 116–123.
24. Jens Meiners, "M-B Changes Product Development," *Automotive News,* September 12, 2005, p. 18.
25. Linda Webb, "Microsoft's New Ergonomic Keyboard More Comfortable," *Cleveland Plain Dealer,* November 7, 2005, p. E4.
26. Based on information from "Welcome to the official Facebook page of American Flatbread," http://www.facebook.com, April 21, 2009; "American Flatbread," FoodGPS.com, February 16, 2008, http://www.foodgps.com/review/american-flatbread-los-alamos-ca-saturday-february-16-2008/; *Pioneering American Flatbread* video by Houghton Mifflin; Andrew Nemethy, "Waitsfield: American Flatbread," *Vermont,* February 21, 2001, seevermont.nybor.com/dining/story/20722.html; www.americanflatbread.com.

Chapter 11

1. Patricia Odell, "Huggies Debuts a New Loyalty Program in 10 Million Mailing," *Promo,* May 20, 2009, www.promo.com; Jack Neff, "'Continuing to Invest' Is Palmer's 'Only Way to Win,'" *Advertising Age,* May 18, 2009, p. 28; Jack Neff, "New Huggies, Old Spices Launches to Go TV-Free," *Advertising Age,* May 4, 2009, p. 3; "K-C Offers New Huggies Line," *Nonwovens Industry,* May 2009, p. 12; Elaine Wong, "Kimberly-Clark Shares Tried-and-True Shopper Marketing Tactics," *Brandweek,* April 2, 2009, www.brandweek.com.
2. Marketing Power (American Marketing Association), http://www.marketingpower.com/AboutAMA/Pages/DefinitionofMarketing.aspx, accessed April 17, 2009.
3. Mya Frazier, James Tenser, and Tricia Despres, "Retail Lesson: Small Programs Best," *Advertising Age,* March 20, 2006, p. S-3.
4. Lynette Ryals and Adrian Payne, "Customer Relationship Management in Financial Services: Towards Information-Enabled Relationship Marketing," *Journal of Strategic Marketing,* March 2001, p. 3.

5. Werner J. Reinartz and V. Kumark, "On the Profitability of Long-Life Customers in a Noncontractual Setting: An Empirical Investigation and Implications for Marketing," *Journal of Marketing,* October 2000, pp. 17–35.

6. Roland T. Rust, Katherine N. Lemon, and Valarie A. Zeithaml, "Return on Marketing: Using Customer Equity to Focus Marketing Strategy," *Journal of Marketing 68,* January 2004, pp. 109–127.

7. Rajkumar Venkatesan and V. Kumar, "A Customer Lifetime Value Framework for Customer Selection and Resource Allocation Strategy," *Journal of Marketing 68,* October 2004, pp. 106–125.

8. Gina Chon, "Toyota's Marketers Get Respect—Now They Want Love," *Wall Street Journal,* January 11, 2006, p. B1.

9. Matthew Boyle, "Best Buy's Giant Gamble," *Fortune,* March 29, 2006, money.cnn.com.

10. "Launch Week Also Marks Debut of Cross Promo Ads," *USA Today,* September 23, 2007, www.usatoday.com/; G. Chambers William III, "2008 Nissan Rogue," *Ft. Worth Star-Telegram,* August 31, 2007, www.star-telegram.com/chambers_williams/story/219830.html.

11. Joseph White, "Detroit Finally Learns Tough Lesson," *Wall Street Journal,* September 11, 2006, online.wsj.com.

12. Ellen Byron, "New Penney: Chain goes for 'Missing Middle,'" *Wall Street Journal,* February 14, 2005, online.wsj.com.

13. Catherine Arnold, "Self-Examination: Researchers Reveal State of MR in Survey," *Marketing News,* February 1, 2005, pp. 55–56.

14. William M. Pride and O. C. Ferrell, *Marketing: Concepts and Strategies,* 15th ed. (Mason, Ohio: South-Western/Cengage Learning, 2010), p. 194.

15. Based in information in http://www.harley-davidson.com, accessed May 19, 2009; Tom Barlow, "Harley-Davidson Earnings Report," Bloggingstocks.com, April 16, 2009, http://www.bloggingstocks.com/2009/04/16/harley-davidson-earnings-report/; Rick Barrett, "A Home for Harley's Heritage," *Milwaukee Journal-Sentinel,* June 29, 2008, www.journalsentinel.com; Matthew Goodman, "Harley-Davidson Chief Jim Ziemer Is Not Enjoying an Easy Ride," *The Sunday Times,* June 29, 2008, business.timesonline.co.uk; Jacqueline Mitchell, "Ten Auto Gifts for Dad," *Forbes,* June 5, 2008, forbes.com.

Chapter 12

1. "Goya Taps into Popularity of Latino Fare, Aims for Universal Appeal," *The Food Institute Report,* February 16, 2009, p. 4; Laurel Wentz, "How Food Giant Goya Plans to Bring Latin Cuisine to the Masses," *Advertising Age,* February 2, 2009, p. 22; Barbara De Lollis, "At Goya, It's All in La Familia," *USA Today,* March 24, 2008, p. 1B; Jenalia Moreno, "Five Questions with Robert Unanue," *Houston Chronicle,* June 21, 2008, p. 2.

2. http://www.apple.com/itunes/marketing/, accessed May 4, 2009.

3. Dennis K. Berman and Ellen Byron, "P&G Sells Sure Deodorant Label to Private Firm Innovative Brands," *Wall Street Journal,* September 26, 2006, p. B2, http://online.wsj.com.

4. Procter & Gamble, www.pg.com, accessed April 17, 2009.

5. www.thecoca-colacompany.com/brands/index.html, www.pepsico.com/Brands.aspx, accessed May 4, 2009.

6. Stephanie Thompson, "Mars to Scale Back M-Azing Brand," *Advertising Age,* October 26, 2006, www.adage.com.

7. "Inside a White-Hot Idea Factory," *BusinessWeek,* January 15, 2007, pp. 72–73.

8. Jathon Sapsford, "Honda Caters to Japan's Pet Population Boom," *Wall Street Journal,* October 5, 2005, p. B1, http://online.wsj.com.

9. "Market Update," www.plma.com, accessed May 4, 2009.

10. "World's Most Valuable Brands," *Interbrand,* www.interbrand.com, September 2008.

11. www.amazon.com, accessed April 17, 2009.

12. Yukari Iwatani Kane and Sarah McBride, "Latest Cut in DVD-Player Duel: Prices," *Wall Street Journal,* November 23, 2007, pp. B1 and B2.

13. Lauren Young, "Candy's Getting Dandy," *BusinessWeek,* February 13, 2006, pp. 88–89.

14. The Verizon website at www.verizon.com, accessed May 4, 2009.

15. Based on information in Steve Miller, "Vroom for Two," *Brandweek,* June 2, 2008, pp. 20; Bill Marsh, "Welcome, Little Smart Car, to the Big American Road," *New York Times,* January 6, 2008, Sec. 4, p. 3; Chris Woodyard, "America Crazy about Breadbox on Wheels Called Smart Car," *USA Today,* November 11, 2007, www.usatoday.com/money/autos/2007-11-11-smartcar_N.html; Royal Ford, "Smallest Car, Biggest Market," *Boston Globe,* December. 6, 2007, p. E1.

Chapter 13

1. Elaine Wong, "Q&A: Best Buy's Barry Judge," June 17, 2009, www.brandweek.com; Jackie Crosby, "Best Buy Turning to Private Labels to Raise Margins," June 17, 2009, www.startribune.com; Jackie Crosby, "Best Buy's Market Share Rise," June 16, 2009, www.startribune.com; Miguel Bustillo, "Wal-Mart Steps Up Its Game in Electronics Aisle," May 18, 2009, www.wsj.com; Eric Morath, "Circuit City Aims to Sell Brand Name to Systemax," April 14, 2009, p. B6.

2. "Industry Report 2008," www.csnews.com.

3. Michael Barbaro, "Readings," January 23, 2005, p. F3; David Moin, "Category Killers' Concerns: Overgrowth and Extinction," January 6, 2005, p. 17.

4. www.dsa.org, accessed April 27, 2009.

5. www.donotcall.gov/faq/faqdefault.aspx; accessed April 27, 2009.

6. John Eggerton, "DirecTV Settles $10 Million in Complaints," December 19, 2005, pp. 4, 30.

7. www.netflix.com; accessed April 27, 2009.

8. Robert McMillan, "Got 796 Quarters Handy? Get Yourself an iPod," January 2006, p. 54.

9. Sandra O'Loughlin, "Out with the Old: Malls versus Centers," May 9, 2005, p. 30.

10. Corinne Kator, "Warehouse Giants," November 2006, www.mmh.com.

11. Robert Coen, "Insider's Report," July 2008, www.universalmccann.com.

12. "The Impact of Direct-to-Consumer Drug Advertising on Seniors' Health," States News Service, October 10, 2005.

13. Paul Sloan, "The Sales Force that Rocks," July 1, 2005, http://cnnmoney.com.

14. Terence Shimp, (Mason, OH: South-Western/Cengage Learning 2010), pp. 454–459.

15. Natalie Schwartz, "Clipping Path," p. 15.

16. Mya Frazier, James Tenser, and Tricia Despres, "Retail Lesson: Small Programs Best," March 20, 2008, pp. S2–S3.

17. "Berry & Homer Wraps Bus Leading Lance Armstrong and Tour of Hope Team on Cross-Country Trek," *Business Wire.*

18. Based on information from David Lieberman, "Netflix, TiVo team up to deliver films on demand via Internet," October 30, 2008, usatoday.com/money/media/2008-10-30-netflix-tivo-films--on-demand_N.htm (accessed November 6, 2008); www.netflix.com, accessed November 5, 2008; Associated Press Staff Writer, "Movie rental giant Netflix rolls out its post-postal plan," May 21, 2008, www.nydailynews.com/money/2008/05/21/2008-05-21_movie_rental_giant_netflix_rolls_out_its-1.html, accessed November 5, 2008; Associated Press Staff Writer, "Microsoft's Xbox 360 to stream Netflix movies," July 14, 2008, www.nydailynews.com/money/2008/07/14/2008-07-14_microsofts_xbox_360_to_stream_netflix_mo.html, accessed November 5, 2008.

Chapter 14

1. Sharon Gaudin, "Facebook Dethrones MySpace in U.S. Popularity Race," *ComputerWorld,* June 16, 2009, www.computerworld.com; "Social-Networking Sites Could Be Embroiled in Privacy Crackdown," *Telegraph (U.K.),* June 18, 2009, www.telegraph.co.uk; Brad Stone, "Is Facebook Growing Up Too Fast?" *New York Times,* March 29, 2009, BU-1-BU-6; "About-Facebook: Zuckerberg Relents on Privacy Rules," *InformationWeek,* February 18, 2009, www.informationweek.com; Randall Stross, "When Everyone's a Friend, Is Anything Private?" *New York Times,* March 8, 2009, p. 3; www.facebook.com.

2. Bradley Mitchell, "Introduction to Network Types," the About.com website at www.about.com, accessed May 4, 2009.

3. Bradley Mitchell, "LAN — Local Area Network," the About.com website at www.about.com, accessed May 4, 2009.

4. Charlene Li and Shar VanBoskirk, "U.S. Online Marketing Forecast: 2005 to 2010," Forrester Research, Inc., website at www.forrester.com, accessed May 5, 2005.

5. The Incisive Interactive Marketing, LLC website at www.clickz.com, accessed May 11, 2009.

6. Ibid.

7. Company website, http://www.manifestdigital.com, accessed May 28, 2009; "No. 752, Manifest Digital," *Inc. 500,* http://www.inc.com, accessed May 28, 2009; "BIA Digital Invests in Manifest Digital," Washington Business Journal, http://www.bizjournals.com, January 26, 2009; "PhizzPop Winner: Manifest Digital," *The*

Chicago Convergence, http://cnms08.typepad.com/cnms08/chicago-2016/, Nov. 26, 2008; information from the video entitled, "Manifest Digital: User-Centered Design," copyright © Cengage Learning.

Chapter 15

1. "Case Study: PriceWaterhouseCoopers," *Marketing Week,* June 25, 2009, www.marketingweek.com; "Prague Out of Race to Host 2020 Summer Olympics," *Associated Press,* June 16, 2009, http://www.theeagle.com/sports/Prague-out-of-race-to-host-2020-Summer-Olympics; Nick Huber, "'Fraud Academy' Launched," *Accountancy Age,* May 21, 2009, pp. 2–3; Lorri Freifeld, "Top 125 2009, No. 1: PWC Does It Again," *Training,* February 16, 2009, n.p.; www.wpc.com.
2. Cathy Booth, "Called to Account," the Time.com website at www.time.com, June 18, 2002.
3. "Andersen Conviction Overturned," The CNNMoney.com website at www.money.cnn.com, May 31, 2005.
4. The American Institute of Certified Public Accountants website at www.aicpa.org, accessed May 16, 2009.
5. John Smith, "Financial Reporting in a Changing World," The International Accounting Standards Board website at www.iasb.org, accessed May 16, 2009.
6. "System Failure," *Fortune,* June 24, 2002, p. 64.
7. The American Institute of Certified Public Accountants website at www.aicpa.org, accessed May 16, 2009.
8. The Bureau of Labor Statistics website at www.bls.gov, May 17, 2009.
9. The American Institute of Certified Public Accountants website at www.aicpa.org, accessed May 16, 2009.
10. Based on information from Jane Sasseen, "White Collar Crime: Who Does Time?" *Business Week,* February 6, 2006, www.businessweek.com; Stephen Labaton, "Four Years Later, Enron's Shadow Lingers as Change Comes Slowly," *New York Times,* January 5, 2008, p. C1; "Making the Numbers at Commodore Appliance," (Houghton Mifflin Video).

Chapter 16

1. Grace Gagliano, "Small Businesses SCORE Relief," *Bradenton Herald,* June 6, 2009, www.bradenton.com; David Port, "Here's an Insider's Guide to 4 of the Best Startup Resources," *Entrepreneur,* April 2009, www.enterpreneur.com; Kelly K. Spors, "Planning a Start-Up? Help and Advice Abound," *Wall Street Journal,* January 18, 2009, www.wsj.com; www.score.org.
2. The Pfizer corporate website at www.pfizer.com, accessed May 21, 2009.
3. The American Bankruptcy Institute website at www.abiworld.org accessed May 21, 2009.

4. Natalie Zmuda, "PepsiCo Launches Massive Overhaul," the Advertising Age website at www.adage.com, October 14, 2008.
5. The Sun Microsystems corporate website at www.sun.com, accessed May 21, 2009.
6. Judith Crown, "ConAgra's New Recipe," the BusinessWeek website at www.businessweek.com accessed March 27, 2008.
7. U.S. Census Bureau, *Statistical Abstract of the United States,* 2009 (Washington, D.C.: U.S. Government Printing Office, 2009), p. 724.
8. Maria Bartiromo, "Black Rock's Peter Fisher on When the Pain Will End," the BusinessWeek website at www.businessweek.com, October 7, 2008.
9. Matthew Boyle, The Fed's Commercial Paper Chase," the BusinessWeek website at www.businessweek.com, October 7, 2008.
10. Giovanny Moreano, "Will Profits Be Written in Rosetta Stone?" the CNBC.com website at www.cnbc.com, accessed April 16, 2009.
11. "Mead Johnson IPO priced at $24 Per Share," the Market Watch website at www.marketwatch.com, accessed May 24, 2009.
12. The Textron corporate website at www.textron.com, accessed May 24, 2009.
13. The IBM corporate website at www.ibm.com, accessed May 25, 2009.
14. *Mergent Transportation Manual* (New York: Mergent, Inc., 2008), p. 604.
15. Based on the video entitled *Pizzeria Uno* © Cengage Learning and the Pizzeria Uno Web site at www.pizzeria-uno.com, accesssed May 25, 2009.

Appendix A

1. "The Regulatory Pyramid," The NYSE website at www.nyse.com, accessed May 26, 2009.
2. Ibid.
3. "Money 101 Lesson 4: Basics of Investing," the CNN/Money website at http://money.cnn.com/magazines/moneymag/money101/lesson4, accessed May 26, 2009.
4. Roger G. Ibbotson, "Predictions of the Past and Forecasts for the Future 1976–2025," Ibbotson Associates website at www.ibbotson.com, accessed April 9, 2005.
5. Suze Orman, *The Road to Wealth* (New York: Riverbend Books, 2001), p. 371.
6. The Treasury Direct website at www.treasurydirect.gov, accessed May 25, 2009.
7. The Investment Company Institute website at www.ici.org, accessed May 26, 2009.
8. The Mutual Fund Education Alliance website at www.mfea.com, accessed October 24, 2008.
9. The Investopedia website at www.investopedia.com, accessed May 27, 2009.

ANSWER KEY

1

1. g **2.** c **3.** j **4.** e **5.** d **6.** b
7. f **8.** a **9.** h **10.** i **11.** F **12.** F
13. T **14.** F **15.** T **16.** T **17.** F
18. T **19.** F **20.** T **21.** a **22.** c
23. d **24.** e **25.** d **26.** b **27.** d
28. c **29.** d **30.** e

2

1. j **2.** g **3.** e **4.** k **5.** a **6.** l
7. d **8.** i **9.** f **10.** b **11.** T
12. F **13.** F **14.** T **15.** F **16.** T
17. T **18.** F **19.** T **20.** F **21.** b
22. e **23.** d **24.** a **25.** d **26.** c
27. e **28.** c **29.** b **30.** d

3

1. i **2.** d **3.** g **4.** j **5.** h **6.** l
7. e **8.** f **9.** a **10.** c **11.** F
12. T **13.** T **14.** F **15.** T **16.** F
17. F **18.** T **19.** F **20.** T **21.** c
22. d **23.** c **24.** c **25.** a **26.** c
27. e **28.** c **29.** b **30.** c

4

1. j **2.** i **3.** k **4.** f **5.** l **6.** h **7.** b
8. d **9.** c **10.** a **11.** F **12.** F
13. T **14.** F **15.** T **16.** F **17.** T
18. F **19.** T **20.** T **21.** d **22.** d
23. c **24.** e **25.** e **26.** c **27.** b
28. a **29.** d **30.** d

5

1. i **2.** e **3.** k **4.** a **5.** d **6.** f
7. b **8.** g **9.** j **10.** l **11.** T
12. F **13.** F **14.** T **15.** F **16.** F
17. F **18.** F **19.** F **20.** T **21.** b
22. e **23.** a **24.** d **25.** c **26.** d
27. e **28.** e **29.** b **30.** c

6

1. h **2.** k **3.** i **4.** f **5.** b **6.** g
7. e **8.** a **9.** c **10.** l **11.** T
12. F **13.** T **14.** F **15.** T **16.** T
17. F **18.** F **19.** T **20.** T **21.** b
22. a **23.** b **24.** d **25.** a **26.** b
27. b **28.** e **29.** a **30.** d

7

1. j **2.** d **3.** l **4.** c **5.** f **6.** e
7. k **8.** a **9.** i **10.** g **11.** T **12.** F
13. T **14.** F **15.** T **16.** F **17.** T
18. F **19.** T **20.** T **21.** a **22.** e
23. c **24.** d **25.** c **26.** c **27.** d
28. a **29.** a **30.** b

8

1. e **2.** a **3.** g **4.** f **5.** l **6.** b
7. k **8.** j **9.** d **10.** i **11.** F
12. T **13.** F **14.** F **15.** T **16.** F
17. F **18.** T **19.** F **20.** T **21.** b
22. b **23.** a **24.** d **25.** e **26.** d
27. c **28.** d **29.** e **30.** c

9

1. h **2.** e **3.** i **4.** k **5.** b **6.** c
7. j **8.** f **9.** a **10.** d **11.** T **12.** F
13. T **14.** F **15.** T **16.** F **17.** T
18. F **19.** T **20.** F **21.** a **22.** d
23. a **24.** d **25.** a **26.** b **27.** a
28. a **29.** d **30.** a

10

1. g **2.** k **3.** d **4.** e **5.** j **6.** c
7. h **8.** b **9.** f **10.** i **11.** T
12. T **13.** F **14.** F **15.** T
16. F **17.** T **18.** F **19.** F
20. T **21.** a **22.** e **23.** a
24. b **25.** c **26.** a **27.** c **28.** b
29. c **30.** a

11

1. f **2.** g **3.** c **4.** e **5.** b **6.** i
7. k **8.** a **9.** l **10.** j **11.** T **12.** F
13. T **14.** T **15.** F **16.** F **17.** T
18. T **19.** T **20.** F **21.** b **22.** b
23. a **24.** c **25.** c **26.** c **27.** e
28. e **29.** a **30.** b

12

1. b **2.** c **3.** a **4.** e **5.** g **6.** f
7. j **8.** i **9.** h **10.** l **11.** F **12.** F
13. F **14.** T **15.** T **16.** T **17.** F
18. T **19.** T **20.** F **21.** a **22.** b
23. c **24.** c **25.** d **26.** b **27.** d
28. c **29.** d **30.** c

13

1. b **2.** a **3.** c **4.** f **5.** e
6. g **7.** j **8.** i **9.** h **10.** k
11. F **12.** F **13.** F **14.** T
15. T **16.** F **17.** T **18.** T
19. F **20.** T **21.** d **22.** c
23. b **24.** b **25.** c **26.** b
27. c **28.** c **29.** c **30.** b

14

1. h **2.** c **3.** k **4.** a **5.** d **6.** f
7. b **8.** j **9.** i **10.** l **11.** T **12.** T
13. F **14.** T **15.** F **16.** F **17.** T
18. F **19.** T **20.** F **21.** b **22.** c
23. e **24.** b **25.** c **26.** d **27.** b
28. a **29.** d **30.** a

15

1. a **2.** g **3.** j **4.** k **5.** b **6.** h
7. c **8.** l **9.** i **10.** e **11.** F **12.** F
13. T **14.** F **15.** T **16.** T **17.** T
18. F **19.** T **20.** T **21.** c **22.** a
23. c **24.** e **25.** d **26.** c **27.** b
28. c **29.** a **30.** b

©Lidija Tomic

16

1. a **2.** e **3.** g **4.** d **5.** l **6.** h

7. b **8.** j **9.** k **10.** c **11.** T **12.** F

13. F **14.** F **15.** T **16.** T **17.** T

18. T **19.** F **20.** F **21.** a **22.** b

23. e **24.** a **25.** d **26.** e **27.** b

28. c **29.** e **30.** d

GLOSSARY

A

absolute advantage the ability to produce a specific product more efficiently than any other nation (68)

accessory equipment standardized equipment used in a firm's production or office activities (317)

account executive an individual, sometimes called a stockbroker or registered representative, who buys and sells securities for clients (A-5)

accountability the obligation of a worker to accomplish an assigned job or task (186)

accounting equation the basis for the accounting process: *assets = liabilities + owners' equity* (423)

accounting the process of systematically collecting, analyzing, and reporting financial information (417)

accounts receivable turnover a financial ratio calculated by dividing net sales by accounts receivable (436)

acid-test ratio a financial ratio calculated by adding cash, marketable securities, and receivables and dividing the total by current liabilities (436)

ad hoc committee a committee created for a specific short-term purpose (196)

administrative manager a manager who is not associated with any specific functional area but who provides overall administrative guidance and leadership (167)

advertising a paid nonpersonal message communicated to a select audience through a mass medium (364)

advertising agency an independent firm that plans, produces, and places advertising for its clients (368)

affirmative action program a plan designed to increase the number of minority employees at all levels within an organization (54)

agent a middleman that expedites exchanges, represents a buyer or a seller, and often is hired permanently on a commission basis (352)

alien corporation a corporation chartered by a foreign government and conducting business in the United States (111)

analytical process a process in operations management in which raw materials are broken into different component parts (207)

annual report a report distributed to stockholders and other interested parties that describes a firm's operating activities and its financial condition (423)

asset allocation the process of spreading your money among several different types of investments to lessen risk (A-8)

assets the resources that a business owns (422)

audit an examination of a company's financial statements and the accounting practices that produced them (418)

authoritarian leader one who holds all authority and responsibility, with communication usually moving from top to bottom (170)

authority the power, within an organization, to accomplish an assigned job or task (187)

automatic vending the use of machines to dispense products (358)

automation the total or near-total use of machines to do work (221)

B

balance of payments the total flow of money into a country minus the total flow of money out of that country over some period of time (71)

balance of trade the total value of a nation's exports minus the total value of its imports over some period of time (70)

balance sheet (or statement of financial position) a summary of the dollar amounts of a firm's assets, liabilities, and owners' equity accounts at the end of a specific accounting period (424)

banker's acceptance a written order for a bank to pay a third party a stated amount of money on a specific date (456)

barter a system of exchange in which goods or services are traded directly for other goods and/or services without using money (23)

behavior modification a systematic program of reinforcement to encourage desirable behavior (273)

bill of lading document issued by a transport carrier to an exporter to prove that merchandise has been shipped (83)

board of directors the top governing body of a corporation, the members of which are elected by the stockholders (112)

bond indenture a legal document that details all the conditions relating to a bond issue (465)

brand a name, term, symbol, design, or any combination of these that identifies a seller's products as distinct from those of other sellers (325)

brand equity marketing and financial value associated with a brand's strength in a market (326)

brand extension using an existing brand to brand a new product in a different product category (328)

brand loyalty extent to which a customer is favorable toward buying a specific brand (326)

brand mark the part of a brand that is a symbol or distinctive design (325)

brand name the part of a brand that can be spoken (325)

breakeven quantity the number of units that must be sold for the total revenue (from all units sold) to equal the total cost (of all units sold) (334)

broadband technology a general term referring to higher-speed Internet connections that deliver data, voice, and video material (389)

broker a middleman that specializes in a particular commodity, represents either a buyer or a seller, and is likely to be hired on a temporary basis (352)

© Bill Noll

budget a financial statement that projects income and/or expenditures over a specified future period (451)

bundle pricing packaging together two or more complementary products and selling them for a single price (338)

bureaucratic structure a management system based on a formal framework of authority that is outlined carefully and followed precisely (192)

business the organized effort of individuals to produce and sell, for a profit, the goods and services that satisfy (8)

business buying behavior the purchasing of products by producers, resellers, governmental units, and institutions (306)

business cycle the recurrence of periods of growth and recession in a nation's economic activity (18)

business ethics the application of moral standards to business situations (35)

business model represents a group of common characteristics and methods of doing business to generate sales revenues and reduce expenses (404)

business plan a carefully constructed guide for the person starting a business (139)

business product a product bought for resale, for making other products, or for use in a firm's operations (316)

business service an intangible product that an organization uses in its operations (317)

business-to-business (or B2B) model a model used by firms that conduct business with other businesses (404)

business-to-consumer (or B2C) model a model used by firms that focus on conducting business with individual consumers (405)

buying allowance a temporary price reduction to resellers for purchasing specified quantities of a product (374)

buying behavior the decisions and actions of people involved in buying and using products (306)

C

capacity the amount of products or services that an organization can produce in a given time (213)

capital budget a financial statement that estimates a firm's expenditures for major assets and its long-term financing needs (451)

capital gain the difference between a security's purchase price and its selling price (A-10)

capital-intensive technology a process in which machines and equipment do most of the work (213)

capitalism an economic system in which individuals own and operate the majority of businesses that provide goods and services (11)

captioned photograph a picture accompanied by a brief explanation (375)

captive pricing pricing the basic product in a product line low, but pricing related items at a higher level (339)

carrier a firm that offers transportation services (361)

cash budget a financial statement that estimates cash receipts and cash expenditures over a specified period (451)

cash flow the movement of money into and out of an organization (446)

catalog marketing a type of marketing in which an organization provides a catalog from which customers make selections and place orders by mail, telephone, or the Internet (356)

category killer a very large specialty store that concentrates on a single product line and competes on the basis of low prices and product availability (356)

caveat emptor a Latin phrase meaning "let the buyer beware" (47)

centralized organization an organization that systematically works to concentrate authority at the upper levels of the organization (187)

certificate of deposit (CD) A document stating that the bank will pay the depositor a guaranteed interest rate on money left on deposit for a specified period of time (453)

certified management accountant (CMA) an accountant who has met the requirements for education and experience, passed a rigorous exam, and is certified by the Institute of Management Accountants (422)

certified public accountant (CPA) an individual who has met state requirements for accounting education and experience and has passed a rigorous accounting examination prepared by the AICPA (422)

chain of command the line of authority that extends from the highest to the lowest levels of an organization (183)

chain retailer a company that operates more than one retail outlet (353)

check a written order for a bank or other financial institution to pay a stated dollar amount to the business or person indicated on the face of the check (453)

chief financial officer (CFO) a high-level corporate executive who manages a firm's finances and reports directly to the company's chief executive officer or president (449)

closed corporation a corporation whose stock is owned by relatively few people and is not sold to the general public (110)

cluster structure an organization that consists primarily of teams with no or very few underlying departments (193)

code of ethics a guide to acceptable and ethical behavior as defined by the organization (39)

collaborative learning system a work environment that allows problem-solving participation by all team members (397)

collateral real estate or property pledged as security for a loan (454)

command economy an economic system in which the government decides what goods and services will be produced, how they will be produced, for whom available goods and services will be produced, and who owns and controls the major factors of production (14)

commercial paper a short-term promissory note issued by a large corporation (458)

commission a payment that is a percentage of sales revenue (245)

common stock stock owned by individuals or firms who may vote on corporate matters but whose claims on profit and assets are subordinate to the claims of others (111)

community shopping center a planned shopping center that includes one or two department stores and some specialty stores, along with convenience stores (358)

comparable worth a concept that seeks equal compensation for jobs requiring about the same level of education, training, and skills (244)

comparative advantage the ability to produce a specific product more efficiently than any other product (68)

comparison discounting setting a price at a specific level and comparing it with a higher price (339)

compensation system the policies and strategies that determine employee compensation (243)

compensation the payment employees receive in return for their labor (243)

competition rivalry among businesses for sales to potential customers (20)

component part an item that becomes part of a physical product and is either a finished item ready for assembly or a product that needs little processing before assembly (317)

computer network a group of two or more computers linked together that allows users to share data and information (399)

computer-aided design (CAD) the use of computers to aid in the development of products (222)

computer-aided manufacturing (CAM) the use of computers to plan and control manufacturing processes (222)

computer-integrated manufacturing (CIM) a computer system that not only helps to design products but also controls the machinery needed to produce the finished product (222)

conceptual skill the ability to think in abstract terms (168)

consumer buying behavior the purchasing of products for personal or household use, not for business purposes (306)

consumer price index (CPI) a monthly index that measures the changes in prices of a fixed basket of goods purchased by a typical consumer in an urban area (18)

consumer product a product purchased to satisfy personal and family needs (316)

consumer sales promotion method a sales promotion method designed to attract consumers to particular retail stores and to motivate them to purchase certain new or established products (372)

consumerism all activities undertaken to protect the rights of consumers (51)

contingency plan a plan that outlines alternative courses of action that may be taken if an organization's other plans are disrupted or become ineffective (163)

continuous process a manufacturing process in which a firm produces the same product(s) over a long period of time (222)

controlling the process of evaluating and regulating ongoing activities to ensure that goals are achieved (164)

convenience product a relatively inexpensive, frequently purchased item for which buyers want to exert only minimal effort (316)

convenience store a small food store that sells a limited variety of products but remains open well beyond normal business hours (354)

convertible preferred stock preferred stock that an owner may exchange for a specified number of shares of common stock (462)

cooperative advertising an arrangement whereby a manufacturer agrees to pay a certain amount of a retailer's media cost for advertising the manufacturer's products (374)

cooperative an association of individuals or firms whose purpose is to perform some business function for its members (117)

corporate bond a corporation's written pledge that it will repay a specified amount of money with interest (465)

corporate culture the inner rites, rituals, heroes, and values of a firm (194)

corporate officers the chairman of the board, president, executive vice presidents, corporate secretary, treasurer, and any other top executive appointed by the board of directors (112)

corporation an artificial person created by law with most of the legal rights of a real person, including the rights to start and operate a business, to buy or sell property, to borrow money, to sue or be sued, and to enter into binding contracts (109)

cost of goods sold the dollar amount equal to beginning inventory *plus* net purchases *less* ending inventory (430)

countertrade an international barter transaction (85)

coupon reduces the retail price of a particular item by a stated amount at the time of purchase (373)

creative selling selling products to new customers and increasing sales to present customers (369)

cross-functional team a team of individuals with varying specialties, expertise, and skills that are brought together to achieve a common task (192)

cultural (or workplace) diversity differences among people in a workforce owing to race, ethnicity, and gender (5)

currency devaluation the reduction of the value of a nation's currency relative to the currencies of other countries (72)

current assets assets that can be converted quickly into cash or that will be used in one year or less (426)

current liabilities debts that will be repaid in one year or less (427)

current ratio a financial ratio computed by dividing current assets by current liabilities (436)

customary pricing pricing on the basis of tradition (338)

customer lifetime value a combination of purchase frequency, average value of purchases, and brand-switching patterns over the entire span of a customer's relationship with a company (292)

customer relationship management (CRM) using information about customers to create marketing strategies that develop and sustain desirable customer relationships (291)

D

data numerical or verbal descriptions that usually result from some sort of measurement (388)

data processing the transformation of data into a form that is useful for a specific purpose (392)

database a single collection of data stored in one place that can be used by people throughout an organization to make decisions (388)

debit card a card that electronically subtracts the amount of a customer's purchase from her or his bank account at the moment the purchase is made (455)

debt capital borrowed money obtained through loans of various types (451)

debt-to-owners'-equity ratio a financial ratio calculated by dividing total liabilities by owners' equity (437)

decentralized organization an organization in which management consciously attempts to spread authority widely across various organization levels (187)

decision making the act of choosing one alternative from a set of alternatives (170)

decisional role a role that involves various aspects of management decision making (168)

decision-support system (DSS) a type of computer program that provides relevant data and information to help a firm's employees make decisions (395)

deflation a general decrease in the level of prices (16)

delegation assigning part of a manager's work and power to other workers (186)

demand the quantity of a product that buyers are willing to purchase at each of various prices (330)

democratic leader one who holds final responsibility but also delegates authority to others, who help to determine work assignments; communication is active upward and downward (170)

department store a retail store that (1) employs twenty-five or more persons and (2) sells at least home furnishings, appliances, family apparel, and household linens and dry goods, each in a different part of the store (353)

departmentalization the process of grouping jobs into manageable units (185)

departmentalization by customer grouping activities according to the needs of various customer populations (186)

departmentalization by function grouping jobs that relate to the same organizational activity (185)

departmentalization by location grouping activities according to the defined geographic area in which they are performed (185)

departmentalization by product grouping activities related to a particular product or service (185)

depreciation the process of apportioning the cost of a fixed asset over the period during which it will be used (426)

depression a severe recession that lasts longer than a recession (19)

design planning the development of a plan for converting a product idea into an actual product or service (212)

direct marketing the use of the telephone, Internet, and nonpersonal media to introduce products to customers, who then can purchase them via mail, telephone, or the Internet (356)

direct selling the marketing of products to customers through face-to-face sales presentations at home or in the workplace (356)

directing the combined processes of leading and motivating (164)

direct-response marketing a type of marketing in which a retailer advertises a product and makes it available through mail, telephone, or online orders (357)

discount a deduction from the price of an item (340)

discount store a self-service general-merchandise outlet that sells products at lower-than-usual prices (353)

discretionary income disposable income *less* savings and expenditures on food, clothing, and housing (307)

disposable income personal income *less* all additional personal taxes (307)

distribution channel (or marketing channel) a sequence of marketing organizations that directs a product from the producer to the ultimate user (347)

dividend a distribution of earnings to the stockholders of a corporation (112)

domestic corporation a corporation in the state in which it is incorporated (111)

domestic system a method of manufacturing in which an entrepreneur distributes raw materials to various homes, where families process them into finished goods to be offered for sale by the merchant entrepreneur (23)

double-entry bookkeeping system a system in which each financial transaction is recorded as two separate accounting entries to maintain the balance shown in the accounting equation (423)

draft issued by the exporter's bank, ordering the importer's bank to pay for the merchandise, thus guaranteeing payment once accepted by the importer's bank (83)

dumping exportation of large quantities of a product at a price lower than that of the same product in the home market (71)

E

earnings per share a financial ratio calculated by dividing net income after taxes by the number of shares of common stock outstanding (435)

e-business (electronic business) the organized effort of individuals to produce and sell, for a profit, the goods and services that satisfy society's needs *through the facilities available on the Internet* (401)

economic community an organization of nations formed to promote the free movement of resources and products among its members and to create common economic policies (79)

economic model of social responsibility the view that society will benefit most when business is left alone to produce and market products that society needs (48)

economics the study of how wealth is created and distributed (10)

economy the way in which people deal with the creation and distribution of wealth (10)

electronic funds transfer (EFT) system a means of performing financial transactions through a computer terminal or telephone hookup (455)

embargo a complete halt to trading with a particular nation or in a particular product (72)

Emergency Economic Stabilization Act a $700 billion bailout plan created to stabilize the nation's economy and restore confidence in the banking and financial industries (10)

employee benefit a reward in addition to regular compensation that is provided indirectly to employees (245)

employee ownership a situation in which employees own the company they work for by virtue of being stockholders (277)

employee training the process of teaching operations and technical employees how to do their present jobs more effectively and efficiently (247)

empowerment making employees more involved in their jobs by increasing their participation in decision making (276)

entrepreneur a person who risks time, effort, and money to start and operate a business (11)

Equal Employment Opportunity Commission (EEOC) a government agency with power to investigate complaints of employment discrimination and power to sue firms that practice it (55)

equity capital money received from the owners or from the sale of shares of ownership in a business (451)

equity theory a theory of motivation based on the premise that people are motivated to obtain and preserve equitable treatment for themselves (269)

esteem needs our need for respect, recognition, and a sense of our own accomplishment and worth (265)

ethics the study of right and wrong and of the morality of the choices individuals make (35)

everyday low prices (EDLPs) setting a low price for products on a consistent basis (338)

exclusive distribution the use of only a single retail outlet for a product in a large geographic area (350)

executive information system (EIS) a computer-based system that facilitates and supports the decision-making needs of top managers and senior executives by providing easy access to both internal and external information (396)

expectancy theory a model of motivation based on the assumption that motivation depends on how much we want something and on how likely we think we are to get it (269)

expert system a type of computer program that uses artificial intelligence to imitate a human's ability to think (396)

Export-Import Bank of the United States an independent agency of the U.S. government whose function it is to assist in financing the exports of American firms (88)

exporting selling and shipping raw materials or products to other nations (69)

express warranty a written explanation of the responsibilities of the producer in the event that a product is found to be defective or otherwise unsatisfactory (329)

external recruiting the attempt to attract job applicants from outside an organization (240)

F

factor a firm that specializes in buying other firms' accounts receivable (459)

factors of production resources used to produce goods and services (10)

factory system a system of manufacturing in which all the materials, machinery, and workers required to manufacture a product are assembled in one place (23)

family branding the strategy in which a firm uses the same brand for all or most of its products (327)

family of funds a group of mutual funds managed by one investment company (A-13)

feature article a piece (of up to 3,000 words) prepared by an organization for inclusion in a particular publication (375)

federal deficit a shortfall created when the federal government spends more in a fiscal year than it receives (19)

financial accounting generates financial statements and reports for interested people outside an organization (421)

financial leverage the use of borrowed funds to increase the return on owners' equity (463)

financial management all the activities concerned with obtaining money and using it effectively (446)

financial manager a manager who is primarily responsible for an organization's financial resources (166)

financial plan a plan for obtaining and using the money needed to implement an organization's goals (450)

financial planner an individual who has had at least two years of training in investments, insurance, taxation, retirement planning, and estate planning and has passed a rigorous examination (A-2)

financial ratio a number that shows the relationship between two elements of a firm's financial statements (434)

first-line manager a manager who coordinates and supervises the activities of operating employees (165)

fiscal policy government influence on the amount of savings and expenditures; accomplished by altering the tax structure and by changing the levels of government spending (19)

fixed assets assets that will be held or used for a period longer than one year (426)

fixed cost a cost incurred no matter how many units of a product are produced or sold (334)

flexible benefit plan compensation plan whereby an employee receives a predetermined amount of benefit dollars to spend on a package of benefits he or she has selected to meet individual needs (246)

flexible manufacturing system (FMS) a single production system that combines robotics and computer-integrated manufacturing (222)

flextime a system in which employees set their own work hours within employer-determined limits (274)

foreign corporation a corporation in any state in which it does business except the one in which it is incorporated (111)

foreign-exchange control a restriction on the amount of a particular foreign currency that can be purchased or sold (72)

form utility utility created by people converting raw materials, finances, and information into finished products (292)

franchise a license to operate an individually owned business as though it were part of a chain of outlets or stores (144)

franchisee a person or organization purchasing a franchise (144)

franchising the actual granting of a franchise (144)

franchisor an individual or organization granting a franchise (144)

free enterprise the system of business in which individuals are free to decide what to produce, how to produce it, and at what price to sell it (3)

frequent-user incentive a program developed to reward customers who engage in repeat (frequent) purchases (373)

full disclosure requirement that investors should have access to all important facts about stocks, bonds, and other securities so that they can make informed decisions (A-7)

full-service wholesaler a middleman that performs the entire range of wholesaler functions (352)

functional middleman a middleman that helps in the transfer of ownership of products but does not take title to the products (348)

G

General Agreement on Tariffs and Trade (GATT) was an international organization of 153 nations dedicated to reducing or eliminating tariffs and other barriers to world trade (78)

general partner a person who assumes full or shared responsibility for operating a business (105)

generally accepted accounting principles (GAAPs) an accepted set of guidelines and practices for companies reporting financial information and for the accounting profession (418)

general-merchandise wholesaler a middleman that deals in a wide variety of products (352)

generic product (or brand) a product with no brand at all

goal an end result that an organization is expected to achieve over a one- to ten-year period (325)

goal-setting theory a theory of motivation suggesting that employees are motivated to achieve goals that they and their managers establish together (271)

grapevine the informal communications network within an organization (198)

gross domestic product (GDP) the total dollar value of all goods and services produced by all people within the boundaries of a country during a one-year period (16)

gross profit a firm's net sales *less* the cost of goods sold (431)

gross sales the total dollar amount of all goods and services sold during the accounting period (430)

groupware one of the latest types of software that facilitates the management of large projects among geographically dispersed employees as well as such group activities as problem solving and brainstorming (396)

H

hard-core unemployed workers with little education or vocational training and a long history of unemployment (55)

high-risk investment an investment made in the uncertain hope of earning a relatively large profit in a short time (A-14)

hostile takeover a situation in which the management and board of directors of a firm targeted for acquisition disapprove of the merger (118)

hourly wage a specific amount of money paid for each hour of work (244)

human resources management (HRM) all the activities involved in acquiring, maintaining, and developing an organization's human resources (234)

human resources manager a person charged with managing an organization's human resources programs (167)

human resources planning the development of strategies to meet a firm's future human resources needs (235)

hygiene factors job factors that reduce dissatisfaction when present to an acceptable degree but that do not necessarily result in high levels of motivation (266)

I

import duty (tariff) a tax levied on a particular foreign product entering a country (71)

import quota a limit on the amount of a particular good that may be imported into a country during a given period of time (72)

importing purchasing raw materials or products in other nations and bringing them into one's own country (69)

incentive payment a payment in addition to wages, salary, or commissions (245)

income statement a summary of a firm's revenues and expenses during a specified accounting period (428)

independent retailer a firm that operates only one retail outlet (353)

individual branding the strategy in which a firm uses a different brand for each of its products (327)

inflation a general rise in the level of prices (16)

informal group a group created by the members themselves to accomplish goals that may or may not be relevant to an organization (197)

informal organization the pattern of behavior and interaction that stems from personal rather than official relationships (197)

information data presented in a form that is useful for a specific purpose (388)

information society a society in which large groups of employees generate or depend on information to perform their jobs (398)

information technology (IT) officer a manager at the executive level who is responsible for ensuring that a firm has the equipment necessary to provide the information the firm's employees and managers need to make effective decisions (389)

informational role a role in which the manager either gathers or provides information (169)

initial public offering (IPO) when a corporation sells common stock to the general public for the first time (460)

inspection the examination of the quality of work in process (220)

institutional advertising advertising designed to enhance a firm's image or reputation (365)

intangible assets assets that do not exist physically but that have a value based on the rights or privileges they confer a firm (426)

integrated marketing communications coordination of promotion efforts to ensure maximal informational and persuasive impact on customers (363)

intensive distribution the use of all available outlets for a product (350)

intermittent process a manufacturing process in which a firm's manufacturing machines and equipment are changed to produce different products (223)

internal recruiting considering present employees as applicants for available positions (240)

international business all business activities that involve exchanges across national boundaries (68)

International Monetary Fund (IMF) an international bank with 185 member nations that makes short-term loans to developing countries experiencing balance-of-payment deficits (89)

Internet a worldwide network of computers linked through telecommunications (398)

Internet service providers (ISPs) provide customers with a connection to the Internet through various phone plugs and cables (398)

interpersonal role a role in which the manager deals with people (169)

interpersonal skill the ability to deal effectively with other people (168)

intranet a smaller version of the Internet for use within a firm's computer network (398)

intrapreneur an employee who pushes an innovative idea, product, or process through an organization (196)

inventory control the process of managing inventories in such a way as to minimize inventory costs, including both holding costs and potential stock-out costs (218)

inventory management the process of managing inventories in such a way as to minimize inventory costs, including both holding costs and potential stock-out costs (359)

inventory turnover a financial ratio calculated by dividing the cost of goods sold in one year by the average value of the inventory (437)

investment banking firm an organization that assists corporations in raising funds, usually by helping to sell new issues of stocks, bonds, or other financial securities (461)

invisible hand a term created by Adam Smith to describe how an individual's own personal gain benefits others and a nation's economy (11)

J

job analysis a systematic procedure for studying jobs to determine their various elements and requirements (238)

job description a list of the elements that make up a particular job (238)

job enlargement expanding a worker's assignments to include additional but similar tasks (272)

job enrichment a motivation technique that provides employees with more variety and responsibility in their jobs (272)

job evaluation the process of determining the relative worth of the various jobs within a firm (244)

job redesign a type of job enrichment in which work is restructured to cultivate the worker-job match (273)

job rotation the systematic shifting of employees from one job to another (185)

job sharing an arrangement whereby two people share one full-time position (275)

job specialization the separation of all organizational activities into distinct tasks and the assignment of different tasks to different people (184)

job specification a list of the qualifications required to perform a particular job (238)

joint venture an agreement between two or more groups to form a business entity in order to achieve a specific goal or to operate for a specific period of time (117)

just-in-time inventory system a system designed to ensure that materials or supplies arrive at a facility just when they are needed so that storage and holding costs are minimized (218)

K

knowledge management (KM) a firm's procedures for generating, using, and sharing the data and information contained in the firm's databases (389)

L

labeling the presentation of information on a product or its package (329)

labor-intensive technology a process in which people must do most of the work (213)

laissez-faire leader one who gives authority to employees and allows subordinates to work as they choose with a minimum of interference; communication flows horizontally among group members (170)

leadership the ability to influence others (169)

leading the process of influencing people to work toward a common goal (163)

letter of credit issued by a bank on request of an importer stating that the bank will pay an amount of money to a stated beneficiary (455)

leveraged buyout (LBO) a purchase arrangement that allows a firm's managers and employees or a group of investors to purchase the company (120)

liabilities a firm's debts and obligations (422)

licensing a contractual agreement in which one firm permits another to produce and market its product and use its brand name in return for a royalty or other compensation (82)

lifestyle shopping center an open air-environment shopping center with upscale chain specialty stores (358)

limit order a request that a security be bought or sold at a price that is equal to or better than some specified price (A-6)

limited liability a feature of corporate ownership that limits each owner's financial liability to the amount of money that he or she has paid for the corporation's stock (103)

limited partner a person who contributes capital to a business but has no management responsibility or liability for losses beyond the amount he or she invested in the partnership (105)

limited-liability company (LLC) a form of business ownership that combines the benefits of a corporation and a partnership while avoiding some of the restrictions and disadvantages of those forms of ownership (115)

limited-line wholesaler a middleman that stocks only a few product lines but carries numerous product items within each line (352)

line extension development of a new product that is closely related to one or more products in the existing product line but designed specifically to meet somewhat different customer needs (321)

line management position a part of the chain of command; it is a position in which a person makes decisions and gives orders to subordinates to achieve the goals of the organization (190)

line of credit a loan that is approved before the money is actually needed (453)

liquidity the ease with which an investment can be converted into cash (426)

local-area network (LAN) a network that connects computers that are in close proximity to each other, such as an office building or a college campus (399)

long-term financing money that will be used for longer than one year (448)

long-term liabilities debts that need not be repaid for at least one year (426)

lump-sum salary increase an entire pay raise taken in one lump sum (245)

M

macroeconomics the study of the national economy and the global economy (10)

major equipment large tools and machines used for production purposes (317)

Malcolm Baldrige National Quality Award an award given by the President of the United States to organizations that apply and are judged to be outstanding in specific managerial tasks that lead to improved quality for both products and services (219)

management by objectives (MBO) a motivation technique in which managers and employees collaborate in setting goals (271)

management development the process of preparing managers and other professionals to assume increased responsibility in both present and future positions (247)

management information system (MIS) a system that provides managers and employees with the information they need to perform their jobs as effectively as possible (389)

management the process of coordinating people and other resources to achieve the goals of an organization (159)

managerial accounting provides managers and employees with the information needed to make decisions about a firm's financing, investing, and operating activities (421)

managerial hierarchy the arrangement that provides increasing authority at higher levels of management (197)

manufacturer (or producer) brand a brand that is owned by a manufacturer (325)

market a group of individuals or organizations, or both, that need products in a given category and that have the ability, willingness, and authority to purchase such products (295)

market economy an economic system in which businesses and individuals decide what to produce and buy, and the market determines quantities sold and prices (12)

market order a request that a security be purchased or sold at the current market price (A-5)

market price the price at which the quantity demanded is exactly equal to the quantity supplied (21)

market segment a group of individuals or organizations within a market that shares one or more common characteristics (297)

market segmentation the process of dividing a market into segments and directing a marketing mix at a particular segment or segments rather than at the total market (297)

market value the price of one share of a stock at a particular time (A-11)

marketing the activity, set of institutions, and processes for creating, communicating, delivering, and exchanging offerings that have value for customers, clients, partners, and society at large (290)

marketing concept a business philosophy that a firm should provide goods and services that satisfy customers' needs through a coordinated set of activities that allows the firm to achieve its objectives (293)

marketing information system a system for managing marketing information that is gathered continually from internal and external sources (303)

marketing manager a manager who is responsible for facilitating the exchange of products between an organization and its customers or clients (167)

marketing mix a combination of product, price, distribution, and promotion developed to satisfy a particular target market (296)

marketing plan a written document that specifies an organization's resources, objectives, strategy, and implementation and control efforts to be used in marketing a specific product or product group (301)

marketing research the process of systematically gathering, recording, and analyzing data concerning a particular marketing problem (303)

marketing strategy a plan that will enable an organization to make the best use of its resources and advantages to meet its objectives (296)

markup the amount a seller adds to the cost of a product to determine its basic selling price (333)

Maslow's hierarchy of needs a sequence of human needs in the order of their importance (264)

mass production a manufacturing process that lowers the cost required to produce a large number of identical or similar products over a long period of time (207)

master limited partnership (MLP) a business partnership that is owned and managed like a corporation but often taxed like a partnership (106)

materials handling the actual physical handling of goods, in warehouses as well as during transportation (361)

materials requirements planning (MRP) a computerized system that integrates production planning and inventory control (218)

matrix structure an organizational structure that combines vertical and horizontal lines of authority, usually by superimposing product departmentalization on a functionally departmentalized organization (192)

maturity date the date on which a corporation is to repay borrowed money (465)

merchant middleman a middleman that actually takes title to products by buying them (348)

merchant wholesaler a middleman that purchases good in large quantities and then sells them to other wholesalers or retailers and to institutional, farm, government, professional, or industrial users (352)

merger the purchase of one corporation by another (118)

microeconomics the study of the decisions made by individuals and businesses (10)

middle manager a manager who implements the strategy and major policies developed by top management (165)

middleman (or marketing intermediary) a marketing organization that links a producer and user within a marketing channel (347)

minority a racial, religious, political, national, or other group regarded as different from the larger group of which it is a part and that is often singled out for unfavorable treatment (54)

mission a statement of the basic purpose that makes an organization different from others (161)

missionary salesperson a salesperson—generally employed by a manufacturer—who visits retailers to persuade them to buy the manufacturer's products (369)

mixed economy an economy that exhibits elements of both capitalism and socialism (12)

monetary policies Federal Reserve decisions that determine the size of the supply of money in the nation and the level of interest rates (19)

monopolistic competition a market situation in which there are many buyers along with a relatively large number of sellers who differentiate their products from the products of competitors (22)

monopoly a market (or industry) with only one seller (22)

morale an employee's feelings about his or her job, superiors, and the firm itself (262)

motivating the process of providing reasons for people to work in the best interests of an organization (164)

motivation the individual internal process that energizes, directs, and sustains behavior; the personal "force" that causes you or me to behave in a particular way (261)

motivation factors job factors that increase motivation but whose absence does not necessarily result in dissatisfaction (266)

motivation-hygiene theory the idea that satisfaction and dissatisfaction are separate and distinct dimensions (266)

multilateral development bank (MDB) an internationally supported bank that provides loans to developing countries to help them grow (89)

multinational enterprise a firm that operates on a worldwide scale without ties to any specific nation or region (85)

multiple-unit pricing the strategy of setting a single price for two or more units (337)

municipal bond sometimes called a muni, a debt security issued by a state or local government (A-10)

mutual fund a company that pools the money of many investors—its shareholders—to invest in a variety of different securities (A-12)

N

National Alliance of Business (NAB) a joint business-government program to train the hard-core unemployed (56)

national debt the total of all federal deficits (20)

natural monopoly an industry requiring huge investments in capital and within which any duplication of facilities would be wasteful and thus not in the public interest (22)

need a personal requirement (264)

negotiated pricing establishing a final price through bargaining (336)

neighborhood shopping center a planned shopping center consisting of several small convenience and specialty stores (358)

net asset value (NAV) is equal to the current market value of a mutual fund's portfolio minus the mutual fund's liabilities divided by the number of outstanding shares (A-12)

net income occurs when revenues exceed expenses (431)

net loss occurs when expenses exceed revenues (431)

net sales the actual dollar amounts received by a firm for the goods and services it has sold after adjustment for returns, allowances, and discounts (430)

network structure an organization in which administration is the primary function, and most other functions are contracted out to other firms (194)

news release a typed page of about 300 words provided by an organization to the media as a form of publicity (375)

nonprice competition competition based on factors other than price (332)

nonstore retailing a type of retailing whereby consumers purchase products without visiting a store (356)

nontariff barrier a nontax measure imposed by a government to favor domestic over foreign suppliers (72)

not-for-profit corporation a corporation organized to provide a social, educational, religious, or other service rather than to earn a profit (116)

O

objective a specific statement detailing what an organization intends to accomplish over a shorter period of time (161)

odd-number pricing the strategy of setting prices using odd numbers that are slightly below whole-dollar amounts (337)

off-price retailer a store that buys manufacturers' seconds, overruns, returns, and off-season merchandise for resale to consumers at deep discounts (355)

oligopoly a market (or industry) in which there are few sellers (22)

online retailing retailing that makes products available to buyers through computer connections (357)

open corporation a corporation whose stock can be bought and sold by any individual (110)

operating expenses all business costs other than the cost of goods sold (431)

operational plan a type of plan designed to implement tactical plans (163)

operations management all activities managers engage in to produce goods and services (206)

operations manager a manager who manages the systems that convert resources into goods and services (166)

order getter a salesperson who is responsible for selling a firm's products to new customers and increasing sales to present customers (369)

order processing activities involved in receiving and filling customers' purchase orders (360)

order taker a salesperson who handles repeat sales in ways that maintain positive relationships with customers (369)

organization a group of two or more people working together to achieve a common set of goals (181)

organization chart a diagram that represents the positions and relationships within an organization (183)

organizational height the number of layers, or levels, of management in a firm (189)

organizing the grouping of resources and activities to accomplish some end result in an efficient and effective manner (163)

orientation the process of acquainting new employees with an organization (243)

outsourcing the process of finding outside vendors and suppliers that provide professional help, parts, or materials at a lower cost (401)

owners' equity the difference between a firm's assets and its liabilities (422)

P

packaging all the activities involved in developing and providing a container with graphics for a product (328)

partnership a voluntary association of two or more persons to act as co-owners of a business for profit (104)

part-time work permanent employment in which individuals work less than a standard work week (275)

penetration pricing the strategy of setting a low price for a new product (336)

perfect (or pure) competition the market situation in which there are many buyers and sellers of a product, and no single buyer or seller is powerful enough to affect the price of that product (20)

performance appraisal the evaluation of employees' current and potential levels of performance to allow managers to make objective human resources decisions (248)

periodic discounting temporary reduction of prices on a patterned or systematic basis (337)

personal budget a specific plan for spending your income (A-2)

personal income the income an individual receives from all sources *less* the Social Security taxes the individual must pay (307)

personal investment the use of your personal funds to earn a financial return (A-2)

personal selling personal communication aimed at informing customers and persuading them to buy a firm's products (364)

physical distribution all those activities concerned with the efficient movement of products from the producer to the ultimate user (359)

physiological needs the things we require for survival (264)

piece-rate system a compensation system under which employees are paid a certain amount for each unit of output they produce (262)

place utility utility created by making a product available at a location where customers wish to purchase it (292)

plan an outline of the actions by which an organization intends to accomplish its goals and objectives (162)

planning establishing organizational goals and deciding how to accomplish them (161)

planning horizon the period during which an operational plan will be in effect (215)

plant layout the arrangement of machinery, equipment, and personnel within a production facility (214)

point-of-purchase display promotional material placed within a retail store (374)

pollution the contamination of water, air, or land through the actions of people in an industrialized society (56)

possession utility utility created by transferring title (or ownership) of a product to a buyer (293)

preferred stock stock owned by individuals or firms who usually do not have voting rights but whose claims on dividends are paid before those of common stock owners (111)

premium a gift that a producer offers a customer in return for buying its product (373)

premium pricing pricing the highest-quality or most-versatile products higher than other models in the product line (339)

press conference a meeting at which invited media personnel hear important news announcements and receive supplementary textual materials and photographs (375)

price competition an emphasis on setting a price equal to or lower than competitors' prices to gain sales or market share (331)

price leaders products priced below the usual markup, near cost, or below cost (339)

price lining the strategy of selling goods only at certain predetermined prices that reflect definite price breaks (339)

price skimming the strategy of charging the highest possible price for a product during the introduction stage of its life cycle (336)

price the amount of money a seller is willing to accept in exchange for a product at a given time and under given circumstances (330)

primary-demand advertising advertising whose purpose is to increase the demand for all brands of a product within a specific industry (364)

private placement occurs when stock and other corporate securities are sold directly to insurance companies, pension funds, or large institutional investors (463)

problem the discrepancy between an actual condition and a desired condition (171)

problem-solving team a team of knowledgeable employees brought together to tackle a specific problem (278)

process material a material that is used directly in the production of another product but is not readily identifiable in the finished product (317)

producer price index (PPI) an index that measures prices at the wholesale level (18)

product deletion the elimination of one or more products from a product line (321)

product design the process of creating a set of specifications from which a product can be produced (212)

product differentiation the process of developing and promoting differences between one's products and all similar products (322)

product everything one receives in an exchange, including all tangible and intangible attributes and expected benefits; it may be a good, service, or idea (315)

product life cycle a series of stages in which a product's sales revenue and profit increase, reach a peak, and then decline (317)

product line a group of similar products that differ only in relatively minor characteristics (320)

product mix all the products a firm offers for sale (320)

product modification the process of changing one or more of a product's characteristics (321)

productivity the average level of output per worker per hour (15)

profit sharing the distribution of a percentage of a firm's profit among its employees (245)

profit what remains after all business expenses have been deducted from sales revenue (9)

promissory note a written pledge by a borrower to pay a certain sum of money to a creditor at a specified future date (457)

promotion communication about an organization and its products that is intended to inform, persuade, or remind target-market members (363)

promotion mix the particular combination of promotion methods a firm uses to reach a target market (364)

prospectus a detailed, written description of a new security, the issuing corporation, and the corporation's top management (A-7)

proxy a legal form listing issues to be decided at a stockholders' meeting and enabling stockholders to transfer their voting rights to some other individual or individuals (112)

proxy fight a technique used to gather enough stockholder votes to control a targeted company (118)

public relations communication activities used to create and maintain favorable relationships between an organization and various public groups, both internal and external (364)

publicity communication in news-story form about an organization, its products, or both (375)

purchasing all the activities involved in obtaining required materials, supplies, components, and parts from other firms (216)

Q

quality circle a team of employees who meet on company time to solve problems of product quality (220)

quality control the process of ensuring that goods and services are produced in accordance with design specifications (219)

R

random discounting temporary reduction of prices on an unsystematic basis (337)

raw material a basic material that actually becomes part of a physical product; usually comes from mines, forests, oceans, or recycled solid wastes (317)

rebate a return of part of the purchase price of a product (372)

recession two or more consecutive three-month periods of decline in a country's GDP (19)

recruiting the process of attracting qualified job applicants (XX)

reference pricing pricing a product at a moderate level and positioning it next to a more expensive model or brand (337)

regional shopping center a planned shopping center containing large department stores, numerous specialty stores, restaurants, movie theaters, and sometimes even hotels (359)

registered bond a bond registered in the owner's name by the issuing company (465)

reinforcement theory a theory of motivation based on the premise that behavior that is rewarded is likely to be repeated, whereas behavior that is punished is less likely to recur (268)

relationship marketing establishing long-term, mutually satisfying buyer-seller relationships (291)

replacement chart a list of key personnel and their possible replacements within a firm (235)

research and development (R&D) a set of activities intended to identify new ideas that have the potential to result in new goods and services (210)

responsibility the duty to do a job or perform a task (186)

retailer a middleman that buys from producers or other middlemen and sells to consumers (348)

retained earnings the portion of a business/corporation's profits not distributed to stockholders (462, 428)

return on owners' equity a financial ratio calculated by dividing net income after taxes by owners' equity (435)

return on sales (or profit margin) a financial ratio calculated by dividing net income after taxes by net sales (435)

revenue stream a source of revenue flowing into a firm (403)

revenues the dollar amounts earned by a firm from selling goods, providing services, or performing business activities (429)

revolving credit agreement a guaranteed line of credit (454)

risk-return ratio a ratio based on the principle that a high-risk decision should generate higher financial returns for a business and more conservative decisions often generate lesser returns (448)

robotics the use of programmable machines to perform a variety of tasks by manipulating materials and tools (222)

S

safety needs the things we require for physical and emotional security (265)

salary a specific amount of money paid for an employee's work during a set calendar period, regardless of the actual number of hours worked (245)

sales forecast an estimate of the amount of a product that an organization expects to sell during a certain period of time based on a specified level of marketing effort (302)

sales promotion the use of activities or materials as direct inducements to customers or salespersons (364)

sales support personnel employees who aid in selling but are more involved in locating prospects, educating customers, building goodwill for the firm, and providing follow-up service (369)

sample a free product given to customers to encourage trial and purchase (373)

Sarbanes-Oxley Act of 2002 provides sweeping new legal protection for employees who report corporate misconduct (39)

scheduling the process of ensuring that materials and other resources are at the right place at the right time (218)

scientific management the application of scientific principles to management of work and workers (262)

S-corporation a corporation that is taxed as though it were a partnership (115)

secondary-market pricing setting one price for the primary target market and a different price for another market (337)

selection the process of gathering information about applicants for a position and then using that information to choose the most appropriate applicant (241)

selective distribution the use of only a portion of the available outlets for a product in each geographic area (350)

selective-demand (or brand) advertising advertising that is used to sell a particular brand of product (364)

self-actualization needs the need to grow and develop and to become all that we are capable of being (265)

self-managed teams groups of employees with the authority and skills to manage themselves (278)

serial bonds bonds of a single issue that mature on different dates (466)

Service Corps of Retired Executives (SCORE) a group of businesspeople who volunteer their services to small businesses through the SBA (142)

service economy an economy in which more effort is devoted to the production of services than to the production of goods (208)

shopping product an item for which buyers are willing to expend considerable effort on planning and making the purchase (316)

short-term financing money that will be used for one year or less (446)

sinking fund a sum of money to which deposits are made each year for the purpose of redeeming a bond issue (466)

Six Sigma a disciplined approach that relies on statistical data and improved methods to eliminate defects for a firm's products and services (220)

skills inventory a computerized data bank containing information on the skills and experience of all present employees (235)

small business one that is independently owned and operated for profit and is not dominant in its field (128)

Small Business Administration (SBA) a governmental agency that assists, counsels, and protects the interests of small businesses in the United States (141)

small-business development centers (SBDCs) university-based groups that provide individual counseling and practical training to owners of small businesses (143)

small-business institutes (SBIs) groups of senior and graduate students in business administration who provide management counseling to small businesses (143)

small-business investment companies (SBICs) privately owned firms that provide venture capital to small enterprises that meet their investment standards (144)

social audit a comprehensive report of what an organization has done and is doing with regard to social issues that affect it (60)

social needs the human requirements for love, affection, and a sense of belonging (265)

social responsibility the recognition that business activities have an impact on society and the consideration of that impact in business decision making (42)

socioeconomic model of social responsibility the concept that business should emphasize not only profits but also the impact of its decisions on society (49)

sole proprietorship a business that is owned (and usually operated) by one person (101)

span of management (or **span of control**) the number of workers who report directly to one manager (188)

special-event pricing advertised sales or price cutting linked to a holiday, season, or event (339)

specialization the separation of a manufacturing process into distinct tasks and the assignment of the different tasks to different individuals (23)

specialty product an item that possesses one or more unique characteristics for which a significant group of buyers is willing to expend considerable purchasing effort (316)

specialty-line wholesaler a middleman that carries a select group of products within a single line (352)

speculative production the time lag between the actual production of goods and when the goods are sold (446)

staff management position a position created to provide support, advice, and expertise within an organization (190)

stakeholders all the different people or groups of people who are affected by the decisions made by an organization (9)

standard of living a loose, subjective measure of how well off an individual or a society is mainly in terms of want satisfaction through goods and services (23)

standing committee a relatively permanent committee charged with performing some recurring task (196)

statement of cash flows a statement that illustrates how the operating, investing, and financing activities of a company affect cash during an accounting period (431)

statistic a measure that summarizes a particular characteristic of an entire group of numbers (392)

stock the shares of ownership of a corporation (109)

stock dividend a dividend in the form of additional stock (A-10)

stock split the division of each outstanding share of a corporation's stock into a greater number of shares (A-11)

stockholder a person who owns a corporation's stock (109)

store (or private) brand a brand that is owned by an individual wholesaler or retailer (325)

strategic alliances a partnership formed to create competitive advantage on a worldwide basis (84)

strategic plan an organization's broadest plan, developed as a guide for major policy setting and decision making (162)

strategic planning the process of establishing an organization's major goals and objectives and allocating the resources to achieve them (161)

supermarket a large self-service store that sells primarily food and household products (354)

superstore a large retail store that carries not only food and nonfood products ordinarily found in supermarkets but also additional product lines (354)

supply the quantity of a product that producers are willing to sell at each of various prices (317)

supply-chain management long-term partnership among channel members working together to create a distribution system that reduces inefficiencies, costs, and redundancies while creating a competitive advantage and satisfying customers (350)

sustainability meeting the needs of the present without compromising the ability of future generations to meet their own needs (27)

syndicate a temporary association of individuals or firms organized to perform a specific task that requires a large amount of capital (117)

synthetic process a process in operations management in which raw materials or components are combined to create a finished product (207)

T

tactical plan a smaller-scale plan developed to implement a strategy (163)

target market a group of individuals or organizations, or both, for which a firm develops and maintains a marketing mix suitable for the specific needs and preferences of that group (296)

task force a committee established to investigate a major problem or pending decision (197)

team a group of workers functioning together as a unit to complete a common goal or purpose (278)

technical salesperson a salesperson who assists a company's current customers in technical matters (370)

technical skill a specific skill needed to accomplish a specialized activity (168)

telecommuting working at home all the time or for a portion of the work week (275)

telemarketing the performance of marketing-related activities by telephone (357)

television home shopping a form of selling in which products are presented to television viewers, who can buy them by calling a toll-free number and paying with a credit card (357)

tender offer an offer to purchase the stock of a firm targeted for acquisition at a price just high enough to tempt stockholders to sell their shares (118)

term-loan agreement a promissory note that requires a borrower to repay a loan in monthly, quarterly, semiannual, or annual installments (464)

Theory X a concept of employee motivation generally consistent with Taylor's scientific management; assumes that employees dislike work and will function only in a highly controlled work environment (267)

Theory Y a concept of employee motivation generally consistent with the ideas of the human relations movement; assumes that employees accept responsibility and work toward organizational goals if by so doing they also achieve personal rewards (267)

Theory Z the belief that some middle ground between Ouchi's type A and type J practices is best for American business (268)

time utility utility created by making a product available when customers wish to purchase it (293)

top manager an upper-level executive who guides and controls the overall fortunes of an organization (165)

total cost the sum of the fixed costs and the variable costs attributed to a product (334)

total quality management (TQM) the coordination of efforts directed at improving customer satisfaction, increasing employee participation, strengthening supplier partnerships, and facilitating an organizational atmosphere of continuous quality improvement (172)

total revenue the total amount received from sales of a product (334)

trade credit a type of short-term financing extended by a seller who does not require immediate payment after delivery of merchandise (457)

trade deficit a negative balance of trade (71)

trade name the complete and legal name of an organization (325)

trade sales promotion method a sales promotion method designed to encourage wholesalers and retailers to stock and actively promote a manufacturer's product (372)

trade salesperson a salesperson—generally employed by a food producer or processor—who assists customers in promoting products, especially in retail stores (370)

trade show an industry-wide exhibit at which many sellers display their products (374)

trademark a brand name or brand mark that is registered with the U.S. Patent and Trademark Office and thus is legally protected from use by anyone except its owner (325)

trading company provides a link between buyers and sellers in different countries (85)

traditional specialty store a store that carries a narrow product mix with deep product lines (355)

transfer pricing prices charged in sales between an organization's units (340)

transportation the shipment of products to customers (361)

trial balance a summary of the balances of all general ledger accounts at the end of the accounting period (423)

trustee an individual or an independent firm that acts as a bond owners' representative (466)

U

undifferentiated approach directing a single marketing mix at the entire market for a particular product (297)

unlimited liability a legal concept that holds a business owner personally responsible for all the debts of the business (103)

unsecured financing financing that is not backed by collateral (457)

utility the ability of a good or service to satisfy a human need (292)

V

variable cost a cost that depends on the number of units produced (334)

venture capital money that is invested in small (and sometimes struggling) firms that have the potential to become very successful (144)

virtual team a team consisting of members who are geographically dispersed but communicate electronically (279)

virtuoso team a team of exceptionally highly skilled and talented individuals brought together to produce significant change (278)

W

wage survey a collection of data on prevailing wage rates within an industry or a geographic area (243)

warehouse club a large-scale members-only establishment that combines features of cash-and-carry wholesaling with discount retailing (355)

warehouse showroom a retail facility in a large, low-cost building with a large on-premises inventory and minimal service (354)

warehousing the set of activities involved in receiving and storing goods and preparing them for reshipment (360)

whistle-blowing informing the press or government officials about unethical practices within one's organization (40)

wholesaler a middleman that sells products to other firms (349)

wide-area network (WAN) a network that connects computers over a large geographic area, such as a city, a state, or even the world (399)

working capital the difference between current assets and current liabilities (435)

World Trade Organization (WTO) powerful successor to GATT that incorporates trade in goods, services, and ideas (79)

World Wide Web (the Web) the Internet's multimedia environment of audio, visual, and text data (398)

De Beers, 326
Deere & Company, 36
Deere, John, 23
Dell Computer, 3, 43, 195, 223, 327, 348, 399, 404
Dell Foundation, 43
Deloitte Touche Tohmatsu, 422
Delphi Automotive Systems Corporation, 59
Demeter, Steve, 128
Department of Justice, 418
Dessauer, Laura, 445
Dick's Sporting Goods, 177
Dingell, John, 35
Disney, 210, 234, 301
Disney, Walt, 110, 181
DiversityBusiness.com, 104
Doctor's Associates, Inc., 147
Dollar General, 347, 354
Donegan, Dan, 227
Dow Chemical Company, 85
Dr Pepper, 326
Dr. Pepper/Seven-Up Companies, 146
Dreese, Mike, 153
Drexel-Heritage, 218
DuBois, Kathleen, 143
Dudley Products, Inc., 3
Dudley, Joe, 3, 4, 7
Dun and Bradstreet (D&B), 133, 304, 434, 464
Dunkin' Donuts, 148, 149
Dunn, Patricia, 35
DuPont, 168–169

E

Eastern Mountain Sports (EMS), 161
Eastman Kodak, 142, 240
eBay, 367, 402, 403, 406, 407
Ebbers, Bernard, 417
Edison, Thomas, 210
Eleftheriou, Kostas, 128
Ellison, Larry, 118, 120
Engibous, Tom, 41
Enron, 9, 38, 40, 418
Environmental Protection Agency (EPA), 56
Equal Employment Opportunity Commission (EEOC), 55, 241, 252
Erb, Joel, 445
Ernst & Young (www.ey.com/global), 422
Ethel's Chocolates, 332
Etsy, Artsy, 137
European Bank for Reconstruction and Development (EBRD), 89
Expedia, 261
Export- Import Bank, 88
Exxon, 325, 397
ExxonMobil, 3, 46, 184, 235, 240

F

Facebook, 304, 386, 399, 416
Fahrenheit 212, 323

Fannie Mae, 38, 134, 417
FBI, 40
Federal Communications Commission (FCC), 368
Federal Reserve Bank, 458
Federal Reserve Bulletin, 392
Federal Reserve System, 19
Federal Trade Commission (FTC), 37, 149, 304, 368
FedEx, 34, 144, 188–189, 192, 261, 430
Ferrari, 278
Fidelity Investments, 396
Field Museum, The, 412
Finagle A Bagel (www.finagleabagel.com), 7, 95–96, 155–156
Financial Accounting Standards Board, 431
Flexible manufacturing system, 222
Food and Drug Administration (FDA), 35, 51, 368
Foot Locker, 177, 355
Ford Motor Company, 16, 22, 101, 135, 166, 184, 192, 197, 222, 236, 294, 334, 366, 405
Ford, Gerald, 52
Ford, Henry, II, 56, 166
Ford, William Clay, Jr., 166
Forrester Research, Inc. (www.forrester.com), 406, 407
Fortune (www.fortune.com), 40, 104, 233, 246, 261, 392
Fortune 500 companies, 240, 241
Fossil, 92–93
Foundations of Business, 7
Fox network, 101
Freddie Mac, 38, 134, 417
Freeport, 135
Friedman, Thomas L., 68
Froogle.google.com, 331
Frosted Flakes, 208, 325
Fry, Art, 196
Fuld, Richard S., Jr., 36

G

Gabhawala, Rekha, 148
Gamble, James, 109
Gap Inc., 6, 355, 373
General Accounting Office (GAO), 73
General Electric (GE), 44, 110, 142, 164, 188, 208, 220, 240, 261, 265, 326, 397, 458
General Mills, 320, 322, 324, 423
General Mills Foundation, 43
General Motors, 22, 84, 366
Georgia coffee, 320
Georgia Pacific, 290
Get Your Share, 6
Giant Food, 392
Gillette, 320, 324
Giorgi, Antoinette, 105

Girl Scouts, 116
Glad Cling Wrap, 208
Glad Products Company, 208
GlaxoSmithKline, 366
Goffee and Jones, 194
Gold Star Appliances, 454–455
Goldman Sachs, 117
Goodrich,Ben, 74
Goodyear, Charles, 210
Google (www.google.com), 44, 161, 164, 221, 233, 246, 400, 407
Goya Foods, 315
Grainger, 351
Grameen Bank, 456
Grameen Danone Foods, 118
Grass, Martin L., 40
Green Mountain Coffee Roasters (www.greenmountaincoffee.com.), 201–202
Greenfield, Jerry, 6
Greyhound, 177
Griswold, Daniel T., 70
Grosnickle, Karolyn, 36
Gross, Al, 136

H

H & R Block, 144
H.J. Heinz Company, 101, 326
Haass, Richard, 26
Habitat for Humanity, 116
Halloween, 292
Halvorsen, Elizabeth, 142
Hard Rock Cafe, 213
Harley Owners Group (HOG), 312
Harley-Davidson (www.harley-davidson.com), 312–313
Harrington, Emily, 143
Harrods, 353
Harvard Business School, 133
Harvey, Bob, 447
Hasbro, 222
Hawthorne plant, 263
Healthcare Financial Management Association, 40
Heinz, 324
Hendricks, Brian, 133
Hershey, 265
Hershey Foods, 424
Hertz Corporation, 146, 301
Herzberg, Frederick, 265–267, 269, 272
Hewlett-Packard (HP), 2, 3, 18, 35, 49, 119, 181, 205, 212, 220, 399
Hicks, Taylor, 403
Hispanic PR Wire, 113
Hitachi, 373
Hog Tales, 312
Holborn, Dean, 349
Holiday Inn, 146, 292
Hollenhorst, Kathy, 196
Home Depot, 182, 219, 351, 353, 356, 390, 420, 442

Home Shopping Network (HSN), 357
Honda, 186, 323, 325, 388
Honeywell, 220
Hoover's Online (www.hoovers.com), 404
Horatio Alger Award, 3
Hotline, 305
Houston Community College System, 161
Howard Johnson Company, 146
Howe, Elias, 23
HR.BLR.COM, 238
Hufbauer, Gary, 74
Huggies, 290
Huiyuan, 308
Huiyuan Juice Group Ltd., 121
Hyatt Corporation, 168

I

IBM, 2, 3, 25, 43, 119, 142, 182, 187, 220, 326, 327, 399, 462
Illumina, Inc., 222
Immelt, Jeffrey R., 164
IncrEdibles Breakaway Foods, 324
Information Resources, Inc., 304
INM United, 445
Innovision Technologies, 132
Institute of Management Accountants, 422
Intel Corporation, 144, 388
Inter-American Development Bank (IDB), 88, 89
Internal Revenue Service, 108, 364
International Bank for Reconstruction and Development (IBRD), 89
International Development Association (IDA), 89
International Financial Reporting Standards (IFRS), 418
International Monetary Fund (IMF), 75
Isle of Capri Casinos, Inc., 265
Ivy Planning Group, 104
Izod, 205

J

J. Crew, 356
Jaguar, 42
JC Penney (www.jcpenney.com), 303, 304, 353, 356
Jefferson Wells, 274
Jell-O, 327
Jobs, Steve, 170
Johnson & Johnson, 101, 110, 366, 397, 416
Johnson, Lyndon, 56
Johnson, S.C., 273
Johnson, Toby, 277
Johnston, Pete, 463

©Bill Noll